Essential C# 7.0

Essential C# 7.0

■ **Mark Michaelis**
with Eric Lippert, Technical Editor

✦✦Addison-Wesley

Boston • Columbus • Indianapolis • New York • San Francisco • Amsterdam • Cape Town
Dubai • London • Madrid • Milan • Munich • Paris • Montreal • Toronto • Delhi • Mexico City
São Paulo • Sydney • Hong Kong • Seoul • Singapore • Taipei • Tokyo

For information about buying this title in bulk quantities, or for special sales opportunities (which may include electronic versions; custom cover designs; and content particular to your business, training goals, marketing focus, or branding interests), please contact our corporate sales department at corpsales@pearsoned.com or (800) 382-3419.

For government sales inquiries, please contact governmentsales@pearsoned.com.

For questions about sales outside the U.S., please contact intlcs@pearson.com.

Visit us on the Web: informit.com/aw

Library of Congress Control Number: 2018933128

ISBN-13: 978-1-5093-0358-8
ISBN-10: 1-5093-0358-8

1   18

To my family: Elisabeth, Benjamin, Hanna, and Abigail.

You have sacrificed a husband and daddy for countless hours of writing, frequently at times when he was needed most.

Thanks!

■

Contents at a Glance

Contents

Figures

Tables

Foreword

WELCOME TO ONE OF THE MOST VENERABLE and trusted franchises you could dream of in the world of C# books—and probably far beyond! Mark Michaelis's Essential C# series has been a classic for years, but it was yet to see the light of day when I first got to know Mark.

In 2005 when LINQ (Language Integrated Query) was disclosed, I had only just joined Microsoft, and I got to tag along to the Microsoft Professional Developers Conference for the big reveal. Despite my almost total lack of contribution to the technology, I thoroughly enjoyed the hype. The talks were overflowing, the printed leaflets were scooped up like free hotcakes: It was a big day for C# and .NET, and I was having a great time.

It was pretty quiet in the hands-on labs area, though, where people could try out the technology preview themselves with nice scripted walkthroughs. That's where I ran into Mark. Needless to say, he wasn't following the script. He was doing his own experiments, combing through the docs, talking to other folks, busily pulling together his own picture.

As a newcomer to the C# community, I think I may have met a lot of people for the first time at that conference—people I have since formed great relationships with. But to be honest, I don't remember it—it's all a blur. The only person I remember is Mark. Here is why: When I asked him if he was liking the new stuff, he didn't just join the rave. He was totally level-headed: *"I don't know yet. I haven't made up my mind about it."* He wanted to absorb and understand the full package, and until then he wasn't going to let anyone tell him what to think.

So instead of the quick sugar rush of affirmation I might have expected, I got to have a frank and wholesome conversation, the first of many over the years, about details, consequences, and concerns with this new technology. And so it remains: Mark is an incredibly valuable community member for us language designers to have, because he is super smart, insists on understanding everything to the core, and has phenomenal insight into how things affect real developers. But perhaps most of all because he is forthright and never afraid to speak his mind. If something passes the Mark Test, then we know we can start feeling pretty good about it!

These are the same qualities that make Mark such a great writer. He goes right to the essence and communicates with great integrity—no sugarcoating—and has a keen eye for practical value and real-world problems. Mark has a great gift for providing clarity and elucidation, and no one will help you get C# 7.0 like he does.

Enjoy!

—Mads Torgersen,
C# Program Manager,
Microsoft

Preface

THROUGHOUT THE HISTORY of software engineering, the methodology used to write computer programs has undergone several paradigm shifts, each building on the foundation of the former by increasing code organization and decreasing complexity. This book takes you through these same paradigm shifts.

The beginning chapters take you through **sequential programming structure** in which statements are executed in the order in which they are written. The problem with this model is that complexity increases exponentially as the requirements increase. To reduce this complexity, code blocks are moved into methods, creating a **structured programming model**. This allows you to call the same code block from multiple locations within a program, without duplicating code. Even with this construct, however, programs quickly become unwieldy and require further abstraction. Object-oriented programming, introduced in Chapter 6, was the response. In subsequent chapters, you will learn about additional methodologies, such as interface-based programming, LINQ (and the transformation it makes to the collection API), and eventually rudimentary forms of declarative programming (in Chapter 18) via attributes.

This book has three main functions.

- It provides comprehensive coverage of the C# language, going beyond a tutorial and offering a foundation upon which you can begin effective software development projects.
- For readers already familiar with C#, this book provides insight into some of the more complex programming paradigms and provides

in-depth coverage of the features introduced in the latest version of the language, C# 7.0 and .NET Framework 4.7/.NET Core 2.0.

- It serves as a timeless reference even after you gain proficiency with the language.

The key to successfully learning C# is to start coding as soon as possible. Don't wait until you are an "expert" in theory; start writing software immediately. As a believer in iterative development, I hope this book enables even a novice programmer to begin writing basic C# code by the end of Chapter 2.

Many topics are not covered in this book. You won't find coverage of topics such as ASP.NET, ADO.NET, Xamarin, smart client development, distributed programming, and so on. Although these topics are relevant to .NET, to do them justice requires books of their own. Fortunately, Addison-Wesley's Microsoft Windows Development Series provides a wealth of writing on these topics. *Essential C# 7.0* focuses on C# and the types within the Base Class Library. Reading this book will prepare you to focus on and develop expertise in any of the areas covered by the rest of the series.

Target Audience for This Book

My challenge with this book was to keep advanced developers awake while not abandoning beginners by using words such as *assembly, link, chain, thread,* and *fusion* as though the topic was more appropriate for blacksmiths than for programmers. This book's primary audience is experienced developers looking to add another language to their quiver. However, I have carefully assembled this book to provide significant value to developers at all levels.

- *Beginners:* If you are new to programming, this book serves as a resource to help transition you from an entry-level programmer to a C# developer, comfortable with any C# programming task that's thrown your way. This book not only teaches you syntax but also trains you in good programming practices that will serve you throughout your programming career.

- *Structured programmers:* Just as it's best to learn a foreign language through immersion, learning a computer language is most effective when you begin using it before you know all the intricacies. In this vein, this book begins with a tutorial that will be comfortable for those familiar with structured programming, and by the end of Chapter 5, developers in this category should feel at home writing basic control flow programs. However, the key to excellence for C# developers is not memorizing syntax. To transition from simple programs to enterprise development, the C# developer must think natively in terms of objects and their relationships. To this end, Chapter 6's Beginner Topics introduce classes and object-oriented development. The role of historically structured programming languages such as C, COBOL, and FORTRAN is still significant but shrinking, so it behooves software engineers to become familiar with object-oriented development. C# is an ideal language for making this transition because it was designed with object-oriented development as one of its core tenets.

- *Object-based and object-oriented developers:* C++, Java, Python, TypeScript, Visual Basic, and Java programmers fall into this category. Many of you are already completely comfortable with semicolons and curly braces. A brief glance at the code in Chapter 1 reveals that, at its core, C# is like other C- and C++-style languages that you already know.

- *C# professionals:* For those already versed in C#, this book provides a convenient reference for less frequently encountered syntax. Furthermore, it provides answers to language details and subtleties that are seldom addressed. Most important, it presents the guidelines and patterns for programming robust and maintainable code. This book also aids in the task of teaching C# to others. With the emergence of C# 3.0 through 7.0, some of the most prominent enhancements are

  - String interpolation (see Chapter 2)
  - Implicitly typed variables (see Chapter 3)
  - Tuples (see Chapter 3)
  - Pattern matching (see Chapter 4)
  - Extension methods (see Chapter 6)
  - Partial methods (see Chapter 6)
  - Anonymous types (see Chapter 12)
  - Generics (see Chapter 12)
  - Lambda statements and expressions (see Chapter 13)
  - Expression trees (see Chapter 13)
  - Standard query operators (see Chapter 15)

- Query expressions (see Chapter 16)
- Dynamic programming (Chapter 18)
- Multithreaded programming with the Task Programming Library and async (Chapter 19)
- Parallel query processing with PLINQ (Chapter 19)
- Concurrent collections (Chapter 20)

These topics are covered in detail for those not already familiar with them. Also pertinent to advanced C# development is the subject of pointers, in Chapter 21. Even experienced C# developers often do not understand this topic well.

Features of This Book

Essential C# 7.0 is a language book that adheres to the core C# Language 7.0 Specification. To help you understand the various C# constructs, it provides numerous examples demonstrating each feature. Accompanying each concept are guidelines and best practices, ensuring that code compiles, avoids likely pitfalls, and achieves maximum maintainability.

To improve readability, code is specially formatted and chapters are outlined using mind maps.

C# Coding Guidelines

One of the more significant enhancements included in *Essential C# 7.0* is C# coding guidelines, as shown in the following example taken from Chapter 17:

> ### Guidelines
>
> **DO** ensure that equal objects have equal hash codes.
>
> **DO** ensure that the hash code of an object never changes while it is in a hash table.
>
> **DO** ensure that the hashing algorithm quickly produces a well-distributed hash.
>
> **DO** ensure that the hashing algorithm is robust in any possible object state.

These guidelines are the key to differentiating a programmer who knows the syntax from an expert who can discern the most effective code to write based on the circumstances. Such an expert not only gets the code to compile but does so while following best practices that minimize bugs and enable maintenance well into the future. The coding guidelines highlight some of the key principles that readers will want to be sure to incorporate into their development.

Code Samples

The code snippets in most of this text can run on most implementations of the Common Language Infrastructure (CLI), but the focus is on the Microsoft .NET Framework and the .NET Core implementation. Platform- or vendor-specific libraries are seldom used except when communicating important concepts relevant only to those platforms (e.g., appropriately handling the single-threaded user interface of Windows). Any code that specifically relates to C# 5.0, 6.0, or 7.0 is called out in the C# version indexes at the end of the book.

Here is a sample code listing.

Begin 2.0

LISTING 1.19: **Commenting Your Code**

```
class Comment Samples
{
  static void Main()
  {

      string firstName; //Variable for storing the first name
      string lastName;  //Variable for storing the last name

      System.Console.WriteLine("Hey you!");

      System.Console.Write /* No new line */ (
          "Enter your first name: ");
      firstName = System.Console.ReadLine();

      System.Console.Write /* No new line */ (
          "Enter your last name: ");
      lastName = System.Console.ReadLine();

      /* Display a greeting to the console
         using composite formatting. */

      System.Console.WriteLine("Your full name is {0} {1}.",
          firstName, lastName);
      // This is the end
      // of the program listing
  }
}
```

The formatting is as follows.

- Comments are shown in italics.

  ```
  /* Display a greeting to the console
     using composite formatting */
  ```

- Keywords are shown in bold.

  ```
  static void Main()
  ```

- Highlighted code calls out specific code snippets that may have changed from an earlier listing, or demonstrates the concept described in the text.

  ```
  System.Console.WriteLine(valerie);
  miracleMax = "It would take a miracle.";
  System.Console.WriteLine(miracleMax);
  ```

  Highlighting can appear on an entire line or on just a few characters within a line.

  ```
  System.Console.WriteLine(
      "Your full name is {0} {1}.", firstName, lastName);
  ```

- Incomplete listings contain an ellipsis to denote irrelevant code that has been omitted.

  ```
  // ...
  ```

- Console output is the output from a particular listing that appears following the listing. User input for the program appears in **boldface.**

OUTPUT 1.7

```
Hey you!
Enter your first name: Inigo
Enter your last name: Montoya
Your full name is Inigo Montoya.
```

Although it might have been convenient to provide full code samples that you could copy into your own programs, doing so would detract from your learning a particular topic. Therefore, you need to modify the code samples before you can incorporate them into your programs. The core omission is error checking, such as exception handling. Also, code samples do not explicitly include using System statements. You need to assume the statement throughout all samples.

You can find sample code at https://IntelliTect.com/EssentialCSharp.

Mind Maps

Each chapter's introduction includes a **mind map,** which serves as an outline that provides an at-a-glance reference to each chapter's content. Here is an example (taken from Chapter 6).

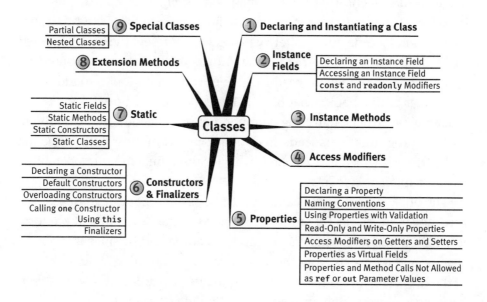

The theme of each chapter appears in the mind map's center. High-level topics spread out from the core. Mind maps allow you to absorb the flow from high-level to more detailed concepts easily, with less chance of encountering very specific knowledge that you might not be looking for.

Helpful Notes

Depending on your level of experience, special features will help you navigate through the text.

- Beginner Topics provide definitions or explanations targeted specifically toward entry-level programmers.
- Advanced Topics enable experienced developers to focus on the material that is most relevant to them.

- Callout notes highlight key principles in callout boxes so that readers easily recognize their significance.
- Language Contrast sidebars identify key differences between C# and its predecessors to aid those familiar with other languages.

How This Book Is Organized

At a high level, software engineering is about managing complexity, and it is toward this end that I have organized *Essential C# 7.0*. Chapters 1–5 introduce structured programming, which enable you to start writing simple functioning code immediately. Chapters 6–10 present the object-oriented constructs of C#. Novice readers should focus on fully understanding this section before they proceed to the more advanced topics found in the remainder of this book. Chapters 12–14 introduce additional complexity-reducing constructs, handling common patterns needed by virtually all modern programs. This leads to dynamic programming with reflection and attributes, which is used extensively for threading and interoperability in the chapters that follow.

The book ends with a chapter on the Common Language Infrastructure, which describes C# within the context of the development platform in which it operates. This chapter appears at the end because it is not C# specific and it departs from the syntax and programming style in the rest of the book. However, this chapter is suitable for reading at any time, perhaps most appropriately immediately following Chapter 1.

Here is a description of each chapter (in this list, chapter numbers shown in **bold** indicate the presence of C# 6.0–7.0 material).

- *Chapter 1—Introducing C#:* After presenting the C# HelloWorld program, this chapter proceeds to dissect it. This should familiarize readers with the look and feel of a C# program and provide details on how to compile and debug their own programs. It also touches on the context of a C# program's execution and its intermediate language.
- *Chapter 2—Data Types:* Functioning programs manipulate data, and this chapter introduces the primitive data types of C#.
- *Chapter 3—More with Data Types:* This chapter includes coverage of two type categories, value types and reference types. From there, it delves into the nullable modifier and a C# 7.0-introduced

feature, tuples. It concludes with an in-depth look at a primitive array structure.

- *Chapter 4—Operators and Control Flow:* To take advantage of the iterative capabilities in a computer, you need to know how to include loops and conditional logic within your program. This chapter also covers the C# operators, data conversion, and preprocessor directives.

- *Chapter 5—Methods and Parameters:* This chapter investigates the details of methods and their parameters. It includes passing by value, passing by reference, and returning data via an out parameter. In C# 4.0, default parameter support was added, and this chapter explains how to use default parameters.

- *Chapter 6—Classes:* Given the basic building blocks of a class, this chapter combines these constructs to form fully functional types. Classes form the core of object-oriented technology by defining the template for an object.

- *Chapter 7—Inheritance:* Although inheritance is a programming fundamental to many developers, C# provides some unique constructs, such as the new modifier. This chapter discusses the details of the inheritance syntax, including overriding.

- *Chapter 8—Interfaces:* This chapter demonstrates how interfaces are used to define the versionable interaction contract between classes. C# includes both explicit and implicit interface member implementation, enabling an additional encapsulation level not supported by most other languages.

- *Chapter 9—Value Types:* Although not as prevalent as defining reference types, it is sometimes necessary to define value types that behave in a fashion similar to the primitive types built into C#. This chapter describes how to define structures while exposing the idiosyncrasies they may introduce.

- *Chapter 10—Well-Formed Types:* This chapter discusses more advanced type definition. It explains how to implement operators, such as + and casts, and describes how to encapsulate multiple classes into a single library. In addition, the chapter demonstrates defining namespaces and XML comments and discusses how to design classes for garbage collection.

- *Chapter 11—Exception Handling:* This chapter expands on the exception-handling introduction from Chapter 5 and describes how exceptions follow a hierarchy that enables creating custom exceptions. It also includes some best practices on exception handling.

- *Chapter 12—Generics:* Generics is perhaps the core feature missing from C# 1.0. This chapter fully covers this 2.0 feature. In addition, C# 4.0 added support for covariance and contravariance—something covered in the context of generics in this chapter.

- *Chapter 13—Delegates and Lambda Expressions:* Delegates begin clearly distinguishing C# from its predecessors by defining patterns for handling events within code. This virtually eliminates the need for writing routines that poll. Lambda expressions are the key concept that make C# 3.0's LINQ possible. This chapter explains how lambda expressions build on the delegate construct by providing a more elegant and succinct syntax. This chapter forms the foundation for the new collection API discussed next.

- *Chapter 14—Events:* Encapsulated delegates, known as events, are a core construct of the Common Language Runtime. Anonymous methods, another C# 2.0 feature, are also presented here.

- *Chapter 15—Collection Interfaces with Standard Query Operators:* The simple and yet elegantly powerful changes introduced in C# 3.0 begin to shine in this chapter as we take a look at the extension methods of the new Enumerable class. This class makes available an entirely new collection API known as the standard query operators and discussed in detail here.

- *Chapter 16—LINQ with Query Expressions:* Using standard query operators alone results in some long statements that are hard to decipher. However, query expressions provide an alternative syntax that matches closely with SQL, as described in this chapter.

- *Chapter 17—Building Custom Collections:* In building custom APIs that work against business objects, it is sometimes necessary to create custom collections. This chapter details how to do this and in the process introduces contextual keywords that make custom collection building easier.

- *Chapter 18—Reflection, Attributes, and Dynamic Programming:* Object-oriented programming formed the basis for a paradigm shift in program structure in the late 1980s. In a similar way, attributes facilitate declarative programming and embedded metadata, ushering in a new paradigm. This chapter looks at attributes and discusses how to retrieve them via reflection. It also covers file input and output via the serialization framework within the Base Class Library. In C# 4.0, a new keyword, dynamic, was added to the language. This removed all type checking until runtime, a significant expansion of what can be done with C#.

- *Chapter 19—Multithreading:* Most modern programs require the use of threads to execute long-running tasks while ensuring active response to simultaneous events. As programs become more sophisticated, they must take additional precautions to protect data in these advanced environments. Programming multithreaded applications is complex. This chapter discusses how to work with threads and provides best practices to avoid the problems that plague multithreaded applications.

- *Chapter 20—Thread Synchronization:* Building on the preceding chapter, this one demonstrates some of the built-in threading pattern support that can simplify the explicit control of multithreaded code.

- *Chapter 21—Platform Interoperability and Unsafe Code:* Given that C# is a relatively young language, far more code is written in other languages than in C#. To take advantage of this preexisting code, C# supports interoperability—the calling of unmanaged code—through P/Invoke. In addition, C# provides for the use of pointers and direct memory manipulation. Although code with pointers requires special privileges to run, it provides the power to interoperate fully with traditional C-based application programming interfaces.

- *Chapter 22—The Common Language Infrastructure:* Fundamentally, C# is the syntax that was designed as the most effective programming language on top of the underlying Common Language Infrastructure. This chapter delves into how C# programs relate to the underlying runtime and its specifications.

- *Indexes of C# 5.0, 6.0, and 7.0 Topics:* These indexes provide quick references for the features added in C# 4.0 through 7.0. They are specifically designed to help programmers quickly update their language skills to a more recent version.

I hope you find this book to be a great resource in establishing your C# expertise and that you continue to reference it for those areas that you use less frequently well after you are proficient in C#.

—Mark Michaelis

IntelliTect.com/mark

Twitter: @Intellitect, @MarkMichaelis

Register your copy of *Essential C# 7.0* on the InformIT site for convenient access to updates and/or corrections as they become available. To start the registration process, go to informit.com/register and log in or create an account. Enter the product ISBN (9781509303588) and click Submit. Look on the Registered Products tab for an Access Bonus Content link next to this product, and follow that link to access any available bonus materials. If you would like to be notified of exclusive offers on new editions and updates, please check the box to receive email from us.

Acknowledgments

No book can be published by the author alone, and I am extremely grateful for the multitude of people who helped me with this one. The order in which I thank people is not significant, except for those who come first. Given that this is now the sixth edition of the book, you can only imagine how much my family has sacrificed to allow me to write over the last 10 years (not to mention the books before that). Benjamin, Hanna, and Abigail often had a Daddy distracted by this book, but Elisabeth suffered even more so. She was often left to take care of things, holding the family's world together on her own. (While on vacation in 2017, I spent days indoors writing while they would much have preferred to go to the beach.) A huge sorry and ginormous Thank You!

Over the years, many technical editors reviewed each chapter in minute detail to ensure technical accuracy. I was often amazed by the subtle errors these folks still managed to catch: Paul Bramsman, Kody Brown, Ian Davis, Doug Dechow, Gerard Frantz, Thomas Heavey, Anson Horton, Brian Jones, Shane Kercheval, Angelika Langer, Eric Lippert, John Michaelis, Jason Morse, Nicholas Paldino, Jon Skeet, Michael Stokesbary, Robert Stokesbary, John Timney, Neal Lundby, Andrew Comb, Jason Peterson, Andrew Scott, Dan Haley, Phil Spokas (who helped with portions of the writing in Chapter 22), and Kevin Bost.

Or course, Eric Lippert is no less than amazing. His grasp of C# is truly astounding, and I am very appreciative of his edits, especially when he pushed for perfection in terminology. His improvements to the C# 3.0 chapters were incredibly significant, and in the second edition my only regret was that I didn't have him review all the chapters. However, that regret is no longer. Eric painstakingly reviewed every *Essential C# 4.0* chapter and even served as a contributing author for *Essential C# 5.0* and *Essential C# 6.0*. I am extremely grateful for his role as a technical editor for *Essential C# 7.0*. Thanks, Eric! I can't imagine anyone better for the job. You deserve all the credit for raising the bar from good to great.

Like Eric and C#, there are fewer than a handful of people who know .NET multithreading as well as Stephen Toub. Accordingly, Stephen concentrated on the two rewritten (for a third time) multithreading chapters and their new focus on async support in C# 5.0. Thanks, Stephen!

Thanks to everyone at Pearson/Addison-Wesley for their patience in working with me in spite of my frequent focus on everything else except the manuscript. Thanks to Trina Fletcher Macdonald, Anna Popick, Julie Nahil, and Carol Lallier. Trina deserves a special medal for putting up with the likes of me when she clearly was juggling myriad other more important things as well. Also, Carol's attention to detail was invaluable, and her ability to improve the writing and red-line potential writing faux pas (even catching them when they occurred in code listings) was so appreciated.

About the Author

Mark Michaelis is the founder of IntelliTect, a high-end software engineering and consulting company where he serves as the chief technical architect and trainer. Mark speaks at developer conferences and has written numerous articles and books. Currently, he is the Essential .NET columnist for *MSDN Magazine*.

Since 1996, Mark has been a Microsoft MVP for C#, Visual Studio Team System, and the Windows SDK. In 2007, he was recognized as a Microsoft Regional Director. He also serves on several Microsoft software design review teams, including C# and VSTS.

Mark holds a bachelor of arts in philosophy from the University of Illinois and a masters in computer science from the Illinois Institute of Technology.

When not bonding with his computer, Mark is busy with his family or playing racquetball (having suspended competing in Ironman back in 2016). Mark lives in Spokane, Washington, with his wife, Elisabeth, and three children, Benjamin, Hanna, and Abigail.

About the Technical Editor

Eric Lippert works on developer tools at Facebook; he is a former member of the C# language design team at Microsoft. When not answering C# questions on StackOverflow or editing programming books, Eric does his best to keep his tiny sailboat upright. He lives in Seattle, Washington, with his wife, Leah.

■ 1 ■
Introducing C#

C# IS NOW A WELL-ESTABLISHED LANGUAGE that builds on features found in its predecessor C-style languages (C, C++, and Java), making it immediately familiar to many experienced programmers.[1] Furthermore, the C# programming language can be used to build software components and applications that run on a wide variety of operating systems (platforms).

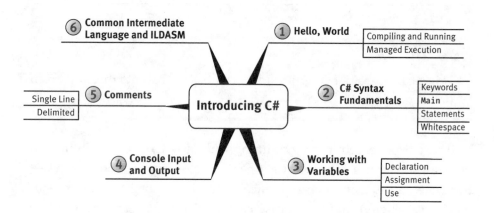

This chapter introduces C# using the traditional HelloWorld program. It focuses on C# syntax fundamentals, including defining an entry point into the C# program, which will familiarize you with the C# syntax style

---

1. The first C# design meeting took place in 1998.

and structure and enable you to produce the simplest of C# programs. Prior to the discussion of C# syntax fundamentals is a summary of managed execution context, which explains how a C# program executes at runtime. This chapter ends with a discussion of variable declaration, writing and retrieving data from the console, and the basics of commenting code in C#.

Hello, World

The best way to learn a new programming language is to write code. The first example is the classic HelloWorld program. In this program, you will display some text to the screen.

Listing 1.1 shows the complete HelloWorld program; in the following sections, you will compile and run the code.

LISTING 1.1: HelloWorld in C#[2]

```
class HelloWorld
{
 static void Main()
 {
    System.Console.WriteLine("Hello. My name is Inigo Montoya.");
 }
}
```

■ NOTE

C# is a case-sensitive language: Incorrect case prevents the code from compiling successfully.

Those experienced in programming with Java, C, or C++ will immediately see similarities. Like Java, C# inherits its basic syntax from C and C++.[3] Syntactic punctuation (such as semicolons and curly braces), features (such as case sensitivity), and keywords (such as class, public, and void) are familiar to programmers experienced in these languages. Beginners and programmers from other languages will quickly find these constructs intuitive.

---

2. Refer to the movie *The Princess Bride* if you're confused about the Inigo Montoya references.

3. When creating C#, the language creators reviewed the specifications for C/C++, literally crossing out the features they didn't like and creating a list of the ones they did like. The group also included designers with strong backgrounds in other languages.

Creating, Editing, Compiling, and Running C# Source Code

Once you have written your C# code, it is time to compile and run it. You have a choice of which .NET implementation(s) to use—sometimes referred to as the **.NET framework**(s). Generally, the implementation is packaged into a **software development kit (SDK)**. The SDK includes the compiler, the runtime execution engine, the framework of pragmatically accessible functionality that the runtime can access (see "Application Programming Interface" later in the chapter), and any additional tooling (such as a build engine for automating build steps) that might be bundled with the SDK. Given that C# has been publicly available since 2000, there are several different .NET frameworks to choose from (see "Multiple .NET Frameworks" later in the chapter).

For each .NET framework, the installation instructions vary depending on which operating system you are developing on and which .NET framework you select. For this reason, I recommend you visit https://www.microsoft.com/net/download for download and installation instructions, selecting first the .NET framework and then the package to download based on which operating system you will be developing for. While I could provide further details here, the .NET download site has the most updated instructions for each combination supported.

If you are unsure about which .NET framework to work with, choose .NET Core by default. It works on Linux, macOS, and Microsoft Windows and is the implementation where the .NET development teams are applying the majority of their investments. Furthermore, because of the cross-platform capabilities, I will favor .NET Core instructions inline within the chapters.

There are also numerous ways to edit your source code, including with the most rudimentary of tools, such as Notepad on Windows, TextEdit on Mac/macOS, or vi on Linux. However, you're likely to want something more advanced so that at least your code is colorized. Any programming editor that supports C# will suffice. If you don't already have a preference, I recommend you consider the open source editor Visual Studio Code (https://code.visualstudio.com). Or, if you are working on Windows or Mac, consider Microsoft Visual Studio 2017 (or later)—see https://www.visualstudio.com. Both are available free of charge.

In the next two sections, I provide instructions for both editors. For Visual Studio Code, we rely on the command line (Dotnet CLI) for creating the initial C# program scaffolding in addition to compiling and running the program. For Windows and Mac, we focus on using Visual Studio 2017.

With Dotnet CLI

Begin 7.0

The Dotnet command, `dotnet.exe`, is the Dotnet command-line interface, or Dotnet CLI, and it may be used to generate the initial code base for a C# program in addition to compiling and running the program. (To avoid ambiguity between CLI referring to the Common Language Infrastructure or the command-line interface, throughout the book I will prefix CLI with Dotnet when referring to the Dotnet CLI. CLI without the Dotnet prefix refers to Common Language Infrastructure.) Once you have completed the installation, verify that `dotnet` is an available command from the command prompt—thus verifying your installation.

Following are the instructions for creating, compiling, and executing the `HelloWorld` program from the command line on Windows, macOS, or Linux:

1. Open a command prompt on Microsoft Windows or the Terminal application on Mac/macOS. (Optionally, consider using the cross-platform command-line interface PowerShell.)[4]

2. Create a new directory where you would like to place the code. Consider a name such as `./HelloWorld` or `./EssentialCSharp/HelloWorld`. From the command line, use

   ```
   mkdir ./HelloWorld
   ```

3. Navigate into the new directory so that it is the command prompt's current location.

   ```
   cd ./HelloWorld
   ```

4. Execute `dotnet new console` from within the `HelloWorld` directory to generate the initial scaffolding for your program. While several files are generated, the two main files are `Program.cs` and the project file:

   ```
   dotnet new console
   ```

5. Run the generated program. This will compile and run the default `Program.cs` created by the `dotnet new console` command. The content of `Program.cs` is similar to Listing 1.1, but it outputs "Hello World!" instead.

   ```
   dotnet run
   ```

---

4. https://github.com/PowerShell/PowerShell

Even though we don't explicitly request the application to compile (or build), that step still occurs because it is invoked implicitly when the `dotnet run` command is executed.

6. Edit the `Program.cs` file and modify the code to match what is shown in Listing 1.1. If you use Visual Studio Code to open and edit `Program.cs`, you will see the advantage of a C#-aware editor, as the code will be colorized indicating the different types of constructs in your program. (Output 1.1 shows an approach using the command line that works for Bash and PowerShell.)

7. Rerun the program:

```
dotnet.exe run
```

Output 1.1 shows the output following the preceding steps.[5]

OUTPUT 1.1

```
1>
2> mkdir ./HelloWorld
3> cd ./HelloWorld/
4> dotnet new console
The template "Console Application" was created successfully.

Processing post-creation actions...
Running 'dotnet restore' on ...\EssentialCSharp\HelloWorld\
↳HelloWorld.csproj...
  Restoring packages for ...\EssentialCSharp\HelloWorld\
↳HelloWorld.csproj...
  Generating MSBuild file ...\EssentialCSharp\HelloWorld\obj\
↳HelloWorld.csproj.nuget.g.props.
  Generating MSBuild file ...\EssentialCSharp\HelloWorld\obj\
↳HelloWorld.csproj.nuget.g.targets.
  Restore completed in 184.46 ms for ...\EssentialCSharp\
↳HelloWorld\HelloWorld.csproj.

Restore succeeded.
5> dotnet run
Hello World!
6> echo '
class HelloWorld
{
  static void Main()
  {
    System.Console.WriteLine("Hello. My name is Inigo Montoya.");
  }
}
' > Program.cs
7> dotnet run
Hello. My name is Inigo Montoya.
8>
```

End 7.0

---

5. The bold formatting in an Output indicates the user-entered content.

With Visual Studio 2017

With Visual Studio 2017, the procedure is similar, but instead of using the command line, you use an **integrated development environment (IDE)**, which has menus you can choose from rather than executing everything from the command line:

1. Launch Visual Studio 2017.
2. Open the New Project dialog using the **File->New Project** (Ctrl+Shift+N) menu.
3. From the **Search box** (Ctrl+E), type *Console App* and select the **Console App (.NET Core)—Visual C#** item. For the **Name** text box, use *HelloWorld*, and for the **Location**, select a working directory of your choosing. See Figure 1.1.

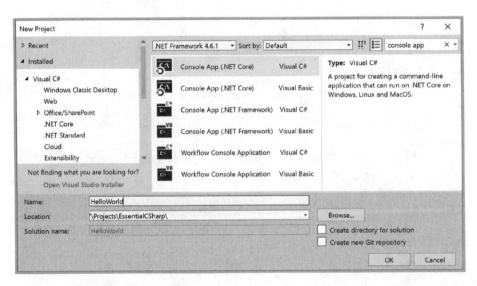

FIGURE 1.1: The New Project Dialog

4. Once the project is created, you should see a `Program.cs` file, as shown in Figure 1.2.
5. Run the generated program using the **Debug->Start Without Debugging** (Ctrl+F5) menu. This will display the command window with the text shown in Output 1.2 except the first line will display only "Hello World!".

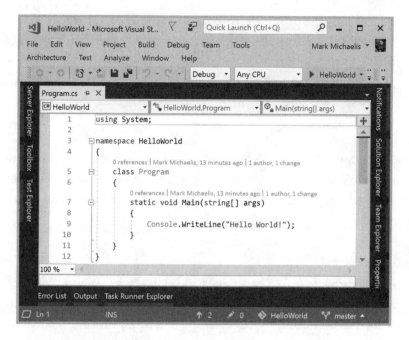

FIGURE 1.2: Dialog That Shows the Program.cs File

6. Modify Program.cs to match Listing 1.1.

7. Rerun the program to see the output shown in Output 1.2.

OUTPUT 1.2

```
> Hello. My name is Inigo Montoya.
Press any key to continue . . .
```

One significant feature of using an IDE is its support for debugging. To try it out, follow these additional steps:

8. Locate your cursor on the System.Console.WriteLine line and click the **Debug->Toggle Breakpoint** menu item to activate a breakpoint on that line.

9. Click the **Debug->Start Debugging** menu to relaunch the application but this time with debugging activated. Note that it will stop execution on the line where you set the breakpoint. You can then hover over a variable (e.g., args) to see its value. You can also move the current

execution of the program from the current line to another line within the method by dragging the yellow arrow in the left margin of the file window.

10. To continue the program execution, use the **Debug->Continue** (Ctrl+F5) menu (or the **Continue** button).

When debugging, you no longer see the "Press any key to continue…" text in the output window. Instead, the console window automatically closes.

Note that Visual Studio Code can also be used as an IDE, as described at https://code.visualstudio.com/docs/languages/csharp—which includes a link for debugging using Visual Studio Code.

Creating a Project

Whether using Dotnet CLI or Visual Studio, there are several files created. The first file is a C# file with the name `Program.cs` by convention. The name *Program* is commonly used as the starting point for a console program even though any name could be used. The `.cs` extension is the standard convention for all C# files and what the compiler expects to compile into the final program by default. To use the code shown in Listing 1.1, open the `Program.cs` file and replace its content with Listing 1.1. Before saving the updated file, observe that the only functional difference between Listing 1.1 and what was generated by default is the text within quotations and a semantic difference of where *System* appears.

While not necessarily required, typically a configuration file called a **project file** is included as part of the generated source code of your C# project. The project file content will vary from one application type and .NET framework to the next. However, at a minimum, it generally identifies what files to include in the compilation, what application type to build (console, Web, mobile, testing project, etc.), which .NET framework to support, potential settings needed to debug or launch the application, along with other dependencies the code may rely on (called *libraries*). For example, a simple .NET Core console application project file appears in Listing 1.2.

LISTING 1.2: Sample .NET Core Console Project File

```
<Project Sdk="Microsoft.NET.Sdk">
  <PropertyGroup>
    <OutputType>Exe</OutputType>
```

```
    <TargetFramework>netcoreapp2.0</TargetFramework>
  </PropertyGroup>
</Project>
```

In Listing 1.2, the application type is identified as a .NET Core version 2.0 (`netcoreapp2.0`) console application (`Exe`). All other settings (such as which C# files to compile) are identified by convention. For example, by default, all `*.cs` files in the same directory (or subdirectory) as the project file are included in the compile. We delve into more details on a project file in Chapter 10.

Compilation and Execution

Begin 7.0

The compiled output created by the `dotnet build` command is an **assembly** called `HelloWorld.dll`.[6] The extension stands for dynamic link library (DLL), and with .NET Core, all assemblies have a .dll extension even if they are console programs, as this one is. By default, the compiled output for a .NET Core application is placed into a subdirectory (`./bin/Debug/netcoreapp2.0/`). The `Debug` directory is used because the default configuration is debug. This configuration causes the output to be optimized for debugging rather than for optimal performance. The compiled output will not execute on its own. Rather, it needs the CLI to host the code. For .NET Core applications, this requires using the `Dotnet.exe` process as a host process for the application.

Instead of creating a console program that can be executed directly using `dotnet run`, developers can create a library of code that can be referenced by another, larger program. A library is also an assembly. In other words, the output from a successful C# compile is an assembly regardless of whether it is a program or a library.

End 7.0

Begin 2.0

Language Contrast: Java—Filename Must Match Class Name

In Java, the filename must follow the name of the class. In C#, this convention is frequently followed but is not required. In C#, it is possible to have two classes in one file, and starting with C# 2.0, it's possible to have a single class span multiple files with a feature called a partial class.

End 2.0

---

6. Note that if you use the Microsoft .NET Framework to create a console program, the compiled code is placed into a HelloWorld.exe file that you can execute directly assuming the Microsoft .NET Framework is installed on the computer.

Essential C# Source Code

The source code[7] associated with the book includes a solution file, EssentialCSharp.sln, which groups together the code from all the chapters. Building, running, and testing the source code is possible with either Visual Studio or Dotnet.exe.

Perhaps the simplest approach is to pass the source code into the HelloWorld program created earlier in the chapter and then execute the source code. Alternatively, the source code contains project files for each chapter and a menu from which it is possible to select which listing to run when executing a program, as shown in the next two sections.

With Dotnet CLI

Begin 7.0

To build and execute the code using the Dotnet CLI, open a command prompt with the current directory set to the same directory as the EssentialCSharp.sln file. From there, use the dotnet build command to compile all the projects.

To run the source code for a particular project, navigate to the directory containing the project file and run the dotnet run command. Alternatively, from any directory, use the dotnet run -p <projectfile> command where the project file is the path to the project file you are trying to execute (e.g., dotnet run -p .\src\Chapter01\Chapter01.csproj). Once executing, the program will prompt for which listing to execute and then proceed with that listing.

Many of the listings have corresponding unit tests in the Chapter[??] .Tests directory where [??] indicates the chapter number. To execute the tests, use the dotnet test command from the project tests directory of the test you are looking execute (or the same command from the

End 7.0

EssentialCSharp.sln file directory to execute them all).

With Visual Studio

After opening the solution file, use the **Build->Build Solution** menu to compile the code with Visual Studio. Before you can execute the source

---

7. The source code available for this book (along with some chapters related to earlier versions of C#) is available for download at https://IntelliTect.com/EssentialCSharp. You can also download the code from GitHub directly at https://github.com/IntelliTect/ EssentialCSharp.

code, you need to select which project to execute by selecting the associated chapter's project as the startup project. For example, to execute the samples in Chapter 1, you would right-click on the **Chapter01** project and choose **Set As Startup Project**. Failure to choose the correct chapter will result in an exception with the message "Error, could not run the Listing…" when you specify the listing number at execution time.

Once you have selected the correct project, you can run the project from the **Debug->Start Without Debugging** menu. Alternatively, if you wish to debug the project, you can use **Debug->Start Debugging**. Once running, the program will prompt for the listing (e.g., 18.33) that you wish to execute. As mentioned earlier, you can enter only listings from the project that was set to start up.

Many of the listings have corresponding unit tests. To execute a test, open the test project and navigate to the test corresponding to the listing you wish to execute. From there, right-click on the test method and choose either **Run Tests** (Ctrl+R, T) or **Debug Tests** (Ctrl+R, Ctrl+T).

C# Syntax Fundamentals

Once you successfully compile and run the `HelloWorld` program, you are ready to start dissecting the code to learn its individual parts. First, consider the C# keywords along with the identifiers that the developer chooses.

■ BEGINNER TOPIC

Keywords

To enable the compiler to interpret the code, certain words within C# have special status and meaning. Known as **keywords**, they provide the concrete syntax that the compiler uses to interpret the expressions the programmer writes. In the `HelloWorld` program, `class`, `static`, and `void` are examples of keywords.

The compiler uses the keywords to identify the structure and organization of the code. Because the compiler interprets these words with elevated significance, C# requires that developers place keywords only in certain locations. When programmers violate these rules, the compiler will issue errors.

C# Keywords

Table 1.1 shows the C# keywords.

TABLE 1.1: C# Keywords

abstract	enum	long	static
add* (1)	equals* (3)	nameof* (6)	string
alias* (2)	event	namespace	struct
as	explicit	new	switch
ascending* (3)	extern	null	this
async* (5)	false	object	throw
await* (5)	finally	on* (3)	true
base	fixed	operator	try
bool	float	orderby* (3)	typeof
break	for	out	uint
by* (3)	foreach	override	ulong
byte	from* (3)	params	unchecked
case	get* (1)	partial* (2)	unsafe
catch	global* (2)	private	ushort
char	goto	protected	using
checked	group* (3)	public	value* (1)
class	if	readonly	var* (3)
const	implicit	ref	virtual
continue	in	remove* (1)	void
decimal	int	return	volatile
default	interface	sbyte	where* (2)
delegate	internal	sealed	when* (6)
descending* (3)	into* (3)	select* (3)	while
do	is	set* (1)	yield* (2)
double	join* (3)	short	
dynamic* (4)	let* (3)	sizeof	
else	lock	stackalloc	

* Contextual keyword. Numbers in parentheses (*n*) identify in which version the contextual keyword was added.

Begin 2.0

Begin 3.0

Begin 4.0

Begin 5.0

Begin 6.0

End 2.0

End 3.0

End 4.0

End 5.0

End 6.0

After C# 1.0, no new **reserved keywords** were introduced to C#. However, some constructs in later versions use **contextual keywords**, which are significant only in specific locations. Outside these designated locations, contextual keywords have no special significance.[8] By this method, most C# 1.0 code is compatible with the later standards.[9]

Begin 2.0

End 2.0

Identifiers

Like other languages, C# includes **identifiers** to identify constructs that the programmer codes. In Listing 1.1, `HelloWorld` and `Main` are examples of identifiers. The identifiers assigned to a construct are used to refer to the construct later, so it is important that the names the developer assigns are meaningful rather than arbitrary.

A keen ability to select succinct and indicative names is an important characteristic of a strong programmer because it means the resultant code will be easier to understand and reuse. Clarity coupled with consistency is important enough that the Framework Design Guidelines (http://bit.ly/dotnetguidelines) advise against the use of abbreviations or contractions in identifier names and even recommend avoiding acronyms that are not widely accepted. If an acronym is sufficiently well established (e.g., HTML), you should use it consistently: Avoid spelling out the accepted acronym in some cases but not in others. Generally, adding the constraint that all acronyms be included in a glossary of terms places enough overhead on the use of acronyms that they are not used flippantly. Ultimately, select clear, possibly even verbose names—especially when working on a team or when developing a library against which others will program.

---

8. For example, early in the design of C# 2.0, the language designers designated `yield` as a keyword, and Microsoft released alpha versions of the C# 2.0 compiler, with `yield` as a designated keyword, to thousands of developers. However, the language designers eventually determined that by using `yield return` rather than `yield`, they could ultimately avoid adding `yield` as a keyword because it would have no special significance outside its proximity to `return`.

9. There are some rare and unfortunate incompatibilities, such as the following:
   - C# 2.0 requires implementation of `IDisposable` with the `using` statement rather than simply using a `Dispose()` method.
   - Some rare generic expressions are different between versions. For example, F(G<A,B>(7)) means F((G<A), (B>7)) in C# 1.0, but in C# 2.0, it means to call generic method G<A,B> with argument 7 and pass the result to F.

There are two basic casing formats for an identifier. **Pascal case** (henceforth PascalCase), as the .NET framework creators refer to it because of its popularity in the Pascal programming language, capitalizes the first letter of each word in an identifier name; examples include `ComponentModel`, `Configuration`, and `HttpFileCollection`. As `HttpFileCollection` demonstrates with HTTP, when using acronyms that are more than two letters long, only the first letter is capitalized. The second format, camel case (henceforth camelCase), follows the same convention except that the first letter is lowercase; examples include `quotient`, `firstName`, `httpFileCollection`, `ioStream`, and `theDreadPirateRoberts`.

Guidelines

DO favor clarity over brevity when naming identifiers.

DO NOT use abbreviations or contractions within identifier names.

DO NOT use any acronyms unless they are widely accepted, and even then, only when necessary.

Notice that although underscores are legal, generally there are no underscores, hyphens, or other nonalphanumeric characters in identifier names. Furthermore, C# doesn't follow its predecessors in that Hungarian notation (prefixing a name with a data type abbreviation) is not used. This convention avoids the variable rename that is necessary when data types change or the inconsistency introduced due to failure to adjust the data type prefix when using Hungarian notation.

In rare cases, some identifiers, such as `Main`, can have a special meaning in the C# language.

Guidelines

DO capitalize both characters in two-character acronyms, except for the first word of a camelCased identifier.

DO capitalize only the first character in acronyms with three or more characters, except for the first word of a camelCased identifier.

DO NOT capitalize any of the characters in acronyms at the beginning of a camelCased identifier.

DO NOT use Hungarian notation (that is, do not encode the type of a variable in its name).

■**ADVANCED TOPIC**

Keywords

Although it is rare, keywords may be used as identifiers if they include @ as a prefix. For example, you could name a local variable @return. Similarly (although it doesn't conform to the casing standards of C# coding standards), it is possible to name a method @throw( ).

There are also four undocumented reserved keywords in the Microsoft implementation: __arglist, __makeref, __reftype, and __refvalue. These are required only in rare interop scenarios, and you can ignore them for all practical purposes. Note that these four special keywords begin with two underscores. The designers of C# reserve the right to make any identifier that begins with two underscores into a keyword in a future version; for safety, avoid ever creating such an identifier yourself.

Type Definition

All executable code in C# appears within a type definition, and the most common type definition begins with the keyword class. A **class definition** is the section of code that generally begins with class identifier { ... }, as shown in Listing 1.3.

LISTING 1.3: Basic Class Declaration

```
class HelloWorld
{
  //...
}
```

The name used for the type (in this case, HelloWorld) can vary, but by convention, it must be PascalCased. For this particular example, therefore, other possible names are Greetings, HelloInigoMontoya, Hello, or simply Program. (Program is a good convention to follow when the class contains the Main( ) method, described next.)

> ### Guidelines
>
> **DO** name classes with nouns or noun phrases.
> **DO** use PascalCasing for all class names.

Generally, programs contain multiple types, each containing multiple methods.

Main Method

▪ **BEGINNER TOPIC**

What Is a Method?

Syntactically, a **method** in C# is a named block of code introduced by a method declaration (e.g., `static void Main()`) and (usually) followed by zero or more statements within curly braces. Methods perform computations and/or actions. Similar to paragraphs in written languages, methods provide a means of structuring and organizing code so that it is more readable. More important, methods can be reused and called from multiple places and so avoid the need to duplicate code. The method declaration introduces the method and defines the method name along with the data passed to and from the method. In Listing 1.4, `Main()` followed by { ... } is an example of a C# method.

The location where C# programs begin execution is the `Main` **method**, which begins with `static void Main()`. When you execute the program by typing `HelloWorld.exe` at the command console, the program starts up, resolves the location of `Main`, and begins executing the first statement within Listing 1.4.

LISTING 1.4: Breaking Apart HelloWorld

```
class HelloWorld
{
    static void Main()  } Method Declaration
    {
        System.Console.WriteLine("Hello, My name is Inigo Montoya");
    }                                         Statement
}
```

Although the `Main` method declaration can vary to some degree, `static` and the method name, `Main`, are always required for a program.

▪ **ADVANCED TOPIC**

Declaration of the `Main` Method

C# requires that the `Main` method return either `void` or `int` and that it take either no parameters or a single array of strings. Listing 1.5 shows the full declaration of the `Main` method.

LISTING 1.5: The Main Method with Parameters and a Return

```
static int Main(string[] args)
{
    //...
}
```

The args parameter is an array of strings corresponding to the command-line arguments. However, the first element of the array is not the program name but the first command-line parameter to appear after the executable name, unlike in C and C++. To retrieve the full command used to execute the program, use System.Environment.CommandLine.

The int returned from Main is the status code, and it indicates the success of the program's execution. A return of a nonzero value generally indicates an error.

Language Contrast: C++/Java—main( ) Is All Lowercase

Unlike its C-style predecessors, C# uses an uppercase *M* for the Main method to be consistent with the PascalCased naming conventions of C#.

The designation of the Main method as static indicates that other methods may call it directly off the class definition. Without the static designation, the command console that started the program would need to perform additional work (known as **instantiation**) before calling the method. (Chapter 6 contains an entire section devoted to the topic of static members.)

Placing void prior to Main( ) indicates that this method does not return any data. (This is explained further in Chapter 2.)

One distinctive C/C++-style characteristic followed by C# is the use of curly braces for the body of a construct, such as the class or the method. For example, the Main method contains curly braces that surround its implementation; in this case, only one statement appears in the method.

Statements and Statement Delimiters

The Main method includes a single statement, System.Console .WriteLine( ), which is used to write a line of text to the console. C# generally uses a semicolon to indicate the end of a **statement**, where a statement comprises one or more actions that the code will perform. Declaring a variable, controlling the program flow, and calling a method are typical uses of statements.

Language Contrast: Visual Basic—Line-Based Statements

Some languages are line based, meaning that without a special annotation, statements cannot span a line. Until Visual Basic 2010, Visual Basic was an example of a line-based language. It required an underscore at the end of a line to indicate that a statement spans multiple lines. Starting with Visual Basic 2010, many cases were introduced where the line continuation character was optional.

■ ADVANCED TOPIC

Statements without Semicolons

Many programming elements in C# end with a semicolon. One example that does not include the semicolon is a `switch` statement. Because curly braces are always included in a `switch` statement, C# does not require a semicolon following the statement. In fact, code blocks themselves are considered statements (they are also composed of statements), and they don't require closure using a semicolon. Similarly, there are cases, such as the `using` declarative, in which a semicolon occurs at the end but it is not a statement.

Since creation of a newline does not separate statements, you can place multiple statements on the same line and the C# compiler will interpret the line as having multiple instructions. For example, Listing 1.6 contains two statements on a single line that, in combination, display Up and Down on two separate lines.

LISTING 1.6: Multiple Statements on One Line

```
System.Console.WriteLine("Up");System.Console.WriteLine("Down");
```

C# also allows the splitting of a statement across multiple lines. Again, the C# compiler looks for a semicolon to indicate the end of a statement (see Listing 1.7).

LISTING 1.7: Splitting a Single Statement across Multiple Lines

```
System.Console.WriteLine(
    "Hello. My name is Inigo Montoya.");
```

In Listing 1.7, the original `WriteLine()` statement from the `HelloWorld` program is split across multiple lines.

■ **BEGINNER TOPIC**

What Is Whitespace?

Whitespace is the combination of one or more consecutive formatting characters such as tab, space, and newline characters. Eliminating all whitespace between words is obviously significant, as is including whitespace within a quoted string.

Whitespace

The semicolon makes it possible for the C# compiler to ignore whitespace in code. Apart from a few exceptions, C# allows developers to insert whitespace throughout the code without altering its semantic meaning. In Listings 1.6 and 1.7, it didn't matter whether a newline was inserted within a statement or between statements, and doing so had no effect on the resultant executable created by the compiler.

Frequently, programmers use whitespace to indent code for greater readability. Consider the two variations on `HelloWorld` shown in Listings 1.8 and 1.9.

LISTING 1.8: No Indentation Formatting

```csharp
class HelloWorld
{
static void Main()
{
System.Console.WriteLine("Hello Inigo Montoya");
}
}
```

LISTING 1.9: Removing Whitespace

```csharp
class HelloWorld{static void Main()
{System.Console.WriteLine("Hello Inigo Montoya");}}
```

Although these two examples look significantly different from the original program, the C# compiler sees them as identical.

■ **BEGINNER TOPIC**

Formatting Code with Whitespace

Indenting the code using whitespace is important for greater readability. As you begin writing code, you need to follow established coding standards and conventions to enhance code readability.

The convention used in this book is to place curly braces on their own line and to indent the code contained between the curly brace pair. If another curly brace pair appears within the first pair, all the code within the second set of braces is also indented.

This is not a uniform C# standard but a stylistic preference.

Working with Variables

Now that you've been introduced to the most basic C# program, it's time to declare a local variable. Once a variable is declared, you can assign it a value, replace that value with a new value, and use it in calculations, output, and so on. However, you cannot change the data type of the variable. In Listing 1.10, `string max` is a variable declaration.

LISTING 1.10: Declaring and Assigning a Variable

```
class miracleMax
{
  static void Main()
  {
        Data Type
        ‾‾‾‾‾‾
        string max;
              ⎵‾‾‾
              Variable
      max = "Have fun storming the castle!";
      System.Console.WriteLine(max);
  }
}
```

■ **BEGINNER TOPIC**

Local Variables

A **variable** is a name that refers to a value that can change over time. *Local* indicates that the programmer **declared** the variable within a method.

To declare a variable is to define it, which you do by

- Specifying the type of data which the variable will contain
- Assigning it an identifier (name)

Data Types

Listing 1.10 declares a variable with the data type `string`. Other common data types used in this chapter are `int` and `char`.

- `int` is the C# designation of an integer type that is 32 bits in size.
- `char` is used for a character type. It is 16 bits, large enough for (non-surrogate) Unicode characters.

The next chapter looks at these and other common data types in more detail.

■ BEGINNER TOPIC

What Is a Data Type?

The type of data that a variable declaration specifies is called a **data type** (or object type). A data type, or simply **type**, is a classification of things that share similar characteristics and behavior. For example, *animal* is a type. It classifies all things (monkeys, warthogs, and platypuses) that have animal characteristics (multicellular, capacity for locomotion, and so on). Similarly, in programming languages, a type is a definition for several items endowed with similar qualities.

Declaring a Variable

In Listing 1.10, `string max` is a variable declaration of a string type whose name is `max`. It is possible to declare multiple variables within the same statement by specifying the data type once and separating each identifier with a comma. Listing 1.11 demonstrates such a declaration.

LISTING 1.11: Declaring Two Variables within One Statement

```
string message1, message2;
```

Because a multivariable declaration statement allows developers to provide the data type only once within a declaration, all variables will be of the same type.

In C#, the name of the variable may begin with any letter or an underscore (_), followed by any number of letters, numbers, and/or underscores. By convention, however, local variable names are camelCased (the first letter in each word is capitalized, except for the first word) and do not include underscores.

Guidelines

DO use camelCasing for local variable names.

Assigning a Variable

After declaring a local variable, you must assign it a value before reading from it. One way to do this is to use the = **operator**, also known as the **simple assignment operator**. Operators are symbols used to identify the function the code is to perform. Listing 1.12 demonstrates how to use the assignment operator to designate the string values to which the variables miracleMax and valerie will point.

LISTING 1.12: Changing the Value of a Variable

```csharp
class StormingTheCastle
{
  static void Main()
  {
      string valerie;
      string miracleMax = "Have fun storming the castle!";

      valerie = "Think it will work?";

      System.Console.WriteLine(miracleMax);
      System.Console.WriteLine(valerie);

      miracleMax = "It would take a miracle.";
      System.Console.WriteLine(miracleMax);
  }
}
```

From this listing, observe that it is possible to assign a variable as part of the variable declaration (as it was for miracleMax) or afterward in a separate statement (as with the variable valerie). The value assigned must always be on the right side of the declaration.

Running the compiled program produces the code shown in Output 1.3.

OUTPUT 1.3

```
>dotnet run
Have fun storming the castle!
Think it will work?
It would take a miracle.
```

In this example, we show the command dotnet run explicitly. In future output listings, we will omit this line unless there is something special about the command used to execute the program.

C# requires that local variables be determined by the compiler to be "definitely assigned" before they are read. Additionally, an assignment results in a value. Therefore, C# allows two assignments within the same statement, as demonstrated in Listing 1.13.

LISTING 1.13: Assignment Returning a Value That Can Be Assigned Again

```csharp
class StormingTheCastle
{
  static void Main()
  {
    // ...
    string requirements, miracleMax;
    requirements = miracleMax = "It would take a miracle.";
    // ...
  }
}
```

Using a Variable

The result of the assignment, of course, is that you can then refer to the value using the variable identifier. Therefore, when you use the variable miracleMax within the System.Console.WriteLine(miracleMax) statement, the program displays Have fun storming the castle!, the value of miracleMax, on the console. Changing the value of miracleMax and executing the same System.Console.WriteLine(miracleMax) statement causes the new miracleMax value, It would take a miracle., to be displayed.

■ADVANCED TOPIC

Strings Are Immutable

All values of type string, whether string literals or otherwise, are immutable (or unmodifiable). For example, it is not possible to change the string Come As You Are. to Come As You Age. A change such as this requires that you reassign the variable instead of modifying the data to which the variable originally referred.

Console Input and Output

This chapter already used System.Console.WriteLine repeatedly for writing out text to the command console. In addition to being able to write out data, a program needs to be able to accept data that a user may enter.

Getting Input from the Console

One way to retrieve text that is entered at the console is to use System.Console.ReadLine(). This method stops the program execution so that the user can enter characters. When the user presses the Enter key, creating a newline, the program continues. The output, also known as the **return**, from the System.Console.ReadLine() method is the string of text that was entered. Consider Listing 1.14 and the corresponding output shown in Output 1.4.

LISTING 1.14: Using System.Console.ReadLine()

```
class HeyYou
{
  static void Main()
  {
      string firstName;
      string lastName;

      System.Console.WriteLine("Hey you!");

      System.Console.Write("Enter your first name: ");
      firstName = System.Console.ReadLine();

      System.Console.Write("Enter your last name: ");
      lastName = System.Console.ReadLine();
  }
}
```

```
Hey you!
Enter your first name: Inigo
Enter your last name: Montoya
```

After each prompt, this program uses the System.Console.ReadLine()
method to retrieve the text the user entered and assign it to an appropriate variable. By the time the second System.Console.ReadLine() assignment completes, firstName refers to the value Inigo and lastName refers
to the value Montoya.

■ ADVANCED TOPIC

System.Console.Read()

In addition to the System.Console.ReadLine() method, there is a
System.Console.Read() method. However, the data type returned by
the System.Console.Read() method is an integer corresponding to the
character value read, or −1 if no more characters are available. To retrieve
the actual character, it is necessary to first cast the integer to a character, as
shown in Listing 1.15.

LISTING 1.15: Using System.Console.Read()

```
int readValue;
char character;
readValue = System.Console.Read();
character = (char) readValue;
System.Console.Write(character);
```

The System.Console.Read() method does not return the input until
the user presses the Enter key; no processing of characters will begin, even
if the user types multiple characters before pressing the Enter key.

In C# 2.0 and above, you can use System.Console.ReadKey(), which,
in contrast to System.Console.Read(), returns the input after a single
keystroke. It allows the developer to intercept the keystroke and perform
actions such as key validation, restricting the characters to numerics.

Begin 2.0

End 2.0

Writing Output to the Console

In Listing 1.14, you prompt the user for his or her first and last names using the method System.Console.Write() rather than System .Console.WriteLine(). Instead of placing a newline character after displaying the text, the System.Console.Write() method leaves the current position on the same line. In this way, any text the user enters will be on the same line as the prompt for input. The output from Listing 1.14 demonstrates the effect of System.Console.Write().

Begin 6.0

The next step is to write the values retrieved using System.Console .ReadLine() back to the console. In the case of Listing 1.16, the program writes out the user's full name. However, instead of using System .Console.WriteLine() as before, this code uses a slight variation that leverages a C# 6.0 feature known as **string interpolation**. Notice the dollar sign preceding the string literal in the call to Console.WriteLine; it indicates that string interpolation will be used. Output 1.5 shows the corresponding output.

LISTING 1.16: Formatting Using String Interpolation

```
class HeyYou
{
  static void Main()
  {
      string firstName;
      string lastName;

      System.Console.WriteLine("Hey you!");

      System.Console.Write("Enter your first name: ");
      firstName = System.Console.ReadLine();

      System.Console.Write("Enter your last name: ");
      lastName = System.Console.ReadLine();

      System.Console.WriteLine(
          $"Your full name is { firstName } { lastName }.");
  }
}
```

OUTPUT 1.5

```
Hey you!
Enter your first name: Inigo
Enter your last name: Montoya
Your full name is Inigo Montoya.
```

Instead of writing out "Your full name is" followed by another `Write` statement for `firstName`, a third `Write` statement for the space, and finally a `WriteLine` statement for `lastName`, Listing 1.16 writes out the entire output using C# 6.0's string interpolation. With string interpolation, the compiler interprets the interior of the curly brackets within the string as regions in which you can embed code (expressions) that the compiler will evaluate and convert to strings. Rather than executing lots of code snippets individually and combining the results as a string at the end, string interpolation allows you to do this in a single step. This makes the code easier to understand.

End 6.0

Prior to C# 6.0, C# used a different approach, that of **composite formatting**. With composite formatting, the code first supplies a **format string** to define the output format—see Listing 1.17.

LISTING 1.17: Formatting Using System.Console.WriteLine( )'s Composite Formatting

```csharp
class HeyYou
{
  static void Main()
  {
    string firstName;
    string lastName;

    System.Console.WriteLine("Hey you!");

    System.Console.Write("Enter your first name: ");
    firstName = System.Console.ReadLine();

    System.Console.Write("Enter your last name: ");
    lastName = System.Console.ReadLine();

    System.Console.WriteLine(
      "Your full name is {0} {1}.", firstName, lastName);
  }
}
```

In this example, the format string is `Your full name is {0} {1}`. It identifies two indexed placeholders for data insertion in the string. Each placeholder corresponds to the order of the arguments that appear after the format string.

Note that the index value begins at zero. Each inserted argument (known as a **format item**) appears after the format string in the order corresponding to the index value. In this example, since `firstName` is the first argument to follow immediately after the format string, it corresponds to index value 0. Similarly, lastName corresponds to index value 1.

Note that the placeholders within the format string need not appear in order. For example, Listing 1.18 switches the order of the indexed placeholders and adds a comma, which changes the way the name is displayed (see Output 1.6).

LISTING 1.18: Swapping the Indexed Placeholders and Corresponding Variables

```
System.Console.WriteLine("Your full name is {1}, {0}",
    firstName, lastName);
```

OUTPUT 1.6

```
Hey you!
Enter your first name: Inigo
Enter your last name: Montoya
Your full name is Montoya, Inigo
```

In addition to not having the placeholders appear consecutively within the format string, it is possible to use the same placeholder multiple times within a format string. Furthermore, it is possible to omit a placeholder. It is not possible, however, to have placeholders that do not have a corresponding argument.

■ **NOTE**

Since C# 6.0-style string interpolation is almost always easier to understand than the alternative composite string approach, throughout the remainder of the book we use string interpolation by default.

Comments

In this section, we modify the program in Listing 1.17 by adding comments. In no way does this modification change the execution of the program; rather, providing comments within the code can simply make the code more understandable in areas where it isn't inherently clear. Listing 1.19 shows the new code, and Output 1.7 shows the corresponding output.

LISTING 1.19: Commenting Your Code

```
class Comment Samples
{
  static void Main()
  {
                                    Single-Line Comment
                          ┌──────────────────────────┴──────────┐
    string firstName; //Variable for storing the first name
    string lastName;  //Variable for storing the last name

    System.Console.WriteLine("Hey you!");
                      Delimited Comment Inside Statement
                      ┌──────────┴──────────┐
    System.Console.Write /* No new line */ (
        "Enter your first name: ");
    firstName = System.Console.ReadLine();

    System.Console.Write /* No new line */ (
        "Enter your last name: ");
    lastName = System.Console.ReadLine();

    /* Display a greeting to the console ⎫
       using composite formatting. */     ⎬ Delimited Comment
                                          ⎭
    System.Console.WriteLine("Your full name is {0} {1}.",
        firstName, lastName);
    // This is the end
    // of the program listing
  }
}
```

OUTPUT 1.7

```
Hey you!
Enter your first name: Inigo
Enter your last name: Montoya
Your full name is Inigo Montoya.
```

In spite of the inserted comments, compiling and executing the new program produces the same output as before.

Programmers use comments to describe and explain the code they are writing, especially where the syntax itself is difficult to understand, or perhaps a particular algorithm implementation is surprising. Since comments are pertinent only to the programmer reviewing the code, the compiler ignores comments and generates an assembly that is devoid of any trace that comments were part of the original source code.

Table 1.2 shows four different C# comment types. The program in Listing 1.18 includes two of these.

TABLE 1.2: C# Comment Types

Begin 2.0

Comment Type	Description	Example
Delimited comments	A forward slash followed by an asterisk, /*, identifies the beginning of a delimited comment. To end the comment, use an asterisk followed by a forward slash: */. Comments of this form may span multiple lines in the code file or appear embedded within a line of code. The asterisks that appear at the beginning of the lines but within the delimiters are simply for formatting.	`/*comment*/`
Single-line comments	Comments may be declared with a delimiter comprising two consecutive forward slash characters: //. The compiler treats all text from the delimiter to the end of the line as a comment. Comments of this form are considered a single line. It is possible, however, to place sequential single-line comments one after another, as is the case with the last comment in Listing 1.18.	`//comment`
XML delimited comments	Comments that begin with /** and end with **/ are called *XML delimited comments*. They have the same characteristics as regular delimited comments, except that instead of ignoring XML comments entirely, the compiler can place them into a separate text file.[†]	`/**comment**/`
XML single-line comments	XML single-line comments begin with /// and continue to the end of the line. In addition, the compiler can save single-line comments into a separate file with the XML delimited comments.	`///comment`

End 2.0

† XML delimited comments were explicitly added only in C# 2.0, but the syntax is compatible with C# 1.0.

A more comprehensive discussion of the XML comments appears in Chapter 10, where we further discuss the various XML tags.

There was a period in programming history when a prolific set of comments implied a disciplined and experienced programmer. This is no longer the case. Instead, code that is readable without comments is more valuable than that which requires comments to clarify what it does. If developers find it necessary to enter comments to clarify what a particular code block is doing, they should favor rewriting the code more clearly over commenting it. Writing comments that simply repeat what the code clearly shows serves only to clutter the code, decrease its readability, and increase the likelihood of the comments going out of date because the code changes without the comments getting updated.

Guidelines

DO NOT use comments unless they describe something that is not obvious to someone other than the developer who wrote the code.

DO favor writing clearer code over entering comments to clarify a complicated algorithm.

■BEGINNER TOPIC

Extensible Markup Language

The Extensible Markup Language (XML) is a simple and flexible text format frequently used within Web applications and for exchanging data between applications. XML is extensible because included within an XML document is information that describes the data, known as **metadata**. Here is a sample XML file:

```xml
<?xml version="1.0" encoding="utf-8" ?>
<body>
  <book title="Essential C# 7.0">
      <chapters>
          <chapter title="Introducing C#"/>
          <chapter title="Data Types"/>
          ...
      </chapters>
  </book>
</body>
```

The file starts with a header indicating the version and character encoding of the XML file. After that appears one main "book" element. Elements begin with a word in angle brackets, such as <body>. To end an element, place the same word in angle brackets and add a forward slash to prefix the word, as in </body>. In addition to elements, XML supports attributes. title="Essential C# 7.0" is an example of an XML attribute. Note that the metadata (book title, chapter, and so on) describing the data ("Essential C# 7.0," "Data Types") is included in the XML file. This can result in rather bloated files, but it offers the advantage that the data includes a description to aid in interpreting it.

Managed Execution and the Common Language Infrastructure

The processor cannot directly interpret an assembly. Assemblies consist mainly of a second language known as **Common Intermediate Language (CIL)**, or **IL** for short.[10] The C# compiler transforms the C# source file into this intermediate language. An additional step, usually performed at execution time, is required to change the CIL code into **machine code** that the processor can understand. This involves an important element in the execution of a C# program: the **Virtual Execution System (VES)**. The VES, also casually referred to as the **runtime,** compiles CIL code as needed (a process known as **just-in-time** compilation or **jitting**). The code that executes under the context of an agent such as the runtime is termed **managed code**, and the process of executing under control of the runtime is called **managed execution**. The code is "managed" because the runtime controls significant portions of the program's behavior by managing aspects such as memory allocation, security, and just-in-time compilation. Code that does not require the runtime to execute is called **native code** (or **unmanaged code**).

The specification for a runtime is included in a broader specification known as the **Common Language Infrastructure (CLI)** specification.[11] An international standard, the CLI includes specifications for the following:

- The VES or runtime
- The CIL
- A type system that supports language interoperability, known as the **Common Type System (CTS)**

---

10. A third term for CIL is Microsoft IL (MSIL). This book uses the term CIL because it is the term adopted by the CLI standard. IL is prevalent in conversation among people writing C# code because they assume that IL refers to CIL rather than other types of intermediate languages.

11. Miller, J., and S. Ragsdale. 2004. *The Common Language Infrastructure Annotated Standard*. Boston: Addison-Wesley.

- Guidance on how to write libraries that are accessible from CLI-compatible languages (available in the **Common Language Specification [CLS]**)

- Metadata that enables many of the services identified by the CLI (including specifications for the layout or file format of assemblies)

▪ NOTE

The term *runtime* can refer to either execution time or the VES. To help clarify the intended meaning, this book uses the term *execution time* to indicate when the program is executing, and it uses the term *runtime* when discussing the agent responsible for managing the execution of a C# program while it executes.

Running within the context of a runtime execution engine enables support for several services and features that programmers do not need to code for directly, including the following:

- *Language interoperability:* Interoperability between different source languages. This is possible because the language compilers translate each source language to the same intermediate language (CIL).

- *Type safety:* Checks for conversion between types, ensuring that only conversions between compatible types will occur. This helps prevent the occurrence of buffer overruns, a leading cause of security vulnerabilities.

- *Code access security:* Certification that the assembly developer's code has permission to execute on the computer.

- *Garbage collection:* Memory management that automatically de-allocates memory previously allocated by the runtime.

- *Platform portability:* Support for potentially running the same assembly on a variety of operating systems. One obvious restriction is that no platform-dependent libraries are used; therefore, platform-dependent idiosyncrasies need to be worked out separately.

- *Base Class Library (BCL):* Provides a foundation of code that developers can depend on (in all .NET frameworks) so that they do not have to develop the code themselves.

> **■ NOTE**
>
> This section gives a brief synopsis of the CLI to familiarize you with the context in which a C# program executes. It also provides a summary of some of the terms that appear throughout this book. Chapter 22 is devoted to the topic of the CLI and its relevance to C# developers. Although the chapter appears last in the book, it does not depend on any earlier chapters, so if you are eager to become more familiar with the CLI, you can jump to it at any time.

Common Intermediate Language and ILDASM

As mentioned in the introduction of this section, the C# compiler converts C# code to CIL code and not to machine code. The processor can directly understand machine code; therefore, CIL code needs to be converted before the processor can execute it. Given an assembly, it is possible to view the CIL code using a CIL disassembler utility to deconstruct the assembly into its CIL representation. (The CIL disassembler is affectionately referred to by its Microsoft .NET Framework specific filename, ILDASM, which stands for IL Disassembler.) ILDASM will disassemble an assembly and extract the CIL generated by the C# compiler into text.

The output that results from disassembling a .NET assembly is significantly easier to understand than machine code. For many developers, this may raise a concern because it is easier for programs to be decompiled and algorithms understood without explicitly redistributing the source code. As with any program, CLI based or not, the only foolproof way of preventing disassembly is to disallow access to the compiled program altogether (e.g., hosting a program only on a website instead of distributing it out to a user's machine). However, if decreased accessibility to the source code is all that is required, there are several obfuscators available. Obfuscators open up the IL code and transform it so that it does the same thing but in a way that is much more difficult to understand. This technique prevents the casual developer from accessing the code and creates assemblies that are much more difficult and tedious to decompile into comprehensible code. Unless a program requires a high degree of algorithm security, obfuscators are generally sufficient.

■ ADVANCED TOPIC

CIL Output for HelloWorld.exe

The exact command used for the CIL disassembler depends on which implementation of the CLI is used. For .NET Core, instructions are available at http://itl.tc/ildasm. Listing 1.20 shows the CIL code created from running ILDASM.

LISTING 1.20: Sample CIL Output

```
.assembly extern System.Runtime
{
  .publickeytoken = ( B0 3F 5F 7F 11 D5 0A 3A )
  .ver 4:2:0:0
}

.assembly extern System.Console
{
  .publickeytoken = ( B0 3F 5F 7F 11 D5 0A 3A )
  .ver 4:1:0:0
}

.assembly 'HelloWorld'
{
  .custom instance void [System.Runtime]System.Runtime.
CompilerServices.CompilationRelaxationsAttribute::.ctor(int32) = ( 01 00 08
00 00 00 00 00 )
  .custom instance void [System.Runtime]System.Runtime.
CompilerServices.RuntimeCompatibilityAttribute::.ctor() = ( 01 00 01 00 54
02 16 57 72 61 70 4E 6F 6E 45 78 63 65 70 74 69 6F 6E 54 68 72 6F 77 73 01 )
  .custom instance void [System.Runtime]System.Runtime.
Versioning.TargetFrameworkAttribute::.ctor(string) = ( 01 00 18 2E 4E 45 54
43 6F 72 65 41 70 70 2C 56 65 72 73 69 6F 6E 3D 76 32 2E 30 01 00 54 0E 14
46 72 61 6D 65 77 6F 72 6B 44 69 73 70 6C 61 79 4E 61 6D 65 00 )
  .custom instance void [System.Runtime]System.
Reflection.AssemblyCompanyAttribute::.ctor(string) = ( 01 00 0A 48 65 6C 6C
6F 57 6F 72 6C 64 00 00 )
  .custom instance void [System.Runtime]System.
Reflection.AssemblyConfigurationAttribute::.ctor(string) = ( 01 00 05 44 65
62 75 67 00 00 )
  .custom instance void [System.Runtime]System.
Reflection.AssemblyDescriptionAttribute::.ctor(string) = ( 01 00 13 50 61 63
6B 61 67 65 20 44 65 73 63 72 69 70 74 69 6F 6E 00 00 )
  .custom instance void [System.Runtime]System.
Reflection.AssemblyFileVersionAttribute::.ctor(string) = ( 01 00 07 31 2E 30
2E 30 2E 30 00 00 )
  .custom instance void [System.Runtime]System.
Reflection.AssemblyInformationalVersionAttribute::.ctor(string) = ( 01 00 05
31 2E 30 2E 30 00 00 )
```

```
    .custom instance void [System.Runtime]System.
↳Reflection.AssemblyProductAttribute::.ctor(string) = ( 01 00 0A 48 65 6C 6C
↳6F 57 6F 72 6C 64 00 00 )
    .custom instance void [System.Runtime]System.
↳Reflection.AssemblyTitleAttribute::.ctor(string) = ( 01 00 0A 48 65 6C 6C 6F
↳57 6F 72 6C 64 00 00 )
    .hash algorithm 0x00008004
    .ver 1:0:0:0
  }

  .module 'HelloWorld.dll'
  // MVID: {c0fe557b-4474-4563-94e1-95c9ead4e3c9}
  .imagebase 0x00400000
  .file alignment 0x00000200
  .stackreserve 0x00100000
  .subsystem 0x0003  // WindowsCui
  .corflags 0x00000001  // ILOnly

  .class private auto ansi beforefieldinit HelloWorld extends [System.
↳Runtime]System.Object
  {

    .method private hidebysig static void Main() cil managed
    {
      .entrypoint
      // Code size 13
      .maxstack 8
      IL_0000: nop
      IL_0001: ldstr "Hello. My name is Inigo Montoya."
      IL_0006: call void [System.Console]System.Console::WriteLine(string)
      IL_000b: nop
      IL_000c: ret
  } // End of method System.Void HelloWorld::Main()

    .method public hidebysig specialname rtspecialname instance void .ctor()
↳cil managed
    {
      // Code size 8
      .maxstack 8
      IL_0000: ldarg.0
      IL_0001: call instance void [System.Runtime]System.Object::.ctor()
      IL_0006: nop
      IL_0007: ret
  } // End of method System.Void HelloWorld::.ctor()
  } // End of class HelloWorld
```

The beginning of the listing is the manifest information. It includes not
only the full name of the disassembled module (HelloWorld.exe) but also
all the modules and assemblies it depends on, along with their version
information.

Perhaps the most interesting thing that you can glean from such a listing is how relatively easy it is to follow what the program is doing compared to trying to read and understand machine code (assembler). In the listing, an explicit reference to `System.Console.WriteLine()` appears. There is a lot of peripheral information to the CIL code listing, but if a developer wanted to understand the inner workings of a C# module (or any CLI-based program) without having access to the original source code, it would be relatively easy unless an obfuscator is used. In fact, several free tools are available (such as Red Gate's Reflector, ILSpy, JustDecompile, dotPeek, and CodeReflect) that can decompile from CIL to C# automatically.

Multiple .NET Frameworks

As briefly mentioned earlier in the chapter, there are multiple .NET frameworks. The large number of offerings is driven mainly by the desire to provide .NET implementations across multiple operating systems and, potentially, even different hardware platforms. Table 1.3 shows those that are predominant.

TABLE 1.3: Predominant .NET Framework Implementations

Comment Type	Description
.NET Core	A truly cross-platform and open source .NET framework that supports a highly modularized set of APIs for both the server and command line applications.
Microsoft .NET Framework	The first, largest, and most widely deployed of the .NET frameworks.
Xamarin	A mobile platform implementation of .NET that works with both iOS and Android and enables the development of mobile applications from a single code base while still enabling access to native platform APIs.
Mono	The oldest open source implementation of .NET that formed the foundation upon which Xamarin and Unity were built. Mono has been replaced by .NET Core for new development.
Unity	A cross-platform game engine used to develop video games for game consoles, PCs, mobile devices, and even websites. (The Unity engine is the first public implementation to support projections into the Microsoft Hololens augmented reality realm.)

All the samples in the book will work for both .NET Core and Microsoft .NET Framework, at a minimum, unless they specifically indicate otherwise. However, because .NET Core is where most of the .NET future investment is occurring, the sample source code that accompanies the book (available from https://IntelliTect.com/EssentialCSharp), will be configured to work with .NET Core by default.

> **■ NOTE**
>
> Throughout the book, *.NET framework* (lowercase) to refers to the framework supported by .NET implementations in general. In contrast, *Microsoft .NET Framework* refers to the specific .NET framework implementation that runs only on Microsoft Windows and was *first* released by Microsoft back in 2001.

Application Programming Interface

All the methods (or more generically, the members) found on a data type such as System.Console are what define the System.Console's **application programming interface (API)**. The API defines how a software program interacts with a component. As such, it is found not just with a single data type, but more generically; the combination of all the APIs for a set of data types are said to create an API for the collective set of components. In .NET, for example, all the types (and the members within those types) in an assembly are said to form the assembly's API. Likewise, given a combination of assemblies, such as those found in .NET Core or the Microsoft .NET Framework, the collective group of assemblies form a larger API. Often, this larger group of APIs is referred to as the **framework**—hence the term .NET *framework* in reference to the APIs exposed by all the assemblies included with the Microsoft .NET Framework. Generically, the API comprises the set of interfaces and protocols (or instructions) for programming against a set of components. In fact, with .NET, the protocols themselves are the rules for how .NET assemblies execute.

C# and .NET Versioning

Since the development life cycle of .NET frameworks is different from that of the C# language, the version of the underlying .NET framework and the corresponding version of the C# language end up with different numbers.

This means that if you compile with the C# 5.0 compiler, it will, by default, compile against the Microsoft .NET Framework version 4.6, for example. Table 1.4 is a brief overview of the C# and .NET releases for the Microsoft .NET Framework and .NET Core.

TABLE 1.4: C# and .NET Versions

Comment Type	Description
C# 1.0 with Microsoft .NET Framework 1.0/1.1 (Visual Studio 2002 and 2003)	The initial release of C#. A language built from the ground up to support .NET programming.
C# 2.0 with Microsoft .NET Framework 2.0 (Visual Studio 2005)	Added generics to the C# language and libraries that supported generics to the Microsoft .NET Framework 2.0.
Microsoft .NET Framework 3.0	An additional set of APIs for distributed commu nications (Windows Communication Foundation [WCF]), rich client presentation (Windows Presentation Foundation [WPF]), workflow (Windows Workflow [WF]), and Web authentication (Cardspaces).
C# 3.0 with Microsoft .NET Framework 3.5 (Visual Studio 2008)	Added support for LINQ, a significant improvement to the APIs used for programming collections. The Microsoft .NET Framework 3.5 provided libraries that extended existing APIs to make LINQ possible.
C# 4.0 with Microsoft .NET Framework 4 (Visual Studio 2010)	Added support for dynamic typing along with significant improvements in the API for writing multithreaded programs that capitalized on multiple processors and cores within those processors.
C# 5.0 with Microsoft .NET Framework 4.5 (Visual Studio 2012) and WinRT integration	Added support for asynchronous method invocation without the explicit registration of a delegate callback. An additional change in the framework was support for interoperability with the Windows Runtime (WinRT).
C# 6.0 with Microsoft .NET Framework 4.6 and .NET Core 1.X (Visual Studio 2015)	Added string interpolation, null propagating member access, exception filters, dictionary initializers, and numerous other features.
C# 7.0 with Microsoft .NET Framework 4.7 and .NET Core 1.1 or 2.0 (Visual Studio 2017)	Added tuples, deconstructors, pattern matching, local functions, return by reference, and more.

Begin 2.0
Begin 3.0
Begin 4.0
Begin 5.0
Begin 6.0
Begin 7.0

End 2.0
End 3.0
End 4.0
End 5.0

Perhaps the most important framework feature added alongside C# 6.0 was support for cross-platform compilation. In other words, not only would the Microsoft .NET Framework run on Windows, but Microsoft also provided the .NET Core implementation that would run on Linux and macOS. Although the .NET Core is not an equivalent feature set to the full Microsoft .NET Framework, it includes enough functionality that entire (ASP.NET) websites can be hosted on operating systems other than Windows and its Internet Information Server (IIS). This means that with the same code base it is possible to compile and execute applications that run across multiple platforms. .NET Core is an entire SDK with everything from the .NET Compiler Platform ("Roslyn"), which itself executes on Linux and macOS, to the .NET Core runtime, along with tools such as the Dotnet command-line utility, `dotnet.exe` (which was introduced around the time of C# 7.0).

End 6.0

End 7.0

.NET Standard

With so many different implementations of .NET, including multiple versions of each individual .NET framework, the frameworks became furcated as each implementation supported a different set of only somewhat overlapping APIs. As a result, writing code that was reusable across multiple .NET frameworks became difficult because it was necessary to litter the code with conditional checks as to whether a particular API was available. To reduce this complexity, the .NET Standard emerged as a means of defining what APIs were supported by which version of the standard. The **.NET Standards**, therefore define what a .NET framework needs to support in order to be compliant with each .NET Standard version number. However, since many of the implementations were already released, the decision tree of identifying which API went into which standard was to some extent based on the existing implementations and the association of those existing implementations with a .NET Standard version number.

The latest release at the time of this writing is .NET Standard 2.0. The advantage of this particular version is that all the base frameworks have implemented (or are working toward implementing) this standard so that, in fact, .NET Standard 2.0 represents a reunification of the furcated APIs found in older versions of each framework.

SUMMARY

This chapter served as a rudimentary introduction to C#. It provided a means of familiarizing you with basic C# syntax. Because of C#'s similarity to C++-style languages, much of this chapter's content might not have been new material to you. However, C# and managed code do have some distinct characteristics, such as compilation down to CIL. Although it is not unique, another key characteristic of C# is its full support for object-oriented programming. Even tasks such as reading and writing data to the console are object oriented. Object orientation is foundational to C#, as you will see throughout this book.

The next chapter examines the fundamental data types that are part of the C# language and discusses how you can use these data types with operands to form expressions.

2

Data Types

$\mathbf{F}$ ROM CHAPTER 1's HelloWorld program, you got a feel for the C# language, its structure, basic syntax characteristics, and how to write the simplest of programs. This chapter continues to discuss the C# basics by investigating the fundamental C# types.

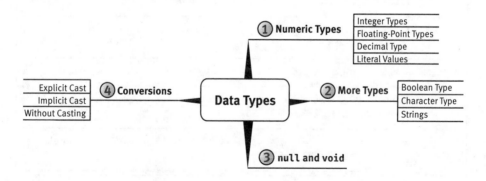

Until now, you have worked with only a few built-in data types, with little explanation. In C# thousands of types exist, and you can combine types to create new types. A few types in C#, however, are relatively simple and are considered the building blocks of all other types. These types are the **predefined types**. The C# language's predefined types include eight integer types, two binary floating-point types for scientific calculations and one decimal float for financial calculations, one Boolean type, and a character type. This chapter investigates these types and looks more closely at the string type.

Fundamental Numeric Types

The basic numeric types in C# have keywords associated with them. These types include integer types, floating-point types, and a special floating-point type called `decimal` to store large numbers with no representation error.

Integer Types

There are eight C# integer types. This variety allows you to select a data type large enough to hold its intended range of values without wasting resources. Table 2.1 lists each integer type.

TABLE 2.1: Integer Types

Type	Size	Range (Inclusive)	BCL Name	Signed	Literal Suffix
sbyte	8 bits	–128 to 127	System.SByte	Yes	
byte	8 bits	0 to 255	System.Byte	No	
short	16 bits	–32,768 to 32,767	System.Int16	Yes	
ushort	16 bits	0 to 65,535	System.UInt16	No	
int	32 bits	–2,147,483,648 to 2,147,483,647	System.Int32	Yes	
uint	32 bits	0 to 4,294,967,295	System.UInt32	No	U or u
long	64 bits	–9,223,372,036,854,775,808 to 9,223,372,036,854,775,807	System.Int64	Yes	L or l
ulong	64 bits	0 to 18,446,744,073,709,551,615	System.UInt64	No	UL or ul

Included in Table 2.1 (and in Tables 2.2 and 2.3) is a column for the full name of each type; we discuss the literal suffix later in the chapter. All the fundamental types in C# have both a short name and a full name. The full name corresponds to the type as it is named in the Base Class Library (BCL). This name, which is the same across all languages, uniquely identifies the type within an assembly. Because of the fundamental nature of these types, C# also supplies keywords as short names or abbreviations to the full names of fundamental types. From the compiler's perspective, both names refer to the same type, producing identical code. In fact, an examination of the resultant Common Intermediate Language (CIL) code would provide no indication of which name was used.

Although C# supports using both the full BCL name and the keyword, as developers we are left with the choice of which to use when. Rather than switching back and forth, it is better to use one or the other consistently. For this reason, C# developers generally use the C# keyword form—choosing, for example, int rather than System.Int32 and string rather than System.String (or a possible shortcut of String).

> ### Guidelines
>
> **DO** use the C# keyword rather than the BCL name when specifying a data type (e.g., string rather than String).
> **DO** favor consistency rather than variety within your code.

The choice for consistency frequently may be at odds with other guidelines. For example, given the guideline to use the C# keyword in place of the BCL name, there may be occasions when you find yourself maintaining a file (or library of files) with the opposite style. In these cases, it would be better to stay consistent with the previous style than to inject a new style and inconsistencies in the conventions. Even so, if the "style" was a bad coding practice that was likely to introduce bugs and obstruct successful maintenance, by all means correct the issue throughout.

> ### Language Contrast: C++—short Data Type
>
> In C/C++, the short data type is an abbreviation for short int. In C#, short on its own is the actual data type.

Floating-Point Types (float, double)

Floating-point numbers have varying degrees of precision, and binary floating-point types can represent numbers exactly only if they are a fraction with a power of 2 as the denominator. If you were to set the value of a floating-point variable to be 0.1, it could very easily be represented as 0.099999999999999 or 0.10000000000000001 or some other number very close to 0.1. Similarly, setting a variable to a large number such as Avogadro's number, 6.02×10^{23}, could lead to a representation error of approximately 10^8, which after all is a tiny fraction of that number. The accuracy of a floating-point number is in proportion to the magnitude of the number it represents. A floating-point number is precise to a certain number of significant digits, not by a fixed value such as ±0.01.

C# supports the two binary floating-point number types listed in Table 2.2.

TABLE 2.2: Floating-Point Types

Type	Size	Range (Inclusive)	BCL Name	Significant Digits	Literal Suffix
float	32 bits	$\pm1.5 \times 10^{-45}$ to $\pm3.4 \times 10^{38}$	System.Single	7	F or f
double	64 bits	$\pm5.0 \times 10^{-324}$ to $\pm1.7 \times 10^{308}$	System.Double	15–16	

Binary numbers appear as base 10 (denary) numbers for human readability. The number of bits (binary digits) converts to 15 decimal digits, with a remainder that contributes to a sixteenth decimal digit as expressed in Table 2.2. Specifically, numbers between 1.7×10^{307} and less than 1×10^{308} have only 15 significant digits. However, numbers ranging from 1×10^{308} to 1.7×10^{308} will have 16 significant digits. A similar range of significant digits occurs with the decimal type as well.

Decimal Type

C# also provides a decimal floating-point type with 128-bit precision (see Table 2.3). This type is suitable for financial calculations.

TABLE 2.3: Decimal Type

Type	Size	Range (Inclusive)	BCL Name	Significant Digits	Literal Suffix
decimal	128 bits	1.0×10^{-28} to approximately 7.9×10^{28}	System.Decimal	28–29	M or m

Unlike binary floating-point numbers, the decimal type maintains exact accuracy for all denary numbers within its range. With the decimal type, therefore, a value of 0.1 is exactly 0.1. However, while the decimal type has greater precision than the floating-point types, it has a smaller range. Thus, conversions from floating-point types to the decimal type may result in overflow errors. Also, calculations with decimal are slightly (generally imperceptibly) slower.

■ ADVANCED TOPIC

Floating-Point Types Dissected

Denary numbers within the range and precision limits of the decimal type are represented exactly. In contrast, the binary floating-point representation of many denary numbers introduces a rounding error. Just as ⅓ cannot be represented exactly in any finite number of decimal digits, so ¹¹⁄₁₀ cannot be represented exactly in any finite number of binary digits. In both cases, we end up with a rounding error of some kind.

A decimal is represented by $\pm N * 10^k$ where the following is true:

- N, the mantissa, is a positive 96-bit integer.
- k, the exponent, is given by -28 <= k <= 0.

In contrast, a binary float is any number $\pm N * 2^k$ where the following is true:

- N is a positive 24-bit (for float) or 53-bit (for double) integer.
- k is an integer ranging from -149 to +104 for float and from -1074 to +970 for double.

Literal Values

A **literal value** is a representation of a constant value within source code. For example, if you want to have System.Console.WriteLine() print out the integer value 42 and the double value 1.618034, you could use the code shown in Listing 2.1.

LISTING 2.1: Specifying Literal Values

```
System.Console.WriteLine(42);
System.Console.WriteLine(1.618034);
```

Output 2.1 shows the results of Listing 2.1.

OUTPUT 2.1

```
42
1.618034
```

■ BEGINNER TOPIC

Use Caution When Hardcoding Values

The practice of placing a value directly into source code is called **hardcoding**, because changing the values requires recompiling the code. Developers must carefully consider the choice between hardcoding values within their code and retrieving them from an external source, such as a configuration file, so that the values are modifiable without recompiling.

By default, when you specify a literal number with a decimal point, the compiler interprets it as a double type. Conversely, a literal value with no decimal point generally defaults to an int, assuming the value is not too large to be stored in an integer. If the value is too large, the compiler will interpret it as a long. Furthermore, the C# compiler allows assignment to a numeric type other than an int, assuming the literal value is appropriate for the target data type. short s = 42 and byte b = 77 are allowed, for example. However, this is appropriate only for constant values; b = s is not allowed without additional syntax, as discussed in the section "Conversions between Data Types" later in this chapter.

As previously discussed in this section, there are many different numeric types in C#. In Listing 2.2, a literal value is placed within C# code. Since numbers with a decimal point will default to the double data type, the output, shown in Output 2.2, is 1.61803398874989 (the last digit, 5, is missing), corresponding to the expected accuracy of a double.

LISTING 2.2: Specifying a Literal double

```
System.Console.WriteLine(1.618033988749895);
```

OUTPUT 2.2

```
1.61803398874989
```

To view the intended number with its full accuracy, you must declare explicitly the literal value as a decimal type by appending an M (or m) (see Listing 2.3 and Output 2.3).

LISTING 2.3: Specifying a Literal decimal

```
System.Console.WriteLine(1.618033988749895M);
```

OUTPUT 2.3

```
1.618033988749895
```

Now the output of Listing 2.3 is as expected: 1.618033988749895. Note that d is the abbreviation for double. To remember that m should be used to identify a decimal, remember that "m is for monetary calculations."

You can also add a suffix to a value to explicitly declare a literal as a float or double by using the F and D suffixes, respectively. For integer data types, the suffixes are U, L, LU, and UL. The type of an integer literal can be determined as follows:

- Numeric literals with no suffix resolve to the first data type that can store the value, in this order: int, uint, long, and ulong.
- Numeric literals with the suffix U resolve to the first data type that can store the value, in the order uint and then ulong.
- Numeric literals with the suffix L resolve to the first data type that can store the value, in the order long and then ulong.
- If the numeric literal has the suffix UL or LU, it is of type ulong.

Note that suffixes for literals are case insensitive. However, uppercase is generally preferred to avoid any ambiguity between the lowercase letter l and the digit 1.

> ## Guidelines
>
> **DO** use uppercase literal suffixes (e.g., 1.618033988749895M).

Begin 7.0

On occasion, numbers can get quite large and difficult to read. To overcome the readability problem, C# 7.0 added support for a **digit separator**, an underscore (_), when expressing a numeric literal, as shown in Listing 2.4.

LISTING 2.4: Specifying Digit Separator

```
System.Console.WriteLine(9_814_072_356);
```

In this case, we separate the digits into thousands (threes), but this is not required by C#. You can use the digit separator to create whatever grouping you like as long as the underscore occurs between the first and the last digit. In fact, you can even have multiple underscores side by side—with

End 7.0

no digit between them.

In addition, you may wish to use exponential notation instead of writing out several zeroes before or after the decimal point (whether using a digit separator or not). To use exponential notation, supply the e or E infix, follow the infix character with a positive or negative integer number, and complete the literal with the appropriate data type suffix. For example, you could print out Avogadro's number as a float, as shown in Listing 2.5 and Output 2.4.

LISTING 2.5: Exponential Notation

```
System.Console.WriteLine(6.023E23F);
```

OUTPUT 2.4

```
6.023E+23
```

■ BEGINNER TOPIC

Hexadecimal Notation

Usually you work with numbers that are represented with a base of 10, meaning there are 10 symbols (0–9) for each place value in the number. If a number is displayed with hexadecimal notation, it is displayed with a base of 16 numbers, meaning 16 symbols are used: 0–9, A–F (lowercase can also be used). Therefore, 0x000A corresponds to the decimal value 10 and 0x002A corresponds to the decimal value 42, being 2 × 16 + 10. The actual number is the same. Switching from hexadecimal to decimal, or vice versa, does not change the number itself, just the representation of the number.

Each hex digit is four bits, so a byte can represent two hex digits.

In all discussions of literal numeric values so far, we have covered only base 10 type values. C# also supports the ability to specify hexadecimal values. To specify a hexadecimal value, prefix the value with 0x and then use any hexadecimal digit, as shown in Listing 2.6.

LISTING 2.6: Hexadecimal Literal Value

```
// Display the value 42 using a hexadecimal literal
System.Console.WriteLine(0x002A);
```

Output 2.5 shows the results of Listing 2.6.

OUTPUT 2.5

```
42
```

Note that this code still displays 42, not 0x002A.

Starting with C# 7.0, you can also represent numbers as binary values (see Listing 2.7).

Begin 7.0

LISTING 2.7: Binary Literal Value

```
// Display the value 42 using a binary literal
System.Console.WriteLine(0b101010);
```

The syntax is like the hexadecimal syntax except with a 0b as the prefix (an uppercase B is also allowed). See the Beginner Topic titled "Bits and Bytes" in Chapter 4 for a full explanation of binary notation and the conversion between binary and decimal.

Note that starting with C# 7.2, you can place the digit separator after the x for a hexadecimal literal or the b for a binary literal.

End 7.0

■ **ADVANCED TOPIC**

Formatting Numbers as Hexadecimal

To display a numeric value in its hexadecimal format, it is necessary to use the x or X numeric formatting specifier. The casing determines whether the hexadecimal letters appear in lowercase or uppercase. Listing 2.8 shows an example of how to do this.

LISTING 2.8: Example of a Hexadecimal Format Specifier

```
// Displays "0x2A"
System.Console.WriteLine($"0x{42:X}");
```

Output 2.6 shows the results.

OUTPUT 2.6

```
0x2A
```

Note that the numeric literal (42) can be in decimal or hexadecimal form. The result will be the same. Also, to achieve the hexadecimal formatting, we rely on the formatting specifier, separated from the string interpolation expression with a colon.

■ **ADVANCED TOPIC**

Round-Trip Formatting

By default, System.Console.WriteLine(1.618033988749895); displays 1.61803398874989, with the last digit missing. To more accurately identify the string representation of the double value, it is possible to convert it using a format string and the round-trip format specifier, R (or r). For example, string.Format("{0:R}", 1.618033988749895) will return the result 1.6180339887498949.

The round-trip format specifier returns a string that, if converted back into a numeric value, will always result in the original value. Listing 2.9 shows the numbers are not equal without use of the round-trip format.

LISTING 2.9: Formatting Using the R Format Specifier

```
// ...
const double number = 1.618033988749895;
double result;
string text;

text = $"{number}";
result = double.Parse(text);
System.Console.WriteLine($"{result == number}: result == number");

text = string.Format("{0:R}", number);
result = double.Parse(text);
System.Console.WriteLine($"{result == number}: result == number");

// ...
```

Output 2.7 shows the resultant output.

OUTPUT 2.7

```
False: result == number
True: result == number
```

When assigning text the first time, there is no round-trip format specifier; as a result, the value returned by double.Parse(text) is not the same as the original number value. In contrast, when the round-trip format specifier is used, double.Parse(text) returns the original value.

For those readers who are unfamiliar with the == syntax from C-based languages, result == number evaluates to true if result is equal to number, while result != number does the opposite. Both assignment and equality operators are discussed in the next chapter.

More Fundamental Types

The fundamental types discussed so far are numeric types. C# includes some additional types as well: bool, char, and string.

Boolean Type (bool)

Another C# primitive is a Boolean or conditional type, bool, which represents true or false in conditional statements and expressions. Allowable values are the keywords `true` and `false`. The BCL name for `bool` is `System.Boolean`. For example, to compare two strings in a case-insensitive manner, you call the `string.Compare()` method and pass a `bool` literal `true` (see Listing 2.10).

LISTING 2.10: A Case-Insensitive Comparison of Two Strings

```
string option;
...
int comparison = string.Compare(option, "/Help", true);
```

In this case, you make a case-insensitive comparison of the contents of the variable `option` with the literal text `/Help` and assign the result to `comparison`.

Although theoretically a single bit could hold the value of a Boolean, the size of `bool` is 1 byte.

Character Type (char)

A `char` type represents 16-bit characters whose set of possible values are drawn from the Unicode character set's UTF-16 encoding. A `char` is the same size as a 16-bit unsigned integer (`ushort`), which represents values between 0 and 65,535. However, `char` is a unique type in C# and code should treat it as such.

The BCL name for `char` is `System.Char`.

■ BEGINNER TOPIC

The Unicode Standard

Unicode is an international standard for representing characters found in most human languages. It provides computer systems with functionality for building **localized** applications—that is, applications that display the appropriate language and culture characteristics for different cultures.

■ ADVANCED TOPIC

16 Bits Is Too Small for All Unicode Characters

Unfortunately, not all Unicode characters can be represented by just one 16-bit `char`. The original Unicode designers believed that 16 bits would be enough, but as more languages were supported, it was realized that this assumption was incorrect. As a result, some (rarely used) Unicode characters are composed of "surrogate pairs" of two char values.

To construct a literal char, place the character within single quotes, as in 'A'. Allowable characters comprise the full range of keyboard characters, including letters, numbers, and special symbols.

Some characters cannot be placed directly into the source code and instead require special handling. These characters are prefixed with a backslash (\) followed by a special character code. In combination, the backslash and special character code constitute an **escape sequence**. For example, \n represents a newline, and \t represents a tab. Since a backslash indicates the beginning of an escape sequence, it can no longer identify a simple backslash; instead, you need to use \\ to represent a single backslash character.

Listing 2.11 writes out one single quote because the character represented by \' corresponds to a single quote.

LISTING 2.11: Displaying a Single Quote Using an Escape Sequence

```
class SingleQuote
{
  static void Main()
  {
      System.Console.WriteLine('\'');
  }
}
```

In addition to showing the escape sequences, Table 2.4 includes the Unicode representation of characters.

TABLE 2.4: Escape Characters

Escape Sequence	Character Name	Unicode Encoding
\'	Single quote	\u0027
\"	Double quote	\u0022
\\	Backslash	\u005C
\0	Null	\u0000

continues

TABLE 2.4: Escape Characters (*continued*)

Escape Sequence	Character Name	Unicode Encoding
`\a`	Alert (system beep)	`\u0007`
`\b`	Backspace	`\u0008`
`\f`	Form feed	`\u000C`
`\n`	Line feed (sometimes referred to as a newline)	`\u000A`
`\r`	Carriage return	`\u000D`
`\t`	Horizontal tab	`\u0009`
`\v`	Vertical tab	`\u000B`
`\uxxxx`	Unicode character in hex	`\u0029`
`\x[n][n][n]n`	Unicode character in hex (first three placeholders are options); variable-length version of `\uxxxx`	`\u3A`
`\Uxxxxxxxx`	Unicode escape sequence for creating surrogate pairs	`\UD840DC01` (𠀁)

You can represent any character using Unicode encoding. To do so, prefix the Unicode value with `\u`. You represent Unicode characters in hexadecimal notation. The letter `A`, for example, is the hexadecimal value `0x41`. Listing 2.12 uses Unicode characters to display a smiley face (:)), and Output 2.8 shows the results.

LISTING 2.12: Using Unicode Encoding to Display a Smiley Face

```
System.Console.Write('\u003A');
System.Console.WriteLine('\u0029');
```

OUTPUT 2.8

```
:)
```

Strings

A finite sequence of zero or more characters is called a **string**. The string type in C# is string, whose BCL name is System.String. The string type includes some special characteristics that may be unexpected to developers familiar with other programming languages. In addition to the string literal format discussed in Chapter 1, strings include a "verbatim string" prefix character of @, support for string interpolation with the $ prefix character, and the potentially surprising fact that strings are immutable.

Literals

You can enter a literal string into code by placing the text in double quotes ("), as you saw in the HelloWorld program. Strings are composed of characters, and consequently, character escape sequences can be embedded within a string.

In Listing 2.13, for example, two lines of text are displayed. However, instead of using System.Console.WriteLine(), the code listing shows System.Console.Write() with the newline character, \n. Output 2.9 shows the results.

LISTING 2.13: **Using the \n Character to Insert a Newline**

```
class DuelOfWits
{
  static void Main()
  {
      System.Console.Write(
          "\"Truly, you have a dizzying intellect.\"");
      System.Console.Write("\n\"Wait 'til I get going!\"\n");
  }
}
```

OUTPUT 2.9

```
"Truly, you have a dizzying intellect."
"Wait 'til I get going!"
```

The escape sequence for double quotes differentiates the printed double quotes from the double quotes that define the beginning and end of the string.

In C#, you can use the @ symbol in front of a string to signify that a backslash should not be interpreted as the beginning of an escape sequence. The resultant **verbatim string literal** does not reinterpret just the backslash character. Whitespace is also taken verbatim when using the @ string syntax. The triangle in Listing 2.14, for example, appears in the console exactly as typed, including the backslashes, newlines, and indentation. Output 2.10 shows the results.

LISTING 2.14: Displaying a Triangle Using a Verbatim String Literal

```
class Triangle
{
  static void Main()
  {
      System.Console.Write(@"begin
           /\
          /  \
         /    \
        /      \
       /_____\
  end");
    }
}
```

OUTPUT 2.10

Without the @ character, this code would not even compile. In fact, even if you changed the shape to a square, eliminating the backslashes, the code still would not compile because a newline cannot be placed directly within a string that is not prefaced with the @ symbol.

The only escape sequence the verbatim string does support is "", which signifies double quotes and does not terminate the string.

Begin 6.0

Language Contrast: C++—String Concatenation at Compile Time

Unlike C++, C# does not automatically concatenate literal strings. You cannot, for example, specify a string literal as follows:

```
"Major Strasser has been shot."
"Round up the usual suspects."
```

Rather, concatenation requires the use of the addition operator. (If the compiler can calculate the result at compile time, however, the resultant CIL code will be a single string.)

If the same literal string appears within an assembly multiple times, the compiler will define the string only once within the assembly and all variables will refer to the same string. That way, if the same string literal containing thousands of characters was placed multiple times into the code, the resultant assembly would reflect the size of only one of them.

String Interpolation

As discussed in Chapter 1, strings can support embedded expressions when using the string interpolation format starting in C# 6.0. The string interpolation syntax prefixes a verbatim string literal with a dollar symbol and then embeds the expressions within curly brackets. The following is an example:

```
System.Console.WriteLine($"Your full name is {firstName} {lastName}.");
```

where firstName and lastName are simple expressions that refer to variables. Note that verbatim string literals can be combined with string interpolation by specifying the $ prior to the @ symbol, as in this example:

```
System.Console.WriteLine($@"Your full name is:
    { firstName } { lastName }");
```

Since this is a verbatim string literal, the text is output on two lines. You can, however, make a similar line break in the code without incurring a line break in the output by placing the line feeds inside the curly braces as follows:

```
System.Console.WriteLine($@"Your full name is: {
    firstName } { lastName }");
```

Note that the @ symbol is still required even when only placing the new lines within the curly braces.

End 6.0

■ ADVANCED TOPIC

Understanding the Internals of String Interpolation

String interpolation is a shorthand for invoking the `string.Format()` method. For example, a statement such as

```
System.Console.WriteLine($"Your full name is {firstName} {lastName}.")
```

will be transformed to the C# equivalent of

```
object[] args = new object[] { firstName, lastName };
Console.WriteLine(string.Format("Your full name is {0} {1}.", args));
```

This leaves in place support for localization in the same way it works with composite string and doesn't introduce any post-compile injection of code via strings.

String Methods

The `string` type, like the `System.Console` type, includes several methods. There are methods, for example, for formatting, concatenating, and comparing strings.

The `Format()` method in Table 2.5 behaves similarly to the `Console.Write()` and `Console.WriteLine()` methods, except that instead of displaying the result in the console window, `string.Format()` returns the result to the caller. Of course, with string interpolation the need for `string.Format()` is significantly reduced (except for localization support). Under the covers, however, string interpolation compiles down to CIL that leverages `string.Format()`.

All of the methods in Table 2.5 are **static**. This means that, to call the method, it is necessary to prefix the method name (e.g., `Concat`) with the type that contains the method (e.g., `string`). As illustrated later in this chapter, however, some of the methods in the string class are **instance** methods. Instead of prefixing the method with the type, instance methods use the variable name (or some other reference to an instance). Table 2.6 shows a few of these methods, along with an example.

TABLE 2.5: string Static Methods

Statement	Example

static string string.
↳Format(
    string format,
    ...)
	string text, firstName, lastName;
	//...
	text = **string**.Format("Your full name is {0} {1}.",
	    firstName, lastName);
	// Display
	// "Your full name is <firstName> <lastName>."
	System.Console.WriteLine(text);

static string string.
↳Concat(
    string str0,
    string str1)
	string text, firstName, lastName;
	//...
	text = string.Concat(firstName, lastName);
	// Display "<firstName><lastName>", notice
	// that there is no space between names
	System.Console.WriteLine(text);

static int string.
↳Compare(
    string str0,
    string str1)
	string option;
	//...
	// String comparison in which case matters
	int result = **string**.Compare(option, "/help");
	
	// Display:
	// 0 if equal
	// negative if option < /help
	// positive if option > /help
	System.Console.WriteLine(result);

	string option;
	//...
	// Case-insensitive string comparison
	int result = **string**.Compare(
	    option, "/Help", **true**);
	
	// Display:
	// 0 if equal
	// < 0 if option < /help
	// > 0 if option > /help
	System.Console.WriteLine(result);

TABLE 2.6: string Methods

Statement	Example

bool StartsWith(
    string value)
bool EndsWith(
    string value)
	string lastName
	//...
	bool isPhd = lastName.EndsWith("Ph.D.");
	bool isDr = lastName.StartsWith("Dr.");

continues

TABLE 2.6: string Methods (*continued*)

Statement	Example

string ToLower()
string ToUpper()
	string severity = "warning";
	// Display the severity in uppercase
	System.Console.WriteLine(severity.ToUpper());

string Trim()
string Trim(...)
string TrimEnd()
string TrimStart()
	// Remove any whitespace at the start or end
	username = username.Trim();

string Replace(
    string oldValue,
    string newValue)
	string filename;
	//...
	// Remove ?'s from the string
	filename = filename.Replace("?", "");;

■ADVANCED TOPIC

using **Directive and** using static **Directive**

Begin 6.0

The invocation of static methods as we have used them so far always involves a prefix of the namespace followed by the type name. When calling System.Console.WriteLine, for example, even though the method invoked is WriteLine() and there is no other method with that name within the context, it is still necessary to prefix the method name with the namespace (System) followed by the type name (Console). On occasion, you may want a shortcut to avoid such explicitness; to do so, you can leverage the C# 6.0 using static directive, as shown in Listing 2.15.

LISTING 2.15: using static Directive

```csharp
// The using directives allow you to drop the namespace
using static System.Console;
class HeyYou
{
  static void Main()
  {
      string firstName;
      string lastName;

      WriteLine("Hey you!");

      Write("Enter your first name: ");
      firstName = ReadLine();
```

```
        Write("Enter your last name: ");
        lastName = ReadLine();

        WriteLine(
            $"Your full name is {firstName} {lastName}.");
    }
}
```

The using static directive needs to appear at the top of the file.[1] Each time we use the System.Console class, it is no longer necessary to also use the System.Console prefix. Instead, we can simply write the method name. An important point to note about the using static directive is that it works only for static methods and properties, not for instance members.

A similar directive, the using directive, allows for eliminating the namespace prefix—for example, System. Unlike the using static directive, the using directive applies universally within the file (or namespace) in which it resides (not just to static members). With the using directive, you can (optionally) eliminate all references to the namespace, whether during instantiation, during static method invocation, or even with the nameof operator found in C# 6.0.

End 6.0

String Formatting

Whether you use string.Format() or the C# 6.0 string interpolation feature to construct complex formatting strings, a rich and complex set of formatting patterns is available to display numbers, dates, times, timespans, and so on. For example, if price is a variable of type decimal, then string.Format("{0,20:C2}", price) or the equivalent interpolation $"{price,20:C2}" both convert the decimal value to a string using the default currency formatting rules, rounded to two figures after the decimal place and right-justified in a 20-character-wide string. Space does not permit a detailed discussion of all the possible formatting strings; consult the MSDN documentation for string.Format() for a complete listing of formatting strings.

If you want an actual left or right curly brace inside an interpolated string or formatted string, you can double the brace to indicate that it is not introducing a pattern. For example, the interpolated string $"{{ {price:C2} }}" might produce the string "{ $1,234.56 }"

---

1. Or at the top of a namespace declaration.

Newline

When writing out a newline, the exact characters for the newline will depend on the operating system on which you are executing. On Microsoft Windows operating systems, the newline is the combination of both the carriage return (\r) and line feed (\n) characters, while a single line feed is used on UNIX. One way to overcome the discrepancy between operating systems is simply to use `System.Console.WriteLine()` to output a blank line. Another approach, which is almost essential for working with newlines from the same code base on multiple operating systems, is to use `System.Environment.NewLine`. In other words, `System.Console.WriteLine("Hello World")` and `System.Console.Write($"Hello World{System.Environment.NewLine}")` are equivalent. However, on Windows, `System.WriteLine()` and `System.Console.Write(System.Environment.NewLine)` are equivalent to `System.Console.Write("\r\n")`—not `System.Console.Write("\n")`. In summary, rely on `System.WriteLine()` and `System.Environment.NewLine` rather than \n to accommodate Windows-specific operating system idiosyncrasies with the same code that runs on Linux and iOS.

Guidelines

DO rely on `System.WriteLine()` and `System.Environment.NewLine` rather than \n to accommodate Windows-specific operating system idiosyncrasies with the same code that runs on Linux and iOS.

■ ADVANCED TOPIC

C# Properties

The `Length` member referred to in the following section is not actually a method, as indicated by the fact that there are no parentheses following its call. `Length` is a property of `string`, and C# syntax allows access to a property as though it were a member variable (known in C# as a **field**). In other words, a property has the behavior of special methods called setters and getters, but the syntax for accessing that behavior is that of a field.

Examining the underlying CIL implementation of a property reveals that it compiles into two methods: `set_<PropertyName>` and `get_<PropertyName>`. Neither of these, however, is directly accessible from C# code, except through the C# property constructs. See Chapter 6 for more details on properties.

String Length

To determine the length of a string, you use a string member called `Length`. This particular member is called a **read-only property**. As such, it cannot be set, nor does calling it require any parameters. Listing 2.16 demonstrates how to use the `Length` property, and Output 2.11 shows the results.

LISTING 2.16: Using string's Length Member

```csharp
class PalindromeLength
{
  static void Main()
  {
      string palindrome;

      System.Console.Write("Enter a palindrome: ");
      palindrome = System.Console.ReadLine();

      System.Console.WriteLine(
          $"The palindrome \"{palindrome}\" is"
          + $" {palindrome.Length} characters.");
  }
}
```

OUTPUT 2.11

```
Enter a palindrome: Never odd or even
The palindrome "Never odd or even" is 17 characters.
```

The length for a string cannot be set directly; it is calculated from the number of characters in the string. Furthermore, the length of a string cannot change because a string is **immutable**.

Strings Are Immutable

A key characteristic of the `string` type is that it is immutable. A string variable can be assigned an entirely new value, but there is no facility for modifying the contents of a `string`. It is not possible, therefore, to convert a `string` to all uppercase letters. It is trivial to create a new string that is composed of an uppercase version of the old string, but the old string is not modified in the process. Consider Listing 2.17 as an example.

LISTING 2.17: Error; string Is Immutable

```
class Uppercase
{
  static void Main()
  {
      string text;

      System.Console.Write("Enter text: ");
      text = System.Console.ReadLine();

      // UNEXPECTED:  Does not convert text to uppercase
      text.ToUpper();

      System.Console.WriteLine(text);
  }
}
```

Output 2.12 shows the results of Listing 2.17.

OUTPUT 2.12

```
Enter text: This is a test of the emergency broadcast system.
This is a test of the emergency broadcast system.
```

At a glance, it would appear that `text.ToUpper()` should convert the characters within `text` to uppercase. However, strings are immutable and, therefore, `text.ToUpper()` will make no such modification. Instead, `text.ToUpper()` returns a new string that needs to be saved into a variable or passed to `System.Console.WriteLine()` directly. The corrected code is shown in Listing 2.18, and its output is shown in Output 2.13.

LISTING 2.18: Working with Strings

```
class Uppercase
{
  static void Main()
  {
      string text, uppercase;

      System.Console.Write("Enter text: ");
      text = System.Console.ReadLine();

      // Return a new string in uppercase
      uppercase = text.ToUpper();

      System.Console.WriteLine(uppercase);
  }
}
```

OUTPUT 2.13

```
Enter text: This is a test of the emergency broadcast system.
THIS IS A TEST OF THE EMERGENCY BROADCAST SYSTEM.
```

If the immutability of a string is ignored, mistakes like those shown in Listing 2.17 can occur with other string methods as well.

To actually change the value of text, assign the value from ToUpper( ) back into text, as in the following code:

```
text = text.ToUpper( );
```

System.Text.StringBuilder

If considerable string modification is needed, such as when constructing a long string in multiple steps, you should use the data type System.Text.StringBuilder rather than string. The StringBuilder type includes methods such as Append( ), AppendFormat( ), Insert( ), Remove( ), and Replace( ), some of which are also available with string. The key difference, however, is that with StringBuilder these methods will modify the data in the StringBuilder itself and will not simply return a new string.

null and void

Two additional keywords relating to types are null and void. The null value, identified with the null keyword, indicates that the variable does not refer to any valid object. void is used to indicate the absence of a type or the absence of any value altogether.

null

null can also be used as a type of string "literal." null indicates that a variable is set to nothing. Reference types, pointer types, and nullable value types can be assigned the value null. The only reference type covered so far in this book is string; Chapter 6 covers the topic of creating classes (which are reference types) in detail. For now, suffice it to say that a variable of reference type contains a reference to a location in memory that is different from the value of the variable. Code that sets a variable to null explicitly assigns the reference to refer to no valid value. In fact, it is even possible to check whether a reference refers to nothing. Listing 2.19 demonstrates assigning null to a string variable.

LISTING 2.19: Assigning null to a String

```
static void Main()
{
    string faxNumber;
    // ...

    // Clear the value of faxNumber
    faxNumber = null;

    // ...
}
```

Assigning the value `null` to a reference type is not equivalent to not assigning it at all. In other words, a variable that has been assigned `null` has still been set, whereas a variable with no assignment has not been set and therefore will often cause a compile error if used prior to assignment.

Assigning the value `null` to a `string` variable is distinctly different from assigning an empty string, `""`. Use of `null` indicates that the variable has no value, whereas `""` indicates that there is a value—an empty string. This type of distinction can be quite useful. For example, the programming logic could interpret a `homePhone` of `null` to mean that the home phone number is unknown, while a `homePhone` value of `""` could indicate that there is no home phone number.

The void "Type"

Sometimes the C# syntax requires a data type to be specified, but no data is actually passed. For example, if no return from a method is needed, C# allows you to specify `void` as the data type instead. The declaration of `Main` within the `HelloWorld` program is an example. The use of `void` as the return type indicates that the method is not returning any data and tells the compiler not to expect a value. `void` is not a data type per se but rather an indication that there is no data being returned.

Language Contrast: C++

In both C++ and C#, void has two meanings: as a marker that a method does not return any data and to represent a pointer to a storage location of unknown type. In C++ programs, it is quite common to see pointer types such as void**. C# can also represent pointers to storage locations of unknown type using the same syntax, but this usage is comparatively rare in C# and typically encountered only when writing programs that interoperate with unmanaged code libraries.

> ## Language Contrast: Visual Basic—Returning void Is Like Defining a Subroutine
>
> The Visual Basic equivalent of returning a void in C# is to define a subroutine (Sub/ End Sub) rather than a function that returns a value.

Conversions between Data Types

Given the thousands of types predefined in the various CLI implementations and the unlimited number of types that code can define, it is important that types support conversion from one type to another where it makes sense. The most common operation that results in a conversion is **casting**.

Consider the conversion between two numeric types: converting from a variable of type long to a variable of type int. A long type can contain values as large as 9,223,372,036,854,775,808; however, the maximum size of an int is 2,147,483,647. As such, that conversion could result in a loss of data—for example, if the variable of type long contains a value greater than the maximum size of an int. Any conversion that could result in a loss of magnitude or an exception because the conversion failed requires an **explicit cast**. Conversely, a conversion operation that will not lose magnitude and will not throw an exception regardless of the operand types is an **implicit conversion**.

Explicit Cast

In C#, you cast using the **cast operator**. By specifying the type you would like the variable converted to within parentheses, you acknowledge that if an explicit cast is occurring, there may be a loss of precision and data, or an exception may result. The code in Listing 2.20 converts a long to an int and explicitly tells the system to attempt the operation.

LISTING 2.20: Explicit Cast Example

```
long longNumber = 50918309109;
int intNumber = (int) longNumber;
                 └──┬──┘
                Cast Operator
```

With the cast operator, the programmer essentially says to the compiler, "Trust me, I know what I am doing. I know that the value will fit into the target type." Making such a choice will cause the compiler to allow the conversion. However, with an explicit conversion, there is still a chance that an error, in the form of an exception, might occur while executing if the data is not converted successfully. It is therefore the programmer's responsibility to ensure the data is successfully converted, or else to provide the necessary error-handling code when the conversion fails.

■ ADVANCED TOPIC

Checked and Unchecked Conversions

C# provides special keywords for marking a code block to indicate what should happen if the target data type is too small to contain the assigned data. By default, if the target data type cannot contain the assigned data, the data will truncate during assignment. For an example, see Listing 2.21.

LISTING 2.21: Overflowing an Integer Value

```
class Program
{
  static void Main()
  {
      // int.MaxValue equals 2147483647
      int n = int.MaxValue;
      n = n + 1 ;
      System.Console.WriteLine(n);
  }
}
```

Output 2.14 shows the results.

OUTPUT 2.14

```
-2147483648
```

Listing 2.21 writes the value -2147483648 to the console. However, placing the code within a checked block, or using the checked option when running the compiler, will cause the runtime to throw an exception of type System.OverflowException. The syntax for a checked block uses the checked keyword, as shown in Listing 2.22.

LISTING 2.22: A Checked Block Example

```
class Program
{
  static void Main()
  {
    checked
    {
      // int.MaxValue equals 2147483647
      int n = int.MaxValue;
      n = n + 1 ;
      System.Console.WriteLine(n);
    }
  }
}
```

Output 2.15 shows the results.

OUTPUT 2.15

```
Unhandled Exception: System.OverflowException: Arithmetic operation
resulted in an overflow at Program.Main() in ...Program.cs:line 12
```

The result is that an exception is thrown if, within the checked block, an overflow assignment occurs at runtime.

The C# compiler provides a command-line option for changing the default checked behavior from unchecked to checked. C# also supports an unchecked block that overflows the data instead of throwing an exception for assignments within the block (see Listing 2.23).

LISTING 2.23: An Unchecked Block Example

```
using System;

class Program
{
  static void Main()
  {
    unchecked
    {
      // int.MaxValue equals 2147483647
      int n = int.MaxValue;
      n = n + 1 ;
      System.Console.WriteLine(n);
    }
  }
}
```

Output 2.16 shows the results.

OUTPUT 2.16

```
-2147483648
```

Even if the checked option is on during compilation, the unchecked keyword in the preceding code will prevent the runtime from throwing an exception during execution.

Readers might wonder why, when adding 1 to `int.MaxValue` unchecked, the result yields –2147483648. The behavior is caused by wraparound semantics. The binary representation of `int.MaxValue` is 01111111111111111111111111111111, where the first digit (0) indicates a positive value. Incrementing this value yields the next value of 10000000000000000000000000000000, the smallest integer (`int.MinValue`), where the first digit (1) signifies the number is negative. Adding 1 to `int.MinValue` would result in 10000000000000000000000000000001 (–2147483647) and so on.

You cannot convert any type to any other type simply because you designate the conversion explicitly using the cast operator. The compiler will still check that the operation is valid. For example, you cannot convert a `long` to a `bool`. No such conversion is defined, and therefore, the compiler does not allow such a cast.

Language Contrast: Converting Numbers to Booleans

It may be surprising to learn that there is no valid cast from a numeric type to a Boolean type, since this is common in many other languages. The reason no such conversion exists in C# is to avoid any ambiguity, such as whether –1 corresponds to true or false. More important, as you will see in the next chapter, this constraint reduces the chance of using the assignment operator in place of the equality operator (e.g., avoiding if(x=42){...} when if(x==42){...} was intended).

Implicit Conversion

In other instances, such as when going from an `int` type to a `long` type, there is no loss of precision, and no fundamental change in the value of the type occurs. In these cases, the code needs to specify only the assignment operator; the conversion is **implicit**. In other words, the compiler is able to determine that such a conversion will work correctly. The code in Listing 2.24 converts from an int to a long by simply using the assignment operator.

LISTING 2.24: Not Using the Cast Operator for an Implicit Conversion

```
int intNumber = 31416;
long longNumber = intNumber;
```

Even when no explicit cast operator is required (because an implicit conversion is allowed), it is still possible to include the cast operator (see Listing 2.25).

LISTING 2.25: Using the Cast Operator for an Implicit Cast

```
int intNumber = 31416;
long longNumber = (long) intNumber;
```

Type Conversion without Casting

No conversion is defined from a string to a numeric type, so methods such as Parse( ) are required. Each numeric data type includes a Parse( ) function that enables conversion from a string to the corresponding numeric type. Listing 2.26 demonstrates this call.

LISTING 2.26: Using float.Parse( ) to Convert a string to a Numeric Data Type

```
string text = "9.11E-31";
float kgElectronMass = float.Parse(text);
```

Another special type is available for converting one type to the next. This type is System.Convert, and an example of its use appears in Listing 2.27.

LISTING 2.27: Type Conversion Using System.Convert

```
string middleCText = "261.626";
double middleC = System.Convert.ToDouble(middleCText);
bool boolean = System.Convert.ToBoolean(middleC);
```

System.Convert supports only a small number of types and is not extensible. It allows conversion from any of the types bool, char, sbyte, short, int, long, ushort, uint, ulong, float, double, decimal, DateTime, and string to any other of those types.

Furthermore, all types support a `ToString()` method that can be used to provide a string representation of a type. Listing 2.28 demonstrates how to use this method. The resultant output is shown in Output 2.17.

LISTING 2.28: Using ToString() to Convert to a string

```csharp
bool boolean = true;
string text = boolean.ToString();
// Display "True"
System.Console.WriteLine(text);
```

OUTPUT 2.17

```
True
```

For the majority of types, the `ToString()` method returns the name of the data type rather than a string representation of the data. The string representation is returned only if the type has an explicit implementation of `ToString()`. One last point to make is that it is possible to code custom conversion methods, and many such methods are available for classes in the runtime.

■ **ADVANCED TOPIC**

Begin 2.0

TryParse()

Starting with C# 2.0 (.NET 2.0), all the numeric primitive types include a static `TryParse()` method. This method is similar to the `Parse()` method, except that instead of throwing an exception if the conversion fails, the `TryParse()` method returns `false`, as demonstrated in Listing 2.29.

LISTING 2.29: Using TryParse() in Place of an Invalid Cast Exception

```csharp
double number;
string input;

System.Console.Write("Enter a number: ");
input = System.Console.ReadLine();
if (double.TryParse(input, out number))
{
    // Converted correctly, now use number
    // ...
}
```

```
    else
    {
        System.Console.WriteLine(
            "The text entered was not a valid number.");
    }
```

Output 2.18 shows the results of Listing 2.29.

OUTPUT 2.18

```
Enter a number: forty-two
The text entered was not a valid number.
```

The resultant value that the code parses from the input string is
returned via an out parameter—in this case, number.

It is worth pointing out that, starting with C# 7.0, it is no longer necessary to declare a variable before using it as an out argument. Using this
feature, the declaration for number is shown in Listing 2.30.

Begin 7.0

LISTING 2.30: Using TryParse() with Inline out Declaration in C# 7.0

```
// double number;
string input;

System.Console.Write("Enter a number: ");
input = System.Console.ReadLine();
if (double.TryParse(input, out double number))
{
    System.Console.WriteLine(
        $"input was parsed successfully to {number}."); }
else
{
    // Note: number scope is here too (although not assigned)
    System.Console.WriteLine(
        "The text entered was not a valid number.");
}
```

Notice that the data type of number is specified following the out modifier and before the variable that it declares. The result is that the number
variable is available from both the true and false consequence of the if
statement but not outside the if statement.

End 7.0

2.0

The key difference between Parse() and TryParse() is that
TryParse() won't throw an exception if it fails. Frequently, the conversion
from a string to a numeric type depends on a user entering the text. It is

expected, in such scenarios, that the user will enter invalid data that will not parse successfully. By using `TryParse()` rather than `Parse()`, you can avoid throwing exceptions in expected situations. (The expected situation in this case is that the user will enter invalid data, and we try to avoid throwing exceptions for expected scenarios.)

End 2.0

SUMMARY

Even for experienced programmers, C# introduces several new programming constructs. For example, as part of the section on data types, this chapter covered the type `decimal`, which can be used to perform financial calculations without floating-point anomalies. In addition, the chapter introduced the fact that the Boolean type, `bool`, does not convert implicitly to or from the integer type, thereby preventing the mistaken use of the assignment operator in a conditional expression. Other characteristics of C# that distinguish it from many of its predecessors are the @ verbatim string qualifier, which forces a string to ignore the escape character, string interpolation that makes code easier to read by embedding it into the string, and the immutable nature of the `string` data type.

In Chapter 3, we continue the topic of data types by elaborating more on the two types of data types: value types and reference types. In addition, we look at combining data elements together into tuples and arrays.

■3■
More with Data Types

I N CHAPTER 2, WE COVERED ALL THE C# predefined types and briefly touched on the topic of reference types versus value types. In this chapter, we continue the discussion of data types with further explanation of the categories of types.

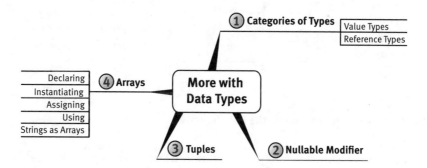

In addition, we delve into the details of combining data elements together into tuples—a feature introduced in C# 7.0—followed by grouping data into sets called **arrays**. To begin, let's delve further into understanding value types and reference types.

Categories of Types

All types fall into one of two categories: **value types** and **reference types**. The differences between the types in each category stem from how they are copied: Value type data is always copied by value, whereas reference type data is always copied by reference.

Value Types

Except for `string`, all the predefined types in the book so far have been value types. Variables of value types contain the value directly. In other words, the variable refers to the same location in memory where the value is stored. Because of this, when a different variable is assigned the same value, a copy of the original variable's value is made to the location of the new variable. A second variable of the same value type cannot refer to the same location in memory as the first variable. Consequently, changing the value of the first variable will not affect the value in the second, as Figure 3.1 demonstrates. In the figure, `number1` refers to a particular location in memory that contains the value `42`. After assigning `number1` to `number2`, both variables will contain the value `42`. However, modifying either variable's value will not affect the other.

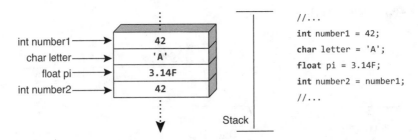

FIGURE 3.1: Value Types Contain the Data Directly

Similarly, passing a value type to a method such as `Console.WriteLine()` will result in a memory copy, and any changes to the parameter inside the method will not affect the original value within the calling function. Since value types require a memory copy, they generally should be defined to consume a small amount of memory; value types should almost always be less than 16 bytes in size.

Reference Types

By contrast, the value of a variable of reference type is a reference to a storage location that contains data. Reference types store the reference where the data is located instead of storing the data directly, as value types do.

Therefore, to access the data, the runtime reads the memory location out of the variable and then "jumps" to the location in memory that contains the data. The memory area of the data a reference type points to is called the **heap** (see Figure 3.2).

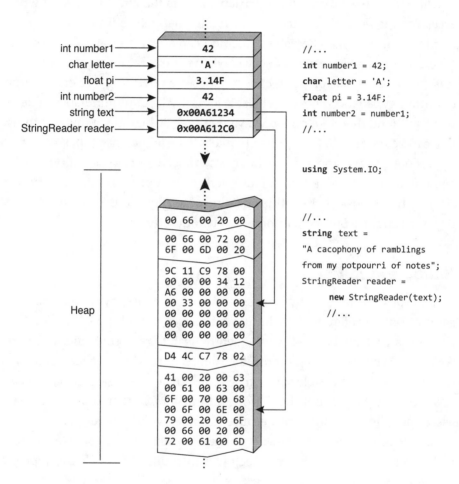

```
//...
int number1 = 42;
char letter = 'A';
float pi = 3.14F;
int number2 = number1;
//...


using System.IO;


//...
string text =
"A cacophony of ramblings
from my potpourri of notes";
StringReader reader =
    new StringReader(text);
//...
```

FIGURE 3.2: Reference Types Point to the Heap

A reference type does not require the same memory copy of the data that a value type does, which makes copying reference types far more efficient than copying large value types. When assigning the value of one reference type variable to another reference type variable, only the reference is copied, not the data referred to. In practice, a reference is always the same size as the "native size" of the processor: A 32-bit processor will copy a 32-bit reference, a 64-bit processor will copy a 64-bit reference, and so on. Obviously, copying the small reference to a large block of data is faster than copying the entire block, as a value type would.

Since reference types copy a reference to data, two different variables can refer to the same data. If two variables refer to the same object, changing a field of the object through one variable causes the effect to be seen when accessing the field via another variable. This happens both for assignment and for method calls. Therefore, a method can affect the data of a reference type, and that change can be observed when control returns to the caller. For this reason, a key factor when choosing between defining a reference type or a value type is whether the object is logically like an immutable value of fixed size (and therefore possibly a value type), or logically a mutable thing that can be referred to (and therefore likely to be a reference type).

Besides `string` and any custom classes such as `Program`, all types discussed so far are value types. However, most types are reference types. Although it is possible to define custom value types, it is relatively rare to do so in comparison to the number of custom reference types.

Nullable Modifier

Begin 2.0

Value types cannot usually be assigned `null` because, by definition, they cannot contain references, including references to nothing. However, this presents a problem because we frequently wish to represent values that are "missing." When specifying a count, for example, what do you enter if the count is unknown? One possible solution is to designate a "magic" value, such as `-1` or `int.MaxValue`, but these are valid integers. Rather, it is desirable to assign `null` to the value type because it is not a valid integer.

To declare variables of value type that can store `null`, you use the nullable modifier, ?. This feature, which was introduced with C# 2.0, appears in Listing 3.1.

LISTING 3.1: Using the Nullable Modifier

```
static void Main()
{
    int? count = null;
    do
    {
        // ...
    }
    while(count == null);
}
```

Assigning null to value types is especially attractive in database programming. Frequently, value type columns in database tables allow null values. Retrieving such columns and assigning them to corresponding fields within C# code is problematic, unless the fields can contain null as well. Fortunately, the nullable modifier is designed to handle such a scenario specifically.

End 2.0

Implicitly Typed Local Variables

Begin 3.0

C# 3.0 added a contextual keyword, var, for declaring an **implicitly typed local variable**. As long as the code initializes a variable at declaration time with an expression of unambiguous type, C# 3.0 and later allow for the variable data type to be implied rather than stated, as shown in Listing 3.2.

LISTING 3.2: Working with Strings

```
class Uppercase
{
  static void Main()
  {
      System.Console.Write("Enter text: ");
      var text = System.Console.ReadLine();

      // Return a new string in uppercase
      var uppercase = text.ToUpper();

      System.Console.WriteLine(uppercase);
  }
}
```

This listing is different from Listing 2.18 in two ways. First, rather than using the explicit data type string for the declaration, Listing 3.2 uses var. The resultant CIL code is identical to using string explicitly. However, var indicates to the compiler that it should determine the data type from the value (System.Console.ReadLine()) that is assigned within the declaration.

Second, the variables text and uppercase are initialized by their declarations. To not do so would result in an error at compile time. As mentioned earlier, the compiler determines the data type of the initializing expression and declares the variable accordingly, just as it would if the programmer had specified the type explicitly.

Although using var rather than the explicit data type is allowed, consider avoiding such use when the data type is known—for example, use string for the declaration of text and uppercase. Not only does this make the code more understandable, but it also verifies that the data type returned by the right-hand side expression is the type expected. When using a var-declared variable, the right-hand side data type should be obvious; if it isn't, use of the var declaration should be avoided.

Guidelines

AVOID using implicitly typed local variables unless the data type of the assigned value is obvious.

Language Contrast: C++/Visual Basic/JavaScript—void*, Variant, and var

An implicitly typed variable is not the equivalent of void* in C++, a Variant in Visual Basic, or var in JavaScript. In each of these cases, the variable declaration is not very restrictive because the variable may be assigned a value of any type, just as can be done in C# with a variable declaration of type object. In contrast, var is definitively typed by the compiler; once established at declaration, the type may not change, and type checks and member calls are verified at compile time.

■ ADVANCED TOPIC

Anonymous Types

Support for var was added to the language in C# 3.0 to permit use of anonymous types. Anonymous types are data types that are declared "on the fly" within a method rather than through explicit class definitions, as shown in Listing 3.3. (See Chapter 15 for more details on anonymous types.)

LISTING 3.3: Implicit Local Variables with Anonymous Types

```
class Program
{
  static void Main()
  {
    var patent1 =
        new { Title = "Bifocals",
        YearOfPublication = "1784" };
    var patent2 =
        new { Title = "Phonograph",
        YearOfPublication = "1877" };
```

```
        System.Console.WriteLine(
            $"{ patent1.Title } ({ patent1.YearOfPublication })");
        System.Console.WriteLine(
            $"{ patent2.Title } ({ patent2.YearOfPublication })");
    }
}
```

The corresponding output is shown in Output 3.1.

OUTPUT 3.1

```
Bifocals (1784)
Phonograph (1877)
```

Listing 3.3 demonstrates the anonymous type assignment to an implicitly typed (var) local variable. This type of operation provided critical functionality in tandem with C# 3.0 support for joining (associating) data types or reducing the size of a particular type down to fewer data elements. However, C# 7.0 introduces syntax for tuples, which all but replaces the need for anonymous types.

End 3.0

Tuples

Begin 7.0

On occasion, you will find it useful to combine data elements together. Consider, for example, information about a country such as the poorest country in the world in 2017: Malawi, whose capital is Lilongwe, with a GDP per capita of $226.50. Given the constructs we have established so far, we could store each data element in individual variables, but the result would be no association of the data elements together. That is, $226.50 would have no association with Malawi except perhaps by a common suffix or prefix in the variable names. Another option would be to combine all the data into a single string with the disadvantage that to work with each data element individually would require parsing it out.

C# 7.0 provides a third option, a tuple. Tuples allow you to combine the assignment to each variable in a single statement as shown here with country data:

```
(string country, string capital, double gdpPerCapita) =
    ("Malawi", "Lilongwe", 226.50);
```

Tuples have several additional syntax possibilities, each shown in Table 3.1.

7.0

TABLE 3.1: Sample Code for Tuple Declaration and Assignment

Example	Description	Example Code
| 1. | Assign a tuple to individually declared variables. | ```csharp
(string country, string capital, double gdpPerCapita) =
    ("Malawi", "Lilongwe", 226.50);
System.Console.WriteLine(
    $@"The poorest country in the world in 2017 was {
    country}, {capital}: {gdpPerCapita}");
``` |
| 2. | Assign a tuple to individually declared variables that are pre-declared. | ```csharp
string country;
string capital;
double gdpPerCapita;

(country, capital, gdpPerCapita) =
    ("Malawi", "Lilongwe", 226.50);
System.Console.WriteLine(
    $@"The poorest country in the world in 2017 was {
    country}, {capital}: {gdpPerCapita}");
``` |
| 3. | Assign a tuple to individually declared and implicitly typed variables. | ```csharp
(var country, var capital, var gdpPerCapita) =
    ("Malawi", "Lilongwe", 226.50);
System.Console.WriteLine(
    $@"The poorest country in the world in 2017 was {
    country}, {capital}: {gdpPerCapita}");
``` |
| 4. | Assign a tuple to individually declared variables that are implicitly typed with a distributive syntax. | ```csharp
var (country, capital, gdpPerCapita) =
    ("Malawi", "Lilongwe", 226.50);
System.Console.WriteLine(
    $@"The poorest country in the world in 2017 was {
    country}, {capital}: {gdpPerCapita}");
``` |
| 5. | Declare a named item tuple and assign it tuple values, and then access the tuple items by name. | ```csharp
(string Name, string Capital, double GdpPerCapita) countryInfo =
    ("Malawi", "Lilongwe", 226.50);
System.Console.WriteLine(
    $@"The poorest country in the world in 2017 was {
    countryInfo.Name}, {countryInfo.Capital}: {
    countryInfo.GdpPerCapita}");
``` |
```

TABLE 3.1: Sample Code for Tuple Declaration and Assignment (*continued*)

Example	Description	Example Code
6.	Assign a named item tuple to a single implicitly typed variable that is implicitly typed, and then access the tuple items by name.	```var countryInfo =
(Name: "Malawi", Capital: "Lilongwe", GdpPerCapita: 226.50);
System.Console.WriteLine(
$@"The poorest country in the world in 2017 was {
countryInfo.Name}, {countryInfo.Capital}: {
countryInfo.gdpPerCapita}");```
7.	Assign an unnamed tuple to a single implicitly typed variable, and then access the tuple elements by their item-number property.	```var countryInfo =
("Malawi", "Lilongwe", 226.50);
System.Console.WriteLine(
$@"The poorest country in the world in 2017 was {
countryInfo.Item1}, {countryInfo.Item2}: {
countryInfo.Item3}");```
8.	Assign a named item tuple to a single implicitly typed variable, and then access the tuple items by their item-number property.	```var countryInfo =
(Name: "Malawi", Capital: "Lilongwe", GdpPerCapita: 226.50);
System.Console.WriteLine(
$@"The poorest country in the world in 2017 was {
countryInfo.Item1}, {countryInfo.Item2}: {
countryInfo.Item3}");```
9.	Discard portions of the tuple with underscores.	```(string name, _, double gdpPerCapita) countryInfo =
("Malawi", "Lilongwe", 226.50);```
10.	Tuple element names can be inferred from variable and property names (starting in C# 7.1).	```string country = "Malawi";
string capital = "Lilongwe";
double gdpPerCapita = 226.50;

var countryInfo =
    (country, capital, gdpPerCapita);
System.Console.WriteLine(
    $@"The poorest country in the world in 2017 was {
    countryInfo.country}, {countryInfo.capital}: {
    countryInfo.gdpPerCapita}");``` |

In the first four examples, and although the right-hand side represents a tuple, the left-hand side still represents individual variables that are assigned together using **tuple syntax**, a syntax involving two or more elements separated by commas and associated together with parentheses. (I use the term *tuple syntax* because the underlying data type that the compiler generates on the left-hand side isn't technically a tuple.) The result is that although we start with values combined as a tuple on the right, the assignment to the left deconstructs the tuple into its constituent parts. In example 2, the left-hand side assignment is to pre-declared variables. However, in examples 1, 3, and 4, the variables are declared within the tuple syntax. Given that we are only declaring variables, the naming and casing convention follows the guidelines we discussed in Chapter 1: "DO use camelCase for local variable names," for example.

Note that although implicit typing (`var`) can be distributed across each variable declaration within the tuple syntax, as shown in example 4, you cannot do the same with an explicit type (such as `string`). Since tuples allow each item to be a different data type, distributing the explicit type name across all elements wouldn't necessarily work unless all the item data types were identical (and even then, the compiler doesn't allow it).

In example 5, we declare a tuple on the left-hand side and then assign the tuple on the right. Note that the tuple has named items, names that we can then reference to retrieve the item values back out of the tuple. This is what enables `countryInfo.Name`, `countryInfo.Capital`, and `countryInfo.GdpPerCapita` syntax in the `System.Console.WriteLine` statement. The result of the tuple declaration on the left is a grouping of the variables into a single variable (`countryInfo`) from which you can then access the constituent parts. This is useful because, as we discuss in Chapter 4, you can then pass this single variable around to other methods, and those methods will also be able to access the individual items within the tuple.

As already mentioned, variables defined using tuple syntax use camelCase. However, the convention for tuple item names is not well defined. Suggestions include using parameter naming conventions when the tuple behaves like a parameter—such as when returning multiple values that before tuple syntax would have used out parameters. The alternative is to use PascalCase, following the naming convention for members of a type (properties, functions, and public fields, as discussed in Chapters 5 and 6). I strongly favor the latter approach of PascalCase, consistent with the casing convention of all member identifiers in C# and .NET. Even so, since the convention isn't broadly agreed upon, I use the word CONSIDER rather than DO in the guideline, "CONSIDER using PascalCasing for all tuple item names."

7.0

> ### Guidelines
>
> DO use camelCasing for variable declarations using tuple syntax.
>
> CONSIDER using PascalCasing for all tuple item names.

Example 6 provides the same functionality as Example 5, although it uses named tuple items on the right-hand side tuple value and an implicit type declaration on the left. The items' names are persisted to the implicitly typed variable, however, so they are still available for the `WriteLine` statement. Of course, this opens up the possibility that you could name the items on the left-hand side with different names than what you use on the right. While the C# compiler allows this, it will issue a warning that the item names on the right will be ignored, as those on the left will take precedence.

If no item names are specified, the individual elements are still available from the assigned tuple variable. However, the names are `Item1`, `Item2, ...`, as shown in Example 7. In fact, the `ItemX` names are always available on the tuple even when custom names are provided (see Example 8). However, when using integrated development environment (IDE) tools such as one of the recent flavors of Visual Studio (one that supports C# 7.0), the `ItemX` property will not appear within the IntelliSense dropdown—a good thing, since presumably the provided name is preferable. As shown in Example 9, portions of a tuple assignment can be discarded using an underscore—referred to as a **discard**.

The ability to infer the tuple item names as shown in example 10 isn't introduced until C# 7.1. As the example demonstrates, the item name within the tuple can be inferred from a variable name or even a property name.

Tuples are a lightweight solution for encapsulating data into a single object in the same way that a bag might capture miscellaneous items you pick up from the store. Unlike arrays (which we discuss next), tuples contain item data types that can vary without constraint[1] except that they are

---

1. Technically, they can't be pointers—a topic we don't introduce until Chapter 21.

identified by the code and cannot be changed at runtime. Also, unlike with arrays, the number of items within the tuple is hardcoded at compile time as well. Lastly, you cannot add custom behavior to a tuple (extension methods notwithstanding). If you need behavior associated with the encapsulated data, then leveraging object-oriented programming and defining a class is the preferred approach—a concept we begin exploring in depth in Chapter 6.

7.0

■ ADVANCED TOPIC

The System.ValueTuple<...> Type

The C# compiler generates code that relies on a set of generic value types (structs), such as `System.ValueTuple<T1, T2, T3>`, as the underlying implementation for the tuple syntax for all tuple instances on the right-hand side of the examples in Table 3.1. Similarly, the same set of `System.ValueTuple<...>` generic value types is used for the left-hand side data type starting with example 5. As we would expect with a tuple type, the only methods included are those related to comparison and equality.

Given that the custom item names and their types are not included in the `System.ValueTuple<...>` definition, how is it possible that each custom item name is seemingly a member of the `System.ValueTuple<...>` type and accessible as a member of that type? What is surprising (particularly for those familiar with the anonymous type implementation) is that the compiler does not generate underlying CIL code for the members corresponding to the custom names. However, even without an underlying member with the custom name, there is (seemingly), from the C# perspective, such a member.

For all the named tuple examples in Table 3.1, it is clearly possible that the names could be known by the compiler for the remainder of the scope of the tuple, since the said scope is bounded within the member in which it is declared. And, in fact, the compiler (and IDE) quite simply rely on this scope to allow accessing each item by name. In other words, the compiler looks at the item names within the tuple declaration and leverages them to allow code that uses those names within the scope. It is for this reason as well that the `ItemX` names are not shown in the IDE IntelliSense as available members on the tuple (the IDE simply ignores them and replaces them with the explicit named items).

Determining the item names from those scoped within a member is reasonable for the compiler, but what happens when a tuple is exposed outside the member, such as a parameter or return from a method that is in a different assembly (for which there is possibly no source code available)? For all tuples that are part of the API (whether a public or private API), the compiler adds item names to the metadata of the member in the form of attributes. For example, the C# equivalent of what the compiler generates for

```
public (string First, string Second) ParseNames(string fullName)
```

is shown in Listing 3.4.

LISTING 3.4: The C# Equivalent of Compiler-Generated CIL Code for a ValueTuple return

```
[return: System.Runtime.CompilerServices.TupleElementNames(new string[]
{"First", "Second"})]
public System.ValueTuple<string, string> ParseNames(string fullName)
{
    // ...
}
```

On a related note, C# 7.0 does not enable the use of custom item names when using the explicit `System.ValueTuple<...>` data type. Therefore, if you replace `var` in Example 8 of Table 3.1, you will end up with warnings that each item name will be ignored.

Here are a few additional miscellaneous facts to keep in mind about `System.ValueTuple<...>`.

- There are eight generic `System.ValueTuple<...>`s corresponding to the possibility of supporting tuple with up to seven items. For the eighth tuple, `System.ValueTuple<T1, T2, T3, T4, T5, T6, T7, TRest>`, the last type parameter allows specifying an additional `ValueTuple`, thus enabling support for *n* items. If, for example, you specify a tuple with 8 parameters, the compiler will automatically generate a `System.ValueTuple<T1, T2, T3, T4, T5, T6, T7, System .ValueTuple<TSub1>>` as the underlying implementing type. (For completeness, the `System.Value<T1>` exists but will rarely be used, since the C# tuple syntax requires a minimum of two items.)
- There is a nongeneric `System.ValueTuple` that serves as a tuple factory with `Create()` methods corresponding to each `ValueTuple` arity. The

ease of using a tuple literal var t1 = ("Inigo Montoya", 42) supersedes the Create() method at least for C# 7.0 (or later) programmers.

- For all practical purposes, C# developers can essentially ignore System.ValueTuple and System.ValueTuple<T>.

Begin 6.0

End 6.0

End 7.0

There is another tuple type that was first included with the Microsoft .NET Framework 4.5: System.Tuple<...>. At the time it was included, it was expected to be the core tuple implementation going forward. However, once C# supported tuple syntax, it was realized that a value type was generally more performant, and so System.ValueTuple<...> was introduced—effectively replacing System.Tuple<...> in all cases except backward compatibility with existing APIs that depend on System.Tuple<...>.

Arrays

One particular aspect of variable declaration that Chapter 1 didn't cover is array declaration. With array declaration, you can store multiple items of the same type using a single variable and still access them individually using the index when required. In C#, the array index starts at zero. Therefore, arrays in C# are zero based.

▪ BEGINNER TOPIC

Arrays

Arrays provide a means of declaring a collection of data items that are of the same type using a single variable. Each item within the array is uniquely designated using an integer value called the **index**. The first item in a C# array is accessed using index 0. Programmers should be careful to specify an index value that is less than the array size. Since C# arrays are zero based, the index for the last element in an array is one less than the total number of items in the array.

For beginners, it is helpful sometimes to think of the index as an offset. The first item is zero away from the start of the array. The second item is one away from the start of the array—and so on.

Arrays are a fundamental part of nearly every programming language, so they are required learning for virtually all developers. Although arrays are frequently used in C# programming, and necessary for the beginner to understand, most programs now use generic collection types rather than arrays when storing collections of data. Therefore, readers should skim over the following section, "Declaring an Array," simply to become familiar with their instantiation and assignment. Table 3.2 provides the highlights of what to note. Generic collections are covered in detail in Chapter 15.

TABLE 3.2: Array Highlights

Description	Example

Declaration
Note that the brackets appear with the data type. Multidimensional arrays are declared using commas, where the comma+1 specifies the number of dimensions.
	``cs
	string[] languages; // one-dimensional
	int[,] cells; // two-dimensional
	``

Assignment
The new keyword and the corresponding data type are optional at declaration time.
Following declaration, the new keyword is required when instantiating an array.
Arrays can be assigned without literal values. As a result, the value of each item in the array is initialized to its default.
If no literal values are provided, the size of the array must be specified. (The size does not have to be a constant; it can be a variable calculated at runtime.)
Starting with C# 3.0, specifying the data type is optional.
	``cs
	string[] languages = { "C#", "COBOL", "Java",
	    "C++", "Visual Basic", "Pascal",
	    "Fortran", "Lisp", "J#"};
	languages = new string[9];
	languages = new string[]{"C#", "COBOL", "Java",
	    "C++", "Visual Basic", "Pascal",
	    "Fortran", "Lisp", "J#" };
	
	// Multidimensional array assignment
	// and initialization
	int[,] cells = int[3,3];
	cells = {
	    {1, 0, 2},
	    {1, 2, 0},
	    {1, 2, 1}
	};
	``

default Keyword
The explicit default of any data type is available using the default operator.
	``cs
	int count = default(int);
	``

continues

TABLE 3.2: Array Highlights (*continued*)

Description	Example

Accessing an Array
Arrays are zero based, so the first element in an array is at index 0.
The square brackets are used to store and retrieve data from an array.
	`string[] languages = new string[9]{`
	`    "C#", "COBOL", "Java",`
	`    "C++", "Visual Basic", "Pascal",`
	`    "Fortran", "Lisp", "J#"};`
	`// Save "C++" to variable called language`
	`string language = languages[3];`
	`// Assign "Java" to the C++ position`
	`languages[3] = languages[2];`
	`// Assign language to location of "Java"`
	`languages[2] = language;`

In addition, the final section of this chapter, "Common Array Errors," provides a review of some of the array idiosyncrasies.

Declaring an Array

In C#, you declare arrays using square brackets. First, you specify the element type of the array, followed by open and closed square brackets; then you enter the name of the variable. Listing 3.5 declares a variable called languages to be an array of strings.

LISTING 3.5: Declaring an Array

```
string[] languages;
```

Obviously, the first part of the array identifies the data type of the elements within the array. The square brackets that are part of the declaration identify the **rank**, or the number of dimensions, for the array; in this case, it is an array of rank 1. These two pieces form the data type for the variable languages.

Language Contrast: C++ and Java—Array Declaration

The square brackets for an array in C# appear immediately following the data type instead of after the variable declaration. This practice keeps all the type information together instead of splitting it up both before and after the identifier, as occurs in C++ and Java.

Listing 3.5 defines an array with a rank of 1. Commas within the square brackets define additional dimensions. Listing 3.6, for example, defines a two-dimensional array of cells for a game of chess or tic-tac-toe.

LISTING 3.6: Declaring a Two-Dimensional Array

```
//     |   |
// ---+---+---
//     |   |
// ---+---+---
//     |   |
int[,] cells;
```

In Listing 3.6, the array has a rank of 2. The first dimension could correspond to cells going across and the second dimension to cells going down. Additional dimensions are added, with additional commas, and the total rank is one more than the number of commas. Note that the number of items that occur for a particular dimension is not part of the variable declaration. This is specified when creating (instantiating) the array and allocating space for each element.

Instantiating and Assigning Arrays

Once an array is declared, you can immediately fill its values using a comma-delimited list of items enclosed within a pair of curly braces. Listing 3.7 declares an array of strings and then assigns the names of nine languages within curly braces.

LISTING 3.7: Array Declaration with Assignment

```
string[] languages = { "C#", "COBOL", "Java",
    "C++", "Visual Basic", "Pascal",
    "Fortran", "Lisp", "J#"};
```

The first item in the comma-delimited list becomes the first item in the array, the second item in the list becomes the second item in the array, and so on. The curly brackets are the notation for defining an array literal.

The assignment syntax shown in Listing 3.6 is available only if you declare and assign the value within one statement. To assign the value after declaration requires the use of the keyword new, as shown in Listing 3.8.

LISTING 3.8: Array Assignment Following Declaration

```
string[] languages;
languages = new string[]{"C#", "COBOL", "Java",
    "C++", "Visual Basic", "Pascal",
    "Fortran", "Lisp", "J#" };
```

Starting in C# 3.0, specifying the data type of the array (`string`) following new is optional as long as the compiler is able to deduce the element type of the array from the types of the elements in the array initializer. The square brackets are still required.

C# also allows use of the new keyword as part of the declaration statement, so it allows the assignment and the declaration shown in Listing 3.9.

LISTING 3.9: Array Assignment with new during Declaration

```
string[] languages = new string[]{
    "C#", "COBOL", "Java",
    "C++", "Visual Basic", "Pascal",
    "Fortran", "Lisp", "J#"};
```

The use of the new keyword tells the runtime to allocate memory for the data type. It instructs the runtime to instantiate the data type—in this case, an array.

Whenever you use the new keyword as part of an array assignment, you may also specify the size of the array within the square brackets. Listing 3.10 demonstrates this syntax.

LISTING 3.10: Declaration and Assignment with the new Keyword

```
string[] languages = new string[9]{
    "C#", "COBOL", "Java",
    "C++", "Visual Basic", "Pascal",
    "Fortran", "Lisp", "J#"};
```

The array size in the initialization statement and the number of elements contained within the curly braces must match. Furthermore, it is possible to assign an array but not specify the initial values of the array, as demonstrated in Listing 3.11.

LISTING 3.11: Assigning without Literal Values

```
string[] languages = new string[9];
```

Assigning an array but not initializing the initial values will still initialize each element. The runtime initializes elements to their default values, as follows:

- Reference types (such as `string`) are initialized to `null`.
- Numeric types are initialized to `0`.
- `bool` is initialized to `false`.
- `char` is initialized to `\0`.

Nonprimitive value types are recursively initialized by initializing each of their fields to their default values. As a result, it is not necessary to individually assign each element of an array before using it.

> **■ NOTE**
>
> In C# 2.0, it is possible to use the `default()` operator to produce the default value of a data type. `default()` takes a data type as a parameter. `default(int)`, for example, produces `0` and `default(bool)` produces `false`.

Begin 2.0

End 2.0

Because the array size is not included as part of the variable declaration, it is possible to specify the size at runtime. For example, Listing 3.12 creates an array based on the size specified in the `Console.ReadLine()` call.

LISTING 3.12: Defining the Array Size at Runtime

```csharp
string[] groceryList;
System.Console.Write("How many items on the list? ");
int size = int.Parse(System.Console.ReadLine());
groceryList = new string[size];
// ...
```

C# initializes multidimensional arrays similarly. A comma separates the size of each rank. Listing 3.13 initializes a tic-tac-toe board with no moves.

LISTING 3.13: Declaring a Two-Dimensional Array

```csharp
int[,] cells = new int[3,3];
```

Initializing a tic-tac-toe board with a specific position could be done as shown in Listing 3.14.

LISTING 3.14: Initializing a Two-Dimensional Array of Integers

```
int[,] cells = {
        {1, 0, 2},
        {1, 2, 0},
        {1, 2, 1}
    };
```

The initialization follows the pattern in which there is an array of three elements of type int[], and each element has the same size; in this example, the size is 3. Note that the sizes of each int[] element must all be identical. The declaration shown in Listing 3.15, therefore, is not valid.

LISTING 3.15: A Multidimensional Array with Inconsistent Size, Causing an Error

```
// ERROR: Each dimension must be consistently sized
int[,] cells = {
        {1, 0, 2, 0},
        {1, 2, 0},
        {1, 2}
        {1}
    };
```

Representing tic-tac-toe does not require an integer in each position. One alternative is to construct a separate virtual board for each player, with each board containing a bool that indicates which positions the players selected. Listing 3.16 corresponds to a three-dimensional board.

LISTING 3.16: Initializing a Three-Dimensional Array

```
bool[,,] cells;
cells = new bool[2,3,3]
    {
        // Player 1 moves              // X |   |
        {  {true, false, false},       // ---+---+---
           {true, false, false},       // X |   |
           {true, false, true} },      // ---+---+---
                                       // X |   | X

        // Player 2 moves              //   |   | O
        {  {false, false, true},       // ---+---+---
           {false, true, false},       //   | O |
           {false, true, false} }      // ---+---+---
                                       //   | O |
    };
```

In this example, the board is initialized and the size of each rank is explicitly identified. In addition to identifying the size as part of the new expression, the literal values for the array are provided. The literal values of type bool[, ,] are broken into two arrays of type bool[,], size 3 × 3. Each two-dimensional array is composed of three bool arrays, size 3.

As already mentioned, each dimension in a multidimensional array must be consistently sized. However, it is also possible to define a **jagged array**, which is an array of arrays. Jagged array syntax is slightly different from that of a multidimensional array; furthermore, jagged arrays do not need to be consistently sized. Therefore, it is possible to initialize a jagged array as shown in Listing 3.17.

LISTING 3.17: Initializing a Jagged Array

```
int[][] cells = {
    new int[]{1, 0, 2, 0},
    new int[]{1, 2, 0},
    new int[]{1, 2},
    new int[]{1}
};
```

A jagged array doesn't use a comma to identify a new dimension. Rather, a jagged array defines an array of arrays. In Listing 3.17, [] is placed after the data type int[], thereby declaring an array of type int[].

Notice that a jagged array requires an array instance (or null) for each internal array. In the preceding example, you use new to instantiate the internal element of the jagged arrays. Leaving out the instantiation would cause a compile error.

Using an Array

You access a specific item in an array using the square bracket notation, known as the **array accessor**. To retrieve the first item from an array, you specify zero as the index. In Listing 3.18, the value of the fifth item (using the index 4 because the first item is index 0) in the languages variable is stored in the variable language.

LISTING 3.18: Declaring and Accessing an Array

```
string[] languages = new string[9]{
    "C#", "COBOL", "Java",
    "C++", "Visual Basic", "Pascal",
    "Fortran", "Lisp", "J#"};
```

```
// Retrieve fifth item in languages array (Visual Basic)
string language = languages[4];
```

The square bracket notation is also used to store data into an array. List-ing 3.19 switches the order of "C++" and "Java".

LISTING 3.19: Swapping Data between Positions in an Array

```
string[] languages = new string[9]{
    "C#", "COBOL", "Java",
    "C++", "Visual Basic", "Pascal",
    "Fortran", "Lisp", "J#"};
// Save "C++" to variable called language
string language = languages[3];
// Assign "Java" to the C++ position
languages[3] = languages[2];
// Assign language to location of "Java"
languages[2] = language;
```

For multidimensional arrays, an element is identified with an index for each dimension, as shown in Listing 3.20.

LISTING 3.20: Initializing a Two-Dimensional Array of Integers

```
int[,] cells = {
        {1, 0, 2},
        {0, 2, 0},
        {1, 2, 1}
    };
// Set the winning tic-tac-toe move to be player 1
cells[1,0] = 1;
```

Jagged array element assignment is slightly different because it is con-sistent with the jagged array declaration. The first element is an array within the array of arrays; the second index specifies the item within the selected array element (see Listing 3.21).

LISTING 3.21: Declaring a Jagged Array

```
int[][] cells = {
    new int[]{1, 0, 2},
    new int[]{0, 2, 0},
    new int[]{1, 2, 1}
};

cells[1][0] = 1;
// ...
```

Length

You can obtain the length of an array, as shown in Listing 3.22.

LISTING 3.22: Retrieving the Length of an Array

```
Console.WriteLine(
    $"There are { languages.Length } languages in the array.");
```

Arrays have a fixed length; they are bound such that the length cannot be changed without re-creating the array. Furthermore, overstepping the **bounds** (or length) of the array will cause the runtime to report an error. This can occur when you attempt to access (either retrieve or assign) the array with an index for which no element exists in the array. Such an error frequently occurs when you use the array length as an index into the array, as shown in Listing 3.23.

LISTING 3.23: Accessing Outside the Bounds of an Array, Throwing an Exception

```
string languages = new string[9];
...
// RUNTIME ERROR: index out of bounds — should
// be 8 for the last element
languages[4] = languages[9];
```

▪ NOTE

The Length member returns the number of items in the array, not the highest index. The Length member for the languages variable is 9, but the highest index for the languages variable is 8, because that is how far it is from the start.

Language Contrast: C++—Buffer Overflow Bugs

Unmanaged C++ does not always check whether you overstep the bounds on an array. Not only can this be difficult to debug, but making this mistake can also result in a potential security error called a **buffer overrun**. In contrast, the Common Language Runtime protects all C# (and Managed C++) code from overstepping array bounds, virtually eliminating the possibility of a buffer overrun issue in managed code.

It is a good practice to use Length in place of the hardcoded array size. To use Length as an index, for example, it is necessary to subtract 1 to avoid an out-of-bounds error (see Listing 3.24).

LISTING 3.24: Using Length - 1 in the Array Index

```
string languages = new string[9];
...
languages[4] = languages[languages.Length - 1];
```

To avoid overstepping the bounds on an array, use a length check to verify that the array has a length greater than 0, and use Length − 1 in place of a hardcoded value when accessing the last item in the array (see Listing 3.24).

Length returns the total number of elements in an array. Therefore, if you had a multidimensional array such as bool cells[,,] of size 2 × 3 × 3, Length would return the total number of elements, 18.

For a jagged array, Length returns the number of elements in the first array. Because a jagged array is an array of arrays, Length evaluates only the outside containing array and returns its element count, regardless of what is inside the internal arrays.

More Array Methods

Arrays include additional methods for manipulating the elements within the array—for example, Sort( ), BinarySearch( ), Reverse( ), and Clear( ) (see Listing 3.25).

LISTING 3.25: Additional Array Methods

```
class ProgrammingLanguages
{
  static void Main()
  {
      string[] languages = new string[]{
        "C#", "COBOL", "Java",
        "C++", "Visual Basic", "Pascal",
        "Fortran", "Lisp", "J#"};

      System.Array.Sort(languages);

      string searchString = "COBOL";
      int index = System.Array.BinarySearch(
        languages, searchString);
      System.Console.WriteLine(
        "The wave of the future, "
        + $"{ searchString }, is at index { index }.");
```

```
        System.Console.WriteLine();
        System.Console.WriteLine(
            $"{ "First Element",-20 }\t{ "Last Element",-20 }");
        System.Console.WriteLine(
            $"{ "------------",-20 }\t{ "------------",-20 }");
        System.Console.WriteLine(
                $"{ languages[0],-20 }\t{ languages[languages.Length-1],-20
🖑}");
        System.Array.Reverse(languages);
        System.Console.WriteLine(
                $"{ languages[0],-20 }\t{ languages[languages.Length-1],-20
🖑}");
        // Note this does not remove all items from the array.
        // Rather, it sets each item to the type's default value.
        System.Array.Clear(languages, 0, languages.Length);
        System.Console.WriteLine(
                $"{ languages[0],-20 }\t{ languages[languages.Length-1],-20
🖑}");
        System.Console.WriteLine(
            $"After clearing, the array size is: { languages.Length }");
    }
}
```

The results of Listing 3.25 are shown in Output 3.2.

OUTPUT 3.2

```
The wave of the future, COBOL, is at index 2.

First Element          Last Element
------------           ------------
C#                     Visual Basic
Visual Basic           C#

After clearing, the array size is: 9
```

Access to these methods is obtained through the System.Array class. For the most part, using these methods is self-explanatory, except for two noteworthy items:

- Before using the BinarySearch() method, it is important to sort the array. If values are not sorted in increasing order, the incorrect index may be returned. If the search element does not exist, the value returned is negative. (Using the complement operator, ~index, returns the first index, if any, that is larger than the searched value.)

- The Clear() method does not remove elements of the array and does not set the length to zero. The array size is fixed and cannot be modified. Therefore, the Clear() method sets each element in the array to its default value (false, 0, or null). This explains why Console.WriteLine() creates a blank line when writing out the array after Clear() is called.

Language Contrast: Visual Basic—Redimensioning Arrays

Visual Basic includes a Redim statement for changing the number of items in an array. Although there is no equivalent C#-specific keyword, there is a method available in .NET 2.0 that will re-create the array and then copy all the elements over to the new array. This method is called System.Array.Resize.

Array Instance Methods

Like strings, arrays have instance members that are accessed not from the data type but directly from the variable. Length is an example of an instance member because access to Length is through the array variable, not the class. Other significant instance members are GetLength(), Rank, and Clone().

Retrieving the length of a particular dimension does not require the Length property. To retrieve the size of a particular rank, an array includes a GetLength() instance method. When calling this method, it is necessary to specify the rank whose length will be returned (see Listing 3.26).

LISTING 3.26: Retrieving a Particular Dimension's Size

```
bool[,,] cells;
cells = new bool[2,3,3];
System.Console.WriteLine(cells.GetLength(0));    // Displays 2
```

The results of Listing 3.26 appear in Output 3.3.

OUTPUT 3.3

```
2
```

Listing 3.26 displays 2 because that is the number of elements in the first dimension.

It is also possible to retrieve the entire array's rank by accessing the array's Rank member. `cells.Rank`, for example, will return 3.

By default, assigning one array variable to another copies only the array reference, not the individual elements of the array. To make an entirely new copy of the array, use the array's `Clone()` method. The `Clone()` method will return a copy of the array; changing any of the members of this new array will not affect the members of the original array.

Strings as Arrays

Variables of type `string` are accessible like an array of characters. For example, to retrieve the fourth character of a string called `palindrome`, you can call `palindrome[3]`. Note, however, that because strings are immutable, it is not possible to assign particular characters within a string. C#, therefore, would not allow `palindrome[3]='a'`, where `palindrome` is declared as a string. Listing 3.27 uses the array accessor to determine whether an argument on the command line is an option, where an option is identified by a dash as the first character.

LISTING 3.27: Looking for Command-Line Options

```
string[] args;
...
if(args[0][0] == '-')
{
    // This parameter is an option
}
```

This snippet uses the `if` statement, which is covered in Chapter 4. In addition, it presents an interesting example because you use the array accessor to retrieve the first element in the array of strings, `args`. Following the first array accessor is a second one, which retrieves the first character of the string. The code, therefore, is equivalent to that shown in Listing 3.28.

LISTING 3.28: Looking for Command-Line Options (Simplified)

```
string[] args;
...
string arg = args[0];
if(arg[0] == '-')
{
    // This parameter is an option
}
```

Not only can string characters be accessed individually using the array accessor, but it is also possible to retrieve the entire string as an array of characters using the string's ToCharArray() method. Using this approach, you could reverse the string with the System.Array.Reverse() method, as demonstrated in Listing 3.29, which determines whether a string is a palindrome.

LISTING 3.29: Reversing a String

```
class Palindrome
{
  static void Main()
  {
      string reverse, palindrome;
      char[] temp;

      System.Console.Write("Enter a palindrome: ");
      palindrome = System.Console.ReadLine();

      // Remove spaces and convert to lowercase
      reverse = palindrome.Replace(" ", "");
      reverse = reverse.ToLower();

      // Convert to an array
      temp = reverse.ToCharArray();

      // Reverse the array
      System.Array.Reverse(temp);

      // Convert the array back to a string and
      // check if reverse string is the same
      if(reverse == new string(temp))
      {
          System.Console.WriteLine(
              $"\"{palindrome}\" is a palindrome.");
      }
      else
      {
          System.Console.WriteLine(
              $"\"{palindrome}\" is NOT a palindrome.");
      }
  }
}
```

The results of Listing 3.29 appear in Output 3.4.

OUTPUT 3.4

```
Enter a palindrome: NeverOddOrEven
"NeverOddOrEven" is a palindrome.
```

This example uses the new keyword; this time, it creates a new string from the reversed array of characters.

Common Array Errors

This section introduced the three types of arrays: single-dimensional, multi-dimensional, and jagged arrays. Several rules and idiosyncrasies govern array declaration and use. Table 3.3 points out some of the most common errors and helps solidify the rules. Try reviewing the code in the Common Mistake column first (without looking at the Error Description and Corrected Code columns) as a way of verifying your understanding of arrays and their syntax.

TABLE 3.3: Common Array Coding Errors

Common Mistake	Error Description	Corrected Code
`int numbers[];`	The square braces for declaring an array appear after the data type, not after the variable identifier.	`int[] numbers;`

`int[] numbers;`
`numbers = {42, 84, 168 };`
	When assigning an array after declaration, it is necessary to use the new keyword and then specify the data type.	`int[] numbers;`
		`numbers = new int[]{`
		`  42, 84, 168 }`

`int[3] numbers =` `  { 42, 84, 168 };`	It is not possible to specify the array size as part of the variable declaration.	`int[] numbers =` `  { 42, 84, 168 };`
`int[] numbers =` `  new int[];`	The array size is required at initialization time unless an array literal is provided.	`int[] numbers =` `  new int[3];`

`int[] numbers =`
`  new int[3]{}`
	The array size is specified as 3, but there are no elements in the array literal. The array size must match the number of elements in the array literal.	`int[] numbers =`
		`  new int[3]`
		`  { 42, 84, 168 };`

continues

TABLE 3.3: Common Array Coding Errors (*continued*)

Common Mistake	Error Description	Corrected Code

`int[] numbers =`
`  new int[3];`
`Console.WriteLine(`
`  numbers[3]);`
	Array indexes start at zero. Therefore, the last item is one less than the array size. (Note that this is a runtime error, not a compile-time error.)	`int[] numbers =`
		`  new int[3];`
		`Console.WriteLine(`
		`  numbers[2]);`

`int[] numbers =`
`  new int[3];`
`numbers[numbers.Length] =`
`  42;`
	Same as previous error: 1 needs to be subtracted from the Length to access the last element. (Note that this is a runtime error, not a compile-time error.)	`int[] numbers =`
		`  new int[3];`
		`numbers[numbers.`
		`⤷Length-1] =`
		`  42;`

`int[] numbers;`
`Console.WriteLine(`
`  numbers[0]);`
	numbers has not yet been assigned an instantiated array, so it cannot be accessed.	`int[] numbers = {42, 84};`
		`Console.WriteLine(`
		`  numbers[0]);`

`int[,] numbers =`
`  { {42},`
`    {84, 42} };`
	Multidimensional arrays must be structured consistently.	`int[,] numbers =`
		`  { {42, 168},`
		`    {84, 42} };`

`int[][] numbers =`
`  { {42, 84},`
`    {84, 42} };`
	Jagged arrays require instantiated arrays to be specified for the arrays within the array.	`int[][] numbers =`
		`  { new int[]{42, 84},`
		`    new int[]{84, 42} };`

SUMMARY

We began the chapter with a discussion of two different categories of types: value types and reference types. These are fundamental concepts that are important for C# programmers to understand because they change the underlying way a type behaves even though it might not be obvious when reading through the code.

Before discussing arrays, we looked at two language constructs that were added in later versions. First, we introduced the nullable modifier, (?), which was added to the language in C# 2.0 and enables value types to store null. Second, we introduced tuples and a new syntax introduced with C# 7.0 that provides language support for working with tuples without having to work explicitly with the underlying data type.

This chapter closed with coverage of C# syntax for arrays, along with the various means of manipulating arrays. For many developers, the syntax can seem rather daunting at first, so the section included a list of the common errors associated with coding arrays.

The next chapter looks at expressions and control flow statements. The `if` statement, which appeared a few times toward the end of this chapter, is discussed as well.

▌4▪

Operators and Control Flow

I N THIS CHAPTER, YOU LEARN about operators, control flow statements, and the C# preprocessor. **Operators** provide syntax for performing different calculations or actions appropriate for the operands within the calculation. **Control flow statements** provide the means for conditional logic within a program or looping over a section of code multiple times. After introducing the `if` control flow statement, the chapter looks at the concept of Boolean expressions, which are embedded within many control flow statements. Included is mention of how integers cannot be converted

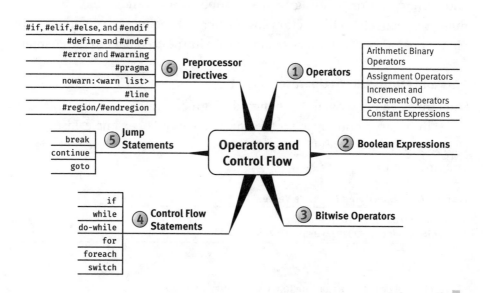

(even explicitly) to bool and the advantages of this restriction. The chapter ends with a discussion of the C# preprocessor directives.

Operators

Now that you have been introduced to the predefined data types (refer to Chapter 2), you can begin to learn more about how to use these data types in combination with operators to perform calculations. For example, you can make calculations on variables that you have declared.

■ BEGINNER TOPIC

Operators

Operators are used to perform mathematical or logical operations on values (or variables) called **operands** to produce a new value, called the **result**. For example, in Listing 4.1 the subtraction operator, -, is used to subtract two operands, the numbers 4 and 2. The result of the subtraction is stored in the variable difference.

LISTING 4.1: **A Simple Operator Example**

```
int difference = 4 - 2;
```

Operators are generally classified into three categories—unary, binary, and ternary, corresponding to the number of operands (one, two, and three, respectively). This section covers some of the most basic unary and binary operators. The ternary operators are introduced later in the chapter.

Plus and Minus Unary Operators (+, -)

Sometimes you may want to change the sign of a numeric value. In these cases, the unary minus operator (-) comes in handy. For example, Listing 4.2 changes the total current U.S. debt to a negative value to indicate that it is an amount owed.

LISTING 4.2: **Specifying Negative Values**[1]

```
// National debt to the penny
decimal debt = -20203668853807.76M;
```

---

1. As of October 1, 2017, according to www.treasurydirect.gov.

Using the minus operator *is equivalent to subtracting the operand from zero*.

The unary plus operator (+) rarely[2] has any effect on a value. It is a superfluous addition to the C# language and was included for the sake of symmetry.

Arithmetic Binary Operators (+, -, *, /, %)

Binary operators require two operands. C# uses infix notation for binary operators: The operator appears between the left and right operands. The result of every binary operator other than assignment must be used somehow—for example, by using it as an operand in another expression such as an assignment.

Language Contrast: C++—Operator-Only Statements

In contrast to the rule mentioned previously, C++ will allow a single binary expression to form the entirety of a statement, such as 4+5;, to compile. In C#, only assignment, call, increment, decrement, await, and object creation expressions are allowed to be the entirety of a statement.

The subtraction example in Listing 4.3 illustrates the use of a binary operator—more specifically, an arithmetic binary operator. The operands appear on each side of the arithmetic operator, and then the calculated value is assigned. The other arithmetic binary operators are addition (+), division (/), multiplication (*), and remainder (% [sometimes called the mod operator]).

LISTING 4.3: Using Binary Operators

```
class Division
{
  static void Main()
  {
      int numerator;
      int denominator;
      int quotient;
      int remainder;
```

---

2. The unary + operator is defined to take operands of type int, uint, long, ulong, float, double, and decimal (and nullable versions of those types). Using it on other numeric types such as short will convert its operand to one of these types as appropriate.

```
        System.Console.Write("Enter the numerator: ");
        numerator = int.Parse(System.Console.ReadLine());

        System.Console.Write("Enter the denominator: ");
        denominator = int.Parse(System.Console.ReadLine());

        quotient = numerator / denominator;
        remainder = numerator % denominator;

        System.Console.WriteLine(
            $"{numerator} / {denominator} = {quotient} with remainder
    {remainder}");
        }
    }
```

Output 4.1 shows the results of Listing 4.3.

OUTPUT 4.1

```
Enter the numerator: 23
Enter the denominator: 3
23 / 3 = 7 with remainder 2
```

In the highlighted assignment statements, the division and remainder operations are executed before the assignments. The order in which operators are executed is determined by their **precedence** and **associativity**. The precedence for the operators used so far is as follows:

1. *, /, and % have highest precedence.
2. + and - have lower precedence.
3. = has the lowest precedence of these six operators.

Therefore, you can assume that the statement behaves as expected, with the division and remainder operators executing before the assignment.

If you forget to assign the result of one of these binary operators, you will receive the compile error shown in Output 4.2.

OUTPUT 4.2

```
... error CS0201: Only assignment, call, increment, decrement,
and new object expressions can be used as a statement
```

■ BEGINNER TOPIC

Parentheses, Associativity, Precedence, and Evaluation

When an expression contains multiple operators, it can be unclear precisely what the operands of each operator are. For example, in the expression x+y*z, clearly the expression x is an operand of the addition and z is an operand of the multiplication. But is y an operand of the addition or the multiplication?

Parentheses allow you to unambiguously associate an operand with its operator. If you wish y to be a summand, you can write the expression as (x+y)*z; if you want it to be a multiplicand, you can write x+(y*z).

However, C# does not require you to parenthesize every expression containing more than one operator; instead, the compiler can use associativity and precedence to figure out from the context which parentheses you have omitted. **Associativity** determines how similar operators are parenthesized; **precedence** determines how dissimilar operators are parenthesized.

A binary operator may be *left-associative* or *right-associative*, depending on whether the expression "in the middle" belongs to the operator on the left or the right. For example, a-b-c is assumed to mean (a-b)-c, and not a-(b-c); subtraction is therefore said to be left-associative. Most operators in C# are left-associative; the assignment operators are right-associative.

When the operators are dissimilar, the **precedence** for those operators is used to determine which side the operand in the middle belongs to. For example, multiplication has higher precedence than addition, and therefore, the expression x+y*z is evaluated as x+(y*z) rather than (x+y)*z.

It is often still a good practice to use parentheses to make the code more readable even when use of parentheses does not change the meaning of the expression. For example, when performing a Celsius-to-Fahrenheit temperature conversion, (c*9.0/5.0)+32.0 is easier to read than c*9.0/5.0+32.0, even though the parentheses are completely unnecessary.

Guidelines

DO use parentheses to make code more readable, particularly if the operator precedence is not clear to the casual reader.

Clearly, operators of higher precedence must execute before adjoining operators of lower precedence: in x+y*z, the multiplication must be executed before the addition because the result of the multiplication is the right-hand operand of the addition. However, it is important to realize that precedence and associativity affect only the order in which the *operators* themselves are executed; they do not in any way affect the order in which the *operands* are evaluated.

Operands are always evaluated from left to right in C#. In an expression with three method calls, such as A( )+B( )*C( ), first A( ) is evaluated, then B( ), then C( ); then the multiplication operator determines the product; and finally the addition operator determines the sum. Just because C( ) is involved in a multiplication and A( ) is involved in a lower-precedence addition does not imply that method invocation C( ) happens before method invocation A( ).

Language Contrast: C++: Evaluation Order of Operands

In contrast to the rule mentioned here, the C++ specification allows an implementation broad latitude to decide the evaluation order of operands. When given an expression such as A( )+B( )*C( ), a C++ compiler can choose to evaluate the function calls in any order, just so long as the product is one of the summands. For example, a legal compiler could evaluate B( ), then A( ), then C( ); then the product; and finally the sum.

Using the Addition Operator with Strings

Operators can also work with non-numeric operands. For example, it is possible to use the addition operator to concatenate two or more strings, as shown in Listing 4.4.

LISTING 4.4: Using Binary Operators with Non-numeric Types

```
class FortyTwo
{
  static void Main()
  {
      short windSpeed = 42;
      System.Console.WriteLine(
          "The original Tacoma Bridge in Washington\nwas "
          + "brought down by a "
          + windSpeed + " mile/hour wind.");
  }
}
```

Output 4.3 shows the results of Listing 4.4.

OUTPUT 4.3

```
The original Tacoma Bridge in Washington
was brought down by a 42 mile/hour wind.
```

Because sentence structure varies among languages in different cultures, developers should be careful not to use the addition operator with strings that possibly will require localization. Similarly, although we can embed expressions within a string using C# 6.0's string interpolation, localization to other languages still requires moving the string to a resource file, neutralizing the string interpolation. For this reason, you should use the addition operator sparingly, favoring composite formatting when localization is a possibility.

Guidelines

DO favor composite formatting over use of the addition operator for concatenating strings when localization is a possibility.

Using Characters in Arithmetic Operations

When introducing the char type in Chapter 2, we mentioned that even though it stores characters and not numbers, the char type is an **integral** type (*integral* means it is based on an integer). It can participate in arithmetic operations with other integer types. However, interpretation of the value of the char type is not based on the character stored within it but rather on its underlying value. The digit 3, for example, is represented by the Unicode value 0x33 (hexadecimal), which in base 10 is 51. The digit 4 is represented by the Unicode value 0x34, or 52 in base 10. Adding 3 and 4 in Listing 4.5 results in a hexadecimal value of 0x67, or 103 in base 10, which is the Unicode value for the letter g.

LISTING 4.5: Using the Plus Operator with the char Data Type

```csharp
int n = '3' + '4';
char c = (char)n;
System.Console.WriteLine(c);  // Writes out g
```

Output 4.4 shows the result of Listing 4.5.

OUTPUT 4.4

```
g
```

You can use this trait of character types to determine how far two characters are from each other. For example, the letter f is three characters away from the letter c. You can determine this value by subtracting the letter c from the letter f, as Listing 4.6 demonstrates.

LISTING 4.6: Determining the Character Difference between Two Characters

```
int distance = 'f' - 'c';
System.Console.WriteLine(distance);
```

Output 4.5 shows the result of Listing 4.6.

OUTPUT 4.5

```
3
```

Special Floating-Point Characteristics

The binary floating-point types, float and double, have some special characteristics, such as the way they handle precision. This section looks at some specific examples, as well as some unique floating-point type characteristics.

A float, with seven decimal digits of precision, can hold the value 1,234,567 and the value 0.1234567. However, if you add these two floats together, the result will be rounded to 1234567, because the exact result requires more precision than the seven significant digits that a float can hold. The error introduced by rounding off to seven digits can become large compared to the value computed, especially with repeated calculations. (See also the Advanced Topic titled "Unexpected Inequality with Floating-Point Types" later in this section.)

Internally, the binary floating-point types actually store a binary fraction, not a decimal fraction. Consequently, "representation error" inaccuracies can occur with a simple assignment, such as double number = 140.6F. The exact value of 140.6 is the fraction 703/5, but the denominator of that fraction is not a power of 2, so it cannot be represented exactly by a binary floating-point number. The value actually represented is the closest fraction with a power of 2 in the denominator that will fit into the 16 bits of a float.

Since the double can hold a more accurate value than the float can store, the C# compiler will actually evaluate this expression to double number = 140.600006103516 because 140.600006103516 is the closest binary fraction to 140.6 as a float. This fraction is slightly larger than 140.6 when represented as a double.

Guidelines

AVOID binary floating-point types when exact decimal arithmetic is required; use the decimal floating-point type instead.

ADVANCED TOPIC

Unexpected Inequality with Floating-Point Types

Because floating-point numbers can be unexpectedly rounded off to non-decimal fractions, comparing floating-point values for equality can be quite confusing. Consider Listing 4.7.

LISTING 4.7: Unexpected Inequality Due to Floating-Point Inaccuracies

```
decimal decimalNumber = 4.2M;
double doubleNumber1 = 0.1F * 42F;
double doubleNumber2 = 0.1D * 42D;
float floatNumber = 0.1F * 42F;

Trace.Assert(decimalNumber != (decimal)doubleNumber1);
// 1. Displays: 4.2 != 4.20000006258488
System.Console.WriteLine(
    $"{decimalNumber} != {(decimal)doubleNumber1}");

Trace.Assert((double)decimalNumber != doubleNumber1);
// 2. Displays: 4.2 != 4.20000006258488
System.Console.WriteLine(
    $"{(double)decimalNumber} != {doubleNumber1}");

Trace.Assert((float)decimalNumber != floatNumber);
// 3. Displays: (float)4.2M != 4.2F
System.Console.WriteLine(
    $"(float){(float)decimalNumber}M != {floatNumber}F");

Trace.Assert(doubleNumber1 != (double)floatNumber);
// 4. Displays: 4.20000006258488 != 4.20000028610229
System.Console.WriteLine(
    $"{doubleNumber1} != {(double)floatNumber}");
```

```
Trace.Assert(doubleNumber1 != doubleNumber2);
// 5. Displays: 4.20000006258488 != 4.2
System.Console.WriteLine(
    $"{doubleNumber1} != {doubleNumber2}");

Trace.Assert(floatNumber != doubleNumber2);
// 6. Displays: 4.2F != 4.2D
System.Console.WriteLine(
    $"{floatNumber}F != {doubleNumber2}D");

Trace.Assert((double)4.2F != 4.2D);
// 7. Displays: 4.19999980926514 != 4.2
System.Console.WriteLine(
    $"{(double)4.2F} != {4.2D}");

Trace.Assert(4.2F != 4.2D);
// 8. Displays: 4.2F != 4.2D
System.Console.WriteLine(
    $"{4.2F}F != {4.2D}D");
```

Output 4.6 shows the results of Listing 4.7.

OUTPUT 4.6

```
4.2 != 4.20000006258488
4.2 != 4.20000006258488
(float)4.2M != 4.2F
4.20000006258488 != 4.20000028610229
4.20000006258488 != 4.2
4.2F != 4.2D
4.19999980926514 != 4.2
4.2F != 4.2D
```

The `Assert()` methods alert the developer whenever arguments evaluate to `false`. However, of all the `Assert()` calls in this code listing, only half have arguments that evaluate to `true`. In spite of the apparent equality of the values in the code listing, they are not actually equivalent due to the inaccuracies associated with `float` values.

> **Guidelines**
>
> **AVOID** using equality conditionals with binary floating-point types. Either subtract the two values and see if their difference is less than a tolerance, or use the `decimal` type.

You should be aware of some additional unique floating-point characteristics as well. For instance, you would expect that dividing an integer by zero would result in an error—and it does with data types such as int and decimal. The float and double types, however, allow for certain special values. Consider Listing 4.8, and its resultant output, Output 4.7.

LISTING 4.8: Dividing a Float by Zero, Displaying NaN

```
float n=0f;
// Displays: NaN
System.Console.WriteLine(n / 0);
```

OUTPUT 4.7

```
NaN
```

In mathematics, certain mathematical operations are undefined, including dividing zero by itself. In C#, the result of dividing the float zero by zero results in a special **Not a Number** value; all attempts to print the output of such a number will result in NaN. Similarly, taking the square root of a negative number with System.Math.Sqrt(-1) will result in NaN.

A floating-point number could overflow its bounds as well. For example, the upper bound of the float type is approximately 3.4×10^{38}. Should the number overflow that bound, the result would be stored as **positive infinity**, and the output of printing the number would be Infinity. Similarly, the lower bound of a float type is -3.4×10^{38}, and computing a value below that bound would result in **negative infinity**, which would be represented by the string -Infinity. Listing 4.9 produces negative and positive infinity, respectively, and Output 4.8 shows the results.

LISTING 4.9: Overflowing the Bounds of a float

```
// Displays: -Infinity
System.Console.WriteLine(-1f / 0);
// Displays: Infinity
System.Console.WriteLine(3.402823E+38f * 2f);
```

OUTPUT 4.8

```
-Infinity
Infinity
```

Further examination of the floating-point number reveals that it can contain a value very close to zero without actually containing zero. If the value exceeds the lower threshold for the float or double type, the value of the number can be represented as **negative zero** or **positive zero**, depending on whether the number is negative or positive, and is represented in output as -0 or 0.

Compound Mathematical Assignment Operators (+=, -=, *=, /=, %=)

Chapter 1 discussed the simple assignment operator, which places the value of the right-hand side of the operator into the variable on the left-hand side. **Compound mathematical assignment operators** combine common binary operator calculations with the assignment operator. For example, consider Listing 4.10.

LISTING 4.10: Common Increment Calculation

```
int x = 123;
x = x + 2;
```

In this assignment, first you calculate the value of x + 2, and then you assign the calculated value back to x. Since this type of operation is performed relatively frequently, an assignment operator exists to handle both the calculation and the assignment with one operator. The += operator increments the variable on the left-hand side of the operator with the value on the right-hand side of the operator, as shown in Listing 4.11.

LISTING 4.11: Using the += Operator

```
int x = 123;
x += 2;
```

This code, therefore, is equivalent to Listing 4.10.

Numerous other compound assignment operators exist to provide similar functionality. You can also use the assignment operator with subtraction, multiplication, division, and remainder operators (as demonstrated in Listing 4.12).

LISTING 4.12: Other Assignment Operator Examples

```
x -= 2;
x /= 2;
x *= 2;
x %= 2;
```

Increment and Decrement Operators (++, --)

C# includes special unary operators for incrementing and decrementing counters. The **increment operator**, ++, increments a variable by one each time it is used. In other words, all of the code lines shown in Listing 4.13 are equivalent.

LISTING 4.13: Increment Operator

```
spaceCount = spaceCount + 1;
spaceCount += 1;
spaceCount++;
```

Similarly, you can decrement a variable by one using the **decrement operator**, --. Therefore, all of the code lines shown in Listing 4.14 are also equivalent.

LISTING 4.14: Decrement Operator

```
lines = lines - 1;
lines -= 1;
lines--;
```

■ BEGINNER TOPIC

A Decrement Example in a Loop

The increment and decrement operators are especially prevalent in loops, such as the while loop described later in the chapter. For example, Listing 4.15 uses the decrement operator to iterate backward through each letter in the alphabet.

LISTING 4.15: Displaying Each Character's Unicode Value in Descending Order

```
char current;
int unicodeValue;

// Set the initial value of current
current = 'z';

do
{
    // Retrieve the Unicode value of current
    unicodeValue = current;
    System.Console.Write($"{current}={unicodeValue}\t");

    // Proceed to the previous letter in the alphabet
    current--;
}
while(current >= 'a');
```

Output 4.9 shows the results of Listing 4.15.

OUTPUT 4.9

```
z=122   y=121   x=120   w=119   v=118   u=117   t=116   s=115   r=114
q=113   p=112   o=111   n=110   m=109   l=108   k=107   j=106   i=105
h=104   g=103   f=102   e=101   d=100   c=99    b=98    a=97
```

The increment and decrement operators are used in Listing 4.15 to control how many times a particular operation is performed. In this example, notice that the increment operator is also used on a character (char) data type. You can use increment and decrement operators on various data types as long as some meaning is assigned to the concept of the "next" or "previous" value for that data type.

We saw that the assignment operator first computes the value to be assigned, and then performs the assignment. The result of the assignment operator is the value that was assigned. The increment and decrement operators are similar: They compute the value to be assigned, perform the assignment, and result in a value. It is therefore possible to use the assignment operator with the increment or decrement operator, though doing so carelessly can be extremely confusing. See Listing 4.16 and Output 4.10 for an example.

LISTING 4.16: Using the Post-Increment Operator

```
int count = 123;
int result;
result = count++;
System.Console.WriteLine(
    $"result = {result} and count = {count}");
```

OUTPUT 4.10

```
result = 123 and count = 124
```

You might be surprised that result was assigned the value that was count *before* count was incremented. Where you place the increment or decrement operator determines whether the assigned value should be the value of the operand before or after the calculation. If you want the value of result to be the value assigned to count, you need to place the operator before the variable being incremented, as shown in Listing 4.17.

LISTING 4.17: Using the Pre-increment Operator

```
int count = 123;
int result;
result = ++count;
System.Console.WriteLine(
  $"result = {result} and count = {count}");
```

Output 4.11 shows the results of Listing 4.17.

OUTPUT 4.11

```
result = 124 and count = 124
```

In this example, the increment operator appears before the operand, so the result of the expression is the value assigned to the variable after the increment. If count is 123, ++count will assign 124 to count and produce the result 124. By contrast, the postfix increment operator count++ assigns 124 to count and produces the value that count held before the increment: 123. Regardless of whether the operator is postfix or prefix, the variable count will be incremented before the value is produced; the only difference is which value is produced. The difference between prefix and postfix behavior is illustrated in Listing 4.18. The resultant output is shown in Output 4.12.

LISTING 4.18: Comparing the Prefix and Postfix Increment Operators

```
class IncrementExample
{
  static void Main()
  {
    int x = 123;
    // Displays 123, 124, 125
    System.Console.WriteLine($"{x++}, {x++}, {x}");
    // x now contains the value 125
    // Displays 126, 127, 127
    System.Console.WriteLine($"{++x}, {++x}, {x}");
    // x now contains the value 127
  }
}
```

OUTPUT 4.12

```
123, 124, 125
126, 127, 127
```

As Listing 4.18 demonstrates, where the increment and decrement operators appear relative to the operand can affect the result produced by the expression. The result of the prefix operators is the value that the variable had before it was incremented or decremented. The result of the postfix operators is the value that the variable had after it was incremented or decremented. Use caution when embedding these operators in the middle of a statement. When in doubt as to what will happen, use these operators independently, placing them within their own statements. This way, the code is also more readable and there is no mistaking the intention.

Language Contrast: C++—Implementation-Defined Behavior

Earlier we discussed how the operands in an expression can be evaluated in any order in C++, whereas they are always evaluated from left to right in C#. Similarly, in C++ an implementation may legally perform the side effects of increments and decrements in any order. For example, in C++ a call of the form M(x++, x++), where x begins as 1, can legally call either M(1,2) or M(2,1) at the whim of the compiler. In contrast, C# will always call M(1,2) because C# makes two guarantees: (1) The arguments to a call are always computed from left to right, and (2) the assignment of the incremented value to the variable always happens before the value of the expression is used. C++ makes neither guarantee.

Guidelines

AVOID confusing usage of the increment and decrement operators.

DO be cautious when porting code between C, C++, and C# that uses increment and decrement operators; C and C++ implementations need not follow the same rules as C#.

■ ADVANCED TOPIC

Thread-Safe Incrementing and Decrementing

In spite of the brevity of the increment and decrement operators, these operators are not atomic. A thread context switch can occur during the execution of the operator and can cause a race condition. You could use a lock statement to prevent the race condition. However, for simple increments and decrements, a less expensive alternative is to use the thread-safe Increment() and Decrement() methods from the System.Threading.Interlocked class. These methods rely on processor functions for performing fast thread-safe increments and decrements. See Chapter 19 for more details.

Constant Expressions and Constant Locals

The preceding chapter discussed literal values, or values embedded directly into the code. It is possible to combine multiple literal values in a **constant expression** using operators. By definition, a constant expression is one that the C# compiler can evaluate at compile time (instead of evaluating it when the program runs) because it is composed entirely of constant operands. Constant expressions can then be used to initialize constant locals, which allow you to give a name to a constant value (similar to the way local variables allow you to give a name to a storage location). For example, the computation of the number of seconds in a day can be a constant expression that is then used in other expressions by name.

The const keyword in Listing 4.19 declares a constant local. Since a constant local is by definition the opposite of a **variable**—*constant* means "not able to vary"—any attempt to modify the value later in the code would result in a compile-time error.

Guidelines

DO NOT use a constant for any value that can possibly change over time. The value of pi and the number of protons in an atom of gold are constants; the price of gold, the name of your company, and the version number of your program can change.

Note that the expression assigned to secondsPerWeek in Listing 4.19 is a constant expression because all the operands in the expression are also constants.

LISTING 4.19: Declaring a Constant

```
// ...
public long Main()
{                                    Constant Expression
    const int secondsPerDay = 60 * 60 * 24;
    const int secondsPerWeek = secondsPerDay * 7;
                   Constant
    // ...
}
```

Introducing Flow Control

Later in this chapter is a code listing (Listing 4.45) that shows a simple way to view a number in its binary form. Even such a simple program, however, cannot be written without using control flow statements. Such statements control the execution path of the program. This section discusses how to change the order of statement execution based on conditional checks. Later on, you will learn how to execute statement groups repeatedly through loop constructs.

A summary of the control flow statements appears in Table 4.1. Note that the General Syntax Structure column indicates common statement use, not the complete lexical structure. An embedded-statement in Table 4.1 may be any statement other than a labeled statement or a declaration, but it is typically a block statement.

Each C# control flow statement in Table 4.1 appears in the tic-tac-toe[3] program and is available in Chapter 4's source code in the file TicTacToe.cs (see http://itl.tc/EssentialCSharpSCC). The program displays the tic-tac-toe board, prompts each player, and updates with each move.

The remainder of this chapter looks at each statement in more detail. After covering the if statement, it introduces code blocks, scope, Boolean expressions, and bitwise operators before continuing with the remaining control flow statements. Readers who find Table 4.1 familiar because of C#'s similarities to other languages can jump ahead to the section titled "C# Preprocessor Directives" or skip to the Summary at the end of the chapter.

---

3. Known as *noughts and crosses* to readers outside the United States.

TABLE 4.1: Control Flow Statements

Statement	General Syntax Structure	Example
if statement	if(*boolean-expression*) *embedded-statement*	```if (input == "quit")
{
System.Console.WriteLine(
"Game end");
return;
}```

	if(*boolean-expression*)
	  embedded-statement
	else
	  embedded-statement
		``if (input == "quit")

{
System.Console.WriteLine(
"Game end");
return;
}
else
GetNextMove();```
while statement	while(*boolean-expression*) *embedded-statement*	```while(count < total)
{
System.Console.WriteLine(
$"count = {count}");
count++;
}```

continues

TABLE 4.1: Control Flow Statements (*continued*)

Statement	General Syntax Structure	Example

do while statement	**do**
	  embedded-statement
	while(*boolean-expression*);
		do
		{
		  System.Console.WriteLine(
		    "Enter name:");
		  input =
		    System.Console.ReadLine();
		}
		while(*input* != "exit");

for statement	**for**(*for-initializer;*
	  boolean-expression;
	  for-iterator)
	  embedded-statement
		for (**int** count = 1;
		  count <= 10;
		  count++)
		{
		  System.Console.WriteLine(
		    $"count = {count}");
		}

foreach statement	**foreach**(*type identifier* **in**
	  expression)
	  embedded-statement
		foreach (**char** letter **in** email)
		{
		  if(!insideDomain)
		  {

continue statement	**continue**;	**if** (letter == '@')
		    {
		      insideDomain = **true**;
		    }
		    continue;
		  }
		  System.Console.Write(
		    letter);
		}

TABLE 4.1: Control Flow Statements *(continued)*

Statement	General Syntax Structure	Example
| switch statement | ```
switch(governing-type-expression)
{
    ...
    case const-expression:
        statement-list
        jump-statement
    default:
        statement-list
        jump-statement
}
``` | ```
switch(input)
{

    case "exit":
    case "quit":
        System.Console.WriteLine(
            "Exiting app....");
        break;
    case "restart":
        Reset();
        goto case "start";
    case "start":
        GetMove();
        break;
    default:
        System.Console.WriteLine(
            input);
        break;
}
``` |
| break statement | ```
break;
``` | |
| goto statement | ```
goto identifier;

goto case const-expression;

goto default;
``` | |

if Statement

The if statement is one of the most common statements in C#. It evaluates a **Boolean expression** (an expression that results in either true or false) called the **condition**. If the condition is true, the **consequence statement** is executed. An if statement may optionally have an else clause that contains an **alternative statement** to be executed if the condition is false. The general form is as follows:

```
if (condition)
    consequence-statement
else
    alternative-statement
```

In Listing 4.20, if the user enters 1, the program displays Play against computer selected. Otherwise, it displays Play against another player.

LISTING 4.20: if/else Statement Example

```
class TicTacToe         // Declares the TicTacToe class
{
    static void Main() // Declares the entry point of the program
    {
        string input;

        // Prompt the user to select a 1- or 2-player game
        System.Console.Write(
            "1 - Play against the computer\n" +
            "2 - Play against another player.\n" +
            "Choose:"
        );
        input = System.Console.ReadLine();

        if(input=="1")
            // The user selected to play the computer
            System.Console.WriteLine(
                "Play against computer selected.");
        else
            // Default to 2 players (even if user didn't enter 2)
            System.Console.WriteLine(
                "Play against another player.");
    }
}
```

Nested if

Sometimes code requires multiple if statements. The code in Listing 4.21 first determines whether the user has chosen to exit by entering a number less than or equal to 0; if not, it checks whether the user knows the maximum number of turns in tic-tac-toe.

LISTING 4.21: Nested if Statements

```
1.    class TicTacToeTrivia
2.    {
3.      static void Main()
4.      {
5.          int input;     // Declare a variable to store the input
6.
7.          System.Console.Write(
8.              "What is the maximum number " +
9.              "of turns in tic-tac-toe?" +
10.             "(Enter 0 to exit.): ");
11.
12.         // int.Parse() converts the ReadLine()
13.         // return to an int data type
14.         input = int.Parse(System.Console.ReadLine());
15.
16.         if (input <= 0) // line 16
17.                 // Input is less than or equal to 0
18.             System.Console.WriteLine("Exiting...");
19.         else
20.             if (input < 9)  // line 20
21.                 // Input is less than 9
22.                 System.Console.WriteLine(
23.                     $"Tic-tac-toe has more than {input}" +
24.                     " maximum turns.");
25.             else
26.                 if(input > 9) // line 26
27.                     // Input is greater than 9
28.                     System.Console.WriteLine(
29.                         $"Tic-tac-toe has fewer than {input}" +
30.                         " maximum turns.");
31.                 else
32.                     // Input equals 9
33.                     System.Console.WriteLine( // line 33
34.                         "Correct, tic-tac-toe " +
35.                         "has a maximum of 9 turns.");
36.      }
37.    }
```

Output 4.13 shows the results of Listing 4.21.

OUTPUT 4.13

```
What is the maximum number of turns in tic-tac-toe? (Enter 0 to exit.): 9
Correct, tic-tac-toe has a maximum of 9 turns.
```

Assume the user enters 9 when prompted at line 14. Here is the execution path:

1. *Line 16:* Check if input is less than 0. Since it is not, jump to line 20.
2. *Line 20:* Check if input is less than 9. Since it is not, jump to line 26.
3. *Line 26:* Check if input is greater than 9. Since it is not, jump to line 33.
4. *Line 33:* Display that the answer was correct.

Listing 4.21 contains nested if statements. To clarify the nesting, the lines are indented. However, as you learned in Chapter 1, whitespace does not affect the execution path. If this code was written without the indenting and without the newlines, the execution would be the same. The code that appears in the nested if statement in Listing 4.22 is equivalent to Listing 4.21.

LISTING 4.22: if/else Formatted Sequentially

```
if (input < 0)
  System.Console.WriteLine("Exiting...");
else if (input < 9)
  System.Console.WriteLine(
      $"Tic-tac-toe has more than {input}" +
      " maximum turns.");
else if(input < 9)
  System.Console.WriteLine(
      $"Tic-tac-toe has less than {input}" +
      " maximum turns.");
else
  System.Console.WriteLine(
      "Correct, tic-tac-toe has a maximum " +
      " of 9 turns.");
```

Although the latter format is more common, in each situation you should use the format that results in the clearest code.

Both of the if statement listings omit the braces. However, as discussed next, this is not in accordance with the guidelines, which advocate the use of code blocks except, perhaps, in the simplest of single-line scenarios.

Code Blocks ({ })

In the previous if statement examples, only one statement follows if and else: a single System.Console.WriteLine(), similar to Listing 4.23.

LISTING 4.23: if Statement with No Code Block

```
if(input < 9)
   System.Console.WriteLine("Exiting");
```

With curly braces, however, we can combine statements into a single statement called a **block statement** or **code block**, allowing the grouping of multiple statements into a single statement that is the consequence. Take, for example, the highlighted code block in the radius calculation in Listing 4.24.

LISTING 4.24: if Statement Followed by a Code Block

```
class CircleAreaCalculator
{
  static void Main()
  {
     double radius;  // Declare a variable to store the radius
     double area;    // Declare a variable to store the area

     System.Console.Write("Enter the radius of the circle: ");

     // double.Parse converts the ReadLine()
     // return to a double
     radius = double.Parse(System.Console.ReadLine());
     if(radius >= 0)
     {
        // Calculate the area of the circle
        area = Math.PI * radius * radius;
        System.Console.WriteLine(
           $"The area of the circle is: { area : 0.00 }");
     }
     else
     {
        System.Console.WriteLine(
           $"{ radius } is not a valid radius.");
     }
  }
}
```

Output 4.14 shows the results of Listing 4.24.

OUTPUT 4.14

```
Enter the radius of the circle: 3
The area of the circle is: 28.27
```

In this example, the if statement checks whether the radius is positive. If so, the area of the circle is calculated and displayed; otherwise, an invalid radius message is displayed.

Notice that in this example, two statements follow the first if. However, these two statements appear within curly braces. The curly braces combine the statements into a code block, which is itself a single statement.

If you omit the curly braces that create a code block in Listing 4.24, only the statement immediately following the Boolean expression executes conditionally. Subsequent statements will execute regardless of the if statement's Boolean expression. The invalid code is shown in Listing 4.25.

LISTING 4.25: Relying on Indentation, Resulting in Invalid Code

```
if(radius >= 0)
   area = Math.PI * radius *radius;
   System.Console.WriteLine(
      $"The area of the circle is: { area:0.00}");
```

In C#, indentation is used solely to enhance the code readability. The compiler ignores it, so the previous code is semantically equivalent to Listing 4.26.

LISTING 4.26: Semantically Equivalent to Listing 4.25 with Curly Braces

```
if(radius >= 0)
{
   area = Math.PI * radius * radius;
}
System.Console.WriteLine(
   $"The area of the circle is:{ area:0.00}");
```

Programmers should take great care to avoid subtle bugs such as this, perhaps even going so far as to always include a code block after a control flow statement, even if there is only one statement. A widely accepted coding guideline is to avoid omitting braces, except possibly for the simplest of single-line if statements.

Although unusual, it is possible to have a code block that is not lexically a direct part of a control flow statement. In other words, placing curly braces on their own (e.g., without a conditional or loop) is legal syntax.

In Listings 4.25 and 4.26, the value of pi was represented by the PI constant in the System.Math class. Instead of hardcoding values for π and e (the base of natural logarithms), code should use System.Math.PI and System.Math.E.

> ### Guidelines
>
> AVOID omitting braces, except for the simplest of single-line if statements.

Code Blocks, Scopes, and Declaration Spaces

Code blocks are often referred to as *scopes*, but the two terms are not exactly interchangeable. The **scope** of a named thing is the region of source code in which it is legal to refer to the thing by its unqualified name. The scope of a local variable, for example, is exactly the text of the code block that encloses it, which explains why it is common to refer to code blocks as scopes.

Scopes are often confused with declaration spaces. A **declaration space** is a logical container of named things in which two things may not have the same name. A code block defines not only a scope but also a local variable declaration space. It is illegal for two local variable declarations with the same name to appear in the same declaration space. Similarly, it is not possible to declare two methods with the signature of Main() within the same class. (This rule is relaxed somewhat for methods: Two methods may have the same name in a declaration space provided that they have different signatures. The signature of a method includes its name and the number and types of its parameters.) Within a block, a local variable can be mentioned by name and must be the unique thing that is declared with that name in the block. Outside the declaring block, there is no way to refer to a local variable by its name; the local variable is said to be "out of scope" outside the block.

In summary, a scope is used to determine what thing a name refers to; a declaration space determines when two things declared with the same name conflict with each other. In Listing 4.27, declaring the local variable message inside the block statement embedded in the if statement restricts its scope to the block statement only; the local variable is out of scope when its name is used later on in the method. To avoid an error, you must declare the variable outside the block.

LISTING 4.27: Variables Inaccessible outside Their Scope

```csharp
class Program
{
    static void Main(string[] args)
    {
        int playerCount;
        System.Console.Write(
            "Enter the number of players (1 or 2):");
        playerCount = int.Parse(System.Console.ReadLine());
        if (playerCount != 1 && playerCount != 2)
        {
            string message =
                "You entered an invalid number of players.";
        }
        else
        {
            // ...
        }
        // Error:  message is not in scope
        System.Console.WriteLine(message);
    }
}
```

Output 4.15 shows the results of Listing 4.27.

OUTPUT 4.15

```
...

...\Program.cs(18,26): error CS0103: The name 'message' does not exist
in the current context
```

The declaration space in which a local variable's name must be unique encompasses all the child code blocks textually enclosed within the block that originally declared the local. The C# compiler prevents the name of a local variable declared immediately within a method code block (or as a parameter) from being reused within a child code block. In Listing 4.27, because args and playerCount are declared within the method code block, they cannot be declared again anywhere within the method.

The name `message` refers to this local variable throughout the scope of the local variable—that is, the block immediately enclosing the declaration. Similarly, `playerCount` refers to the same variable throughout the block containing the declaration, including within both of the child blocks that are the consequence and the alternative of the `if` statement.

Language Contrast: C++—Local Variable Scope

In C++, a local variable declared in a block is in scope from the point of the declaration statement through the end of the block. Thus an attempt to refer to the local variable before its declaration will fail to find the local variable because that variable is not in scope. If there is another thing with that name "in scope," the C++ language will resolve the name to that thing, which might not be what you intended. In C#, the rule is subtly different: A local variable is in scope throughout the entire block in which it is declared, but it is illegal to refer to the local variable before its declaration. That is, the attempt to find the local variable will succeed, and the usage will then be treated as an error. This is just one of C#'s many rules that attempt to prevent errors common in C++ programs.

Boolean Expressions

The parenthesized condition of the `if` statement is a **Boolean expression**. In Listing 4.28, the condition is highlighted.

LISTING 4.28: Boolean Expression

```
if (input < 9)
{
    // Input is less than 9
    System.Console.WriteLine(
        $"Tic-tac-toe has more than { input }" +
        " maximum turns.");
}
// ...
```

Boolean expressions appear within many control flow statements. Their key characteristic is that they always evaluate to `true` or `false`. For `input < 9` to be allowed as a Boolean expression, it must result in a `bool`. The compiler disallows `x = 42`, for example, because this expression assigns `x` and results in the value that was assigned instead of checking whether the value of the variable is 42.

Language Contrast: C++—Mistakenly Using = in Place of ==

C# eliminates a coding error commonly found in C and C++. In C++, Listing 4.29 is allowed.

LISTING 4.29: C++, But Not C#, Allows Assignment as a Condition

```
if (input = 9)     // Allowed in C++, not in C#
   System.Console.WriteLine(
      "Correct, tic-tac-toe has a maximum of 9 turns.");
```

Although at first glance this code appears to check whether input equals 9, Chapter 1 showed that = represents the assignment operator, not a check for equality. The return from the assignment operator is the value assigned to the variable—in this case, 9. However, 9 is an int, and as such it does not qualify as a Boolean expression and is not allowed by the C# compiler. The C and C++ languages treat integers that are nonzero as true and integers that are zero as false. C#, by contrast, requires that the condition actually be of a Boolean type; integers are not allowed.

Relational and Equality Operators

Relational and **equality operators** determine whether a value is greater than, less than, or equal to another value. Table 4.2 lists all the relational and equality operators. All are binary operators.

TABLE 4.2: Relational and Equality Operators

Operator	Description	Example
<	Less than	input < 9;
>	Greater than	input > 9;
<=	Less than or equal to	input <= 9;
>=	Greater than or equal to	input >= 9;
==	Equality operator	input == 9;
!=	Inequality operator	input != 9;

The C# syntax for equality uses ==, just as many other programming languages do. For example, to determine whether input equals 9, you use input == 9. The equality operator uses two equal signs to distinguish it from the assignment operator, =. The exclamation point signifies NOT in C#, so to test for inequality you use the inequality operator, !=.

Relational and equality operators always produce a `bool` value, as shown in Listing 4.30.

LISTING 4.30: Assigning the Result of a Relational Operator to a bool Variable

```
bool result = 70 > 7;
```

In the full tic-tac-toe program listing, you use the equality operator to determine whether a user has quit. The Boolean expression of Listing 4.31 includes an OR (||) logical operator, which the next section discusses in detail.

LISTING 4.31: Using the Equality Operator in a Boolean Expression

```
if (input == "" || input == "quit")
{
    System.Console.WriteLine($"Player {currentPlayer} quit!!");
    break;
}
```

Logical Boolean Operators

The **logical operators** have Boolean operands and produce a Boolean result. Logical operators allow you to combine multiple Boolean expressions to form more complex Boolean expressions. The logical operators are |, ||, &, &&, and ^, corresponding to OR, AND, and exclusive OR. The | and & versions of OR and AND are rarely used for Boolean logic, for reasons which we discuss in this section.

OR Operator (||)

In Listing 4.31, if the user enters `quit` or presses the Enter key without typing in a value, it is assumed that she wants to exit the program. To enable two ways for the user to resign, you can use the logical OR operator, ||. The || operator evaluates Boolean expressions and results in a `true` value if *either* operand is `true` (see Listing 4.32).

LISTING 4.32: Using the OR Operator

```
if ((hourOfTheDay > 23) || (hourOfTheDay < 0))
    System.Console.WriteLine("The time you entered is invalid.");
```

It is not necessary to evaluate both sides of an OR expression, because if either operand is `true`, the result is known to be `true` regardless of the value of the other operand. Like all operators in C#, the left operand is evaluated before the right one, so if the left portion of the expression evaluates to `true`, the right portion is ignored. In the example in Listing 4.32, if `hourOfTheDay` has the value 33, then (`hourOfTheDay > 23`) will evaluate to `true` and the OR operator will ignore the second half of the expression, **short-circuiting** it. Short-circuiting an expression also occurs with the Boolean AND operator. (Note that the parentheses are not necessary here; the logical operators are of higher precedence than the relational operators. However, it is clearer to the novice reader to parenthesize the subexpressions for clarity.)

AND Operator (&&)

The Boolean AND operator, &&, evaluates to `true` only if both operands evaluate to `true`. If either operand is `false`, the result will be `false`. Listing 4.33 writes a message if the given variable is both greater than 10 and less than 24.[4] Similarly to the OR operator, the AND operator will not always evaluate the right side of the expression. If the left operand is determined to be `false`, the overall result will be `false` regardless of the value of the right operand, so the runtime skips evaluating the right operand.

LISTING 4.33: Using the AND Operator

```
if ((10 < hourOfTheDay) && (hourOfTheDay < 24))
  System.Console.WriteLine(
  "Hi-Ho, Hi-Ho, it's off to work we go.");
```

Exclusive OR Operator (^)

The caret symbol, ^, is the exclusive OR (XOR) operator. When applied to two Boolean operands, the XOR operator returns `true` only if exactly one of the operands is true, as shown in Table 4.3.

---

4. The typical hours that programmers work each day.

TABLE 4.3: Conditional Values for the XOR Operator

Left Operand	Right Operand	Result
True	True	False
True	False	True
False	True	True
False	False	False

Unlike the Boolean AND and Boolean OR operators, the Boolean XOR operator does not short-circuit: It always checks both operands, because the result cannot be determined unless the values of both operands are known. Note that the XOR operator is exactly the same as the Boolean inequality operator.

Logical Negation Operator (!)

The **logical negation operator**, or **NOT operator**, !, inverts a bool value. This operator is a unary operator, meaning it requires only one operand. Listing 4.34 demonstrates how it works, and Output 4.16 shows the result.

LISTING 4.34: Using the Logical Negation Operator

```
bool valid = false;
bool result = !valid;
// Displays "result = True"
System.Console.WriteLine($"result = { result }");
```

OUTPUT 4.16

```
result = True
```

At the beginning of Listing 4.34, valid is set to false. You then use the negation operator on valid and assign the value to result.

Conditional Operator (?:)

In place of an `if-else` statement used to select one of two values, you can use the **conditional operator**. The conditional operator uses both a question mark and a colon; the general format is as follows:

```
condition ? consequence : alternative
```

The conditional operator is a ternary operator because it has three operands: `condition`, `consequence`, and `alternative`. (As it is the only ternary operator in C#, it is often called the *ternary operator*, but it is clearer to refer to it by its name than by the number of operands it takes.) Like the logical operators, the conditional operator uses a form of short-circuiting. If the condition evaluates to `true`, the conditional operator evaluates only `consequence`. If the conditional evaluates to `false`, it evaluates only `alternative`. The result of the operator is the evaluated expression.

Listing 4.35 illustrates the use of the conditional operator. The full listing of this program appears in `Chapter04\TicTacToe.cs` of the source code.

LISTING 4.35: Conditional Operator

```csharp
class TicTacToe
{
  static string Main()
  {
    // Initially set the currentPlayer to Player 1
    int currentPlayer = 1;

    // ...

    for (int turn = 1; turn <= 10; turn++)
    {
      // ...

      // Switch players
      currentPlayer = (currentPlayer == 2) ? 1 : 2;
    }
  }
}
```

The program swaps the current player. To do so, it checks whether the current value is 2. This is the *conditional* portion of the conditional expression. If the result of the condition is `true`, the conditional operator results in the *consequence* value, 1. Otherwise, it results in the *alternative* value, 2. Unlike an `if` statement, the result of the conditional operator must be assigned (or passed as a parameter); it cannot appear as an entire statement on its own.

The C# language requires that the consequence and alternative expressions in a conditional operator be consistently typed and that the consistent type be determined without examination of the surrounding context of the expression. For example, f ? "abc" : 123 is not a legal conditional expression because the consequence and alternative are a string and a number, neither of which is convertible to the other. Even if you say object result = f ? "abc" : 123;, the C# compiler will flag this expression as illegal because the type that is consistent with both expressions (i.e., object) is found outside the conditional expression.

Null-Coalescing Operator (??)

The **null-coalescing operator** is a concise way to express "If this value is null, then use this other value." It has the following form:

```
expression1 ?? expression2
```

The null-coalescing operator also uses a form of short-circuiting. If expression1 is not null, its value is the result of the operation and the other expression is not evaluated. If expression1 does evaluate to null, the value of expression2 is the result of the operator. Unlike the conditional operator, the null-coalescing operator is a binary operator.

Listing 4.36 illustrates the use of the null-coalescing operator.

LISTING 4.36: Null-Coalescing Operator

```
string fileName = GetFileName();
// ...
string fullName = fileName ?? "default.txt";
// ...
```

In this listing, we use the null-coalescing operator to set fullName to "default.txt" if fileName is null. If fileName is not null, fullName is simply assigned the value of fileName.

The null-coalescing operator "chains" nicely. For example, an expression of the form x ?? y ?? z results in x if x is not null; otherwise, it results in y if y is not null; otherwise, it results in z. That is, it goes from left to right and picks out the first non-null expression, or uses the last expression if all the previous expressions were null.

The null-coalescing operator was added to C# in version 2.0, along with nullable value types. This operator works on both operands of nullable value types and reference types.

Null-Conditional Operator (?.)

Begin 6.0

Whenever you invoke a method on a value that is null, the runtime will throw a `System.NullReferenceException`, which almost always indicates an error in the programming logic. In recognition of the frequency of this pattern (i.e., checking for null before invoking a member), C# 6.0 introduces the `?.` operator, known as the **null-conditional operator**, as shown in Listing 4.37.

LISTING 4.37: **Null-Conditional Operator**

```
class Program
{
  static void Main(string[] args)
  {
      if (args?.Length == 0)
      {
          System.Console.WriteLine(
              "ERROR: File missing. "
              + "Use:\n\tfind.exe file:<filename>");
      }
      else
      {
          if (args[0]?.ToLower().StartsWith("file:")??false)
          {
              string fileName = args[0]?.Remove(0, 5);
              // ...
          }
      }
  }
}
```

The null-conditional operator checks whether the operand (the first `args` in Listing 4.37) is null prior to invoking the method or property (`Length` in the first example in this listing). The logically equivalent explicit code would be the following (although in the C# 6.0 syntax, the value of `args` is evaluated only once):

```
(args != null) ? (int?)args.Length : null
```

What makes the null-conditional operator especially convenient is that it can be chained. If, for example, you invoke
`args[0]?.ToLower().StartsWith("file:")`, both `ToLower()` and
`StartsWith()` will be invoked only if `args[0]` is not null. When expressions are chained, if the first operand is null, the expression evaluation is
short-circuited, and no further invocation within the expression call chain
will occur.

Be careful, however, that you don't unintentionally neglect additional
null-conditional operators. Consider, for example, what would happen if
(hypothetically, in this case) `args[0]?.ToLower()` could also return null.
In this scenario, a `NullReferenceException` would occur upon invocation of `StartsWith()`. This doesn't mean you must use a chain of null-
conditional operators but rather that you should be intentional about the
logic. In this example, because `ToLower()` can never be null, no additional
null-conditional operator is necessary.

An important thing to note about the null-conditional operator is that,
when utilized with a member that returns a value type, it always returns a
nullable version of that type. For example, `args?.Length` returns an `int?`,
not simply an `int`. Similarly, `args[0]?.ToLower().StartsWith("file:")`
returns a `bool?` (a `Nullable<bool>`). Also, because an `if` statement
requires a `bool` data type, it is necessary to follow the `StartsWith()`
expression with the null-coalescing operator (`??`).

Although perhaps a little peculiar (in comparison to other operator
behavior), the return of a nullable value type is produced only at the end of
the call chain. Consequently, calling the dot (`.`) operator on `Length` allows
invocation of only `int` (not `int?`) members. However, encapsulating
`args?.Length` in parentheses—thereby forcing the `int?` result via parentheses operator precedence—will invoke the `int?` return and make the
`Nullable<T>` specific members (`HasValue` and `Value`) available.

Null-conditional operators can also be used in combination with an
index operator, as shown in Listing 4.38.

LISTING 4.38: Null-Conditional Operator with Index Operator

```
class Program
{
  public static void Main(string[] args)
  {
    // CAUTION: args?.Length not verified
```

```
        string directoryPath = args?[0];
        string searchPattern = args?[1];
        // ...
    }
}
```

In this listing, the first and second elements of args are assigned to their respective variables only if args is not null. If it is, null will be assigned instead.

Unfortunately, this example is naïve, if not dangerous, because the null-conditional operator gives a false sense of security, implying that if args isn't null, then the element must exist. Of course, this isn't the case: The element may not exist even if args isn't null. Also, because checking for the element count with args?.Length verifies that args isn't null, you never really need to use the null-conditional operator when indexing the collection after checking the length.

In conclusion, you should avoid using the null-conditional operator in combination with the index operator if the index operator throws an IndexOutOfRangeException for nonexistent indexes. Doing so leads to a false sense of code validity.

■ ADVANCED TOPIC

Leveraging the Null-Conditional Operator with Delegates

The null-conditional operator is a great feature on its own. However, using it in combination with a delegate invocation resolves a C# pain point that has existed since C# 1.0. Notice below how the PropertyChange event handler is assigned to a local copy (propertyChanged) before we check the value for null and finally fire the event. This is the easiest thread-safe way to invoke events without running the risk that an event unsubscribe will occur between the time when the check for null occurs and the time when the event is fired. Unfortunately, this approach is nonintuitive, and frequently developers neglect to follow this pattern—with the result of throwing inconsistent NullReferenceExceptions. Fortunately, with the introduction of the null-conditional operator in C# 6.0, this issue has been resolved.

With C# 6.0, the check for a delegate value changes from

```
PropertyChangedEventHandler propertyChanged =
  PropertyChanged;
if (propertyChanged != null)
{
  propertyChanged(this,
      new PropertyChangedEventArgs(nameof(Name)));
}
```

to simply

```
PropertyChanged?.Invoke(propertyChanged(
  this, new PropertyChangedEventArgs(nameof(Name)));
```

Because an event is just a delegate, the same pattern of invoking a delegate via the null-conditional operator and an `Invoke( )` is always possible.

End 6.0

Bitwise Operators (<<, >>, |, &, ^, ~)

An additional set of operators that is common to virtually all programming languages is the set of operators for manipulating values in their binary formats: the bit operators.

◼ BEGINNER TOPIC

Bits and Bytes

All values within a computer are represented in a binary format of 1s and 0s, called **binary digits (bits)**. Bits are grouped together in sets of eight, called **bytes**. In a byte, each successive bit corresponds to a value of 2 raised to a power, starting from 2^0 on the right and moving to 2^7 on the left, as shown in Figure 4.1.

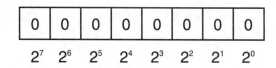

FIGURE 4.1: Corresponding Placeholder Values

In many scenarios, particularly when dealing with low-level or system services, information is retrieved as binary data. To manipulate these devices and services, you need to perform manipulations of binary data.

In Figure 4.2, each box corresponds to a value of 2 raised to the power shown. The value of the byte (8-bit number) is the sum of the powers of 2 of all of the eight bits that are set to 1.

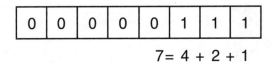

$$7 = 4 + 2 + 1$$

FIGURE 4.2: Calculating the Value of an Unsigned Byte

The binary translation just described is significantly different for signed numbers. Signed numbers (long, short, int) are represented using a *two's complement* notation. This practice ensures that addition continues to work when adding a negative number to a positive number, as though both were positive operands. With this notation, negative numbers behave differently from positive numbers. Negative numbers are identified by a 1 in the leftmost location. If the leftmost location contains a 1, you add the locations with 0s rather than the locations with 1s. Each location corresponds to the negative power of 2 value. Furthermore, from the result, it is also necessary to subtract 1. This is demonstrated in Figure 4.3.

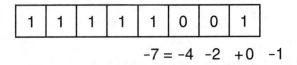

$$-7 = -4 \quad -2 \quad +0 \quad -1$$

FIGURE 4.3: Calculating the Value of a Signed Byte

Therefore, 1111 1111 1111 1111 corresponds to –1, and 1111 1111 1111 1001 holds the value –7. The binary representation 1000 0000 0000 0000 corresponds to the lowest negative value that a 16-bit integer can hold.

Shift Operators (<<, >>, <<=, >>=)

Sometimes you want to shift the binary value of a number to the right or left. In executing a left shift, all bits in a number's binary representation are shifted to the left by the number of locations specified by the operand on the right of the shift operator. Zeroes are then used to backfill the locations on the right side of the binary number. A right-shift operator does almost the same thing in the opposite direction. However, if the number is a negative value of a signed type, the values used to backfill the left side of the binary number are 1s and not 0s. The shift operators are >> and <<, known as the right-shift and left-shift operators, respectively. In addition, there are combined shift and assignment operators, <<= and >>=.

Consider the following example. Suppose you had the int value -7, which would have a binary representation of 1111 1111 1111 1111 1111 1111 1111 1001. In Listing 4.39, you right-shift the binary representation of the number –7 by two locations.

LISTING 4.39: Using the Right-Shift Operator

```
int x;
x = (-7 >> 2); // 11111111111111111111111111111001 becomes
            // 11111111111111111111111111111110
// Write out "x is -2."
System.Console.WriteLine($"x = { x }.");
```

Output 4.17 shows the results of Listing 4.39.

OUTPUT 4.17

```
x = -2.
```

Because of the right shift, the value of the bit in the rightmost location has "dropped off" the edge, and the negative bit indicator on the left shifts by two locations to be replaced with 1s. The result is -2.

Although legend has it that x << 2 is faster than x * 4, you should not use bit-shift operators for multiplication or division. This difference might have held true for certain C compilers in the 1970s, but modern compilers and modern microprocessors are perfectly capable of optimizing arithmetic. Using shifting for multiplication or division is confusing and frequently leads to errors when code maintainers forget that the shift operators are lower precedence than the arithmetic operators.

Bitwise Operators (&, |, ^)

In some instances, you might need to perform logical operations, such as AND, OR, and XOR, on a bit-by-bit basis for two operands. You do this via the &, |, and ^ operators, respectively.

■ BEGINNER TOPIC

Logical Operators Explained

If you have two numbers, as shown in Figure 4.4, the bitwise operations will compare the values of the locations beginning at the leftmost significant value and continuing right until the end. The value of "1" in a location is treated as "true," and the value of "0" in a location is treated as "false."

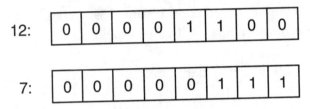

FIGURE 4.4: The Numbers 12 and 7 Represented in Binary

Therefore, the bitwise AND of the two values in Figure 4.4 would entail the bit-by-bit comparison of bits in the first operand (12) with the bits in the second operand (7), resulting in the binary value 000000100, which is 4. Alternatively, a bitwise OR of the two values would produce 00001111, the binary equivalent of 15. The XOR result would be 00001011, or decimal 11.

Listing 4.40 demonstrates the use of these bitwise operators. The results of Listing 4.40 appear in Output 4.18.

LISTING 4.40: Using Bitwise Operators

```
byte and, or, xor;
and = 12 & 7;   // and = 4
or = 12 | 7;    // or = 15
xor = 12 ^ 7;   // xor = 11
System.Console.WriteLine(
    $"and = { and } \nor = { or }\nxor = { xor }");
```

OUTPUT 4.18

```
and = 4
or = 15
xor = 11
```

In Listing 4.40, the value 7 is the **mask**; it is used to expose or eliminate specific bits within the first operand using the particular operator expression. Note that, unlike the AND (&&) operator, the & operator always evaluates *both* sides even if the left portion is false. Similarly, the | version of the OR operator is *not* "short-circuiting." It always evaluates both operands even if the left operand is true. The bit versions of the AND and OR operators, therefore, are not short-circuiting.

To convert a number to its binary representation, you need to iterate across each bit in a number. Listing 4.41 is an example of a program that converts an integer to a string of its binary representation. The results of Listing 4.41 appear in Output 4.19.

LISTING 4.41: Getting a String Representation of a Binary Display

```csharp
class BinaryConverter
{
  static void Main()
  {
      const int size = 64;
      ulong value;
      char bit;

      System.Console.Write ("Enter an integer: ");
      // Use long.Parse() to support negative numbers
      // Assumes unchecked assignment to ulong
      value = (ulong)long.Parse(System.Console.ReadLine());

      // Set initial mask to 100...
      ulong mask = 1UL << size - 1;
      for (int count = 0; count < size; count++)
      {
          bit = ((mask & value) != 0) ? '1': '0';
          System.Console.Write(bit);
          // Shift mask one location over to the right
          mask >>= 1;
      }
      System.Console.WriteLine();
  }
}
```

OUTPUT 4.19

```
Enter an integer: 42
0000000000000000000000000000000000000000000000000000000000101010
```

Within each iteration of the for loop in Listing 4.41 (as discussed later in this chapter), we use the right-shift assignment operator to create a mask corresponding to each bit position in value. By using the & bit operator to mask a particular bit, we can determine whether the bit is set. If the mask test produces a nonzero result, we write 1 to the console; otherwise, we write 0. In this way, we create output describing the binary value of an unsigned long.

Note also that the parentheses in (mask & value) != 0 are necessary because inequality is higher precedence than the AND operator. Without the explicit parentheses, this expression would be equivalent to mask & (value != 0), which does not make any sense; the left side of the & is a ulong and the right side is a bool.

This particular example is provided for learning purposes only. There is actually a built-in CLR method, System.Convert.ToString(value, 2) that does such a conversion. In fact, the second argument specifies the base (e.g., 2 for binary, 10 for decimal, or 16 for hexadecimal), allowing for more than just conversion to binary.

Bitwise Compound Assignment Operators (&=, |=, ^=)

Not surprisingly, you can combine these bitwise operators with assignment operators as follows: &=, |=, and ^=. As a result, you could take a variable, OR it with a number, and assign the result back to the original variable, which Listing 4.42 demonstrates.

LISTING 4.42: Using Logical Assignment Operators

```
byte and = 12, or = 12, xor = 12;
and &= 7;    // and = 4
or  |= 7;    // or = 15
xor ^= 7;    // xor = 11
System.Console.WriteLine(
    $"and = { and } \nor = { or }\nxor = { xor }");
```

The results of Listing 4.42 appear in Output 4.20.

OUTPUT 4.20

```
and = 4
or = 15
xor = 11
```

Combining a bitmap with a mask using something like `fields &= mask` clears the bits in `fields` that are not set in the `mask`. The opposite, `fields &= ~mask`, clears the bits in `fields` that are set in `mask`.

Bitwise Complement Operator (~)

The **bitwise complement operator** takes the complement of each bit in the operand, where the operand can be an `int`, `uint`, `long`, or `ulong`. The expression `~1`, therefore, returns the value with binary notation 1111 1111 1111 1111 1111 1111 1111 1110, and `~(1<<31)` returns the number with binary notation 0111 1111 1111 1111 1111 1111 1111 1111.

Control Flow Statements, Continued

Now that we've described Boolean expressions in more detail, we can more clearly describe the control flow statements supported by C#. Many of these statements will be familiar to experienced programmers, so you can skim this section looking for details specific to C#. Note in particular the `foreach` loop, as it may be new to many programmers.

The `while` and `do/while` Loops

Thus far you have learned how to write programs that do something only once. However, computers can easily perform similar operations multiple times. To do so, you need to create an instruction loop. The first instruction loop we discuss is the `while` loop, because it is the simplest conditional loop. The general form of the `while` statement is as follows:

```
while (condition)
    statement
```

The computer will repeatedly execute the statement that is the "body" of the loop as long as the condition (which must be a Boolean expression) evaluates to `true`. If the condition evaluates to `false`, code execution skips the body and executes the code following the loop statement. Note that `statement` will continue to execute even if it causes the condition to become `false`. The loop exits only when the condition is reevaluated "at the top of the loop." The Fibonacci calculator shown in Listing 4.43 demonstrates the `while` loop.

LISTING 4.43: while Loop Example

```
class FibonacciCalculator
{
  static void Main()
  {
      decimal current;
      decimal previous;
      decimal temp;
      decimal input;

      System.Console.Write("Enter a positive integer:");

      // decimal.Parse converts the ReadLine to a decimal
      input = decimal.Parse(System.Console.ReadLine());

      // Initialize current and previous to 1, the first
      // two numbers in the Fibonacci series
      current = previous = 1;

      // While the current Fibonacci number in the series is
      // less than the value input by the user
      while (current <= input)
      {
          temp = current;
          current = previous + current;
          previous = temp; // Executes even if previous
          // statement caused current to exceed input
      }

      System.Console.WriteLine(
          $"The Fibonacci number following this is { current }");
  }
}
```

A **Fibonacci number** is a member of the **Fibonacci series**, which includes all numbers that are the sum of the previous two numbers in the series, beginning with 1 and 1. In Listing 4.43, you prompt the user for an integer. Then you use a while loop to find the first Fibonacci number that is greater than the number the user entered.

■ BEGINNER TOPIC

When to Use a while Loop

The remainder of this chapter considers other statements that cause a block of code to execute repeatedly. The term *loop body* refers to the statement (frequently a code block) that is to be executed within the while statement, since the code is executed in a "loop" until the exit condition is achieved. It is important to understand which loop construct to select. You use a while construct to iterate while the condition evaluates to true. A for loop is used most appropriately whenever the number of repetitions is known, such as when counting from 0 to n. A do/while is similar to a while loop, except that it will always execute the loop body at least once.

The do/while loop is very similar to the while loop except that a do/while loop is preferred when the number of repetitions is from 1 to n and n is not known when iterating begins. This pattern frequently occurs when prompting a user for input. Listing 4.44 is taken from the tic-tac-toe program.

LISTING 4.44: do/while Loop Example

```
// Repeatedly request player to move until he
// enters a valid position on the board
bool valid;
do
{
    valid = false;

    // Request a move from the current player
    System.Console.Write(
        $"\nPlayer {currentPlayer}: Enter move:");
    input = System.Console.ReadLine();

    // Check the current player's input
    // ...

} while (!valid);
```

In Listing 4.44, you initialize valid to false at the beginning of each **iteration**, or loop repetition. Next, you prompt and retrieve the number the user input. Although not shown here, you then check whether the input was correct, and if it was, you assign valid equal to true. Since the code uses a do/while statement rather than a while statement, the user will be prompted for input at least once.

The general form of the do/while loop is as follows:

```
do
    statement
while (condition);
```

As with all the control flow statements, a code block is generally used as the single statement to allow multiple statements to be executed as the

loop body. However, any single statement except for a labeled statement or
a local variable declaration can be used.

The for Loop

The for loop iterates a code block until a specified condition is reached. In
that way, it is very similar to the while loop. The difference is that the for
loop has built-in syntax for initializing, incrementing, and testing the value
of a counter, known as the **loop variable**. Because there is a specific location
in the loop syntax for an increment operation, the increment and decrement operators are frequently used as part of a for loop.

Listing 4.45 shows the for loop used to display an integer in binary
form. The results of this listing appear in Output 4.21.

LISTING 4.45: Using the for Loop

```csharp
class BinaryConverter
{
  static void Main()
  {
      const int size = 64;
      ulong value;
      char bit;

      System.Console.Write("Enter an integer: ");
      // Use long.Parse()to support negative numbers
      // Assumes unchecked assignment to ulong
      value = (ulong)long.Parse(System.Console.ReadLine());

      // Set initial mask to 100...
      ulong mask = 1UL << size - 1;
      for (int count = 0; count < size; count++)
      {
          bit = ((mask & value) > 0) ? '1': '0';
          System.Console.Write(bit);
          // Shift mask one location over to the right
          mask >>= 1;
      }
  }
}
```

OUTPUT 4.21

```
Enter an integer: -42
1111111111111111111111111111111111111111111111111111111111010110
```

Listing 4.45 performs a bit mask 64 times, once for each bit in the number. The three parts of the for loop header first declare and initialize the variable count, then describe the condition that must be met for the loop body to be executed, and finally describe the operation that updates the loop variable. The general form of the for loop is as follows:

```
for (initial ; condition ; loop)
    statement
```

Here is a breakdown of the for loop:

- The initial section performs operations that precede the first iteration. In Listing 4.45, it declares and initializes the variable count. The initial expression does not have to be a declaration of a new variable (though it frequently is). It is possible, for example, to declare the variable beforehand and simply initialize it in the for loop, or to skip the initialization section entirely by leaving it blank. Variables declared here are in scope throughout the header and body of the for statement.

- The condition portion of the for loop specifies an end condition. The loop exits when this condition is false, exactly like the while loop does. The for loop will execute the body only as long as the condition evaluates to true. In the preceding example, the loop exits when count is greater than or equal to 64.

- The loop expression executes after each iteration. In the preceding example, count++ executes after the right shift of the mask (mask >>= 1) but before the condition is evaluated. During the 64th iteration, count is incremented to 64, causing the condition to become false and therefore terminating the loop.

- The statement portion of the for loop is the "loop body" code that executes while the conditional expression remains true.

If you wrote out each for loop execution step in pseudocode without using a for loop expression, it would look like this:

1. Declare and initialize count to 0.
2. If count is less than 64, continue to step 3; otherwise, go to step 7.
3. Calculate bit and display it.

4. Shift the mask.

5. Increment `count` by 1.

6. Jump back to line 2.

7. Continue the execution of the program after the loop.

The `for` statement doesn't require any of the elements in its header. The expression `for(;;){ ... }` is perfectly valid, although there still needs to be a means to escape from the loop so that it will not continue to execute indefinitely. (If the condition is missing, it is assumed to be the constant `true`.)

The initial and loop expressions have an unusual syntax to support loops that require multiple loop variables, as shown in Listing 4.46.

LISTING 4.46: `for` Loop Using Multiple Expressions

```
for (int x = 0, y = 5; ((x <= 5) && (y >=0 )); y--, x++)
{
  System.Console.Write(
     $"{ x }{ ((x > y) ? '>' : '<' )}{ y }\t";
}
```

The results of Listing 4.46 appear in Output 4.22.

OUTPUT 4.22

```
0<5    1<4    2<3    3>2    4>1    5>0
```

Here the initialization clause contains a complex declaration that declares and initializes two loop variables, but this is at least similar to a declaration statement that declares multiple local variables. The loop clause is quite unusual, as it can consist of a comma-separated list of expressions, not just a single expression.

Guidelines

CONSIDER refactoring the method to make the control flow easier to understand if you find yourself writing `for` loops with complex conditionals and multiple loop variables.

The `for` loop is little more than a more convenient way to write a `while` loop; you can always rewrite a `for` loop like this:

```
{
  initial;
  while (condition)
  {
    statement;
    loop;
  }
}
```

> ### Guidelines
>
> **DO** use the `for` loop when the number of loop iterations is known in advance and the "counter" that gives the number of iterations executed is needed in the loop.
>
> **DO** use the `while` loop when the number of loop iterations is not known in advance and a counter is not needed.

The foreach Loop

The last loop statement in the C# language is `foreach`. The `foreach` loop iterates through a collection of items, setting a loop variable to represent each item in turn. In the body of the loop, operations may be performed on the item. A nice property of the `foreach` loop is that every item is iterated over exactly once; it is not possible to accidentally miscount and iterate past the end of the collection, as can happen with other loops.

The general form of the `foreach` statement is as follows:

```
foreach(type variable in collection)
  statement
```

Here is a breakdown of the `foreach` statement:

- `type` is used to declare the data type of the variable for each item within the collection. It may be `var`, in which case the compiler infers the type of the item from the type of the collection.
- `variable` is a read-only variable into which the `foreach` loop will automatically assign the next item within the collection. The scope of the variable is limited to the body of the loop.
- `collection` is an expression, such as an array, representing any number of items.
- `statement` is the loop body that executes for each iteration of the loop.

Consider the foreach loop in the context of the simple example shown in Listing 4.47.

LISTING 4.47: Determining Remaining Moves Using the foreach Loop

```csharp
class TicTacToe        // Declares the TicTacToe class
{
  static void Main() // Declares the entry point of the program
  {
      // Hardcode initial board as follows:
      // ---+---+---
      //  1 | 2 | 3
      // ---+---+---
      //  4 | 5 | 6
      // ---+---+---
      //  7 | 8 | 9
      // ---+---+---
      char[] cells = {
        '1', '2', '3', '4', '5', '6', '7', '8', '9'
      };

      System.Console.Write(
          "The available moves are as follows: ");

      // Write out the initial available moves
      foreach (char cell in cells)
      {
        if (cell != 'O' && cell != 'X')
        {
            System.Console.Write($"{ cell } ");
        }
      }
  }
}
```

Output 4.23 shows the results of Listing 4.47.

OUTPUT 4.23

```
The available moves are as follows: 1 2 3 4 5 6 7 8 9
```

When the execution engine reaches the foreach statement, it assigns to the variable cell the first item in the cells array—in this case, the value '1'. It then executes the code within the block that makes up the foreach loop body. The if statement determines whether the value of cell is 'O' or 'X'. If it is neither, the value of cell is written out to the console. The next iteration then assigns the next array value to cell, and so on.

Note that the compiler prevents modification of the variable (cell) during the execution of a foreach loop. Also, the loop variable has a subtly different behavior starting in C# 5 than it did in previous versions; the difference is apparent only when the loop body contains a lambda expression or anonymous method that uses the loop variable. See Chapter 13 for details.

■ BEGINNER TOPIC

Where the switch Statement Is More Appropriate

Sometimes you might compare the same value in several continuous if statements, as shown with the input variable in Listing 4.48.

LISTING 4.48: Checking the Player's Input with an if Statement

```csharp
// ...

bool valid = false;

// Check the current player's input
if( (input == "1") ||
  (input == "2") ||
  (input == "3") ||
  (input == "4") ||
  (input == "5") ||
  (input == "6") ||
  (input == "7") ||
  (input == "8") ||
  (input == "9") )
{
    // Save/move as the player directed
    // ...

    valid = true;
}
else if( (input == "") || (input == "quit") )
{
    valid = true;
}
else
{
    System.Console.WriteLine(
      "\nERROR:  Enter a value from 1-9. "
      + "Push ENTER to quit");
}

// ...
```

This code validates the text entered to ensure that it is a valid tic-tac-toe move. If the value of input were 9, for example, the program would have to perform nine different evaluations. It would be preferable to jump to the correct code after only one evaluation. To enable this, you use a switch statement.

The Basic switch Statement

A basic switch statement is simpler to understand than a complex if statement when you have a value that must be compared against different constant values. The switch statement looks like this:

```
switch (expression)
{
    case constant:
      statements
    default:
      statements
}
```

Here is a breakdown of the switch statement:

- expression is the value that is being compared against the different constants. The type of this expression determines the "governing type" of the switch. Allowable governing data types are bool, sbyte, byte, short, ushort, int, uint, long, ulong, char, any enum type (covered in Chapter 9), the corresponding nullable types of each of those value types, and string.
- constant is any constant expression compatible with the governing type.
- A group of one or more case labels (or the default label) followed by a group of one or more statements is called a **switch section**. The pattern given previously has two switch sections; Listing 4.49 shows a switch statement with three switch sections.
- statements is one or more statements to be executed when the expression equals one of the constant values mentioned in a label in the switch section. The end point of the group of statements must not be reachable. Typically, the last statement is a jump statement such as a break, return, or goto statement.

A `switch` statement should have at least one switch section; `switch(x){}` is legal but will generate a warning. Also, the guideline provided earlier was to avoid omitting braces in general. One exception to this rule of thumb is to omit braces for `case` and `break` statements because they serve to indicate the beginning and end of a block.

Listing 4.49, with a `switch` statement, is semantically equivalent to the series of `if` statements in Listing 4.48.

LISTING 4.49: Replacing the if Statement with a switch Statement

```
static bool ValidateAndMove(
  int[] playerPositions, int currentPlayer, string input)
{
  bool valid = false;

  // Check the current player's input
  switch (input)
  {
    case "1" :
    case "2" :
    case "3" :
    case "4" :
    case "5" :
    case "6" :
    case "7" :
    case "8" :
    case "9" :
      // Save/move as the player directed
      ...
      valid = true;
      break;

    case "" :
    case "quit" :
      valid = true;
      break;
    default :
      // If none of the other case statements
      // is encountered, then the text is invalid
```

```
        System.Console.WriteLine(
          "\nERROR:  Enter a value from 1-9. "
          + "Push ENTER to quit");
        break;
    }

    return valid;
}
```

In Listing 4.49, input is the test expression. Since input is a string, the governing type is string. If the value of input is one of the strings 1, 2, 3, 4, 5, 6, 7, 8, or 9, the move is valid and you change the appropriate cell to match that of the current user's token (X or O). Once execution encounters a break statement, control leaves the switch statement.

The next switch section describes how to handle the empty string or the string quit; it sets valid to true if input equals either value. The default switch section is executed if no other switch section had a case label that matched the test expression.

Language Contrast: C++—switch Statement Fall-Through

In C++, if a switch section does not end with a jump statement, control "falls through" to the next switch section, executing its code. Because unintended fall-through is a common error in C++, C# does not allow control to accidentally fall through from one switch section to the next. The C# designers believed it was better to prevent this common source of bugs and encourage better code readability than to match the potentially confusing C++ behavior. If you do want one switch section to execute the statements of another switch section, you may do so explicitly with a goto statement, as demonstrated later in this chapter.

There are several things to note about the switch statement:

- A switch statement with no switch sections will generate a compiler warning, but the statement will still compile.
- Switch sections can appear in any order; the default section does not have to appear last. In fact, the default switch section does not have to appear at all—it is optional.
- The C# language requires that every switch section, including the last section, ends with a jump statement (see next section). This means that switch sections usually end with a break, return, throw, or goto.

C# 7.0 introduced an improvement to the switch statement that enables pattern matching so that any data type, not just the limited few identified earlier, can be used for the switch expression. Pattern matching enables the use of switch statements based on the type of the switch expression and the use of case labels that also declare variables. Lastly, pattern matching switch statements support conditional expressions so that not only the type but also a Boolean expression at the end of the case label can identify which case label should execute. For more information on pattern matching switch statements, see Chapter 7.

Begin 7.0

End 7.0

Jump Statements

It is possible to alter the execution path of a loop. In fact, with jump statements, it is possible to escape out of the loop or to skip the remaining portion of an iteration and begin with the next iteration, even when the loop condition remains true. This section considers some of the ways to jump the execution path from one location to another.

The break Statement

To escape out of a loop or a switch statement, C# uses a break statement. Whenever the break statement is encountered, control immediately leaves the loop or switch. Listing 4.50 examines the foreach loop from the tic-tac-toe program.

LISTING 4.50: Using break to Escape Once a Winner Is Found

```csharp
class TicTacToe        // Declares the TicTacToe class
{
  static void Main() // Declares the entry point of the program
  {
      int winner = 0;
      // Stores locations each player has moved
      int[] playerPositions = { 0, 0 };

      // Hardcoded board position:
      // X | 2 | 0
      // ---+----+---
      // 0 | 0 | 6
      // ---+----+---
      // X | X | X
      playerPositions[0] = 449;
      playerPositions[1] = 28;
```

```csharp
// Determine if there is a winner
int[] winningMasks = {
    7, 56, 448, 73, 146, 292, 84, 273 };

// Iterate through each winning mask to determine
// if there is a winner
foreach (int mask in winningMasks)
{
    if ((mask & playerPositions[0]) == mask)
    {
        winner = 1;
        break;
    }
    else if ((mask & playerPositions[1]) == mask)
    {
        winner = 2;
        break;
    }
}

System.Console.WriteLine(
    $"Player { winner } was the winner");
}
}
```

Output 4.24 shows the results of Listing 4.50.

OUTPUT 4.24

```
Player 1 was the winner
```

Listing 4.50 uses a break statement when a player holds a winning position. The break statement forces its enclosing loop (or a switch statement) to cease execution, and control moves to the next line outside the loop. For this listing, if the bit comparison returns true (if the board holds a winning position), the break statement causes control to jump and display the winner.

■ BEGINNER TOPIC

Bitwise Operators for Positions

The full tic-tac-toe listing uses the bitwise operators to determine which player wins the game. First, the code saves the positions of each player into a bitmap called playerPositions. (It uses an array so that the positions for both players can be saved.)

To begin, both playerPositions are 0. As each player moves, the bit corresponding to the move is set. If, for example, the player selects cell 3, shifter is set to 3 − 1. The code subtracts 1 because C# is zero based and you need to adjust for 0 as the first position instead of 1. Next, the code sets position, the bit corresponding to cell 3, using the shift operator 000000000000001 << shifter, where shifter now has a value of 2. Lastly, it sets playerPositions for the current player (subtracting 1 again to shift to zero based) to 0000000000000100. Listing 4.51 uses |= so that previous moves are combined with the current move.

LISTING 4.51: Setting the Bit That Corresponds to Each Player's Move

```
int shifter;   // The number of places to shift
               // over to set a bit
int position;  // The bit that is to be set

// int.Parse() converts "input" to an integer.
// int.Parse(input) - 1 because arrays
// are zero based.
shifter = int.Parse(input) - 1;

// Shift mask of 00000000000000000000000000000001
// over by cellLocations
position = 1 << shifter;

// Take the current player cells and OR them to set the
// new position as well.
// Since currentPlayer is either 1 or 2,
// subtract 1 to use currentPlayer as an
// index in a zero-based array.
playerPositions[currentPlayer-1] |= position;
```

Later in the program, you can iterate over each mask corresponding to winning positions on the board to determine whether the current player has a winning position, as shown in Listing 4.50.

The continue Statement

You might have a block containing a series of statements within a loop. If you determine that some conditions warrant executing only a portion of these statements for some iterations, you can use the continue statement to jump to the end of the current iteration and begin the next iteration. The continue statement exits the current iteration (regardless of whether additional statements remain) and jumps to the loop condition. At that point, if the loop conditional is still true, the loop will continue execution.

Listing 4.52 uses the `continue` statement so that only the letters of the domain portion of an email are displayed. Output 4.25 shows the results of Listing 4.52.

LISTING 4.52: Determining the Domain of an Email Address

```csharp
class EmailDomain
{
  static void Main()
  {
      string email;
      bool insideDomain = false;
      System.Console.WriteLine("Enter an email address: ");

      email = System.Console.ReadLine();

      System.Console.Write("The email domain is: ");

      // Iterate through each letter in the email address
      foreach (char letter in email)
      {
          if (!insideDomain)
          {
              if (letter == '@')
              {
                  insideDomain = true;
              }
              continue;
          }

          System.Console.Write(letter);
      }
  }
}
```

OUTPUT 4.25

```
Enter an email address:
mark@dotnetprogramming.com
The email domain is: dotnetprogramming.com
```

In Listing 4.52, if you are not yet inside the domain portion of the email address, you can use a `continue` statement to move control to the end of the loop, and process the next character in the email address.

You can almost always use an `if` statement in place of a `continue` statement, and this is usually more readable. The problem with the `continue` statement is that it provides multiple flows of control within a single itera-tion, which compromises readability. In Listing 4.53, the sample has been rewritten, replacing the `continue` statement with the `if`/`else` construct to demonstrate a more readable version that does not use the `continue` statement.

LISTING 4.53: Replacing a continue Statement with an if Statement

```
foreach (char letter in email)
{
  if (insideDomain)
  {
      System.Console.Write(letter);
  }
  else
  {
      if (letter == '@')
      {
          insideDomain = true;
      }
  }
}
```

The goto Statement

Early programming languages lacked the relatively sophisticated "struc-tured" control flows that modern languages such as C# have as a mat-ter of course and instead relied on simple conditional branching (`if`) and unconditional branching (`goto`) statements for most of their control flow needs. The resultant programs were often hard to understand. The contin-ued existence of a `goto` statement within C# seems like an anachronism to many experienced programmers. However, C# supports `goto`, and it is the only method for supporting fall-through within a `switch` statement. In Listing 4.54, if the `/out` option is set, code execution jumps to the `default` case using the `goto` statement, and similarly for `/f`.

LISTING 4.54: Demonstrating a switch with goto Statements

```
// ...
static void Main(string[] args)
{
  bool isOutputSet = false;
  bool isFiltered = false;
```

```
    foreach (string option in args)
    {
        switch (option)
        {
            case "/out":
                isOutputSet = true;
                isFiltered = false;
                goto default;
            case "/f":
                isFiltered = true;
                isRecursive = false;
                goto default;
            default:
                if (isRecursive)
                {
                    // Recurse down the hierarchy
                    // ...

                }
                else if (isFiltered)
                {
                    // Add option to list of filters
                    // ...
                }
                break;
        }
    }

    // ...

}
```

Output 4.26 shows how to execute the code shown in Listing 4.54.

OUTPUT 4.26

```
C:\SAMPLES>Generate /out fizbottle.bin /f "*.xml" "*.wsdl"
```

To branch to a switch section label other than the default label, you can use the syntax goto case constant;, where constant is the constant associated with the case label you wish to branch to. To branch to a statement that is not associated with a switch section, precede the target statement with any identifier followed by a colon; you can then use that identifier with the goto statement. For example, you could have a labeled statement myLabel : Console.WriteLine();. The statement goto myLabel; would then branch to the labeled statement. Fortunately,

C# prevents you from using goto to branch *into* a code block; instead, goto may be used only to branch within a code block or to an enclosing code block. By making these restrictions, C# avoids most of the serious goto abuses possible in other languages.

In spite of the improvements, use of goto is generally considered to be inelegant, difficult to understand, and symptomatic of poorly structured code. If you need to execute a section of code multiple times or under different circumstances, either use a loop or extract code to a method of its own.

Guidelines

AVOID using goto.

C# Preprocessor Directives

Control flow statements evaluate expressions at runtime. In contrast, the C# preprocessor is invoked during compilation. The preprocessor commands are directives to the C# compiler, specifying the sections of code to compile or identifying how to handle specific errors and warnings within the code. C# preprocessor commands can also provide directives to C# editors regarding the organization of code.

Language Contrast: C++—Preprocessing

Languages such as C and C++ use a **preprocessor** to perform actions on the code based on special tokens. Preprocessor directives generally tell the compiler how to compile the code in a file and do not participate in the compilation process itself. In contrast, the C# compiler handles "preprocessor" directives as part of the regular lexical analysis of the source code. As a result, C# does not support preprocessor macros beyond defining a constant. In fact, the term *preprocessor* is generally a misnomer for C#.

Each preprocessor directive begins with a hash symbol (#), and all preprocessor directives must appear on one line. A newline rather than a semicolon indicates the end of the directive.

A list of each preprocessor directive appears in Table 4.4.

TABLE 4.4: **Preprocessor Directives**

Statement or Expression	General Syntax Structure	Example

#if directive	**#if** preprocessor-expression
	    code
	#endif
		#if CSHARP2PLUS
		    Console.Clear( );
		#endif

#elif directive	**#if** preprocessor-expression1
	    code
	#elif preprocessor-expression2
	    code
	#endif
		#if LINUX
		...
		#elif WINDOWS
		...
		#endif

#else directive	**#if**
	    code
	#else
	    code
	#endif
		#if CSHARP1
		...
		#else
		...
		#endif

#define directive	**#define** conditional-symbol	**#define** CSHARP2PLUS
#undef directive	**#undef** conditional-symbol	**#undef** CSHARP2PLUS
#error directive	**#error** preproc-message	**#error** Buggy implementation
#warning directive	**#warning** preproc-message	**#warning** Needs code review
#pragma directive	**#pragma** warning	**#pragma** warning disable 1030
#line directive	**#line** org-line new-line ─────────────── **#line default**	**#line** 467 "TicTacToe.cs" ... **#line default**
#region directive	**#region** pre-proc-message code **#endregion**	**#region** Methods ... **#endregion**

Excluding and Including Code (#if, #elif, #else, #endif)

Perhaps the most common use of preprocessor directives is in controlling when and how code is included. For example, to write code that could be compiled by both C# 2.0 and later compilers and the prior version 1.0 compilers, you would use a preprocessor directive to exclude C# 2.0–specific code when compiling with a version 1.0 compiler. You can see this in the tic-tac-toe example and in Listing 4.55.

LISTING 4.55: Excluding C# 2.0 Code from a C# 1.x Compiler

```
#if CSHARP2PLUS
System.Console.Clear();
#endif
```

In this case, you call the `System.Console.Clear()` method. Using the `#if` and `#endif` preprocessor directives, this line of code will be compiled only if the preprocessor symbol `CSHARP2PLUS` is defined.

Another use of the preprocessor directive would be to handle differences among platforms, such as surrounding Windows- and Linux-specific APIs with `WINDOWS` and `LINUX` `#if` directives. Developers often use these directives in place of multiline comments (`/*...*/`) because they are easier to remove by defining the appropriate symbol or via a search and replace.

A final common use of the directives is for debugging. If you surround code with an `#if DEBUG`, you will remove the code from a release build on most IDEs. The IDEs define the `DEBUG` symbol by default in a debug compile and `RELEASE` by default for release builds.

To handle an else-if condition, you can use the `#elif` directive within the `#if` directive instead of creating two entirely separate `#if` blocks, as shown in Listing 4.56.

LISTING 4.56: Using #if, #elif, and #endif Directives

```
#if LINUX
...
#elif WINDOWS
...
#endif
```

Defining Preprocessor Symbols (#define, #undef)

You can define a preprocessor symbol in two ways. The first is with the `#define` directive, as shown in Listing 4.57.

LISTING 4.57: A #define Example

```
#define CSHARP2PLUS
```

The second method uses the `define` command line. Output 4.27 demonstrates this with Dotnet command-line interface.

OUTPUT 4.27

```
>dotnet.exe -define:CSHARP2PLUS TicTacToe.cs
```

Output 4.28 shows the same functionality using the csc.exe compiler directly.

OUTPUT 4.28

```
>csc.exe -define:CSHARP2PLUS TicTacToe.cs
```

To add multiple definitions, separate them with a semicolon. The advantage of the define compiler option is that no source code changes are required, so you may use the same source files to produce two different binaries.

To undefine a symbol, you use the #undef directive in the same way you use #define.

Emitting Errors and Warnings (#error, #warning)

Sometimes you may want to flag a potential problem with your code. You do this by inserting #error and #warning directives to emit an error or a warning, respectively. Listing 4.58 uses the tic-tac-toe sample to warn that the code does not yet prevent players from entering the same move multiple times. The results of Listing 4.58 appear in Output 4.29.

LISTING 4.58: Defining a Warning with #warning

```
#warning    "Same move allowed multiple times."
```

OUTPUT 4.29

```
Performing main compilation...
...\tictactoe.cs(471,16): warning CS1030: #warning: '"Same move allowed
↳multiple times."'

Build complete -- 0 errors, 1 warnings
```

By including the #warning directive, you ensure that the compiler will report a warning, as shown in Output 4.29. This particular warning is a way of flagging the fact that there is a potential enhancement or bug within the code. It could be a simple way of reminding the developer of a pending task.

Turning Off Warning Messages (#pragma)

Begin 2.0

Warnings are helpful because they point to code that could potentially be troublesome. However, sometimes it is preferred to turn off particular warnings explicitly because they can be ignored legitimately. C# 2.0 and later compilers provide the preprocessor #pragma directive for just this purpose (see Listing 4.59).

LISTING 4.59: Using the Preprocessor #pragma Directive to Disable the #warning Directive

```
#pragma warning disable  1030
```

Note that warning numbers are prefixed with the letters *CS* in the compiler output. However, this prefix is not used in the #pragma warning directive. The number corresponds to the warning error number emitted by the compiler when there is no preprocessor command.

To reenable the warning, #pragma supports the restore option following the warning, as shown in Listing 4.60.

LISTING 4.60: Using the Preprocessor #pragma Directive to Restore a Warning

```
#pragma warning restore  1030
```

In combination, these two directives can surround a particular block of code where the warning is explicitly determined to be irrelevant.

Perhaps one of the most common warnings to disable is CS1591. This warning appears when you elect to generate XML documentation using the /doc compiler option, but you neglect to document all of the public items within your program.

nowarn:<warn list> Option

In addition to the #pragma directive, C# compilers generally support the nowarn:<warn list> option. This achieves the same result as #pragma, except that instead of adding it to the source code, you can insert the command as a compiler option. The nowarn option affects the entire compilation, whereas the #pragma option affects only the file in which it appears.

Turning off the CS1591 warning, for example, would appear on the command line as shown in Output 4.30.

OUTPUT 4.30

End 2.0

```
> csc /doc:generate.xml /nowarn:1591 /out:generate.exe Program.cs
```

Specifying Line Numbers (#line)

The #line directive controls on which line number the C# compiler reports an error or warning. It is used predominantly by utilities and designers that emit C# code. In Listing 4.61, the actual line numbers within the file appear on the left.

LISTING 4.61: The #line Preprocessor Directive

```
124        #line 113 "TicTacToe.cs"
125        #warning "Same move allowed multiple times."
126        #line default
```

Including the #line directive causes the compiler to report the warning found on line 125 as though it were on line 113, as shown in the compiler error message in Output 4.31.

OUTPUT 4.31

```
Performing main compilation...
...\tictactoe.cs(113,18): warning CS1030: #warning: '"Same move allowed
⤷multiple times."'

Build complete -- 0 errors, 1 warnings
```

Following the #line directive with default reverses the effect of all prior #line directives and instructs the compiler to report true line numbers rather than the ones designated by previous uses of the #line directive.

Hints for Visual Editors (#region, #endregion)

C# contains two preprocessor directives, #region and #endregion, that are useful only within the context of visual code editors. Code editors, such as Microsoft Visual Studio, can search through source code and find these directives to provide editor features when writing code. C# allows you to declare a region of code using the #region directive. You must pair the #region directive with a matching #endregion directive, both of which may optionally include a descriptive string following the directive. In addition, you may nest regions within one another.

Listing 4.62 shows the tic-tac-toe program as an example.

LISTING 4.62: #region and #endregion Preprocessor Directives

```
...
#region Display Tic-tac-toe Board

#if CSHARP2PLUS
  System.Console.Clear();
#endif

// Display the current board
border = 0;    // set the first border (border[0] = "|")

// Display the top line of dashes
// ("\n---+---+---\n")
System.Console.Write(borders[2]);
foreach (char cell in cells)
{
  // Write out a cell value and the border that comes after it
  System.Console.Write($" { cell } { borders[border] }");

  // Increment to the next border
  border++;

  // Reset border to 0 if it is 3
  if (border == 3)
  {
      border = 0;
  }
}
#endregion Display Tic-tac-toe Board
...
```

These preprocessor directives are used, for example, with Microsoft Visual Studio. Visual Studio examines the code and provides a tree control to open and collapse the code (on the left-hand side of the code editor window) that matches the region demarcated by the #region directives (see Figure 4.5).

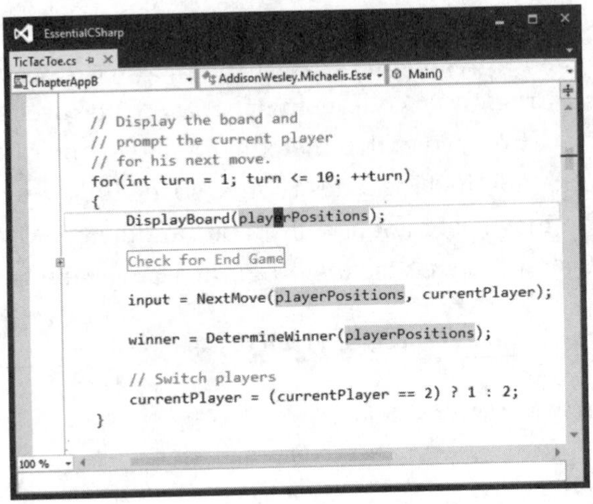

FIGURE 4.5: Collapsed Region in Microsoft Visual Studio .NET

SUMMARY

This chapter began by introducing the C# operators related to assignment and arithmetic. Next, we used the operators along with the `const` keyword to declare constants. Coverage of all the C# operators was not sequential, however. Before discussing the relational and logical comparison operators, the chapter introduced the `if` statement and the important concepts of code blocks and scope. To close out the coverage of operators, we discussed the bitwise operators, especially regarding masks. We also discussed other control flow statements such as loops, `switch`, and `goto`, and ended the chapter with a discussion of the C# preprocessor directives.

Operator precedence was discussed earlier in the chapter; Table 4.5 summarizes the order of precedence across all operators, including several that are not yet covered.

TABLE 4.5: Operator Order of Precedence*

Category	Operators

Primary	`x.y  f(x)  a[x]  x++  x--  new`
	`typeof(T)  checked(x)  unchecked(x) default(T)`
	`nameof(x) delegate{}   ()`

Unary	`+   -   !   ~   ++x   --x  (T)x await x`

TABLE 4.5: Operator Order of Precedence* (*continued*)

Category	Operators
Multiplicative	`*  /  %`
Additive	`+  -`
Shift	`<<  >>`
Relational and type testing	`<  >  <=  >=  is  as`
Equality	`==  !=`
Logical AND	`&`
Logical XOR	`^`
Logical OR	`|`
Conditional AND	`&&`
Conditional OR	`||`
Null coalescing	`??`
Conditional	`?:`
Assignment and lambda	`=  *=  /=  %=  +=  -=  <<=  >>=  &=  ^=  |=  =>`

* Rows appear in order of precedence from highest to lowest.

Perhaps one of the best ways to review all of the content covered in Chapters 1, 2, and 3 is to look at the tic-tac-toe program found in `Chapter04\TicTacToe.cs`. By reviewing this program, you can see one way in which you can combine all that you have learned into a complete program.

5

Methods and Parameters

FROM WHAT YOU HAVE LEARNED about C# programming so far, you should be able to write straightforward programs consisting of a list of statements, similar to the way programs were created in the 1970s. Programming has come a long way since the 1970s, however; as programs have become more complex, new paradigms have emerged to manage that complexity. *Procedural* or *structured* programming provides constructs by which statements are grouped together to form units. Furthermore, with structured programming, it is possible to pass data to a group of statements and then have data returned once the statements have executed.

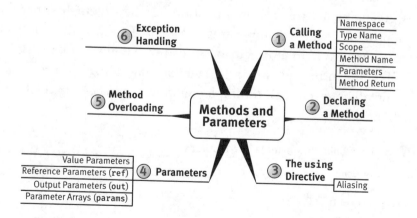

Besides the basics of calling and defining methods, this chapter covers some slightly more advanced concepts—namely, recursion, method overloading, optional parameters, and named arguments. All method calls discussed so far and through the end of this chapter are static (a concept that Chapter 6 explores in detail).

Even as early as the `HelloWorld` program in Chapter 1, you learned how to define a method. In that example, you defined the `Main()` method. In this chapter, you will learn about method creation in more detail, including the special C# syntaxes (`ref` and `out`) for parameters that pass variables rather than values to methods. Lastly, we will touch on some rudimentary error handling.

Calling a Method

■ **BEGINNER TOPIC**

What Is a Method?

Up to this point, all of the statements in the programs you have written have appeared together in one grouping called a `Main()` method. When programs become any more complex than those we have seen thus far, a single method implementation quickly becomes difficult to maintain and complex to read through and understand.

A **method** is a means of grouping together a sequence of statements to perform a particular action or compute a particular result. This provides greater structure and organization for the statements that comprise a program. Consider, for example, a `Main()` method that counts the lines of source code in a directory. Instead of having one large `Main()` method, you can provide a shorter version that allows you to hone in on the details of each method implementation as necessary. Listing 5.1 shows an example.

LISTING 5.1: **Grouping Statements into Methods**

```
class LineCount
{
  static void Main()
  {
      int lineCount;
      string files;
```

```
        DisplayHelpText();
        files = GetFiles();
        lineCount = CountLines(files);
        DisplayLineCount(lineCount);
    }
    // ...
}
```

Instead of placing all of the statements into `Main()`, the listing breaks them into groups called methods. The `System.Console.WriteLine()` statements that display the help text have been moved to the `DisplayHelpText()` method. All of the statements used to determine which files to count appear in the `GetFiles()` method. To actually count the files, the code calls the `CountLines()` method before displaying the results using the `DisplayLineCount()` method. With a quick glance, it is easy to review the code and gain an overview, because the method name describes the purpose of the method.

Guidelines

DO give methods names that are verbs or verb phrases.

A method is always associated with a type—usually a **class**—that provides a means of grouping related methods together.

Methods can receive data via **arguments** that are supplied for their **parameters**. Parameters are variables used for passing data from the **caller** (the code containing the method call) to the invoked method (`Write()`, `WriteLine()`, `GetFiles()`, `CountLines()`, and so on). In Listing 5.1, `files` and `lineCount` are examples of arguments passed to the `CountLines()` and `DisplayLineCount()` methods via their parameters. Methods can also return data to the caller via a **return value** (in Listing 5.1, the `GetFiles()` method call has a return value that is assigned to `files`).

To begin, we reexamine `System.Console.Write()`, `System.Console.WriteLine()`, and `System.Console.ReadLine()` from Chapter 1. This time we look at them as examples of method calls in general instead of looking at the specifics of printing and retrieving data from the console. Listing 5.2 shows each of the three methods in use.

LISTING 5.2: A Simple Method Call

```csharp
class HeyYou
{
  static void Main()
  {
      string firstName;
      string lastName;

      System.Console.WriteLine("Hey you!");

      System.Console.Write("Enter your first name: ");

      firstName = System.Console.ReadLine();
      System.Console.Write("Enter your last name: ");
      lastName = System.Console.ReadLine();
      System.Console.WriteLine(
          $"Your full name is { firstName } { lastName }.");
  }
}
```

The parts of the method call include the method name, argument list, and returned value. A fully qualified method name includes a namespace, type name, and method name; a period separates each part of a fully qualified method name. As we will see, methods are often called with only a part of their fully qualified name.

Namespaces

Namespaces are a categorization mechanism for grouping all types related to a particular area of functionality. Namespaces are hierarchical and can have arbitrarily many levels in the hierarchy, though namespaces with more than half a dozen levels are rare. Typically the hierarchy begins with a company name, and then a product name, and then the functional area. For example, in `Microsoft.Win32.Networking`, the outermost namespace is `Microsoft`, which contains an inner namespace `Win32`, which in turn contains an even more deeply nested `Networking` namespace.

Namespaces are primarily used to organize types by area of functionality so that they can be more easily found and understood. However, they can also be used to avoid type name collisions. For example, the compiler can distinguish between two types with the name `Button` as long as each type has a different namespace. Thus you can disambiguate types `System.Web.UI.WebControls.Button` and `System.Windows.Controls.Button`.

In Listing 5.2, the `Console` type is found within the `System` namespace. The `System` namespace contains the types that enable the programmer to perform many fundamental programming activities. Almost all C# programs use types within the `System` namespace. Table 5.1 provides a listing of other common namespaces.

TABLE 5.1: Common Namespaces

Namespace	Description
System	Contains the fundamental types and types for conversion between types, mathematics, program invocation, and environment management.
System.Collections.Generics	Contains strongly typed collections that use generics.
System.Data	Contains types used for working with databases.
System.Drawing	Contains types for drawing to the display device and working with images.
System.IO	Contains types for working with directories and manipulating, loading, and saving files.
System.Linq	Contains classes and interfaces for querying data in collections using a Language Integrated Query.
System.Text	Contains types for working with strings and various text encodings, and for converting between those encodings.
System.Text.RegularExpressions	Contains types for working with regular expressions.
System.Threading	Contains types for multithreaded programming.
System.Threading.Tasks	Contains types for task-based asynchrony.
System.Web	Contains types that enable browser-to-server communication, generally over HTTP. The functionality within this namespace is used to support ASP.NET.

Begin 4.0

continues

TABLE 5.1: Common Namespaces (*continued*)

Namespace	Description
System.Windows	Contains types for creating rich user interfaces starting with .NET 3.0 using a UI technology called Windows Presentation Framework (WPF) that leverages Extensible Application Markup Language (XAML) for declarative design of the UI.
System.Xml	Contains standards-based support for XML processing.

End 4.0

It is not always necessary to provide the namespace when calling a method. For example, if the call expression appears in a type in the same namespace as the called method, the compiler can infer the namespace to be the namespace that contains the type. Later in this chapter, you will see how the using directive eliminates the need for a namespace qualifier as well.

Guidelines

DO use PascalCasing for namespace names.

CONSIDER organizing the directory hierarchy for source code files to match the namespace hierarchy.

Type Name

Calls to static methods require the type name qualifier as long as the target method is not within the same type.[1] (As discussed later in the chapter, a using static directive allows you to omit the type name.) For example, a call expression of Console.WriteLine() found in the method HelloWorld.Main() requires the type, Console, to be stated. However, just as with the namespace, C# allows the omission of the type name from a method call whenever the method is a member of the type containing the call expression. (Examples of method calls such as this appear in Listing 5.4.) The type name is unnecessary in such cases because the compiler

---

1. Or base class.

infers the type from the location of the call. If the compiler can make no such inference, the name must be provided as part of the method call.

At their core, types are a means of grouping together methods and their associated data. For example, `Console` is the type that contains the `Write()`, `WriteLine()`, and `ReadLine()` methods (among others). All of these methods are in the same *group* because they belong to the `Console` type.

Scope

In the previous chapter, you learned that the *scope* of a program element is the region of text in which it can be referred to by its unqualified name. A call that appears inside a type declaration to a method declared in that type does not require the type qualifier because the method is in scope throughout its containing type. Similarly, a type is in scope throughout the namespace that declares it; therefore, a method call that appears in a type in a particular namespace need not specify that namespace in the method call name.

Method Name

Every method call contains a method name, which might or might not be qualified with a namespace and type name, as we have discussed. After the method name comes the argument list; the argument list is a parenthesized, comma-separated list of the values that correspond to the parameters of the method.

Parameters and Arguments

A method can take any number of parameters, and each parameter is of a specific data type. The values that the caller supplies for parameters are called the **arguments**; every argument must correspond to a particular parameter. For example, the following method call has three arguments:

```
System.IO.File.Copy(
    oldFileName, newFileName, false)
```

The method is found on the class `File`, which is located in the namespace `System.IO`. It is declared to have three parameters, with the first and second being of type `string` and the third being of type `bool`. In this example, we use variables (`oldFileName` and `newFileName`) of type `string` for the old and new filenames, and then specify `false` to indicate that the copy should fail if the new filename already exists.

Method Return Values

In contrast to `System.Console.WriteLine()`, the method call `System.Console.ReadLine()` in Listing 5.2 does not have any arguments because the method is declared to take no parameters. However, this method happens to have a **method return value**. The method return value is a means of transferring results from a called method back to the caller. Because `System.Console.ReadLine()` has a return value, it is possible to assign the return value to the variable `firstName`. In addition, it is possible to pass this method return value itself as an argument to another method call, as shown in Listing 5.3.

LISTING 5.3: Passing a Method Return Value as an Argument to Another Method Call

```
class Program
{
  static void Main()
  {
    System.Console.Write("Enter your first name: ");
    System.Console.WriteLine("Hello {0}!",
       System.Console.ReadLine());
  }
}
```

Instead of assigning the returned value to a variable and then using that variable as an argument to the call to `System.Console.WriteLine()`, Listing 5.3 calls the `System.Console.ReadLine()` method within the call to `System.Console.WriteLine()`. At execution time, the `System.Console.ReadLine()` method executes first, and its return value is passed directly into the `System.Console.WriteLine()` method, rather than into a variable.

Not all methods return data. Both versions of `System.Console.Write()` and `System.Console.WriteLine()` are examples of such methods. As you will see shortly, these methods specify a return type of `void`, just as the `HelloWorld` declaration of `Main` returned `void`.

Statement versus Method Call

Listing 5.3 provides a demonstration of the difference between a statement and a method call. Although `System.Console.WriteLine("Hello {0}!", System.Console.ReadLine());` is a single statement, it contains two method calls. A statement often contains one or more expressions, and in this example, two of those expressions are method calls. Therefore, method calls form parts of statements.

Although coding multiple method calls in a single statement often reduces the amount of code, it does not necessarily increase the readability and seldom offers a significant performance advantage. Developers should favor readability over brevity.

> ■ **NOTE**
>
> In general, developers should favor readability over brevity. Readability is critical to writing code that is self-documenting and therefore more maintainable over time.

Declaring a Method

Begin 6.0

This section expands on the explanation of declaring a method to include parameters or a return type. Listing 5.4 contains examples of these concepts, and Output 5.1 shows the results.

LISTING 5.4: Declaring a Method

```csharp
class IntroducingMethods
{
  public static void Main()
  {
      string firstName;
      string lastName;
      string fullName;
      string initials;

      System.Console.WriteLine("Hey you!");

      firstName = GetUserInput("Enter your first name: ");
      lastName = GetUserInput("Enter your last name: ");

      fullName = GetFullName(firstName, lastName);
      initials = GetInitials(firstName, lastName);
      DisplayGreeting(fullName, initials);
  }

  static string GetUserInput(string prompt)
  {
      System.Console.Write(prompt);
      return System.Console.ReadLine();
  }

  static string GetFullName(  // C# 6.0 expression-bodied method
      string firstName, string lastName) =>
          $"{ firstName } { lastName }";
```

```
static void DisplayGreeting(string fullName, string initials)
{
    System.Console.WriteLine(
        $"Hello { fullName }! Your initials are { initials }");
    return;
}

static string GetInitials(string firstName, string lastName)
{
    return $"{ firstName[0] }. { lastName[0] }.";
}
}
```

OUTPUT 5.1

```
Hey you!
Enter your first name: Inigo
Enter your last name: Montoya
Your full name is Inigo Montoya.
```

End 6.0

Five methods are declared in Listing 5.4. From Main() the code calls GetUserInput(), followed by a call to GetFullName() and GetInitials(). All of the last three methods return a value and take arguments. In addition, the listing calls DisplayGreeting(), which doesn't return any data. No method in C# can exist outside the confines of an enclosing type; in this case, the enclosing type is the IntroducingMethods class. Even the Main method examined in Chapter 1 must be within a type.

Language Contrast: C++/Visual Basic—Global Methods

C# provides no global method support; everything must appear within a type declaration. This is why the Main() method was marked as static—the C# equivalent of a C++ global and Visual Basic "shared" method.

■ BEGINNER TOPIC

Refactoring into Methods

Moving a set of statements into a method instead of leaving them inline within a larger method is a form of **refactoring**. Refactoring reduces code duplication, because you can call the method from multiple places instead of duplicating the code. Refactoring also increases code readability. As part of the coding process, it is a best practice to continually review your code and look for opportunities to refactor. This involves looking for blocks of code that are difficult to understand at a glance and moving them into a method with a name that clearly defines the code's behavior. This practice is often preferred over commenting a block of code, because the method name serves to describe what the implementation does.

For example, the Main() method that is shown in Listing 5.4 results in the same behavior as does the Main() method that is shown in Listing 1.16 in Chapter 1. Perhaps even more noteworthy is that although both listings are trivial to follow, Listing 5.4 is easier to grasp at a glance by just viewing the Main() method and not worrying about the details of each called method's implementation.

In earlier versions of Visual Studio, you can select a group of statements, right-click on it, and then select the Extract Method refactoring from the Refactoring section of the context menu to automatically move a group of statements to a new method. In Visual Studio 2015, the refactorings are available from the Quick Actions section of the context menu.

Formal Parameter Declaration

Consider the declarations of the DisplayGreeting(), GetFullName(), and the GetInitials() methods. The text that appears between the parentheses of a method declaration is the **formal parameter list**. (As we will see when we discuss generics, methods may also have a **type parameter list**. When it is clear from context which kind of parameters we are discussing, we simply refer to them as *parameters* in a *parameter list*.) Each parameter in the parameter list includes the type of the parameter along with the parameter name. A comma separates each parameter in the list.

Behaviorally, most parameters are virtually identical to local variables, and the naming convention of parameters follows accordingly. Therefore, parameter names use camelCase. Also, it is not possible to declare a local variable (a variable declared inside a method) with the same name as a parameter of the containing method, because this would create two *local variables* of the same name.

Guidelines

DO use camelCasing for parameter names.

Method Return Type Declaration

In addition to `GetUserInput()`, `GetFullName()`, and the `GetInitials()` methods requiring parameters to be specified, each of these methods also includes a **method return type**. You can tell that a method returns a value because a data type appears immediately before the method name in the method declaration. Each of these method examples specifies a `string` return type. Unlike with parameters, of which there can be any number, only one method return type is allowable.

As with `GetUserInput()` and `GetInitials()`, methods with a return type almost always contain one or more `return` statements that return control to the caller. A `return` statement consists of the `return` keyword followed by an expression that computes the value the method is returning. For example, the `GetInitials()` method's `return` statement is `return $"{ firstName[0] }. { lastName[0] }.";`. The expression (an interpolated string in this case) following the `return` keyword must be compatible with the stated return type of the method.

If a method has a return type, the block of statements that makes up the body of the method must have an *unreachable end point*. That is, there must be no way for control to "fall off the end" of a method without it returning a value. Often the easiest way to ensure that this condition is met is to make the last statement of the method a `return` statement. However, `return` statements can appear in locations other than at the end of a method implementation. For example, an `if` or `switch` statement in a method implementation could include a `return` statement within it; see Listing 5.5 for an example.

LISTING 5.5: A `return` Statement before the End of a Method

```
class Program
{
    static bool MyMethod()
    {
        string command = ObtainCommand();
        switch(command)
        {
            case "quit":
                return false;
            // ... omitted, other cases
            default:
                return true;
        }
    }
}
```

(Note that a `return` statement transfers control out of the `switch`, so no break statement is required to prevent illegal fall-through in a switch section that ends with a `return` statement.)

In Listing 5.5, the last statement in the method is not a `return` statement; it is a `switch` statement. However, the compiler can deduce that every possible code path through the method results in a `return`, so that the end point of the method is not reachable. Thus this method is legal even though it does not end with a `return` statement.

If particular code paths include unreachable statements following the `return`, the compiler will issue a warning that indicates the additional statements will never execute.

Though C# allows a method to have multiple `return` statements, code is generally more readable and easier to maintain if there is a single exit location rather than multiple returns sprinkled through various code paths of the method.

Specifying `void` as a return type indicates that there is no return value from the method. As a result, a call to the method may not be assigned to a variable or used as a parameter type at the call site. A `void` method call may be used only as a statement. Furthermore, within the body of the method the `return` statement becomes optional, and when it is specified, there must be no value following the `return` keyword. For example, the return of `Main()` in Listing 5.4 is `void`, and there is no `return` statement within the method. However, `DisplayGreeting()` includes an (optional) `return` statement that is not followed by any returned result.

Although, technically, a method can have only one return type, the return type could be a tuple. As a result, starting with C# 7.0, it is possible to return multiple values packaged as a tuple using C# tuple syntax. For example, you could declare a `GetName()` method, as shown in Listing 5.6.

Begin 7.0

LISTING 5.6: Returning Multiple Values Using a Tuple

```
class Program
{
    static string GetUserInput(string prompt)
    {
        System.Console.Write(prompt);
        return System.Console.ReadLine();
    }
    static (string First, string Last) GetName()
    {
        string firstName, lastName;
        firstName = GetUserInput("Enter your first name: ");
```

```
        lastName = GetUserInput("Enter your last name: ");
        return (firstName, lastName);
    }
    static public void Main()
    {
        (string First, string Last) name = GetName();
        System.Console.WriteLine($"Hello { name.First } { name.Last }!");
    }
}
```

Technically, of course, we are still returning only one data type, a `ValueTuple<string, string>`; however, effectively, you can return any (preferably reasonable) number you like.

Expression Bodied Methods

To support the simplest of method declarations without the formality of a method body, C# 6.0 introduced **expression bodied methods**, which are declared using an expression rather than a full method body. Listing 5.4's `GetFullName()` method provides an example of the expression bodied method:

```
static string GetFullName( string firstName, string lastName) =>
        $"{ firstName } { lastName }";
```

In place of the curly brackets typical of a method body, an expression bodied method uses the "goes to" operator (fully introduced in Chapter 13), for which the resulting data type must match the return type of the method. In other words, even though there is no explicit `return` statement in the expression bodied method implementation, it is still necessary that the return type from the expression match the method declaration's return type.

Expression bodied methods are syntactic shortcuts to the fuller method body declaration. As such, their use should be limited to the simplest of method implementations—generally expressible on a single line.

Language Contrast: C++—Header Files

Unlike in C++, C# classes never separate the implementation from the declaration. In C#, there is no header (`.h`) file or implementation (`.cpp`) file. Instead, declaration and implementation appear together in the same file. (C# does support an advanced feature called *partial methods*, in which the method's defining declaration is separate from its implementation, but for the purposes of this chapter, we consider only nonpartial methods.) The lack of separate declaration and implementation in C# removes the requirement to maintain redundant declaration information in two places found in languages that have separate header and implementation files, such as C++.

■**BEGINNER TOPIC**

Namespaces

As described earlier, **namespaces** are an organizational mechanism for categorizing and grouping together related types. Developers can discover related types by examining other types within the same namespace as a familiar type. Additionally, through namespaces, two or more types may have the same name as long as they are disambiguated by different namespaces.

The using Directive

Fully qualified namespace names can become quite long and unwieldy. It is possible, however, to import all the types from one or more namespaces into a file so that they can be used without full qualification. To achieve this, the C# programmer includes a using directive, generally at the top of the file. For example, in Listing 5.7, Console is not prefixed with System. The namespace may be omitted because of the using System directive that appears at the top of the listing.

LISTING 5.7: using Directive Example

```
// The using directive imports all types from the
// specified namespace into the entire file
using System;

class HelloWorld
{
  static void Main()
  {
    // No need to qualify Console with System
    // because of the using directive above
    Console.WriteLine("Hello, my name is Inigo Montoya");
  }
}
```

The results of Listing 5.7 appear in Output 5.2.

OUTPUT 5.2

```
Hello, my name is Inigo Montoya
```

A using directive such as using System does not enable you to omit System from a type declared within a child namespace of System. For example, if your code accessed the StringBuilder type from the System.Text namespace, you would have to either include an additional using System.Text; directive or fully qualify the type as System.Text .StringBuilder, not just Text.StringBuilder. In short, a using directive does not import types from any **nested namespaces**. Nested namespaces, which are identified by the period in the namespace, always need to be imported explicitly.

Language Contrast: Java—Wildcards in import Directive

Java allows for importing namespaces using a wildcard such as the following:

```
import javax.swing.*;
```

In contrast, C# does not support a wildcard using directive but instead requires each namespace to be imported explicitly.

Language Contrast: Visual Basic .NET—Project Scope Imports Directive

Unlike C#, Visual Basic .NET supports the ability to specify the using directive equivalent, Imports, for an entire project rather than for just a specific file. In other words, Visual Basic .NET provides a command-line means of the using directive that will span an entire compilation.

Frequent use of types within a particular namespace implies that the addition of a using directive for that namespace is a good idea, instead of fully qualifying all types within the namespace. Accordingly, almost all C# files include the using System directive at the top. Throughout the remainder of this book, code listings often omit the using System directive. Other namespace directives are included explicitly, however.

One interesting effect of the using System directive is that the string data type can be identified with varying case: String or string. The former version relies on the using System directive and the latter uses the string keyword. Both are valid C# references to the System.String data type, and the resultant Common Intermediate Language (CIL) code is unaffected by which version is chosen.[2]

■ ADVANCED TOPIC

Nested using Directives

Not only can you have using directives at the top of a file, but you also can include them at the top of a namespace declaration. For example, if a new namespace, EssentialCSharp, were declared, it would be possible to add a using declarative at the top of the namespace declaration (see Listing 5.8).

LISTING 5.8: Specifying the using Directive inside a Namespace Declaration

```csharp
namespace EssentialCSharp
{
  using System;

  class HelloWorld
  {
    static void Main()
    {
        // No need to qualify Console with System
        // because of the using directive above
        Console.WriteLine("Hello, my name is Inigo Montoya");
    }
  }
}
```

The results of Listing 5.8 appear in Output 5.3.

OUTPUT 5.3

```
Hello, my name is Inigo Montoya
```

The difference between placing the using directive at the top of a file and placing it at the top of a namespace declaration is that the directive is active only within the namespace declaration. If the code includes a new

---

2. I prefer the string keyword, but whichever representation a programmer selects, the code within a project ideally should be consistent.

namespace declaration above or below the `EssentialCSharp` declaration, the `using System` directive within a different namespace would not be active. Code seldom is written this way, especially given the standard practice of providing a single type declaration per file.

using static **Directive**

Begin 6.0

The `using` directive allows you to abbreviate a type name by omitting the namespace portion of the name—such that just the type name can be specified for any type within the stated namespace. In contrast, the `using static` directive allows you to omit both the namespace and the type name from any member of the stated type. A `using static System.Console` directive, for example, allows you to specify `WriteLine()` rather than the fully qualified method name of `System.Console.WriteLine()`. Continuing with this example, we can update Listing 5.2 to leverage the `using static System.Console` directive to create Listing 5.9.

LISTING 5.9: using static **Directive**

```csharp
using static System.Console;

class HeyYou
{
    static void Main()
    {
        string firstName;
        string lastName;

        WriteLine("Hey you!");

        Write("Enter your first name: ");

        firstName = ReadLine();
        Write("Enter your last name: ");
        lastName = ReadLine();
        WriteLine(
            $"Your full name is { firstName } { lastName }.");
    }
}
```

In this case, there is no loss of readability of the code: `WriteLine()`, `Write()`, and `ReadLine()` all clearly relate to a console directive. In fact, one could argue that the resulting code is simpler and therefore clearer than before.

However, sometimes this is not the case. For example, if your code uses classes that have overlapping behavior names, such as an `Exists()` method on a file and an `Exists()` method on a directory, then perhaps a `using static` directive would reduce clarity when you invoke `Exists()`. Similarly, if the class you were writing had its own members with overlapping behavior names—for example, `Display()` and `Write()`—then perhaps clarity would be lost to the reader.

This ambiguity would not be allowed by the compiler. If two members with the same signature were available (through either `using static` directives or separately declared members), any invocation of them that was ambiguous would result in a compile error.

End 6.0

Aliasing

The `using` directive also allows **aliasing** a namespace or type. An alias is an alternative name that you can use within the text to which the `using` directive applies. The two most common reasons for aliasing are to disambiguate two types that have the same name and to abbreviate a long name. In Listing 5.10, for example, the `CountDownTimer` alias is declared as a means of referring to the type `System.Timers.Timer`. Simply adding a `using System.Timers` directive will not sufficiently enable the code to avoid fully qualifying the `Timer` type. The reason is that `System.Threading` also includes a type called `Timer`; therefore, using just `Timer` within the code will be ambiguous.

LISTING 5.10: Declaring a Type Alias

```
using System;
using System.Threading;
using CountDownTimer = System.Timers.Timer;

class HelloWorld
{
  static void Main()
  {
      CountDownTimer timer;

      // ...
  }
}
```

Listing 5.10 uses an entirely new name, `CountDownTimer`, as the alias. It is possible, however, to specify the alias as `Timer`, as shown in Listing 5.11.

LISTING 5.11: Declaring a Type Alias with the Same Name

```
using System;
using System.Threading;

// Declare alias Timer to refer to System.Timers.Timer to
// avoid code ambiguity with System.Threading.Timer
using Timer = System.Timers.Timer;

class HelloWorld
{
  static void Main()
  {
      Timer timer;

      // ...
  }
}
```

Because of the alias directive, "Timer" is not an ambiguous reference. Furthermore, to refer to the `System.Threading.Timer` type, you will have to either qualify the type or define a different alias.

Returns and Parameters on `Main()`

So far, declaration of an executable's `Main()` method has been the simplest declaration possible. You have not included any parameters or non-`void` return type in your `Main()` method declarations. However, C# supports the ability to retrieve the command-line arguments when executing a program, and it is possible to return a status indicator from the `Main()` method.

The runtime passes the command-line arguments to `Main()` using a single `string` array parameter. All you need to do to retrieve the parameters is to access the array, as demonstrated in Listing 5.12. The purpose of this program is to download a file whose location is given by a URL. The first command-line argument identifies the URL, and the optional second argument is the filename to which to save the file. The listing begins with a `switch` statement that evaluates the number of parameters (`args.Length`) as follows:

1. If there are not two parameters, display an error indicating that it is necessary to provide the URL and filename.
2. The presence of two arguments indicates the user has provided both the URL of the resource and the download target filename.

LISTING 5.12: Passing Command-Line Arguments to Main

```csharp
using System;
using System.Net;

class Program
{
    static int Main(string[] args)
    {
        int result;
        string targetFileName;
        string url;
        switch (args.Length)
        {
            default:
                // Exactly two arguments must be specified; give an error
                Console.WriteLine(
                    "ERROR:  You must specify the "
                    + "URL and the file name");
                targetFileName = null;
                url = null;
                break;
            case 2:
                url = args[0];
                targetFileName = args[1];
                break;
        }

        if (targetFileName != null && url != null)
        {
            WebClient webClient = new WebClient();
            webClient.DownloadFile(url, targetFileName);
            result = 0;
        }
        else
        {
            Console.WriteLine(
                "Usage: Downloader.exe <URL> <TargetFileName>");
            result = 1;
        }
        return result;
    }
}
```

The results of Listing 5.12 appear in Output 5.4.

OUTPUT 5.4

```
>Downloader.exe
ERROR:  You must specify the URL to be downloaded
Downloader.exe <URL> <TargetFileName>
```

If you were successful in calculating the target filename, you would use it to save the downloaded file. Otherwise, you would display the help text. The `Main()` method also returns an `int` rather than a `void`. This is optional for a `Main()` declaration, but if it is used, the program can return a status code to a caller (such as a script or a batch file). By convention, a return other than zero indicates an error.

Although all command-line arguments can be passed to `Main()` via an array of strings, sometimes it is convenient to access the arguments from inside a method other than `Main()`. The `System.Environment` `.GetCommandLineArgs()` method returns the command-line arguments array in the same form that `Main(string[] args)` passes the arguments into `Main()`.

■ ADVANCED TOPIC

Disambiguate Multiple `Main()` Methods
If a program includes two classes with `Main()` methods, it is possible to specify on the command line which class to use for the `Main()` declaration. `csc.exe` includes an `/m` option to specify the fully qualified class name of `Main()`.

■ BEGINNER TOPIC

Call Stack and Call Site
As code executes, methods call more methods, which in turn call additional methods, and so on. In the simple case of Listing 5.4, `Main()` calls `GetUserInput()`, which in turn calls `System.Console.ReadLine()`, which in turn calls even more methods internally. Every time a new method is invoked, the runtime creates an *activation frame* that contains information about the arguments passed to the new call, the local variables of the new call, and information about where control should resume when the new method returns. The set of calls within calls within calls, and so on, produces a series of activation frames that is termed the **call stack**.[3]

---

3. Except for async or iterator methods, which move their activator records onto the heap.

As program complexity increases, the call stack generally gets larger and larger as each method calls another method. As calls complete, however, the call stack shrinks until another method is invoked. The process of removing activation frames from the call stack is termed **stack unwinding**. Stack unwinding always occurs in the reverse order of the method calls. When the method completes, execution returns to the **call site**—that is, the location from which the method was invoked.

Advanced Method Parameters

So far this chapter's examples have returned data via the method return value. This section demonstrates how methods can return data via their method parameters and how a method may take a variable number of arguments.

Value Parameters

Arguments to method calls are usually **passed by value**, which means the value of the argument expression is copied into the target parameter. For example, in Listing 5.13, the value of each variable that Main() uses when calling Combine() will be copied into the parameters of the Combine() method. Output 5.5 shows the results of this listing.

LISTING 5.13: Passing Variables by Value

```
class Program
{
  static void Main()
  {
    // ...
    string fullName;
    string driveLetter = "C:";
    string folderPath  = "Data";
    string fileName     = "index.html";

    fullName = Combine(driveLetter, folderPath, fileName);

    Console.WriteLine(fullName);
    // ...
  }

  static string Combine(
      string driveLetter, string folderPath, string fileName)
```

```
    {
        string path;
        path = string.Format("{1}{0}{2}{0}{3}",
            System.IO.Path.DirectorySeparatorChar,
            driveLetter, folderPath, fileName);
        return path;
    }
}
```

OUTPUT 5.5

```
C:\Data\index.html
```

Even if the Combine() method assigns null to driveLetter, folderPath, and fileName before returning, the corresponding variables within Main() will maintain their original values because the variables are copied when calling a method. When the call stack unwinds at the end of a call, the copied data is thrown away.

■ BEGINNER TOPIC

Matching Caller Variables with Parameter Names

In Listing 5.13, the variable names in the caller exactly matched the parameter names in the called method. This matching is provided simply for readability purposes; whether names match is entirely irrelevant to the behavior of the method call. The parameters of the called method and the local variables of the calling method are found in different declaration spaces and have nothing to do with each other.

■ ADVANCED TOPIC

Reference Types versus Value Types

For the purposes of this section, it is inconsequential whether the parameter passed is a value type or a reference type. Rather, the important issue is whether the called method can write a value into the caller's original variable. Since a copy of the caller variable's value is made, the caller's variable cannot be reassigned. Nevertheless, it is helpful to understand the difference between a variable that contains a value type and a variable that contains a reference type.

The value of a reference type variable is, as the name implies, a reference to the location where the data associated with the object is stored. How the runtime chooses to represent the value of a reference type variable is an implementation detail of the runtime; typically it is represented as the address of the memory location in which the object's data is stored, but it need not be.

If a reference type variable is passed by value, the reference itself is copied from the caller to the method parameter. As a result, the target method cannot update the caller variable's value but it may update the data referred to by the reference.

Alternatively, if the method parameter is a value type, the value itself is copied into the parameter, and changing the parameter in the called method will not affect the original caller's variable.

Reference Parameters (ref)

Consider Listing 5.14, which calls a function to swap two values, and Output 5.6, which shows the results.

LISTING 5.14: Passing Variables by Reference

```csharp
class Program
{
  static void Main()
  {
      // ...
      string first = "hello";
      string second = "goodbye";
      Swap(ref first, ref second);

      Console.WriteLine(
          $@"first = ""{ first }"", second = ""{ second }""" );
      // ...
  }

  static void Swap(ref string x, ref string y)
  {
      string temp = x;
      x = y;
      y = temp;
  }
}
```

OUTPUT 5.6

```
first = "goodbye", second = "hello"
```

The values assigned to first and second are successfully switched. To do this, the variables are **passed by reference**. The obvious difference between the call to Swap() and Listing 5.13's call to Combine() is the inclusion of the keyword ref in front of the parameter's data type. This keyword changes the call such that the variables used as arguments are passed by reference, so the called method can update the original caller's variables with new values.

When the called method specifies a parameter as ref, the caller is required to supply a variable, not a value, as an argument and to place ref in front of the variables passed. In so doing, the caller explicitly recognizes that the target method could reassign the values of the variables associated with any ref parameters it receives. Furthermore, it is necessary to initialize any local variables passed as ref because target methods could read data from ref parameters without first assigning them. In Listing 5.14, for example, temp is assigned the value of first, assuming that the variable passed in first was initialized by the caller. Effectively, a ref parameter is an alias for the variable passed. In other words, it is essentially giving a parameter name to an existing variable, rather than creating a new variable and copying the value of the argument into it.

Output Parameters (out)

Begin 7.0

As mentioned earlier, a variable used as a ref parameter must be assigned before it is passed to the called method, because the called method might read from the variable. The "swap" example given previously must read and write from both variables passed to it. However, it is often the case that a method that takes a reference to a variable intends to write to the variable but not to read from it. In such cases, clearly it could be safe to pass an uninitialized local variable by reference.

To achieve this, code needs to decorate parameter types with the keyword out. This is demonstrated in the TryGetPhoneButton() method in Listing 5.15, which returns the phone button corresponding to a character.

LISTING 5.15: Passing Variables Out Only

```
class ConvertToPhoneNumber
{
  static int Main(string[] args)
  {
      if(args.Length == 0)
```

```
        {
            Console.WriteLine(
                "ConvertToPhoneNumber.exe <phrase>");
            Console.WriteLine(
                "'_' indicates no standard phone button");
            return 1;
        }
        foreach(string word in args)
        {
            foreach(char character in word)
            {
                if(TryGetPhoneButton(character, out char button))
                {
                    Console.Write(button);
                }
                else
                {
                    Console.Write('_');
                }
            }
        }
        Console.WriteLine();
        return 0;
    }

    static bool TryGetPhoneButton(char character, out char button)
    {
        bool success = true;
        switch( char.ToLower(character) )
        {
            case '1':
                button = '1';
                break;
            case '2': case 'a': case 'b': case 'c':
                button = '2';
                break;

            // ...

            case '-':
                button = '-';
                break;
            default:
                // Set the button to indicate an invalid value
                button = '_';
                success = false;
                break;
        }
        return success;
    }
}
```

Output 5.7 shows the results of Listing 5.15.

OUTPUT 5.7

7.0

```
>ConvertToPhoneNumber.exe CSharpIsGood
274277474663
```

In this example, the `TryGetPhoneButton()` method returns `true` if it can successfully determine the `character`'s corresponding phone button. The function also returns the corresponding button by using the `button` parameter, which is decorated with `out`.

An `out` parameter is functionally identical to a `ref` parameter; the only difference is which requirements the language enforces regarding how the aliased variable is read from and written to. Whenever a parameter is marked with `out`, the compiler checks that the parameter is set for all code paths within the method that return normally (i.e., the code paths that do not throw an exception). If, for example, the code does not assign `button` a value in some code path, the compiler will issue an error indicating that the code didn't initialize `button`. Listing 5.15 assigns `button` to the underscore character because even though it cannot determine the correct phone button, it is still necessary to assign a value.

A common coding error when working with `out` parameters is to forget to declare the `out` variable before you use it. Starting with C# 7.0, it is possible to declare the `out` variable inline when invoking the function. Listing 5.15 uses this feature with the statement `TryGetPhoneButton(character, out char button)` without ever declaring the `button` variable beforehand. Prior to C# 7.0, it would be necessary to first declare the `button` variable and then invoke the function with `TryGetPhoneButton(character, out button)`.

Another C# 7.0 feature is the ability to discard an `out` parameter entirely. If, for example, you simply wanted to know whether a character was a valid phone button but not actually return the numeric value, you could discard the `button` parameter using an underscore: `TryGetPhoneButton(character, out _)`.

Prior to C# 7.0's tuple syntax, a developer of a method might declare one or more `out` parameters to get around the restriction that a method may have only one return type; a method that needs to return two values can do so by returning one value normally, as the return value of the method, and a second value by writing it into an aliased variable passed as an out parameter. Although this pattern is both common and legal, there are usually better ways to achieve that aim. For example, if you are considering returning two or more values from a method and C# 7.0 is available, it is likely preferable to use C# 7.0 tuple syntax. Prior to that, consider writing two methods, one for each value, or still using the System.ValueTuple type (which would require referencing the System.ValueTuple NuGet package) but without C# 7.0 syntax.

> **▪ NOTE**
>
> Each and every normal code path must result in the assignment of all out parameters.

Read-Only Pass by Reference (in)

In C# 7.2, support was added for passing a value type by reference that was read only. Rather than passing the value type to a function so that it could be changed, read-only pass by reference was added so that the value type could be passed by reference so that not only copy of the value type occurred but, in addition, the invoked method could not change the value type. In other words, the purpose of the feature is to reduce the memory copied when passing a value while still identifying it as read only, thus improving the performance. This syntax is to add an in modifier to the parameter. For example:

```
int Method(in int number) { ... }
```

With the in modifier, any attempts to reassign number (number++, for example) will result in a compile error indicating that number is read only.

Return by Reference

Another C# 7.0 addition is support for returning a reference to a variable. Consider, for example, a function that returns the first pixel in an image that is associated with red-eye, as shown in Listing 5.16.

LISTING 5.16: ref Return and ref Local Declaration

```
// Returning a reference
public static ref byte FindFirstRedEyePixel(byte[] image)
```

7.0

```csharp
{
  // Do fancy image detection perhaps with machine learning
  for (int counter = 0; counter < image.Length; counter++)
  {
    if(image[counter] == (byte)ConsoleColor.Red)
    {
      return ref image[counter];
    }
  }
  throw new InvalidOperationException("No pixels are red.");
}
public static void Main()
{
  byte[] image = new byte[254];
  // Load image
  int index = new Random().Next(0, image.Length - 1);
  image[index] =
      (byte)ConsoleColor.Red;
  System.Console.WriteLine(
      $"image[{index}]={(ConsoleColor)image[index]}");
  // ...

  // Obtain a reference to the first red pixel
  ref byte redPixel = ref FindFirstRedEyePixel(image);
  // Update it to be Black
  redPixel = (byte)ConsoleColor.Black;
  System.Console.WriteLine(
      $"image[{index}]={(ConsoleColor)image[redPixel]}");
}
```

By returning a reference to the variable, the caller is then able to update the pixel to a different color, as shown in the highlighted line of Listing 5.16. Checking for the update via the array shows that the value is now black.

There are two important restrictions on return by reference—both due to object lifetime: Object references shouldn't be garbage collected while they're still referenced, and they shouldn't consume memory when they no longer have any references. To enforce these restrictions, you can only return the following from a reference-returning function:

- References to fields or array elements
- Other reference-returning properties or functions
- References that were passed in as parameters to the by-reference-returning function

For example, `FindFirstRedEyePixel()` returns a reference to an item in the image array, which was a parameter to the function. Similarly, if the image was stored as a field within the class, you could return the field by reference:

```
byte[] _Image;
public ref byte[] Image { get { return ref _Image; } }
```

Second, `ref` locals are initialized to refer to a particular variable and can't be modified to refer to a different variable.

There are several return-by-reference characteristics of which to be cognizant:

- If you're returning a reference, you obviously must return it. This means, therefore, that in the example in Listing 5.16, even if no red-eye pixel exists, you still need to return a reference byte. The only workaround would be to throw an exception. In contrast, the by-reference parameter approach allows you to leave the parameter unchanged and return a `bool` indicating success. In many cases, this might be preferable.

- When declaring a reference local variable, initialization is required. This involves assigning it a `ref` return from a function or a reference to a variable:

  ```
  ref string text;  // Error
  ```

- Although it's possible in C# 7.0 to declare a reference local variable, declaring a field of type `ref` isn't allowed:

  ```
  class Thing { ref string _Text;  /* Error */ }
  ```

- You can't declare a by-reference type for an auto-implemented property:

  ```
  class Thing { ref string Text { get;set; }  /* Error */ }
  ```

- Properties that return a reference are allowed:

  ```
  class Thing { string _Text = "Inigo Montoya";
      ref string Text { get { return ref _Text; } } }
  ```

- A reference local variable can't be initialized with a value (such as null or a constant). It must be assigned from a by-reference-returning member or a local variable, field, or array element:

  ```
  ref int number = null; ref int number = 42;  // ERROR
  ```

End 7.0

Parameter Arrays (params)

In the examples so far, the number of arguments that must be passed has been fixed by the number of parameters declared in the target method declaration. However, sometimes it is convenient if the number of arguments may vary. Consider the Combine( ) method from Listing 5.13. In that method, you passed the drive letter, folder path, and filename. What if the path had more than one folder, and the caller wanted the method to join additional folders to form the full path? Perhaps the best option would be to pass an array of strings for the folders. However, this would make the calling code a little more complex, because it would be necessary to construct an array to pass as an argument.

To make it easier on the callers of such a method, C# provides a keyword that enables the number of arguments to vary in the calling code instead of being set by the target method. Before we discuss the method declaration, observe the calling code declared within Main( ), as shown in Listing 5.17.

LISTING 5.17: **Passing a Variable Parameter List**

```
using System;
using System.IO;
class PathEx
{
  static void Main()
  {
      string fullName;

      // ...

      // Call Combine() with four arguments
      fullName = Combine(
          Directory.GetCurrentDirectory(),
          "bin", "config", "index.html");
      Console.WriteLine(fullName);

      // ...

      // Call Combine() with only three arguments
      fullName = Combine(
          Environment.SystemDirectory,
          "Temp", "index.html");
      Console.WriteLine(fullName);

      // ...
```

```
        // Call Combine() with an array
        fullName = Combine(
            new string[] {
                "C:\\", "Data",
                "HomeDir", "index.html"} );
        Console.WriteLine(fullName);
        // ...
    }

    static string Combine(params string[] paths)
    {
        string result = string.Empty;
        foreach (string path in paths)
        {
            result = Path.Combine(result, path);
        }
        return result;
    }
}
```

Output 5.8 shows the results of Listing 5.17.

OUTPUT 5.8

```
C:\Data\mark\bin\config\index.html
C:\WINDOWS\system32\Temp\index.html
C:\Data\HomeDir\index.html
```

In the first call to Combine(), four arguments are specified. The second call contains only three arguments. In the final call, a single argument is passed using an array. In other words, the Combine() method takes a variable number of arguments—presented either as any number of string arguments separated by commas or as a single array of strings. The former syntax is called the *expanded* form of the method call, and the latter form is called the *normal* form.

To allow invocation using either form, the Combine() method does the following:

1. Places params immediately before the last parameter in the method declaration
2. Declares the last parameter as an array

With a **parameter array** declaration, it is possible to access each corresponding argument as a member of the params array. In the Combine()

method implementation, you iterate over the elements of the `paths` array and call `System.IO.Path.Combine()`. This method automatically combines the parts of the path, appropriately using the platform-specific directory-separator character. Note that `PathEx.Combine()` is identical to `Path.Combine()` except that `PathEx.Combine()` handles a variable number of parameters rather than simply two.

There are a few notable characteristics of the parameter array:

- The parameter array is not necessarily the only parameter on a method.
- The parameter array must be the last parameter in the method declaration. Since only the last parameter may be a parameter array, a method cannot have more than one parameter array.
- The caller can specify zero arguments that correspond to the parameter array parameter, which will result in an array of zero items being passed as the parameter array.
- Parameter arrays are type-safe: The arguments given must be compatible with the element type of the parameter array.
- The caller can use an explicit array rather than a comma-separated list of parameters. The resulting CIL code is identical.
- If the target method implementation requires a minimum number of parameters, those parameters should appear explicitly within the method declaration, forcing a compile error instead of relying on run-time error handling if required parameters are missing. For example, if you have a method that requires one or more integer arguments, declare the method as `int Max(int first, params int[] operands)` rather than as `int Max(params int[] operands)` so that at least one value is passed to `Max()`.

Using a parameter array, you can pass a variable number of arguments of the same type into a method. The section "Method Overloading," which appears later in this chapter, discusses a means of supporting a variable number of arguments that are not necessarily of the same type.

Guidelines

DO use parameter arrays when a method can handle any number—including zero—of additional arguments.

Recursion

Calling a method **recursively** or implementing the method using **recursion** refers to use of a method that calls itself. Recursion is sometimes the simplest way to implement a particular algorithm. Listing 5.18 counts the lines of all the C# source files (*.cs) in a directory and its subdirectory.

LISTING 5.18: Counting the Lines within *.cs Files, Given a Directory

```csharp
using System.IO;

public static class LineCounter
{
    // Use the first argument as the directory
    // to search, or default to the current directory
    public static void Main(string[] args)
    {
        int totalLineCount = 0;
        string directory;
        if (args.Length > 0)
        {
            directory = args[0];
        }
        else
        {
            directory = Directory.GetCurrentDirectory();
        }
        totalLineCount = DirectoryCountLines(directory);
        System.Console.WriteLine(totalLineCount);
    }

    static int DirectoryCountLines(string directory)
    {
        int lineCount = 0;
        foreach (string file in
            Directory.GetFiles(directory, "*.cs"))
        {
            lineCount += CountLines(file);
        }

        foreach (string subdirectory in
            Directory.GetDirectories(directory))
        {
            lineCount += DirectoryCountLines(subdirectory);
        }

        return lineCount;
    }
```

```
private static int CountLines(string file)
{
    string line;
    int lineCount = 0;
    FileStream stream =
        new FileStream(file, FileMode.Open);⁴
    StreamReader reader = new StreamReader(stream);
    line = reader.ReadLine();

    while(line != null)
    {
        if (line.Trim() != "")
        {
            lineCount++;
        }
        line = reader.ReadLine();
    }

    reader.Close();   // Automatically closes the stream
    return lineCount;
}
}
```

Output 5.9 shows the results of Listing 5.18.

OUTPUT 5.9

```
104
```

The program begins by passing the first command-line argument to
DirectoryCountLines() or by using the current directory if no argument
is provided. This method first iterates through all the files in the current
directory and totals the source code lines for each file. After processing each
file in the directory, the code processes each subdirectory by passing the
subdirectory back into the DirectoryCountLines() method, rerunning the
method using the subdirectory. The same process is repeated recursively
through each subdirectory until no more directories remain to process.

Readers unfamiliar with recursion may find it confusing at first.
Regardless, it is often the simplest pattern to code, especially with hierarchical type data such as the filesystem. However, although it may be the
most readable approach, it is generally not the fastest implementation. If

---

4. This code could be improved with a using statement, a construct that we have avoided
   because it has not yet been introduced.

performance becomes an issue, developers should seek an alternative solution to a recursive implementation. The choice generally hinges on balancing readability with performance.

Infinite Recursion Error

A common programming error in recursive method implementations appears in the form of a stack overflow during program execution. This usually happens because of **infinite recursion**, in which the method continually calls back on itself, never reaching a point that triggers the end of the recursion. It is a good practice for programmers to review any method that uses recursion and to verify that the recursion calls are finite.

A common pattern for recursion using pseudocode is as follows:

```
M(x)
{
  if x is trivial
    return the result
  else
    a. Do some work to make the problem smaller
    b. Recursively call M to solve the smaller problem
    c. Compute the result based on a. and b.
    return the result
}
```

Things go wrong when this pattern is not followed. For example, if you don't make the problem smaller or if you don't handle all possible "smallest" cases, the recursion never terminates.

Method Overloading

Listing 5.18 called `DirectoryCountLines()`, which counted the lines of *.cs files. However, if you want to count code in *.h/*.cpp files or in *.vb files, `DirectoryCountLines()` will not work. Instead, you need a method that takes the file extension but still keeps the existing method definition so that it handles *.cs files by default.

All methods within a class must have a unique signature, and C# defines uniqueness by variation in the method name, parameter data types, or number of parameters. This does not include method return data types; defining two methods that differ only in their return data types will cause a compile error. This is true even if the return type is two different tuples. **Method overloading** occurs when a class has two or more methods with the same name and the parameter count and/or data types vary between the overloaded methods.

■ **NOTE**

A method is considered unique as long as there is variation in the method name, parameter data types, or number of parameters.

Method overloading is a type of **operational polymorphism**. Polymorphism occurs when the same logical operation takes on many ("poly") forms ("morphs") because the data varies. Calling `WriteLine()` and passing a format string along with some parameters is implemented differently than calling `WriteLine()` and specifying an integer. However, logically, to the caller, the method takes care of writing the data, and it is somewhat irrelevant how the internal implementation occurs. Listing 5.19 provides an example, and Output 5.10 shows the results.

LISTING 5.19: Counting the Lines within `*.cs` Files Using Overloading

```csharp
using System.IO;

public static class LineCounter
{
  public static void Main(string[] args)
  {
    int totalLineCount;

    if (args.Length > 1)
    {
      totalLineCount =
        DirectoryCountLines(args[0], args[1]);
    }
    if (args.Length > 0)
    {
      totalLineCount = DirectoryCountLines(args[0]);
    }
    else
    {
      totalLineCount  = DirectoryCountLines();
    }

    System.Console.WriteLine(totalLineCount);
  }
```

```csharp
static int DirectoryCountLines()
{
    return DirectoryCountLines(
        Directory.GetCurrentDirectory());
}


static int DirectoryCountLines(string directory)
{
    return DirectoryCountLines(directory, "*.cs");
}

static int DirectoryCountLines(
    string directory, string extension)
{
    int lineCount = 0;
    foreach (string file in
        Directory.GetFiles(directory, extension))
    {
        lineCount += CountLines(file);
    }

    foreach (string subdirectory in
        Directory.GetDirectories(directory))
    {
        lineCount += DirectoryCountLines(subdirectory);
    }

    return lineCount;
}

private static int CountLines(string file)
{
    int lineCount = 0;
    string line;
    FileStream stream =
        new FileStream(file, FileMode.Open);⁵
    StreamReader reader = new StreamReader(stream);
    line = reader.ReadLine();
    while(line != null)
    {
        if (line.Trim() != "")
        {
            lineCount++;
        }
        line = reader.ReadLine();
    }
}
```

---

5. This code could be improved with a using statement, a construct that we have avoided because it has not yet been introduced.

```
        reader.Close();  // Automatically closes the stream
        return lineCount;
    }
}
```

OUTPUT 5.10

```
>LineCounter.exe .\ *.cs
28
```

The effect of method overloading is to provide optional ways to call the method. As demonstrated inside Main(), you can call the DirectoryCountLines() method with or without passing the directory to search and the file extension.

Notice that the parameterless implementation of DirectoryCountLines() was changed to call the single-parameter version (int DirectoryCountLines (string directory)). This is a common pattern when implementing overloaded methods. The idea is that developers implement only the core logic in one method, and all the other overloaded methods will call that single method. If the core implementation changes, it needs to be modified in only one location rather than within each implementation. This pattern is especially prevalent when using method overloading to enable optional parameters that do not have values determined at compile time, so they cannot be specified using optional parameters.

> **■ NOTE**
>
> Placing the core functionality into a single method that all other overloading methods invoke means that you can make changes in implementation in just the core method, which the other methods will automatically take advantage of.

Optional Parameters

Begin 4.0

Starting with C# 4.0, the language designers added support for **optional parameters**. By allowing the association of a parameter with a constant value as part of the method declaration, it is possible to call a method without passing an argument for every parameter of the method (see Listing 5.20).

LISTING 5.20: Methods with Optional Parameters

```csharp
using System.IO;

public static class LineCounter
{
  public static void Main(string[] args)
  {
      int totalLineCount;

      if (args.Length > 1)
      {
          totalLineCount =
              DirectoryCountLines(args[0], args[1]);
      }
      if (args.Length > 0)
      {
          totalLineCount = DirectoryCountLines(args[0]);
      }
      else
      {
          totalLineCount  = DirectoryCountLines();
      }

      System.Console.WriteLine(totalLineCount);
  }

  static int DirectoryCountLines()
  {
      // ...
  }

/*
  static int DirectoryCountLines(string directory)
  { ... }
*/

  static int DirectoryCountLines(
      string directory, string extension = "*.cs")
  {
      int lineCount = 0;
      foreach (string file in
          Directory.GetFiles(directory, extension))
      {
          lineCount += CountLines(file);
      }

      foreach (string subdirectory in
          Directory.GetDirectories(directory))
      {
          lineCount += DirectoryCountLines(subdirectory);
      }

      return lineCount;
  }
```

4.0

```
private static int CountLines(string file)
{
    // ...
}
}
```

In Listing 5.20, the DirectoryCountLines() method declaration with a single parameter has been removed (commented out), but the call from Main() (specifying one parameter) remains. When no extension parameter is specified in the call, the value assigned to extension within the declaration (*.cs in this case) is used. This allows the calling code to not specify a value if desired, and it eliminates the additional overload that would be required in C# 3.0 and earlier. Note that optional parameters must appear after all required parameters (those that don't have default values). Also, the fact that the default value needs to be a constant, compile-time–resolved value is fairly restrictive. You cannot, for example, declare a method like

```
DirectoryCountLines(
    string directory = Environment.CurrentDirectory,
    string extension = "*.cs")
```

because Environment.CurrentDirectory is not a constant. In contrast, because "*.cs" is a constant, C# does allow it for the default value of an optional parameter.

Guidelines

DO provide good defaults for all parameters where possible.

DO provide simple method overloads that have a small number of required parameters.

CONSIDER organizing overloads from the simplest to the most complex.

A second method call feature made available in C# 4.0 is the use of **named arguments**. With named arguments, it is possible for the caller to explicitly identify the name of the parameter to be assigned a value rather than relying solely on parameter and argument order to correlate them (see Listing 5.21).

LISTING 5.21: Specifying Parameters by Name

```
class Program
{
```

```
static void Main()
{
    DisplayGreeting(
        firstName: "Inigo", lastName: "Montoya");
}

public static void DisplayGreeting(
    string firstName,
    string middleName = default(string),
    string lastName = default(string))
{

    // ...

}
}
```

In Listing 5.21, the call to `DisplayGreeting()` from within `Main()` assigns a value to a parameter by name. Of the two optional parameters (`middleName` and `lastName`), only `lastName` is given as an argument. For cases where a method has lots of parameters and many of them are optional (a common occurrence when accessing Microsoft COM libraries), using the named argument syntax is certainly a convenience. However, along with the convenience comes an impact on the flexibility of the method interface. In the past, parameter names could be changed without causing C# code that invokes the method to no longer compile. With the addition of named parameters, the parameter name becomes part of the interface because changing the name would cause code that uses the named parameter to no longer compile.

4.0

Guidelines

DO treat parameter names as part of the API, and avoid changing the names if version compatibility between APIs is important.

For many experienced C# developers, this is a surprising restriction. However, the restriction has been imposed as part of the Common Language Specification ever since .NET 1.0. Moreover, Visual Basic has always supported calling methods with named arguments. Therefore, library developers should already be following the practice of not changing parameter names to successfully interoperate with other .NET languages from version to version. In essence, C# 4.0 now imposes the same restriction on changing parameter names that many other .NET languages already require.

Given the combination of method overloading, optional parameters, and named parameters, resolving which method to call becomes less obvious. A call is **applicable** (compatible) with a method if all parameters have exactly one corresponding argument (either by name or by position) that is type compatible, unless the parameter is optional (or is a parameter array). Although this restricts the possible number of methods that will be called, it doesn't identify a unique method. To further distinguish which specific method will be called, the compiler uses only explicitly identified parameters in the caller, ignoring all optional parameters that were not specified at the caller. Therefore, if two methods are applicable because one of them has an optional parameter, the compiler will resolve to the method without the optional parameter.

End 4.0

■ ADVANCED TOPIC

Method Resolution

When the compiler must choose which of several applicable methods is the best one for a particular call, the one with the *most specific* parameter types is chosen. Assuming there are two applicable methods, each requiring an implicit conversion from an argument to a parameter type, the method whose parameter type is the more derived type will be used.

For example, a method that takes a `double` parameter will be chosen over a method that takes an `object` parameter if the caller passes an argument of type `int`. This is because `double` is more specific than `object`. There are objects that are not doubles, but there are no doubles that are not objects, so `double` must be more specific.

If more than one method is applicable and no unique best method can be determined, the compiler will issue an error indicating that the call is ambiguous.

For example, given the following methods:

```
static void Method(object thing){}
static void Method(double thing){}
static void Method(long thing){}
static void Method(int thing){}
```

a call of the form `Method(42)` will resolve as `Method(int thing)` because that is an exact match from the argument type to the parameter type. Were that method to be removed, overload resolution would choose the `long` version, because `long` is more specific than either `double` or `object`.

The C# specification includes additional rules governing implicit conversion between `byte`, `ushort`, `uint`, `ulong`, and the other numeric types. In general, though, it is better to use a cast to make the intended target method more recognizable.

Basic Error Handling with Exceptions

This section examines how to handle error reporting via a mechanism known as **exception handling**.

With exception handling, a method is able to pass information about an error to a calling method without using a return value or explicitly providing any parameters to do so. Listing 5.22 contains a slight modification to Listing 1.16, the HeyYou program from Chapter 1. Instead of requesting the last name of the user, it prompts for the user's age.

LISTING 5.22: Converting a string to an int

```csharp
using System;

class ExceptionHandling
{
  static void Main()
  {
      string firstName;
      string ageText;
      int age;

      Console.WriteLine("Hey you!");

      Console.Write("Enter your first name: ");
      firstName = System.Console.ReadLine();

      Console.Write("Enter your age: ");
      ageText = Console.ReadLine();
      age = int.Parse(ageText);

      Console.WriteLine(
          $"Hi { firstName }!  You are { age*12 } months old.");
  }
}
```

Output 5.11 shows the results of Listing 5.22.

OUTPUT 5.11

```
Hey you!
Enter your first name: Inigo
Enter your age: 42
Hi Inigo!  You are 504 months old.
```

The return value from `System.Console.ReadLine()` is stored in a variable called `ageText` and is then passed to a method with the `int` data type, called `Parse()`. This method is responsible for taking a string value that represents a number and converting it to an `int` type.

■ BEGINNER TOPIC

42 as a String versus 42 as an Integer

C# requires that every non-null value have a well-defined type associated with it. Therefore, not only the data value but also the type associated with the data is important. A string value of 42, therefore, is distinctly different from an integer value of 42. The string is composed of the two characters 4 and 2, whereas the `int` is the number 42.

Given the converted string, the final `System.Console.WriteLine()` statement will print the age in months by multiplying the age value by 12.

But what happens if the user does not enter a valid integer string? For example, what happens if the user enters "forty-two"? The `Parse()` method cannot handle such a conversion. It expects the user to enter a string that contains only digits. If the `Parse()` method is sent an invalid value, it needs some way to report this fact back to the caller.

Trapping Errors

To indicate to the calling method that the parameter is invalid, `int.Parse()` will **throw an exception**. Throwing an exception halts further execution in the current control flow and jumps into the first code block within the call stack that handles the exception.

Since you have not yet provided any such handling, the program reports the exception to the user as an **unhandled exception**. Assuming there is no registered debugger on the system, the error will appear on the console with a message such as that shown in Output 5.12.

OUTPUT 5.12

```
Hey you!
Enter your first name: Inigo
Enter your age: forty-two

Unhandled Exception: System.FormatException: Input string was
    not in a correct format.
   at System.Number.ParseInt32(String s, NumberStyles style,
      NumberFormatInfo info)
   at ExceptionHandling.Main()
```

Obviously, such an error is not particularly helpful. To fix this, it is necessary to provide a mechanism that handles the error, perhaps reporting a more meaningful error message back to the user.

This process is known as **catching an exception**. The syntax is demonstrated in Listing 5.23, and the output appears in Output 5.13.

LISTING 5.23: Catching an Exception

```csharp
using System;

class ExceptionHandling
{
  static int Main()
  {
      string firstName;
      string ageText;
      int age;
      int result = 0;

      Console.Write("Enter your first name: ");
      firstName = Console.ReadLine();

      Console.Write("Enter your age: ");
      ageText = Console.ReadLine();

      try
      {
          age = int.Parse(ageText);
          Console.WriteLine(
              $"Hi { firstName }! You are { age*12 } months old.");
      }
      catch (FormatException )
      {
          Console.WriteLine(
              $"The age entered, { ageText }, is not valid.");
          result = 1;
      }
```

```csharp
    catch(Exception exception)
    {
        Console.WriteLine(
            $"Unexpected error:  { exception.Message }");
        result = 1;
    }
    finally
    {
        Console.WriteLine($"Goodbye { firstName }");
    }

    return result;
  }
}
```

OUTPUT 5.13

```
Enter your first name: Inigo
Enter your age: forty-two
The age entered, forty-two, is not valid.
Goodbye Inigo
```

To begin, surround the code that could potentially throw an exception (age = int.Parse()) with a **try block**. This block begins with the try keyword. It indicates to the compiler that the developer is aware of the possibility that the code within the block might throw an exception, and if it does, one of the **catch blocks** will attempt to handle the exception.

One or more catch blocks (or the finally block) must appear immediately following a try block. The catch block header (see the Advanced Topic titled "General Catch" later in this chapter) optionally allows you to specify the data type of the exception, and as long as the data type matches the exception type, the catch block will execute. If, however, there is no appropriate catch block, the exception will fall through and go unhandled as though there were no exception handling. The resultant control flow appears in Figure 5.1.

For example, assume the user enters "forty-two" for the age in the previous example. In this case, int.Parse() will throw an exception of type System.FormatException, and control will jump to the set of catch blocks. (System.FormatException indicates that the string was not of the correct format to be parsed appropriately.) Since the first catch block matches the type of exception that int.Parse() threw, the code inside this block will execute. If a statement within the try block threw a different exception,

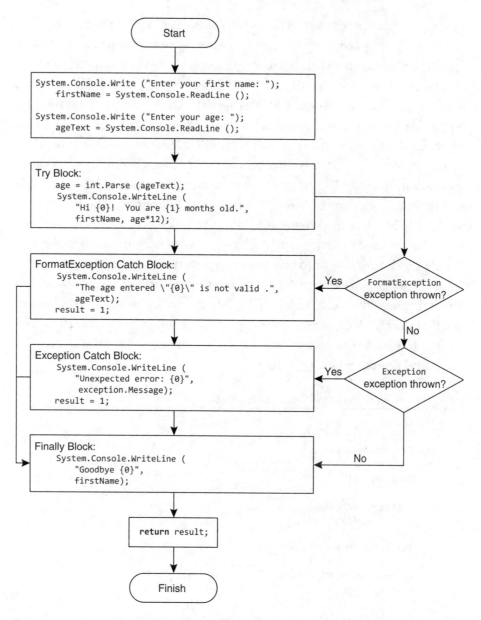

FIGURE 5.1: Exception-Handling Control Flow

the second catch block would execute because all exceptions are of type
System.Exception.

If there were no System.FormatException catch block, the System
.Exception catch block would execute even though int.Parse throws a

System.FormatException. This is because a System.FormatException
is also of type System.Exception. (System.FormatException is a more
specific implementation of the generic exception, System.Exception.)

The order in which you handle exceptions is significant. Catch blocks
must appear from most specific to least specific. The System.Exception data
type is least specific, so it appears last. System.FormatException appears
first because it is the most specific exception that Listing 5.23 handles.

Regardless of whether control leaves the try block normally or because
the code in the try block throws an exception, the **finally block** of code
will execute after control leaves the try-protected region. The purpose of
the finally block is to provide a location to place code that will execute
regardless of how the try/catch blocks exit—with or without an exception.
Finally blocks are useful for cleaning up resources regardless of whether
an exception is thrown. In fact, it is possible to have a try block with a
finally block and no catch block. The finally block executes regardless of
whether the try block throws an exception or whether a catch block is even
written to handle the exception. Listing 5.24 demonstrates the try/finally
block, and Output 5.14 shows the results.

LISTING 5.24: Finally Block without a Catch Block

```csharp
using System;

class ExceptionHandling
{
  static int Main()
  {
      string firstName;
      string ageText;
      int age;
      int result = 0;

      Console.Write("Enter your first name: ");
      firstName = Console.ReadLine();

      Console.Write("Enter your age: ");
      ageText = Console.ReadLine();

      try
      {
          age = int.Parse(ageText);
          Console.WriteLine(
              $"Hi { firstName }! You are { age*12 } months old.");
      }
```

```
        finally
        {
            Console.WriteLine($"Goodbye { firstName }");
        }

        return result;
    }
}
```

OUTPUT 5.14

```
Enter your first name: Inigo
Enter your age: forty-two

Unhandled Exception: System.FormatException: Input string was not in a
↳correct format.
    at System.Number.StringToNumber(String str, NumberStyles options,
↳NumberBuffer& number, NumberFormatInfo info, Boolean parseDecimal)
    at System.Number.ParseInt32(String s, NumberStyles style,
↳NumberFormatInfo info)
    at ExceptionHandling.Main()
Goodbye Inigo
```

The attentive reader will have noticed something interesting here: The runtime first reported the unhandled exception and then ran the finally block. What explains this unusual behavior?

First, the behavior is legal because when an exception is unhandled, the behavior of the runtime is implementation defined; any behavior is legal! The runtime chooses this particular behavior because it knows before it chooses to run the finally block that the exception will be unhandled; the runtime has already examined all of the activation frames on the call stack and determined that none of them is associated with a catch block that matches the thrown exception.

As soon as the runtime determines that the exception will be unhandled, it checks whether a debugger is installed on the machine, because you might be the software developer who is analyzing this failure. If a debugger is present, it offers the user the chance to attach the debugger to the process *before* the finally block runs. If there is no debugger installed or if the user declines to debug the problem, the default behavior is to print the unhandled exception to the console and then see if there are any finally blocks that could run. Due to the "implementation-defined" nature of the situation, the runtime is not required to run finally blocks in this situation; an implementation may choose to do so or not.

> ## Guidelines
>
> **AVOID** explicitly throwing exceptions from finally blocks. (Implicitly thrown exceptions resulting from method calls are acceptable.)
>
> **DO** favor try/finally and avoid using try/catch for cleanup code.
>
> **DO** throw exceptions that describe which exceptional circumstance occurred, and if possible, how to prevent it.

■ ADVANCED TOPIC

Exception Class Inheritance

Starting in C# 2.0, all objects thrown as exceptions derive from `System.Exception`. (Objects thrown from other languages that do not derive from `System.Exception` are automatically "wrapped" by an object that does.) Therefore, they can be handled by the `catch(System.Exception exception)` block. It is preferable, however, to include a catch block that is specific to the most derived type (e.g., `System.FormatException`), because then it is possible to get the most information about an exception and handle it less generically. In so doing, the `catch` statement that uses the most derived type is able to handle the exception type specifically, accessing data related to the exception thrown and avoiding conditional logic to determine what type of exception occurred.

This is why C# enforces the rule that catch blocks appear from most derived to least derived. For example, a `catch` statement that catches `System.Exception` cannot appear before a statement that catches `System.FormatException` because `System.FormatException` derives from `System.Exception`.

A method could throw many exception types. Table 5.2 lists some of the more common ones within the framework.

TABLE 5.2: Common Exception Types

Exception Type	Description
`System.Exception`	The "base" exception from which all other exceptions derive.

TABLE 5.2: Common Exception Types (*continued*)

Exception Type	Description
System.ArgumentException	Indicates that one of the arguments passed into the method is invalid.
System.ArgumentNullException	Indicates that a particular argument is null and that this is not a valid value for that parameter.
System.ApplicationException	To be avoided. The original idea was that you might want to have one kind of handling for system exceptions and another for application exceptions, which, although plausible, doesn't actually work well in the real world.
System.FormatException	Indicates that the string format is not valid for conversion.
System.IndexOutOfRangeException	Indicates that an attempt was made to access an array or other collection element that does not exist.
System.InvalidCastException	Indicates that an attempt to convert from one data type to another was not a valid conversion.
System.InvalidOperationException	Indicates that an unexpected scenario has occurred such that the application is no longer in a valid state of operation.
System.NotImplementedException	Indicates that although the method signature exists, it has not been fully implemented.
System.NullReferenceException	Thrown when code tries to find the object referred to by a reference that is null.
System.ArithmeticException	Indicates an invalid math operation, not including divide by zero.
System.ArrayTypeMismatchException	Occurs when attempting to store an element of the wrong type into an array.
System.StackOverflowException	Indicates an unexpectedly deep recursion.

■ADVANCED TOPIC

General Catch

It is possible to specify a catch block that takes no parameters, as shown in Listing 5.25.

LISTING 5.25: **General Catch Blocks**

```
...
try
{
    age = int.Parse(ageText);
    System.Console.WriteLine(
        $"Hi { firstName }!  You are { age*12 } months old.");
}
catch (System.FormatException exception)
{
    System.Console.WriteLine(
        $"The age entered ,{ ageText }, is not valid.");
    result = 1;
}
catch(System.Exception exception)
{
    System.Console.WriteLine(
        $"Unexpected error:  { exception.Message }");
    result = 1;
}
catch
{
    System.Console.WriteLine("Unexpected error!");
    result = 1;
}
finally
{
    System.Console.WriteLine($"Goodbye { firstName }");
}
...
```

A catch block with no data type, called a **general catch block**, is equivalent to specifying a catch block that takes an object data type—for instance, catch(object exception){...}. Because all classes ultimately derive from object, a catch block with no data type must appear last.

General catch blocks are rarely used because there is no way to capture any information about the exception. In addition, C# doesn't support the ability to throw an exception of type object. (Only libraries written in languages such as C++ allow exceptions of any type.)

The behavior starting in C# 2.0 varies slightly from the earlier C# behavior. In C# 2.0, if a language allows throwing non-`System.Exceptions`, the object of the thrown exception will be wrapped in a `System.Runtime.CompilerServices.RuntimeWrappedException` that does derive from `System.Exception`. Therefore, all exceptions, whether derived from `System.Exception` or not, will propagate into C# assemblies as if they were derived from `System.Exception`.

Begin 2.0

The result is that `System.Exception` catch blocks will catch all exceptions not caught by earlier blocks, and a general catch block, following a `System.Exception` catch block, will never be invoked. Consequently, following a `System.Exception` catch block with a general catch block in C# 2.0 or later will result in a compiler warning indicating that the general catch block will never execute.

End 2.0

Guidelines

AVOID general catch blocks and replace them with a catch of `System.Exception`.

AVOID catching exceptions for which the appropriate action is unknown. It is better to let an exception go unhandled than to handle it incorrectly.

AVOID catching and logging an exception before rethrowing it. Instead, allow the exception to escape until it can be handled appropriately.

Reporting Errors Using a throw Statement

C# allows developers to throw exceptions from their code, as demonstrated in Listing 5.26 and Output 5.15.

Listing 5.26: Throwing an Exception

```csharp
using System;
public class ThrowingExceptions
{
  public static void Main()
  {
    try
    {
      Console.WriteLine("Begin executing");
```

```
        Console.WriteLine("Throw exception");
        throw new Exception("Arbitrary exception");
        Console.WriteLine("End executing");
    }
    catch(FormatException exception)
    {
        Console.WriteLine(
            "A FormateException was thrown");
    }
    catch(Exception exception)
    {
        Console.WriteLine(
            $"Unexpected error: { exception.Message }");
    }
    catch
    {
        Console.WriteLine("Unexpected error!");
    }

    Console.WriteLine(
        "Shutting down...");
}
}
```

OUTPUT 5.15

```
Begin executing
Throw exception...
Unexpected error:  Arbitrary exception
Shutting down...
```

As the arrows in Listing 5.26 depict, throwing an exception causes execution to jump from where the exception is thrown into the first catch block within the stack that is compatible with the thrown exception type.[6] In this case, the second catch block handles the exception and writes out an error message. In Listing 5.26, there is no finally block, so execution falls through to the System.Console.WriteLine() statement following the try/catch block.

To throw an exception, it is necessary to have an instance of an exception. Listing 5.26 creates an instance using the keyword new followed by the type of the exception. Most exception types allow a message to be generated as part of throwing the exception, so that when the exception occurs, the message can be retrieved.

---

6. Technically it could be caught by a compatible catch filter as well.

Sometimes a catch block will trap an exception but be unable to handle it appropriately or fully. In these circumstances, a catch block can rethrow the exception using the `throw` statement without specifying any exception, as shown in Listing 5.27.

LISTING 5.27: Rethrowing an Exception

```
...
    catch(Exception exception)
    {
        Console.WriteLine(
            $@"Rethrowing unexpected error:  {
                exception.Message }");
        throw;
    }
...
```

In Listing 5.27, the `throw` statement is "empty" rather than specifying that the exception referred to by the `exception` variable is to be thrown. This illustrates a subtle difference: `throw;` preserves the *call stack* information in the exception, whereas `throw exception;` replaces that information with the current call stack information. For debugging purposes, it is usually better to know the original call stack.

Guidelines

DO prefer using an empty throw when catching and rethrowing an exception so as to preserve the call stack.

DO report execution failures by throwing exceptions rather than returning error codes.

DO NOT have public members that return exceptions as return values or an out parameter. Throw exceptions to indicate errors; do not use them as return values to indicate errors.

Avoid Using Exception Handling to Deal with Expected Situations

Developers should make an effort to avoid throwing exceptions for expected conditions or normal control flow. For example, developers should not expect users to enter valid text when specifying their age.[7]

---

7. In general, developers should expect their users to perform unexpected actions; in turn, they should code defensively to handle "stupid user tricks."

Therefore, instead of relying on an exception to validate data entered by the user, developers should provide a means of checking the data before attempting the conversion. (Better yet, they should prevent the user from entering invalid data in the first place.) Exceptions are designed specifically for tracking exceptional, unexpected, and potentially fatal situations. Using them for an unintended purpose such as expected situations will cause your code to be hard to read, understand, and maintain.

Additionally, like most languages, C# incurs a slight performance hit when throwing an exception—taking microseconds compared to the nanoseconds most operations take. This delay is generally not noticeable in human time—except when the exception goes unhandled. For example, when Listing 5.22 is executed and the user enters an invalid age, the exception is unhandled and there is a noticeable delay while the runtime searches the environment to see whether there is a debugger to load. Fortunately, slow performance when a program is shutting down isn't generally a factor to be concerned with.

Guidelines

DO NOT use exceptions for handling normal, expected conditions; use them for exceptional, unexpected conditions.

Begin 2.0

■ **ADVANCED TOPIC**

Numeric Conversion with TryParse( )

One of the problems with the Parse( ) method is that the only way to determine whether the conversion will be successful is to attempt the cast and then catch the exception if it doesn't work. Because throwing an exception is a relatively expensive operation, it is better to attempt the conversion without exception handling. In the first release of C#, the only data type that enabled this behavior was a double method called double.TryParse( ). However, this method is included with all numeric primitive types starting with the Microsoft .NET Framework 2.0. It requires the use of the out keyword because the return from the TryParse( ) function is a bool rather than the converted value. Listing 5.28 is a code snippet that demonstrates the conversion using int.TryParse( ).

LISTING 5.28: Conversion Using int.TryParse()

```
if (int.TryParse(ageText, out int age))
{
    Console.WriteLine(
        $"Hi { firstName }!  "
        + $"You are { age*12 } months old.");
}
else
{
    Console.WriteLine(
        $"The age entered, { ageText }, is not valid.");
}
```

With the Microsoft .NET Framework 4, a `TryParse()` method was also added to enum types.

With the `TryParse()` method, it is no longer necessary to include a try/catch block simply for the purpose of handling the string-to-numeric conversion.

End 2.0

SUMMARY

This chapter discussed the details of declaring and calling methods, including the use of the keywords `out` and `ref` to pass and return variables rather than their values. In addition to method declaration, this chapter introduced exception handling.

A method is a fundamental construct that is a key to writing readable code. Instead of writing large methods with lots of statements, you should use methods to create "paragraphs" of roughly 10 or fewer statements within your code. The process of breaking large functions into smaller pieces is one of the ways you can refactor your code to make it more readable and maintainable.

The next chapter considers the class construct and describes how it encapsulates methods (behavior) and fields (data) into a single unit.

◼6◾
Classes

YOU BRIEFLY SAW IN CHAPTER 1 how to declare a new class called HelloWorld. In Chapters 2 and 3, you learned about the built-in primitive types included with C#. Since you have now also learned about control flow and how to declare methods, it is time to discuss defining your own types. Type definition is a core construct of any C# program; this support for classes and the objects created from them is what makes C# an object-oriented language.

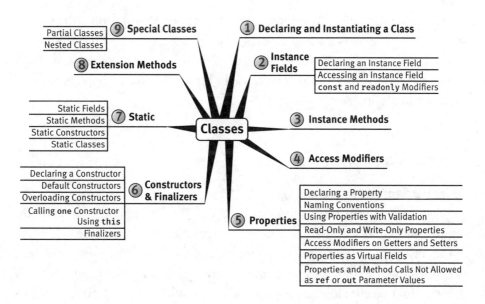

This chapter introduces the basics of object-oriented programming using C#. A key focus is on how to define **classes**, which are the templates for objects themselves.

All of the constructs of structured programming from the previous chapters still apply within object-oriented programming. However, by wrapping those constructs within classes, you can create larger, more organized programs that are more maintainable. The transition from structured, control-flow-based programs to object-oriented programs revolutionized programming because it provided an extra level of organization. The result was that smaller programs were simplified somewhat. Even more important, it was easier to create much larger programs because the code within those programs was better organized.

One of the key advantages of object-oriented programming is that instead of creating new programs entirely from scratch, you can assemble a collection of existing objects from prior work, extending the classes with new features, adding more classes, and thereby providing new functionality.

Readers unfamiliar with object-oriented programming should read the Beginner Topic blocks for an introduction. The general text outside the Beginner Topics focuses on using C# for object-oriented programming with the assumption that readers are already familiar with object-oriented concepts.

This chapter delves into how C# supports encapsulation through its support of constructs such as classes, properties, and access modifiers; we covered methods in Chapter 5. Chapter 7 builds on this foundation with the introduction of inheritance and the polymorphism that object-oriented programming enables.

■ BEGINNER TOPIC

Object-Oriented Programming

The key to programming successfully today lies in the ability to provide organization and structure to the implementation of the complex requirements of large applications. Object-oriented programming provides one of the key methodologies in accomplishing this goal, to the point that it is difficult for object-oriented programmers to envision transitioning back to structured programming, except for the most trivial programs.

The most fundamental construct in object-oriented programming is the class. A group of classes form a programming abstraction, model, or template of what is often a real-world concept. The class `OpticalStorageMedia`, for example, may have an `Eject()` method on it that causes a disk to eject from the player. The `OpticalStorageMedia` class is the programming abstraction of the real-world object of a CD or DVD player.

Classes exhibit the three principal characteristics of object-oriented programming: encapsulation, inheritance, and polymorphism.

Encapsulation

Encapsulation allows you to hide details. The details can still be accessed when necessary, but by intelligently encapsulating the details, large programs are made easier to understand, data is protected from inadvertent modification, and code becomes easier to maintain because the effects of a code change are limited to the scope of the encapsulation. Methods are examples of encapsulation. Although it is possible to take the code from a method and embed it directly inline with the caller's code, refactoring of code into a method provides encapsulation benefits.

Inheritance

Consider the following example: A DVD drive is a type of optical media device. It has a specific storage capacity along with the ability to hold a digital movie. A CD drive is also a type of optical media device, but it has different characteristics. The copy protection on CDs is different from DVD copy protection, and the storage capacity is different as well. Both CD drives and DVD drives are different from hard drives, USB drives, and floppy drives (remember those?). All fit into the category of storage devices, but each has special characteristics, even for fundamental functions such as the supported filesystems and whether instances of the media are read-only or read/write.

Inheritance in object-oriented programming allows you to form "is a kind of" relationships between these similar but different items. It is reasonable to say that a DVD drive "is a kind of" storage media and that a CD drive "is a kind of" storage media, and as such, that each has storage capacity. We could also reasonably say that both have an "is a kind of" relationship with "optical storage media," which in turn "is a kind of" storage media.

If you define classes corresponding to each type of storage device mentioned, you will have defined a **class hierarchy**, which is a series of "is a kind of" relationships. The base class, from which all storage devices derive, could be the class `StorageMedia`. As such, classes that represent CD drives, DVD drives, hard drives, USB drives, and floppy drives are derived from the class `StorageMedia`. However, the classes for CD and DVD drives don't need to derive from `StorageMedia` directly. Instead, they can derive from an intermediate class, `OpticalStorageMedia`. You can view the class hierarchy graphically using a Unified Modeling Language (UML)–like class diagram, as shown in Figure 6.1.

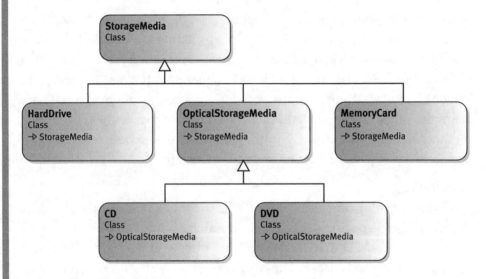

FIGURE 6.1: Class Hierarchy

The inheritance relationship involves a minimum of two classes, such that one class is a more specific kind of the other; in Figure 6.1, `HardDrive` is a more specific kind of `StorageMedia`. Although the more specialized type, `HardDrive`, is a kind of `StorageMedia`, the reverse is not true—that is, an instance of `StorageMedia` is not necessarily a `HardDrive`. As Figure 6.1 shows, inheritance can involve more than two classes.

The more specialized type is called the **derived type** or the **subtype**. The more general type is called the **base type** or the **super type**. The base type is also often called the *parent* type, and its derived types are often called its *child* types. Though this usage is common, it can be confusing: After all, a child is not a kind of parent! In this book, we stick to *derived type* and *base type*.

To **derive** or **inherit** from another type is to **specialize** that type, which means to customize the base type so that it is more suitable for a specific purpose. The base type may contain those implementation details that are common to all of the derived types.

The key feature of inheritance is that all derived types inherit the members of the base type. Often, the implementation of the base members can be modified, but regardless, the derived type contains the base type's members in addition to any other members that the derived type contains explicitly.

Derived types allow you to organize your classes into a coherent hierarchy where the derived types have greater specificity than their base types.

Polymorphism

Polymorphism is formed from *poly*, meaning "many," and *morph*, meaning "form." In the context of objects, polymorphism means that a single method or type can have many forms of implementation.

Suppose you have a media player that can play both music CDs and DVDs containing MP3s. However, the exact implementation of the Play() method will vary depending on the media type. Calling Play() on an object representing a music CD or on an object representing a music DVD will play music in both cases, because each object's type understands the intricacies of playing. All that the media player knows about is the common base type, OpticalStorageMedia, and the fact that it defines the Play() method. Polymorphism is the principle that a type can take care of the exact details of a method's implementation because the method appears on multiple derived types, each of which shares a common base type (or interface) that also contains the same method signature.

Declaring and Instantiating a Class

Defining a class involves first specifying the keyword class, followed by an identifier, as shown in Listing 6.1.

LISTING 6.1: Defining a Class

```
class Employee
{
}
```

All code that belongs to the class will appear between the curly braces following the class declaration. Although not a requirement, generally you place each class into its own file. This makes it easier to find the code that defines a particular class, because the convention is to name the file using the class name.

> **Guidelines**
>
> **DO NOT** place more than one class in a single source file.
> **DO** name the source file with the name of the public type it contains.

Once you have defined a new class, you can use that class as though it were built into the framework. In other words, you can declare a variable of that type or define a method that takes a parameter of the new class type. Listing 6.2 demonstrates such declarations.

LISTING 6.2: Declaring Variables of the Class Type

```
class Program
{
  static void Main()
  {
      Employee employee1, employee2;
      // ...
  }

  static void IncreaseSalary(Employee employee)
  {
      // ...
  }
}
```

■ BEGINNER TOPIC

Objects and Classes Defined

In casual conversation, the terms *class* and *object* appear interchangeably. However, object and class have distinct meanings. A **class** is a template for what an object will look like at instantiation time. An **object**, therefore, is an instance of a class. Classes are like the mold for what a widget will look like. Objects correspond to widgets created by the mold. The process of creating an object from a class is called **instantiation** because an object is an instance of a class.

Now that you have defined a new class type, it is time to instantiate an object of that type. Mimicking its predecessors, C# uses the new keyword to instantiate an object (see Listing 6.3).

LISTING 6.3: Instantiating a Class

```
class Program
{
  static void Main()
  {
      Employee employee1 = new Employee();
      Employee employee2;
      employee2 = new Employee();

      IncreaseSalary(employee1);
  }
}
```

Not surprisingly, the assignment can occur in the same statement as the declaration or in a separate statement.

Unlike the primitive types you have worked with so far, there is no literal way to specify an Employee. Instead, the new operator provides an instruction to the runtime to allocate memory for an Employee object, instantiate the object, and return a reference to the instance.

Although an explicit operator for allocating memory exists, there is no such operator for de-allocating the memory. Instead, the runtime automatically reclaims the memory sometime after the object becomes inaccessible. The **garbage collector** is responsible for the automatic de-allocation. It determines which objects are no longer referenced by other active objects and then de-allocates the memory for those objects. The result is that there is no compile-time–determined program location where the memory will be collected and restored to the system.

In this trivial example, no explicit data or methods are associated with an Employee, which renders the object essentially useless. The next section focuses on adding data to an object.

■ **BEGINNER TOPIC**

Encapsulation Part 1: Objects Group Data with Methods

If you received a stack of index cards with employees' first names, a stack of index cards with their last names, and a stack of index cards with their salaries, the cards would be of little value unless you knew that the cards were in the same order in each stack. Even so, the data would be difficult to work with because determining a person's full name would require searching through two stacks. Worse, if you dropped one of the stacks, there would be no way to reassociate the first name with the last name and the salary. Instead, you would need one stack of employee cards in which the data for each employee is grouped on one card. With this approach, first names, last names, and salaries will be encapsulated together.

Outside the object-oriented programming context, to **encapsulate** a set of items is to enclose those items within a capsule. Similarly, object-oriented programming encapsulates methods and data together into an object. This provides a grouping of all of the class **members** (the data and methods within a class) so that they no longer need to be handled individually. Instead of passing a first name, a last name, and a salary as three separate parameters to a method, objects enable a call to pass a reference to an employee object. Once the called method receives the object reference, it can send a message (e.g., it can call a method such as `AdjustSalary()`) to the object to perform a particular operation.

Language Contrast: C++—The `delete` Operator

C# programmers should view the new operator as a call to instantiate an object, not as a call to allocate memory. Both objects allocated on the heap and objects allocated on the stack support the new operator, emphasizing the point that new is not about how memory allocation should take place and whether de-allocation is necessary.

Thus C# does not need the `delete` operator found in C++. Memory allocation and de-allocation are details that the runtime manages, allowing the developer to focus more on domain logic. However, though memory is managed by the runtime, the runtime does not manage other resources such as database connections, network ports, and so on. Unlike C++, C# does not support **implicit deterministic resource cleanup** (the occurrence of implicit object destruction at a compile-time–defined location in the code). Fortunately, C# does support **explicit deterministic resource cleanup** via a `using` statement and **implicit nondeterministic resource cleanup** using finalizers.

Instance Fields

One of the key aspects of object-oriented design is the grouping of data to provide structure. This section discusses how to add data to the Employee class. The general object-oriented term for a variable that stores data within a class is **member variable**. This term is well understood in C#, but the more standard term and the one used in the specification is **field**, which is a named unit of storage associated with the containing type. **Instance fields** are variables declared at the class level to store data associated with an object. Hence, **association** is the relationship between the field data type and the containing field.

Declaring an Instance Field

In Listing 6.4, the class Employee has been modified to include three fields: FirstName, LastName, and Salary.

LISTING 6.4: Declaring Fields

```
class Employee
{
  public string FirstName;
  public string LastName;
  public string Salary;
}
```

With these fields added, it is possible to store some fundamental data with every Employee instance. In this case, you prefix the fields with an access modifier of public. The use of public on a field indicates that the data within the field is accessible from classes other than Employee (see the section "Access Modifiers" later in this chapter).

As with local variable declarations, a field declaration includes the data type to which the field refers. Furthermore, it is possible to assign fields an initial value at declaration time, as demonstrated with the Salary field in Listing 6.5.

LISTING 6.5: Setting Initial Values of Fields at Declaration Time

```
class Employee
{
  public string FirstName;
  public string LastName;
  public string Salary = "Not enough";
}
```

We delay the guidelines of naming and coding fields until later in the chapter, after C# properties have been introduced. Suffice it to say, Listing 6.5 does *not* follow the general convention.

Accessing an Instance Field

You can set and retrieve the data within fields. However, the fact that a field does not include a `static` modifier indicates that it is an instance field. You can access an instance field only from an instance of the containing class (an object). You cannot access it from the class directly (without first creating an instance, in other words).

Listing 6.6 shows an updated look at the `Program` class and its utilization of the `Employee` class, and Output 6.1 shows the results.

LISTING 6.6: Accessing Fields

```
class Program
{
  static void Main()
  {
      Employee employee1 = new Employee();
      Employee employee2;
      employee2 = new Employee();

      employee1.FirstName = "Inigo";
      employee1.LastName = "Montoya";
      employee1.Salary = "Too Little";
      IncreaseSalary(employee1);
      Console.WriteLine(
          "{0} {1}: {2}",
          employee1.FirstName,
          employee1.LastName,
          employee1.Salary);
      // ...
  }

  static void IncreaseSalary(Employee employee)
  {
      employee.Salary = "Enough to survive on";
  }
}
```

OUTPUT 6.1

```
Inigo Montoya: Enough to survive on
```

Listing 6.6 instantiates two `Employee` objects, as you saw earlier. It then sets each field, calls `IncreaseSalary()` to change the salary, and displays each field associated with the object referenced by `employee1`.

Notice that you first have to specify which `Employee` instance you are working with. Therefore, the `employee1` variable appears as a prefix to the field name when assigning and accessing the field.

Instance Methods

One alternative to formatting the names in the `WriteLine()` method call within `Main()` is to provide a method in the `Employee` class that takes care of the formatting. Changing the functionality to be within the `Employee` class rather than a member of `Program` is consistent with the encapsulation of a class. Why not group the methods relating to the employee's full name with the class that contains the data that forms the name?

Listing 6.7 demonstrates the creation of such a method.

LISTING 6.7: Accessing Fields from within the Containing Class

```
class Employee
{
  public string FirstName;
  public string LastName;
  public string Salary;

  public string GetName()
  {
      return $"{ FirstName } { LastName }";
  }
}
```

There is nothing particularly special about this method compared to what you learned in Chapter 4, except that now the `GetName()` method accesses fields on the object instead of just local variables. In addition, the method declaration is not marked with `static`. As you will see later in this chapter, static methods cannot directly access instance fields within a class. Instead, it is necessary to obtain an instance of the class to call any instance member, whether a method or a field.

Given the addition of the `GetName()` method, you can update `Program.Main()` to use the method, as shown in Listing 6.8 and Output 6.2.

LISTING 6.8: Accessing Fields from outside the Containing Class

```
class Program
{
  static void Main()
  {
      Employee employee1 = new Employee();
      Employee employee2;
      employee2 = new Employee();

      employee1.FirstName = "Inigo";
      employee1.LastName = "Montoya";
      employee1.Salary = "Too Little";
      IncreaseSalary(employee1);
      Console.WriteLine(
          $"{ employee1.GetName() }: { employee1.Salary }");
      // ...
  }
  // ...
}
```

OUTPUT 6.2

```
Inigo Montoya: Enough to survive on
```

Using the this Keyword

You can obtain the reference to a class from within instance members that belong to the class. To indicate explicitly that the field or method accessed is an instance member of the containing class in C#, you use the keyword this. Use of this is implicit when calling any instance member, and it returns an instance of the object itself.

For example, consider the SetName() method shown in Listing 6.9.

LISTING 6.9: Using this to Identify the Field's Owner Explicitly

```
class Employee
{
  public string FirstName;
  public string LastName;
  public string Salary;

  public string GetName()
  {
      return $"{ FirstName }  { LastName }";
  }
```

```
    public void SetName(
        string newFirstName, string newLastName)
    {
        this.FirstName = newFirstName;
        this.LastName = newLastName;
    }
}
```

This example uses the keyword this to indicate that the fields FirstName and LastName are instance members of the class.

Although the this keyword can prefix any and all references to local class members, the general guideline is not to clutter code when there is no additional value. Therefore, you should avoid using the this keyword unless it is required. Listing 6.12 (later in this chapter) is an example of one of the few circumstances when such a requirement exists. Listings 6.9 and 6.10, however, are not good examples. In Listing 6.9, this can be dropped entirely without changing the meaning of the code. And in Listing 6.10 (presented next), by changing the naming convention for fields, we can avoid any ambiguity between local variables and fields.

■ BEGINNER TOPIC

Relying on Coding Style to Avoid Ambiguity

In the SetName() method, you did not have to use the this keyword because FirstName is obviously different from newFirstName. But suppose that, instead of calling the parameter "newFirstName," you called it "FirstName" (using PascalCase), as shown in Listing 6.10.

LISTING 6.10: Using this to Avoid Ambiguity

```
class Employee
{
  public string FirstName;
  public string LastName;
  public string Salary;

  public string GetName()
  {
      return $"{ FirstName }  { LastName }";
  }

  // Caution:  Parameter names use PascalCase
```

```
public void SetName(string FirstName, string LastName)
{
    this.FirstName = FirstName;
    this.LastName = LastName;
}
}
```

In this example, it is not possible to refer to the FirstName field without explicitly indicating that the Employee object owns the variable. this acts just like the employee1 variable prefix used in the Program.Main() method (see Listing 6.8); it identifies the reference as the one on which SetName() was called.

Listing 6.10 does not follow the C# naming convention in which parameters are declared like local variables, using camelCase. This can lead to subtle bugs, because assigning FirstName (intending to refer to the field) to FirstName (the parameter) will lead to code that still compiles and even runs. To avoid this problem, it is a good practice to have a different naming convention for parameters and local variables than the naming convention for fields. We demonstrate one such convention later in this chapter.

Language Contrast: Visual Basic—Accessing a Class Instance with Me

The C# keyword this is identical to the Visual Basic keyword Me.

In Listings 6.9 and 6.10, the this keyword is not used in the GetName() method—it is optional. However, if local variables or parameters exist with the same name as the field (see the SetName() method in Listing 6.10), omitting this would result in accessing the local variable/parameter when the intention was the field; given this scenario, use of this is required.

You also can use the keyword this to access a class's methods explicitly. For example, this.GetName() is allowed within the SetName() method, permitting you to print out the newly assigned name (see Listing 6.11 and Output 6.3).

LISTING 6.11: Using this with a Method

```csharp
class Employee
{
  // ...

  public string GetName()
  {
      return $"{ FirstName }  { LastName }";
  }

  public void SetName(string newFirstName, string newLastName)
  {
      this.FirstName = newFirstName;
      this.LastName = newLastName;
      Console.WriteLine(
          $"Name changed to '{ this.GetName() }'");
  }
}
```

```csharp
class Program
{
  static void Main()
  {
      Employee employee = new Employee();

      employee.SetName("Inigo", "Montoya");
      // ...
  }
  // ...
}
```

OUTPUT 6.3

```
Name changed to 'Inigo Montoya'
```

Sometimes it may be necessary to use this to pass a reference to the currently executing object. Consider the Save() method in Listing 6.12.

LISTING 6.12: Passing this in a Method Call

```csharp
class Employee
{
  public string FirstName;
  public string LastName;
  public string Salary;
```

```
    public void Save()
    {
        DataStorage.Store(this);
    }
}


class DataStorage
{
    // Save an employee object to a file
    // named with the Employee name
    public static void Store(Employee employee)
    {
        // ...
    }
}
```

The Save() method in Listing 6.12 calls a method on the DataStorage class, called Store(). The Store() method, however, needs to be passed the Employee object, which needs to be persisted. This is done using the keyword this, which passes the instance of the Employee object on which Save() was called.

Storing and Loading with Files

The actual implementation of the Store() method inside DataStorage involves classes within the System.IO namespace, as shown in Listing 6.13. Inside Store(), you begin by instantiating a FileStream object that you associate with a file corresponding to the employee's full name. The FileMode.Create parameter indicates that you want a new file to be created if there isn't already one with the <firstname><lastname>.dat name; if the file exists already, it will be overwritten. Next, you create a StreamWriter class. The StreamWriter class is responsible for writing text into the FileStream. You write the data using WriteLine() methods, just as though writing to the console.

LISTING 6.13: Data Persistence to a File

```
using System;
// IO namespace
using System.IO;

class DataStorage
{
    // Save an employee object to a file
    // named with the Employee name.
    // Error handling not shown.
```

```
public static void Store(Employee employee)
{
    // Instantiate a FileStream using FirstNameLastName.dat
    // for the filename. FileMode.Create will force
    // a new file to be created or override an
    // existing file.
    FileStream stream = new FileStream(
        employee.FirstName + employee.LastName + ".dat",
        FileMode.Create);1

    // Create a StreamWriter object for writing text
    // into the FileStream
    StreamWriter writer = new StreamWriter(stream);

    // Write all the data associated with the employee
    writer.WriteLine(employee.FirstName);
    writer.WriteLine(employee.LastName);
    writer.WriteLine(employee.Salary);

    // Close the StreamWriter and its stream
    writer.Dispose();  // Automatically closes the stream
}
// ...
}
```

Once the write operations are completed, both the FileStream and the StreamWriter need to be closed so that they are not left open indefinitely while waiting for the garbage collector to run. Listing 6.13 does not include any error handling, so if an exception is thrown, neither Close() method will be called.

The load process is similar (see Listing 6.14).

LISTING 6.14: Data Retrieval from a File

```
class Employee
{
    // ...
}
```

```
// IO namespace
using System;
using System.IO;

class DataStorage
{
    // ...
```

---

1. This code could be improved with a using statement, a construct that we have avoided because it has not yet been introduced.

```
public static Employee Load(string firstName, string lastName)
{
    Employee employee = new Employee();

    // Instantiate a FileStream using FirstNameLastName.dat
    // for the filename. FileMode.Open will open
    // an existing file or else report an error.
    FileStream stream = new FileStream(
        firstName + lastName + ".dat", FileMode.Open);²

    // Create a StreamReader for reading text from the file
    StreamReader reader = new StreamReader(stream);

    // Read each line from the file and place it into
    // the associated property
    employee.FirstName = reader.ReadLine();
    employee.LastName = reader.ReadLine();
    employee.Salary = reader.ReadLine();

    // Close the StreamReader and its stream
    reader.Dispose();   // Automatically closes the stream

    return employee;
    }
}
```

```
class Program
{
  static void Main()
  {
      Employee employee1;

      Employee employee2 = new Employee();
      employee2.SetName("Inigo", "Montoya");
      employee2.Save();

      // Modify employee2 after saving
      IncreaseSalary(employee2);

      // Load employee1 from the saved version of employee2
      employee1 = DataStorage.Load("Inigo", "Montoya");

      Console.WriteLine(
          $"{ employee1.GetName() }: { employee1.Salary }");

      // ...
  }
  // ...
}
```

---

2. This code could be improved with a using statement, a construct that we have avoided because it has not yet been introduced.

Output 6.4 shows the results.

OUTPUT 6.4

```
Name changed to 'Inigo Montoya'
Inigo Montoya:
```

The reverse of the save process appears in Listing 6.14, which uses a `StreamReader` rather than a `StreamWriter`. Again, `Close()` needs to be called on both `FileStream` and `StreamReader` once the data has been read.

Output 6.4 does not show any salary after `Inigo Montoya:` because `Salary` was not set to `Enough to survive on` by a call to `IncreaseSalary()` until after the call to `Save()`.

Notice in `Main()` that we can call `Save()` from an instance of an employee, but to load a new employee we call `DataStorage.Load()`. To load an employee, we generally don't already have an employee instance to load into, so an instance method on `Employee` would be less than ideal. An alternative to calling `Load` on `DataStorage` would be to add a static `Load()` method (see the section "Static Members" later in this chapter) to `Employee` so that it would be possible to call `Employee.Load()` (using the `Employee` class, not an instance of `Employee`).

Notice the inclusion of the `using System.IO` directive at the top of the listing. This directive makes each `IO` class accessible without prefixing it with the full namespace.

Access Modifiers

When declaring a field earlier in the chapter, you prefixed the field declaration with the keyword `public`. `public` is an **access modifier** that identifies the level of encapsulation associated with the member it decorates. Five access modifiers are available: `public`, `private`, `protected`, `internal`, and `protected internal`. This section considers the first two.

■ **BEGINNER TOPIC**

Encapsulation Part 2: Information Hiding

Besides wrapping data and methods together into a single unit, encapsulation deals with hiding the internal details of an object's data and behavior.

To some degree, methods do this; from outside a method, all that is visible to a caller is the method declaration. None of the internal implementation is visible. Object-oriented programming enables this further, however, by providing facilities for controlling the extent to which members are visible from outside the class. Members that are not visible outside the class are **private members**.

In object-oriented programming, *encapsulation* is the term for not only grouping data and behavior but also hiding data and behavior implementation details within a class (the capsule) so that the inner workings of a class are not exposed. This reduces the chance that callers will modify the data inappropriately or program according to the implementation, only to have it change in the future.

The purpose of an access modifier is to provide encapsulation. By using `public`, you explicitly indicate that it is acceptable that the modified fields are accessible from outside the `Employee` class—in other words, that they are accessible from the `Program` class, for example.

Consider an `Employee` class that includes a `Password` field, however. It should be possible to call an `Employee` object and verify the password using a `Logon()` method. Conversely, it should not be possible to access the `Password` field on an `Employee` object from outside the class.

To define a `Password` field as hidden and inaccessible from outside the containing class, you use the keyword `private` for the access modifier, in place of `public` (see Listing 6.15). As a result, the `Password` field is not accessible from inside the `Program` class, for example.

LISTING 6.15: Using the private Access Modifier

```
class Employee
{
  public string FirstName;
  public string LastName;
  public string Salary;
  private string Password;
  private bool IsAuthenticated;

  public bool Logon(string password)
  {
      if(Password == password)
      {
          IsAuthenticated = true;
      }
      return IsAuthenticated;
  }
}
```

```
    public bool GetIsAuthenticated()
    {
        return IsAuthenticated;
    }
    // ...
}
```

```
class Program
{
    static void Main()
    {
        Employee employee = new Employee();

        employee.FirstName = "Inigo";
        employee.LastName = "Montoya";

        // ...

        // Password is private, so it cannot be
        // accessed from outside the class
        // Console.WriteLine(
        //     $"Password = { employee.Password}");
    }
    // ...
}
```

Although this option is not shown in Listing 6.15, it is possible to decorate a method with an access modifier of `private` as well.

If no access modifier is placed on a class member, the declaration defaults to `private`. In other words, members are private by default and programmers need to specify explicitly that a member is to be public.

Properties

The preceding section, "Access Modifiers," demonstrated how you can use the `private` keyword to encapsulate a password, preventing access from outside the class. This type of encapsulation is often too strict, however. For example, sometimes you might need to define fields that external classes can only read but whose values you can change internally. Alternatively, perhaps you want to allow access to write some data in a class, but you need to be able to validate changes made to the data. In yet another scenario, perhaps you need to construct the data on the fly. Traditionally, languages enabled the features found in these examples by marking fields as private and then providing getter and setter methods for accessing and modifying the data. The code in Listing 6.16 changes both `FirstName` and `LastName` to private fields. Public getter and setter methods for each field allow their values to be accessed and changed.

LISTING 6.16: Declaring Getter and Setter Methods

```csharp
class Employee
{

    private string FirstName;
    // FirstName getter
    public string GetFirstName()
    {
        return FirstName;
    }
    // FirstName setter
    public void SetFirstName(string newFirstName)
    {
        if(newFirstName != null && newFirstName != "")
        {
            FirstName = newFirstName;
        }
    }

    private string LastName;
    // LastName getter
    public string GetLastName()
    {
        return LastName;
    }
    // LastName setter
    public void SetLastName(string newLastName)
    {
        if(newLastName != null && newLastName != "")
        {
            LastName = newLastName;
        }
    }
    // ...
}
```

Unfortunately, this change affects the programmability of the `Employee` class. No longer can you use the assignment operator to set data within the class, nor can you access the data without calling a method.

Declaring a Property

Recognizing the frequency of this type of pattern, the C# designers provided explicit syntax for it. This syntax is called a **property** (see Listing 6.17 and Output 6.5).

LISTING 6.17: Defining Properties

```csharp
class Program
{
  static void Main()
  {
      Employee employee = new Employee();

      // Call the FirstName property's setter
      employee.FirstName = "Inigo";

      // Call the FirstName property's getter
      System.Console.WriteLine(employee.FirstName);
  }
}
```

```csharp
class Employee
{
    // FirstName property
    public string FirstName
    {
       get
       {
           return _FirstName;
       }
       set
       {
           _FirstName = value;
       }
    }
    private string _FirstName;

    // ...
}
```

OUTPUT 6.5

```
Inigo
```

The first thing to notice in Listing 6.17 is not the property code itself, but rather the code within the Program class. Although you no longer have the fields with the FirstName and LastName identifiers, you cannot see this by looking at the Program class. The API for accessing an employee's first and last names has not changed at all. It is still possible to assign the parts of the name using a simple assignment operator, for example (employee.FirstName = "Inigo").

The key feature is that properties provide an API that looks programmatically like a field. In actuality, no such fields exist. A property declaration looks exactly like a field declaration, but following it are curly braces in which to place the property implementation. Two optional parts make up the property implementation. The `get` part defines the getter portion of the property. It corresponds directly to the `GetFirstName()` and `GetLastName()` functions defined in Listing 6.16. To access the `FirstName` property, you call `employee.FirstName`. Similarly, setters (the `set` portion of the implementation) enable the calling syntax of the field assignment:

```
employee.FirstName = "Inigo";
```

Property definition syntax uses three contextual keywords. You use the `get` and `set` keywords to identify either the retrieval or the assignment portion of the property, respectively. In addition, the setter uses the `value` keyword to refer to the right side of the assignment operation. When `Program.Main()` calls `employee.FirstName = "Inigo"`, therefore, `value` is set to `"Inigo"` inside the setter and can be used to assign `_FirstName`. Listing 6.17's property implementations are the most commonly used. When the getter is called (such as in `Console.WriteLine(employee.FirstName)`), the value from the field (`_FirstName`) is obtained and written to the console.

Starting with C# 7.0, it is also possible to declare property getters and setters using expression-bodied members, as shown in Listing 6.18.

Begin 7.0

LISTING 6.18: Defining Properties

```
class Employee
{
    // FirstName property
    public string FirstName
    {
        get
        {
            return _FirstName;
        }
        set
        {
            _FirstName = value;
        }
    }

    // LastName property
    public string LastName
    {
        get => _FirstName;
```

```
        set => _FirstName = value;
    }
    private string _LastName;
    // ...
}
```

In Listing 6.18 we use two different syntaxes for an identical property implementation. In real-world code, try to be consistent in your choice of syntax.

Automatically Implemented Properties

In C# 3.0, property syntax included another syntax shortcut. Since a property with a single backing field that is assigned and retrieved by the get and set accessors is so trivial and common (see the implementations of FirstName and LastName), the C# 3.0 compiler (and higher) allows the declaration of a property without any accessor implementation or backing field declaration. Listing 6.19 demonstrates the syntax with the Title and Manager properties, and Output 6.6 shows the results.

LISTING 6.19: Automatically Implemented Properties

```
class Program
{
  static void Main()
  {
        Employee employee1 =
            new Employee();
        Employee employee2 =
            new Employee();

        // Call the FirstName property's setter
        employee1.FirstName = "Inigo";

        // Call the FirstName property's getter
        System.Console.WriteLine(employee1.FirstName);

        // Assign an auto-implemented property
        employee2.Title = "Computer Nerd";
        employee1.Manager = employee2;

        // Print employee1's manager's title
        System.Console.WriteLine(employee1.Manager.Title);
  }
}

class Employee
{
  // FirstName property
```

End 7.0

Begin 3.0

```csharp
    public string FirstName
    {
        get
        {
            return _FirstName;
        }
        set
        {
            _FirstName = value;
        }
    }
    private string _FirstName;

    // LastName property
    public string LastName
    {
        get => _FirstName;
        set => _FirstName = value;
    }
    private string _LastName;

    public string Title { get; set; }

    public Employee Manager { get; set; }

    public string Salary { get; set; } = "Not Enough";
    // ...
}
```

OUTPUT 6.6

```
Inigo
Computer Nerd
```

Auto-implemented properties provide for a simpler way of writing properties in addition to reading them. Furthermore, when it comes time to add something such as validation to the setter, any existing code that calls the property will not have to change, even though the property declaration will have changed to include an implementation.

Throughout the remainder of the book, we frequently use this C# 3.0 or later syntax without indicating that it is a feature introduced in C# 3.0.

End 3.0

One final thing to note about automatically declared properties is that in C# 6.0, it is possible to initialize them as Listing 6.19 does for Salary:

Begin 6.0

```csharp
public string Salary { get; set; } = "Not Enough";
```

Prior to C# 6.0, property initialization was possible only via a method (including the constructor, as we discuss later in the chapter). However, with C# 6.0, you can initialize automatically implemented properties at declaration time using a syntax much like that used for field initialization.

Property and Field Guidelines

Given that it is possible to write explicit setter and getter methods rather than properties, on occasion a question may arise as to whether it is better to use a property or a method. The general guideline is that methods should represent actions and properties should represent data. Properties are intended to provide simple access to simple data with a simple computation. The expectation is that invoking a property will not be significantly more expensive than accessing a field.

With regard to naming, notice that in Listing 6.19 the property name is FirstName, and the field name changed from earlier listings to _FirstName—that is, PascalCase with an underscore prefix. Other common naming conventions for the private field that backs a property are _firstName and m_FirstName (a holdover from C++, where the *m* stands for member variable), and on occasion the camelCase convention, just like with local variables.[3] The camelCase convention should be avoided, however. The camelCase used for property names is the same as the naming convention used for local variables and parameters, meaning that overlaps in names become highly probable. Also, to respect the principles of encapsulation, fields should not be declared as public or protected.

Guidelines

DO use properties for simple access to simple data with simple computations.

AVOID throwing exceptions from property getters.

DO preserve the original property value if the property throws an exception.

DO favor automatically implemented properties over properties with simple backing fields when no additional logic is required.

---

3. We prefer _FirstName because the *m* in front of the name is unnecessary when compared with an underscore (_). Also, by using the same casing as the property, it is possible to have only one string within the Visual Studio code template expansion tools instead of having one for both the property name and the field name.

Regardless of which naming pattern you use for private fields, the coding standard for properties is PascalCase. Therefore, properties should use the `LastName` and `FirstName` pattern with names that represent nouns, noun phrases, or adjectives. It is not uncommon, in fact, that the property name is the same as the type name. Consider an `Address` property of type `Address` on a `Person` object, for example.

Guidelines

CONSIDER using the same casing on a property's backing field as that used in the property, distinguishing the backing field with an "_" prefix. Do not, however, use two underscores; identifiers beginning with two underscores are reserved for the use of the C# compiler itself.

DO name properties using a noun, noun phrase, or adjective.

CONSIDER giving a property the same name as its type.

AVOID naming fields with camelCase.

DO favor prefixing Boolean properties with "Is," "Can," or "Has," when that practice adds value.

DO NOT declare instance fields that are public or protected. (Instead, expose them via a property.)

DO name properties with PascalCase.

DO favor automatically implemented properties over fields.

DO favor automatically implemented properties over using fully expanded ones if there is no additional implementation logic.

Using Properties with Validation

Notice in Listing 6.20 that the `Initialize()` method of `Employee` uses the property rather than the field for assignment as well. Although this is not required, the result is that any validation within the property setter will be invoked both inside and outside the class. Consider, for example, what would happen if you changed the `LastName` property so that it checked `value` for `null` or an empty string before assigning it to `_LastName`.

LISTING 6.20: Providing Property Validation

```
class Employee
{
  // ...
  public void Initialize(
      string newFirstName, string newLastName)
  {
      // Use property inside the Employee
```

```
            // class as well
            FirstName = newFirstName;
            LastName = newLastName;
        }


        // LastName property
        public string LastName
        {
            get => _LastName;
            set
            {
                // Validate LastName assignment
                if(value == null)
                {
                    // Report error
                    // In C# 6.0 replace "value" with nameof(value)
                    throw new ArgumentNullException("value");
                }
                else
                {
                    // Remove any whitespace around
                    // the new last name
                    value = value.Trim();
                    if(value == "")
                    {
                        // Report error
                        // In C# 6.0 replace "value" with nameof(value)
                        throw new ArgumentException(
                            "LastName cannot be blank.", "value");⁴
                    }
                    else
                        _LastName = value;
                }
            }
        }
        private string _LastName;
        // ...
    }
```

With this new implementation, the code throws an exception if LastName is assigned an invalid value, either from another member of the same class or via a direct assignment to LastName from inside Program.Main(). The ability to intercept an assignment and validate the parameters by providing a field-like API is one of the advantages of properties.

---

4. Apologies to Teller, Cher, Sting, Madonna, Bono, Prince, Liberace, et al.

It is a good practice to access a property-backing field only from inside the property implementation. In other words, you should always use the property rather than calling the field directly. In many cases, this principle holds even from code within the same class as the property. If you follow this practice, when you add code such as validation code, the entire class immediately takes advantage of it.[5]

Although rare, it is possible to assign value inside the setter, as Listing 6.20 does. In this case, the call to value.Trim() removes any whitespace surrounding the new last name value.

> ## Guidelines
>
> **AVOID** accessing the backing field of a property outside the property, even from within the containing class.
>
> **DO** use "value" for the paramName argument when creating ArgumentException() or ArgumentNullException() type exceptions ("value" is the implicit name of the parameter on property setters).

Begin 6.0

■ ADVANCED TOPIC

nameof Operator

If during property validation you determine that the new value assignment is invalid, it is necessary to throw an exception—generally of type ArgumentException() or ArgumentNullException(). Both exceptions take an argument of type string called paramName that identifies the name of the parameter that is invalid. In Listing 6.20, we pass "value" as the argument for this parameter, but C# 6.0 provides an improvement with the nameof operator. The nameof operator takes an identifier, like the value variable, and returns a string representation of that name—in this case, "value".

---

5. As described later in the chapter, one exception to this occurs when the field is marked as read-only, because then the value can be set only in the constructor. In C# 6.0, you can directly assign the value of a read-only property, completely eliminating the need for the read-only field.

The advantage of using the nameof operator is that if the identifier name changes, then refactoring tools will automatically change the argument to nameof as well. If no refactoring tool is used, the code will no longer compile, forcing the developer to change the argument manually.

In the case of a property validator, the parameter is always value and cannot be changed, so the benefits of leveraging the nameof operator are arguably lost. Nonetheless, consider continued use of the nameof operator in all cases of the paramName argument to remain consistent with the guideline: Always use nameof for the paramName argument passed into exceptions like ArgumentNullException and ArgumentNullException that take such a parameter.

End 6.0

Read-Only and Write-Only Properties

By removing either the getter or the setter portion of a property, you can change a property's accessibility. Properties with only a setter are write-only, which is a relatively rare occurrence. Similarly, providing only a getter will cause the property to be read-only; any attempts to assign a value will cause a compile error. To make Id read-only, for example, you would code it as shown in Listing 6.21.

LISTING 6.21: Defining a Read-Only Property Prior to C# 6.0

```csharp
class Program
{
  static void Main()
  {
      Employee employee1 = new Employee();
      employee1.Initialize(42);

      // ERROR:  Property or indexer 'Employee.Id'
      // cannot be assigned to; it is read-only
      // employee1.Id = "490";
  }
}

class Employee
{
  public void Initialize(int id)
  {
      // Use field because Id property has no setter;
      // it is read-only
      _Id = id.ToString();
  }
```

```
// ...
// Id property declaration
public string Id
{
    get => _Id;
    // No setter provided
}
private string _Id;


}
```

Listing 6.21 assigns the field from within the Employee Initialize() method rather than the property (_Id = id). Assigning via the property causes a compile error, as it does in Program.Main().

Starting in C# 6.0, there is also support for read-only, **automatically implemented properties** as follows:

```
public bool[,,] Cells { get; } = new bool[2, 3, 3];
```

This is clearly a significant improvement over the pre-C# 6.0 approach, especially given the commonality of read-only properties for something like an array of items or the Id in Listing 6.21.

One important note about a read-only automatically implemented property is that, like read-only fields, the compiler requires that it be initialized via an initializer (or in the constructor). In the preceding snippet we use an initializer, but the assignment of Cells from within the constructor is also permitted, as we shall see shortly.

Given the guideline that fields should not be accessed from outside their wrapping property, those programming in a C# 6.0 world will discover that there is virtually no need to ever use pre-C# 6.0 syntax; instead, the programmer can always use a read-only, automatically implemented property. The only exception might be when the data type of the read-only modified field does not match the data type of the property—for example, if the field was of type int and the read-only property was of type double.

Guidelines

DO create read-only properties if the property value should not be changed.

DO create read-only automatically implemented properties in C# 6.0 (or later) rather than read-only properties with a backing field if the property value should not be changed.

Properties as Virtual Fields

As you have seen, properties behave like virtual fields. In some instances, you do not need a backing field at all. Instead, the property getter returns a calculated value, while the setter parses the value and persists it to some other member fields (if it even exists). Consider, for example, the `Name` property implementation shown in Listing 6.22. Output 6.7 shows the results.

LISTING 6.22: **Defining Properties**

```csharp
class Program
{
  static void Main()
  {
      Employee employee1 = new Employee();

      employee1.Name = "Inigo Montoya";
      System.Console.WriteLine(employee1.Name);

      // ...
  }
}


class Employee
{
  // ...

  // FirstName property
  public string FirstName
  {
      get
      {
          return _FirstName;
      }
      set
      {
          _FirstName = value;
      }
  }
  private string _FirstName;

  // LastName property
  public string LastName
  {
      get => _LastName;
      set => _LastName = value;
  }
  private string _LastName;
  // ...
```

```csharp
        // Name property
        public string Name
        {
            get
            {
                return $"{ FirstName } { LastName }";
            }
            set
            {

                // Split the assigned value into
                // first and last names
                string[] names;
                names = value.Split(new char[]{' '});
                if(names.Length == 2)
                {
                    FirstName = names[0];
                    LastName = names[1];
                }
                else
                {
                    // Throw an exception if the full
                    // name was not assigned
                    throw new System. ArgumentException (
                        $"Assigned value '{ value }' is invalid", "value");6
                }
            }
        }
        public string Initials => $"{ FirstName[0] } { LastName[0] }";
        // ...
    }
```

OUTPUT 6.7

```
Inigo Montoya
```

The getter for the Name property concatenates the values returned from the FirstName and LastName properties. In fact, the name value assigned is not actually stored. When the Name property is assigned, the value on the right side is parsed into its first and last name parts.

Access Modifiers on Getters and Setters

Begin 2.0

As previously mentioned, it is a good practice not to access fields from outside their properties because doing so circumvents any validation or additional logic that may be inserted. Unfortunately, C# 1.0 did not allow

---

6. See the section "nameof Operator" in Chapter 18.

different levels of encapsulation between the getter and setter portions of a property. It was not possible, therefore, to create a public getter and a private setter so that external classes would have read-only access to the property while code within the class could write to the property.

In C# 2.0, support was added for placing an access modifier on either the get or the set portion of the property implementation (not on both), thereby overriding the access modifier specified on the property declaration. Listing 6.23 demonstrates how to do this.

Listing 6.23: Placing Access Modifiers on the Setter

```csharp
class Program
{
  static void Main()
  {
      Employee employee1 = new Employee();
      employee1.Initialize(42);
      // ERROR: The property or indexer 'Employee.Id'
      // cannot be used in this context because the set
      // accessor is inaccessible
      employee1.Id = "490";
  }
}


class Employee
{
  public void Initialize(int id)
  {
      // Set Id property
      Id = id.ToString();
  }

  // ...
  // Id property declaration
  public string Id
  {
      get => _Id;
      // Providing an access modifier is possible in C# 2.0
      // and higher only
      private set => _Id = value;
  }
  private string _Id;

}
```

2.0

By using `private` on the setter, the property appears as read-only to classes other than `Employee`. From within `Employee`, the property appears as read/write, so you can assign the property within the class itself. When specifying an access modifier on the getter or setter, take care that the access modifier is more restrictive than the access modifier on the property as a whole. It is a compile error, for example, to declare the property as `private` and the setter as `public`.

Guidelines

DO apply appropriate accessibility modifiers on implementations of getters and setters on all properties.

DO NOT provide set-only properties or properties with the setter having broader accessibility than the getter.

Properties and Method Calls Not Allowed as `ref` or `out` Parameter Values

C# allows properties to be used identically to fields, except when they are passed as `ref` or `out` parameter values. `ref` and `out` parameter values are internally implemented by passing the memory address to the target method. However, because properties can be virtual fields that have no backing field or can be read-only or write-only, it is not possible to pass the address for the underlying storage. As a result, you cannot pass properties as `ref` or `out` parameter values. The same is true for method calls. Instead, when code needs to pass a property or method call as a `ref` or `out` parameter value, the code must first copy the value into a variable and then pass the variable. Once the method call has completed, the code must assign the variable back into the property.

▪ ADVANCED TOPIC

Property Internals

Listing 6.24 shows that getters and setters are exposed as `get_FirstName()` and `set_FirstName()` in the Common Intermediate Language (CIL).

LISTING 6.24: CIL Code Resulting from Properties

```
// ...

.field private string _FirstName
.method public hidebysig specialname instance string
        get_FirstName() cil managed
```

```
{
  // Code size       12 (0xc)
  .maxstack  1
  .locals init (string V_0)
  IL_0000:  nop
  IL_0001:  ldarg.0
  IL_0002:  ldfld       string Employee::_FirstName
  IL_0007:  stloc.0
  IL_0008:  br.s        IL_000a

  IL_000a:  ldloc.0
  IL_000b:  ret
} // End of method Employee::get_FirstName

.method public hidebysig specialname instance void
      set_FirstName(string 'value') cil managed
{
  // Code size       9 (0x9)
  .maxstack  8
  IL_0000:  nop
  IL_0001:  ldarg.0
  IL_0002:  ldarg.1
  IL_0003:  stfld       string Employee::_FirstName
  IL_0008:  ret
} // End of method Employee::set_FirstName

.property instance string FirstName()
{
  .get instance string Employee::get_FirstName()
  .set instance void Employee::set_FirstName(string)
} // End of property Employee::FirstName

// ...
```

Just as important to their appearance as regular methods is the fact that properties are an explicit construct within the CIL, too. As Listing 6.25 shows, the getters and setters are called by CIL properties, which are an explicit construct within the CIL code. Because of this, languages and compilers are not restricted to always interpreting properties based on a naming convention. Instead, CIL properties provide a means for compilers and code editors to provide special syntax.

LISTING 6.25: Properties Are an Explicit Construct in CIL

```
.property instance string FirstName()
{
  .get instance string Program::get_FirstName()
  .set instance void Program::set_FirstName(string)
} // End of property Program::FirstName
```

Notice in Listing 6.24 that the getters and setters that are part of the property include the specialname metadata. This modifier is what IDEs, such as Visual Studio, use as a flag to hide the members from IntelliSense.

Begin 3.0

An automatically implemented property is almost identical to one for which you define the backing field explicitly. In place of the manually defined backing field, the C# compiler generates a field with the name <PropertyName>k_BackingField in CIL. This generated field includes an attribute (see Chapter 18) called System.Runtime .CompilerServices.CompilerGeneratedAttribute. Both the getters and the setters are decorated with the same attribute because they, too, are generated—with the same implementation as in Listings 5.23 and 5.24.

End 3.0

Constructors

Now that you have added fields to a class and can store data, you need to consider the validity of that data. As you saw in Listing 6.3, it is possible to instantiate an object using the new operator. The result, however, is the ability to create an employee with invalid data. Immediately following the assignment of employee, you have an Employee object whose name and salary are not initialized. In this particular listing, you assigned the uninitialized fields immediately following the instantiation of an employee, but if you failed to do the initialization, you would not receive a warning from the compiler. As a result, you could end up with an Employee object with an invalid name.

Declaring a Constructor

To correct this problem, you need to provide a means of specifying the required data when the object is created. You do this using a constructor, as demonstrated in Listing 6.26.

LISTING 6.26: Defining a Constructor

```
class Employee
{
    // Employee constructor
    public Employee(string firstName, string lastName)
    {
        FirstName = firstName;
        LastName = lastName;
    }
```

```csharp
public string FirstName{ get; set; }
public string LastName{ get; set; }
public string Salary{ get; set; } = "Not Enough";

// ...
}
```

As shown here, to define a constructor you create a method with no return type, whose method name is identical to the class name.

The constructor is the method that the runtime calls to initialize an instance of the object. In this case, the constructor takes the first name and the last name as parameters, allowing the programmer to specify these names when instantiating the Employee object. Listing 6.27 is an example of how to call a constructor.

LISTING 6.27: Calling a Constructor

```csharp
class Program
{
  static void Main()
  {
      Employee employee;
      employee = new Employee("Inigo", "Montoya");
      employee.Salary = "Too Little";

      System.Console.WriteLine(
          "{0} {1}: {2}",
          employee.FirstName,
          employee.LastName,
          employee.Salary);
  }
  // ...
}
```

Notice that the new operator returns the type of the object being instantiated (even though no return type or return statement was specified explicitly in the constructor's declaration or implementation). In addition, you have removed the initialization code for the first and last names because that initialization takes place within the constructor. In this example, you don't initialize Salary within the constructor, so the code assigning the salary still appears.

Developers should take care when using both assignment at declaration time and assignment within constructors. Assignments within the constructor will occur after any assignments are made when a field is declared (such as string Salary = "Not enough" in Listing 6.5). There-fore, assignment within a constructor will override any value assigned at declaration time. This subtlety can lead to a misinterpretation of the code by a casual reader who assumes the value after instantiation is the one assigned in the field declaration. Therefore, it is worth considering a cod-ing style that does not mix both declaration assignment and constructor assignment within the same class.

■ ADVANCED TOPIC

Implementation Details of the new Operator

Internally, the interaction between the new operator and the constructor is as follows. The new operator retrieves "empty" memory from the memory manager and then calls the specified constructor, passing a reference to the empty memory to the constructor as the implicit this parameter. Next, the remainder of the constructor chain executes, passing around the refer-ence between constructors. None of the constructors have a return type; behaviorally they all return void. When execution of the constructor chain is complete, the new operator returns the memory reference, now referring to the memory in its initialized form.

Default Constructors

When you add a constructor explicitly, you can no longer instantiate an Employee from within Main() without specifying the first and last names. The code shown in Listing 6.28, therefore, will not compile.

LISTING 6.28: Default Constructor No Longer Available

```csharp
class Program
{
    static void Main()
    {
        Employee employee;
        // ERROR: No overload because method 'Employee'
        // takes '0' arguments
        employee = new Employee();

        // ...
    }
}
```

If a class has no explicitly defined constructor, the C# compiler adds one during compilation. This constructor takes no parameters and therefore is the **default constructor** by definition. As soon as you add an explicit constructor to a class, the C# compiler no longer provides a default constructor. Therefore, with Employee(string firstName, string lastName) defined, the default constructor, Employee(), is not added by the compiler. You could manually add such a constructor, but then you would again be allowing construction of an Employee without specifying the employee name.

It is not necessary to rely on the default constructor defined by the compiler. It is also possible for programmers to define a default constructor explicitly—perhaps one that initializes some fields to particular values. Defining the default constructor simply involves declaring a constructor that takes no parameters.

Object Initializers

Begin 3.0

Starting with C# 3.0, the C# language team added functionality to initialize an object's accessible fields and properties using an **object initializer**. The object initializer consists of a set of member initializers enclosed in curly braces following the constructor call to create the object. Each member initializer is the assignment of an accessible field or property name with a value (see Listing 6.29).

LISTING 6.29: Calling an Object Initializer

```
class Program
{
  static void Main()
  {
       Employee employee1 = new Employee("Inigo", "Montoya")
          { Title = "Computer Nerd", Salary = "Not enough"};
      // ...
  }
}
```

Notice that the same constructor rules apply even when using an object initializer. In fact, the resultant CIL is exactly the same as it would be if the fields or properties were assigned within separate statements immediately following the constructor call. The order of member initializers in C# provides the sequence for property and field assignment in the statements following the constructor call within CIL.

In general, all properties should be initialized to reasonable default values by the time the constructor exits. Moreover, by using validation logic on the setter, it is possible to restrict the assignment of invalid data to a property. On occasion, the values on one or more properties may cause other properties on the same object to contain invalid values. When this occurs, exceptions from the invalid state should be postponed until the invalid interrelated property values become relevant.

Guidelines

DO provide sensible defaults for all properties, ensuring that defaults do not result in a security hole or significantly inefficient code. For automatically implemented properties, set the default via the constructor.

DO allow properties to be set in any order, even if this results in a temporarily invalid object state.

■ ADVANCED TOPIC

Collection Initializers

Using a similar syntax to that of object initializers, collection initializers were added in C# 3.0. Collection initializers support a similar feature set as object initializers, only with collections. Specifically, a collection initializer allows the assignment of items within the collection at the time of the collection's instantiation. Borrowing on the same syntax used for arrays, the collection initializer initializes each item within the collection as part of collection creation. Initializing a list of Employees, for example, involves specifying each item within curly braces following the constructor call, as Listing 6.30 shows.

LISTING 6.30: Calling an Object Initializer

```
class Program
{
  static void Main()
  {
      List<Employee> employees = new List<Employee>()
          {
              new Employee("Inigo", "Montoya"),
```

```
        new Employee("Kevin", "Bost")
    };
    // ...
}
}
```

After the assignment of a new collection instance, the compiler-generated code instantiates each object in sequence and adds them to the collection via the Add( ) method.

End 3.0

■ **ADVANCED TOPIC**

Begin 7.0

Finalizers

Constructors define what happens during the instantiation process of a class. To define what happens when an object is destroyed, C# provides the finalizer construct. Unlike destructors in C++, finalizers do not run immediately after an object goes out of scope. Rather, the finalizer executes at some unspecified time after an object is determined to be "unreachable." Specifically, the garbage collector identifies objects with finalizers during a garbage collection cycle, and instead of immediately de-allocating those objects, it adds them to a finalization queue. A separate thread runs through each object in the finalization queue and calls the object's finalizer before removing it from the queue and making it available for the garbage collector again. Chapter 10 discusses this process, along with resource cleanup, in depth. Parenthetically, C# 7.0 allows finalizers to be implemented as expression-bodied members.

End 7.0

Overloading Constructors

Constructors can be overloaded—you can have more than one constructor as long as the number or types of the parameters vary. For example, as Listing 6.31 shows, you could provide a constructor that has an employee ID with first and last names, or even just the employee ID.

LISTING 6.31: Overloading a Constructor

```
class Employee
{
    public Employee(string firstName, string lastName)
```

```
        {
            FirstName = firstName;
            LastName = lastName;
        }

        public Employee(
            int id, string firstName, string lastName )
        {
            Id = id;
            FirstName = firstName;
            LastName = lastName;
        }

        public Employee(int id) => Id = id;

        public int Id
        {
            get => Id;
            private set
            {
                // Look up employee name...
                // ...
            }
        }
        public string FirstName { get; set; }
        public string LastName { get; set; }
        public string Salary { get; set; } = "Not Enough";

        // ...
    }
```

This approach enables Program.Main() to instantiate an employee
from the first and last names either by passing in the employee ID only
or by passing both the names and the IDs. You would use the constructor
with both the names and the IDs when creating a new employee in the
system. You would use the constructor with only the ID to load up the
employee from a file or a database.

As is the case with method overloading, multiple constructors are used
to support simple scenarios using a small number of parameters and complex scenarios with additional parameters. Consider using optional parameters in favor of overloading so that the default values for "defaulted"
properties are visible in the API. For example, a constructor signature of
Person(string firstName, string lastName, int? age = null)
provides signature documentation that if the Age of a Person is not specified,
it will default to null.

Notice also that, starting with C# 7.0, it is possible to have expression-bodied member implementations of constructors, as in

Begin 7.0

End 7.0

```
public Employee(int id) => Id = id;
```

Guidelines

DO use the same name for constructor parameters (camelCase) and properties (PascalCase) if the constructor parameters are used to simply set the property.

DO provide constructor optional parameters and/or convenience constructor overloads that initialize properties with good defaults.

DO allow properties to be set in any order, even if this results in a temporarily invalid object state.

Constructor Chaining: Calling Another Constructor Using `this`

Notice in Listing 6.31 that the initialization code for the `Employee` object is now duplicated in multiple places and therefore has to be maintained in multiple places. The amount of code is small, but there are ways to eliminate the duplication by calling one constructor from another—**constructor chaining**—using **constructor initializers**. Constructor initializers determine which constructor to call before executing the implementation of the current constructor (see Listing 6.32).

LISTING 6.32: Calling One Constructor from Another

```
class Employee
{
    public Employee(string firstName, string lastName)
    {
        FirstName = firstName;
        LastName = lastName;
    }

    public Employee(
        int id, string firstName, string lastName )
        : this(firstName, lastName)
    {
        Id = id;
    }
```

```csharp
    public Employee(int id)
    {
        Id = id;

        // Look up employee name...
        // ...

            // NOTE: Member constructors cannot be
            // called explicitly inline
            // this(id, firstName, lastName);
    }

    public int Id { get; private set; }
    public string FirstName { get; set; }
    public string LastName { get; set; }
    public string Salary { get; set; } = "Not Enough";

    // ...
}
```

To call one constructor from another within the same class (for the same object instance), C# uses a colon followed by the this keyword, followed by the parameter list on the callee constructor's declaration. In this case, the constructor that takes all three parameters calls the constructor that takes two parameters. Often, this calling pattern is reversed—that is, the constructor with the fewest parameters calls the constructor with the most parameters, passing defaults for the parameters that are not known.

■ BEGINNER TOPIC

Centralizing Initialization

Notice that in the Employee(int id) constructor implementation from Listing 6.32, you cannot call this(firstName, LastName) because no such parameters exist on this constructor. To enable such a pattern in which all initialization code happens through one method, you must create a separate method, as shown in Listing 6.33.

LISTING 6.33: Providing an Initialization Method

```csharp
class Employee
{
  public Employee(string firstName, string lastName)
  {
      int id;
      // Generate an employee ID...
```

```
        // ...
        Initialize(id, firstName, lastName);
    }


    public Employee(int id, string firstName, string lastName )
    {
        Initialize(id, firstName, lastName);
    }


    public Employee(int id)
    {
        string firstName;
        string lastName;
        Id = id;

        // Look up employee data
        // ...

        Initialize(id, firstName, lastName);
    }


    private void Initialize(
        int id, string firstName, string lastName)
    {

        Id = id;
        FirstName = firstName;
        LastName = lastName;
    }
    // ...
}
```

In this case, the method is called `Initialize()`, and it takes both the names and the employee IDs. Note that you can continue to call one constructor from another, as shown in Listing 6.32.

Deconstructors

Constructors allow you to take multiple parameters and encapsulate them all into a single object. Up until C# 7.0, there was no explicit construct for implementing the reverse—unwrapping the encapsulated item into its constituent parts. Sure, you could manually assign each property to a variable; however, if there were a significant number of such variables, it would require many separate statements. With C#'s 7.0 syntax for tuples this becomes significantly easier. You could, for example, declare a method like the `Deconstruct()` method shown in Listing 6.34.

Begin 7.0

LISTING 6.34: Providing an Initialization Method

```csharp
class Employee
{
    public void Deconstruct(
        out int id, out string firstName,
        out string lastName, out string salary)
    {
        (id, firstName, lastName, salary) =
            (Id, FirstName, LastName, Salary);
    }
    // ...
}
```

```csharp
class Program
{
    static void Main()
    {
        Employee employee;
        employee = new Employee("Inigo", "Montoya");
        employee.Salary = "Too Little";

        employee.Deconstruct(out _, out string firstName,
            out string lastName, out string salary)

        System.Console.WriteLine(
            "{0} {1}: {2}",
            firstName, lastName, salary);
    }
}
```

Such a method could be invoked directly, as one would expect from Chapter 5, declaring the out parameters inline.

Starting with C# 7.0, it is possible to invoke the Deconstruct() method—the **deconstructor**—implicitly by assigning the object instance to a tuple directly (this time assuming the assigned variables are already declared):

```csharp
(_, firstName, lastName, salary) = employee;
```

The syntax results in the identical CIL code as that highlighted in Listing 6.34—it is just a simpler syntax (and a little less indicative that the Deconstruct() method is invoked).

Note that the syntax allows for variables matching the out parameter assignments using tuple syntax. It does not allow for the assignment of a tuple type, either

```csharp
(int, string, string, string) tuple = employee;
```

or with named items as in

```
(int id, string firstName, string lastName, string salary) tuple = employee
```

To declare a deconstructor, the method name must be `Deconstruct` and with a signature that returns void and exclusively accepts two or more `out` parameters. And, given such a signature, it is possible to assign an object instance directly to a tuple without the explicit method invocation.

End 7.0

Static Members

The `HelloWorld` example in Chapter 1 briefly touched on the keyword `static`. This section defines the `static` keyword more fully.

First, let's consider an example. Assume that the employee `Id` value needs to be unique for each employee. One way to accomplish this is to store a counter to track each employee ID. If the value is stored as an instance field, however, every time you instantiate an object, a new `NextId` field will be created such that every instance of the `Employee` object will consume memory for that field. The biggest problem is that each time an `Employee` object is instantiated, the `NextId` value on all of the previously instantiated `Employee` objects needs to be updated with the next ID value. In this case, what you need is a single field that all `Employee` object instances share.

Language Contrast: C++/Visual Basic—Global Variables and Functions

Unlike many of the languages that came before it, C# does not have global variables or global functions. All fields and methods in C# appear within the context of a class. The equivalent of a global field or function within the realm of C# is a static field or function. There is no functional difference between global variables/functions and C# static fields/methods, except that static fields/methods can include access modifiers, such as private, that can limit the access and provide better encapsulation.

Static Fields

To define data that is available across multiple instances, you use the `static` keyword, as demonstrated in Listing 6.35.

LISTING 6.35: **Declaring a Static Field**

```csharp
class Employee
{
  public Employee(string firstName, string lastName)
  {
      FirstName = firstName;
      LastName = lastName;
      Id = NextId;
      NextId++;
  }

  // ...

  public static int NextId;
  public int Id { get; set; }
  public string FirstName { get; set; }
  public string LastName { get; set; }
  public string Salary { get; set; } = "Not Enough";

  // ...
}
```

In this example, the NextId field declaration includes the static modifier and therefore is called a **static field**. Unlike Id, a single storage location for NextId is shared across all instances of Employee. Inside the Employee constructor, you assign the new Employee object's Id the value of NextId immediately before incrementing the Id. When another Employee class is created, NextId will be incremented and the new Employee object's Id field will hold a different value.

Just as **instance fields** (nonstatic fields) can be initialized at declaration time, so can static fields, as demonstrated in Listing 6.36.

LISTING 6.36: **Assigning a Static Field at Declaration**

```csharp
class Employee
{
  // ...
  public static int NextId = 42;
  // ...
}
```

Unlike with instance fields, if no initialization for a static field is provided, the static field will automatically be assigned its default value (0, null, false, and so on)—the equivalent of default(T), where T is the name of the type. As a result, it will be possible to access the static field even if it has never been explicitly assigned in the C# code.

Nonstatic fields, or instance fields, provide a new storage location for each object to which they belong. In contrast, static fields don't belong to the instance, but rather to the class itself. As a result, you access a static field from outside a class via the class name. Consider the new `Program` class shown in Listing 6.37 (using the `Employee` class from Listing 6.35).

LISTING 6.37: Accessing a Static Field

```
using System;

class Program
{
  static void Main()
  {
      Employee.NextId = 1000000;

      Employee employee1 = new Employee(
          "Inigo", "Montoya");
      Employee employee2 = new Employee(
          "Princess", "Buttercup");

      Console.WriteLine(
          "{0} {1} ({2})",
          employee1.FirstName,
          employee1.LastName,
          employee1.Id);
      Console.WriteLine(
          "{0} {1} ({2})",
          employee2.FirstName,
          employee2.LastName,
          employee2.Id);

      Console.WriteLine(
          $"NextId = { Employee.NextId }");
  }

  // ...
}
```

Output 6.8 shows the results of Listing 6.37.

OUTPUT 6.8

```
Inigo Montoya (1000000)
Princess Buttercup (1000001)
NextId = 1000002
```

To set and retrieve the initial value of the `NextId` static field, you use the class name, `Employee`, rather than a reference to an instance of the type. The only place you can omit the class name is within the class itself (or a derived class). In other words, the `Employee(...)` constructor did not need to use `Employee.NextId` because the code appeared within the context of the `Employee` class itself, and therefore, the context was already understood. The scope of a variable is the program text in which the variable can be referred to by its unqualified name; the scope of a static field is the text of the class (and any derived classes).

Even though you refer to static fields slightly differently than you refer to instance fields, it is not possible to define a static field and an instance field with the same name in the same class. The possibility of mistakenly referring to the wrong field is high, so the C# designers decided to prevent such code. Overlap in names, therefore, introduces conflict within the declaration space.

■ **BEGINNER TOPIC**

Data Can Be Associated with Both a Class and an Object

Both classes and objects can have associated data, just as can the molds and the widgets created from them.

For example, a mold could have data corresponding to the number of widgets it created, the serial number of the next widget, the current color of the plastic injected into the mold, and the number of widgets it produces per hour. Similarly, a widget has its own serial number, its own color, and perhaps the date and time when the widget was created. Although the color of the widget corresponds to the color of the plastic within the mold at the time the widget was created, it obviously does not contain data corresponding to the color of the plastic currently in the mold, or the serial number of the next widget to be produced.

In designing objects, programmers should take care to declare both fields and methods appropriately, as static or instance based. In general, you should declare methods that don't access any instance data as static methods, and methods that access instance data (where the instance is not passed in as a parameter) as instance methods. Static fields store data corresponding to the class, such as defaults for new instances or the number of instances that have been created. Instance fields store data associated with the object.

Static Methods

Just as with static fields, you access static methods directly off the class name—for example, as `Console.ReadLine()`. Furthermore, it is not necessary to have an instance to access the method.

Listing 6.38 provides another example of both declaring and calling a static method.

LISTING 6.38: Defining a Static Method on `DirectoryInfo`

```
public static class DirectoryInfoExtension
{
    public static void CopyTo(
        DirectoryInfo sourceDirectory, string target,
        SearchOption option, string searchPattern)
    {
        if (target[target.Length - 1] !=
            Path.DirectorySeparatorChar)
        {
            target += Path.DirectorySeparatorChar;
        }
        if (!Directory.Exists(target))
        {
            Directory.CreateDirectory(target);
        }

        for (int i = 0; i < searchPattern.Length; i++)
        {
            foreach (string file in
                Directory.GetFiles(
                    sourceDirectory.FullName, searchPattern))
            {
                File.Copy(file,
                    target + Path.GetFileName(file), true);
            }
        }

        // Copy subdirectories (recursively)
        if (option == SearchOption.AllDirectories)
        {
            foreach(string element in
                Directory.GetDirectories(
                    sourceDirectory.FullName))
            {
                Copy(element,
                    target + Path.GetFileName(element),
                    searchPattern);
            }
        }
    }
}
```

```
// ...
DirectoryInfo directory = new DirectoryInfo(".\\Source");
directory.MoveTo(".\\Root");
DirectoryInfoExtension.CopyTo(
    directory, ".\\Target",
    SearchOption.AllDirectories, "*");
// ...
```

In Listing 6.38, the `DirectoryInfoExtension.Copy()` method takes a `DirectoryInfo` object and copies the underlying directory structure to a new location.

Because static methods are not referenced through a particular instance, the `this` keyword is invalid inside a static method. In addition, it is not possible to access either an instance field or an instance method directly from within a static method without a reference to the particular instance to which the field or method belongs. (Note that `Main()` is another example of a static method.)

One might have expected this method on the `System.IO.Directory` class or as an instance method on `System.IO.DirectoryInfo`. Since neither exists, Listing 6.38 defines such a method on an entirely new class. In the section "Extension Methods" later in this chapter, we show how to make it appear as an instance method on `DirectoryInfo`.

Static Constructors

In addition to static fields and methods, C# supports **static constructors**. Static constructors are provided as a means to initialize the class itself rather than the instances of a class. Such constructors are not called explicitly; instead, the runtime calls static constructors automatically upon first access to the class, whether by calling a regular constructor or by accessing a static method or field on the class. Because the static constructor cannot be called explicitly, no parameters are allowed on static constructors.

You use static constructors to initialize the static data within the class to a particular value, primarily when the initial value involves more complexity than a simple assignment at declaration time. Consider Listing 6.39.

LISTING 6.39: Declaring a Static Constructor

```
class Employee
{
  static Employee()
  {
      Random randomGenerator = new Random();
```

```
        NextId = randomGenerator.Next(101, 999);
    }

    // ...
    public static int NextId = 42;
    // ...
}
```

Listing 6.39 assigns the initial value of NextId to be a random integer between 100 and 1,000. Because the initial value involves a method call, the NextId initialization code appears within a static constructor and not as part of the declaration.

If assignment of NextId occurs within both the static constructor and the declaration, it is not obvious what the value will be when initialization concludes. The C# compiler generates CIL in which the declaration assignment is moved to be the first statement within the static constructor. Therefore, NextId will contain the value returned by randomGenerator.Next(101, 999) instead of a value assigned during NextId's declaration. Assignments within the static constructor, therefore, will take precedence over assignments that occur as part of the field declaration, as was the case with instance fields. Note that there is no support for defining a static finalizer.

Be careful not to throw an exception from a static constructor, as this will render the type unusable for the remainder of the application's lifetime.[7]

▪ ADVANCED TOPIC

Favor Static Initialization during Declaration

Static constructors execute before the first access to any member of a class, whether it is a static field, another static member, or an instance constructor. To support this practice, the compiler injects a check into all type static members and constructors to ensure that the static constructor runs first.

Without the static constructor, the compiler initializes all static members to their default values and avoids adding the static constructor check. The result is that static assignment initialization is called before any static fields are accessed but not necessarily before all static methods or

---

7. Technically the application domain's lifetime—the Common Language Runtime's virtual equivalent of an operating system process.

any instance constructor is invoked. This might provide a performance improvement if initialization of static members is expensive and is not needed before accessing a static field. For this reason, you should consider either initializing static fields inline rather than using a static constructor or initializing them at declaration time.

> ### Guidelines
>
> **CONSIDER** initializing static fields inline rather than explicitly using static constructors or declaration assigned values.

Static Properties

Begin 2.0

You also can declare properties as static. For example, Listing 6.40 wraps the data for the next ID into a property.

LISTING 6.40: Declaring a Static Property

```
class Employee
{
    // ...
    public static int NextId
    {
        get
        {
            return _NextId;
        }
        private set
        {
            _NextId = value;
        }
    }
    public static int _NextId = 42;
    // ...
}
```

It is almost always better to use a static property rather than a public static field, because public static fields are callable from anywhere, whereas a static property offers at least some level of encapsulation.

Begin 6.0

In C# 6.0, the entire NextId implementation—including an inaccessible backing field—can be simplified down to an automatically implemented

End 6.0

property with an initializer:

```
public static int NextId { get; private set; } = 42;
```

Static Classes

Some classes do not contain any instance fields. Consider, for example, a
Math class that has functions corresponding to the mathematical operations Max( ) and Min( ), as shown in Listing 6.41.

LISTING 6.41: Declaring a Static Class

```csharp
// Static class introduced in C# 2.0
public static class SimpleMath
{
  // params allows the number of parameters to vary
  public static int Max(params int[] numbers)
  {
    // Check that there is at least one item in numbers
    if(numbers.Length == 0)
    {
        throw new ArgumentException(
            "numbers cannot be empty", "numbers");
    }

    int result;
    result = numbers[0];
    foreach (int number in numbers)
    {
        if(number > result)
        {
            result = number;
        }
    }
    return result;
  }

  // params allows the number of parameters to vary
  public static int Min(params int[] numbers)
  {
    // Check that there is at least one item in numbers
    if(numbers.Length == 0)
    {
        throw new ArgumentException(
            "numbers cannot be empty", "numbers");
    }

    int result;
    result = numbers[0];
    foreach (int number in numbers)
    {
        if(number < result)
        {
            result = number;
        }
    }
```

2.0

```
            return result;
        }
    }
```

```
    public class Program
    {
        public static void Main(string[] args)
        {
            int[] numbers = new int[args.Length];
            for (int count = 0; count < args.Length; count++)
            {
                numbers[count] = args[count].Length;
            }

            Console.WriteLine(
                $@"Longest argument length = {
                    SimpleMath.Max(numbers) }");
            Console.WriteLine(
                $@"Shortest argument length = {
                    SimpleMath.Min(numbers) }");
        }
    }
```

This class does not have any instance fields (or methods), so creation of such a class would be pointless. Consequently, the class is decorated with the static keyword. The static keyword on a class provides two facilities. First, it prevents a programmer from writing code that instantiates the SimpleMath class. Second, it prevents the declaration of any instance fields or methods within the class. Because the class cannot be instantiated, instance members would be pointless. The Program class in prior listings is another good candidate for a static class because it too contains only static members.

One more distinguishing characteristic of the static class is that the C# compiler automatically marks it as abstract and sealed within the CIL. This designates the class as **inextensible**; in other words, no class can be derived from this class or even instantiate it.

In the previous chapter, we saw that the using static directive can be used with static classes such as SimpleMath. For example, adding a using static SimpleMath; declarative at the top of Listing 6.41 would allow you to invoke Max without the SimpleMath prefix:

```
            Console.WriteLine(
                $@"Longest argument length = { Max(numbers) }");
```

Extension Methods

Consider the `System.IO.DirectoryInfo` class, which is used to manipulate filesystem directories. This class supports functionality to list the files and subdirectories (`DirectoryInfo.GetFiles()`) as well as the capability to move the directory (`DirectoryInfo.Move()`). One feature it doesn't support directly is the copy feature. If you needed such a method, you would have to implement it, as shown earlier in Listing 6.38.

The `DirectoryInfoExtension.Copy()` method is a standard static method declaration. However, notice that calling this `Copy()` method is different from calling the `DirectoryInfo.Move()` method. This is unfortunate. Ideally, we want to add a method to `DirectoryInfo` so that, given an instance, we could call `Copy()` as an instance method: `directory.Copy()`.

C# 3.0 simulates the creation of an instance method on a different class via **extension methods**. To do this, we simply change the signature of our static method so that the first parameter—that is, the data type we are extending—is prefixed with the `this` keyword (see Listing 6.42).

LISTING 6.42: Static Copy Method for `DirectoryInfo`

```
public static class DirectoryInfoExtension
{
  public static void CopyTo(
      this DirectoryInfo sourceDirectory, string target,
      SearchOption option, string searchPattern)
  {
    // ...
  }
}


// ...
    DirectoryInfo directory = new DirectoryInfo(".\\Source");
    directory.CopyTo(".\\Target",
        SearchOption.AllDirectories, "*");
  // ...
```

3.0

With this simple addition to C# 3.0, it is now possible to add "instance methods" to any class, including classes that are not within the same assembly. The resultant CIL code, however, is identical to what the compiler creates when calling the extension method as a normal static method.

Extension method requirements are as follows:

- The first parameter corresponds to the type that the method extends or on which it operates.
- To designate the extension method, prefix the extended type with the `this` modifier.
- To access the method as an extension method, import the extending type's namespace via a `using` directive (or place the extending class in the same namespace as the calling code).

If the extension method signature matches a signature already found on the extended type (i.e., if `CopyTo()` already existed on `DirectoryInfo`), the extension method will never be called except as a normal static method.

Note that specializing a type via inheritance (covered in detail in Chapter 7) is preferable to using an extension method. Extension methods do not provide a clean versioning mechanism, because the addition of a matching signature to the extended type will take precedence over the extension method without warning of the change. The subtlety of this behavior is more pronounced for extended classes whose source code you don't control. Another minor point is that, although development IDEs support IntelliSense for extension methods, simply reading through the calling code does not make it obvious that a method is an extension method.

In general, you should use extension methods sparingly. Do not, for example, define them on type `object`. Chapter 8 discusses how to use extension methods in association with an interface. Without such an association, defining extension methods is rare.

Guidelines

AVOID frivolously defining extension methods, especially on types you don't own.

Encapsulating the Data

In addition to properties and the access modifiers we looked at earlier in the chapter, there are several other specialized ways of encapsulating the data within a class. For instance, there are two more field modifiers. The first is the `const` modifier, which you already encountered when declaring local variables. The second is the capability of fields to be defined as read-only.

const

Just as with `const` values, a `const` field contains a compile-time–determined value that cannot be changed at runtime. Values such as pi make good candidates for constant field declarations. Listing 6.43 shows an example of declaring a `const` field.

LISTING 6.43: Declaring a Constant Field

```
class ConvertUnits
{
   public const float CentimetersPerInch = 2.54F;
   public const int CupsPerGallon = 16;
   // ...
}
```

Constant fields are static automatically, since no new field instance is required for each object instance. Declaring a constant field as `static` explicitly will cause a compile error. Also, constant fields are usually declared only for types that have literal values (e.g., `string`, `int`, and `double`). Types such as `Program` or `System.Guid` cannot be used for constant fields.

It is important that the types of values used in `public` constant expressions are permanent in time. Values such as pi, Avogadro's number, and the circumference of the Earth are good examples. However, values that could potentially change over time are not. Build numbers, population counts, and exchange rates would be poor choices for constants.

■ **Guidelines**

DO use constant fields for values that will never change.
DO NOT use constant fields for values that will change over time.

■ **ADVANCED TOPIC**

Public Constants Should Be Permanent Values

Publicly accessible constants should be permanent, because changing the value of a constant will not necessarily take effect in the assemblies that use it. If an assembly references a constant from a different assembly, the value of the constant is compiled directly into the referencing assembly. Therefore, if the value in the referenced assembly is changed but the referencing assembly is not recompiled, the referencing assembly will still use the original value, not the new value. Values that could potentially change in the future should be specified as `readonly` instead.

readonly

Unlike `const`, the `readonly` modifier is available only for fields (not for local variables). It declares that the field value is modifiable only from inside the constructor or via an initializer during declaration. Listing 6.44 demonstrates how to declare a read-only field.

LISTING 6.44: Declaring a Field as readonly

```
class Employee
{
  public Employee(int id)
  {
      _Id = id;
  }

  // ...

  public readonly int _Id;
  public int Id
  {
      get { return _Id; }
  }

  // Error: A readonly field cannot be assigned to (except
  // in a constructor or a variable initializer)
  // public void SetId(int id) =>
  //          _Id = id;

  // ...
}
```

Unlike constant fields, `readonly`-decorated fields can vary from one instance to the next. In fact, a read-only field's value can change within the constructor. Furthermore, read-only fields occur as either instance or static fields. Another key distinction is that you can assign the value of a read-only field at execution time rather than just at compile time. Given that read-only fields must be set in the constructor or initializer, such fields are the one case where the compiler requires the fields be accessed from code outside their corresponding property. Besides this one exception, you should avoid accessing a backing field from anywhere other than its wrapping property.

Another important feature of `readonly`-decorated fields over `const` fields is that read-only fields are not limited to types with literal values. It is possible, for example, to declare a `readonly` `System.Guid` instance field:

```
public static readonly Guid ComIUnknownGuid =
    new Guid("00000000-0000-0000-C000-000000000046");
```

The same, however, is not possible using a constant because of the fact that there is no C# literal representation of a GUID.

Given the guideline that fields should not be accessed from outside their wrapping property, those programming in a C# 6.0 (or later) world will discover that that there is almost never a need to use the `readonly` modifier. Instead, it is preferable to use a read-only automatically implemented property, as discussed earlier in the chapter.

Begin 6.0

Consider Listing 6.45 for one more read-only example.

LISTING 6.45: Declaring a Read-Only Automatically Implemented Property

```
class TicTacToeBoard
{
  // Set both players' moves to all false (blank)
  //    |   |
  // ---+---+---
  //    |   |
  // ---+---+---
  //    |   |
  public bool[,,] Cells { get; } = new bool[2, 3, 3];
  // Error: The property Cells cannot
  // be assigned to because it is read-only
  // public void SetCells(bool[,,] value) =>
  //         Cells = new bool[2, 3, 3];

  // ...
}
```

Whether implemented using C# 6.0 read-only automatically implemented properties or the readonly modifier on a field, ensuring immutability of the array reference is a useful defensive coding technique. It ensures that the array instance remains the same, while allowing the elements within the array to change. Without the read-only constraint, it would be all too easy to mistakenly assign a new array to the member, thereby discarding the existing array rather than updating individual array elements. In other words, using a read-only approach with an array does not freeze the contents of the array. Rather, it freezes the array instance (and therefore the number of elements in the array) because it is not possible to reassign the value to a new instance. The elements of the array are still writeable.

Guidelines

DO favor read-only automatically implemented properties in C# 6.0 (or later) over read-only fields.

DO use public static readonly modified fields for predefined object instances prior to C# 6.0.

AVOID changing a public readonly modified field in pre-C# 6.0 to a read-only automatically implemented property in C# 6.0 (or later) if version API compatibility is required.

End 6.0

Nested Classes

In addition to defining methods and fields within a class, it is possible to define a class within a class. Such classes are called **nested classes**. You use a nested class when the class makes little sense outside the context of its containing class.

Consider a class that handles the command-line options of a program. Such a class is generally unique to each program, so there is no reason to make a CommandLine class accessible from outside the class that contains Main(). Listing 6.46 demonstrates such a nested class.

LISTING 6.46: Defining a Nested Class

```
// CommandLine is nested within Program
class Program
{
```

```csharp
// Define a nested class for processing the command line
private class CommandLine
{
    public CommandLine(string[] arguments)
    {
        for(int argumentCounter=0;
            argumentCounter<arguments.Length;
            argumentCounter++)
        {
            switch (argumentCounter)
            {
                case 0:
                    Action = arguments[0].ToLower();
                    break;
                case 1:
                    Id = arguments[1];
                    break;
                case 2:
                    FirstName = arguments[2];
                    break;
                case 3:
                    LastName = arguments[3];
                    break;
            }
        }
    }
    public string Action;
    public string Id;
    public string FirstName;
    public string LastName;
}

static void Main(string[] args)
{
    CommandLine commandLine = new CommandLine(args);

    switch (commandLine.Action)
    {
        case "new":
            // Create a new employee
            // ...
            break;
        case "update":
            // Update an existing employee's data
            // ...
            break;
        case "delete":
            // Remove an existing employee's file
            // ...
            break;
```

```
            default:
                Console.WriteLine(
                    "Employee.exe " +
            "new|update|delete <id> [firstname] [lastname]");
                break;
        }
    }
}
```

The nested class in this example is `Program.CommandLine`. As with all class members, no containing class identifier is needed from inside the containing class, so you can simply refer to it as `CommandLine`.

One unique characteristic of nested classes is the ability to specify `private` as an access modifier for the class itself. Because the purpose of this class is to parse the command line and place each argument into a separate field, `Program.CommandLine` is relevant only to the `Program` class in this application. The use of the `private` access modifier defines the intended accessibility of the class and prevents access from outside the class. You can do this only if the class is nested.

The `this` member within a nested class refers to an instance of the nested class, not the containing class. One way for a nested class to access an instance of the containing class is if the containing class instance is explicitly passed, such as via a constructor or a method parameter.

Another interesting characteristic of nested classes is that they can access any member on the containing class, including private members. The converse is not true, however: It is not possible for the containing class to access a private member of the nested class.

Nested classes are rare. They should not be defined if they are likely to be referenced outside the containing type. Furthermore, treat `public` nested classes with suspicion; they indicate potentially poor code that is likely to be confusing and hard to discover.

Guidelines

AVOID publicly exposed nested types. The only exception is if the declaration of such a type is unlikely or pertains to an advanced customization scenario.

Partial Classes

Begin 2.0

Another language feature added in C# 2.0 is **partial classes**. Partial classes are portions of a class that the compiler can combine to form a complete class. Although you could define two or more partial classes within the same file, the general purpose of a partial class is to allow the splitting of a class definition across multiple files. Primarily this is useful for tools that are generating or modifying code. With partial classes, the tools can work on a file separate from the one the developer is manually coding.

Defining a Partial Class

C# 2.0 (and later) allows declaration of a partial class by prepending a contextual keyword, `partial`, immediately before `class`, as Listing 6.47 shows.

LISTING 6.47: Defining a Partial Class

```
// File: Program1.cs
partial class Program
{
}
```

```
// File: Program2.cs
partial class Program
{
}
```

In this case, each portion of `Program` is placed into a separate file, as identified by the comment.

Besides their use with code generators, another common use of partial classes is to place any nested classes into their own files. This is in accordance with the coding convention that places each class definition within its own file. For example, Listing 6.48 places the `Program.CommandLine` class into a file separate from the core `Program` members.

LISTING 6.48: Defining a Nested Class in a Separate Partial Class

```csharp
// File: Program.cs
partial class Program
{
    static void Main(string[] args)
    {
        CommandLine commandLine = new CommandLine(args);

        switch (commandLine.Action)
        {
            // ...
        }
    }
}
```

```csharp
// File: Program+CommandLine.cs
partial class Program
{
    // Define a nested class for processing the command line
    private class CommandLine
    {
        // ...
    }
}
```

Partial classes do not allow for extending compiled classes or classes in other assemblies. They are simply a means of splitting a class implementation across multiple files within the same assembly.

End 2.0

Partial Methods

Begin 3.0

Beginning with C# 3.0, the language designers added the concept of partial methods, extending the partial class concept of C# 2.0. Partial methods are allowed only within partial classes, and like partial classes, their primary purpose is to accommodate code generation.

Consider a code generation tool that generates the `Person.Designer.cs` file for the `Person` class based on a `Person` table within a database. This tool examines the table and creates properties for each column in the table. The problem, however, is that frequently the tool cannot generate any validation logic that may be required because this logic is based on business rules that are not embedded into the database table definition. To overcome this difficulty, the developer of the `Person` class needs to add the validation logic. It is undesirable to modify `Person.Designer.cs` directly, because if the file is regenerated (e.g., to accommodate an additional column in the database), the changes would be lost. Instead, the structure of the code for `Person` needs to be separated out so that the generated code appears in one file and the custom code (with business rules) is placed into a separate file unaffected by any regeneration. As we saw in the preceding section, partial classes are well suited for the task of splitting a class across multiple files, but they are not always sufficient. In many cases, we also need **partial methods**.

Partial methods allow for a declaration of a method without requiring an implementation. However, when the optional implementation is included, it can be located in one of the sister partial class definitions, likely in a separate file. Listing 6.49 shows the partial method declaration and the implementation for the `Person` class.

LISTING 6.49: Defining a Nested Class in a Separate Partial Class

```csharp
// File: Person.Designer.cs
public partial class Person
{
    #region Extensibility Method Definitions
    partial void OnLastNameChanging(string value);
    partial void OnFirstNameChanging(string value);
    #endregion

    // ...
    public System.Guid PersonId
    {
        // ...
    }
    private System.Guid _PersonId;

    // ...
    public string LastName
    {
        get
        {
            return _LastName;
        }
        set
        {
            if ((_LastName != value))
            {
```

3.0

```
                OnLastNameChanging(value);
                _LastName = value;
            }
        }
    }
    private string _LastName;

    // ...
    public string FirstName
    {
        get
        {
            return _FirstName;
        }
        set
        {
            if ((_FirstName != value))
            {
                OnFirstNameChanging(value);
                _FirstName = value;
            }
        }
    }
    private string _FirstName;

}
```

```
// File: Person.cs
partial class Person
{
    partial void OnLastNameChanging(string value)
    {
        if (value == null)
        {
            throw new ArgumentNullException("value");
        }
        if(value.Trim().Length == 0)
        {
            throw new ArgumentException(
                "LastName cannot be empty.",
                "value");
        }
    }
}
```

In the listing of Person.Designer.cs are declarations for the OnLastNameChanging() and OnFirstNameChanging() methods. Furthermore, the properties for the last and first names make calls to their corresponding changing methods. Even though the declarations of the changing methods contain no implementation, this code will successfully compile. The key is that the method declarations are prefixed with the contextual keyword `partial` in addition to the class that contains such methods.

In Listing 6.49, only the `OnLastNameChanging()` method is implemented. In this case, the implementation checks the suggested new `LastName` value and throws an exception if it is not valid. Notice that the signatures for `OnLastNameChanging()` between the two locations match.

Any partial method must return `void`. If the method didn't return `void` and the implementation was not provided, what would the expected return be from a call to a nonimplemented method? To avoid any invalid assumptions about the return, the C# designers decided to prohibit methods with returns other than `void`. Similarly, `out` parameters are not allowed on partial methods. If a return value is required, `ref` parameters may be used.

In summary, partial methods allow generated code to call methods that have not necessarily been implemented. Furthermore, if there is no implementation provided for a partial method, no trace of the partial method appears in the CIL. This helps keep code size small while keeping flexibility high.

End 3.0

SUMMARY

This chapter explained C# constructs for classes and object orientation in C#. Its coverage included a discussion of declaring fields, and how to access them on a class instance.

This chapter also discussed the key decision of whether to store data on a per-instance basis or across all instances of a type. Static data is associated with the class, and instance data is stored on each object.

In addition, the chapter explored encapsulation in the context of access modifiers for methods and data. The C# construct of properties was introduced, and you saw how to use it to encapsulate private fields.

The next chapter focuses on how to associate classes with each other via inheritance and explores the benefits derived from this object-oriented construct.

■7■
Inheritance

C HAPTER 6 DISCUSSED HOW ONE CLASS can reference other classes via fields and properties. This chapter discusses how to use the inheritance relationship between classes to build class hierarchies that form an "is a" relationship.

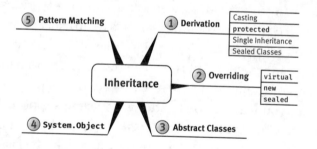

■BEGINNER TOPIC

Inheritance Definitions

The preceding chapter provided an overview of inheritance. Here's a review of the defined terms:

* *Derive/inherit:* Specialize a base class to include additional members or customization of the base class members.

- *Derived/sub/child type:* The specialized type that inherits the members of the more general type.
- *Base/super/parent type:* The general type whose members a derived type inherits.

Inheritance forms an "is a kind of" relationship. The derived type is always implicitly also of the base type. Just as a hard drive is a kind of storage device, so any other type derived from the storage device type is a kind of storage device. Notice that the converse is not necessarily true: A storage device is not necessarily a hard drive.

> ■ **NOTE**
>
> Inheritance within code is used to define an "is a kind of" relationship between two classes where the derived class is a specialization of the base class.

Derivation

It is common to want to extend a given type to add features, such as behavior and data. The purpose of inheritance is to do exactly that. Given a `Person` class, you create an `Employee` class that additionally contains `EmployeeId` and `Department` properties. The reverse approach may also be applied. Given, for example, a `Contact` class within a personal digital assistant (PDA), you may decide to add calendaring support. Toward this effort, you create an `Appointment` class. However, instead of redefining the methods and properties that are common to both classes, you might choose to **refactor** the `Contact` class. Specifically, you could move the common methods and properties on `Contact` into a base class called `PdaItem` from which both `Contact` and `Appointment` derive, as shown in Figure 7.1.

The common items in this case are `Created`, `LastUpdated`, `Name`, `ObjectKey`, and the like. Through derivation, the methods defined on the base class, `PdaItem`, are accessible from all classes derived from `PdaItem`.

When declaring a derived class, follow the class identifier with a colon and then the base class, as Listing 7.1 demonstrates.

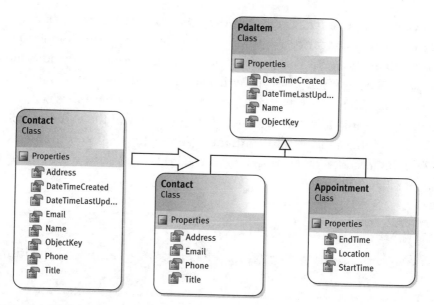

FIGURE 7.1: Refactoring into a Base Class

LISTING 7.1: Deriving One Class from Another

```
public class PdaItem
{
  public string Name { get; set; }

  public DateTime LastUpdated { get; set; }
}
```

```
// Define the Contact class as inheriting the PdaItem class
public class Contact : PdaItem
{
  public string Address { get; set; }
  public string Phone { get; set; }
}
```

Listing 7.2 shows how to access the properties defined in Contact.

LISTING 7.2: Using Inherited Methods

```
public class Program
{
  public static void Main()
  {
    Contact contact = new Contact();
    contact.Name = "Inigo Montoya";

    // ...
  }
}
```

Even though Contact does not directly have a property called Name, all instances of Contact can still access the Name property from PdaItem and use it as though it was part of Contact. Furthermore, any additional classes that derive from Contact will also inherit the members of PdaItem or any class from which PdaItem was derived. The inheritance chain has no practical limit, and each derived class will have all the members of its base class inheritance chain combined (see Listing 7.3). In other words, although Customer doesn't derive from PdaItem directly, it still inherits the members of PdaItem.

> ■ **NOTE**
>
> Via inheritance, each member of a base class will also appear within the chain of derived classes.

LISTING 7.3: Classes Deriving from One Another to Form an Inheritance Chain

```csharp
public class PdaItem : object
{
  // ...
}
```

```csharp
public class Appointment : PdaItem
{
  // ...
}
```

```csharp
public class Contact : PdaItem
{
  // ...
}
```

```csharp
public class Customer : Contact
{
  // ...
}
```

In Listing 7.3, PdaItem is shown explicitly to derive from object. Although C# allows such syntax, it is unnecessary because all classes that don't have some other derivation will derive from object, regardless of whether it is specified.

> **▪ NOTE**
>
> Unless an alternative base class is specified, all classes will derive from
> object by default.

Casting between Base and Derived Types

As Listing 7.4 shows, because derivation forms an "is a" relationship, a
derived type value can always be directly assigned to a base type variable.

LISTING 7.4: Implicit Base Type Casting

```csharp
public class Program
{
  public static void Main()
  {
      // Derived types can be implicitly converted to
      // base types
      Contact contact = new Contact();
      PdaItem item = contact;
      // ...

      // Base types must be cast explicitly to derived types
      contact = (Contact)item;
      // ...
  }
}
```

The derived type, Contact, is a PdaItem and can be assigned directly
to a variable of type PdaItem. This is known as an **implicit conversion**
because no cast operator is required and the conversion will, on principle,
always succeed; that is, it will not throw an exception.

The reverse, however, is not true. A PdaItem is not necessarily a Contact;
it could be an Appointment or some other derived type. Therefore, casting
from the base type to the derived type requires an **explicit cast**, which
could fail at runtime. To perform an explicit cast, you identify the target type within parentheses prior to the original reference, as Listing 7.4
demonstrates.

With the explicit cast, the programmer essentially communicates to
the compiler to trust her—she knows what she is doing—and the C#
compiler allows the conversion to proceed if the target type is derived
from the originating type. Although the C# compiler allows an explicit

conversion at compile time between potentially compatible types, the Common Language Runtime (CLR) will still verify the explicit cast at execution time, throwing an exception if the object instance is not actually of the targeted type.

The C# compiler allows the cast operator even when the type hierarchy allows an implicit conversion. For example, the assignment from `contact` to `item` could use a cast operator as follows:

```
item = (PdaItem)contact;
```

or even when no conversion is necessary:

```
contact = (Contact)contact;
```

> ■ **NOTE**
>
> A derived object can be implicitly converted to its base class. In contrast, converting from the base class to the derived class requires an explicit cast operator, as the conversion could fail. Although the compiler will allow an explicit cast if it is potentially valid, the runtime will still prevent an invalid cast at execution time by throwing an exception.

■ **BEGINNER TOPIC**

Casting within the Inheritance Chain

An implicit conversion to a base class does not instantiate a new instance. Instead, the same instance is simply referred to as the base type, and the capabilities (the accessible members) are those of the base type. It is just like referring to a CD-ROM drive as a "storage device." Since not all storage devices support an eject operation, a CD-ROM drive that is viewed as a storage device cannot be ejected either, and a call to `storageDevice.Eject()` would not compile even though the instantiated object may have been a CDROM object that supported the `Eject()` method.

Similarly, casting down from the base class to the derived class simply begins referring to the type more specifically, expanding the available operations. The restriction is that the actual instantiated type must be an instance of the targeted type (or something derived from it).

Defining Custom Conversions

Conversion between types is not limited to types within a single inheritance chain. It is possible to convert between unrelated types as well, such as converting from an `Address` to `string`, and vice versa. The key is the provision of a conversion operator between the two types. C# allows types to include either explicit or implicit conversion operators. If the operation could possibly fail, such as in a cast from `long` to `int`, developers should choose to define an explicit conversion operator. This warns developers performing the conversion to do so only when they are certain the conversion will succeed, or else to be prepared to catch the exception if it doesn't. They should also use an explicit conversion over an implicit conversion when the conversion is lossy. Converting from a `float` to an `int`, for example, truncates the decimal, which a return cast (from `int` back to `float`) would not recover.

Listing 7.5 shows an example of an implicit conversion operator signature.

LISTING 7.5: **Defining Cast Operators**

```
class GPSCoordinates
{
  // ...

  public static implicit operator UTMCoordinates(
      GPSCoordinates coordinates)
  {
      // ...
  }
}
```

In this case, you have an implicit conversion from `GPSCoordinates` to `UTMCoordinates`. A similar conversion could be written to reverse the process. Note that an explicit conversion could also be written by replacing `implicit` with `explicit`.

private **Access Modifier**

All members of a base class, except for constructors and destructors, are inherited by the derived class. However, just because a member is inherited, that does not mean it is accessible. For example, in Listing 7.6, the private field, _Name, is not available on Contact because private members are accessible only at code locations inside the type that declares them.

LISTING 7.6: Private Members Are Inherited but Not Accessible

```
public class PdaItem
{
  private string _Name;
  // ...
}
```

```
public class Contact : PdaItem
{
  // ...
}
```

```
public class Program
{
  public static void Main()
  {
    Contact contact = new Contact();

    // ERROR:  'PdaItem._Name' is inaccessible
    // due to its protection level
    // contact._Name = "Inigo Montoya";
  }
}
```

As part of respecting the principle of encapsulation, derived classes cannot access members declared as private.[1] This forces the base class developer to make an explicit choice as to whether a derived class gains access to a member. In this case, the base class is defining an API in which _Name can be changed only via the Name property. That way, if validation is added, the derived class will gain the validation benefit automatically because it was unable to access _Name directly from the start.

> ■ **NOTE**
> Derived classes cannot access members declared as private in a base class.

---

1. Except for the corner case when the derived class is also a nested class of the base class.

protected Access Modifier

Encapsulation is finer grained than just `public` or `private`, however. It is possible to define members in base classes that only derived classes can access. As an example, consider the `ObjectKey` property shown in Listing 7.7.

LISTING 7.7: protected Members Are Accessible Only from Derived Classes

```
public class Program
{
  public static void Main()
  {
      Contact contact = new Contact();
      contact.Name = "Inigo Montoya";

      // ERROR:  'PdaItem.ObjectKey' is inaccessible
      // due to its protection level
      // contact.ObjectKey = Guid.NewGuid();
  }
}


public class PdaItem
{
  protected Guid ObjectKey { get; set; }
  // ...
}


public class Contact : PdaItem
{
  void Save()
  {
      // Instantiate a FileStream using <ObjectKey>.dat
      // for the filename
      FileStream stream = System.IO.File.OpenWrite(
          ObjectKey + ".dat");
  }

  void Load(PdaItem pdaItem)
  {
      // ERROR:  'pdaItem.ObjectKey' is inaccessible
      // due to its protection level
      // pdaItem.ObjectKey = ...;

      Contact contact = pdaItem as Contact;
      if(contact != null)
      {
          contact.ObjectKey = ...;
      }

      // ...
  }
}
```

ObjectKey is defined using the protected access modifier. The result is that it is accessible outside of PdaItem only from classes that derive from PdaItem. Contact derives from PdaItem, so all members of Contact have access to ObjectKey. In contrast, Program does not derive from PdaItem, so using the ObjectKey property within Program results in a compile-time error.

> **■ NOTE**
>
> Protected members in the base class are accessible only from the base class and other classes within the derivation chain.

A subtlety shown in the Contact.Load() method is worth noting. Developers are often surprised that it is not possible to access the protected ObjectKey of an explicit PdaItem from code within Contact, even though Contact derives from PdaItem. The reason is that a PdaItem could potentially be an Address, and Contact should not be able to access protected members of Address. Therefore, encapsulation prevents Contact from potentially modifying the ObjectKey of an Address. A successful cast to Contact will bypass the restriction as shown. The governing rule is that accessing a protected member from a derived class requires compile-time determination that the protected member is an instance of the derived class (or a class further derived from it).

Extension Methods

Begin 3.0

Extension methods are technically not members of the type they extend and therefore are not inherited. Nevertheless, because every derived class may be used as an instance of any of its base classes, an extension method on one type also extends every derived type. If we extend a base class such as PdaItem, all the extension methods will also be available in the derived classes. However, as with all extension methods, priority is given to instance methods. If a compatible signature appears anywhere within the inheritance chain, it will take precedence over an extension method.

Requiring extension methods on base types is rare. As with extension methods in general, if the base type's code is available, it is preferable to modify the base type directly. Even in cases where the base type's code is unavailable, programmers should consider whether to add extension methods to an interface that the base type or individual derived types implement. We cover interfaces and how to use them with extension methods in the next chapter.

End 3.0

Single Inheritance

In theory, you can place an unlimited number of classes in an inheritance tree. For example, `Customer` derives from `Contact`, which derives from `PdaItem`, which derives from `object`. However, C# is a **single-inheritance** programming language (as is the CIL language to which C# compiles). This means that a class cannot derive from two classes directly. It is not possible, for example, to have `Contact` derive from both `PdaItem` and `Person`.

Language Contrast: C++—Multiple Inheritance

C#'s single inheritance is one of its major object-oriented differences from C++.

For the rare cases that require a multiple-inheritance class structure, one solution is to use **aggregation**; instead of one class inheriting from another, one class contains an instance of the other. Figure 7.2 shows an example of this class structure. Aggregation occurs when the association relationship defines a core part of the containing object. For multiple inheritance, this involves picking one class as the primary base class (`PdaItem`) and deriving a new class (`Contact`) from that. The second desired base class (`Person`) is added as a field in the derived class (`Contact`). Next, all the nonprivate members on the field (`Person`) are redefined on the derived class (`Contact`), which then delegates the calls out to the field (`Person`). Some code duplication occurs because methods are redeclared; however, this is minimal, since the real method body is implemented only within the aggregated class (`Person`).

In Figure 7.2, `Contact` contains a private property called `InternalPerson` that is drawn as an association to the `Person` class. `Contact` also contains the `FirstName` and `LastName` properties but with no corresponding fields. Instead, the `FirstName` and `LastName` properties simply delegate their

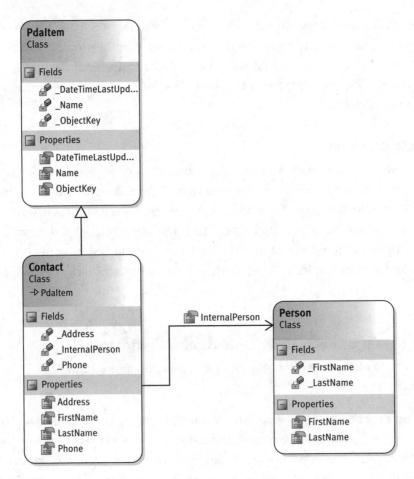

FIGURE 7.2: Simulating Multiple Inheritance Using Aggregation

calls out to `InternalPerson.FirstName` and `InternalPerson.LastName`, respectively. Listing 7.8 shows the resultant code.

LISTING 7.8: Working around Single Inheritance Using Aggregation

```
public class PdaItem
{
  // ...
}

public class Person
{
  // ...
}
```

```
public class Contact : PdaItem
{
   private Person InternalPerson { get; set; }

   public string FirstName
   {
      get { return InternalPerson.FirstName; }
      set { InternalPerson.FirstName = value; }
   }

   public string LastName
   {
      get { return InternalPerson.LastName; }
      set { InternalPerson.LastName = value; }
   }

   // ...
}
```

Besides the added complexity of delegation, another drawback is that any methods added to the field class (`Person`) will require manual addition to the derived class (`Contact`); otherwise, `Contact` will not expose the added functionality.

Sealed Classes

To design a class correctly that others can extend via derivation can be a tricky task that requires testing with examples to verify the derivation will work successfully. Listing 7.9 shows how to avoid unexpected derivation scenarios and problems by marking classes as **sealed**.

LISTING 7.9: Preventing Derivation with Sealed Classes

```
public sealed class CommandLineParser
{
  // ...
}
```

```
// ERROR:  Sealed classes cannot be derived from
public sealed class DerivedCommandLineParser :
  CommandLineParser
{
  // ...
}
```

Sealed classes include the `sealed` modifier, and the result is that they cannot be derived from. The `string` type is an example of a type that uses the `sealed` modifier to prevent derivation.

Overriding the Base Class

All members of a base class are inherited in the derived class, except for constructors and destructors. However, sometimes the base class does not have the optimal implementation of a particular member. Consider the Name property on PdaItem, for example. The implementation is probably acceptable when inherited by the Appointment class. For the Contact class, however, the Name property should return the FirstName and LastName properties combined. Similarly, when Name is assigned, it should be split across FirstName and LastName. In other words, the base class property declaration is appropriate for the derived class, but the implementation is not always valid. There needs to be a mechanism for **overriding** the base class implementation with a custom implementation in the derived class.

virtual Modifier

C# supports overriding on instance methods and properties but not on fields or on any static members. It requires an explicit action within both the base class and the derived class. The base class must mark each member for which it allows overriding as virtual. If public or protected members do not include the virtual modifier, subclasses will not be able to override those members.

Language Contrast: Java—Virtual Methods by Default

By default, methods in Java are virtual, and they must be explicitly sealed if nonvirtual behavior is preferred. In contrast, C# defaults to nonvirtual.

Listing 7.10 shows an example of property overriding.

LISTING 7.10: **Overriding a Property**

```
public class PdaItem
{
    public virtual string Name { get; set; }
    // ...
}
```

```csharp
public class Contact : PdaItem
{
    public override string Name
    {
        get
        {
            return $"{ FirstName } { LastName }";
        }

        set
        {
            string[] names = value.Split(' ');
            // Error handling not shown
            FirstName = names[0];
            LastName = names[1];
        }
    }

    public string FirstName { get; set; }
    public string LastName { get; set; }

    // ...
}
```

Not only does PdaItem include the virtual modifier on the
Name property, but Contact's Name property is also decorated with the keyword override. Eliminating virtual would result in an error, and omitting
override would cause a warning to be generated, as you will see shortly.
C# requires the overriding methods to use the override keyword explicitly.
In other words, virtual identifies a method or property as available for
replacement (overriding) in the derived type.

Language Contrast: Java and C++—Implicit Overriding

Unlike with Java and C++, the override keyword is required on the derived class. C#
does not allow implicit overriding. To override a method, both the base class and the
derived class members must match and have corresponding virtual and override
keywords. Furthermore, when the override keyword is specified, the derived implementation is assumed to replace the base class implementation.

Overloading a member causes the runtime to call the most derived
implementation (see Listing 7.11).

LISTING 7.11: Runtime Calling the Most Derived Implementation of a Virtual Method

```
public class Program
{
  public static void Main()
  {
      Contact contact;
      PdaItem item;

      contact = new Contact();
      item = contact;

      // Set the name via PdaItem variable
      item.Name = "Inigo Montoya";

      // Display that FirstName & LastName
      // properties were set
      Console.WriteLine(
          $"{ contact.FirstName } { contact.LastName }");
  }
}
```

Output 7.1 shows the results of Listing 7.11.

OUTPUT 7.1

```
Inigo Montoya
```

In Listing 7.11, item.Name is called; item is declared as a PdaItem there. However, the contact's FirstName and LastName are still set. The rule is that whenever the runtime encounters a virtual method, it calls the most derived and overriding implementation of the virtual member. In this case, the code instantiates a Contact and calls Contact.Name because Contact contains the most derived implementation of Name.

In creating a class, programmers should be careful when choosing to allow overriding a method, since they cannot control the derived implementation. Virtual methods should not include critical code because such methods may never be called if the derived class overrides them. Furthermore, converting a method from a virtual method to a nonvirtual method could break derived classes that override the method. You should avoid such a code-breaking change, especially for assemblies intended for use by third parties.

Listing 7.12 includes a virtual Run() method. If the Controller programmer calls Run() with the expectation that the critical Start() and Stop() methods will be called, he will run into a problem.

LISTING 7.12: Carelessly Relying on a Virtual Method Implementation

```
public class Controller
{
  public void Start()
  {
      // Critical code
  }
  public virtual void Run()
  {
      Start();
      Stop();
  }
  public void Stop()
  {
      // Critical code
  }
}
```

In overriding Run( ), a developer could perhaps not call the critical Start( ) and Stop( ) methods. To force the Start( )/Stop( ) expectation, the Controller programmer should define the class, as shown in Listing 7.13.

LISTING 7.13: Forcing the Desirable Run( ) Semantics

```
public class Controller
{
    public void Start()
    {
        // Critical code
    }

    private void Run()
    {
        Start();
        InternalRun();
        Stop();
    }

    protected virtual void InternalRun()
    {
        // Default implementation
    }

    public void Stop()
    {
        // Critical code
    }
}
```

With this new listing, on the one hand, the `Controller` programmer prevents users from mistakenly calling `InternalRun()`, because it is protected. On the other hand, declaring `Run()` as `public` ensures that `Start()` and `Stop()` are invoked appropriately. It is still possible for users to modify the default implementation of how the `Controller` executes by overriding the protected `InternalRun()` member from within the derived class.

Virtual methods provide default implementations only—that is, implementations that derived classes could override entirely. However, because of the complexities of inheritance design, it is important to consider (and preferably to implement) a specific scenario that requires the virtual method definition rather than declaring members as `virtual` by default.

Language Contrast: C++—Dispatch Method Calls during Construction

In C++, methods called during construction will not dispatch the virtual method. Instead, during construction, the type is associated with the base type rather than the derived type, and virtual methods call the base implementation. In contrast, C# dispatches virtual method calls to the most derived type. This is consistent with the principle of calling the most derived virtual member, even if the derived constructor has not completely executed. Regardless, in C# the situation should be avoided.

Finally, only instance members can be `virtual`. The CLR uses the concrete type, specified at instantiation time, to determine where to dispatch a `virtual` method call, so `static virtual` methods are meaningless and the compiler prohibits them.

new Modifier

When an overriding method does not use `override`, the compiler issues a warning similar to that shown in Output 7.2 or Output 7.3.

OUTPUT 7.2

```
warning CS0114: '<derived method name>' hides inherited member
'<base method name>'. To make the current member override that
implementation, add the override keyword. Otherwise add the new
keyword.
```

OUTPUT 7.3

```
warning CS0108: The keyword new is required on '<derived property
name>' because it hides inherited member '<base property name>'
```

The obvious solution is to add the override modifier (assuming the base member is virtual). However, as the warnings point out, the new modifier is also an option. Consider the scenario shown in Table 7.1—a specific example of the more general problem known as the **brittle base class** or **fragile base class** problem.

TABLE 7.1: Why the New Modifier?

Activity	Code

Programmer A defines class Person that includes properties FirstName and LastName.	```public class Person```
	 ```{```
	   ```public string FirstName { get; set; }```
	   ```public string LastName { get; set; }```
	 ```}```

Programmer B derives from Person and defines Contact with the additional property Name. In addition, he defines the Program class whose Main() method instantiates Contact, assigns Name, and then prints out the name.	```public class Contact : Person```
	 ```{```
	   ```public string Name```
	   ```{```
	     ```get```
	     ```{```
	       ```return FirstName + " " + LastName;```
	     ```}```
	
	     ```set```
	     ```{```
	       ```string[] names = value.Split(' ');```
	       ```// Error handling not shown```
	       ```FirstName = names[0];```
	       ```LastName = names[1];```
	     ```}```
	   ```}```
	 ```}```

continues

TABLE 7.1: Why the New Modifier? (*continued*)

Activity	Code
Later, Programmer A adds the Name property, but instead of implementing the getter as FirstName + " " + LastName, she implements it as LastName + ", " + FirstName. Furthermore, she doesn't define the property as virtual, and she uses the property in a DisplayName() method.	```// ...``` ```public class Person``` ``{`` `public string Name` `{` `get` `{` `return LastName + ", " + FirstName;` `}` `set` `{` `string[] names = value.Split(", ");` `// Error handling not shown` `LastName = names[0];` `FirstName = names[1];` `}` `}` `public static void Display(Person person)` `{` `// Display <LastName>, <FirstName>` `Console.WriteLine( person.Name );` `}` `}`

Because Person.Name is not virtual, Programmer A will expect Display() to use the Person implementation, even if a Person-derived data type, Contact, is passed in. However, Programmer B would expect Contact.Name to be used in all cases where the variable data type is a Contact. (Programmer B would have no code where Person.Name was used, since no Person.Name property existed initially.) To allow the addition of Person.Name without breaking either programmer's expected behavior, you cannot assume virtual was intended. Furthermore, because C# requires an override member to explicitly use the override modifier, some other semantic must be assumed instead of allowing the addition of a member in the base class to cause the derived class to no longer compile.

This semantic is the new modifier, and it hides a redeclared member of the derived class from the base class. Instead of calling the most derived member, a member of the base class calls the most derived member in the inheritance chain prior to the member with the new modifier. If the inheritance chain contains only two classes, a member in the base class will behave as though no method was declared on the derived class (if the derived implementation overrides the base class member). Although the compiler will report the warning shown in either Output 7.2 or Output 7.3, if neither override nor new is specified, new will be assumed, thereby maintaining the desired version safety.

Consider Listing 7.14 as an example. Its output appears in Output 7.4.

LISTING 7.14: override versus new Modifier

```
public class Program
{
  public class BaseClass
  {
     public void DisplayName()
     {
        Console.WriteLine("BaseClass");
     }
  }

     public class DerivedClass : BaseClass
     {
        // Compiler WARNING: DisplayName() hides inherited
        // member. Use the new keyword if hiding was intended.
        public virtual void DisplayName()
        {
           Console.WriteLine("DerivedClass");
        }
     }

  public class SubDerivedClass : DerivedClass
  {
     public override void DisplayName()
     {
        Console.WriteLine("SubDerivedClass");
     }
  }

  public class SuperSubDerivedClass : SubDerivedClass
  {
     public new void DisplayName()
     {
        Console.WriteLine("SuperSubDerivedClass");
     }
  }
```

```csharp
public static void Main()
{
    SuperSubDerivedClass superSubDerivedClass
        = new SuperSubDerivedClass();

    SubDerivedClass subDerivedClass = superSubDerivedClass;
    DerivedClass derivedClass = superSubDerivedClass;
    BaseClass baseClass = superSubDerivedClass;

    superSubDerivedClass.DisplayName();
    subDerivedClass.DisplayName();
    derivedClass.DisplayName();
    baseClass.DisplayName();
}
}
```

OUTPUT 7.4

```
SuperSubDerivedClass
SubDerivedClass
SubDerivedClass
BaseClass
```

These results occur for the following reasons:

- SuperSubDerivedClass: SuperSubDerivedClass.DisplayName() displays SuperSubDerivedClass because there is no derived class and therefore no overload.
- SubDerivedClass: SubDerivedClass.DisplayName() is the most derived member to override a base class's virtual member. SuperSubDerivedClass.DisplayName() is hidden because of its new modifier.
- SubDerivedClass: DerivedClass.DisplayName() is virtual and SubDerivedClass.DisplayName() is the most derived member to override it. As before, SuperSubDerivedClass.DisplayName() is hidden because of the new modifier.
- BaseClass: BaseClass.DisplayName() does not redeclare any base class member and it is not virtual; therefore, it is called directly.

When it comes to the CIL, the new modifier has no effect on which statements the compiler generates. However, a "new" method results in the generation of the newslot metadata attribute on the method. From the C# perspective, its only effect is to remove the compiler warning that would appear otherwise.

sealed Modifier

Just as you can prevent inheritance using the `sealed` modifier on a class, so virtual members may be `sealed` as well (see Listing 7.15). This approach prevents a subclass from overriding a base class member that was originally declared as `virtual` higher in the inheritance chain. Such a situation arises when a subclass B overrides a base class A's member and then needs to prevent any further overriding below subclass B.

LISTING 7.15: Sealing Members

```csharp
class A
{
  public virtual void Method()
  {
  }
}
class B : A
{
  public override sealed void Method()
  {
  }
}

class C : B
{
  // ERROR:  Cannot override sealed members
  // public override void Method()
  // {
  // }
}
```

In this example, the use of the `sealed` modifier on class B's `Method()` declaration prevents class C from overriding `Method()`.

In general, marking a class as `sealed` is rarely done and should be reserved only for those situations in which there are strong reasons favoring such a restriction. In fact, leaving types unsealed is increasingly desirable, as unit testing has become prominent because of the need to support mock (test double) object creation in place of real implementations. One possible scenario when sealing a class might be warranted is when the cost of sealing individual virtual members outweighs the benefits of leaving the class unsealed. However, a more targeted sealing of individual members—perhaps because there are dependencies in the base implementation for correct behavior—is likely to be preferable.

base Member

In choosing to override a member, developers often want to invoke the member on the base class (see Listing 7.16).

LISTING 7.16: Accessing a Base Member

```
using static System.Environment;

public class Address
{
    public string StreetAddress;
    public string City;
    public string State;
    public string Zip;

    public override string ToString()
    {
        return $"{ StreetAddress + NewLine }"
            + $"{ City }, { State }  { Zip }";
    }
}

public class InternationalAddress : Address
{
    public string Country;

    public override string ToString()
    {
        return base.ToString() +
            NewLine + Country;
    }
}
```

In Listing 7.16, InternationalAddress inherits from Address and implements ToString(). To call the parent class's implementation, you use the base keyword. The syntax is virtually identical to this, including support for using base as part of the constructor (discussed shortly).

Parenthetically, in the Address.ToString() implementation, you are required to override because ToString() is also a member of object. Any members that are decorated with override are automatically designated as virtual, so additional child classes may further specialize the implementation.

> ## ■ **NOTE**
>
> Any methods decorated with `override` are automatically virtual. A base class method can be overridden only if it is virtual, and the overriding method is therefore virtual as well.

Constructors

When instantiating a derived class, the runtime first invokes the base class's constructor so that the base class initialization is not circumvented. However, if there is no accessible (nonprivate) default constructor on the base class, it is not clear how to construct the base class; in turn, the C# compiler reports an error.

To avoid the error caused by the lack of an accessible default constructor, programmers need to designate explicitly, in the derived class constructor header, which base constructor to run (see Listing 7.17).

LISTING 7.17: Specifying Which Base Constructor to Invoke

```csharp
public class PdaItem
{
    public PdaItem(string name)
    {
        Name = name;
    }

    // ...
}
```

```csharp
public class Contact : PdaItem
{
    public Contact(string name) :
        base(name)
    {
        Name = name;
    }

    public string Name { get; set; }
    // ...
}
```

By identifying the base constructor in the code, you let the runtime know which base constructor to invoke before invoking the derived class constructor.

Abstract Classes

Many of the inheritance examples so far have defined a class called PdaItem that defines the methods and properties common to Contact, Appointment, and so on, which are type objects that derive from PdaItem. PdaItem is not intended to be instantiated itself, however. A PdaItem instance has no meaning by itself; it has meaning only when it is used as a base class—to share default method implementations across the set of data types that derive from it. These characteristics are indicative of the need for PdaItem to be an **abstract** class rather than a **concrete** class. Abstract classes are designed for derivation only. It is not possible to instantiate an abstract class, except in the context of instantiating a class that derives from it. Classes that are not abstract and can instead be instantiated directly are concrete classes.

■ BEGINNER TOPIC

Abstract Classes

Abstract classes represent abstract entities. Their **abstract members** define what an object derived from an abstract entity should contain, but they don't include the implementation. Often, much of the functionality within an abstract class is unimplemented. Before a class can successfully derive from an abstract class, however, it needs to provide the implementation for the abstract methods in its abstract base class.

To define an abstract class, C# requires the abstract modifier to the class definition, as shown in Listing 7.18.

LISTING 7.18: Defining an Abstract Class

```
// Define an abstract class
public abstract class PdaItem
{
  public PdaItem(string name)
  {
      Name = name;
  }

  public virtual string Name { get; set; }
}
```

```csharp
public class Program
{
  public static void Main()
  {
    PdaItem item;
    // ERROR:  Cannot create an instance of the abstract class
    // item = new PdaItem("Inigo Montoya");
  }
}
```

Although abstract classes cannot be instantiated, this restriction is a minor characteristic of an abstract class. Their primary significance is achieved when abstract classes include **abstract members**. An abstract member is a method or property that has no implementation. Its purpose is to force all derived classes to provide the implementation.

Consider Listing 7.19 as an example.

LISTING 7.19: Defining Abstract Members

```csharp
// Define an abstract class
public abstract class PdaItem
{
  public PdaItem(string name)
  {
    Name = name;
  }

  public virtual string Name { get; set; }
  public abstract string GetSummary();
}

using static System.Environment;

public class Contact : PdaItem
{
    public override string Name
    {
        get
        {
            return $"{ FirstName } { LastName }";
        }

        set
        {
            string[] names = value.Split(' ');
            // Error handling not shown
            FirstName = names[0];
            LastName = names[1];
        }
    }
```

```csharp
    public string FirstName { get; set; }
    public string LastName { get; set; }
    public string Address { get; set; }

    public override string GetSummary()
    {
        return @"FirstName: { FirstName + NewLine }"
          + $"LastName: { LastName + NewLine }"
          + $"Address: { Address + NewLine }";
    }

  // ...
}

public class Appointment : PdaItem
{
  public Appointment(string name) :
    base(name)
  {
    Name = name;
  }

  public DateTime StartDateTime  { get; set; }
  public DateTime EndDateTime    { get; set; }
  public string Location    { get; set; }

  // ...

  public override string GetSummary()
  {
      return $"Subject: { Name + NewLine }"
        + $"Start: { StartDateTime + NewLine }"
        + $"End: { EndDateTime + NewLine }"
        + $"Location: { Location }";
  }
}
```

Listing 7.19 defines the GetSummary() member as abstract, so it doesn't include any implementation. The code then overrides this member within Contact and provides the implementation. Because abstract members are supposed to be overridden, such members are automatically virtual and cannot be declared so explicitly. In addition, abstract members cannot be private because derived classes would not be able to see them.

It is surprisingly difficult to develop a well-designed object hierarchy. For this reason, when programming abstract types, you should be sure to implement at least one (and preferably more) concrete type that derives from the abstract type to validate the design.

> **NOTE**
>
> Abstract members must be overridden, so they are automatically virtual and cannot be declared so explicitly.

Language Contrast: C++—Pure Virtual Functions

C++ allows for the definition of abstract functions using the cryptic notation =0. These functions are called pure virtual functions in C++. In contrast with C#, however, C++ does not require the class itself to have any special declaration. Unlike C#'s `abstract` class modifier, C++ has no class declaration change when the class includes pure virtual functions.

If you provide no `GetSummary()` implementation in `Contact`, the compiler will report an error.

> **NOTE**
>
> By declaring an abstract member, the abstract class programmer states that to form an "is a" relationship between a concrete class and an abstract base class (that is, a `PdaItem`), it is necessary to implement the abstract members, the members for which the abstract class could not provide an appropriate default implementation.

BEGINNER TOPIC

Polymorphism

When the implementation for the same member signature varies between two or more classes, the scenario demonstrates a key object-oriented principle: **polymorphism**. *Poly* means "many" and *morph* means "form," so polymorphism refers to the fact that there are multiple implementations of the same signature. Also, because the same signature cannot be used multiple times within a single class, each implementation of the member signature occurs on a different class.

The idea behind polymorphism is that the object itself knows best how to perform a particular operation. Moreover, by enforcing common ways to invoke those operations, polymorphism is a technique that encourages code reuse when taking advantage of the commonalities. Given multiple types of documents, each document type class knows best how to perform a `Print()` method for its corresponding document type. Therefore, instead of defining a single print method that includes a `switch` statement with the special logic to print each document type, with polymorphism you call the `Print()` method corresponding to the specific type of document you wish to print. For example, calling `Print()` on a word processing document class behaves according to word processing specifics, whereas calling the same method on a graphics document class will result in print behavior specific to the graphic. Given the document types, however, all you have to do to print a document is call `Print()`, regardless of the type.

Moving the custom print implementation out of a `switch` statement offers a number of maintenance advantages. First, the implementation appears in the context of each document type's class rather than in a location far removed; this is in keeping with encapsulation. Second, adding a new document type doesn't require a change to the `switch` statement. Instead, all that is necessary is for the new document type class to implement the `Print()` signature.

Abstract members are intended to be a way to enable polymorphism. The base class specifies the signature of the method, and the derived class provides the implementation (see Listing 7.20).

LISTING 7.20: Using Polymorphism to List the PdaItems

```
public class Program
{
  public static void Main()
  {
      PdaItem[] pda = new PdaItem[3];

      Contact contact = new Contact("Sherlock Holmes");
      contact.Address = "221B Baker Street, London, England";
      pda[0] = contact;

      Appointment appointment =
          new Appointment("Soccer tournament");
      appointment.StartDateTime = new DateTime(2008, 7, 18);
```

```
        appointment.EndDateTime = new DateTime(2008, 7, 19);
        appointment.Location = "Estádio da Machava";
        pda[1] = appointment;

        contact = new Contact("Hercule Poirot");
        contact.Address =
            "Apt 56B, Whitehaven Mansions, Sandhurst Sq, London";
        pda[2] = contact;

        List(pda);
    }

    public static void List(PdaItem[] items)
    {
        // Implemented using polymorphism. The derived
        // type knows the specifics of implementing
        // GetSummary().
        foreach (PdaItem item in items)
        {
            Console.WriteLine("_____");
            Console.WriteLine(item.GetSummary());
        }
    }
}
```

The results of Listing 7.20 appear in Output 7.5.

OUTPUT 7.5

```
_____
FirstName: Sherlock
LastName: Holmes
Address: 221B Baker Street, London, England

_____
Subject: Soccer tournament
Start: 7/18/2008 12:00:00 AM
End: 7/19/2008 12:00:00 AM
Location: Estádio da Machava

_____
FirstName: Hercule
LastName: Poirot
Address: Apt 56B, Whitehaven Mansions, Sandhurst Sq, London
```

In this way, you can call the method on the base class, but the implementation is specific to the derived class. Output 7.5 shows that the List() method from Listing 7.20 is able to successfully display both Contacts and Addresses, and display them in a way custom to each. The invocation of the abstract GetSummary() method actually invokes the overriding method specific to the instance.

All Classes Derive from `System.Object`

Given any class, whether a custom class or one built into the system, the methods shown in Table 7.2 will be defined.

TABLE 7.2: Members of `System.Object`

Method Name	Description
public virtual bool `Equals(object o)`	Returns `true` if the object supplied as a parameter is equal in *value*, not necessarily in reference, to the instance.
public virtual int `GetHashCode()`	Returns an integer corresponding to an evenly spread hash code. This is useful for collections such as `HashTable` collections.
public `Type GetType()`	Returns an object of type `System.Type` corresponding to the type of the object instance.
public static bool `ReferenceEquals(` **object** a, **object** b`)`	Returns `true` if the two supplied parameters refer to the same object.
public virtual string `ToString()`	Returns a string representation of the object instance.
public virtual void `Finalize()`	An alias for the destructor; informs the object to prepare for termination. C# prevents you from calling this method directly.
protected object `MemberwiseClone()`	Clones the object in question by performing a shallow copy; references are copied, but not the data within a referenced type.

All of the methods listed in Table 7.2 appear on all objects through inheritance; all classes derive (either directly or via an inheritance chain) from `object`. Even literals include these methods, enabling somewhat peculiar-looking code such as this:

```
Console.WriteLine( 42.ToString() );
```

Even class definitions that don't have any explicit derivation from `object` derive from `object` anyway. The two declarations for `PdaItem` in Listing 7.21, therefore, result in identical CIL.

LISTING 7.21: System.Object Derivation Implied When No Derivation Is Specified Explicitly

```csharp
public class PdaItem
{
    // ...
}
```

```csharp
public class PdaItem : object
{
    // ...
}
```

When the `object`'s default implementation isn't sufficient, programmers can override one or more of the three virtual methods. Chapter 10 describes the details involved in doing so.

Verifying the Underlying Type with the `is` Operator

Because C# allows casting down the inheritance chain, it is sometimes desirable to determine what the underlying type is before attempting a conversion. Also, checking the type may be necessary for type-specific actions where polymorphism was not implemented. To determine the underlying type, C# provides the `is` operator (see Listing 7.22).

LISTING 7.22: is Operator Determining the Underlying Type

```csharp
public static void Save(object data)
{
    if (data is string)
    {
        string text = (string)data;
        if (text.Length > 0)
        {
            data = Encrypt(text);
            // ...
        }
    }
    else if (data == null)
    {
        throw new ArgumentNullException(nameof(data));
    }
    // ...
}
```

Listing 7.22 encrypts the data if the underlying type is a `string`. This is significantly different from encrypting any data type that successfully converts to a string, since many types support conversion to a string, and yet their underlying type is not a string.

While it might be clearer to check for null at the start of the method, in this case we check later to demonstrate that even if the target is null, the is operator will return false, and so the null check will still execute.

Note that with an explicit cast, it is the programmer's responsibility to understand the code logic sufficiently to avoid an invalid cast exception. If there is the possibility of an invalid cast occurring, then it would be preferable to leverage an is operator and avoid the exception entirely. The advantage is that the is operator enables a code path for when the explicit cast might fail without the expense of exception handling.

Although the is operator capability is important, you should consider issues related to polymorphism prior to using the is operator. Polymorphism supports the expansion of a behavior to other data types without requiring any modification of the implementation that defines the behavior. For example, deriving from a common base type and then using that type as the parameter to the Save() method avoids the need to check for string explicitly and enables other data types to support encryption during the save operation by deriving from the same base type.

Pattern Matching with the is Operator

Begin 7.0

Starting with C# 7.0, the is operator has been improved to support a concept known as pattern matching. The problem with the is operator described previously is that after checking that data is indeed a string, we still must cast it to a string (assuming we want to access it as a string). A preferable approach would be to both check and, if the check is true, assign the result to a new variable. With C# 7.0's introduction of **pattern matching**, this becomes possible, as shown in Listing 7.23. Effectively, the pattern-matching is operator replaces the more basic is operator in the vast majority of scenarios.

LISTING 7.23: **is Operator Determining the Underlying Type**

```
public static void Save(object data)
{
    if (data is string text && text.Length > 0)
    {
        data = Encrypt(text);
        // ...
    }
}
```

```
    else if (data is null)
    {
        throw new ArgumentNullException(nameof(data));
    }
    // ...
}
```

Notice how the is operator with pattern matching includes checking whether the type is string, declaring a new variable (text), and casting data into a string, which the code then leverages to check that the length is greater than 0.

Also notice that with pattern matching, it is possible to use the is operator to check for null. There is no readability difference between using the is operator and using the equality operator to check for null. My recommendation is to choose one or the other consistently, however.

Pattern Matching within a switch Statement

Listing 7.23 is a simple if-else statement, but you can imagine a similar example in which we check for more than just a string. And, while an if statement would work, a switch statement with a match expression in which the match expression works with any type can provide significantly better readability. Listing 7.24 provides an example using a Storage class.

LISTING 7.24: Pattern Matching within a switch Statement

```
static public void Eject(Storage storage)
{
  switch (storage)
  {
      case null: // The location of case null doesn't matter
          throw new ArgumentNullException(nameof(storage));
      // ** Causes compile error because case statments below
      // ** are unreachable
      // case Storage tempStorage:
      //    throw new Exception();
      //    break;
      case UsbKey usbKey when usbKey.IsPluggedIn:
          usbKey.Unload();
          Console.WriteLine("USB Drive Unloaded!");
          break;
      case Dvd dvd when dvd.IsInserted:
          dvd.Eject();
          Console.WriteLine("DVD Ejected!");
          break;
```

```
    case Dvd dvd when !dvd.IsInserted:
        throw new ArgumentException(
            "There was no DVD present.", nameof(storage));
    case HardDrive hardDrive:
        throw new InvalidOperationException();
    default:   // The location of case default doesn't matter
        throw new ArgumentException(nameof(storage));
    }
}
```

The `switch` statement pattern-matching support provides a significant amount of functionality (especially compared to the **basic `switch` statement** of earlier C# language versions introduced in Chapter 4).

- Unlike basic switch statements, pattern-matching case clauses are *not* limited to types with constant values (`string`, `int`, `long`, `enum`, and so on). Rather, any type can be used.

- The pattern-matching case labels include the declaration of a variable following the type. For example,

  ```
  case HardDrive hardDrive:
  ```

  The scope of this variable is limited to the scope of the switch section (the case label followed by one or more statements ending in a jump statement).

- Pattern-matching case labels support a condition that allows code to further filter out the type condition with an additional expression. For example,

  ```
  case Usbkey usbKey when usbKey.IsPluggedIn:
  ```

- With pattern-matching switch sections, the order of the sections becomes significant. A case label for a base class with no condition (such as `case Storage storage`) will block the execution of any later switch blocks for derived classes. If there is no filter condition, the compiler will flag the problem as an error. However, if the case label for the base class has a condition (that can't be trivially resolved at compile time), then any later case label for a derived type will be eclipsed.[2]

---

2. Apropos because, at least in the United States, there was a full eclipse on the day this section was written—August 21, 2017.

- The location of the switch section for null is not significant, as the condition in which it resolves to true is always unique. (As with a basic switch statement, the default case label location continues to not be significant either.)

- Multiple pattern-matching case labels for the same type are allowable if no more than one of them has no filter condition. For example,

```
case Dvd dvd ...
```

- You can mix constant switch sections with pattern-matching switch sections, although simplicity is clearly preferable. For example,

```
case 42
```

and

```
case int i when i == 42
```

- Switch sections for pattern-matching switch statements still require a jump statement. For example,

```
case HardDrive hardDrive:
    throw new InvalidOperationException();
```

- Nullable types (e.g., int?) are not allowed in a case clause. Use the non-nullable version instead. This makes sense because the null value would be matched by case null and never by the case clause for the nullable type.

Just like with the is operator, pattern matching should be used only when polymorphism is not an option. Assume, therefore, for purposes of this sample, that we don't have the source code for the storage classes and there is no common appropriate base method—hence polymorphism is not a viable approach.

End 7.0

Conversion Using the as Operator

The advantage of the is operator is that it enables verification that a data item is of a particular type. The as operator goes one step further: It attempts a conversion to a particular data type and assigns null if the source type is not inherently (within the inheritance chain) of the target type. This strategy is significant because it avoids the exception that could result from casting. Listing 7.25 demonstrates use of the as operator.

LISTING 7.25: Data Conversion Using the as Operator

```
object Print(IDocument document)
{
  if(thing != null)
  {
      // Print document...
  }
  else
  {
  }
}

static void Main()
{
  object data;

  // ...

  Print(data as Document);
}
```

By using the as operator, you can avoid additional try/catch handling code if the conversion is invalid, because the as operator provides a way to attempt a cast without throwing an exception if the cast fails.

One advantage of the is operator over the as operator is that the latter cannot successfully determine the underlying type. The as operator may implicitly cast up or down an inheritance chain as well as to types supporting the cast operator. Unlike the as operator, the is operator can determine the underlying type.

More important, the as operator generally requires the additional step of checking the assigned variable for null. Since the pattern-matching is operator includes this conditional check automatically, it *effectively* eliminates the need for the as operator—assuming C# 7.0 or later is available.

SUMMARY

This chapter discussed how to specialize a class by deriving from it and adding additional methods and properties. This coverage included a discussion of the private and protected access modifiers that control the level of encapsulation.

The chapter also investigated the details of overriding the base class implementation and, alternatively, hiding it using the new modifier. To control overriding, C# provides the `virtual` modifier, which identifies to the deriving class developer which members she intends for derivation. To prevent any derivation, the `sealed` modifier may be used on the class. Similarly, placing the `sealed` modifier on a member prevents further overriding from subclasses.

This chapter included a brief discussion of how all types derive from `object`. Chapter 10 discusses this derivation further, with a look at how `object` includes three virtual methods with specific rules and guidelines that govern overloading. Before you get there, however, you need to consider another programming paradigm that builds on object-oriented programming: interfaces. This is the subject of Chapter 8.

The chapter ended with the details of type conversion using the `is` and `as` operators. It included a discussion of C# 7.0 pattern-matching capability and its use in both `if` and `switch` statements.

8

Interfaces

POLYMORPHISM IS AVAILABLE not only via inheritance (as discussed in Chapter 7) but also via interfaces. Unlike abstract classes, interfaces cannot include any implementation. Like abstract classes, however, interfaces define a set of members that callers can rely on being implemented.

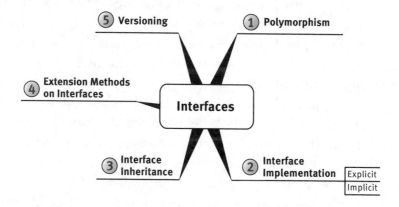

By implementing an interface, a type defines its capabilities. **The interface implementation relationship is a "can do" relationship.** The type can do what the interface requires an implementing type to do. The interface defines the contract between the types that implement the interface and the code that uses the interface. Types that implement interfaces must declare methods with the same signatures as the methods declared by the implemented interfaces. This chapter discusses implementing and using interfaces.

Introducing Interfaces

▪ BEGINNER TOPIC

Why Interfaces?

Interfaces are useful because—unlike abstract classes—they enable the complete separation of implementation details from services provided. For a real-world example, consider the "interface" that is an electrical wall socket. How the electrical power gets to the socket is an implementation detail: It might be generated by chemical, nuclear, or solar energy; the generator might be in the next room or far away; and so on. The socket provides a "contract": It agrees to supply a particular voltage at a specific frequency, and in return it requires that the appliance using that interface provide a compatible plug. The appliance need not care anything about the implementation details that get power to the socket; all it needs to worry about is that it provides a compatible plug.

Consider the following example: A huge number of file compression formats are available (`.zip`, `.7-zip`, `.cab`, `.lha`, `.tar`, `.tar.gz`, `.tar.bz2`, `.bh`, `.rar`, `.arj`, `.arc`, `.ace`, `.zoo`, `.gz`, `.bzip2`, `.xxe`, `.mime`, `.uue`, and `.yenc`, just to name a few). If you created classes for each compression format, you could end up with different method signatures for each compression implementation and no ability to apply a standard calling convention across them. The desired method could be declared as abstract in the base class. However, deriving from a common base class uses up a class's one and only opportunity for inheritance. It is unlikely that there is any code common to various compression implementations that can be put in the base class, thereby ruling out the potential benefits of having a base class implementation. The key point is that base classes let you share implementation along with the member signatures, whereas interfaces allow you to share the member signatures without the implementation.

Instead of sharing a common base class, each compression class needs to implement a common interface. Interfaces define the contract that a class supports to interact with the other classes that expect the interface. If all the classes implemented the `IFileCompression` interface and its `Compress()` and `Uncompress()` methods, the code for calling the algorithm on any particular compression class would simply involve a conversion to the `IFileCompression` interface and a call to the members. The result is polymorphism because each compression class has the same method signature but individual implementations of that signature.

The `IFileCompression` interface shown in Listing 8.1 is an example of an interface implementation. By convention—a convention so strong it is universal—the interface name is PascalCase with a capital "I" prefix.

LISTING 8.1: Defining an Interface

```
interface IFileCompression
{
  void Compress(string targetFileName, string[] fileList);
  void Uncompress(
      string compressedFileName, string expandDirectoryName);
}
```

`IFileCompression` defines the methods a type must implement to be used in the same manner as other compression-related classes. The power of interfaces is that they grant the ability to callers to switch among implementations without modifying the calling code.

One key characteristic of an interface is that it has no implementation and no data. Method declarations in an interface have a single semicolon in place of curly braces after the header. Fields (data) cannot appear in an interface declaration. When an interface requires the derived class to have certain data, it declares a property rather than a field. Since the property does not contain any implementation as part of the interface declaration, it doesn't reference a backing field.

The declared members of an interface describe the members that must be accessible on an implementing type. The purpose of nonpublic members is to make those members inaccessible to other code. Therefore, C# does not allow access modifiers on interface members; instead, it automatically defines them as public.

Guidelines

DO use PascalCasing and an "I" prefix for interface names.

Polymorphism through Interfaces

Consider another example, as shown in Listing 8.2: `IListable` defines the members that a class needs to support for the `ConsoleListControl` class to display it. As such, any class that implements `IListable` can use the

ConsoleListControl to display itself. The IListable interface requires a
read-only property, ColumnValues.

LISTING 8.2: Implementing and Using Interfaces

```csharp
interface IListable
{
    // Return the value of each column in the row
    string[] ColumnValues
    {
        get;
    }
}
```

```csharp
public abstract class PdaItem
{
    public PdaItem(string name)
    {
        Name = name;
    }

    public virtual string Name{get;set;}
}
```

```csharp
class Contact : PdaItem, IListable
{
    public Contact(string firstName, string lastName,
        string address, string phone) : base(null)
    {
        FirstName = firstName;
        LastName = lastName;
        Address = address;
        Phone = phone;
    }

    public string FirstName { get; set; }
    public string LastName { get; set; }
    public string Address { get; set; }
    public string Phone { get; set; }

    public string[] ColumnValues
    {
        get
        {
            return new string[]
            {
                FirstName,
                LastName,
                Phone,
                Address
            };
        }
    }
}
```

```csharp
    public static string[] Headers
    {
        get
        {
            return new string[] {
                "First Name", "Last Name     ",
                "Phone         ",
                "Address                       " };
        }
    }

    // ...
}
```

```csharp
class Publication : IListable
{
    public Publication(string title, string author, int year)
    {
        Title = title;
        Author = author;
        Year = year;
    }

    public string Title { get; set; }
    public string Author { get; set; }
    public int Year { get; set; }

    public string[] ColumnValues
    {
        get
        {
            return new string[]
            {
                Title,
                Author,
                Year.ToString()
            };
        }
    }

    public static string[] Headers
    {
        get
        {
            return new string[] {
                "Title                         ",
                "Author          ",
                "Year" };
        }
    }

    // ...
}
```

```csharp
class Program
{
  public static void Main()
  {
      Contact[] contacts = new Contact[]
      {
          new Contact(
              "Dick", "Traci",
              "123 Main St., Spokane, WA  99037",
              "123-123-1234"),
          new Contact(
              "Andrew", "Littman",
              "1417 Palmary St., Dallas, TX 55555",
              "555-123-4567"),
          new Contact(
              "Mary", "Hartfelt",
              "1520 Thunder Way, Elizabethton, PA 44444",
              "444-123-4567"),
          new Contact(
              "John", "Lindherst",
              "1 Aerial Way Dr., Monteray, NH 88888",
              "222-987-6543"),
          new Contact(
              "Pat", "Wilson",
              "565 Irving Dr., Parksdale, FL 22222",
              "123-456-7890"),
          new Contact(
              "Jane", "Doe",
              "123 Main St., Aurora, IL 66666",
              "333-345-6789")
      };

      // Classes are implicitly convertable to
      // their supported interfaces
      ConsoleListControl.List(Contact.Headers, contacts);

      Console.WriteLine();

      Publication[] publications = new Publication[3] {
          new Publication(
              "The End of Poverty: Economic Possibilities for Our Time",
              "Jeffrey Sachs", 2006),
          new Publication("Orthodoxy",
              "G.K. Chesterton", 1908),
          new Publication(
              "The Hitchhiker's Guide to the Galaxy",
              "Douglas Adams", 1979)
          };
      ConsoleListControl.List(
          Publication.Headers, publications);
  }
}
```

```csharp
class ConsoleListControl
{
    public static void List(string[] headers, IListable[] items)
    {
        int[] columnWidths = DisplayHeaders(headers);

        for (int count = 0; count < items.Length; count++)
        {
            string[] values = items[count].ColumnValues;
            DisplayItemRow(columnWidths, values);
        }
    }

    /// <summary>Displays the column headers</summary>
    /// <returns>Returns an array of column widths</returns>
    private static int[] DisplayHeaders(string[] headers)
    {
        // ...
    }

    private static void DisplayItemRow(
        int[] columnWidths, string[] values)
    {
        // ...
    }
}
```

The results of Listing 8.2 appear in Output 8.1.

OUTPUT 8.1

```
First Name  Last Name       Phone         Address
Dick        Traci           123-123-1234  123 Main St., Spokane, WA  99037
Andrew      Littman         555-123-4567  1417 Palmary St., Dallas, TX 55555
Mary        Hartfelt        444-123-4567  1520 Thunder Way, Elizabethton, PA 44444
John        Lindherst       222-987-6543  1 Aerial Way Dr., Monteray, NH 88888
Pat         Wilson          123-456-7890  565 Irving Dr., Parksdale, FL 22222
Jane        Doe             333-345-6789  123 Main St., Aurora, IL 66666

Title                                               Author           Year
The End of Poverty: Economic Possibilities for Our Time  Jeffrey Sachs    2006
Orthodoxy                                           G.K. Chesterton  1908
The Hitchhiker's Guide to the Galaxy                Douglas Adams    1979
```

In Listing 8.2, the ConsoleListControl can display seemingly unrelated classes (Contact and Publication). Any class can be displayed provided that it implements the required interface. As a result, the ConsoleListControl.List() method relies on polymorphism to appropriately display whichever set of objects it is passed. Each class has its own

implementation of ColumnValues, and converting a class to IListable
still allows the particular class's implementation to be invoked.

Interface Implementation

Declaring a class to implement an interface is similar to deriving from a
base class: The implemented interfaces appear in a comma-separated list
along with the base class. The base class specifier (if there is one) must
come first, but otherwise order is not significant. Classes can implement
multiple interfaces but may derive directly from only one base class. An
example appears in Listing 8.3.

LISTING 8.3: **Implementing an Interface**

```csharp
public class Contact : PdaItem, IListable, IComparable
{
    // ...

    #region IComparable Members
    /// <summary>
    ///
    /// </summary>
    /// <param name="obj"></param>
    /// <returns>
    /// Less than zero:     This instance is less than obj
    /// Zero                This instance is equal to obj
    /// Greater than zero   This instance is greater than obj
    /// </returns>
    public int CompareTo(object obj)
    {
        int result;
        Contact contact = obj as Contact;

        if (obj == null)
        {
            // This instance is greater than obj
            result = 1;
        }
        else if (obj.GetType() != typeof(Contact))
        {
            // Use C# 6.0 nameof operator in message to
            // ensure consistency in the Type name
            throw new ArgumentException(
                $"The parameter is not a value of type { nameof(Contact) }",
                nameof(obj));
        }
```

```
        else if (Contact.ReferenceEquals(this, obj))
        {
            result = 0;
        }
        else
        {
            result = LastName.CompareTo(contact.LastName);
            if (result == 0)
            {
                result = FirstName.CompareTo(contact.FirstName);
            }
        }
        return result;
    }
    #endregion

    #region IListable Members
    string[] IListable.ColumnValues
    {
        get
        {
            return new string[]
            {
                FirstName,
                LastName,
                Phone,
                Address
            };
        }
    }
    #endregion
}
```

Once a class declares that it implements an interface, all members of the interface must be implemented. An abstract class is permitted to supply an abstract implementation of an interface member. A nonabstract implementation may throw a NotImplementedException type exception in the method body, but somehow an implementation of the member must be supplied.

One important characteristic of interfaces is that they can never be instantiated; you cannot use new to create an interface, so interfaces do not have constructors or finalizers. Interface instances are available only by instantiating a type that implements the interface. Furthermore, interfaces cannot include static members. One key interface purpose is polymorphism, and polymorphism without an instance of the implementing type has little value.

Each interface member behaves like an abstract method, forcing the derived class to implement the member. Therefore, it is not possible to use the abstract modifier on interface members explicitly.

When implementing an interface member in a type, there are two ways to do so: **explicitly** or **implicitly.** So far we've seen only implicit implementations, where the type member that implements the interface member is a public member of the implementing type.

Explicit Member Implementation

Explicitly implemented methods are available only by calling them through the interface itself; this is typically achieved by casting an object to the interface. For example, to call `IListable.ColumnValues` in Listing 8.4, you must first cast the contact to `IListable` because of `ColumnValues'` explicit implementation.

LISTING 8.4: Calling Explicit Interface Member Implementations

```
string[] values;
Contact contact1, contact2;

// ...

// ERROR:  Unable to call ColumnValues() directly
//         on a contact
// values = contact1.ColumnValues;

// First cast to IListable
values = ((IListable)contact2).ColumnValues;
// ...
```

The cast and the call to `ColumnValues` occur within the same statement in this case. Alternatively, you could assign `contact2` to an `IListable` variable before calling `ColumnValues`.

To declare an explicit interface member implementation, prefix the member name with the interface name (see Listing 8.5).

LISTING 8.5: Explicit Interface Implementation

```
public class Contact : PdaItem, IListable, IComparable
{
    // ...

    public int CompareTo(object obj)
    {
        // ...
    }
```

```
    #region IListable Members
    string[] IListable.ColumnValues
    {
        get
        {
            return new string[]
            {
                FirstName,
                LastName,
                Phone,
                Address
            };
        }
    }
    #endregion
}
```

Listing 8.5 implements ColumnValues explicitly by prefixing the property name with IListable. Furthermore, since explicit interface implementations are directly associated with the interface, there is no need to modify them with virtual, override, or public. In fact, these modifiers are not allowed. The method is not treated as a public member of the class, so marking it as public would be misleading.

Implicit Member Implementation

Notice that CompareTo() in Listing 8.5 does not include the IComparable prefix; it is implemented implicitly. With implicit member implementation, it is necessary only for the member to be public and for the member's signature to match the interface member's signature. Interface member implementation does not require use of the override keyword or any indication that this member is tied to the interface. Furthermore, since the member is declared just like any other class member, code that calls implicitly implemented members can do so directly, just as it would any other class member:

```
result = contact1.CompareTo(contact2);
```

In other words, implicit member implementation does not require a cast because the member is not hidden from direct invocation on the implementing class.

Many of the modifiers disallowed on an explicit member implementation are required or are optional on an implicit implementation. For example, implicit member implementations must be public. Furthermore, virtual is optional depending on whether derived classes may override the implementation. Eliminating virtual will cause the member to behave as though it is sealed.

Explicit versus Implicit Interface Implementation

The key difference between implicit and explicit member interface implementation lies not in the syntax of the method declaration but in the ability to access the method by name through an instance of the type rather than via the interface.

When building a class hierarchy, it's desirable to model real-world "is a" relationships—a giraffe is a mammal, for example. These are *semantic* relationships. Interfaces are often used to model *mechanism* relationships. A PdaItem "is not a" "comparable," but it might well be IComparable. This interface has nothing to do with the semantic model; it's a detail of the implementation mechanism. Explicit interface implementation is a technique for enabling the separation of mechanism concerns from model concerns. Forcing the caller to convert the object to an interface such as IComparable before treating the object as comparable explicitly separates out in the code when you are talking to the model and when you are dealing with its implementation mechanisms.

In general, it is preferable to limit the public surface area of a class to be "all model" with as little extraneous mechanism as possible. (Unfortunately, some mechanisms are unavoidable in .NET. In the real world, for example, you cannot get a giraffe's hash code or convert a giraffe to a string. However, you can get a Giraffe's hash code [GetHashCode()] and convert it to a string [ToString()] in .NET. By using object as a common base class, .NET mixes model code with mechanism code, even if only to a limited extent.)

Here are several guidelines that will help you choose between an explicit implementation and an implicit implementation.

- Is the member a core part of the class functionality?

  Consider the ColumnValues property implementation on the Contact class. This member is not an integral part of a Contact type but rather a peripheral member probably accessed only by the ConsoleListControl class. As such, it doesn't make sense for the member to be immediately visible on a Contact object, cluttering up what could potentially already be a large list of members.

Alternatively, consider the `IFileCompression.Compress()` member. Including an implicit `Compress()` implementation on a `ZipCompression` class is a perfectly reasonable choice: `Compress()` is a core part of the `ZipCompression` class's behavior, so it should be directly accessible from the `ZipCompression` class.

- Is the interface member name appropriate as a class member?

  Consider an `ITrace` interface with a member called `Dump()` that writes out a class's data to a trace log. Implementing `Dump()` implicitly on a `Person` or `Truck` class would result in confusion as to which operation the method performs. Instead, it is preferable to implement the member explicitly so that only from a data type of `ITrace`, where the meaning is clearer, can the `Dump()` method be called. Consider using an explicit implementation if a member's purpose is unclear on the implementing class.

- Does a class member with the same signature already exist?

  Explicit interface member implementation does not add a named element to the type's declaration space. Therefore, if there is already a potentially conflicting member of a type, a second one can be provided with the same name or signature as long as it is an explicit interface member.

Much of the decision making regarding implicit versus explicit interface member implementation comes down to intuition. However, these questions provide suggestions about which issues to consider when making your choice. Since changing an implementation from implicit to explicit results in a version-breaking change, it is better to err on the side of defining interfaces explicitly, allowing them to be changed to implicit implementations later. Furthermore, since the decision between implicit and explicit does not have to be consistent across all interface members, defining some methods as explicit and others as implicit is fully supported.

Guidelines

AVOID implementing interface members explicitly without a good reason. However, if you're unsure, favor explicit implementation.

Converting between the Implementing Class and Its Interfaces

Just as with a derived type and a base class, a conversion from an implementing type to its implemented interface is an implicit conversion. No cast operator is required because an instance of the implementing type will always provide all the members in the interface; therefore, the object can always be converted successfully to the interface type.

Although the conversion will always be successful from the implementing type to the implemented interface, many different types could implement a particular interface. Consequently, you can never be certain that a "downward" cast from an interface to one of its implementing types will be successful. Therefore, converting from an interface to one of its implementing types requires an explicit cast.

Interface Inheritance

Interfaces can derive from each other, resulting in an interface that inherits all the members in its base interfaces. As shown in Listing 8.6, the interfaces directly derived from `IReadableSettingsProvider` are the explicit base interfaces.

LISTING 8.6: Deriving One Interface from Another

```
interface IReadableSettingsProvider
{
    string GetSetting(string name, string defaultValue);
}


interface ISettingsProvider : IReadableSettingsProvider
{
    void SetSetting(string name, string value);
}


class FileSettingsProvider : ISettingsProvider
{
    #region ISettingsProvider Members
    public void SetSetting(string name, string value)
    {
        // ...
    }
    #endregion
```

```
        #region IReadableSettingsProvider Members
        public string GetSetting(string name, string defaultValue)
        {
            // ...
        }
        #endregion
    }
```

In this case, ISettingsProvider is derived from IReadableSettingsProvider and therefore inherits its members. If IReadableSettingsProvider also had an explicit base interface, ISettingsProvider would inherit those members as well, and the full set of interfaces in the derivation hierarchy would simply be the accumulation of base interfaces.

Note that if GetSetting() is implemented explicitly, it must be done using IReadableSettingsProvider. The declaration with ISettingsProvider in Listing 8.7 will not compile.

LISTING 8.7: Explicit Member Declaration without the Containing Interface (Failure)

```
// ERROR: GetSetting() not available on ISettingsProvider
string ISettingsProvider.GetSetting(
    string name, string defaultValue)
{
    // ...
}
```

The results of Listing 8.7 appear in Output 8.2.

OUTPUT 8.2

```
'ISettingsProvider.GetSetting' in explicit interface declaration
is not a member of interface.
```

This output appears in addition to an error indicating that IReadableSettingsProvider.GetSetting() is not implemented. The fully qualified interface member name used for explicit interface member implementation must reference the interface name in which it was originally declared.

Even though a class implements an interface (ISettingsProvider) that is derived from a base interface (IReadableSettingsProvider), the class can still declare an implementation of both interfaces overtly, as Listing 8.8 demonstrates.

LISTING 8.8: Using a Base Interface in the Class Declaration

```
class FileSettingsProvider : ISettingsProvider,
    IReadableSettingsProvider
{
    #region ISettingsProvider Members
    public void SetSetting(string name, string value)
    {
        // ...
    }
    #endregion

    #region IReadableSettingsProvider Members
    public string GetSetting(string name, string defaultValue)
    {
        // ...
    }
    #endregion
}
```

In this listing, there is no change to the interface's implementations on the class. Although the additional interface implementation declaration on the class header is superfluous, it provides for better readability.

The decision to provide multiple interfaces rather than just one combined interface depends largely on what the interface designer wants to require of the implementing class. By providing an IReadableSettingsProvider interface, the designer communicates that implementers are required only to implement a settings provider that retrieves settings. They do not have to be able to write to those settings. This reduces the implementation burden by not imposing the complexities of writing settings as well.

In contrast, implementing ISettingsProvider assumes that there is never a reason to have a class that can write settings without reading them. The inheritance relationship between ISettingsProvider and IReadableSettingsProvider, therefore, forces the combined total of both interfaces on the ISettingsProvider class.

One final but important note: Although *inheritance* is the correct term, conceptually it is more accurate to say that an interface represents a contract, and one contract can specify that the provisions of another contract must also be followed. So, the code ISettingsProvider : IReadableSettingsProvider conceptually states that the ISettingsProvider contract requires also respecting the IReadableSettingsProvider contract rather than that the ISettingsProvider "is a kind of" IReadableSettingsProvider. That being said, the remainder of the chapter will continue using the inheritance relationship terminology in accordance with the standard C# terminology.

Multiple Interface Inheritance

Just as classes can implement multiple interfaces, so interfaces can inherit from multiple interfaces. The syntax used for this purpose is consistent with class derivation and implementation, as shown in Listing 8.9.

LISTING 8.9: Multiple Interface Inheritance

```csharp
interface IReadableSettingsProvider
{
  string GetSetting(string name, string defaultValue);
}

interface IWriteableSettingsProvider
{
  void SetSetting(string name, string value);
}

interface ISettingsProvider : IReadableSettingsProvider,
    IWriteableSettingsProvider
{
}
```

It is unusual to have an interface with no members, but if implementing both interfaces together is predominant, it is a reasonable choice for this case. The difference between Listing 8.9 and Listing 8.6 is that it is now possible to implement IWriteableSettingsProvider without supplying any read capability. Listing 8.6's FileSettingsProvider is unaffected, but if it used explicit member implementation, specifying the interface to which a member belongs changes slightly.

Extension Methods on Interfaces

Begin 3.0

Perhaps one of the most important features of extension methods is the fact that they work with interfaces in addition to classes. The syntax used is identical to that used for extension methods for classes. The extended type (the first parameter and the parameter prefixed with this) is the interface

that we extend. Listing 8.10 shows an extension method for IListable().
It is declared on the Listable class.

LISTING 8.10: Interface Extension Methods

```
class Program
{
  public static void Main()
  {
      Contact[] contacts = new Contact[] {
          new Contact(
              "Dick", "Traci",
              "123 Main St., Spokane, WA  99037",
              "123-123-1234")
          // ...
      };

          // Classes are implicitly converted to
          // their supported interfaces
          contacts.List(Contact.Headers);

      Console.WriteLine();

      Publication[] publications = new Publication[3] {
          new Publication(
              "The End of Poverty: Economic Possibilities for Our Time",
              "Jeffrey Sachs", 2006),
          new Publication("Orthodoxy",
              "G.K. Chesterton", 1908),
          new Publication(
              "The Hitchhiker's Guide to the Galaxy",
              "Douglas Adams", 1979)
          };
      publications.List(Publication.Headers);
  }
}


static class Listable
{
  public static void List(
      this IListable[] items, string[] headers)
  {
      int[] columnWidths = DisplayHeaders(headers);

      for (int itemCount = 0; itemCount < items.Length; itemCount++)
      {
          string[] values = items[itemCount].ColumnValues;

          DisplayItemRow(columnWidths, values);
      }
  }
  // ...
}
```

3.0

In this example, the extension method is not on for an `IListable` parameter (although it could have been) but rather for an `IListable[]` parameter. This demonstrates that C# allows extension methods not only on an instance of a particular type but also on a collection of those objects. Support for extension methods is the foundation on which Language Integrated Query (LINQ) is implemented. `IEnumerable` is the fundamental interface that all collections implement. By defining extension methods for `IEnumerable`, LINQ support was added to all collections. This radically changed programming with collections; we explore this topic in detail in Chapter 15.

End 3.0

Implementing Multiple Inheritance via Interfaces

As Listing 8.3 demonstrated, a single class can implement any number of interfaces in addition to deriving from a single class. This feature provides a possible workaround for the lack of multiple inheritance support in C# classes. The process uses aggregation as described in Chapter 7, but you can vary the structure slightly by adding an interface to the mix, as shown in Listing 8.11.

LISTING 8.11: Working around Single Inheritance Using Aggregation with Interfaces

```csharp
public class PdaItem
{
  // ...
}
```

```csharp
interface IPerson
{
    string FirstName
    {
        get;
        set;
    }

    string LastName
    {
        get;
        set;
    }
}
```

```csharp
public class Person : IPerson
{
  // ...
}
```

```
public class Contact : PdaItem, IPerson
{
    private Person Person
    {
        get { return _Person; }
        set { _Person = value; }
    }
    private Person _Person;

    public string FirstName
    {
        get { return _Person.FirstName; }
        set { _Person.FirstName = value; }
    }

    public string LastName
    {
        get { return _Person.LastName; }
        set { _Person.LastName = value; }
    }

    // ...
}
```

IPerson ensures that the signatures between the Person members and the same members duplicated onto Contact are consistent. The implementation is still not synonymous with multiple inheritance, however, because new members added to Person will not be added to Contact.

One possible improvement that works if the implemented members are methods (not properties) is to define interface extension methods for the additional functionality "derived" from the second base class. An extension method on IPerson could provide a method called VerifyCredentials(), for example, and all classes that implement IPerson—even an IPerson interface that had no members but just extension methods—would have a default implementation of VerifyCredentials(). What makes this approach viable is that polymorphism is still available, as is overriding. Overriding is supported because any instance implementation of a method will take priority over an extension method with the equivalent static signature.

Guidelines

CONSIDER defining interfaces to achieve a similar effect to that of multiple inheritance.

■ BEGINNER TOPIC

Interface Diagramming

Interfaces in a UML-like[1] figure take two possible forms. First, you can show the interface as though it is an inheritance relationship similar to a class inheritance, as demonstrated in Figure 8.1 between IPerson and IContact. Alternatively, you can show the interface using a small circle, often referred to as a *lollipop*, exemplified by IPerson and IContact in Figure 8.1.

In Figure 8.1, Contact derives from PdaItem and implements IContact. In addition, it aggregates the Person class, which implements IPerson. Although the Visual Studio Class Designer does not support this practice, interfaces are sometimes shown as using a derivation-type arrow to a class. For example, Person could have an arrow to IPerson instead of a lollipop.

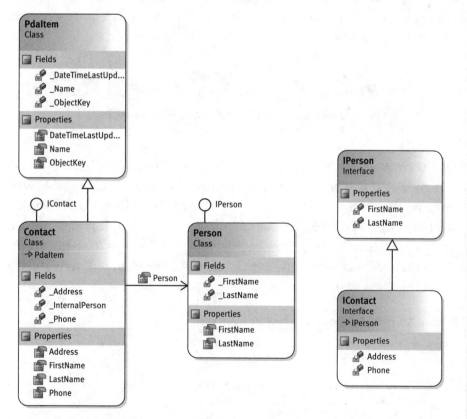

FIGURE 8.1: Working around Single Inheritances with Aggregation and Interface

---

1. Unified Modeling Language (UML), a standard specification for modeling object design using graphical notation.

Versioning

When creating a new version of a component or application that other developers have programmed against, you should not change interfaces. Because interfaces define a contract between the implementing class and the class using the interface, changing the interface is equivalent to changing the contract, which will possibly break any code written against the interface.

Changing or removing an interface member signature is obviously a code-breaking change, as any call to that member will no longer compile without modification. The same is true when you change public or protected member signatures on a class. However, unlike with classes, adding members to an interface could also prevent code from compiling without additional changes. The problem is that any class implementing the interface must do so entirely, and implementations for all members must be provided. With new interface members, the compiler will require that developers add new interface members to the class implementing the interface.

> **Guidelines**
>
> **DO NOT add members to an interface that has already shipped.**

The creation of `IDistributedSettingsProvider` in Listing 8.12 serves as a good example of extending an interface in a version-compatible way. Imagine that at first, only the `ISettingsProvider` interface is defined (as it was in Listing 8.6). In the next version, however, it is determined that per-machine settings are required. To enable this constraint, the `IDistributedSettingsProvider` interface is created, and it derives from `ISettingsProvider`.

LISTING 8.12: Deriving One Interface from Another

```csharp
interface IDistributedSettingsProvider : ISettingsProvider
{
    /// <summary>
    /// Get the settings for a particular machine.
    /// </summary>
    /// <param name="machineName">
    /// The machine name the setting is related to.</param>
    /// <param name="name">The name of the setting.</param>
    /// <param name="defaultValue">
    /// The value returned if the setting is not found.</param>
    /// <returns>The specified setting.</returns>
```

```
    string GetSetting(
        string machineName, string name, string defaultValue);

    /// <summary>
    /// Set the settings for a particular machine.
    /// </summary>
    /// <param name="machineName">
    /// The machine name the setting is related to.</param>
    /// <param name="name">The name of the setting.</param>
    /// <param name="value">The value to be persisted.</param>
    /// <returns>The specified setting.</returns>
    void SetSetting(
        string machineName, string name, string value);
}
```

The important issue is that programmers with classes that implement ISettingsProvider can choose to upgrade the implementation to include IDistributedSettingsProvider, or they can ignore it.

If instead of creating a new interface, the machine-related methods are added to ISettingsProvider, classes implementing this interface will no longer successfully compile with the new interface definition. Instead, a version-breaking change will occur.

Changing interfaces during the development phase is obviously acceptable, although perhaps laborious if implemented extensively. However, once an interface is released, it should not be changed. Instead, a second interface should be created, possibly deriving from the original interface.

(Listing 8.12 includes XML comments describing the interface members, as discussed further in Chapter 10.)

Interfaces Compared with Classes

Interfaces introduce another category of data types. (They are one of the few categories of types that don't extend System.Object.)[2] Unlike classes, however, interfaces can never be instantiated. An interface instance is accessible only via a reference to an object that implements the interface. It is not possible to use the new operator with an interface; therefore, interfaces cannot contain any constructors or finalizers. Furthermore, static members are not allowed on interfaces.

---

2. The others being pointer types and type parameter types. However, every interface type is convertible to System.Object, and it is permissible to call the methods of System.Object on any instance of an interface, so perhaps this is a hairsplitting distinction.

Interfaces are closer to abstract classes, sharing such features as the lack of instantiation capability. Table 8.1 lists additional comparisons.

Given that abstract classes and interfaces have their own sets of advantages and disadvantages, you must make a cost–benefit decision based on the comparisons in Table 8.1 and the guidelines that follow to make the right choice.

Guidelines

DO generally favor classes over interfaces. Use abstract classes to decouple contracts (what the type does) from implementation details (how the type does it.)

CONSIDER defining an interface if you need to support its functionality on types that already inherit from some other type.

TABLE 8.1: Comparing Abstract Classes and Interfaces

Abstract Classes	Interfaces
Cannot be instantiated directly, only by instantiating a derived class.	Cannot be instantiated directly, only by instantiating an implementing type.
Derived classes either must be abstract themselves or must implement all abstract members.	Implementing types must implement all interface members.
Can add additional nonabstract members that all derived classes can inherit without breaking cross-version compatibility.	Adding additional members to interfaces breaks the version compatibility.
Can declare methods, properties, and fields (along with all other member types including constructors and finalizer).	Can declare only methods and properties, not fields, constructors, or finalizers.
Members may be instance, virtual, abstract, or static and may provide implementations for nonabstract members that can be used by derived classes.	All members are instance based (not static) and are automatically treated as though they were abstract, so they cannot include any implementation.
A derived class may derive from only a single base class.	An implementing type may arbitrarily implement many interfaces.

Interfaces Compared with Attributes

Interfaces with no members at all, inherited or otherwise, are sometimes used to represent information about a type. For example, you might create a marker IObsolete interface to indicate that a type has been replaced by another type. This is generally considered to be an abuse of the interface mechanism; interfaces should be used to represent which functions a type can perform, not to indicate facts about particular types. Instead of marker interfaces, use attributes for this purpose. See Chapter 18 for more details.

Guidelines

AVOID using "marker" interfaces with no members; use attributes instead.

SUMMARY

Interfaces are a key element of object-oriented programming in C#. They provide functionality similar to abstract classes but without using up the single-inheritance option. Classes also implement multiple interfaces.

In C#, the implementation of interfaces can be either explicit or implicit, depending on whether the implementing class is to expose an interface member directly or only via a conversion to the interface. Furthermore, the granularity of whether the implementation is explicit or implicit is at the member level: One member may be implicitly implemented, while another member of the same interface is explicitly implemented.

The next chapter looks at value types and discusses the importance of defining custom value types. At the same time, the chapter points out the subtle problems that such types can introduce.

9.
Value Types

YOU HAVE USED VALUE TYPES throughout this book; for example, int is a value type. This chapter discusses not only using value types but also defining custom value types. There are two categories of custom value types: structs and enums. This chapter discusses how structs enable programmers to define new value types that behave very similarly to most of the predefined types discussed in Chapter 2. The key is that all newly defined value types have their own custom data and methods. The chapter also discusses how to use enums to define sets of constant values.

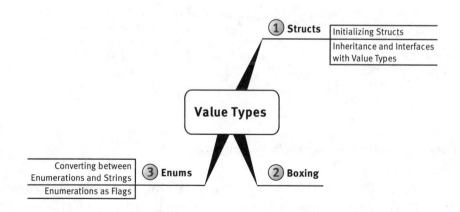

■ BEGINNER TOPIC

Categories of Types

All types discussed so far have fallen into one of two categories: reference types and value types. The differences between the types in each category stem from differences in copying strategies, which in turn result in each type being stored differently in memory. As a review, this Beginner Topic reintroduces the value type/reference type discussion for those readers who are unfamiliar with these issues.

Value Types

Variables of **value types** directly contain their values, as shown in Figure 9.1. The variable name is associated directly with the storage location in memory where the value is stored. Because of this, when a second variable is assigned the value of an original variable, a copy of the original variable's value is made to the storage location associated with the second variable. Two variables never refer to the same storage location (unless one or both are `out` or `ref` parameters, which are, by definition, aliases for another variable). Changing the value of the original variable will not affect the value in the second variable, because each variable is associated with a different storage location. Consequently, changing the value of one value type variable cannot affect the value of any other value type variable.

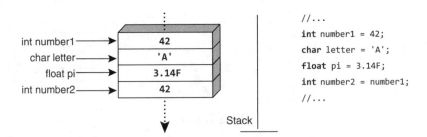

FIGURE 9.1: Value Types Contain the Data Directly

A value type variable is like a piece of paper that has a number written on it. If you want to change the number, you can erase it and replace it with a different number. If you have a second piece of paper, you can copy the number from the first piece of paper, but the two pieces of paper are then independent; erasing and replacing the number on one of them does not change the other.

Similarly, passing an instance of a value type to a method such as `Console.WriteLine()` will also result in a memory copy from the storage location associated with the argument to the storage location associated with the parameter, and any changes to the parameter variable inside the method will not affect the original value within the caller. Since value types require a memory copy, they generally should be defined to consume a small amount of memory (typically 16 bytes or less).

Guidelines

DO NOT create value types that consume more than 16 bytes of memory.

Values of value types are often short-lived; in many situations, a value is needed only for a portion of an expression or for the activation of a method. In these cases, variables and temporary values of value types can often be stored on the **temporary storage pool**, called the *stack*. (This term is actually a misnomer: There is no requirement that the temporary pool allocates its storage off the stack. In fact, as an implementation detail, it frequently chooses to allocate storage out of available registers instead.)

The temporary pool is less costly to clean up than the garbage-collected heap; however, value types tend to be copied more than reference types, and that copying can impose a performance cost of its own. Do not fall into the trap of believing that value types are faster because they can be allocated on the stack.

Reference Types

In contrast, the value of a reference type variable is a reference to an instance of an object (see Figure 9.2). Variables of reference type store the reference (typically implemented as the memory address) where the data for the object instance is located instead of storing the data directly, as a variable of value type does. Therefore, to access the data, the runtime reads the reference out of the variable and then dereferences it to reach the location in memory that actually contains the data for the instance.

A reference type variable, therefore, has two storage locations associated with it: the storage location directly associated with the variable and the storage location referred to by the reference that is the value stored in the variable.

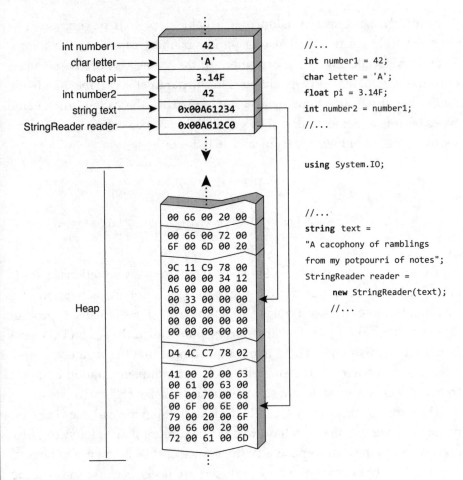

FIGURE 9.2: Reference Types Point to the Heap

A reference type variable is, again, like a piece of paper that always has something written on it. Imagine a piece of paper that has a house address written on it—for example, "123 Sesame Street, New York City." The piece of paper is a variable; the address is a reference to a building. Neither the paper nor the address written on it is the building, and the location of the paper need not have anything whatsoever to do with the location of the building to which its contents refer. If you make a copy of that reference on another piece of paper, the contents of both pieces of paper refer to the same building. If you then paint that building green, the building referred to by both pieces of paper can be observed to be green, because the references refer to the same thing.

The storage location directly associated with the variable (or temporary value) is treated no differently than the storage location associated with a value type variable: If the variable is known to be short-lived, it is allocated on the short-term storage pool. The value of a reference type variable is always either a reference to a storage location in the garbage-collected heap or null.

Compared to a variable of value type, which stores the data of the instance directly, accessing the data associated with a reference involves an extra hop: First the reference must be dereferenced to find the storage location of the actual data, and then the data can be read or written. Copying a reference type value copies only the reference, which is small. (A reference is guaranteed to be no larger than the bit size of the processor; a 32-bit machine has 4-byte references, a 64-bit machine has 8-byte references, and so on.) Copying the value of a value type copies all the data, which could be large. Therefore, in some circumstances, reference types are more efficient to copy. This is why the guideline for value types is to ensure that they are never more than 16 bytes or thereabouts; if a value type is more than four times as expensive to copy as a reference, it probably should simply be a reference type.

Since reference types copy only a reference to the data, two different variables can refer to the same data. In such a case, changing the data through one variable will be observed to change the data for the other variable as well. This happens both for assignments and for method calls.

To continue our previous analogy, if you pass the address of a building to a method, you make a copy of the paper containing the reference and hand the copy to the method. The method cannot change the contents of the original paper to refer to a different building. If the method paints the referred-to building, however, when the method returns, the caller can observe that the building to which the caller is still referring is now a different color.

Structs

All the C# built-in types, such as `bool` and `decimal`, are value types, except for `string` and `object`, which are reference types. Numerous additional value types are provided within the framework. It is also possible for developers to define their own value types.

To define a custom value type, you use a syntax similar to the syntax you would use to define class and interface types. The key difference in the syntax is that value types use the keyword `struct`, as shown in Listing 9.1. Here we have a value type that describes a high-precision angle in terms of its degrees, minutes, and seconds. (A *minute* is one-sixtieth of a degree, and a *second* is one-sixtieth of a minute. This system is used in navigation because it has the nice property that an arc of one minute over the surface of the ocean at the equator is exactly one nautical mile.)

LISTING 9.1: Declaring a struct

Begin 6.0

```csharp
// Use keyword struct to declare a value type
struct Angle
{
    public Angle(int degrees, int minutes, int seconds)
    {
        Degrees = degrees;
        Minutes = minutes;
        Seconds = seconds;
    }

    // Using C# 6.0 read-only, automatically implemented properties
    public int Degrees { get; }
    public int Minutes { get; }
    public int Seconds { get; }

    public Angle Move(int degrees, int minutes, int seconds)
    {
        return new Angle(
            Degrees + degrees,
            Minutes + minutes,
            Seconds + seconds);
    }
}
```

```csharp
// Declaring a class as a reference type
// (declaring it as a struct would create a value type
// larger than 16 bytes)
class Coordinate
{
    public Angle Longitude { get; set; }

    public Angle Latitude { get; set; }
}
```

This listing defines `Angle` as a value type that stores the degrees, minutes, and seconds of an angle, either longitude or latitude. The resultant C# type is a **struct**.

Note that the `Angle` struct in Listing 9.1 is immutable because all properties are declared using C# 6.0's read-only, automatically implemented property capability. To create a read-only property without C# 6.0, programmers will need to declare a property with only a getter that accesses its data from a `readonly` modified field (see Listing 9.3). C# 6.0 provides a noticeable code reduction when it comes to defining immutable types.

Starting with C# 7.2, you can verify that, in fact, you have successfully defined a struct that is read only by declaring it as such:

```
readonly struct Angle {}
```

Now the compiler will verify that the entire struct is immutable, reporting an error if there is a field that is not read only or a property that has a setter.

Begin 7.2

6.0

End 7.2

■ NOTE

Although nothing in the language requires it, a good guideline is for value types to be immutable: Once you have instantiated a value type, you should not be able to modify the same instance. In scenarios where modification is desirable, you should create a new instance. Listing 9.1 supplies a `Move()` method that doesn't modify the instance of `Angle`, but instead returns an entirely new instance.

There are two good reasons for this guideline. First, value types should represent values. One does not think of adding two integers together as mutating either of them; rather, the two addends are immutable and a third value is produced as the result.

Second, because value types are copied by value, not by reference, it is very easy to get confused and incorrectly believe that a mutation to one value type variable can be observed to cause a mutation in another, as it would with a reference type.

Guidelines

DO create value types that are immutable.

Initializing Structs

In addition to properties and fields, structs may contain methods and constructors. However, no default constructor may be defined. Instead, the C#

compiler automatically generates a default constructor that initializes all fields to their default values. The default value is null for a field of reference type data, a zero value for a field of numeric type, false for a field of Boolean type, and so on.

To ensure that a local value type variable can be fully initialized by a constructor, every constructor in a struct must initialize all fields (and read-only, automatically implemented properties) within the struct. (In C# 6.0, initialization via a read-only, automatically implemented property is sufficient because the backing field is unknown and its initialization would not be possible.) Failure to initialize all data within the struct causes a compile-time error. To complicate matters slightly, C# disallows field initializers in a struct. Listing 9.2, for example, would not compile if the line _Degrees = 42 was uncommented.

LISTING 9.2: Initializing a struct Field within a Declaration, Resulting in an Error

```
struct Angle
{
  // ...
  // ERROR:  Fields cannot be initialized at declaration time
  // int _Degrees = 42;
  // ...
}
```

If not explicitly instantiated via the new operator's call to the constructor, all data contained within the struct is implicitly initialized to that data's default value. However, all data within a value type must be explicitly initialized to avoid a compiler error. This raises a question: When might a value type be implicitly initialized but not explicitly instantiated? This situation occurs when instantiating a reference type that contains an unassigned field of value type as well as when instantiating an array of value types without an array initializer.

To fulfill the initialization requirement on a struct, all explicitly declared fields must be initialized. Such initialization must be done directly. For example, in Listing 9.3, the constructor that initializes the property (if uncommented out) rather than the field produces a compile error.

LISTING 9.3: Accessing Properties before Initializing All Fields

```
struct Angle
  {
  // ERROR:  The "this" object cannot be used before
```

```
//        all of its fields are assigned to
// public Angle(int degrees, int minutes, int seconds)
// {
//     Degrees = degrees;
//     Minutes = minutes;
//     Seconds = seconds;
// }

public Angle(int degrees, int minutes, int seconds)
{
    _Degrees = degrees;
    _Minutes = minutes;
    _Seconds = seconds;
}

public int Degrees { get { return _Degrees; } }
readonly private int _Degrees;

public int Minutes { get { return _Minutes; } }
readonly private int _Minutes;

public int Seconds { get { return _Seconds; } }
readonly private int _Seconds;

// ...
}
```

6.0

It is not legal to access this until the compiler knows that all fields have been initialized; the use of Degrees is implicitly this.Degrees. To resolve this issue, you need to initialize the fields directly, as demonstrated in the constructor of Listing 9.3 that is not commented out.

Because of the struct's field initialization requirement, the succinctness of C# 6.0's read-only, automatically implemented property support, and the guideline to avoid accessing fields from outside of their wrapping property, you should favor read-only, automatically implemented properties over fields within structs starting with C# 6.0.

Guidelines

DO ensure that the default value of a struct is valid; it is always possible to obtain the default "all zero" value of a struct.

■ ADVANCED TOPIC

Using new with Value Types

Invoking the new operator with a reference type causes the runtime to create a new instance of the object on the garbage-collected heap, initialize all of its fields to their default values, and call the constructor, passing a reference to the instance as this. The result is the reference to the instance, which can then be copied to its final destination. In contrast, invoking the new operator with a value type causes the runtime to create a new instance of the object on the temporary storage pool, initialize all of its fields to their default values, and call the constructor (passing the temporary storage location as a ref variable as this), resulting in the value being stored in the temporary storage location, which can then be copied to its final destination.

Unlike classes, structs do not support finalizers. Structs are copied by value; they do not have referential identity, as reference types do. Therefore, it is hard to know when it would be safe to execute the finalizer and free an unmanaged resource owned by the struct. The garbage collector knows when there are no "live" references to an instance of reference type and can choose to run the finalizer for an instance of reference type at any time after there are no more live references. Nevertheless, no part of the runtime tracks how many copies of a given value type exist at any moment.

Language Contrast: C++—struct Defines Type with Public Members

In C++, the difference between a type declared with struct and one declared with class is whether the default accessibility is public or private. The contrast is far greater in C#, where the difference is whether instances of the type are copied by value or by reference.

Using the default Operator

As described earlier, no default constructor may be defined on a struct. Instead, all value types have an automatically defined default constructor that initializes the storage of a value type to its default state. Therefore, it is always legal to use the new operator to create a value type instance. As an alternative syntax, you can use the default operator to produce the default value for a struct. In Listing 9.4, we add a second constructor to the Angle struct that uses the default operator on int as an argument to the previously declared three-argument constructor.

LISTING 9.4: Using the default Operator to Obtain the Default Value of a Type

```csharp
// Use keyword struct to declare a value type
struct Angle
{
  public Angle(int degrees, int minutes)
      : this( degrees, minutes, default(int) )
  {
  }

  // ...
}
```

The expressions `default(int)` and `new int()` both produce the same value. Furthermore, accessing the implicitly initialized value type is a valid operation; accessing the default value of a reference type, in contrast, would produce a `NullReferenceException`. For this reason, you should take care to explicitly initialize value types following instantiation if the `default(T)` value is not a valid state for the type.

End 6.0

Note that in C# 7.1, `default` can be used without `(int)`, as in

Begin 7.0

```csharp
public Angle(int degrees, int minutes)
: this( degrees, minutes, default ) { ... }
```

End 7.0

For more information about the `default` operator, see Chapter 12.

Inheritance and Interfaces with Value Types

All value types are implicitly sealed. In addition, all non-enum value types derive from `System.ValueType`. As a consequence, the inheritance chain for structs is always from `object` to `System.ValueType` to the struct.

Value types can implement interfaces, too. Many of those built into the framework implement interfaces such as `IComparable` and `IFormattable`.

`System.ValueType` brings with it the behavior of value types, but it does not include any additional members. The `System.ValueType` customizations focus on overriding all of `object`'s virtual members. The rules for overriding these methods in a struct are almost the same as those for classes (see Chapter 10). However, one difference is that with value types, the default implementation for `GetHashCode()` is to forward the call to the first non-null field within the struct. Also, `Equals()` makes significant use of reflection. Therefore, if a value type is used frequently inside collections, especially dictionary-type collections that use hash codes, the value type should include overrides for both `Equals()` and `GetHashCode()` to ensure good performance. See Chapter 10 for more details.

> ### Guidelines
>
> **DO** overload the equality operators (`Equals()`, `==`, and `!=`) on value types if equality is meaningful. (Also consider implementing the `IEquatable<T>` interface.)

Boxing

We know that variables of value type directly contain their data, whereas variables of reference type contain a reference to another storage location. But what happens when a value type is converted to one of its implemented interfaces or to its root base class, `object`? The result of the conversion has to be a reference to a storage location that contains something that looks like an instance of a reference type, but the variable contains a value of value type. Such a conversion, which is known as **boxing**, has special behavior. Converting a variable of value type that directly refers to its data to a reference type that refers to a location on the garbage-collected heap involves several steps.

1. Memory is allocated on the heap that will contain the value type's data and the other overhead necessary to make the object look like every other instance of a managed object of reference type (namely, a `SyncBlockIndex` and method table pointer).
2. The value of the value type is copied from its current storage location into the newly allocated location on the heap.
3. The result of the conversion is a reference to the new storage location on the heap.

The reverse operation is **unboxing**. The unboxing conversion checks whether the type of the boxed value is compatible with the type to which the value is being unboxed, and then results in a copy of the value stored in the heap location.

Boxing and unboxing are important to consider because boxing has some performance and behavioral implications. Besides learning how to recognize these conversions within C# code, a developer can count the box/unbox instructions in a particular snippet of code by looking through the Common Intermediate Language (CIL). Each operation has specific instructions, as shown in Table 9.1.

TABLE 9.1: Boxing Code in CIL

C# Code	CIL Code
`static void Main()`	`.method private hidebysig`
	`        static void  Main() cil managed`
`{`	`{`
	`  .entrypoint`
	`  // Code size        21 (0x15)`
	`  .maxstack  1`
`    int number;`	`  .locals init ([0] int32 number,`
`    object thing;`	`             [1] object thing)`
	`  IL_0000:  nop`
`    number = 42;`	`  IL_0001:  ldc.i4.s    42`
	`  IL_0003:  stloc.0`
`    // Boxing`	`  IL_0004:  ldloc.0`
`    thing = number;`	`  IL_0005:  box         [mscorlib]System.Int32`
	`  IL_000a:  stloc.1`
`    // Unboxing`	`  IL_000b:  ldloc.1`
`    number = (int)thing;`	`  IL_000c:  unbox.any   [mscorlib]System.Int32`
	`  IL_0011:  stloc.0`
	`  IL_0012:  br.s        IL_0014`
`return;`	`  IL_0014:  ret`
`}`	`} // end of method Program::Main`

When boxing and unboxing occur infrequently, their implications for performance are irrelevant. However, boxing can occur in some unexpected situations, and frequent occurrences can have a significant impact on performance. Consider Listing 9.5 and Output 9.1. The `ArrayList` type maintains a list of references to objects, so adding an integer or floating-point number to the list will box the value so that a reference can be obtained.

LISTING 9.5: Subtle Box and Unbox Instructions

```
class DisplayFibonacci
{
  static void Main()
  {

    int totalCount;
    System.Collections.ArrayList list =
```

```
          new System.Collections.ArrayList();

      Console.Write("Enter a number between 2 and 1000:");
      totalCount = int.Parse(Console.ReadLine());

      // Execution-time error:
      // list.Add(0);  // Cast to double or 'D' suffix required.
                       // Whether cast or using 'D' suffix,
                       // CIL is identical.
      list.Add((double)0);
      list.Add((double)1);
      for (int count = 2; count < totalCount; count++)
      {
          list.Add(
              ((double)list[count - 1] +
              (double)list[count - 2]) );
      }

      foreach (double count in list)
      {
          Console.Write("{0}, ", count);
      }
    }
  }
```

OUTPUT 9.1

```
Enter a number between 2 and 1000:42
0, 1, 1, 2, 3, 5, 8, 13, 21, 34, 55, 89, 144, 233, 377, 610, 987, 1597,
2584, 4181, 6765, 10946, 17711, 28657, 46368, 75025, 121393, 196418,
317811, 514229, 832040, 1346269, 2178309, 3524578, 5702887, 9227465,
14930352, 24157817, 39088169, 63245986, 102334155, 165580141,
```

The code shown in Listing 9.5, when compiled, produces five box and three unbox instructions in the resultant CIL.

1. The first two box instructions occur in the initial calls to list.Add(). The signature for the ArrayList method is int Add(object value). As such, any value type passed to this method is boxed.

2. Next are two unbox instructions in the call to Add() within the for loop. The return from an ArrayList's index operator is always object because that is what ArrayList contains. To add the two values, you need to cast them back to doubles. This cast from a reference to an object to a value type is implemented as an unbox call.

3. Now you take the result of the addition and place it into the ArrayList instance, which again results in a box operation. Note that the first two unbox instructions and this box instruction occur within a loop.

4. In the `foreach` loop, you iterate through each item in `ArrayList` and assign the items to `count`. As you saw earlier, the items within `ArrayList` are references to `object`s, so assigning them to a `double` is, in effect, unboxing each of them.

5. The signature for `Console.WriteLine()`, which is called within the `foreach` loop, is `void Console.Write(string format, object arg)`. As a result, each call to it boxes the `double` to `object`.

Every boxing operation involves both an allocation and a copy; every unboxing operation involves a type check and a copy. Doing the equivalent work using the unboxed type would eliminate the allocation and type check. Obviously, you can easily improve this code's performance by eliminating many of the boxing operations. Using an `object` rather than `double` in the last `foreach` loop is one such improvement. Another would be to change the `ArrayList` data type to a generic collection (see Chapter 12). The point being made here is that boxing can be rather subtle, so developers need to pay special attention and notice situations where it could potentially occur repeatedly and affect performance.

Another unfortunate boxing-related problem also occurs at runtime: If you wanted to change the initial two `Add()` calls so that they did not use a cast (or a `double` literal), you would have to insert integers into the array list. Since `int`s will implicitly be converted to `double`s, this would appear to be an innocuous modification. However, the casts to `double` from within the `for` loop, and again in the assignment to `count` in the `foreach` loop, would fail. The problem is that immediately following the unbox operation is an attempt to perform a memory copy of the value of the boxed `int` into a `double`. You cannot do this without first casting to an `int`, because the code will throw an `InvalidCastException` at execution time. Listing 9.6 shows a similar error commented out and followed by the correct cast.

LISTING 9.6: Unboxing Must Be to the Underlying Type

```
// ...
int number;
object thing;
double bigNumber;

number = 42;
thing = number;
```

```
// ERROR: InvalidCastException
// bigNumber = (double)thing;
bigNumber = (double)(int)thing;
// ...
```

▪ ADVANCED TOPIC

Value Types in the lock Statement

C# supports a lock statement for synchronizing code. The statement compiles down to System.Threading.Monitor's Enter() and Exit() methods. These two methods must be called in pairs. Enter() records the unique reference argument passed so that when Exit() is called with the same reference, the lock can be released. The trouble with using value types is the boxing. Therefore, each time Enter() or Exit() is called, a new value is created on the heap. Comparing the reference of one copy to the reference of a different copy will always return false, so you cannot hook up Enter() with the corresponding Exit(). Therefore, value types in the lock() statement are not allowed.

Listing 9.7 points out a few more runtime boxing idiosyncrasies, and Output 9.2 shows the results.

LISTING 9.7: **Subtle Boxing Idiosyncrasies**

```
interface IAngle
{
    void MoveTo(int degrees, int minutes, int seconds);
}
```

```
struct Angle : IAngle
{
  // ...

  // NOTE:  This makes Angle mutable, against the general
  //        guideline
  public void MoveTo(int degrees, int minutes, int seconds)
  {
        _Degrees = degrees;
        _Minutes = minutes;
        _Seconds = seconds;
  }
}
```

```csharp
class Program
{
  static void Main()
  {
      // ...

      Angle angle = new Angle(25, 58, 23);
      // Example 1: Simple box operation
      object objectAngle = angle;  // Box
      Console.Write( ((Angle)objectAngle).Degrees);

      // Example 2: Unbox, modify unboxed value, and discard value
      ((Angle)objectAngle).MoveTo(26, 58, 23);
      Console.Write(", " + ((Angle)objectAngle).Degrees);

      // Example 3: Box, modify boxed value, and discard reference to box
      ((IAngle)angle).MoveTo(26, 58, 23);
      Console.Write(", " + ((Angle)angle).Degrees);

      // Example 4: Modify boxed value directly
      ((IAngle)objectAngle).MoveTo(26, 58, 23);
      Console.WriteLine(", " + ((Angle)objectAngle).Degrees);

      // ...
  }
}
```

OUTPUT 9.2

```
25, 25, 25, 26
```

Listing 9.7 uses the `Angle` struct and `IAngle` interface. Note also that the `IAngle.MoveTo()` interface changes `Angle` to be mutable. This change brings out some of the idiosyncrasies of mutable value types and, in so doing, demonstrates the importance of the guideline to make structs immutable.

In Example 1 of Listing 9.7, after you initialize `angle`, you then box it into a variable called `objectAngle`. Next, Example 2 calls `MoveTo()` to change `Hours` to 26. However, as the output demonstrates, no change actually occurs the first time. The problem is that to call `MoveTo()`, the compiler unboxes `objectAngle` and (by definition) makes a copy of the value. Value types are copied by value—that is why they are called value types. Although the resultant value is successfully modified at execution time, this copy of the value is discarded and no change occurs on the heap location referenced by `objectAngle`.

Recall our analogy that suggested variables of value type are like pieces of paper with the value written on them. When you box a value, you make a photocopy of the paper and put the copy in a box. When you unbox the value, you make a photocopy of the paper in the box. Making an edit to this second copy does not change the copy that is in the box.

In Example 3, a similar problem occurs in reverse. Instead of calling `MoveTo()` directly, the value is cast to `IAngle`. The conversion to an interface type boxes the value, so the runtime copies the data in `angle` to the heap and provides a reference to that box. Next, the method call modifies the value in the referenced box. The value stored in variable `angle` remains unmodified.

In the last case, the cast to `IAngle` is a reference conversion, not a boxing conversion. The value has already been boxed by the conversion to `object` in this case, so no copy of the value occurs on this conversion. The call to `MoveTo()` updates the `_Hours` value stored in the box, and the code behaves as desired.

As you can see from this example, mutable value types are quite confusing because it is often unclear when you are mutating a copy of the value rather than the storage location you actually intend to change. By avoiding mutable value types in the first place, you can eliminate this sort of confusion.

Guidelines

AVOID mutable value types.

■ ADVANCED TOPIC

How Boxing Can Be Avoided during Method Calls

Anytime a method is called on a value type, the value type receiving the call (represented by `this` in the body of the method) must be a variable, not a value, because the method might be trying to mutate the receiver. Clearly, it must be mutating the receiver's storage location, rather than mutating a copy of the receiver's value and then discarding it. Examples 2 and 4 of Listing 9.7 illustrate how this fact affects the performance of a method invocation on a boxed value type.

In Example 2, the unboxing conversion logically produces the boxed value, not a reference to the storage location on the heap that contains the boxed copy. Which storage location, then, is passed as the `this` to the mutating method call? It cannot be the storage location from the box on the heap, because the unboxing conversion produces a copy of that value, not a reference to that storage location.

When this situation arises—a variable of value type is required but only a value is available—one of two things happens: Either the C# compiler generates code that makes a new, temporary storage location and copies the value from the box into the new location, resulting in the temporary storage location becoming the needed variable, or the compiler produces an error and disallows the operation. In this case, the former strategy is used. The new temporary storage location is then the receiver of the call; after it is mutated, the temporary storage location is discarded.

This process—performing a type check of the boxed value, unboxing to produce the storage location of the boxed value, allocating a temporary variable, copying the value from the box to the temporary variable, and then calling the method with the location of the temporary storage—happens every time you use the unbox-and-then-call pattern, regardless of whether the method actually mutates the variable. Clearly, if it does not mutate the variable, some of this work could be avoided. Because the C# compiler does not know whether any particular method you call will try to mutate the receiver, it must err on the side of caution.

These expenses are all eliminated when calling an interface method on a boxed value type. In such a case, the expectation is that the receiver will be the storage location in the box; if the interface method mutates the storage location, it is the boxed location that should be mutated. Therefore, the expense of performing a type check, allocating new temporary storage, and making a copy is avoided. Instead, the runtime simply uses the storage location in the box as the receiver of the call to the struct's method.

In Listing 9.8, we call the two-argument version of `ToString()` that is found on the `IFormattable` interface, which is implemented by the `int` value type. In this example, the receiver of the call is a boxed value type, but it is not unboxed to make the call to the interface method.

LISTING 9.8: Avoiding Unboxing and Copying

```
int number;
object thing;
number = 42;
```

```
// Boxing
thing = number;
// No unboxing conversion
string text = ((IFormattable)thing).ToString(
    "X", null);
Console.WriteLine(text);
```

You might now wonder: Suppose that we had instead called the virtual ToString() method declared by object with an instance of a value type as the receiver. What happens then? Is the instance boxed, unboxed, or what? A number of different scenarios are possible depending on the details:

- If the receiver is unboxed and the struct overrides ToString(), the overridden method is called directly. There is no need for a virtual call because the method cannot be overridden further by a more derived class; all value types are automatically sealed.

- If the receiver is unboxed and the struct does not override ToString(), the base class implementation must be called, and it expects a reference to an object as its receiver. Therefore, the receiver is boxed.

- If the receiver is boxed and the struct overrides ToString(), the storage location in the box is passed to the overriding method without unboxing it.

- If the receiver is boxed and the struct does not override ToString(), the reference to the box is passed to the base class's implementation of the method, which is expecting a reference.

Enums

Compare the two code snippets shown in Listing 9.9.

LISTING 9.9: Comparing an Integer Switch to an Enum Switch

```
int connectionState;
// ...
switch (connectionState)
{
    case 0:
        // ...
        break;
```

```
    case 1:
        // ...
        break;
    case 2:
        // ...
        break;
    case 3:
        // ...
        break;
}
```

```
ConnectionState connectionState;
// ...
switch (connectionState)
{
    case ConnectionState.Connected:
        // ...
        break;
    case ConnectionState.Connecting:
        // ...
        break;
    case ConnectionState.Disconnected:
        // ...
        break;
    case ConnectionState.Disconnecting:
        // ...
        break;
}
```

Obviously, the difference in terms of readability is tremendous—in the second snippet, the cases are self-documenting. However, the performance at runtime is identical. To achieve this outcome, the second snippet uses **enum values** in each case.

An enum is a value type that the developer can declare. The key characteristic of an enum is that it declares at compile time a set of possible constant values that can be referred to by name, thereby making the code easier to read. The syntax for a typical enum declaration is shown in Listing 9.10.

LISTING 9.10: Defining an Enum

```
enum ConnectionState
{
  Disconnected,
  Connecting,
  Connected,
  Disconnecting
}
```

> ■ **NOTE**
>
> An enum can be used as a more readable replacement for Boolean values as well. For example, a method call such as `SetState(true)` is less readable than `SetState(DeviceState.On)`.

You use an enum value by prefixing it with the enum name. To use the `Connected` value, for example, you would use the syntax `ConnectionState.Connected`. Do not make the enum type name a part of the value's name so as to avoid the redundancy of something such as `ConnectionState.ConnectionStateConnected`. By convention, the enum name itself should be singular (unless the enums are bit flags, as discussed shortly). That is, the nomenclature should be `ConnectionState`, not `ConnectionStates`.

Enum values are actually implemented as nothing more than integer constants. By default, the first enum value is given the value 0, and each subsequent entry increases by 1. However, you can assign explicit values to enums, as shown in Listing 9.11.

LISTING 9.11: Defining an Enum Type

```
enum ConnectionState : short
{
  Disconnected,
  Connecting = 10,
  Connected,
  Joined = Connected,
  Disconnecting
}
```

In this code, `Disconnected` has a default value of 0 and `Connecting` has been explicitly assigned 10; consequently, `Connected` will be assigned 11. `Joined` is assigned 11, the value assigned to `Connected`. (In this case, you do not need to prefix `Connected` with the enum name, since it appears within its scope.) `Disconnecting` is 12.

An enum always has an underlying type, which may be any integral type other than `char`. In fact, the enum type's performance is identical to that of the underlying type. By default, the underlying value type is `int`, but you can specify a different type using inheritance type syntax. Instead of `int`, for example, Listing 9.11 uses a `short`. For consistency, the syntax for enums emulates the syntax of inheritance, but this doesn't actually make an inheritance relationship. The base class for all enums is System.Enum, which in turn is derived from System.ValueType. Furthermore, these classes are sealed; you can't derive from an existing enum type to add additional members.

An enum is really nothing more than a set of names thinly layered on top of the underlying type; there is no mechanism that restricts the value of a variable of enumerated type to just the values named in the declaration. For example, because it is possible to cast the integer 42 to short, it is also possible to cast the integer 42 to the ConnectionState type, even though there is no corresponding ConnectionState enum value. If the value can be converted to the underlying type, the conversion to the enum type will also be successful.

The advantage of this odd feature is that enums can have new values added in later API releases, without breaking earlier versions. Additionally, the enum values provide names for the known values while still allowing unknown values to be assigned at runtime. The burden is that developers must code defensively for the possibility of unnamed values. It would be unwise, for example, to replace case ConnectionState.Disconnecting with default and expect that the only possible value for the default case was ConnectionState.Disconnecting. Instead, you should handle the Disconnecting case explicitly, and the default case should report an error or behave innocuously. As indicated earlier, however, conversion between the enum and the underlying type, and vice versa, requires an explicit cast; it is not an implicit conversion. For example, code cannot call ReportState(10) if the method's signature is void ReportState(ConnectionState state). The only exception occurs when passing 0, because there is an implicit conversion from 0 to any enum.

Although you can add more values to an enum in a later version of your code, you should do so with care. Inserting an enum value in the middle of an enum will bump the values of all later enums (adding Flooded or Locked before Connected will change the Connected value, for example). This will affect the versions of all code that is recompiled against the new version. However, any code compiled against the old version will continue to use the old values, making the intended values entirely different. Besides inserting an enum value at the end of the list, one way to avoid changing enum values is to assign values explicitly.

Guidelines

CONSIDER adding new members to existing enums, but keep in mind the compatibility risk.

AVOID creating enums that represent an "incomplete" set of values, such as product version numbers.

AVOID creating "reserved for future use" values in an enum.

AVOID enums that contain a single value.

DO provide a value of 0 (none) for simple enums, knowing that 0 will be the default value when no explicit initialization is provided.

Enums are slightly different from other value types because they derive from System.Enum before deriving from System.ValueType.

Type Compatibility between Enums

C# also does not support a direct cast between arrays of two different enums. However, the CLR does, provided that both enums share the same underlying type. To work around this restriction of C#, the trick is to cast first to System.Array, as shown at the end of Listing 9.12.

LISTING 9.12: Casting between Arrays of Enums

```
enum ConnectionState1
{
  Disconnected,
  Connecting,
  Connected,
  Disconnecting
}
```

```
enum ConnectionState2
{
  Disconnected,
  Connecting,
  Connected,
  Disconnecting
}
```

```
class Program
{
  static void Main()
  {
      ConnectionState1[] states =
          (ConnectionState1[])(Array)new ConnectionState2[42];
  }
}
```

This example exploits the fact that the CLR's notion of assignment compatibility is more lenient than C#'s concept. (The same trick is possible for other illegal conversions, such as int[] to uint[].) However, use this approach cautiously because there is no C# specification requiring that this behavior work across different CLR implementations.

Converting between Enums and Strings

One of the conveniences associated with enums is that the ToString() method, which is called by methods such as System.Console.WriteLine(), writes out the enum value identifier:

```
System.Diagnostics.Trace.WriteLine(
    $"The connection is currently { ConnectionState.Disconnecting }");
```

The preceding code will write the text in Output 9.3 to the trace buffer.

OUTPUT 9.3

```
The connection is currently Disconnecting.
```

Conversion from a string to an enum is a little more difficult to achieve, because it involves a static method on the System.Enum base class. Listing 9.13 provides an example of how to do it without generics (see Chapter 12), and Output 9.4 shows the results.

LISTING 9.13: Converting a String to an Enum Using Enum.Parse()

```
ThreadPriorityLevel priority = (ThreadPriorityLevel)Enum.Parse(
    typeof(ThreadPriorityLevel), "Idle");
Console.WriteLine(priority);
```

OUTPUT 9.4

```
Idle
```

In this code, the first parameter to Enum.Parse() is the type, which you specify using the keyword typeof(). This example depicts a compile-time way of identifying the type, like a literal for the type value (see Chapter 18).

Until Microsoft .NET Framework 4, there was no TryParse() method, so code written to target prior versions needs to include appropriate exception handling if there is a chance the string will not correspond to an enum value identifier. Microsoft .NET Framework 4's TryParse<T>() method uses generics, but the type parameters can be inferred, resulting in the to-enum conversion behavior shown in Listing 9.14.

LISTING 9.14: Converting a String to an Enum Using Enum.TryParse<T>()

```
System.Diagnostics.ThreadPriorityLevel priority;
if(Enum.TryParse("Idle", out priority))
{
    Console.WriteLine(priority);
}
```

This technique eliminates the need to use exception handling if the string might not convert successfully. Instead, code can check the Boolean result returned from the call to TryParse<T>().

Regardless of whether the code uses the "Parse" or "TryParse" approach, the key caution about converting from a string to an enum is that such a cast is not localizable. Therefore, developers should use this type of cast only for messages that are not exposed to users (assuming localization is a requirement).

> ### Guidelines
>
> **AVOID** direct enum/string conversions where the string must be localized into the user's language.

Enums as Flags

Many times, developers not only want enum values to be unique but also want to be able to represent a combination of values. For example, consider System.IO.FileAttributes. This enum, shown in Listing 9.15, indicates various attributes on a file: read-only, hidden, archive, and so on. Unlike with the ConnectionState attribute, where each enum value was mutually exclusive, the FileAttributes enum values can and are intended for combination: A file can be both read-only and hidden. To support this behavior, each enum value is a unique bit.

LISTING 9.15: Using Enums as Flags

```
[Flags] public enum FileAttributes
{
    ReadOnly =          1<<0,    // 000000000000000001
    Hidden =            1<<1,    // 000000000000000010
    System =            1<<2,    // 000000000000000100
    Directory =         1<<4,    // 000000000000010000
    Archive =           1<<5,    // 000000000000100000
    Device =            1<<6,    // 000000000001000000
    Normal =            1<<7,    // 000000000010000000
    Temporary =         1<<8,    // 000000000100000000
    SparseFile =        1<<9,    // 000000001000000000
    ReparsePoint =      1<<10,   // 000000010000000000
    Compressed =        1<<11,   // 000000100000000000
    Offline =           1<<12,   // 000001000000000000
    NotContentIndexed = 1<<13,   // 000010000000000000
    Encrypted =         1<<14,   // 000100000000000000
    IntegrityStream =   1<<15,   // 001000000000000000
    NoScrubData  =      1<<17,   // 100000000000000000
}
```

> **■ NOTE**
>
> Note that the name of a bit flags enum is usually pluralized, indicating that a value of the type represents a set of flags.

To join enum values, you use a bitwise OR operator. To test for the existence of a particular flag, use the HasFlags() method (which was added with Microsoft .NET Framework 4.0) or use the bitwise AND operator. Both cases are illustrated in Listing 9.16.

LISTING 9.16: Using Bitwise OR and AND with Flag Enums[1]

```csharp
using System;
using System.IO;

public class Program
{
  public static void Main()
  {
      // ...

      string fileName = @"enumtest.txt";

      System.IO.FileInfo file =
          new System.IO.FileInfo(fileName);

      file.Attributes = FileAttributes.Hidden |
          FileAttributes.ReadOnly;

      Console.WriteLine($"{file.Attributes} = {(int)file.Attributes}");

        // Added in C# 4.0/Microsoft .NET Framwork 4.0
      if (!file.Attributes.HasFlag(FileAttributes.Hidden))
      {
          throw new Exception("File is not hidden.");
      }
      // Use bit operators prior to C# 4.0/.NET 4.0
      if (( file.Attributes & FileAttributes.ReadOnly) !=
          FileAttributes.ReadOnly)
      {
          throw new Exception("File is not read-only.");
      }

      // ...
  }
}
```

The results of Listing 9.16 appear in Output 9.5.

OUTPUT 9.5

```
Hidden | ReadOnly = 3
```

Using the bitwise OR operator allows you to set the file to both read-only and hidden.

Each value within the enum does not need to correspond to only one flag. It is perfectly reasonable to define additional flags that correspond to frequent combinations of values. Listing 9.17 shows an example.

---

1. Note that the `FileAttributes.Hidden` value does not work on Linux.

LISTING 9.17: Defining Enum Values for Frequent Combinations

```
[Flags] enum DistributedChannel
{
  None = 0,
  Transacted = 1,
  Queued = 2,
  Encrypted = 4,
  Persisted = 16,
  FaultTolerant =
      Transacted | Queued | Persisted
}
```

It is a good practice to have a zero `None` member in a flags enum because the initial default value of a field of enum type or an element of an array of enum type is 0. Avoid enum values corresponding to items such as `Maximum` as the last enum, because `Maximum` could be interpreted as a valid enum value. To check whether a value is included within an enum, use the `System.Enum.IsDefined()` method.

Guidelines

DO use the `FlagsAttribute` to mark enums that contain flags.

DO provide a None value equal to 0 for all flag enums.

AVOID creating flag enums where the zero value has a meaning other than "no flags are set."

CONSIDER providing special values for commonly used combinations of flags.

DO NOT include "sentinel" values (such as a value called `Maximum`); such values can be confusing to the user.

DO use powers of 2 to ensure that all flag combinations are represented uniquely.

■ ADVANCED TOPIC

FlagsAttribute

If you decide to use bit flag enums, the declaration of the enum should be marked with `FlagsAttribute`. In such a case, the attribute appears in square brackets (see Chapter 18) just prior to the enum declaration, as shown in Listing 9.18.

LISTING 9.18: Using FlagsAttribute

```
// FileAttributes defined in System.IO

[Flags] // Decorating an enum with FlagsAttribute
public enum FileAttributes
{
  ReadOnly =            1<<0,      // 000000000000001
  Hidden =              1<<1,      // 000000000000010
  // ...
}
```

```
using System;
using System.Diagnostics;
using System.IO;

class Program
{
  public static void Main()
  {
      string fileName = @"enumtest.txt";
      FileInfo file = new FileInfo(fileName);
      file.Open(FileMode.Create).Close();

      FileAttributes startingAttributes =
          file.Attributes;

      file.Attributes = FileAttributes.Hidden |
          FileAttributes.ReadOnly;

      Console.WriteLine("\"{0}\" outputs as \"{1}\"",
          file.Attributes.ToString().Replace(",", " |"),
          file.Attributes);

      FileAttributes attributes =
          (FileAttributes) Enum.Parse(typeof(FileAttributes),
          file.Attributes.ToString());

      Console.WriteLine(attributes);

      File.SetAttributes(fileName,
          startingAttributes);
      file.Delete();
  }
}
```

The results of Listing 9.18 appear in Output 9.6.

OUTPUT 9.6

```
"ReadOnly | Hidden" outputs as "ReadOnly, Hidden"
ReadOnly, Hidden
```

The attribute documents that the enum values can be combined. Furthermore, it changes the behavior of the `ToString()` and `Parse()` methods. For example, calling `ToString()` on an enum that is decorated with `FlagsAttribute` writes out the strings for each enum flag that is set. In Listing 9.18, `file.Attributes.ToString()` returns `ReadOnly, Hidden` rather than the 3 it would have returned without the `FileAttributes` flag. If two enum values are the same, the `ToString()` call would return the first value. As mentioned earlier, however, you should use caution when relying on this behavior because it is not localizable.

Parsing a value from a string to the enum also works. Each enum value identifier is separated from the others by a comma.

Note that `FlagsAttribute` does not automatically assign unique flag values or check that they have unique values. Doing this wouldn't make sense, given that duplicates and combinations are often desirable. Instead, you must assign the values of each enum item explicitly.

SUMMARY

This chapter began with a discussion of how to define custom value types. Because it is easy to write confusing or buggy code when mutating value types, and because value types are typically used to model immutable values, it is a good idea to make value types immutable. We also described how value types are boxed when they must be treated polymorphically as reference types.

The idiosyncrasies introduced by boxing are subtle, and the vast majority of them lead to problematic issues at execution time rather than at compile time. Although it is important to know about these quirks so as to try to avoid them, in many ways paying too much attention to the potential pitfalls overshadows the usefulness and performance advantages of value types. Programmers should not be overly concerned about using value types. Value types permeate virtually every chapter of this book, yet the idiosyncrasies associated with them come into play infrequently. We have staged the code surrounding each issue to demonstrate the concern, but in reality these types of patterns rarely occur. The key to avoiding most of them is to follow the guideline of not creating mutable value types, and following this constraint explains why you don't encounter them within the built-in value types.

Perhaps the only issue to occur with some frequency is repetitive boxing operations within loops. However, generics greatly reduce boxing, and even without them, performance is rarely affected enough to warrant their avoidance until a particular algorithm with boxing is identified as a bottleneck.

Furthermore, custom-built structs are relatively rare. They obviously play an important role within C# development, but the number of custom-built structs declared by typical developers is usually tiny compared to the number of custom-built classes. Heavy use of custom-built structs is most common in code targeted at interoperating with unmanaged code.

> **Guidelines**
>
> **DO NOT** define a struct unless it logically represents a single value, consumes 16 bytes or less of storage, is immutable, and is infrequently boxed.

This chapter also introduced enums. Enumerated types are a standard construct available in many programming languages. They help improve both API usability and code readability.

The next chapter presents more guidelines for creating well-formed types—both value types and reference types. It begins by looking at overriding the virtual members of objects and defining operator-overloading methods. These two topics apply to both structs and classes, but they are somewhat more important when completing a struct definition and making it well formed.

■ 10 ■
Well-Formed Types

THE PREVIOUS CHAPTERS COVERED MOST OF THE CONSTRUCTS for defining classes and structs. However, several details remain to round out the type definition with fit-and-finish-type functionality. This chapter explains how to put the final touches on a type declaration.

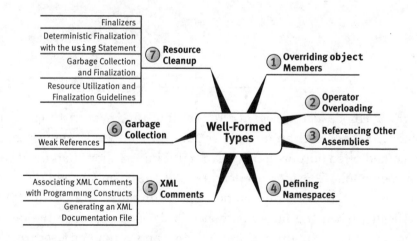

Overriding object Members

Chapter 6 discussed how all classes and structs derive from object. In addition, it reviewed each method available on object and discussed how some of them are virtual. This section discusses the details concerning overriding the virtual methods.

Overriding ToString()

By default, calling ToString() on any object will return the fully quali-fied name of the class. Calling ToString() on a System.IO.FileStream object will return the string System.IO.FileStream, for example. For some classes, however, ToString() can be more meaningful. On string, for example, ToString() returns the string value itself. Similarly, return-ing a Contact's name would make more sense. Listing 10.1 overrides ToString() to return a string representation of Coordinate.

LISTING 10.1: Overriding ToString()

```
public struct Coordinate
{
  public Coordinate(Longitude longitude, Latitude latitude)
  {
      Longitude = longitude;
      Latitude = latitude;
  }

  public Longitude Longitude { get; }
  public Latitude Latitude { get; }

  public override string ToString()
  {
      return $"{ Longitude } { Latitude }";
  }

  // ...
}
```

Write methods such as Console.WriteLine() and System.Diagnostics .Trace.Write() call an object's ToString() method, so overloading the method often outputs more meaningful information than the default implementation. Consider overloading the ToString() method when-ever relevant diagnostic information can be provided from the output—specifically, when the target audience is developers, since the default object.ToString() output is a type name and is not end-user friendly. ToString() is useful for debugging from within a developer IDE or writing to a log file. For this reason, you should keep the strings relatively short (one screen length) so that they are not cut off. However, the lack of localization and other advanced formatting features makes this approach less suitable for general end-user text display.

Guidelines

DO override `ToString()` whenever useful developer-oriented diagnostic strings can be returned.

DO try to keep the string returned from `ToString()` short.

DO NOT return an empty string or null from `ToString()`.

AVOID throwing exceptions or making observable side effects (changing the object state) from `ToString()`.

DO provide an overloaded `ToString(string format)` or implement `IFormattable` if the return value is culture-sensitive or requires formatting (e.g., `DateTime`).

CONSIDER returning a unique string from `ToString()` so as to identify the object instance.

Overriding `GetHashCode()`

Overriding `GetHashCode()` is more complex than overriding `ToString()`. Even so, you should override `GetHashCode()` when you are overriding `Equals()`, and there is a compiler warning to indicate this step is recommended if you don't. Overriding `GetHashCode()` is also a good practice when you are using it as a key into a hash table collection (e.g., `System.Collections.Hashtable` and `System.Collections.Generic.Dictionary`).

The purpose of the hash code is to *efficiently balance a hash table* by generating a number that corresponds to the value of an object. Here are some implementation principles for a good `GetHashCode()` implementation:

- *Required:* Equal objects must have equal hash codes (if `a.Equals(b)`, then `a.GetHashCode() == b.GetHashCode()`).
- *Required:* `GetHashCode()`'s returns over the life of a particular object should be constant (the same value), even if the object's data changes. In many cases, you should cache the method return to enforce this constraint.
- *Required:* `GetHashCode()` should not throw any exceptions; `GetHashCode()` must always successfully return a value.
- *Performance:* Hash codes should be unique whenever possible. However, since hash codes return only an `int`, there inevitably will be an overlap in hash codes for objects that have potentially more values than an `int` can hold, which is virtually all types. (An obvious example is

long, since there are more possible `long` values than an `int` could uniquely identify.)

- *Performance:* The possible hash code values should be distributed evenly over the range of an `int`. For example, creating a hash that doesn't consider the fact that distribution of a string in Latin-based languages primarily centers on the initial 128 ASCII characters would result in a very uneven distribution of string values and would not be a strong `GetHashCode()` algorithm.

- *Performance:* `GetHashCode()` should be optimized for performance. `GetHashCode()` is generally used in `Equals()` implementations to short-circuit a full equals comparison if the hash codes are different. As a result, it is frequently called when the type is used as a key type in dictionary collections.

- *Performance:* Small differences between two objects should result in large differences between hash code values—ideally, a 1-bit difference in the object should result in approximately 16 bits of the hash code changing, on average. This helps ensure that the hash table remains balanced no matter how it is "bucketing" the hash values.

- *Security:* It should be difficult for an attacker to craft an object that has a particular hash code. The attack is to flood a hash table with large amounts of data that all hash to the same value. The hash table implementation can become inefficient, resulting in a possible denial-of-service attack.

These guidelines and rules are, of course, contradictory: It is very difficult to come up with a hash algorithm that is fast and meets all of these guidelines. As with any design problem, you'll need to use a combination of good judgment and realistic performance measurements to come up with a good solution.

Consider the `GetHashCode()` implementation for the `Coordinate` type shown in Listing 10.2.

LISTING 10.2: Implementing `GetHashCode()`

```csharp
public struct Coordinate
{
  public Coordinate(Longitude longitude, Latitude latitude)
  {
      Longitude = longitude;
      Latitude = latitude;
  }
```

```
public Longitude Longitude { get; }
public Latitude Latitude { get; }

public override int GetHashCode()
{
    int hashCode = Longitude.GetHashCode();
    // As long as the hash codes are not equal
    if(Longitude.GetHashCode() != Latitude.GetHashCode())
    {
        hashCode ^= Latitude.GetHashCode();  // eXclusive OR
    }
    return hashCode;
}

// ...
}
```

Generally, the key is to use the XOR operator over the hash codes from the relevant types and to make sure the XOR operands are not likely to be close or equal—or else the result will be all zeroes. (In those cases where the operands are close or equal, consider using bit shifts and adds instead.) The alternative operands, AND and OR, have similar restrictions, but those restrictions come into play more frequently. Applying AND multiple times tends toward all 0 bits, and applying OR tends toward all 1 bits.

For finer-grained control, split larger-than-int types using the shift operator. For example, GetHashCode() for a long called value is implemented as follows:

```
int GetHashCode() { return ((int)value ^ (int)(value >> 32)) };
```

Also, if the base class is not object, base.GetHashCode() should be included in the XOR assignment.

Finally, Coordinate does not cache the value of the hash code. Since each field in the hash code calculation is readonly, the value can't change. However, implementations should cache the hash code if calculated values could change or if a cached value could offer a significant performance advantage.

Overriding Equals()

Overriding Equals() without overriding GetHashCode() results in a warning such as that shown in Output 10.1.

OUTPUT 10.1

```
warning CS0659: '<Class Name>' overrides Object.Equals(object o) but
does not override Object.GetHashCode()
```

Generally, developers expect overriding `Equals()` to be trivial, but it includes a surprising number of subtleties that require careful thought and testing.

Object Identity versus Equal Object Values

Two references are identical if both refer to the same instance. `object` (and, by inheritance, all derived types) includes a static method called `ReferenceEquals()` that explicitly checks for this object identity (see Figure 10.1).

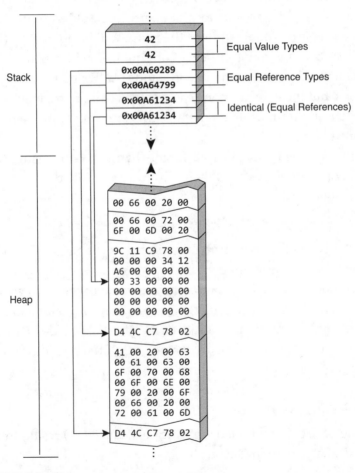

FIGURE 10.1: Identity

However, reference equality is not the only type of equality. Two object instances can also be called equal if the values of some or all of their members are equal. Consider the comparison of two ProductSerialNumbers shown in Listing 10.3.

LISTING 10.3: Overriding the Equality Operator

```
public sealed class ProductSerialNumber
{
  // ...
}
```

```
class Program
{
  static void Main()
  {
      ProductSerialNumber serialNumber1 =
          new ProductSerialNumber("PV", 1000, 09187234);
      ProductSerialNumber serialNumber2 = serialNumber1;
      ProductSerialNumber serialNumber3 =
          new ProductSerialNumber("PV", 1000, 09187234);

      // These serial numbers ARE the same object identity
      if(!ProductSerialNumber.ReferenceEquals(serialNumber1,
          serialNumber2))
      {
          throw new Exception(
              "serialNumber1 does NOT " +
              "reference equal serialNumber2");
      }
      // And, therefore, they are equal
      else if(!serialNumber1.Equals(serialNumber2))
      {
          throw new Exception(
              "serialNumber1 does NOT equal serialNumber2");
      }
      else
      {
          Console.WriteLine(
              "serialNumber1 reference equals serialNumber2");
          Console.WriteLine(
              "serialNumber1 equals serialNumber2");
      }


      // These serial numbers are NOT the same object identity
      if (ProductSerialNumber.ReferenceEquals(serialNumber1,
              serialNumber3))
      {
          throw new Exception(
              "serialNumber1 DOES reference " +
              "equal serialNumber3");
      }
```

```
        // But they are equal (assuming Equals is overloaded)
        else if(!serialNumber1.Equals(serialNumber3) ||
            serialNumber1 != serialNumber3)
        {
            throw new Exception(
                "serialNumber1 does NOT equal serialNumber3");
        }

        Console.WriteLine( "serialNumber1 equals serialNumber3" );
    }
}
```

The results of Listing 10.3 appear in Output 10.2.

OUTPUT 10.2

```
serialNumber1 reference equals serialNumber2
serialNumber1 equals serialNumber3
```

As the last assertion demonstrates with `ReferenceEquals()`, `serialNumber1` and `serialNumber3` are not the same reference. However, the code constructs them with the same values, and both are logically associated with the same physical product. If one instance was created from data in the database and another was created from manually entered data, you would expect that the instances would be equal and, therefore, that the product would not be duplicated (reentered) in the database. Two identical references are obviously equal; however, two different objects could be equal but not reference equal. Such objects will not have identical object identities, but they may have key data that identifies them as being equal objects.

Only reference types can be reference equal, thereby supporting the concept of identity. Calling `ReferenceEquals()` on value types will always return `false` because value types are boxed when they are converted to `object` for the call. Even when the same variable is passed in both (value type) parameters to `ReferenceEquals()`, the result will still be `false` because the values are boxed independently. Listing 10.4 demonstrates this behavior: Because each argument is put into a "different box" in this example, they are never reference equal.

■ NOTE

Calling `ReferenceEquals()` on value types will always return `false`.

LISTING 10.4: Value Types Never Reference Equal Themselves

```csharp
public struct Coordinate
{
    public Coordinate(Longitude longitude, Latitude latitude)
    {
        Longitude = longitude;
        Latitude = latitude;
    }

    public Longitude Longitude { get; }
    public Latitude Latitude { get; }
    // ...
}
```

```csharp
class Program
{
    public void Main()
    {
        //...

        Coordinate coordinate1 =
            new Coordinate( new Longitude(48, 52),
                            new Latitude(-2, -20));

        // Value types will never be reference equal
        if ( Coordinate.ReferenceEquals(coordinate1,
            coordinate1) )
        {
            throw new Exception(
                "coordinate1 reference equals coordinate1");
        }

        Console.WriteLine(
            "coordinate1 does NOT reference equal itself" );
    }
}
```

In contrast to the definition of `Coordinate` as a reference type in Chapter 9, the definition going forward is that of a value type (`struct`) because the combination of `Longitude` and `Latitude` data is logically thought of as a value and its size is less than 16 bytes. (In Chapter 9, `Coordinate` aggregated `Angle` rather than `Longitude` and `Latitude`.) A contributing factor to declaring `Coordinate` as a value type is that it is a (complex) numeric value that has operations on it. In contrast, a reference type such as `Employee` is not a value that you manipulate numerically, but rather refers to an object in real life.

Implementing Equals()

To determine whether two objects are equal (i.e., if they have the same identifying data), you use an object's `Equals()` method. The implementation of this virtual method on `object` uses `ReferenceEquals()` to evaluate equality. Since this implementation is often inadequate, it is sometimes necessary to override `Equals()` with a more appropriate implementation.

> **■ NOTE**
>
> The implementation of `object.Equals()`, the default implementation on all objects before overloading, relies on `ReferenceEquals()` alone.

For objects to *equal* one another, the expectation is that the identifying data within them will be equal. For `ProductSerialNumbers`, for example, the `ProductSeries`, `Model`, and `Id` must be the same; however, for an `Employee` object, perhaps comparing `EmployeeIds` would be sufficient for equality. To correct the `object.Equals()` implementation it is necessary to override it. Value types, for example, override the `Equals()` implementation to instead use the fields that the type includes.

The steps for overriding `Equals()` are as follows:

1. Check for `null`.
2. Check for reference equality if the type is a reference type.
3. Check for equivalent types.
4. Invoke a typed helper method that can treat the operand as the compared type rather than an object (see the `Equals(Coordinate obj)` method in Listing 10.5).
5. Possibly check for equivalent hash codes to short-circuit an extensive, field-by-field comparison. (Two objects that are equal cannot have different hash codes.)
6. Check `base.Equals()` if the base class overrides `Equals()`.
7. Compare each identifying field for equality.
8. Override `GetHashCode()`.
9. Override the `==` and `!=` operators (see the next section).

Listing 10.5 shows a sample `Equals()` implementation.

LISTING 10.5: Overriding `Equals()`

```csharp
public struct Longitude
{
  // ...
}
```

```csharp
public struct Latitude
{
  // ...
}
```

```csharp
public struct Coordinate: IEquatable<T>
{
  public Coordinate(Longitude longitude, Latitude latitude)
  {
      Longitude = longitude;
      Latitude = latitude;
  }

  public Longitude Longitude { get; }
  public Latitude Latitude { get; }

  public override bool Equals(object obj)
  {
      // STEP 1: Check for null
      if (obj == null)
      {
          return false;
      }
      // STEP 3: Equivalent data types;
      // can be avoided if type is sealed
      if (this.GetType() != obj.GetType())
      {
          return false;
      }
      return Equals((Coordinate)obj);
  }
  public bool Equals(Coordinate obj)
  {
      // STEP 1: Check for null if a reference type
      // (e.g., a reference type)
      // if (ReferenceEquals(obj, null))
      // {
      //     return false;
      // }
```

```
            // STEP 2: Check for ReferenceEquals if this
            // is a reference type
            // if (ReferenceEquals(this, obj))
            // {
            //    return true;
            // }

            // STEP 4: Possibly check for equivalent hash codes
            // if (this.GetHashCode() != obj.GetHashCode())
            // {
            //    return false;
            // }

            // STEP 5: Check base.Equals if base overrides Equals()
            // System.Diagnostics.Debug.Assert(
            //    base.GetType() != typeof(object) );
            // if ( !base.Equals(obj) )
            // {
            //    return false;
            // }

            // STEP 6: Compare identifying fields for equality
            // using an overload of Equals on Longitude
            return ( (Longitude.Equals(obj.Longitude)) &&
                (Latitude.Equals(obj.Latitude)) );
        }

        // STEP 7: Override GetHashCode
        public override int GetHashCode()
        {
            int hashCode = Longitude.GetHashCode();
            hashCode ^= Latitude.GetHashCode(); // Xor (eXclusive OR)
            return hashCode;
        }

    }
```

In this implementation, the first two checks are relatively obvious. However, it is interesting to point out that step 3 can be avoided if the type is sealed.

Steps 4 to 6 occur in an overload of Equals() that takes the Coordinate data type specifically. This way, a comparison of two Coordinates will avoid Equals(object obj) and its GetType() check altogether.

Since GetHashCode() is not cached and is no more efficient than step 5, the GetHashCode() comparison is commented out. Similarly, base.Equals() is not used, since the base class is not overriding Equals(). (The assertion checks that base is not of type object but does not verify whether the base class overrides Equals(), which is required to appropriately call base.Equals( ).) Regardless, because GetHashCode( ) does not necessarily return a unique value (it simply identifies when operands are different), on its own it does not conclusively identify equal objects.

Like GetHashCode( ), Equals( ) should never throw any exceptions. It is valid to compare any object with any other object, and doing so should never result in an exception.

Guidelines

DO implement GetHashCode( ), Equals( ), the == operator, and the != operator together—not one of these without the other three.

DO use the same algorithm when implementing Equals( ), ==, and !=.

AVOID throwing exceptions from implementations of GetHashCode( ), Equals( ), ==, and !=.

AVOID overloading equality operators on mutable reference types or if the implementation would be significantly slower.

DO implement all the equality-related methods when implementing IComparable.

Overriding GetHashCode( ) and Equals( ) with Tuple

As shown in the previous two sections, the implementation of Equals( ) and GetHashCode( ) were fairly complex, yet the actual code is generally boilerplate. For Equals() it's necessary to compare all the contained identifying data structures while avoiding infinite recursion or null reference exceptions. For GetHashCode( ) it's necessary to combine the unique hash code of each of the non-null-contained identifying data structures in an exclusive OR operation. With C# 7.0 tuples, this turns out to be quite simple.

For Equals(Coordinate coordinate) you can group each of the identifying members into a tuple and compare them to the target argument of the same type:

```
public bool Equals(Coordinate coordinate) =>
  return (Longitude, Latitude).Equals(
    (coordinate.Longitude, coordinate.Latitude));
```

(One might argue that this is more readable if each identifying member were explicitly compared instead, but I leave that for the reader to arbitrate.) Internally the tuple (System.ValueTuple<...>) uses EqualityComparer<T>, which relies on the type parameters implementation of IEquatable<T> (which only contains a single Equals<T>(T other) member). Therefore, to correctly override `Equals`, you need to follow the guideline: DO implement `IEquatable<T>` when overriding `Equals()`. That way your own custom data types will leverage your custom implementation of `Equals()` rather than `Object.Equals()`.

Perhaps the more compelling of the two overloads is `GetHashCode()` and its use of the tuple. Rather than engage in the complex gymnastics of an exclusive OR operation of the non-null identifying members, you can simply instantiate a tuple of all identifying members and return the `GetHashCode()` value for the said tuple, like so:

```
public override int GetHashCode() =>
    return (Radius, StartAngle, SweepAngle).GetHashCode();
```

Note that in C# 7.3, the tuple now implements `==` and `!=`, which it should have when it was first implemented, a topic we investigate next.

Operator Overloading

The preceding section looked at overriding `Equals()` and provided the guideline that the class should also implement `==` and `!=`. Implementing any operator is called *operator overloading*. This section describes how to perform such overloading not only for `==` and `!=` but also for other supported operators.

For example, `string` provides a `+` operator that concatenates two strings. This is perhaps not surprising, because `string` is a predefined type, so it could possibly have special compiler support. However, C# provides for adding `+` operator support to a class or struct. In fact, all operators are supported except `x.y`, `f(x)`, `new`, `typeof`, `default`, `checked`, `unchecked`, `delegate`, `is`, `as`, `=`, and `=>`. One particularly noteworthy operator that cannot be implemented is the assignment operator; there is no way to change the behavior of the `=` operator.

Before going through the exercise of implementing an operator overload, consider the fact that such operators are not discoverable through IntelliSense. Unless the intent is for a type to act like a primitive type (e.g., a numeric type), you should avoid overloading an operator.

Comparison Operators (==, !=, <, >, <=, >=)

Once `Equals()` is overridden, there is a possible inconsistency. That is, two objects could return `true` for `Equals()` but `false` for the `==` operator because == performs a reference equality check by default. To correct this flaw, it is important to overload the equals (==) and not equals (!=) operators as well.

For the most part, the implementation for these operators can delegate the logic to Equals(), or vice versa. However, for reference types, some initial null checks are required first (see Listing 10.6).

LISTING 10.6: Implementing the == and != Operators

```csharp
public sealed class ProductSerialNumber
{
  // ...

  public static bool operator ==(
      ProductSerialNumber leftHandSide,
      ProductSerialNumber rightHandSide)
  {

      // Check if leftHandSide is null
      // (operator== would be recursive)
      if(ReferenceEquals(leftHandSide, null))
      {
          // Return true if rightHandSide is also null
          // and false otherwise
          return ReferenceEquals(rightHandSide, null);
      }

      return (leftHandSide.Equals(rightHandSide));
  }

  public static bool operator !=(
      ProductSerialNumber leftHandSide,
      ProductSerialNumber rightHandSide)
  {
      return !(leftHandSide == rightHandSide);
  }
}
```

Note that in this example, we use ProductSerialNumber rather than Coordinate to demonstrate the logic for a reference type, which has the added complexity of a null value.

Be sure to avoid the null checks with an equality operator (leftHandSide == null). Doing so would recursively call back into the method, resulting in a loop that continues until the stack overflows. To avoid this problem, you can call ReferenceEquals() to check for null.

> ## Guidelines
>
> **AVOID** using the equality comparison operator (==) from within the implementation of the == operator overload.

Binary Operators (+, -, *, /, %, &, |, ^, <<, >>)

You can add an `Arc` to a `Coordinate`. However, the code so far provides no support for the addition operator. Instead, you need to define such a method, as Listing 10.7 demonstrates.

LISTING 10.7: Adding an Operator

```csharp
struct Arc
{
  public Arc(
      Longitude longitudeDifference,
      Latitude latitudeDifference)
  {
      LongitudeDifference = longitudeDifference;
      LatitudeDifference = latitudeDifference;
  }

  public Longitude LongitudeDifference { get; }
  public Latitude LatitudeDifference { get; }
}
```

```csharp
struct Coordinate
{
  // ...
  public static Coordinate operator +(
      Coordinate source, Arc arc)
  {
      Coordinate result = new Coordinate(
          new Longitude(
              source.Longitude + arc.LongitudeDifference),
          new Latitude(
              source.Latitude + arc.LatitudeDifference));
      return result;
  }
}
```

The +, -, *, /, %, &, |, ^, <<, and >> operators are implemented as binary static methods where at least one parameter is of the containing type. The method name is the operator prefixed by the word *operator* as a keyword. As shown in Listing 10.8, given the definition of the - and + binary operators, you can add and subtract an Arc to and from the coordinate. Note that Longitude and Latitude will also require implementations of the + operator because they are called by source.Longitude + arc.LongitudeDifference and source.Latitude + arc.LatitudeDifference.

LISTING 10.8: Calling the – and + Binary Operators

```
public class Program
{
  public static void Main()
  {
      Coordinate coordinate1,coordinate2;
      coordinate1 = new Coordinate(
          new Longitude(48, 52), new Latitude(-2, -20));
      Arc arc = new Arc(new Longitude(3), new Latitude(1));

      coordinate2 = coordinate1 + arc;
      Console.WriteLine(coordinate2);

      coordinate2 = coordinate2 - arc;
      Console.WriteLine(coordinate2);

      coordinate2 += arc;
      Console.WriteLine(coordinate2);
  }
}
```

The results of Listing 10.8 appear in Output 10.3.

OUTPUT 10.3

```
51° 52' 0 E  -1° -20' 0 N
48° 52' 0 E  -2° -20' 0 N
51° 52' 0 E  -1° -20' 0 N
```

For Coordinate, you implement the – and + operators to return coordinate locations after adding/subtracting Arc. This allows you to string multiple operators and operands together, as in result = ((coordinate1 + arc1) + arc2) + arc3. Moreover, by supporting the same operators (+/-) on Arc (see Listing 10.9), you could eliminate the parentheses. This approach works because the result of the first operand (arc1 + arc2) is another Arc, which you can then add to the next operand of type Arc or Coordinate.

In contrast, consider what would happen if you provided a – operator that had two Coordinates as parameters and returned a double corresponding to the distance between the two coordinates. Adding a double to a Coordinate is undefined, so you could not string together operators and operands. Caution is in order when defining operators that return a different type, because doing so is counterintuitive.

Combining Assignment with Binary Operators (+=, -=, *=, /=, %=, &=, ...)

As previously mentioned, there is no support for overloading the assignment operator. However, assignment operators in combination with binary operators (+=, -=, *=, /=, %=, &=, |=, ^=, <<=, and >>=) are effectively overloaded when overloading the binary operator. Given the definition of a binary operator without the assignment, C# automatically allows for assignment in combination with the operator. Using the definition of Coordinate in Listing 10.7, therefore, you can have code such as

```
coordinate += arc;
```

which is equivalent to the following:

```
coordinate = coordinate + arc;
```

Conditional Logical Operators (&&, ||)

Like assignment operators, conditional logical operators cannot be overloaded explicitly. However, because the logical operators & and | can be overloaded, and the conditional operators comprise the logical operators, effectively it is possible to overload conditional operators. x && y is processed as x & y, where y must evaluate to true. Similarly, x || y is processed as x | y only if x is false. To enable support for evaluating a type to true or false—in an if statement, for example—it is necessary to override the true/false unary operators.

Unary Operators (+, -, !, ~, ++, --, true, false)

Overloading unary operators is very similar to overloading binary operators, except that they take only one parameter, also of the containing type. Listing 10.9 overloads the + and – operators for Longitude and Latitude and then uses these operators when overloading the same operators in Arc.

LISTING 10.9: Overloading the – and + Unary Operators

```csharp
public struct Latitude
{
    // ...
    public static Latitude operator -(Latitude latitude)
    {
        return new Latitude(-latitude.DecimalDegrees);
    }
    public static Latitude operator +(Latitude latitude)
    {
        return latitude;
    }
}

public struct Longitude
{
    // ...
    public static Longitude operator -(Longitude longitude)
    {
        return new Longitude(-longitude.DecimalDegrees);
    }
    public static Longitude operator +(Longitude longitude)
    {
        return longitude;
    }
}

public struct Arc
{
    // ...
    public static Arc operator -(Arc arc)
    {
        // Uses unary - operator defined on
        // Longitude and Latitude
        return new Arc(-arc.LongitudeDifference,
            -arc.LatitudeDifference);
    }
    public static Arc operator +(Arc arc)
    {
        return arc;
    }
}
```

Just as with numeric types, the + operator in this listing doesn't have any effect and is provided for symmetry.

Overloading `true` and `false` is subject to the additional requirement that both must be overloaded—not just one of the two. The signatures are the same as with other operator overloads; however, the return must be a `bool`, as demonstrated in Listing 10.10.

LISTING 10.10: Overloading the true and false Operators

```
public static bool operator false(IsValid item)
{
    // ...
}
public static bool operator true(IsValid item)
{
    // ...
}
```

You can use types with overloaded `true` and `false` operators in `if`, `do`, `while`, and `for` controlling expressions.

Conversion Operators

Currently, there is no support in `Longitude`, `Latitude`, and `Coordinate` for casting to an alternative type. For example, there is no way to cast a `double` into a `Longitude` or `Latitude` instance. Similarly, there is no support for assigning a `Coordinate` using a `string`. Fortunately, C# provides for the definition of methods specifically intended to handle the converting of one type to another. Furthermore, the method declaration allows for specifying whether the conversion is implicit or explicit.

■ **ADVANCED TOPIC**

Cast Operator (( ))

Implementing the explicit and implicit conversion operators is not technically overloading the cast operator (( )). However, this action is effectively what takes place, so *defining a cast operator* is common terminology for implementing explicit or implicit conversion.

Defining a conversion operator is similar in style to defining any other operator, except that the "operator" is the resultant type of the conversion. Additionally, the `operator` keyword follows a keyword that indicates whether the conversion is implicit or explicit (see Listing 10.11).

LISTING 10.11: Providing an Implicit Conversion between Latitude and double

```
public struct Latitude
{
    // ...
```

```csharp
    public Latitude(double decimalDegrees)
    {
        DecimalDegrees = Normalize(decimalDegrees);
    }

    public double DecimalDegrees { get; }

    // ...

    public static implicit operator double(Latitude latitude)
    {
        return latitude.DecimalDegrees;
    }
    public static implicit operator Latitude(double degrees)
    {
        return new Latitude(degrees);
    }

    // ...
}
```

With these conversion operators, you now can convert doubles implicitly to and from Latitude objects. Assuming similar conversions exist for Longitude, you can simplify the creation of a Coordinate object by specifying the decimal degrees portion of each coordinate portion (e.g., coordinate = new Coordinate(43, 172);).

> **⬛ NOTE**
>
> When implementing a conversion operator, either the return or the parameter must be of the enclosing type—in support of encapsulation. C# does not allow you to specify conversions outside the scope of the converted type.

Guidelines for Conversion Operators

The difference between defining an implicit and an explicit conversion operator centers on preventing an unintentional implicit conversion that results in undesirable behavior. You should be aware of two possible consequences of using the explicit conversion operator. First, conversion operators that throw exceptions should always be explicit. For example, it is highly likely that a string will not conform to the format that a conversion from string to Coordinate requires. Given the chance of a failed conversion, you should define the particular conversion operator as explicit, thereby requiring that you be intentional about the conversion and ensure that the format is correct or, alternatively, that you provide code to handle the possible exception. Frequently, the pattern for conversion is that one direction (`string` to `Coordinate`) is explicit and the reverse (`Coordinate` to `string`) is implicit.

A second consideration is that some conversions will be lossy. Converting from a `float` (`4.2`) to an `int` is entirely valid, assuming an awareness of the fact that the decimal portion of the `float` will be lost. Any conversions that will lose data and will not successfully convert back to the original type should be defined as explicit. If an explicit cast is unexpectedly lossy or invalid, consider throwing a `System.InvalidCastException`.

> ■
> ## Guidelines
> **DO NOT** provide an implicit conversion operator if the conversion is lossy.
> **DO NOT** throw exceptions from implicit conversions.

Referencing Other Assemblies

Instead of placing all code into one monolithic binary file, C# and the underlying CLI framework allow you to spread code across multiple assemblies. This approach enables you to reuse assemblies across multiple executables.

■ **BEGINNER TOPIC**

Class Libraries

The `HelloWorld` program is one of the most trivial programs you can write. Real-world programs are more complex, and as complexity increases, it helps to organize the complexity by breaking programs into multiple parts. To do this, developers move portions of a program into separate compiled units called **class libraries** or, simply, **libraries**. Programs then reference and rely on class libraries to provide parts of their functionality. The power of this concept is that two programs can rely on the same class library, thereby sharing the functionality of that class library across both programs and reducing the total amount of code needed.

In other words, it is possible to write features once, place them into a class library, and allow multiple programs to include those features by referencing the same class library. Later in the development cycle, when developers fix a bug or add functionality to the class library, all the programs will have access to the increased functionality, just because they continue to reference the now improved class library.

Frequently, the code we write could be useful to more than one program. Imagine, for example, using the Longitude, Latitude, and Coordinate classes from a mapping program and a digital photo geo-coding program or writing a command-line parser class. Classes and sets of classes like these can be written once and then reused from many different programs. As such, they need to be grouped together into an assembly called a *library* or *class library* and written for the purposes of reuse rather than only within a single program.

To create a library rather than a console project, follow the same directions as provided in Chapter 1 except for Dotnet CLI use Class Library or classlib for the template.

Similarly, with Visual Studio 2017, from the **File->New Project...** menu item (Ctrl+Shift+N) use the **Search** text box to find all Class Library templates, and then select **Class Library (.NET Standard)**—the Visual C# version, of course. Use *GeoCoordinates* for the project name. From the **Solution** combo text box, select **Add to solution**. This last step is important because it simplifies adding a project reference from the program project (such as the HelloWorld project)

Next, place the source code from Listing 10.9 into separate files for each struct and name the file after the struct name and build the project. Building the project will compile the C# code into an assembly— a GeoCoordinates.dll file—and place it into a subdirectory of .\bin\.

Referencing a Library

Given the library, we need to **reference** it from a program. Given a new console program using the Program class from Listing 10.8, we need to add a reference to the GeoCoordinates.dll assembly, identifying where the library is located and embedding metadata that uniquely identifies the library into the program. There are several ways to do this. First, you can reference the library project file, thus identifying which project contains the library source code and forming a dependency between the two projects. You can't compile the program referencing the library until the library is compiled. This dependency causes the library to compile (if it isn't compiled already) when the program compiles.

The second approach is to reference the assembly file itself. In other words, reference the compiled library rather than the project. This makes sense when the library is compiled separately from the program, such as by another team within your organization.

Third, you can reference a NuGet package, as described in the next section.

Note that it isn't only console programs that can reference libraries and packages. In fact, any assembly can reference any other assembly. Frequently, one library will reference another library, creating a chain of dependencies.

Referencing a Project or Library with Dotnet CLI

In Chapter 1 we discussed creating a console program. This created a program that included a `Main` method—the entry point at which the program will begin executing. To add a reference to the newly created assembly, we continue where we left off with an additional command for adding a reference:

```
dotnet add .\HelloWorld\HelloWord.csproj package .\GeoCordinates\bin\
  Debug\netcoreapp2.0\GeoCoordinates.dll
```

Following the add argument is a file path for the compiled assembly referenced by the project.

Rather than referencing the assembly, you can reference the project file. As already mentioned, this chains the projects together so that building the program will trigger the class library to compile first if it hasn't compiled already. The advantage is that as the program compiles, it will automatically locate the compiled class library assembly—whether it be in the debug or release directory, for example. The command for referencing a project file is:

```
dotnet add .\HelloWorld\HelloWord.csproj reference .\GeoCoordinates \
  GeoCoordinates.csproj
```

If you have the source code for a class library and source code changes frequently, consider referencing the class library using the class library project file rather than the compiled assembly.

Upon completion of either the project or the compiled assembly reference, your project can compile with the `Program` class source code found in Listing 10.8.

Referencing a Project or Library with Visual Studio 2017

Likewise, in Chapter 1 we discussed creating a console program with Visual Studio. This created a program that included a `Main`. To add a reference to the `GeoCoordinates` assembly, click the **Project->Add Reference...** menu item. Next, from the **Projects\Solution** tab, select the **GeoCoordinates** project and **OK** to confirm the reference.

Similarly, to add an assembly reference, follow the same process as before, clicking the **Project->Add Reference...** menu item. However, this time click the **Browse...** button and navigate to and select the `GeoCordinates.dll` assembly.

As with Dotnet CLI, you can compile the program project with the `Program` class source code found in Listing 10.8.

NuGet Packaging

Starting with Visual Studio 2010, Microsoft introduced a library packaging system called NuGet. The purpose of the system is to provide a means for libraries to be easily shared across projects and between companies. Frequently, a library assembly is more than just a single compiled file. It might have configuration files, additional resources, and metadata associated with it. Unfortunately, however, before NuGet, there was no manifest that identified all the dependencies. Furthermore, there was no standard provider or package library for where the referenced assemblies could be found.

NuGet addresses both issues. Not only does NuGet include a manifest that identifies the author(s), companies, dependencies, and more, it also comes with a default package provider at NuGet.org where packages can be uploaded, updated, indexed, and then downloaded by projects that are looking to leverage them. With NuGet, you can reference a **NuGet package** (*.nupkg) and have it automatically installed from one of your preconfigured NuGet provider URLs.

Begin 4.0

With the NuGet package is a manifest (a `*.nuspec` file) that contains all the additional metadata that is included in the package. Additionally, it provides all the additional resources you may want—localization files, config files, content files, and so on. In the end, the NuGet package is an archive of all the individual resources combined into a single ZIP file—albeit with the `.nupkg` extension. Therefore, if you rename the file with a `*.ZIP` extension, you can open and examine the file using any common compression utility.

NuGet References with Dotnet CLI

Begin 7.0

To add a NuGet package to your project using Dotnet CLI requires executing a single command:

```
>dotnet add .\HelloWorld\HelloWorld.csproj package Microsoft.Extensions.
↳CommandLineUtils
```

This command checks each of the registered NuGet package providers for the specified package and downloads it. (You can also trigger the download explicitly using the command `dotnet restore`.)

To create a local NuGet package, use the `dotnet pack` command. This command generates a `GeoCoordinates.1.0.0.nupkg` file, which you can reference using the `add ... package` command.

4.0

The digits following the assembly name correspond to the package version number. To specify the version number explicitly, edit the project file (`*.csproj`) and add a `<Version>...</Version>` child element to the `PropertyGroup` element.

End 7.0

NuGet References with Visual Studio 2017

Following the instructions laid out in Chapter 1, you already have a HelloWorld project. Starting with that project, you can add a NuGet package using Visual Studio 2017 as follows:

1. Click the **Project->Manage NuGet Packages...** menu item (see Figure 10.2).

2. Select the **Browse** filter, and then enter *Microsoft.Extensions .CommandLineUtils* into the **Search** (Ctrl+E) text box. Note that a partial name such as *CommandLineUtils* will also filter the list (see Figure 10.3).

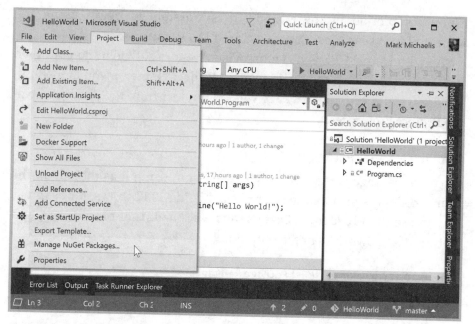

FIGURE 10.2: The Project Menu

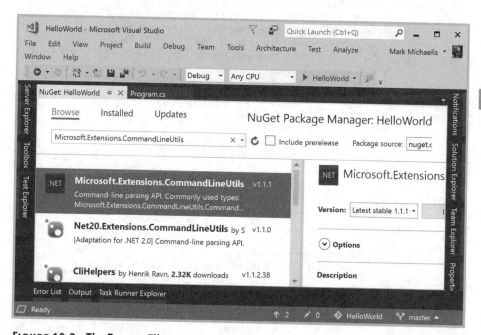

4.0

FIGURE 10.3: The Browse Filter

3. Click the **Install** button to install the package into the project.

Upon completion of these steps, it is possible to begin using the `Microsoft.Extensions.CommandLineUtils` library.

As with Dotnet CLI, you can use Visual Studio 2017 to build your own NuGet package using the **Build->Pack <Project Name>** menu item. Similarly, you can specify the package version number from the **Package** tab of the **Project Properties**.

Invoking a NuGet Package

Once the package is referenced, you can begin using it as though all the source code was included in the project. Listing 10.12 shows, for example, how to use the `Microsoft.Extensions.CommandLineUtils` library, and Output 10.4 shows the sample output.

LISTING 10.12: Invoking a NuGet Package Reference

```
public class Program
{
  public static void Main(string[] args)
  {
      CommandLineApplication commandLineApplication =
          new CommandLineApplication(throwOnUnexpectedArg: false);
      CommandArgument name = commandLineApplication.Argument(
          "name", "Enter the full name of the person to be greeted.");
      CommandOption greeting = commandLineApplication.Option(
        "-$|-g |--greeting <greeting>",
        "The greeting to display. The greeting supports"
        + " a format string where '{name}' will be "
        + "substituted with the name.",
        CommandOptionType.SingleValue);
      commandLineApplication.HelpOption("-? | -h | --help");
      commandLineApplication.Execute(args);
      if (!greeting.HasValue())
      {
          Console.WriteLine($"Hello { name.Value }.");
      }
      else
      {
          Console.WriteLine(
              greeting.Value().Replace("{name}", name.Value));
      }
  }
}
```

OUTPUT 10.4

```
>dotnet run "Inigo Montoya" -g "Hello {name}. Welcome!"
Hello Inigo Montoya.  Welcome!"
```

4.0

This library is used to parse both arguments and options from the command line where options have switches to identify them, while arguments are void of such switches. See Table 10.1 for examples.

TABLE 10.1: `Microsoft.Extension.CommandUtils` Examples

Argument Type	Example	Explanation
Options	`Program.exe -f=Inigo,` `-l Montoya —hello`	Option `-f` with value `"Inigo"` Option `-l` with value `"Montoya"` Option `—hello` with value `"on"`
Command with argument	`Program.exe "hello",` `"Inigo", "Montoya"`	Command `"hello"` Argument `"Inigo"` Argument `"Montoya"`
Symbols	`Program.exe -?`	Display help

End 4.0

■ ADVANCED TOPIC

Encapsulation of Types

Just as classes serve as an encapsulation boundary for behavior and data, so assemblies provide for similar boundaries among groups of types. Developers can break a system into assemblies and then share those assemblies with multiple applications or integrate them with assemblies provided by third parties.

`public` or `internal` Access Modifiers on Type Declarations

By default, a class without any access modifier is defined as `internal`.[1] The result is that the class is inaccessible from outside the assembly. Even though another assembly references the assembly containing the class, all internal classes within the referenced assemblies will be inaccessible.

Just as `private` and `protected` provide levels of encapsulation to members within a class, so C# supports the use of access modifiers at the class level for control over the encapsulation of the classes within an assembly. The access modifiers available are `public` and `internal`. To expose a class outside the assembly, the assembly must be marked as `public`. Therefore,

---

1. Excluding nested types, which are `private` by default.

before compiling the Coordinates.dll assembly, it is necessary to modify the type declarations as public (see Listing 10.13).

LISTING 10.13: Making Types Available outside an Assembly

```
public struct Coordinate
{
  // ...
}
```

```
public struct Latitude
{
  // ...
}
```

```
public struct Longitude
{
  // ...
}
```

```
public struct Arc
{
  // ...
}
```

Similarly, declarations such as class and enum can be either public or internal.[2]

The internal access modifier is not limited to type declarations; that is, it is also available on type members. Consequently, you can designate a type as public but mark specific methods within the type as internal so that the members are available only from within the assembly. It is not possible for the members to have a greater accessibility than the type. If the class is declared as internal, public members on the type will be accessible only from within the assembly.

The protected internal Type Modifier

Another type member access modifier is protected internal. Members with an accessibility modifier of protected internal will be accessible from all locations within the containing assembly *and* from classes that

---

2. You can decorate nested classes with any access modifier available to other class members (e.g., private). However, outside the class scope, the only access modifiers that are available are public and internal.

derive from the type, even if the derived class is not in the same assembly. The default state is `private`, so when you add an access modifier (other than `public`), the member becomes slightly more visible. Adding two modifiers compounds this effect.

> ■ **NOTE**
>
> Members with an accessibility modifier of `protected internal` will be accessible from all locations within the containing assembly *and* from classes that derive from the type, even if the derived class is not in the same assembly.

■ **BEGINNER TOPIC**

Begin 7.2

Type Member Accessibility Modifiers

The full list of access modifiers appears in Table 10.2.

TABLE 10.2: Accessibility Modifiers

Modifier	Description
public	Declares that the member is accessible anywhere the type is accessible. If the class is `internal`, the member will be internally visible. Public members will be accessible from outside the assembly if the containing type is public.
internal	The member is accessible from within the assembly only.
private	The member is accessible from within the containing type but inaccessible otherwise.
protected	The member is accessible within the containing type and any subtypes derived from it, regardless of assembly.
protected internal	The member is accessible from anywhere within the containing assembly *and* from any types derived from the containing type, even if the derived types are within a different assembly.
private protected	The member is accessible from any types derived from the containing type that are also in the same assembly. (This feature was added in C# 7.2.)

End 7.2

Defining Namespaces

As mentioned in Chapter 2, all data types are identified by the combination of their namespace and their name. However, in the CLR, there is no such thing as a "namespace." The type's name actually is the fully qualified type name, including the namespace. For the classes you defined earlier, there was no explicit namespace declaration. Classes such as these are automatically declared as members of the default global namespace. It is likely that such classes will experience a name collision, which occurs when you attempt to define two classes with the same name. Once you begin referencing other assemblies from third parties, the likelihood of a name collision increases even further.

More important, there are thousands of types in the CLI framework and multiple orders of magnitude more outside the framework. Finding the right type for a particular problem, therefore, could potentially be a significant battle.

The resolution to both of these problems is to organize all the types, grouping them into logical related categories called namespaces. For example, classes outside the System namespace are generally placed into a namespace corresponding with the company, product name, or both. Classes from Addison-Wesley, for example, are placed into an Awl or AddisonWesley namespace, and classes from Microsoft (not System classes) are located in the Microsoft namespace. The second level of a namespace should be a stable product name that will not vary between versions. Stability, in fact, is key at all levels. Changing a namespace name is a version-incompatible change that should be avoided. For this reason, avoid using volatile names (organization hierarchy, fleeting brands, and so on) within a namespace name.

Namespaces should be PascalCase, but if your brand uses nontraditional casing, it is acceptable to use the brand casing. (Consistency is key, so if that will be problematic—with Pascal or brand-based casing—favor the use of whichever convention will produce the greater consistency.) You should use the namespace keyword to create a namespace and to assign a class to it, as shown in Listing 10.14.

LISTING 10.14: Defining a Namespace

```csharp
// Define the namespace AddisonWesley
namespace AddisonWesley
{
  class Program
  {
    // ...
  }
}
// End of AddisonWesley namespace declaration
```

All content between the namespace declaration's curly braces will then belong within the specified namespace. In Listing 10.14, for example, `Program` is placed into the namespace `AddisonWesley`, making its full name `AddisonWesley.Program`.

■ NOTE

In the CLR there is no such thing as a "namespace." Rather, the type's name is the fully qualified type name.

Like classes, namespaces support nesting. This provides for a hierarchical organization of classes. All the `System` classes relating to network APIs are in the namespace `System.Net`, for example, and those relating to the Web are in `System.Web`.

There are two ways to nest namespaces. The first approach is to nest them within one another (similar to classes), as demonstrated in Listing 10.15.

LISTING 10.15: Nesting Namespaces within One Another

```csharp
// Define the namespace AddisonWesley
namespace AddisonWesley
{
  // Define the namespace AddisonWesley.Michaelis
  namespace Michaelis
  {
    // Define the namespace
    // AddisonWesley.Michaelis.EssentialCSharp
    namespace EssentialCSharp
    {
      // Declare the class
      // AddisonWesley.Michaelis.EssentialCSharp.Program
      class Program
      {
```

```
        // ...
    }
  }
 }
}
// End of AddisonWesley namespace declaration
```

Such a nesting will assign the `Program` class to the `AddisonWesley` `.Michaelis.EssentialCSharp` namespace.

The second approach is to use the full namespace in a single namespace declaration in which a period separates each identifier, as shown in Listing 10.16.

LISTING 10.16: Nesting Namespaces Using a Period to Separate Each Identifier

```
// Define the namespace AddisonWesley.Michaelis.EssentialCSharp
namespace AddisonWesley.Michaelis.EssentialCSharp
{
  class Program
  {
      // ...
  }
}
// End of AddisonWesley namespace declaration
```

Regardless of whether a namespace declaration follows the pattern shown in Listing 10.15, that in Listing 10.16, or a combination of the two, the resultant CIL code will be identical. The same namespace may occur multiple times, in multiple files, and even across assemblies. For example, with the convention of one-to-one correlation between files and classes, you can define each class in its own file and surround it with the same namespace declaration.

Given that namespaces are key for organizing types, it is frequently helpful to use the namespace for organizing all the class files. For this reason, it is helpful to create a folder for each namespace, placing a class such as `AddisonWesley.Fezzik.Services.Registration` into a folder hierarchy corresponding to the name.

When using Visual Studio projects, if the project name is `AddisonWesley.Fezzik`, you should create one subfolder called `Services` into which `RegistrationService.cs` is placed. You would then create another subfolder—Data, for example—into which you place classes relating to entities within the program—`RealestateProperty`, `Buyer`, and `Seller`, for example.

> **Guidelines**
>
> **DO** prefix namespace names with a company name to prevent name-spaces from different companies having the same name.
>
> **DO** use a stable, version-independent product name at the second level of a namespace name.
>
> **DO NOT** define types without placing them into a namespace.
>
> **CONSIDER** creating a folder structure that matches the namespace hierarchy.

XML Comments

Chapter 1 introduced comments. However, you can use XML comments for more than just notes to other developers reviewing the source code. XML-based comments follow a practice popularized with Java. Although the C# compiler ignores all comments as far as the resultant executable goes, the developer can use command-line options to instruct the compiler[3] to extract the XML comments into a separate XML file. By taking advantage of the XML file generation, the developer can generate documentation of the API from the XML comments. In addition, C# editors can parse the XML comments in the code and display them to developers as distinct regions (e.g., as a different color from the rest of the code) or parse the XML comment data elements and display them to the developer.

Figure 10.4 demonstrates how an IDE can take advantage of XML comments to assist the developer with a tip about the code he is trying to write. Such coding tips offer significant assistance in large programs, especially when multiple developers share code. For this to work, however, the developer obviously must take the time to enter the XML comments within the code and then direct the compiler to create the XML file. The next section explains how to accomplish this.

---

3. The C# standard does not specify whether the C# compiler or a separate utility should take care of extracting the XML data. However, all mainstream C# compilers include the necessary functionality via a compile switch instead of within an additional utility.

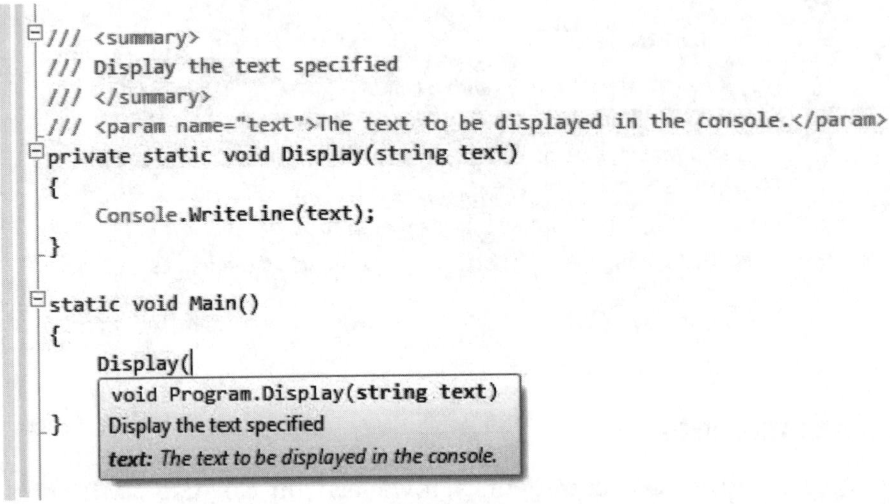

```
/// <summary>
/// Display the text specified
/// </summary>
/// <param name="text">The text to be displayed in the console.</param>
private static void Display(string text)
{
    Console.WriteLine(text);
}

static void Main()
{
    Display(|
```

```
void Program.Display(string text)
Display the text specified
text: The text to be displayed in the console.
```

```
}
```

FIGURE 10.4: XML Comments as Tips in Visual Studio IDE

Associating XML Comments with Programming Constructs

Begin 2.0

Consider the listing of the DataStorage class, as shown in Listing 10.17.

LISTING 10.17: Commenting Code with XML Comments

```
/// <summary>
/// DataStorage is used to persist and retrieve
/// employee data from the files
/// </summary>
class DataStorage
{
    /// <summary>
    /// Save an employee object to a file
    /// named with the employee name
    /// </summary>
    /// <remarks>
    /// This method uses                         Single-Line XML
    /// <seealso cref="System.IO.FileStream"/>    Comment
    /// in addition to
    /// <seealso cref="System.IO.StreamWriter"/>
    /// </remarks>
    /// <param name="employee">
    /// The employee to persist to a file</param>
    /// <data>January 1, 2000</date>
    public static void Store(Employee employee)
    {
        // ...
    }
```

```
      /**  <summary>
       *   Loads up an employee object
       *   </summary>
       *   <remarks>
       *   This method uses
       *   <seealso cref="System.IO.FileStream"/>
       *   in addition to
       *   <seealso cref="System.IO.StreamReader"/>       XML Delimited
       *   </remarks>                                      Comment
       *   <param name="firstName">                        (C# 2.0)
       *   The first name of the employeee</param>
       *   <param name="lastName">
       *   The last name of the employee</param>
       *   <returns>
       *   The employee object corresponding to the names
       *   </returns>
       *   <date>January 1, 2000</date>**/
      public static Employee Load(
          string firstName, string lastName)
      {
          // ...
      }
  }

  class Program
  {
      // ...
  }
```

Listing 10.17 uses both XML-delimited comments that span multiple lines and single-line XML comments in which each line requires a separate three-forward-slash delimiter (///).

Given that XML comments are designed to document the API, they are intended for use only in association with C# declarations, such as the class or method shown in Listing 10.17. Any attempt to place an XML comment inline with the code, unassociated with a declaration, will result in a warning by the compiler. The compiler makes the association simply because the XML comment appears immediately before the declaration.

Although C# allows any XML tag to appear in comments, the C# standard explicitly defines a set of tags to be used. `<seealso cref="System .IO.StreamWriter"/>` is an example of using the seealso tag. This tag creates a link between the text and the System.IO.StreamWriter class.

End 2.0

Generating an XML Documentation File

The compiler checks that the XML comments are well formed and issues a warning if they are not. To generate the XML file, add a `DocumentationFile` subelement to the `ProjectProperties` element:

```
<DocumentationFile>$(OutputPath)\$(TargetFramework)\$(AssemblyName).
⤷xml</DocumentationFile>
```

This subelement causes an XML file to be generated during build into the output directory using the `<assemblyname>.xml` as the filename. Using the `CommentSamples` class listed earlier and the compiler options listed here, the resultant `CommentSamples.XML` file appears as shown in Listing 10.18.

LISTING 10.18: `Comments.xml`

```xml
<?xml version="1.0"?>
<doc>
    <assembly>
        <name>DataStorage</name>
    </assembly>
    <members>
        <member name="T:DataStorage">
            <summary>
            DataStorage is used to persist and retrieve
            employee data from the files.
            </summary>
        </member>
        <member name="M:DataStorage.Store(Employee)">
            <summary>
            Save an employee object to a file
            named with the Employee name.
            </summary>
            <remarks>
            This method uses
            <seealso cref="T:System.IO.FileStream"/>
            in addition to
            <seealso cref="T:System.IO.StreamWriter"/>
            </remarks>
            <param name="employee">
            The employee to persist to a file</param>
            <date>January 1, 2000</date>
        </member>
        <member name="M:DataStorage.Load(
                System.String,System.String)">
            <summary>
```

```
        Loads up an employee object
        </summary>
        <remarks>
        This method uses
        <seealso cref="T:System.IO.FileStream"/>
        in addition to
        <seealso cref="T:System.IO.StreamReader"/>
        </remarks>
        <param name="firstName">
        The first name of the employee</param>
        <param name="lastName">
        The last name of the employee</param>
        <returns>
        The employee object corresponding to the names
        </returns>
        <date>January 1, 2000</date>*
      </member>
    </members>
  </doc>
```

The resultant file includes only the amount of metadata that is necessary to associate an element back to its corresponding C# declaration. This is important to note, because in general, it is necessary to use the XML output in combination with the generated assembly to produce any meaningful documentation. Fortunately, tools such as the free GhostDoc[4] and the open source project NDoc[5] can generate documentation.

Guidelines

DO provide XML comments on public APIs when they provide more context than the API signature alone. This includes member descriptions, parameter descriptions, and examples of calling the API.

Garbage Collection

Garbage collection is obviously a core function of the runtime. Its purpose is to restore memory consumed by objects that are no longer referenced. The emphasis in this statement is on memory and references: The garbage collector is responsible only for restoring memory; it does not handle other

---

4. See http://submain.com/ to learn more about GhostDoc.
5. See http://ndoc.sourceforge.net to learn more about NDoc.

resources such as database connections, handles (files, windows, etc.), network ports, and hardware devices such as serial ports. Also, the garbage collector determines what to clean up based on whether any references remain. Implicitly, this means that the garbage collector works with reference objects and restores memory on the heap only. Additionally, it means that maintaining a reference to an object will delay the garbage collector from reusing the memory consumed by the object.

■ **ADVANCED TOPIC**

Garbage Collection in .NET

Many details about the garbage collector pertain to the specific CLI framework and therefore could vary. This section discusses the Microsoft .NET framework implementations, because they are the most prevalent.

In .NET, the garbage collector uses a mark-and-compact algorithm. At the beginning of an iteration, it identifies all **root references** to objects. Root references are any references from static variables, CPU registers, and local variables or parameter instances (and f-reachable objects, as described later in this section). Given this list, the garbage collector is able to walk through the tree identified by each root reference and determine recursively all the objects to which the root references point. In this manner, the garbage collector creates a graph of all reachable objects.

Instead of enumerating all the inaccessible objects, the garbage collector performs garbage collection by compacting all reachable objects next to one another, thereby overwriting any memory consumed by objects that are inaccessible (and therefore qualify as garbage).

Locating and moving all reachable objects requires that the system maintain a consistent state while the garbage collector runs. To achieve this, all managed threads within the process halt during garbage collection. Obviously, this behavior can result in brief pauses in an application, which are generally insignificant unless a particularly large garbage collection cycle is necessary. To reduce the likelihood of a garbage collection cycle occurring at an inopportune time, the `System.GC` object includes a `Collect()` method, which can be called immediately before the critical performing code. This method does not prevent the garbage collector from running, but it does reduce the probability that it will run, assuming no intense memory utilization occurs during the critical performance code.

One perhaps surprising aspect of .NET garbage collection behavior is that not all garbage is necessarily cleaned up during an iteration. Studies of object lifetimes reveal that recently created objects are more likely to need garbage collection than long-standing objects. Capitalizing on this behavior, the .NET garbage collector is generational, attempting to clean up short-lived objects more frequently than objects that have already survived a previous garbage collection iteration. Specifically, objects are organized into three generations. Each time an object survives a garbage collection cycle, it is moved to the next generation, until it ends up in generation 2 (counting starts from zero). The garbage collector, then, runs more frequently for objects in generation 0 than it does for objects in generation 2.

Over time, in spite of the trepidation that .NET stirred during its early beta releases when compared with unmanaged code, .NET's garbage collection has proved extremely efficient. More important, the gains realized in development productivity have far outweighed the costs in development for the few cases where managed code is dropped to optimize particular algorithms.

Weak References

All references discussed so far are **strong references** because they maintain an object's accessibility and prevent the garbage collector from cleaning up the memory consumed by the object. The framework also supports the concept of **weak references**. Weak references do not prevent garbage collection on an object, but they do maintain a reference so that if the garbage collector does not clean up the object, it can be reused.

Weak references are designed for objects that are expensive to create, yet too expensive to keep around. Consider, for example, a large list of objects loaded from a database and displayed to the user. The loading of this list is potentially expensive, and once the user closes the list, it should be available for garbage collection. However, if the user requests the list multiple times, a second expensive load call will always be required. With weak references, it becomes possible to use code to check whether the list has been cleaned up, and if not, to re-reference the same list. In this way, weak references serve as a memory cache for objects. Objects within the cache are retrieved quickly, but if the garbage collector has recovered the memory of these objects, they will need to be re-created.

Once an object (or collection of objects) is recognized as worthy of potential weak reference consideration, it needs to be assigned to `System .WeakReference` (see Listing 10.19).

LISTING 10.19: Using a Weak Reference

```csharp
// ...

private WeakReference Data;

public FileStream GetData()
{
    FileStream data = (FileStream)Data.Target;
    if (data != null)
    {
        return data;
    }
    else
    {
        // Load data
        // ...

        // Create a weak reference
        // to data for use later
        Data.Target = data;
    }
    return data;
}

// ...
```

Given the assignment of `WeakReference` (Data), you can check for garbage collection by seeing if the weak reference is set to `null`. The key when doing so is to first assign the weak reference to a strong reference (`FileStream data = Data`) to avoid the possibility that between checking for `null` and accessing the data, the garbage collector will run and clean up the weak reference. The strong reference obviously prevents the garbage collector from cleaning up the object, so it must be assigned first (instead of checking `Target` for `null`).

Resource Cleanup

Garbage collection is a key responsibility of the runtime. Nevertheless, it is important to recognize that the garbage collection process centers on the code's memory utilization. It is not about the cleaning up of file handles, database connection strings, ports, or other limited resources.

Finalizers

Finalizers allow developers to write code that will clean up a class's resources. Unlike constructors that are called explicitly using the new operator, finalizers cannot be called explicitly from within the code. There is no new equivalent such as a `delete` operator. Rather, the garbage collector is responsible for calling a finalizer on an object instance. Therefore, developers cannot determine at compile time exactly when the finalizer will execute. All they know is that the finalizer will run sometime between when an object was last used and when the application shuts down normally. (Finalizers might not execute if the process is terminated abnormally. For instance, events such as the computer being turned off or a forced termination of the process will prevent the finalizer from running.)

> **■ NOTE**
>
> You cannot determine at compile time exactly when the finalizer will execute.

The finalizer declaration is identical to the destructor syntax of C#'s predecessor—namely, C++. As shown in Listing 10.20, the finalizer declaration is prefixed with a tilde before the name of the class.

LISTING 10.20: Defining a Finalizer

```csharp
using System.IO;

class TemporaryFileStream
{
  public TemporaryFileStream(string fileName)
  {
      File = new FileInfo(fileName);
      Stream = new FileStream(
          File.FullName, FileMode.OpenOrCreate,
          FileAccess.ReadWrite);
  }

  public TemporaryFileStream()
      : this(Path.GetTempFileName()) { }

  // Finalizer
  ~TemporaryFileStream()
  {
      Close();
  }
```

```
    public FileStream Stream { get; }
    public FileInfo File { get; }

    public void Close()
    {
        Stream?.Close();
        File?.Delete();
    }
}
```

Finalizers do not allow any parameters to be passed, so they cannot be overloaded. Furthermore, finalizers cannot be called explicitly—that is, only the garbage collector can invoke a finalizer. Access modifiers on finalizers are therefore meaningless, and as such, they are not supported. Finalizers in base classes will be invoked automatically as part of an object finalization call.

> **■ NOTE**
>
> Finalizers cannot be called explicitly; only the garbage collector can invoke a finalizer.

Because the garbage collector handles all memory management, finalizers are not responsible for de-allocating memory. Rather, they are responsible for freeing up resources such as database connections and file handles—resources that require an explicit activity that the garbage collector doesn't know about.

Finalizers execute on their own thread, making their execution even less deterministic. This indeterminate nature makes an unhandled exception within a finalizer (outside of the debugger) difficult to diagnose because the circumstances that led to the exception are not clear. From the user's perspective, the unhandled exception will be thrown relatively randomly and with little regard for any action the user was performing. For this reason, you should take care to avoid exceptions within finalizers. Instead, you should use defensive programming techniques such as checking for nulls (refer to Listing 10.20).

Deterministic Finalization with the using Statement

The problem with finalizers on their own is that they don't support **deterministic finalization** (the ability to know when a finalizer will run).

Rather, finalizers serve the important role of being a backup mechanism for cleaning up resources if a developer using a class neglects to call the requisite cleanup code explicitly.

For example, consider the `TemporaryFileStream`, which includes not only a finalizer but also a `Close()` method. This class uses a file resource that could potentially consume a significant amount of disk space. The developer using `TemporaryFileStream` can explicitly call `Close()` to restore the disk space.

Providing a method for deterministic finalization is important because it eliminates a dependency on the indeterminate timing behavior of the finalizer. Even if the developer fails to call `Close()` explicitly, the finalizer will take care of the call. In such a case, the finalizer will run later than if it was called explicitly—but it will be called eventually.

Because of the importance of deterministic finalization, the base class library includes a specific interface for the pattern and C# integrates the pattern into the language. The `IDisposable` interface defines the details of the pattern with a single method called `Dispose()`, which developers call on a resource class to "dispose" of the consumed resources. Listing 10.21 demonstrates the `IDisposable` interface and some code for calling it.

LISTING 10.21: Resource Cleanup with `IDisposable`

```csharp
using System;
using System.IO;

class Program
{
  // ...
  static void Search()
  {
      TemporaryFileStream fileStream =
          new TemporaryFileStream();

      // Use temporary file stream
      // ...

      fileStream.Dispose();

      // ...
  }
}
```

```csharp
class TemporaryFileStream : IDisposable
{
  public TemporaryFileStream(string fileName)
  {
      File = new FileInfo(fileName);
      Stream = new FileStream(
          File.FullName, FileMode.OpenOrCreate,
          FileAccess.ReadWrite);
  }

  public TemporaryFileStream()
      : this(Path.GetTempFileName()) { }

  ~TemporaryFileStream()
  {
      Dispose(false);
  }

  public FileStream Stream { get; }
  public FileInfo File { get; }

  public void Close()
  {
      Dispose();
  }

  #region IDisposable Members
  public void Dispose()
  {
      Dispose(true);

      // Turn off calling the finalizer
      System.GC.SuppressFinalize(this);
  }
  #endregion
  public void Dispose(bool disposing)
  {
      // Do not dispose of an owned managed object (one with a
      // finalizer) if called by member finalize,
      // as the owned managed objects finalize method
      // will be (or has been) called by finalization queue
      // processing already
      if (disposing)
      {
          Stream?.Close();
      }
      File?.Delete();
  }
}
```

From `Program.Search()`, there is an explicit call to `Dispose()` after using the `TemporaryFileStream`. `Dispose()` is the method responsible for cleaning up the resources (in this case, a file) that are not related to memory and therefore are subject to cleanup implicitly by the garbage collector. Nevertheless, the execution here contains a hole that would prevent execution of `Dispose()`—namely, the chance that an exception will occur between the time when `TemporaryFileStream` is instantiated and the time when `Dispose()` is called. If this happens, `Dispose()` will not be invoked and the resource cleanup will have to rely on the finalizer. To avoid this problem, callers need to implement a try/finally block. Instead of requiring programmers to code such a block explicitly, C# provides a `using` statement expressly for the purpose (see Listing 10.22).

LISTING 10.22: Invoking the using Statement

```csharp
class Program
{
    // ...

    static void Search()
    {
        using (TemporaryFileStream fileStream1 =
            new TemporaryFileStream(),
            fileStream2 = new TemporaryFileStream())
        {
            // Use temporary file stream
        }
    }
}
```

The resultant CIL code is identical to the code that would be created if the programmer specified an explicit try/finally block, where `fileStream.Dispose()` is called in the finally block. The `using` statement, however, provides a syntax shortcut for the try/finally block.

Within a `using` statement, you can instantiate more than one variable by separating each variable from the others with a comma. The key considerations are that all variables must be of the same type and that they implement `IDisposable`. To enforce the use of the same type, the data type is specified only once rather than before each variable declaration.

Garbage Collection, Finalization, and IDisposable

There are several additional noteworthy items to point out in Listing 10.21. First, the IDisposable.Dispose() method contains an important call to System.GC.SuppressFinalize(). Its purpose is to remove the TemporaryFileStream class instance from the **finalization (f-reachable) queue.** This is possible because all cleanup was done in the Dispose() method rather than waiting for the finalizer to execute.

Without the call to SuppressFinalize(), the instance of the object will be included in the f-reachable queue—a list of all the objects that are mostly ready for garbage collection except they also have finalization implementations. The runtime cannot garbage-collect objects with finalizers until after their finalization methods have been called. However, garbage collection itself does not call the finalization method. Rather, references to finalization objects are added to the f-reachable queue and are processed by an additional thread at a time deemed appropriate based on the execution context. In an ironic twist, this approach delays garbage collection for the managed resources—when it is mostly likely that these very resources should likely be cleaned up earlier. The reason for the delay is that the f-reachable queue is a list of "references"; as such, the objects are not considered garbage until after their finalization methods are called and the object references are removed from the f-reachable queue.

> ■ **NOTE**
>
> Objects with finalizers that are not explicitly disposed will end up with an extended object lifetime. Even after all explicit references have gone out of scope, the f-reachable queue will have references, keeping the object alive until the f-reachable queue processing is complete.

It is for this reason that Dispose() invokes System.GC.SuppressFinalize. Invoking this method informs the runtime not to add this object to the finalization queue but instead to allow the garbage collector to de-allocate the object when it no longer has any references (including any f-reachable references).

Second, `Dispose()` calls `Dispose(bool disposing)` with an argument of `true`. The result is that the `Dispose()` method on `Stream` is invoked (cleaning up its resources and suppressing its finalization). Next, the temporary file itself is deleted immediately upon calling `Dispose()`. This important call eliminates the need to wait for the finalization queue to be processed before cleaning up potentially expensive resources.

Third, rather than calling `Close()`, the finalizer now calls `Dispose(bool disposing)` with an argument of `false`. The result is that `Stream` is not closed (disposed) even though the file is deleted. The condition around closing `Stream` ensures that if `Dispose(bool disposing)` is called from the finalizer, the `Stream` instance itself will also be queued up for finalization processing (or possibly it would have already run depending on the order). Therefore, when executing the finalizer, objects owned by the managed resource should not be cleaned up, as this action will be the responsibility of the finalization queue.

Fourth, you should use caution when creating both a `Close()` type and a `Dispose()` method. It is not clear by looking at only the API that `Close()` calls `Dispose()`, so developers will be left wondering whether they need to explicitly call `Close()` and `Dispose()`.

Guidelines

DO implement a finalizer method only on objects with resources that are scarce or expensive, even though finalization delays garbage collection.

DO implement `IDisposable` to support deterministic finalization on classes with finalizers.

DO implement a finalizer method on classes that implement `IDisposable` in case `Dispose()` is not invoked explicitly.

DO refactor a finalization method to call the same code as `IDisposable`, perhaps simply calling the `Dispose()` method.

DO NOT throw exceptions from finalizer methods.

DO call `System.GC.SuppressFinalize()` from `Dispose()` to avoid repeating resource cleanup and delaying garbage collection on an object.

DO ensure that `Dispose()` is idempotent (it should be possible to call `Dispose()` multiple times).

continues

DO keep `Dispose()` simple, focusing on resource cleanup required by finalization.

AVOID calling `Dispose()` on owned objects that have a finalizer. Instead, rely on the finalization queue to clean up the instance.

AVOID referencing other objects that are not being finalized during finalization.

DO invoke a base class's `Dispose()` method when overriding `Dispose()`.

CONSIDER ensuring that an object becomes unusable after `Dispose()` is called. After an object has been disposed, methods other than `Dispose()` (which could potentially be called multiple times) should throw an `ObjectDisposedException`.

DO implement `IDisposable` on types that own disposable fields (or properties) and dispose of said instances.

Language Contrast: C++—Deterministic Destruction

Although finalizers are similar to destructors in C++, the fact that their execution cannot be determined at compile time makes them distinctly different. The garbage collector calls C# finalizers some time after they were last used but before the program shuts down; C++ destructors are automatically called when the object (not a pointer) goes out of scope.

Although running the garbage collector can be a relatively expensive process, the fact that garbage collection is intelligent enough to delay running until process utilization is somewhat reduced offers an advantage over deterministic destructors, which will run at compile-time–defined locations, even when a processor is in high demand.

■ ADVANCED TOPIC

Exception Propagating from Constructors

Even when an exception propagates out of a constructor, the object is still instantiated, although no new instance is returned by the new operator. If the type defines a finalizer, the method will run when the object becomes eligible for garbage collection (providing additional motivation to ensure the finalize method can run on partially constructed objects). Also note that if a constructor prematurely shares its this reference, it will still be accessible even if the constructor throws an exception. Do not allow this scenario to occur.

Resurrecting Objects

By the time an object's finalization method is called, all references to the object have disappeared and the only step before garbage collection is running the finalization code. Even so, it is possible to add a reference inadvertently for a finalization object back into the root reference's graph. In such a case, the re-referenced object will no longer be inaccessible; in turn, it will not be ready for garbage collection. However, if the finalization method for the object has already run, it will not necessarily run again unless it is explicitly marked for finalization (using the GC.ReRegisterFinalize() method).

Obviously, resurrecting objects in this manner is peculiar behavior, and you should generally avoid it. Finalization code should be simple and should focus on cleaning up only the resources that it references.

Lazy Initialization

In the preceding section, we discussed how to deterministically dispose of an object with a using statement and how the finalization queue will dispose of resources in the event that no deterministic approach is used.

A related pattern is called **lazy initialization** or **lazy loading**. Using lazy initialization, you can create (or obtain) objects when you need them rather than beforehand—the latter can be an especially problematic situation when those objects are never used. Consider the FileStream property of Listing 10.23.

LISTING 10.23: Lazy Loading a Property

```
using System.IO;

class DataCache
{
    // ...

        public TemporaryFileStream FileStream =>
            InternalFileStream??(InternalFileStream =
                new TemporaryFileStream());
```

```
        private TemporaryFileStream InternalFileStream
            { get; set; } = null;
    // ...
    }
```

In the `FileStream` expression-bodied property, we check whether
`InternalFileStream` is null or not null before returning its value
directly. If `InternalFileStream` is null, we first instantiate the
`TemporaryFileStream` object and assign it to `InternalFileStream` before
returning the new instance. Thus, the `TemporaryFileStream` required in
the `FileStream` property is created only when the getter on the property
is called. If the getter is never invoked, the `TemporaryFileStream` object
would not be instantiated and we would save whatever execution time
such an instantiation would cost. Obviously, if the instantiation is negligible or inevitable (and postponing the inevitable is less desirable), simply
assigning it during declaration or in the constructor makes sense.

Begin 4.0

■ ADVANCED TOPIC

Lazy Loading with Generics and Lambda Expressions
Starting with Microsoft .NET Framework 4.0, a new class was added to
the CLR to assist with lazy initialization: `System.Lazy<T>`. Listing 10.24
demonstrates how to use it.

LISTING 10.24: Lazy Loading a Property with System.Lazy<T>

```
using System.IO;

class DataCache
{
  // ...

 public TemporaryFileStream FileStream =>
     InternalFileStream.Value;
 private Lazy<TemporaryFileStream> InternalFileStream { get; }
     = new Lazy<TemporaryFileStream>(
         () => new TemporaryFileStream() );

  // ...
  }
```

The `System.Lazy<T>` class takes a type parameter (T) that identifies
which type the `Value` property on `System.Lazy<T>` will return. Instead of

assigning a fully constructed `TemporaryFileStream` to the `_FileStream` field, an instance of `Lazy<TemporaryFileStream>` is assigned (a lightweight call), delaying the instantiation of the `TemporaryFileStream` itself until the `Value` property (and therefore the `FileStream` property) is accessed.

If in addition to type parameters (generics) you use delegates, you can even provide a function for how to initialize an object when the `Value` property is accessed. Listing 10.24 demonstrates passing the delegate—a lambda expression in this case—into the constructor for `System.Lazy<T>`.

Note that the lambda expression itself, `()` `=>` `new TemporaryFileStream(FileStreamName)`, does not execute until `Value` is called. Rather, the lambda expression provides a means of passing the instructions for what will happen; it does not actually execute those instructions until explicitly requested to do so.

One obvious question is when you should use the `System.Lazy<T>` rather than the approach outlined in Listing 10.23. The difference is negligible: In fact, Listing 10.23 may actually be simpler. That is, it is simpler until there are multiple threads involved, such that a race condition might occur regarding the instantiation. In Listing 10.23, more than one check for null might potentially occur before instantiation, resulting in multiple instances being created. In contrast, `System.Lazy<T>` provides a thread-safe mechanism ensuring that one and only one object will be created.

End 4.0

SUMMARY

This chapter provided a whirlwind tour of many topics related to building solid class libraries. All the topics pertain to internal development as well, but they are much more critical to building robust classes. Ultimately, the focus here was on forming more robust and programmable APIs. In the category of robustness, we can include namespaces and garbage collection. Both of these topics fit in the programmability category as well, along with overriding `object`'s virtual members, operator overloading, and XML comments for documentation.

Exception handling uses inheritance heavily by defining an exception hierarchy and enforcing custom exceptions to fit within this hierarchy. Furthermore, the C# compiler uses inheritance to verify catch block order. In the next chapter, you will see why inheritance is such a core part of exception handling.

■ 11 ■
Exception Handling

CHAPTER 5 DISCUSSED USING THE TRY/CATCH/FINALLY BLOCKS for standard exception handling. In that chapter, the catch block always caught exceptions of type System.Exception. This chapter defines some additional details of exception handling—specifically, details surrounding additional exception types, defining custom exceptions, and multiple catch blocks for handling each type. This chapter also details exceptions because of their reliance on inheritance.

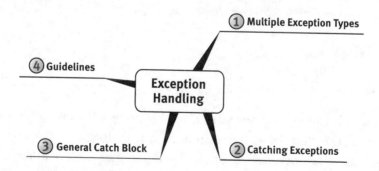

Multiple Exception Types

Listing 11.1 throws a System.ArgumentException, not the System .Exception type demonstrated in Chapter 5. C# allows code to throw any type that derives (perhaps indirectly) from System.Exception.

To throw an exception, you simply prefix the exception instance with the keyword throw. The type of exception used is obviously the type that best describes the circumstances surrounding the error that caused the exception.

For example, consider the TextNumberParser.Parse() method in Listing 11.1.

LISTING 11.1: Throwing an Exception

Begin 6.0
Begin 7.0

```
public sealed class TextNumberParser
{
  public static int Parse(string textDigit)
  {
      string[] digitTexts =
          { "zero", "one", "two", "three", "four",
              "five", "six", "seven", "eight", "nine" };

      int result = Array.IndexOf(
          digitTexts,
              // Leveraging C# 2.0's null coelesce operator
          (textDigit??
              // Leveraging C# 7.0's throw expression
              throw new ArgumentNullException(nameof(textDigit))
          ).ToLower());
      if (result < 0)
      {
          // Leveraging C# 6.0's nameof operator
          throw new ArgumentException(
              "The argument did not represent a digit",
              nameof(textDigit));
      }

      return result;
  }
}
```

End 7.0

In the call to Array.IndexOf(), we leverage a C# 7.0 throw expression when the textDigit argument is null. Prior to C# 7.0, throw expressions were not allowed; only throw statements were allowed. As a result, two separate statements were required: one checking for null and the other to throw the exception. You could not embed the throw within the same statement as a null coalescing operator, for example.

Instead of throwing System.Exception, it is more appropriate to throw ArgumentException because the type itself indicates what went wrong and includes special parameters for identifying which parameter was at fault.

Two similar exceptions are `ArgumentNullException` and `NullReferenceException`. `ArgumentNullException` should be thrown for the inappropriate passing of null arguments. This is a special case of an invalid parameter exception that would more generally (when it isn't null) be thrown as an `ArgumentException` or an `ArgumentOutOfRangeException`. `NullReferenceException` is generally an exception that the underlying runtime will throw only with an attempt to dereference a null value—that is, an attempt to call a member on an object whose value is null. Instead of triggering a `NullReferenceException` to be thrown, programmers should check parameters for `null` before accessing them and then throw an `ArgumentNullException`, which can provide more contextual information, such as the parameter name. If there is an innocuous way to proceed even if an argument is null, be sure to use the C# 6.0 null propagation operator to avoid the runtime throwing a `NullReferenceException`.

One important characteristic of the argument exception types (including `ArgumentNullException`, `ArgumentNullException`, and `ArgumentOutOfRangeException`) is that each has a constructor parameter that allows identification of the argument name as a string. Prior to C# 6.0, this meant hardcoding a magic string (e.g., "textDigit") to identify the parameter name. The problem with this approach is that if the parameter name ever changed, developers had to remember to update the magic string. Fortunately, C# 6.0 and later provides a `nameof` operator, which takes the parameter name identifier and generates the parameter name at compile time (see `nameof(textDigit)` in Listing 11.1). The advantage of this approach is that now the IDE can use refactoring tools (such as automatic renaming) to change the identifier everywhere, including when it is used as an argument to the `nameof` operator. Additionally, if the parameter name changes (without the use of a refactoring tool), the compiler will generate an error if the identifier passed to the `nameof` operator no longer exists. Moving forward, with C# 6.0 (and later), the general guideline is to always use the `nameof` operator for the parameter name of an argument type exception. Chapter 18 provides a full explanation for the `nameof` operator. Until then, it is sufficient to understand that `nameof` simply returns the name of the argument identified.

6.0

Several other exceptions are intended only for the runtime and derive (sometimes indirectly) from `System.SystemException`. They include `System.StackOverflowException`, `System.OutOfMemoryException`, `System.Runtime.InteropServices.COMException`, `System.ExecutionEngineException`, and `System.Runtime.InteropServices.SEHException`. Do not throw exceptions of these types. Similarly, you should avoid throwing a `System.Exception` or `System.ApplicationException`, as these exceptions are so general that they provide little indication of the cause of or resolution to the problem. Instead, throw the most derived exception that fits the scenario. Obviously, developers should avoid creating APIs that could potentially result in a system failure. However, if the executing code reaches a certain state such that continuing to execute is unsafe or unrecoverable, it should call `System.Environment.FailFast()`. This will immediately terminate the process after writing a message to the Windows Application event log, and will even include the message as part of Windows Error Reporting if the user so chooses.

Guidelines

DO throw an `ArgumentException` or one of its subtypes if bad arguments are passed to a member. Prefer the most derived exception type (e.g., `ArgumentNullException`), if applicable.

DO set the `ParamName` property when throwing an `ArgumentException` or one of the subclasses.

DO throw the most specific (most derived) exception that makes sense.

DO NOT throw a `NullReferenceException`. Instead, throw `ArgumentNullException` when a value is unexpectedly null.

DO NOT throw a `System.SystemException` or an exception type that derives from it.

DO NOT throw a `System.Exception` or `System.ApplicationException`.

CONSIDER terminating the process by calling `System.Environment.FailFast()` if the program encounters a scenario where it is unsafe for further execution.

DO use `nameof` for the `paramName` argument passed into argument exception types that take such a parameter. Examples of such exceptions include `ArgumentException`, `ArgumentOutOfRangeException`, and `ArgumentNullException`.

End 6.0

Catching Exceptions

Throwing a particular exception type enables the catcher to use the exception's type itself to identify the problem. It is not necessary, in other words, to catch the exception and use a `switch` statement on the exception message to determine which action to take in light of the exception. Instead, C# allows for multiple catch blocks, each targeting a specific exception type, as Listing 11.2 shows.

LISTING 11.2: Catching Different Exception Types

```csharp
using System;

public sealed class Program
{
    public static void Main(string[] args)
    {
        try
        {
            // ...
            throw new InvalidOperationException(
                "Arbitrary exception");
            // ...
        }
        catch(Win32Exception exception)
            when(exception.NativeErrorCode == 42)
        {
            // Handle Win32Exception where
            // ErrorCode is 42
        }
        catch (NullReferenceException exception)
        {
            // Handle NullReferenceException
        }
        catch (ArgumentException exception)
        {
            // Handle ArgumentException
        }
        catch (InvalidOperationException exception)
        {
            bool exceptionHandled=false;
            // Handle InvalidOperationException
            // ...
            if(!exceptionHandled)
            {
                throw;
            }
        }
    }
}
```

```
        catch (Exception exception)
        {
            // Handle Exception
        }
        finally
        {
            // Handle any cleanup code here as it runs
            // regardless of whether there is an exception
        }
    }
}
```

Listing 11.2 includes five catch blocks, each handling a different type of exception. When an exception occurs, the execution will jump to the catch block with the exception type that most closely matches the exception. The closeness of a match is determined by the inheritance chain. For example, even though the exception thrown is of type System.Exception, this "is a" relationship occurs through inheritance because System.InvalidOperationException ultimately derives from System.Exception. Since the exception type InvalidOperationException most closely matches the exception thrown, the catch(InvalidOperationException...) block will catch the exception and not the catch(Exception...) block.

Starting with C# 6.0, an additional conditional expression is available for catch blocks. Rather than limiting whether a catch block matches based only on an exception type match, C# 6.0 and later provides support for a conditional clause. The when clause allows you to supply a Boolean expression; the catch block handles the exception only if the condition is true. In Listing 11.2, this is an equality comparison operator. Nevertheless, you could, for example, make a method call to validate a condition.

Of course, you could also simply place the conditional check as an if block within the catch body. However, doing so causes the catch block to become the handler for the exception before the condition is checked. It is difficult to write code that allows a different catch block to handle the exception in the scenario where the condition is not met. However, with the **exception condition**, it is now possible to examine the program state (including the exception) without having to catch and rethrow the exception.

Begin 6.0

End 6.0

Use conditional clauses with caution; if the conditional expression itself throws an exception, then that new exception is ignored and the condition is treated as false. For this reason, you should avoid throwing exceptions for the exception conditional expression.

Catch blocks must appear in order, from most specific to most general, to avoid a compile-time error. For example, moving the catch(Exception...) block before any of the other exceptions will result in a compile error, since all prior exceptions derive from System.Exception at some point in their inheritance chain.

As shown with the catch (SystemException){ }) block, a named parameter for the catch block is not required. In fact, a final catch without even the type parameter is allowable, as you will see in the next section.

Rethrowing an Existing Exception

In the InvalidOperationException catch block, a throw statement appears without any identification of the exception to throw (throw is on its own), even though an exception instance (exception) appears in the catch block scope that could be rethrown. Throwing a specific exception would update all the stack information to match the new throw location. As a result, all the stack information indicating the call site where the exception originally occurred would be lost, making it significantly more difficult to diagnose the problem. For this reason, C# supports a throw statement or expression (C# 7.0 or later) without the explicit exception reference as long as it occurs within a catch block. This way, code can examine the exception to determine if it is possible to fully handle it, and if not, rethrow the exception (even though not specified explicitly) as though it was never caught and without replacing any stack information.

■ ADVANCED TOPIC

Begin 5.0

Throwing Existing Exceptions without Replacing Stack Information

In C# 5.0, a mechanism was added that enables the throwing of a previously thrown exception without losing the stack trace information in the original exception. This allows you to rethrow exceptions, for example, even from outside a catch block and, therefore, without using throw;. Although it is fairly rare to need to do this, on some occasions exceptions are wrapped or saved until the program execution moves outside the catch block. For example, multithreaded code might wrap an exception with an AggregateException. The Microsoft .NET Framework 4.5 provides a System.Runtime.ExceptionServices.ExceptionDispatchInfo class specifically to handle this scenario through the use of its static Catch() and instance Throw() methods. (Unfortunately, this class is not available in .NET Core as of version 2.0.) Listing 11.3 demonstrates rethrowing the exception without resetting the stack trace information or using an empty throw statement.

LISTING 11.3: Using ExceptionDispatchInfo to Rethrow an Exception

```
using System
using System.Runtime.ExceptionServices;
using System.Threading.Tasks;
Task task = WriteWebRequestSizeAsync(url);
try
{
  while (!task.Wait(100))
  {
      Console.Write(".");
  }
}
catch(AggregateException exception)
{
    exception = exception.Flatten();
    ExceptionDispatchInfo.Capture(
        exception.InnerException).Throw();
}
```

With the ExceptionDispatchInfo.Throw() method, the compiler doesn't treat it as a return statement in the same way that it might a normal throw statement. For example, if the method signature returned a value but no value was returned from the code path with ExceptionDispatchInfo.Throw(), the compiler would issue an error indicating no value was returned. On occasion, therefore, developers may be forced to follow ExceptionDispatchInfo.Throw() with a return statement even though such a statement would never execute at runtime—the exception would be thrown instead.

End 5.0

Begin 2.0

> ## Language Contrast: Java—Exception Specifiers
>
> C# has no equivalent to Java's exception specifiers. With exception specifiers, the Java compiler is able to verify that all possible exceptions thrown within a function (or a function's call hierarchy) are either caught or declared as possibly rethrown. The C# team considered this option and concluded that the maintenance burden that it imposed was not worth the perceived benefit. Therefore, it is not necessary to maintain a list of all possible exceptions throughout a particular call stack, but neither is it feasible to easily determine the possible exceptions. (As it turns out, this wasn't possible for Java, either. Calling virtual methods or using late binding, such as reflection, made it impossible to fully resolve at compile time which exceptions a method could possibly throw.)

General Catch Block

C# requires that any object that code throws must derive from `System.Exception`. However, this requirement is not universal to all languages. C and C++, for example, allow any object type to be thrown, including managed exceptions that don't derive from `System.Exception`. Starting with C# 2.0, all exceptions, whether deriving from `System.Exception` or not, will propagate into C# assemblies as derived from `System.Exception`. The result is that `System.Exception` catch blocks will catch all exceptions not caught by earlier blocks.

C# also supports a **general catch block** (`catch{ }`) that behaves identically to the `catch(System.Exception exception)` block except that there is no type or variable name. Also, the general catch block must appear last within the list of catch blocks. Since the general catch block is identical to the `catch(System.Exception exception)` block and the general catch block must appear last, the compiler issues a warning if both exist within the same try/catch statement because the general catch block will never be invoked (see the Advanced Topic titled "General Catch Blocks in C# 1.0" for more information on general catch blocks).

■ ADVANCED TOPIC

General Catch Blocks in C# 1.0

In C# 1.0, if a non–`System.Exception`-derived exception was thrown from a method call (residing in an assembly not written in C#), the exception would not be caught by a catch(System.Exception) block. If a different language throws a string, for example, the exception could go unhandled. To avoid this, C# includes a catch block that takes no parameters. The term for such a catch block is *general catch block*, and Listing 11.4 includes one.

LISTING 11.4: Catching Any Exception

```csharp
using System

public sealed class Program
{
  public static void Main()
  {
      try
      {
          // ...
          throw new InvalidOperationException (
              "Arbitrary exception");
          // ...
      }
      catch (NullReferenceException exception)
      {
          // Handle NullReferenceException
      }
      catch (ArgumentException exception)
      {
          // Handle ArgumentException
      }
      catch (InvalidOperationException exception)
      {
          // Handle ApplicationException
       }
      catch (Exception exception)
      {
          // Handle Exception
      }
      catch
      {
          // Any unhandled exception
      }
      finally
      {
          // Handle any cleanup code here as it runs
          // regardless of whether there is an exception
      }
  }
}
```

The general catch block will catch all exceptions, regardless of whether they derive from System.Exception, assuming an earlier catch block does not catch them. The disadvantage of such a block is simply that there is no exception instance to access and therefore no way to know the appropriate course of action. It wouldn't even be possible to recognize the unlikely case where such an exception is innocuous. The best course of action is to handle the exception with some cleanup code before shutting down the application. The catch block could save any volatile data, for example, before shutting down the application or rethrowing the exception.

End 2.0

■ ADVANCED TOPIC

General Catch Block Internals

The Common Intermediate Language (CIL) code corresponding to a general catch block is, in fact, a catch(object) block. Thus, regardless of the type thrown, the general catch block will catch it. Interestingly, it is not possible to explicitly declare a catch(object) exception block within C# code. Therefore, there is no means of catching a non–System.Exception-derived exception and having an exception instance to scrutinize.

In fact, unmanaged exceptions from languages such as C++ generally result in System.Runtime.InteropServices.SEHException-type exceptions, which derive from the System.Exception type. Therefore, not only can the unmanaged type exceptions be caught using a general catch block, but the non–System.Exception-managed types that are thrown can be caught as well—for instance, types such as string.

Guidelines for Exception Handling

Exception handling provides much-needed structure to the error-handling mechanisms that preceded it. However, it can still lead to some unwieldy results if used haphazardly. The following guidelines offer some best practices for exception handling.

- *Catch only the exceptions that you can handle.*

  Generally it is possible to handle some types of exceptions but not others. For example, opening a file for exclusive read-write access may throw a System.IO.IOException because the file is already in use. In catching this type of exception, the code can report to the user that the file is in use and allow the user the option of canceling the operation or retrying it. Only exceptions for which there is a known action should be caught. Other exception types should be left for callers higher in the stack.

- *Don't hide (bury) exceptions you don't fully handle.*

  New programmers are often tempted to catch all exceptions and then continue executing instead of reporting an unhandled exception to the user. However, this practice may result in a critical system problem going undetected. Unless code takes explicit action to handle an exception or explicitly determines certain exceptions to be innocuous, catch blocks should rethrow exceptions instead of catching them and hiding them from the caller. In most cases, catch(System.Exception) and general catch blocks should occur higher in the call stack unless the block ends by rethrowing the exception.

- *Use System.Exception and general catch blocks rarely.*

Begin 4.0

  Almost all exceptions derive from System.Exception. However, the best way to handle some System.Exceptions is to allow them to go unhandled or to gracefully shut down the application sooner rather than later. These exceptions include things such as System.OutOfMemoryException and System.StackOverflowException. In Common Language Runtime (CLR) 4, such exceptions defaulted to nonrecoverable, such that catching them without rethrowing them would cause the CLR to rethrow them anyway. These exceptions are runtime exceptions that the developer cannot write code to recover from. Therefore, the best course of action is to shut down the application—something the runtime will force in CLR 4 and later. Code prior to CLR 4 should catch such exceptions only to run cleanup or emergency code (such as saving any volatile data) before shutting down the application or rethrowing the exception with throw;.

End 4.0

- *Avoid exception reporting or logging lower in the call stack.*

  Often, programmers are tempted to log exceptions or report exceptions to the user at the soonest possible location in the call stack.

However, these locations are seldom able to handle the exception fully; instead, they resort to rethrowing the exception. Such catch blocks should not log the exception or report it to a user while in the bowels of the call stack. If the exception is logged and rethrown, the callers higher in the call stack may do the same, resulting in duplicate log entries of the exception. Worse, displaying the exception to the user may not be appropriate for the type of application. (Using `System.Console.WriteLine()` in a Windows application will never be seen by the user, for example, and displaying a dialog in an unattended command-line process may go unnoticed and freeze the application.) Logging- and exception-related user interfaces should be reserved for use higher up in the call stack.

- *Use* `throw;` *rather than* `throw <exception object>` *inside a catch block.*

It is possible to rethrow an exception inside a catch block. For example, the implementation of `catch(ArgumentNullException exception)` could include a call to `throw exception`. However, rethrowing the exception like this will reset the stack trace to the location of the rethrown call instead of reusing the original throw point location. Therefore, unless you are rethrowing with a different exception type or intentionally hiding the original call stack, use `throw;` to allow the same exception to propagate up the call stack.

- *Favor exception conditions to avoid rethrowing an exception inside a catch block.*

Begin 6.0

On occasions when you find yourself catching an exception that you can't, in fact, handle appropriately and therefore need to rethrow, favor using an exception condition to avoid catching the exception in the first place.

- *Avoid throwing exceptions from exception conditionals.*

When providing an exception conditional, avoid code that throws an exception. Throwing an exception from an exception conditional will result in a false condition, and the exception occurrence will be ignored. For this reason, consider placing complicated conditional checks into a separate method that is wrapped in a try/catch block that handles the exception explicitly.

- *Avoid exception conditionals that might change over time.*

  If an exception conditional evaluates conditions such as exception messages that could potentially change with localization or changed message, the expected exception condition will not get caught, unexpectedly changing the business logic. For this reason, ensure exception conditions are valid over time.

- *Use caution when rethrowing different exceptions.*

  From inside a catch block, rethrowing a different exception will not only reset the throw point but also hide the original exception. To preserve the original exception, set the new exception's `InnerException` property, generally assignable via the constructor. Rethrowing a different exception should be reserved for the following situations:

  1. *Changing the exception type clarifies the problem.*

     For example, in a call to `Logon(User user)`, rethrowing a different exception type is perhaps more appropriate than propagating `System.IO.IOException` when the file with the user list is inaccessible.

  2. *Private data is part of the original exception.*

     In the preceding scenario, if the file path is included in the original `System.IO.IOException`, thereby exposing private security information about the system, the exception should be wrapped. This assumes, of course, that `InnerException` is not set with the original exception. (Funnily enough, a very early version of CLR v1 [pre-alpha, even] had an exception that said something like "Security exception: You do not have permission to determine the path of `c:\temp\foo.txt`".)

  3. *The exception type is too specific for the caller to handle appropriately.*

     For example, instead of throwing an exception specific to a particular database system, a more generic exception is used so that database-specific code higher in the call stack can be avoided.

End 6.0

Guidelines

AVOID exception reporting or logging lower in the call stack.

DO NOT over-catch. Exceptions should be allowed to propagate up the call stack unless it is clearly understood how to programmatically address those errors lower in the stack.

CONSIDER catching a specific exception when you understand why it was thrown in a given context and can respond to the failure programmatically.

AVOID catching System.Exception or System.SystemException except in top-level exception handlers that perform final cleanup operations before rethrowing the exception.

DO use throw rather than throw <exception object> inside a catch block.

DO use exception conditions to avoid rethrowing an exception from within a catch block.

DO use caution when rethrowing different exceptions.

DO NOT throw a NullReferenceException, favoring ArgumentNullException instead when a value is unexpectedly null.

AVOID throwing exceptions from exception conditionals.

AVOID exception conditionals that might change over time.

Defining Custom Exceptions

Once throwing an exception becomes the best course of action, it is preferable to use framework exceptions because they are well established and understood. Instead of throwing a custom invalid argument exception, for example, it is preferable to use the System.ArgumentException type. However, if the developers using a particular API will take special action—the exception-handling logic will vary to handle a custom exception type, for instance—it is appropriate to define a custom exception. For example, if a mapping API receives an address for which the ZIP code is invalid, instead of throwing System.ArgumentException, it may be better to throw a custom InvalidAddressException. The key is whether the caller is likely to write a specific InvalidAddressException catch block with special handling rather than just a generic System.ArgumentException catch block.

Defining a custom exception simply involves deriving from System
.Exception or some other exception type. Listing 11.5 provides an example.

LISTING 11.5: Creating a Custom Exception

```
class DatabaseException : System.Exception
{
  public DatabaseException(
      System.Data.SqlClient.SQLException exception)
  {
      InnerException = exception;
      // ...
  }

  public DatabaseException(
      System.Data.OracleClient.OracleException exception)
  {
      InnerException = exception;
      // ...
  }

  public DatabaseException()
  {
      // ...
  }

  public DatabaseException(string message)
  {
      // ...
  }

  public DatabaseException(
      string message, Exception innerException)
  {
      InnerException = innerException;
      // ...
  }
}
```

This custom exception might be created to wrap proprietary database
exceptions. Since Oracle and SQL Server (for example) throw different exceptions for similar errors, an application could define a custom exception that
standardizes the database-specific exceptions into a common exception wrapper that the application can handle in a standard manner. That way, whether
the application was using an Oracle or a SQL Server back-end database, the
same catch block could be used to handle the error higher up the stack.

The only requirement for a custom exception is that it derives from
System.Exception or one of its descendants. However, there are several
more good practices for custom exceptions:

- All exceptions should use the "Exception" suffix. This way, their purpose is easily established from their name.
- Generally, all exceptions should include constructors that take no parameters, a string parameter, and a parameter set consisting of a string and an inner exception. Furthermore, since exceptions are usually constructed within the same statement in which they are thrown, any additional exception data should also be allowed as part of the constructor. (The obvious exception to creating all these constructors is if certain data is required and a constructor circumvents the requirements.)
- The inheritance chain should be kept relatively shallow (with fewer than approximately five levels).

The inner exception serves an important purpose when rethrowing an exception that is different from the one that was caught. For example, if a `System.Data.SqlClient.SqlException` is thrown by a database call but is caught within the data access layer to be rethrown as a `DatabaseException`, the `DatabaseException` constructor that takes the `SqlException` (or inner exception) will save the original `SqlException` in the `InnerException` property. That way, when requiring additional details about the original exception, developers can retrieve the exception from the `InnerException` property (e.g., `exception.InnerException`).

Guidelines

DO NOT create a new exception type if the exception would not be handled differently than an existing CLR exception. Throw the existing framework exception instead.

DO create a new exception type to communicate a unique program error that cannot be communicated using an existing CLR exception and can be programmatically handled in a different way than any other existing CLR exception type.

DO provide a parameterless constructor on all custom exception types. Also provide constructors that take a message and an inner exception.

DO end exception class names with the "Exception" suffix.

DO make exceptions runtime-serializable.

CONSIDER providing exception properties for programmatic access to extra information relevant to the exception.

AVOID deep exception hierarchies.

■ ADVANCED TOPIC

Serializable Exceptions

Serializable objects are objects that the runtime can persist into a stream—a
file stream, for example—and then be reinstantiated out of the stream. In the
case of exceptions, this behavior may be necessary for certain distributed
communication technologies. To support serialization, exception declarations should either include the `System.SerializableAttribute` attribute
or implement `ISerializable`. Furthermore, they must include a constructor that takes `System.Runtime.Serialization.SerializationInfo`
and `System.Runtime.Serialization.StreamingContext`. Listing 11.6
shows an example of using `System.SerializableAttribute`.

LISTING 11.6: **Defining a Serializable Exception**

```
// Supporting serialization via an attribute
[Serializable]
class DatabaseException : System.Exception
{
  // ...

  // Used for deserialization of exceptions
  public DatabaseException(
      SerializationInfo serializationInfo,
      StreamingContext context)
  {
    // ...
  }

}
```

The preceding `DatabaseException` example demonstrates both
the attribute and the constructor requirement for making an exception
serializable.

Note that for .NET Core, `System.SerializableAttribute` was
not available until it supported .NET Standard 2.0. If you are writing code that will compile across multiple frameworks including
a .NET Standard version less than 2.0, consider defining your own
`System.SerializableAttribute` as a **polyfill**. A polyfill is code that fills
a hole in a particular version of technology and thereby adds the functionality or at least provides a shim for what is missing.

Rethrowing a Wrapped Exception

On occasion, an exception thrown at a lower level in the stack will no longer make sense when caught at a higher level. For example, consider a `System.IO.IOException` that occurs because a system is out of disk space on the server. A client catching such an exception would not necessarily be able to understand the context of why there was even I/O activity. Similarly, consider a geographic coordinate request API that throws a `System.UnauthorizedAccessException` (an exception totally unrelated to the API called). In this second example, the caller has no context for understanding what the API call has to do with security. From the perspective of the code that invokes the API, these exceptions cause more confusion than they help diagnose. Instead of exposing such exceptions to the client, it might make sense to first catch the exception and then throw a different exception, such as `InvalidOperationException` (or even perhaps a custom exception), as a means of communicating that the system is in an invalid state. In such scenarios, be sure to set the `InnerException` property of the wrapping exception (generally via the constructor call such as `new InvalidOperationException(String, Exception)`) so that there is additional context that can be used for diagnostic purposes by someone closer to the framework that was invoked.

An important detail to remember when considering whether to wrap and rethrow an exception is the fact that the original stack trace—which provides the context of where the exception was thrown—will be replaced with the new stack trace of where the wrapping exception is thrown (assuming `ExceptionDispatchInfo` is not used). Fortunately, when the original exception is embedded into the wrapping exception, the original stack trace is still available.

Guidelines

CONSIDER wrapping specific exceptions thrown from the lower layer in a more appropriate exception if the lower-layer exception does not make sense in the context of the higher-layer operation.

DO specify the inner exception when wrapping exceptions.

DO target developers as the audience for exceptions, identifying both the problem and the mechanism to resolve it, where possible.

Ultimately, the intended recipient of the exception is the programmer writing code that calls your API—possibly incorrectly. Therefore, you should provide as much information to her that indicates both what the programmer did wrong and—perhaps more important—how to fix it. The exception type is a critical piece of the communication mechanism. Therefore, you must choose the type carefully.

■ **BEGINNER TOPIC**

Checked and Unchecked Conversions

As we first discussed in a Chapter 2 Advanced Topic, C# provides special keywords for marking a code block with instructions to the runtime for what should happen if the target data type is too small to contain the assigned data. By default, if the target data type cannot contain the assigned data, the data will truncate during assignment. For an example, see Listing 11.7.

LISTING 11.7: Overflowing an Integer Value

```
using System;

public class Program
{
  public static void Main()
  {
      // int.MaxValue equals 2147483647
      int n = int.MaxValue;
      n = n + 1 ;
      System.Console.WriteLine(n);
  }
}
```

The results of Listing 11.7 appear in Output 11.1.

OUTPUT 11.1

```
-2147483648
```

The code in Listing 11.7 writes the value -2147483648 to the console. However, placing the code within a checked block or using the checked option when running the compiler will cause the runtime to throw an exception of type System.OverflowException. The syntax for a checked block uses the checked keyword, as shown in Listing 11.8.

LISTING 11.8: A Checked Block Example

```
using System;

public class Program
{
  public static void Main()
  {
      checked
      {
          // int.MaxValue equals 2147483647
          int n = int.MaxValue;
          n = n + 1 ;
          System.Console.WriteLine(n);
      }
  }
}
```

If the calculation involves only constants, the calculation will be checked by default. The results of Listing 11.8 appear in Output 11.2.

OUTPUT 11.2

```
Unhandled Exception: System.OverflowException: Arithmetic operation
resulted in an overflow. at Program.Main() in ...Program.cs:line 12
```

In addition, depending on the version of Windows and whether a debugger is installed, a dialog may appear that prompts the user to send an error message to Microsoft, check for a solution, or debug the application. Also, the location information (`Program.cs:line X`) will appear only in debug compilations—that is, compilations using the /Debug option of the Microsoft `csc.exe` compiler. The result is that an exception is thrown if, within the checked block, an overflow assignment occurs at runtime.

The C# compiler provides a command-line option for changing the default checked behavior from unchecked to checked. C# also supports an unchecked block that truncates the data instead of throwing an exception for assignments within the block (see Listing 11.9).

LISTING 11.9: An Unchecked Block Example

```
using System;

public class Program
{
  public static void Main()
```

```
    {
        unchecked
        {
            // int.MaxValue equals 2147483647
            int n = int.MaxValue;
            n = n + 1 ;
            System.Console.WriteLine(n);
        }
    }
}
```

The results of Listing 11.9 appear in Output 11.3.

OUTPUT 11.3

```
-2147483648
```

Even if the checked option is on during compilation, the unchecked keyword in the code in Listing 11.9 will prevent the runtime from throwing an exception during execution.

Equivalent checked and unchecked expressions are available for cases where statements are not allowed. For example, a field initializer may consist of an expression rather than a statement:

```
int _Number = unchecked(int.MaxValue + 1);
```

SUMMARY

Throwing an exception causes a significant performance hit. A single exception causes lots of runtime stack information to be loaded and processed—data that would not otherwise be loaded—and it takes a considerable amount of time to handle. As pointed out in Chapter 5, you should use exceptions only to handle exceptional circumstances; APIs should provide mechanisms to check whether an exception will be thrown instead of forcing a particular API to be called to determine whether an exception will be thrown.

The next chapter introduces generics—a C# 2.0 feature that significantly enhances code written in C# 1.0. In fact, it essentially deprecates any use of the System.Collections namespace, which was formerly used in nearly every project.

◼ 12 ◼
Generics

AS YOUR PROJECTS BECOME MORE SOPHISTICATED, you will need a better way to reuse and customize existing software. To facilitate code reuse, especially the reuse of algorithms, C# includes a feature called **generics**. Just as methods are powerful because they can take arguments, so types and methods that take type arguments have significantly more functionality.

Generics are lexically like generic types in Java and templates in C++. In all three languages, these features enable the implementation of algorithms and patterns once, rather than requiring separate implementations for each type the algorithm or pattern operates on. However, C# generics are very different from both Java generics and C++ templates in the details of their implementation and impact on the type system of their respective languages. Generics were added to the runtime and C# in version 2.0.

Begin 2.0

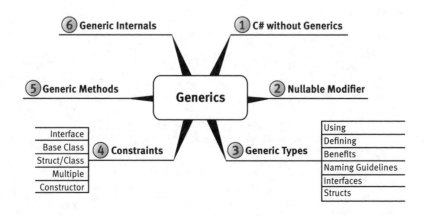

◼ **487**

C# without Generics

We begin the discussion of generics by examining a class that does not use generics. This class, System.Collections.Stack, represents a collection of objects such that the last item to be added to the collection is the first item retrieved from the collection (last in, first out [LIFO]). Push() and Pop(), the two main methods of the Stack class, add items to the stack and remove them from the stack, respectively. The declarations for the methods on the Stack class appear in Listing 12.1.

LISTING 12.1: The System.Collections.Stack Method Signatures

```
public class Stack
{
    public virtual object Pop() { ... }
    public virtual void Push(object obj) { ... }
    // ...
}
```

Programs frequently use stack type collections to facilitate multiple undo operations. For example, Listing 12.2 uses the System.Collections .Stack class for undo operations within a program that simulates the Etch A Sketch game.

LISTING 12.2: Supporting Undo in a Program Similar to the Etch A Sketch Game

```
using System;
using System.Collections;

class Program
{
  // ...

  public void Sketch()
  {
      Stack path = new Stack();
      Cell currentPosition;
      ConsoleKeyInfo key;  // Added in C# 2.0

      do
      {
          // Etch in the direction indicated by the
          // arrow keys that the user enters
          key = Move();
```

2.0

```
                switch (key.Key)
                {
                    case ConsoleKey.Z:
                        // Undo the previous Move
                        if (path.Count >= 1)
                        {
                            currentPosition = (Cell)path.Pop();
                            Console.SetCursorPosition(
                                currentPosition.X, currentPosition.Y);
                            Undo();
                        }
                        break;

                    case ConsoleKey.DownArrow:
                    case ConsoleKey.UpArrow:
                    case ConsoleKey.LeftArrow:
                    case ConsoleKey.RightArrow:
                        // SaveState()
                        currentPosition = new Cell(
                            Console.CursorLeft, Console.CursorTop);
                        path.Push(currentPosition);
                        break;

                    default:
                        Console.Beep();  // Added in C# 2.0
                        break;
                }

            }
        while (key.Key != ConsoleKey.X);  // Use X to quit

    }
}

public struct Cell
{
    // Use read-only field prior to C# 6.0
    public int X { get; }
    public int Y { get; }
    public Cell(int x, int y)
    {
        X = x;
        Y = y;
    }
}
```

The results of Listing 12.2 appear in Output 12.1.

2.0

OUTPUT 12.1

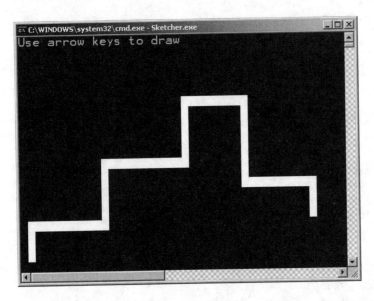

Using the variable path, which is declared as a System.Collections .Stack, you save the previous move by passing a custom type, Cell, into the Stack.Push() method using path.Push(currentPosition). If the user enters a Z (or presses Ctrl+Z), you undo the previous move by retrieving it from the stack using a Pop() method, setting the cursor position to be the previous position, and calling Undo().

Although this code is functional, there is a fundamental shortcoming in the System.Collections.Stack class. As shown in Listing 12.1, the Stack class collects values of type object. Because every object in the Common Language Runtime (CLR) derives from object, Stack provides no validation that the elements you place into it are homogenous or are of the intended type. For example, instead of passing currentPosition, you can pass a string in which X and Y are concatenated with a decimal point between them. However, the compiler must allow the inconsistent data types because the stack class is written to take any object, regardless of its more specific type.

Furthermore, when retrieving the data from the stack using the Pop() method, you must cast the return value to a Cell. But if the type of the value returned from the Pop() method is not Cell, an exception is thrown. By deferring type checking until runtime by using a cast, you make the

2.0

program more brittle. The fundamental problem with creating classes that can work with multiple data types without generics is that they must work with a common base class (or interface), usually `object`.

Using value types, such as a struct or an integer, with classes that use `object` exacerbates the problem. If you pass a value type to the `Stack` `.Push()` method, for example, the runtime automatically boxes it. Similarly, when you retrieve a value type, you need to explicitly unbox the data and cast the `object` reference you obtain from the `Pop()` method into a value type. Casting a reference type to a base class or interface has a negligible performance impact, but the box operation for a value type introduces more overhead, because it must allocate memory, copy the value, and then later garbage-collect that memory.

C# is a language that encourages *type safety*: The language is designed so that many type errors, such as assigning an integer to a variable of type `string`, can be caught at compile time. The fundamental problem is that the `stack` class is not as type-safe as one expects a C# program to be. To change the `stack` class to enforce type safety to restrict the contents of the stack to be a particular data type (without using generic types), you must create a specialized `stack` class, as in Listing 12.3.

LISTING 12.3: Defining a Specialized Stack Class

```
public class CellStack
{
  public virtual Cell Pop();
  public virtual void Push(Cell cell);
  // ...
}
```

Because `CellStack` can store only objects of type `Cell`, this solution requires a custom implementation of the stack methods, which is less than ideal. Implementing a type-safe stack of integers would require yet another custom implementation; each implementation would look remarkably like every other one. There would be lots of duplicated, redundant code.

2.0

■ BEGINNER TOPIC

Another Example: Nullable Value Types

Chapter 3 introduced the capability of declaring variables that could contain null by using the nullable modifier, ?, when declaring a value type variable. C# began supporting this functionality only in version 2.0 because the right implementation required generics. Prior to the introduction of generics, programmers faced essentially two options.

The first option was to declare a nullable data type for each value type that needs to handle null values, as shown in Listing 12.4.

LISTING 12.4: Declaring Versions of Various Value Types That Store null

```csharp
struct NullableInt
{
    /// <summary>
    /// Provides the value when HasValue returns true
    /// </summary>
    public int Value{ get; private set; }

    /// <summary>
    /// Indicates whether there is a value or whether
    /// the value is "null"
    /// </summary>
    public bool HasValue{ get; private set; }

    // ...
}

struct NullableGuid
{
    /// <summary>
    /// Provides the value when HasValue returns true
    /// </summary>
    public Guid Value{ get; private set; }

    /// <summary>
    /// Indicates whether there is a value or whether
    /// the value is "null"
    /// </summary>
    public bool HasValue{ get; private set; }

    ...
}
...
```

2.0

Listing 12.4 shows possible implementations of NullableInt and NullableGuid. If a program required additional nullable value types, you would have to create yet another struct with the properties modified to use the desired value type. Any improvement of the implementation (e.g., adding a user-defined implicit conversion from the underlying type to the nullable type) would require modifying all the nullable type declarations.

An alternative strategy for implementing a nullable type without generics is to make a single type with a Value property of type object, as shown in Listing 12.5.

LISTING 12.5: Declaring a Nullable Type That Contains a Value Property of Type object

```
struct Nullable
{
    /// <summary>
    /// Provides the value when HasValue returns true
    /// </summary>
    public object Value{ get; private set; }

    /// <summary>
    /// Indicates whether there is a value or whether
    /// the value is "null"
    /// </summary>
    public bool HasValue{ get; private set; }

    ...
}
```

Although this option requires only one implementation of a nullable type, the runtime always boxes value types when setting the Value property. Furthermore, retrieving the underlying value from the Value property requires a cast operation, which might potentially be invalid at runtime.

Neither option is particularly attractive. To eliminate this problem, C# 2.0 introduced generics to C#. (And, in fact, nullable types are implemented as the generic type Nullable<T>.)

Introducing Generic Types

Generics provide a facility for creating data structures that can be specialized to handle specific types. Programmers define these **parameterized types** so that each variable of a particular generic type has the same internal algorithm, but the types of data and method signatures can vary on the basis of the type arguments provided for the type parameters.

2.0

To minimize the learning curve for developers, C# designers chose syntax that superficially resembles C++ templates. In C#, the syntax for generic classes and structures uses angle brackets to both declare the generic type parameters in the type declaration and specify the generic type arguments when the type is used.

Using a Generic Class

Listing 12.6 shows how you can specify the actual type argument used by the generic class. You instruct the path variable to be the "Stack of Cell" type by specifying Cell within angle bracket notation in both the object creation expression and the declaration statement. In other words, when declaring a variable (path in this case) using a generic data type, C# requires the developer to identify the actual type arguments used by the generic type. Listing 12.6 illustrates this process with the new generic Stack class.

LISTING 12.6: Implementing Undo with a Generic Stack Class

```
using System;
using System.Collections.Generic;

class Program
{
  // ...

  public void Sketch()
  {
      Stack<Cell> path;            // Generic variable declaration
      path = new Stack<Cell>();    // Generic object instantiation
      Cell currentPosition;
      ConsoleKeyInfo key;

      do
      {
        // Etch in the direction indicated by the
        // arrow keys entered by the user
        key = Move();

        switch (key.Key)
        {
            case ConsoleKey.Z:
                // Undo the previous Move
                if (path.Count >= 1)
                {
                    // No cast required
                    currentPosition = path.Pop();
```

2.0

```
                Console.SetCursorPosition(
                    currentPosition.X, currentPosition.Y);
                Undo();
            }
            break;

        case ConsoleKey.DownArrow:
        case ConsoleKey.UpArrow:
        case ConsoleKey.LeftArrow:
        case ConsoleKey.RightArrow:
            // SaveState()
            currentPosition = new Cell(
                Console.CursorLeft, Console.CursorTop);
            // Only type Cell allowed in call to Push()
            path.Push(currentPosition);
            break;

        default:
            Console.Beep();  // Added in C# 2.0
            break;
        }

    } while (key.Key != ConsoleKey.X);  // Use X to quit
    }
}
```

The results of Listing 12.6 appear in Output 12.2.

OUTPUT 12.2

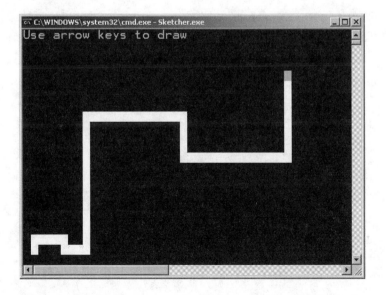

In the path declaration shown in Listing 12.6, you declare a variable and initialize it with a new instance of the System.Collections .Generic.Stack<Cell> class. You specify in angle brackets that the data type of the stack's elements is Cell. As a result, every object added to and retrieved from path is of type Cell. In turn, you no longer need to cast the return of path.Pop() or ensure that only Cell type objects are added to path in the Push() method.

Defining a Simple Generic Class

Generics allow you to author algorithms and patterns and to reuse the code for different data types. Listing 12.7 creates a generic Stack<T> class similar to the System.Collections.Generic.Stack<T> class used in the code in Listing 12.6. You specify a **type parameter** (in this case, T) within angle brackets after the class name. The generic Stack<T> can then be supplied with a single type argument that is substituted everywhere T appears in the class. Thus, the stack can store items of any stated type, without duplicating code or converting the item to type object. The type parameter T is a placeholder that must be supplied with a type argument. In Listing 12.7, you can see that the type parameter will be used for the internal Items array, the type for the parameter to the Push() method, and the return type for the Pop() method.

LISTING 12.7: Declaring a Generic Class, Stack<T>

```
public class Stack<T>
{
    // Use read-only field prior to C# 6.0
    private T[] InternalItems { get; }

    public void Push(T data)
    {
        ...
    }

    public T Pop()
    {
        ...
    }
}
```

2.0

Benefits of Generics

There are several advantages to using a generic class over a nongeneric version (such as the System.Collections.Generic.Stack<T> class used earlier instead of the original System.Collections.Stack type):

1. Generics facilitate increased type safety, preventing data types other than those explicitly intended by the members within the parameterized class. In Listing 12.7, the parameterized stack class restricts you to the Cell data type when using Stack<Cell>. For example, the statement path.Push("garbage") produces a compile-time error indicating that there is no overloaded method for System.Collections.Generic.Stack<T>.Push(T) that can work with the string, because it cannot be converted to a Cell.

2. Compile-time type checking reduces the likelihood of InvalidCastException type errors at runtime.

3. Using value types with generic class members no longer causes a boxing conversion to object. For example, path.Pop() and path.Push() do not require an item to be boxed when added or unboxed when removed.

4. Generics in C# reduce code bloat. Generic types retain the benefits of specific class versions, without the overhead. For example, it is no longer necessary to define a class such as CellStack.

5. Performance improves because casting from an object is no longer required, thereby eliminating a type check operation. Also, performance improves because boxing is no longer necessary for value types.

6. Generics reduce memory consumption by avoiding boxing and, therefore, consuming less memory on the heap.

7. Code becomes more readable because of fewer casting checks and because of the need for fewer type-specific implementations.

8. Editors that assist coding via some type of IntelliSense work directly with return parameters from generic classes. There is no need to cast the return data for IntelliSense to work.

At their core, generics offer the ability to code pattern implementations and then reuse those implementations wherever the patterns appear. Patterns describe problems that occur repeatedly within code, and templates provide a single implementation for these repeating patterns.

2.0

Type Parameter Naming Guidelines

Just as when you name a method's formal parameter, so you should be as descriptive as possible when naming a type parameter. Furthermore, to distinguish the parameter as being a type parameter, its name should include a *T* prefix. For example, in defining a class such as `EntityCollection<TEntity>`, you use the type parameter name "TEntity."

The only time you would not use a descriptive type parameter name is when such a description would not add any value. For example, using *T* in the `Stack<T>` class is appropriate, since the indication that *T* is a type parameter is sufficiently descriptive; the stack works for any type.

In the next section, you will learn about constraints. It is a good practice to use constraint-descriptive type names. For example, if a type parameter must implement `IComponent`, consider a type name of "TComponent."

Guidelines

DO choose meaningful names for type parameters and prefix the name with *T*.

CONSIDER indicating a constraint in the name of a type parameter.

Generic Interfaces and Structs

C# supports the use of generics throughout the language, including interfaces and structs. The syntax is identical to that used by classes. To declare an interface with a type parameter, place the type parameter in angle brackets immediately after the interface name, as shown in the example of `IPair<T>` in Listing 12.8.

LISTING 12.8: Declaring a Generic Interface

```
interface IPair<T>
{
    T First { get; set; }
    T Second { get; set; }
}
```

2.0

This interface represents pairs of like objects, such as the coordinates of a point, a person's genetic parents, or nodes of a binary tree. The type contained in the pair is the same for both items.

To implement the interface, you use the same syntax as you would for a nongeneric class. Note that it is legal, and indeed common, for the type argument for one generic type to be a type parameter of another, as shown in Listing 12.9. The type argument of the interface is the type parameter declared by the class. In addition, this example uses a struct rather than a class, demonstrating that C# supports custom generic value types.

LISTING 12.9: Implementing a Generic Interface

```
public struct Pair<T>: IPair<T>
{
    public T First { get; set; }
    public T Second { get; set; }
}
```

Support for generic interfaces is especially important for collection classes, where generics are most prevalent. Before generics, developers relied on a series of interfaces within the System.Collections namespace. Like their implementing classes, these interfaces worked only with type object, and as a result, the interface forced all access to and from these collection classes to require a cast. By using type-safe generic interfaces, you can avoid cast operations.

■ ADVANCED TOPIC

Implementing the Same Interface Multiple Times on a Single Class

Two different constructions of the same generic interface are considered different types. Consequently, "the same" generic interface can be implemented multiple times by a class or struct. Consider the example in Listing 12.10.

LISTING 12.10: Duplicating an Interface Implementation on a Single Class

```
public interface IContainer<T>
{
    ICollection<T> Items  { get; set; }
}
```

2.0

```
public class Person: IContainer<Address>,
    IContainer<Phone>, IContainer<Email>
{
    ICollection<Address> IContainer<Address>.Items
    {
        get{...}
        set{...}
    }
    ICollection<Phone> IContainer<Phone>.Items
    {
        get{...}
        set{...}
    }
    ICollection<Email> IContainer<Email>.Items
    {
        get{...}
        set{...}
    }
}
```

In this example, the `Items` property appears multiple times using an explicit interface implementation with a varying type parameter. Without generics, this would not be possible; instead, the compiler would allow only one explicit `IContainer.Items` property.

However, this technique of implementing multiple versions of the same interface is considered by many to be a "bad code smell" because it is potentially confusing (particularly if the interface permits covariant or contravariant conversions). Moreover, the `Person` class here seems potentially badly designed; one does not normally think of a person as being "a thing that can provide a set of email addresses." When you feel tempted to make a class implement three versions of the same interface, consider whether it might be better to make it instead implement three properties—for example, `EmailAddresses`, `PhoneNumbers`, and `MailingAddresses`—each of which returns the appropriate construction of the generic interface.

Guidelines

AVOID implementing multiple constructions of the same generic interface in one type.

Defining a Constructor and a Finalizer

Perhaps surprisingly, the constructors (and finalizer) of a generic class or struct do not require type parameters; in other words, they do not require Pair<T>(){...}. In the pair example in Listing 12.11, the constructor is declared using public Pair(T first, T second).

LISTING 12.11: Declaring a Generic Type's Constructor

```csharp
public struct Pair<T>: IPair<T>
{
    public Pair(T first, T second)
    {
        First = first;
        Second = second;
    }

    public T First  { get; set; }
    public T Second  { get; set; }
}
```

Specifying a Default Value

Listing 12.11 included a constructor that takes the initial values for both First and Second and assigns them to First and Second. Since Pair<T> is a struct, any constructor you provide must initialize all fields and automatically implemented properties. This presents a problem, however. Consider a constructor for Pair<T> that initializes only half of the pair at instantiation time.

Defining such a constructor, as shown in Listing 12.12, causes a compile-time error because the field Second is still uninitialized at the end of the constructor. Providing initialization for Second presents a problem because you don't know the data type of T. If it is a reference type, null would work, but this approach would not work if T were a non-nullable value type.

LISTING 12.12: Not Initializing All Fields, Causing a Compile-Time Error

```csharp
public struct Pair<T>: IPair<T>
{
    // ERROR:  Field 'Pair<T>.Second' must be fully assigned
    //         before control leaves the constructor
    // public Pair(T first)
    // {
    //     First = first;
    // }

    // ...
}
```

2.0

To deal with this scenario, C# provides the `default` operator, first discussed in Chapter 9. There, we showed how the default value of `int` could be specified with `default(int)`. In the case of T, which `Second` requires, you can use `default(T)`, as shown in Listing 12.13.

LISTING 12.13: Initializing a Field with the default Operator

```csharp
public struct Pair<T>: IPair<T>
{
  public Pair(T first)
  {
    First = first;
    Second = default(T);
  }

  // ...
}
```

The `default` operator can provide the default value for any type, including type parameters.

C# 7.1 includes the option to use default without specifying a parameter as long as it is possible to infer the data type. For example, with variable initialization or assignment, you can use `Pair<T> pair = default` in place of `Pair<T> pair = default(Pair<T>)`. Furthermore, if a method returns an `int`, it is possible to simply use `return default` and have the compiler infer a `default(int)` from the return of the method. Other scenarios where such inference is possible are default parameter (optional) values and method call arguments.

Multiple Type Parameters

Generic types may declare any number of type parameters. The initial `Pair<T>` example contains only one type parameter. To enable support for storing a dichotomous pair of objects, such as a name/value pair, you could create a new version of the type that declares two type parameters, as shown in Listing 12.14.

LISTING 12.14: Declaring a Generic with Multiple Type Parameters

```csharp
interface IPair<TFirst, TSecond>
{
  TFirst First { get; set; }
  TSecond Second { get; set; }
}
```

```
public struct Pair<TFirst, TSecond>: IPair<TFirst, TSecond>
{
    public Pair(TFirst first, TSecond second)
    {
        First = first;
        Second = second;
    }

    public TFirst First { get; set; }
    public TSecond Second { get; set; }
}
```

When you use the `Pair<TFirst, TSecond>` class, you supply multiple type parameters within the angle brackets of the declaration and instantiation statements; you then supply matching types to the parameters of the methods when you call them. Listing 12.15 illustrates this approach.

LISTING 12.15: Using a Type with Multiple Type Parameters

```
Pair<int, string> historicalEvent =
    new Pair<int, string>(1914,
        "Shackleton leaves for South Pole on ship Endurance");
Console.WriteLine("{0}: {1}",
    historicalEvent.First, historicalEvent.Second);
```

The number of type parameters—that is, the **arity**—uniquely distinguishes the class from others of the same name. Therefore, it is possible to define both `Pair<T>` and `Pair<TFirst, TSecond>` within the same namespace because of the arity variation. Furthermore, because of their close semantic relationship, generics that differ only by arity should be placed into the same C# file.

Guidelines

DO place multiple generic classes into a single file if they differ only by the number of generic parameters.

■ BEGINNER TOPIC

Tuples: Where Arity is in Abundance

We introduced C# 7.0's support for tuple syntax back in Chapter 3. Internally, the underlying type that implements the tuple syntax is, in fact, a generic—specifically a `System.ValueTuple`. As with `Pair<...>`, it was

Begin 7.0

2.0

possible to reuse the same name because of the variation in arity (each class had a different number of type parameters), as shown in Listing 12.16.

LISTING 12.16: Using Arity to Overload a Type Definition

```
public class ValueTuple { ... }
public class ValueTuple<T1>:
    IStructuralEquatable, IStructuralComparable, IComparable {...}
public class ValueTuple<T1, T2>: ... {...}
public class ValueTuple<T1, T2, T3>: ... {...}
public class ValueTuple<T1, T2, T3, T4>: ... {...}
public class ValueTuple<T1, T2, T3, T4, T5>: ... {...}
public class ValueTuple<T1, T2, T3, T4, T5, T6>: ... {...}
public class ValueTuple<T1, T2, T3, T4, T5, T6, T7>: ... {...}
public class ValueTuple<T1, T2, T3, T4, T5, T6, T7, TRest>: ... {...}
```

The ValueTuple<...> set of classes was designed for the same purpose as the Pair<T> and Pair<TFirst, TSecond> classes, except together they can handle eight type arguments. In fact, using the last ValueTuple shown in Listing 12.16, TRest can be used to store another ValueTuple, making the number of elements of the tuple practically unlimited. And, if you define such a tuple using C# 7.0's tuple syntax, that is what the compiler will generate.

Another interesting member of the tuple family of classes is the nongeneric ValueTuple class. This class has eight static factory methods for instantiating the various generic tuple types. Although each generic type could be instantiated directly using its constructor, the ValueTuple type's factory methods allow for inference of the type arguments via the Create() method. This is insignificant in C# 7.0 because the code is as simple as var keyValuePair = ("555-55-5555", new Contact("Inigo Montoya")) (assuming no named items). However, as shown in Listing 12.17, using the Create() method in combination with type inference is simpler for C# 6.0.

LISTING 12.17: Comparing System.ValueTuple Instantiation Approaches

```
#if !PRECSHARP7
    (string, Contact) keyValuePair;
    keyValuePair =
        ("555-55-5555", new Contact("Inigo Montoya"));
#else  // Use System.ValueTupe<string,Contact> prior to C# 7.0
    ValueTuple<string, Contact> keyValuePair;
    keyValuePair =
        ValueTuple.Create(
            "555-55-5555", new Contact("Inigo Montoya"));
```

```
        keyValuePair =
            new ValueTuple<string, Contact>(
                "555-55-5555", new Contact("Inigo Montoya"));
    #endif // !PRECSHARP7
```

Obviously, when the `ValueTuple` gets large, the number of type parameters to specify could be cumbersome without the `Create()` factory methods.

Note that a similar tuple class was added in C# 4.0: `System.Tuple`. However, it was determined that abundant use of C# 7.0's tuple syntax and the resulting prevalence of tuples it would introduce warranted creating the `System.ValueTuple` type because of the performance improvements it provided.

Begin 4.0

End 4.0

End 7.0

As you might have deduced from the fact that the framework libraries declare eight different generic `System.ValueTuple` types, there is no support in the CLR type system for *variadic* generic types. Methods can take an arbitrary number of arguments by using *parameter arrays*, but there is no corresponding technique for generic types; every generic type must be of a specific arity. (See the Beginner Topic titled "Tuples: Where Arity is in Abundance" for an example where you might imagine such a feature.)

Nested Generic Types

Type parameters on a containing generic type will "cascade" down to any nested types automatically. If the containing type declares a type parameter T, for example, all nested types will also be generic and type parameter T will be available on the nested type as well. If the nested type includes its own type parameter named T, this will hide the type parameter within the containing type, and any reference to T in the nested type will refer to the nested T type parameter. Fortunately, reuse of the same type parameter name within the nested type will cause a compiler warning to prevent accidental overlap (see Listing 12.18).

LISTING 12.18: Nested Generic Types

```
class Container<T, U>
{
    // Nested classes inherit type parameters.
    // Reusing a type parameter name will cause
    // a warning.
```

2.0

```
class Nested<U>
{
    void Method(T param0, U param1)
    {
    }
}
}
```

The containing type's type parameters are accessible in the nested type the same way that members of the containing type are also accessible from the nested type. The rule is simply that a type parameter is available anywhere within the body of the type that declares it.

> **Guidelines**
>
> AVOID shadowing a type parameter of an outer type with an identically named type parameter of a nested type.

Constraints

Generics support the ability to define constraints on type parameters. These constraints ensure that the types provided as type arguments conform to various rules. Take, for example, the BinaryTree<T> class shown in Listing 12.19.

LISTING 12.19: Declaring a BinaryTree<T> Class with No Constraints

```
public class BinaryTree<T>
{
    public BinaryTree ( T item)
    {
        Item = item;
    }

    public T Item { get; set; }
    public Pair<BinaryTree<T>> SubItems { get; set; }
}
```

(An interesting side note is that BinaryTree<T> uses Pair<T> internally, which is possible because Pair<T> is simply another type.)

Suppose you want the tree to sort the values within the Pair<T> value as it is assigned to the SubItems property. To achieve the sorting,

2.0

the SubItems set accessor uses the CompareTo( ) method of the supplied
key, as shown in Listing 12.20.

LISTING 12.20: Needing the Type Parameter to Support an Interface

```
public class BinaryTree<T>
{
    public T Item { get; set; }
    public Pair<BinaryTree<T>> SubItems
    {
        get{ return _SubItems; }
        set
        {
            IComparable<T> first;
            // ERROR: Cannot implicitly convert type...
            first = value.First;  // Explicit cast required

            if (first.CompareTo(value.Second) < 0)
            {
                // first is less than second
                // ...
            }
            else
            {
                // first and second are the same or
                // second is less than first
                // ...
            }
            _SubItems = value;
        }
    }
    private Pair<BinaryTree<T>> _SubItems;
}
```

At compile time, the type parameter T is an unconstrained generic.
When the code is written as shown in Listing 12.20, the compiler
assumes that the only members available on T are those inherited from
the base type object, since every type has object as a base class. Only
methods such as ToString( ), therefore, are available to call on an
instance of the type parameter T. As a result, the compiler displays a
compilation error because the CompareTo( ) method is not defined on
type object.

You can cast the T parameter to the IComparable<T> interface to access
the CompareTo( ) method, as shown in Listing 12.21.

2.0

LISTING 12.21: Needing the Type Parameter to Support an Interface or Exception Thrown

```
public class BinaryTree<T>
{
    public T Item { get; set; }
    public Pair<BinaryTree<T>> SubItems
    {
        get{ return _SubItems; }
        set
        {
            IComparable<T> first;
            first = (IComparable<T>)value.First.Item;

            if (first.CompareTo(value.Second.Item) < 0)
            {
                // first is less than second
                ...
            }
            else
            {
                // second is less than or equal to first
                ...
            }
            _SubItems = value;
        }
    }
    private Pair<BinaryTree<T>> _SubItems;
}
```

Unfortunately, if you now declare a `BinaryTree<SomeType>` class variable but the type argument does not implement the `IComparable<SomeType>` interface, you will encounter an execution-time error—specifically, an `InvalidCastException`. This eliminates a key reason for having generics in the first place: to improve type safety.

To avoid this exception and instead generate a compile-time error if the type argument does not implement the interface, C# allows you to supply an optional list of **constraints** for each type parameter declared in the generic type. A constraint declares the characteristics that the generic type requires of the type argument supplied for each type parameter. You declare a constraint using the where keyword, followed by a parameter–requirements pair, where the parameter must be one of those declared in the generic type and the requirements describe the class or interfaces to which the type argument must be convertible, the presence of a default constructor, or a reference/value type restriction.

2.0

Interface Constraints

To ensure that a binary tree has its nodes correctly ordered, you can use the CompareTo() method in the BinaryTree class. To do this most effectively, you should impose a constraint on the T type parameter. That is, you need the T type parameter to implement the IComparable<T> interface. The syntax for declaring this constraint appears in Listing 12.22.

LISTING 12.22: **Declaring an Interface Constraint**

```
public class BinaryTree<T>
    where T: System.IComparable<T>
{
    public T Item { get; set; }
    public Pair<BinaryTree<T>> SubItems
    {
        get{ return _SubItems; }
        set
        {
            IComparable<T> first;
            // Notice that the cast can now be eliminated
            first = value.First.Item;

            if (first.CompareTo(value.Second.Item) < 0)
            {
                // first is less than second
                ...
            }
            else
            {
                // second is less than or equal to first
                ...
            }
            _SubItems = value;
        }
    }
    private Pair<BinaryTree<T>> _SubItems;
}
```

When given the interface constraint addition in Listing 12.22, the compiler ensures that each time you use the BinaryTree<T> class, you specify a type parameter that implements the corresponding construction of the IComparable<T> interface. Furthermore, you no longer need to explicitly cast the variable to an IComparable<T> interface before calling the CompareTo() method. Casting is not even required to access members that use explicit interface implementation, which in other contexts would hide the member without a cast. When calling a method on a value typed

2.0

as a generic type parameter, the compiler checks whether the method matches any method on any of the interfaces declared as constraints.

If you tried to create a `BinaryTree<T>` variable using `System .Text.StringBuilder` as the type parameter, you would receive a compiler error because `StringBuilder` does not implement `IComparable<StringBuilder>`. The error is similar to the one shown in Output 12.3.

OUTPUT 12.3

```
error CS0311: The type 'System.Text.StringBuilder' cannot be used as type
parameter 'T' in the generic type or method 'BinaryTree<T>'. There is no
implicit reference conversion from 'System.Text.StringBuilder' to
'System.IComparable<System.Text.StringBuilder>'.
```

To specify an interface for the constraint, you declare an **interface type constraint**. This constraint even circumvents the need to cast to call an explicit interface member implementation.

Class Type Constraints

Sometimes you might want to constrain a type argument to be convertible to a particular class type. You do this using a **class type constraint**, as shown in Listing 12.23.

LISTING 12.23: Declaring a Class Type Constraint

```
public class EntityDictionary<TKey, TValue>
    : System.Collections.Generic.Dictionary<TKey, TValue>
    where TValue : EntityBase
{
    ...
}
```

In Listing 12.23, `EntityDictionary<TKey, TValue>` requires that all type arguments provided for the type parameter `TValue` be implicitly convertible to the `EntityBase` class. By requiring the conversion, it becomes possible to use the members of `EntityBase` on values of type `TValue` within the generic implementation, because the constraint will ensure that all type arguments can be implicitly converted to the `EntityBase` class.

The syntax for the class type constraint is the same as that for the interface type constraint, except that class type constraints must appear before any interface type constraints (just as the base class must appear before implemented interfaces in a class declaration). However, unlike interface constraints, multiple base class constraints are not allowed, since it is not possible to derive from multiple unrelated classes. Similarly, base class constraints cannot specify sealed classes or nonclass types. For example, C# does not allow a type parameter to be constrained to `string` or `System.Nullable<T>` because there would then be only one possible type argument for that type parameter—that's hardly "generic." If the type parameter is constrained to a single type, there is no need for the type parameter in the first place; just use that type directly.

Certain "special" types are not legal as class type constraints. See the Advanced Topic titled "Constraint Limitations," later in this chapter, for details.

struct/class Constraints

Another valuable generic constraint is the ability to restrict type arguments to be any non-nullable value type or any reference type. Rather than specifying a class from which T must derive, you simply use the keyword `struct` or `class`, as shown in Listing 12.24.

LISTING 12.24: Specifying the Type Parameter as a Value Type

```
public struct Nullable<T> :
    IFormattable, IComparable,
    IComparable<Nullable<T>>, INullable
    where T : struct
{
    // ...
}
```

Note that the `class` constraint—somewhat confusingly—does not restrict the type argument to class types; rather, it restricts it to reference types. A type argument supplied for a type parameter constrained with the `class` constraint may be any class, interface, delegate, or array type.

Because a class type constraint requires a reference type, using a `struct` constraint with a class type constraint would be contradictory. Therefore, you cannot combine `struct` and `class` constraints.

The `struct` constraint has one special characteristic: Nullable value types do not satisfy the constraint. Why? Nullable value types are implemented as the generic type `Nullable<T>`, which itself applies the `struct`

2.0

constraint to T. If nullable value types satisfied that constraint, it would be possible to define the nonsense type `Nullable<Nullable<int>>`. A doubly nullable integer is confusing to the point of being meaningless. (As expected, the shorthand syntax `int??` is also disallowed.)

Multiple Constraints

For any given type parameter, you may specify any number of interface type constraints, but no more than one class type constraint (just as a class may implement any number of interfaces but inherit from only one other class). Each new constraint is declared in a comma-delimited list following the generic type parameter and a colon. If there is more than one type parameter, each must be preceded by the `where` keyword. In Listing 12.25, the generic `EntityDictionary` class declares two type parameters: `TKey` and `TValue`. The `TKey` type parameter has two interface type constraints, and the `TValue` type parameter has one class type constraint.

LISTING 12.25: Specifying Multiple Constraints

```
public class EntityDictionary<TKey, TValue>
    : Dictionary<TKey, TValue>
    where TKey : IComparable<TKey>, IFormattable
    where TValue : EntityBase
{
    ...
}
```

In this case, there are multiple constraints on `TKey` itself and an additional constraint on `TValue`. When specifying multiple constraints on one type parameter, an AND relationship is assumed. If a type `C` is supplied as the type argument for `TKey`, `C` must implement `IComparable<C>` and `IFormattable`, for example.

Notice there is no comma between each `where` clause.

Constructor Constraints

In some cases, it is desirable to create an instance of the type argument's type inside the generic class. In Listing 12.26, for example, the `MakeValue()` method for the `EntityDictionary<TKey, TValue>` class must create an instance of the type argument corresponding to type parameter `TValue`.

2.0

LISTING 12.26: Requiring a Default Constructor Constraint

```csharp
public class EntityBase<TKey>
{
    public TKey Key { get; set; }
}

public class EntityDictionary<TKey, TValue> :
    Dictionary<TKey, TValue>
    where TKey: IComparable<TKey>, IFormattable
    where TValue : EntityBase<TKey>, new()
{
    // ...

    public TValue MakeValue(TKey key)
    {
        TValue newEntity = new TValue();
        newEntity.Key = key;
        Add(newEntity.Key, newEntity);
        return newEntity;
    }

    // ...
}
```

Because not all objects are guaranteed to have public default constructors, the compiler does not allow you to call the default constructor on an unconstrained type parameter. To override this compiler restriction, you can add the text new() after all other constraints are specified. This text is a **constructor constraint**, and it requires the type argument corresponding to the constrained type parameter to have a public default constructor. Only the default constructor constraint is available. You cannot specify a constraint that ensures that the type argument supplied provides a constructor that takes formal parameters.

Constraint Inheritance

Neither generic type parameters nor their constraints are inherited by a derived class, because generic type parameters are not members. (Remember, class inheritance is the property that the derived class has all the members of the base class.) It is a common practice to make new generic types that inherit from other generic types. In such a case, because the type parameters of the derived generic type become the type arguments of the generic base class, the type parameters must have constraints equal to (or stronger than) those on the base class. Confused? Consider Listing 12.27.

2.0

LISTING 12.27: Inherited Constraints Specified Explicitly

```
class EntityBase<T> where T : IComparable<T>
{
  // ...
}
```

```
// ERROR:
// The type 'U' must be convertible to
// 'System.IComparable<U>' to use it as parameter
// 'T' in the generic type or method
// class Entity<U> : EntityBase<U>
// {
//    ...
// }
```

In Listing 12.27, EntityBase<T> requires that the type argument U supplied for T by the base class specifier EntityBase<U> implement IComparable<U>. Therefore, the Entity<U> class needs to require the same constraint on U. Failure to do so will result in a compile-time error. This pattern increases a programmer's awareness of the base class's type constraint in the derived class, avoiding the confusion that might otherwise occur when the programmer uses the derived class and discovers the constraint but does not understand where it comes from.

We have not covered generic methods yet; we'll get to them later in this chapter. For now, simply recognize that methods may also be generic and may also place constraints on the type arguments supplied for their type parameters. How, then, are constraints handled when a virtual generic method is inherited and overridden? In contrast to the situation with type parameters declared on a generic class, constraints on overriding virtual generic methods (or explicit interface) methods are inherited implicitly and may not be restated (see Listing 12.28).

LISTING 12.28: Repeating Inherited Constraints on Virtual Members Is Prohibited

```
class EntityBase
{
  public virtual void Method<T>(T t)
      where T : IComparable<T>
  {
    // ...
  }
}
```

```
class Order : EntityBase
{
  public override void Method<T>(T t)
  //    Constraints may not be repeated on overriding
  //    members
  //    where T : IComparable<T>
  {
      // ...
  }
}
```

In the generic class inheritance case, the type parameter on the derived class can be further constrained by adding not only the constraints on the base class (required), but also other constraints. However, overriding virtual generic methods need to conform exactly to the constraints defined by the base class method. Additional constraints could break polymorphism, so they are not allowed and the type parameter constraints on the overriding method are implied.

▪ ADVANCED TOPIC

Constraint Limitations

Constraints are appropriately limited to avoid nonsensical code. For example, you cannot combine a class type constraint with a `struct` or `class` constraint. Also, you cannot specify constraints to restrict inheritance to special types such as `object`, arrays, `System.ValueType`, `System.Enum` (enum), `System.Delegate`, or `System.MulticastDelegate`.

In some cases, constraint limitations are perhaps more desirable, but they still are not supported. The following subsections provide some additional examples of constraints that are not allowed.

Operator Constraints Are Not Allowed

You cannot constrain a type parameter to a type that implements a particular method or operator, except via interface type constraints (for methods) or class type constraints (for methods and operators). Because of this, the generic `Add( )` in Listing 12.29 does not work.

LISTING 12.29: Constraint Expressions Cannot Require Operators

```
public abstract class MathEx<T>
{
```

2.0

```
    public static T Add(T first, T second)
    {
        // Error: Operator '+' cannot be applied to
        // operands of type 'T' and 'T'
        // return first + second;
    }
}
```

In this case, the method assumes that the + operator is available on all types that could be supplied as type arguments for T. But there is no constraint that prevents you from supplying a type argument that does not have an associated addition operator, so an error occurs. Unfortunately, there is no way to specify that an addition operator is required within a constraint, aside from using a class type constraint where the class type implements an addition operator.

More generally, there is no way to constrain a type to have a static method.

OR Criteria Are Not Supported

If you supply multiple interfaces or class constraints for a type parameter, the compiler always assumes an AND relationship between constraints. For example, where T : IComparable<T>, IFormattable requires that both IComparable<T> and IFormattable are supported. There is no way to specify an OR relationship between constraints. Hence, an equivalent of Listing 12.30 is not supported.

LISTING 12.30: **Combining Constraints Using an OR Relationship Is Not Allowed**

```
    public class BinaryTree<T>
        // Error: OR is not supported
        // where T: System.IComparable<T> || System.IFormattable
    {
        ...
    }
```

Supporting this functionality would prevent the compiler from resolving which method to call at compile time.

Constraints of Type Delegate and Enum Are Not Valid

Delegate types, array types, and enumerated types may not be used as class type constraints, because they are all effectively "sealed" types. (If you are not familiar with delegate types, see Chapter 13.) Their base types—System.Delegate, System.MultiCastDelegate, System.Array, and `System.Enum`—may also not be used as constraints. For example, the compiler will generate an error when it encounters the class declaration in Listing 12.31.

LISTING 12.31: Inheritance Constraints Cannot Be of Type System.Delegate

```
// Error:  Constraint cannot be special class 'System.Delegate'
public class Publisher<T>
    where T : System.Delegate
{
    public event T Event;
    public void Publish()
    {
        if (Event != null)
        {
            Event(this, new EventArgs());
        }
    }
}
```

All delegate types are considered special classes that cannot be specified as type parameters. Doing so would prevent compile-time validation of the call to `Event()` because the signature of the event firing is unknown with the data types `System.Delegate` and `System.MulticastDelegate`. The same restriction applies to any enum type.

Constructor Constraints Are Allowed Only for Default Constructors

Listing 12.26 includes a constructor constraint that forces the type argument supplied for `TValue` to provide a public parameterless constructor. There is no constraint to force the type argument to provide a constructor that takes other formal parameters. For example, you might want to constrain `TValue` so that the type argument provided for it must provide a constructor that takes the type argument provided for `TKey`, but this is not possible. Listing 12.32 demonstrates the invalid code.

LISTING 12.32: Constructor Constraints Can Be Specified Only for Default Constructors

```
public TValue New(TKey key)
{
    // Error: 'TValue': Cannot provide arguments
    // when creating an instance of a variable type
    TValue newEntity = null;
    // newEntity = new TValue(key);
    Add(newEntity.Key, newEntity);
    return newEntity;
}
```

2.0

One way to circumvent this restriction is to supply a factory interface that includes a method for instantiating the type. The factory implementing the interface takes responsibility for instantiating the entity rather than the EntityDictionary itself (see Listing 12.33).

LISTING 12.33: Using a Factory Interface in Place of a Constructor Constraint

```
public class EntityBase<TKey>
{
  public EntityBase(TKey key)
  {
      Key = key;
  }
  public TKey Key { get; set; }
}

public class EntityDictionary<TKey, TValue, TFactory> :
      Dictionary<TKey, TValue>
  where TKey : IComparable<TKey>, IFormattable
  where TValue : EntityBase<TKey>
  where TFactory : IEntityFactory<TKey, TValue>, new()
{
  ...
  public TValue New(TKey key)
  {
      TFactory factory = new TFactory();
      TValue newEntity = factory.CreateNew(key);
      Add(newEntity.Key, newEntity);
      return newEntity;
  }
  ...
}

public interface IEntityFactory<TKey, TValue>
{
    TValue CreateNew(TKey key);
}
...
```

A declaration such as this allows you to pass the new key to a TValue factory method that takes parameters, rather than forcing you to rely on the default constructor. It no longer uses the constructor constraint on TValue because TFactory is responsible for instantiating value. (One modification to the code in Listing 12.33 would be to cache a reference to the factory method—possibly leveraging Lazy<T> if multithreaded support was needed. This would enable you to reuse the factory method instead of reinstantiating it every time.)

2.0

A declaration for a variable of type EntityDictionary<TKey, TValue, TFactory> would result in an entity declaration similar to the Order entity in Listing 12.34.

LISTING 12.34: Declaring an Entity to Be Used in EntityDictionary<...>

```csharp
public class Order : EntityBase<Guid>
{
  public Order(Guid key) :
      base(key)
  {
      // ...
  }
}

public class OrderFactory : IEntityFactory<Guid, Order>
{
  public Order CreateNew(Guid key)
  {
      return new Order(key);
  }
}
```

Generic Methods

Earlier, you saw that it is a relatively simple matter to add a method to a type when the type is generic; such a method can use the generic type parameters declared by the type. You did this, for example, in the generic class examples we have seen so far.

Generic methods use generic type parameters, much as generic types do. They can be declared in generic or nongeneric types. If declared in a generic type, their type parameters are distinct from those of their containing generic type. To declare a generic method, you specify the generic type parameters the same way you do for generic types: Add the type parameter declaration syntax immediately following the method name, as shown in the MathEx.Max<T> and MathEx.Min<T> examples in Listing 12.35.

LISTING 12.35: Defining Generic Methods

```csharp
public static class MathEx
{
  public static T Max<T>(T first, params T[] values)
      where T : IComparable<T>
  {
      T maximum = first;
```

2.0

```
            foreach (T item in values)
            {
                if (item.CompareTo(maximum) > 0)
                {
                    maximum = item;
                }
            }
            return maximum;
    }

    public static T Min<T>(T first, params T[] values)
        where T : IComparable<T>
    {
        T minimum = first;

            foreach (T item in values)
            {
                if (item.CompareTo(minimum) < 0)
                {
                    minimum = item;
                }
            }
            return minimum;
    }
}
```

In this example, the method is static, although C# does not require this.

Generic methods, like generic types, can include more than one type parameter. The arity (the number of type parameters) is an additional distinguishing characteristic of a method signature. That is, it is legal to have two methods that are identical in their names and formal parameter types, as long as they differ in method type parameter arity.

Generic Method Type Inference

Just as type arguments are provided after the type name when using a generic type, so the method type arguments are provided after the method type name. The code used to call the Min<T> and Max<T> methods looks like that shown in Listing 12.36.

LISTING 12.36: Specifying the Type Parameter Explicitly

```
Console.WriteLine(
    MathEx.Max<int>(7, 490));
Console.WriteLine(
    MathEx.Min<string>("R.O.U.S.", "Fireswamp"));
```

2.0

The output to Listing 12.36 appears in Output 12.4.

OUTPUT 12.4

```
490
Fireswamp
```

Not surprisingly, the type arguments, int and string, correspond to the actual types used in the generic method calls. However, specifying the type arguments is redundant because the compiler can infer the type parameters from the formal parameters passed to the method. Clearly, the caller of Max in Listing 12.36 intends the type argument to be int because both of the method arguments are of type int. To avoid redundancy, you can exclude the type parameters from the call in all cases when the compiler is able to logically infer which type arguments you must have intended. An example of this practice, which is known as **method type inference**, appears in Listing 12.37. The output appears in Output 12.5.

LISTING 12.37: Inferring the Type Argument from the Arguments

```
Console.WriteLine(
    MathEx.Max(7, 490)); // No type arguments!
Console.WriteLine(
    MathEx.Min("R.O.U.S'", "Fireswamp"));
```

OUTPUT 12.5

```
490
Fireswamp
```

For method type inference to succeed, the types of the arguments must be "matched" with the formal parameters of the generic method in such a way that the desired type arguments can be inferred. An interesting question to consider is what happens when contradictory inferences are made. For example, when you call the Max<T> method using MathEx .Max(7.0, 490), the compiler could deduce from the first argument that the type argument should be double, and it could deduce from the second argument that the type argument is int, a contradiction. In C# 2.0, this would have produced an error. A more sophisticated analysis would notice that the contradiction can be resolved because every int can be converted

2.0

to double, so double is the best choice for the type argument. C# 3.0 and C# 4.0 both included improvements to the method type inferencing algorithm that permit the compiler to make these more sophisticated analyses.

In cases where method type inference is still not sophisticated enough to deduce the type arguments, you can resolve the error either by inserting casts on the arguments that clarify to the compiler the argument types that should be used in the inferences or by giving up on type inferencing and including the type arguments explicitly.

Notice that the method type inference algorithm, when making its inferences, considers only the arguments, the arguments' types, and the formal parameter types of the generic method. Other factors that could, in practice, be used in the analysis—such as the return type of the generic method, the type of the variable that the method's returned value is being assigned to, or the constraints on the method's generic type parameters—are not considered at all by the method type inference algorithm.

Specifying Constraints

Type parameters of generic methods may be constrained in the same way that type parameters of generic types are constrained. For example, you can restrict a method's type parameter to implement an interface or to be convertible to a class type. The constraints are specified between the argument list and the method body, as shown in Listing 12.38.

LISTING 12.38: Specifying Constraints on Generic Methods

```csharp
public class ConsoleTreeControl
{
    // Generic method Show<T>
    public static void Show<T>(BinaryTree<T> tree, int indent)
        where T :  IComparable<T>
    {
        Console.WriteLine("\n{0}{1}",
            "+ --".PadLeft(5*indent, ' '),
            tree.Item.ToString());
        if (tree.SubItems.First != null)
            Show(tree.SubItems.First, indent+1);
        if (tree.SubItems.Second != null)
            Show(tree.SubItems.Second, indent+1);
    }
}
```

2.0

Here, the Show<T> implementation itself does not directly use any member of the IComparable<T> interface, so you might wonder why the constraint is required. Recall, however, that the BinaryTree<T> class did require this constraint (see Listing 12.39).

LISTING 12.39: BinaryTree<T> Requiring IComparable<T> Type Parameters

```
public class BinaryTree<T>
    where T: System.IComparable<T>
{
    ...
}
```

Because the BinaryTree<T> class requires this constraint on its T, and because Show<T> uses its T as a type argument corresponding to a constrained type parameter, Show<T> needs to ensure that the constraint on the class's type parameter is met on its method type argument.

■ **ADVANCED TOPIC**

Casting inside a Generic Method

Sometimes you should be wary of using generics—for instance, when using them specifically to bury a cast operation. Consider the following method, which converts a stream into an object of a given type:

```
public static T Deserialize<T>(
    Stream stream, IFormatter formatter)
{
    return (T)formatter.Deserialize(stream);
}
```

The formatter is responsible for removing data from the stream and converting it to an object. The Deserialize() call on the formatter returns data of type object. A call to use the generic version of Deserialize() looks something like this:

```
string greeting =
    Deserialization.Deserialize<string>(stream, formatter);
```

The problem with this code is that to the caller of the method, Deserialize<T>() appears to be type-safe. However, a cast operation

2.0

is still performed on behalf of the caller, as in the case of the nongeneric equivalent shown here:

```
string greeting =
    (string)Deserialization.Deserialize(stream, formatter);
```

The cast could fail at runtime; the method might not be as type-safe as it appears. The `Deserialize<T>` method is generic solely so that it can hide the existence of the cast from the caller, which seems dangerously deceptive. It might be better for the method to be nongeneric and return `object`, making the caller aware that it is not type-safe. Developers should use care when casting in generic methods if there are no constraints to verify cast validity.

> **Guidelines**
>
> **AVOID** misleading the caller with generic methods that are not as type-safe as they appear.

Covariance and Contravariance

A question often asked by new users of generic types is why an expression of type `List<string>` may not be assigned to a variable of type `List<object>`—if a `string` may be converted to type `object`, surely a list of strings is similarly compatible with a list of objects. But this is not, generally speaking, either type-safe or legal. If you declare two variables with different type parameters using the same generic class, the variables are not type-compatible even if they are assigning from a more specific type to a more generic type—in other words, they are not **covariant**.

Covariant is a technical term from category theory, but its underlying idea is straightforward: Suppose two types X and Y have a special relationship—namely, that every value of the type X may be converted to the type Y. If the types I<X> and I<Y> always also have that same special relationship, we say, "I<T> is covariant in T." When dealing with simple generic types with only one type parameter, the type parameter can be understood and we simply say, "I<T> is covariant." The conversion from I<X> to I<Y> is called a **covariant conversion**.

2.0

For example, instances of a generic class, `Pair<Contact>` and `Pair<PdaItem>`, are not type-compatible even when the type arguments are themselves compatible. In other words, the compiler prevents the conversion (implicit or explicit) of `Pair<Contact>` to `Pair<PdaItem>`, even though `Contact` derives from `PdaItem`. Similarly, converting `Pair<Contact>` to the interface type `IPair<PdaItem>` will also fail. See Listing 12.40 for an example.

LISTING 12.40: Conversion between Generics with Different Type Parameters

```
// ...
// Error: Cannot convert type ...
Pair<PdaItem> pair = (Pair<PdaItem>) new Pair<Contact>();
IPair<PdaItem> duple = (IPair<PdaItem>) new Pair<Contact>();
```

But why is this not legal? Why are `List<T>` and `Pair<T>` not covariant? Listing 12.41 shows what would happen if the C# language allowed unrestricted generic covariance.

LISTING 12.41: Preventing Covariance Maintains Homogeneity

```
//...
Contact contact1 = new Contact("Princess Buttercup"),
Contact contact2 = new Contact("Inigo Montoya");
Pair<Contact> contacts = new Pair<Contact>(contact1, contact2);

// This gives an error: Cannot convert type ...,
// but suppose it did not
// IPair<PdaItem> pdaPair = (IPair<PdaItem>) contacts;
// This is perfectly legal but not type-safe
// pdaPair.First = new Address("123 Sesame Street");
...
```

An `IPair<PdaItem>` can contain an address, but the object is really a `Pair<Contact>` that can contain only contacts, not addresses. Type safety is completely violated if unrestricted generic covariance is allowed.

Now it should also be clear why a list of strings may not be used as a list of objects. You cannot insert an integer into a list of strings, but you can insert an integer into a list of objects; thus it must be illegal to cast a list of strings to a list of objects, an error the compiler can enforce.

2.0

Begin 4.0

Enabling Covariance with the out Type Parameter Modifier in C# 4.0 (and Later)

You might have noticed that both problems described earlier as consequences of unrestricted covariance arise because the generic pair and the generic list allow their contents to be written. Suppose we eliminated this possibility by making a read-only IReadOnlyPair<T> interface that exposes T only as coming "out" of the interface (i.e., used as the return type of a method or read-only property) and never going "into" it (i.e., used as a formal parameter or writeable property type). If we restricted ourselves to an "out only" interface with respect to T, the covariance problem just described would not occur (see Listing 12.42).

LISTING 12.42: Potentially Possible Covariance

```csharp
interface IReadOnlyPair<T>
{
  T First { get; }
  T Second { get; }
}
```

```csharp
interface IPair<T>
{
  T First { get; set; }
  T Second { get; set; }
}
```

```csharp
public struct Pair<T> : IPair<T>, IReadOnlyPair<T>
{
  // ...
}
```

```csharp
class Program
{
  static void Main()
  {
    // Error: Only theoretically possible without
    // the out type parameter modifier
    Pair<Contact> contacts =
        new Pair<Contact>(
            new Contact("Princess Buttercup"),
            new Contact("Inigo Montoya") );
    IReadOnlyPair<PdaItem> pair = contacts;
    PdaItem pdaItem1 = pair.First;
    PdaItem pdaItem2 = pair.Second;
  }
}
```

2.0

When we restrict the generic type declaration to expose data only as it comes out of the interface, there is no reason for the compiler to prevent covariance. All operations on an `IReadOnlyPair<PdaItem>` instance would convert `Contacts` (from the original `Pair<Contact>` object) up to the base class `PdaItem`—a perfectly valid conversion. There is no way to "write" an address into the object that is really a pair of contacts, because the interface does not expose any writeable properties.

The code in Listing 12.42 still does not compile. However, support for safe covariance was added to C# 4. To indicate that a generic interface is intended to be covariant in one of its type parameters, you can declare the type parameter with the `out` type parameter modifier. Listing 12.43 shows how to modify the interface declaration to indicate that it should be allowed to be covariant.

LISTING 12.43: Covariance Using the out Type Parameter Modifier

```
...
interface IReadOnlyPair<out T>
{
  T First { get; }
  T Second { get; }
}
```

Modifying the type parameter on the `IReadOnlyPair<out T>` interface with `out` will cause the compiler to verify that `T` is, indeed, used only for "outputs"—method return types and read-only property return types—and never for formal parameters or property setters. From then on, the compiler will allow any covariant conversions involving the interface to succeed. When this modification is made to the code in Listing 12.42, it will compile and execute successfully.

Several important restrictions are placed on covariant conversions:

- Only generic interfaces and generic delegates (described in Chapter 13) may be covariant. Generic classes and structs are never covariant.
- The varying type arguments of both the source and target generic types must be reference types, not value types. That is, an `IReadOnlyPair<string>` may be converted covariantly to `IReadOnlyPair<object>` because both `string` and `IReadOnlyPair<object>` are reference types. An `IReadOnlyPair<int>` may not be converted to `IReadOnlyPair<object>` because `int` is not a reference type.

4.0

2.0

- The interface or delegate must be declared as supporting covariance, and the compiler must be able to verify that the annotated type parameters are, in fact, used in only "output" positions.

Enabling Contravariance with the `in` Type Parameter Modifier in C# 4.0 (and Later)

Covariance that "goes backward" is called **contravariance**. Again, suppose two types X and Y are related such that every value of the type X may be converted to the type Y. If the types I<X> and I<Y> always have that same special relationship "backward"—that is, every value of the type I<Y> can be converted to the type I<X>—we say, "I<T> is contravariant in T."

Most people find that contravariance is much harder to comprehend than covariance is. The canonical example of contravariance is a comparer. Suppose you have a derived type, Apple, and a base type, Fruit. Clearly, they have the special relationship: Every value of type Apple may be converted to Fruit.

Now suppose you have an interface ICompareThings<T> that has a method bool FirstIsBetter(T t1, T t2) that takes two Ts and returns a bool saying whether the first one is better than the second one.

What happens when we provide type arguments? An ICompareThings<Apple> has a method that takes two Apples and compares them. An ICompareThings<Fruit> has a method that takes two Fruits and compares them. But since every Apple is a Fruit, clearly a value of type ICompareThings<Fruit> can be safely used anywhere that an ICompareThings<Apple> is needed. The direction of the convertibility has been reversed; hence the term *contravariance*.

Perhaps unsurprisingly, the opposite of the restrictions on a covariant interface are necessary to ensure safe contravariance. An interface that is contravariant in one of its type parameters must use that type parameter only in input positions such as formal parameters (or in the types of write-only properties, which are extremely rare). You can mark an interface as being contravariant by declaring the type parameter with the in modifier, as shown in Listing 12.44.

LISTING 12.44: Contravariance Using the `in` Type Parameter Modifier

```
class Fruit {}
class Apple : Fruit {}
class Orange : Fruit {}
```

```
interface ICompareThings<in T>
{
  bool FirstIsBetter(T t1, T t2);

}
```

```
class Program
{
  class FruitComparer : ICompareThings<Fruit>
  { ... }
  static void Main()
  {
      // Allowed in C# 4.0 and later
      ICompareThings<Fruit> fc = new FruitComparer();
      Apple apple1 = new Apple();
      Apple apple2 = new Apple();
      Orange orange = new Orange();
      // A fruit comparer can compare apples and oranges:
      bool b1 = fc.FirstIsBetter(apple1, orange);
      // or apples and apples:
      bool b2 = fc.FirstIsBetter(apple1, apple2);
      // This is legal because the interface is
      // contravariant
      ICompareThings<Apple> ac = fc;
      // This is really a fruit comparer, so it can
      // still compare two apples
      bool b3 = ac.FirstIsBetter(apple1, apple2);
  }
}
```

4.0

Like covariance support, contravariance uses a type parameter modifier: in, which appears in the interface's type parameter declaration. This instructs the compiler to check that T never appears on a property getter or as the return type of a method, thereby enabling contravariant conversions for this interface.

Contravariant conversions have all the analogous restrictions as described earlier for covariant conversions: They are valid only for generic interface and delegate types, the varying type arguments must be reference types, and the compiler must be able to verify that the interface is safe for the contravariant conversions.

An interface can be covariant in one type parameter and contravariant in another, but this seldom arises in practice except with delegates. The Func<A1, A2, ..., R> family of delegates, for example, are covariant in the return type, R, and contravariant in all the argument types.

2.0

Lastly, note that the compiler will check the validity of the covariance and contravariance type parameter modifiers throughout the source. Consider the `PairInitializer<in T>` interface in Listing 12.45.

LISTING 12.45: Compiler Validation of Variance

```
// ERROR:  Invalid variance; the type parameter 'T' is not
//         invariantly valid
interface IPairInitializer<in T>
{
  void Initialize(IPair<T> pair);
}
```

```
// Suppose the code above were legal, and see what goes
// wrong:
class FruitPairInitializer : IPairInitializer<Fruit>
{
  // Let's initiaize our pair of fruit with an
  // apple and an orange:
  public void Initialize(IPair<Fruit> pair)
  {
    pair.First = new Orange();
    pair.Second = new Apple();
  }
}
```

```
// ... later ...
var f = new FruitPairInitializer();
// This would be legal if contravariance were legal:
IPairInitializer<Apple> a = f;
// And now we write an orange into a pair of apples:
a.Initialize(new Pair<Apple>());
```

A casual observer might be tempted to think that since `IPair<T>` is used only as an input formal parameter, the contravariant `in` modifier on `IPairInitializer` is valid. However, the `IPair<T>` interface cannot safely vary, so it cannot be constructed with a type argument that can vary. As you can see, this would not be type-safe and, in turn, the compiler disallows the `IPairInitializer<T>` interface from being declared as contravariant in the first place.

Support for Unsafe Covariance in Arrays

So far, we have described covariance and contravariance as being properties of generic types. Of all the nongeneric types, arrays are most like generics; that is, just as we think of a generic "list of T" or a generic "pair of T," so we can think of an "array of T" as being the same sort of pattern. Since arrays clearly support both reading and writing, given what you know about covariance and contravariance, you probably would suppose that arrays may be neither safely contravariant nor covariant. That is, you might imagine that an array can be safely covariant only if it is never written to and safely contravariant only if it is never read from—though neither seems like a realistic restriction.

Unfortunately, C# does support array covariance, even though doing so is not type-safe. For example, `Fruit[] fruits = new Apple[10];` is perfectly legal in C#. If you then include the expression `fruits[0] = new Orange();`, the runtime will issue a type safety violation in the form of an exception. It is deeply disturbing that it is not always legal to assign an `Orange` into an array of `Fruit` because it might really be an array of `Apples`, but that is the situation not just in C# but in all CLR languages that use the runtime's implementation of arrays.

Try to avoid using unsafe array covariance. Every array is convertible to the read-only (and therefore safely covariant) interface `IEnumerable<T>`; that is, `IEnumerable<Fruit> fruits = new Apple[10]` is both safe and legal because there is no way to insert an `Orange` into the array if all you have is the read-only interface.

Guidelines

AVOID unsafe array covariance. Instead, **CONSIDER** converting the array to the read-only interface `IEnumerable<T>`, which can be safely converted via covariant conversions.

End 4.0

Generic Internals

Given the discussions in earlier chapters about the prevalence of objects within the CLI type system, it should come as no surprise to learn that generics are also objects. In fact, the type parameter on a generic class becomes metadata that the runtime uses to build appropriate classes when needed. Generics, therefore, support inheritance, polymorphism, and encapsulation. With generics, you can define methods, properties, fields, classes, interfaces, and delegates.

2.0

To achieve this, generics require support from the underlying runtime. In turn, the addition of generics to the C# language is a feature of both the compiler and the framework. To avoid boxing, for example, the implementation of generics is different for value-based type parameters than for generics with reference type parameters.

■ **ADVANCED TOPIC**

CIL Representation of Generics

When a generic class is compiled, it is not significantly different from a nongeneric class. The result of the compilation is nothing but metadata and CIL. The CIL is parameterized to accept a user-supplied type somewhere in code. As an example, suppose you had a simple Stack class declared as shown in Listing 12.46.

LISTING 12.46: Stack<T> Declaration

```
public class Stack<T> where T : IComparable
{
    T[] items;
    // rest of the class here
}
```

When you compile the class, the generated CIL is parameterized and looks something like Listing 12.47.

LISTING 12.47: CIL Code for Stack<T>

```
.class private auto ansi beforefieldinit
    Stack'1<([mscorlib]System.IComparable)T>
    extends [mscorlib]System.Object
{
    ...
}
```

The first notable item is the '1 that appears following Stack on the second line. That number is the arity. It declares the number of type parameters that the generic class will require type arguments for. A declaration such as EntityDictionary<TKey, TValue> would have an arity of 2.

The second line of the generated CIL shows the constraints imposed upon the class. The T type parameter is decorated with an interface declaration for the IComparable constraint.

If you continue looking through the CIL, you will find that the item's array declaration of type T is altered to contain a type parameter using *exclamation point notation*, which is featured in the generics-capable version of the CIL. The exclamation point denotes the presence of the first type parameter specified for the class, as shown in Listing 12.48.

LISTING 12.48: CIL with Exclamation Point Notation to Support Generics

```
.class public auto ansi beforefieldinit
    'Stack'1'<([mscorlib]System.IComparable) T>
    extends [mscorlib]System.Object
{
    .field private !0[ ] items
    ...
}
```

Beyond the inclusion of the arity and type parameter in the class header and the type parameter denoted with exclamation points in code, there is little difference between the CIL generated for a generic class and the CIL generated for a nongeneric class.

▪ ADVANCED TOPIC

Instantiating Generics Based on Value Types

When a generic type is first constructed with a value type as a type parameter, the runtime creates a specialized generic type with the supplied type parameter(s) placed appropriately in the CIL. Therefore, the runtime creates new specialized generic types for each new parameter value type.

For example, suppose some code declared a Stack constructed of integers, as shown in Listing 12.49.

LISTING 12.49: Stack<int> Definition

```
Stack<int> stack;
```

When using this type, Stack<int>, for the first time, the runtime generates a specialized version of the Stack class with the type argument int substituted for its type parameter. From then on, whenever the code uses a Stack<int>, the runtime reuses the generated specialized Stack<int> class. In Listing 12.50, you declare two instances of a Stack<int>, both using the code already generated by the runtime for a Stack<int>.

2.0

LISTING 12.50: Declaring Variables of Type Stack<T>

```
Stack<int> stackOne = new Stack<int>();
Stack<int> stackTwo = new Stack<int>();
```

If later in the code, you create another Stack with a different value type substituted for the type parameter (such as a long or a user-defined struct) the runtime will generate another version of the generic type. The benefit of specialized value type classes is better performance. Furthermore, the code can avoid conversions and boxing because each specialized generic class natively contains the value type.

■ **ADVANCED TOPIC**

Instantiating Generics Based on Reference Types

Generics work slightly differently for reference types. The first time a generic type is constructed with a reference type, the runtime creates a specialized generic type with object references substituted for type parameters in the CIL, not a specialized generic type based on the type argument. Each subsequent time a constructed type is instantiated with a reference type parameter, the runtime reuses the previously generated version of the generic type even if the reference type is different from the first reference type.

For example, suppose you have two reference types: a Customer class and an Order class. Next, you create an EntityDictionary of Customer types:

```
EntityDictionary<Guid, Customer> customers;
```

Prior to accessing this class, the runtime generates a specialized version of the EntityDictionary class that, instead of storing Customer as the specified data type, stores object references. Suppose the next line of code creates an EntityDictionary of another reference type, called Order:

```
EntityDictionary<Guid, Order> orders =
    new EntityDictionary<Guid, Order>();
```

Unlike with value types, no new specialized version of the EntityDictionary class is created for the EntityDictionary that uses the Order type. Instead, an instance of the version of EntityDictionary that uses object references is instantiated and the orders variable is set to reference it.

To still gain the advantage of type safety, for each object reference substituted in place of the type parameter, an area of memory for an `Order` type is specifically allocated and the pointer is set to that memory reference.

Suppose you then encountered a line of code to instantiate an `EntityDictionary` of a `Customer` type as follows:

```
customers = new EntityDictionary<Guid, Customer>();
```

As with the previous use of the `EntityDictionary` class created with the `Order` type, another instance of the specialized `EntityDictionary` class (the one based on `object` references) is instantiated and the pointers contained therein are set to reference a `Customer` type specifically. This implementation of generics greatly reduces code bloat by reducing to one the number of specialized classes created by the compiler for generic classes of reference types.

Even though the runtime uses the same internal generic type definition when the type parameter on a generic reference type varies, this behavior is superseded if the type parameter is a value type. `Dictionary<int, Customer>`, `Dictionary<Guid, Order>`, and `Dictionary<long, Order>` will require new internal type definitions, for example.

Language Contrast: Java—Generics

The implementation of generics in Java occurs entirely within the compiler, not within the Java Virtual Machine. Sun Microsystems, who originally developed Java long before Oracle took it over, adopted this approach to ensure that no updated Java Virtual Machine would need to be distributed because generics were used.

The Java implementation uses syntax like the templates in C++ and the generics in C#, including type parameters and constraints. Because it does not treat value types differently from reference types, however, the unmodified Java Virtual Machine cannot support generics for value types. As such, generics in Java do not offer the same gains in execution efficiency as they do in C#. Indeed, whenever the Java compiler needs to return data, it injects automatic downcasts from the specified constraint, if one is declared, or the base `Object` type, if it is not declared. Further, the Java compiler generates a single specialized type at compile time, which it then uses to instantiate any constructed type. Finally, because the Java Virtual Machine does not support generics natively, there is no way to ascertain the type parameter for an instance of a generic type at execution time, and other uses of reflection are severely limited.

2.0

SUMMARY

The addition of generic types and methods to C# 2.0 fundamentally transformed the coding style of C# developers. In almost all cases in which programmers used object within C# 1.0 code, generics became a better choice in C# 2.0. In modern C# programs, using object (particularly in the context of any collection type) should make you consider whether the problem would be better solved with generics. The increased type safety enabled by elimination of casts, the elimination of the boxing performance penalty, and reduction of repeated code are all significant improvements.

Chapter 15 looks more at the most pervasive generic namespaces, System.Collections.Generic. As its name implies, this namespace is composed almost exclusively of generic types. It provides clear examples of how some types that originally used objects were then converted to use generics. However, before we tackle these topics, we will investigate expressions, which provide a significant C# 3.0 (and later) improvement for working with collections.

End 2.0

■ 13 ■
Delegates and Lambda Expressions

Begin 3.0

PREVIOUS CHAPTERS DISCUSSED extensively how to create classes to encapsulate data and operations on data. As you create more and more classes, you will see common patterns in the relationships among them. One common pattern is to pass an object to a method solely so that the method can, in turn, call a method on the object. For example, if you pass to a method a reference to IComparer<int>, odds are good that the called method will itself call the Compare() method on the object you provided. In this case, the interface is nothing more than a way to pass a reference to a single method that can be invoked. Consider a second example in which you invoke a new process. Rather than blocking or repeatedly checking (polling) when the process has completed, ideally you would like to have the method run asynchronously and then invoke a **callback** function, which the called method will invoke to notify the caller when the asynchronous invocation completes.

It seems unnecessary to have to define a new interface every time you want to pass a method around. In this chapter we describe how to create and use a special kind of class called a *delegate* that enables you to treat references to methods as you would any other data. We then show how to create custom delegate instances quickly and easily with *lambda expressions*.

Lambda expressions were added to the language in C# 3.0; the previous version, C# 2.0, supported a less elegant syntax for custom delegate creation called *anonymous methods*. Every version of C# after C# 2.0 supports anonymous methods for backward compatibility, but in new code they should be deprecated in favor of using lambda expressions. This chapter includes Advanced Topic blocks that describe how to use anonymous methods should you need to work with legacy C# 2.0 code; you can largely ignore these sections if you are working only with newer code.

We conclude the chapter with a discussion of *expression trees*, which enable you to use the compiler's analysis of a lambda expression at execution time.

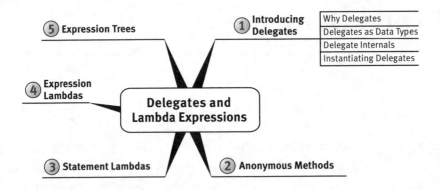

Introducing Delegates

Veteran C and C++ programmers have long used function pointers as a mechanism for passing a reference to one method as an argument to another method. C# achieves similar functionality by using **delegates**. Delegates allow you to capture a reference to a method and pass it around like any other object, and to call the captured method like any other method. Let's consider an example illustrating how this technique might be useful.

Defining the Scenario

Although it is not very efficient, one of the simplest sort routines is the bubble sort. Listing 13.1 shows the `BubbleSort()` method.

LISTING 13.1: BubbleSort() Method

```csharp
static class SimpleSort1
{
    public static void BubbleSort(int[] items)
    {
        int i;
        int j;
```

```
        int temp;

        if(items==null)
        {
          return;
        }

        for (i = items.Length - 1; i >= 0; i--)
        {
            for (j = 1; j <= i; j++)
            {
                if (items[j - 1] > items[j])
                {
                    temp = items[j - 1];
                    items[j - 1] = items[j];
                    items[j] = temp;
                }
            }
        }
    }
    // ...
}
```

This method will sort an array of integers in ascending order.

Suppose you need to sort the integers in Listing 13.1 in either ascending or descending order. You could duplicate the code and replace the greater-than operator with a less-than operator, but it seems like a bad idea to replicate several dozen lines of code merely to change a single operator. As a less verbose alternative, you could pass in an additional parameter indicating how to perform the sort, as shown in Listing 13.2.

LISTING 13.2: BubbleSort( ) Method, Ascending or Descending

```
class SimpleSort2
{
  public enum SortType
  {
      Ascending,
      Descending
  }

  public static void BubbleSort(int[] items, SortType sortOrder)
  {
      int i;
      int j;
      int temp;

      if(items==null)
      {
        return;
      }
```

3.0

```
for (i = items.Length - 1; i >= 0; i--)
{
    for (j = 1; j <= i; j++)
    {
        bool swap = false;
        switch (sortOrder)
        {
            case SortType.Ascending :
                swap = items[j - 1] > items[j];
                break;

            case SortType.Descending :
                swap = items[j - 1] < items[j];
                break;
        }
        if (swap)
        {
            temp = items[j - 1];
            items[j - 1] = items[j];
            items[j] = temp;
        }
    }
}
// ...
}
```

However, this code handles only two of the possible sort orders. If you wanted to sort them lexicographically (that is, 1, 10, 11, 12, 2, 20, ...), or order them via some other criterion, it would not take long before the number of SortType values and the corresponding switch cases would become cumbersome.

Delegate Data Types

To increase flexibility and reduce code duplication in the previous code listings, you can make the comparison method a parameter to the BubbleSort() method. To pass a method as an argument, a data type is required to represent that method; this data type is generally called a *delegate* because it "delegates" the call to the method referred to by the object. You can use the name of a method as a delegate instance. And, since C# 3.0, you can also use a lambda expression as a delegate, to express a short piece of code "in place" rather than creating a method for it. (In C# 7.0, you can create local function and then use the function name for the delegate as well.) Listing 13.3 includes a modification to the

BubbleSort() method that takes a lambda expression parameter. In this case, the delegate data type is Func<int, int, bool>.

LISTING 13.3: BubbleSort() with Delegate Parameter

```csharp
class DelegateSample
{
    // ...

    public static void BubbleSort(
        int[] items, Func<int, int, bool> compare)
    {
        int i;
        int j;
        int temp;

        if(compare == null)
        {
            throw new ArgumentNullException(nameof(compare));
        }

        if(items==null)
        {
          return;
        }

        for (i = items.Length - 1; i >= 0; i--)
        {
            for (j = 1; j <= i; j++)
            {
                if (compare(items[j - 1], items[j]))
                {
                    temp = items[j - 1];
                    items[j - 1] = items[j];
                    items[j] = temp;
                }
            }
        }
    }
    // ...
}
```

3.0

The delegate of type Func<int, int, bool> represents a method that compares two integers. Within the BubbleSort() method, you then use the instance of the Func<int, int, bool>, referred to by the compare parameter, to determine which integer is greater. Since compare represents a method, the syntax to invoke the method is identical to calling any other method. In this case, the Func<int, int, bool> delegate takes two integer

parameters and returns a Boolean value that indicates whether the first
integer is greater than the second one:

```
if (compare(items[j - 1], items[j])) { ... }
```

Note that the `Func<int, int, bool>` delegate is strongly typed to
represent a method that returns a `bool` and accepts exactly two integer
parameters. Just as with any other method call, the call to a delegate is
strongly typed, and if the data types for the arguments are not compatible
with the parameters, the C# compiler reports an error.

Declaring Delegate Types

You just saw how to define a method that uses a delegate, and you learned
how to invoke a call to the delegate simply by treating the delegate variable as a method. However, you have yet to learn how to declare a delegate
type. To declare a delegate type, you use the `delegate` keyword and follow
it with what looks like a method declaration. The signature of that method is
the signature of the method that the delegate can refer to, and the name
of the delegate type appears where the name of the method would appear
in a method declaration. The `Fun<...>` delegate in Listing 13.3, for example, is declared as

```
public delegate TResult Func<in T1, in T2, out TResult>(
    in T1 arg1, in T2 arg2)
```

(The `in`/`out` type modifiers were not added until C# 4.0, and we will discuss them later in the chapter.)

General Purpose Delegate Types: `System.Func` and `System.Action`

3.0

Fortunately, starting with C# 3.0, it turns out you rarely, if ever, need to
declare your own delegates. The need to define your own custom delegate types was effectively eliminated with the .NET 3.5 runtime library
(which corresponds to C# 3.0) because it included a set of general-purpose
delegates, most of them generic. The `System.Func` family of delegates is
for referring to methods that return a value; the `System.Action` family of
delegates is for referring to `void`-returning methods. The signatures for
these delegates are shown in Listing 13.4.

LISTING 13.4: Func and Action Delegate Declarations

```
public delegate void Action ();
public delegate void Action<in T>(T arg)
public delegate void Action<in T1, in T2>(
    in T1 arg1, in T2 arg2)
public delegate void Action<in T1, in T2, in T3>(
    T1 arg1, T2 arg2, T3 arg3)
public delegate void Action<in T1, in T2, in T3, in T4(
    T1 arg1, T2 arg2, T3 arg3, T4 arg4)
...
public delegate void Action<
    in T1, in T2, in T3, in T4, in T5, in T6, in T7, in T8,
    in T9, in T10, in T11, in T12, in T13, in T14, in T16(
        T1 arg1, T2 arg2, T3 arg3, T4 arg4,
        T5 arg5, T6 arg6, T7 arg7, T8 arg8,
        T9 arg9, T10 arg10, T11 arg11, T12 arg12,
        T13 arg13, T14 arg14, T15 arg15, T16 arg16)
```

```
public delegate TResult Func<out TResult>();
public delegate TResult Func<in T, out TResult>(T arg)
public delegate TResult Func<in T1, in T2, out TResult>(
    in T1 arg1, in T2 arg2)
public delegate TResult Func<in T1, in T2, in T3, out TResult>(
    T1 arg1, T2 arg2, T3 arg3)
public delegate TResult Func<in T1, in T2, in T3, in T4,
    out TResult>(T1 arg1, T2 arg2, T3 arg3, T4 arg4)
...
public delegate TResult Func<
    in T1, in T2, in T3, in T4, in T5, in T6, in T7, in T8,
    in T9, in T10, in T11, in T12, in T13, in T14, in T16,
    out TResult>(
        T1 arg1, T2 arg2, T3 arg3, T4 arg4,
        T5 arg5, T6 arg6, T7 arg7, T8 arg8,
        T9 arg9, T10 arg10, T11 arg11, T12 arg12,
        T13 arg13, T14 arg14, T15 arg15, T16 arg16)
```

```
public delegate bool Predicate<in T>( T obj)
```

3.0

Since the delegate definitions are generic, it is possible to use them instead of defining your own custom delegate (which we discuss shortly).

The first delegate type in Listing 13.4 is an Action<...>. It is used to represent a method for which there is no return and supports methods of up to 16 parameters. For delegates that need to return a result, there is the Func<...> delegate. The last type parameter of Func<...> is TResult—the type of the return. The other type parameters on Func<...> correspond in sequence to the types of the delegate parameters. The

BubbleSort method in Listing 13.3, for example, requires a delegate that returns bool and takes two int parameters.

The last delegate listed is the Predicate<int T>. When a lambda is used to return a bool, the lambda is called a **predicate**. However, this predicate is generally used to filter or identify items from a collection—you pass it an item and it returns true or false to indicate whether or not to filter the item. In contrast, our BubbleSort() example accepted two parameters for the purpose of comparing them, and so Func<int, int, bool> was used instead of a predicate type.

> ### Guidelines
>
> **CONSIDER** whether the readability benefit of defining your own delegate type outweighs the convenience of using a predefined generic delegate type.

■ ADVANCED TOPIC

Declaring a Delegate Type

As stated, in many cases, the inclusion of Func and Action delegates in the Microsoft .NET Framework 3.5, and later in the .NET Standard, virtually eliminates the need to define your own delegate types. However, you should consider declaring your own delegate types when doing so significantly increases the readability of the code. A delegate named Comparer, for example, provides an explicit indication of what the delegate is used for, whereas using Func<int, int, bool> only identifies a delegate's parameters and return type. Listing 13.5 shows how to declare the Comparer delegate type to require two integers and return a Boolean value.

LISTING 13.5: Declaring a Delegate Type

```
public delegate bool Comparer (
    int first, int second);
```

Given the new delegate data type, you can update Listing 13.3 with a signature that replaces Func<int, int, bool> with Comparer:

```
public static void BubbleSort(int[] items, Comparer compare)
```

Just as classes can be nested in other classes, so delegates can also be nested in classes. If the delegate declaration appeared within another class, the delegate type would be a nested type, as shown in Listing 13.6.

LISTING 13.6: Declaring a Nested Delegate Type

```
class DelegateSample
{
  public delegate bool ComparisonHandler (
    int first, int second);
}
```

In this case, the data type would be DelegateSample.ComparisonHandler because it is defined as a nested type within DelegateSample. Nesting should be considered when utilization is expected to be needed only from within the containing class.

Instantiating a Delegate

In this final step of implementing the BubbleSort() method with a delegate, you will learn how to call the method and pass a delegate instance—specifically, an instance of type Func<int, int, bool>. To instantiate a delegate, you need a method with parameters and a return type that matches the signature of the delegate type itself. The name of the method need not match the name of the delegate, but the rest of the method signature must be compatible with the delegate signature. Listing 13.7 shows the code for a greater-than method compatible with the delegate type.

LISTING 13.7: Declaring a Func<int, int, bool>-Compatible Method

```
class DelegateSample
{
  public static void BubbleSort(
    int[] items, Func<int, int, bool> compare)
  {
    // ...
  }

  public static bool GreaterThan(int first, int second)
  {
    return first > second;
  }
  // ...
}
```

3.0

With this method defined, you can call `BubbleSort()` and supply as the argument the name of the method that is to be captured by the delegate, as shown in Listing 13.8.

LISTING 13.8: Using a Method Name as an Argument

```
class DelegateSample
{
  public static void BubbleSort(
      int[] items, Func<int, int, bool> compare)
  {
      // ...
  }

  public static bool GreaterThan(int first, int second)
  {
      return first > second;
  }

  static void Main()
  {
      int i;
      int[] items = new int[5];

      for (i=0; i < items.Length; i++)
      {
          Console.Write("Enter an integer: ");
          items[i] = int.Parse(Console.ReadLine());
      }

      BubbleSort(items, GreaterThan);

      for (i = 0; i < items.Length; i++)
      {
          Console.WriteLine(items[i]);
      }
  }
}
```

3.0

Note that delegates are reference types, but you do not necessarily use new to instantiate them. The conversion from the **method group**—the expression that names the method—to the delegate type automatically creates a new delegate object in C# 2.0 and later.

■ ADVANCED TOPIC

Delegate Instantiation in C# 1.0

In Listing 13.8, the delegate was instantiated by simply passing the name of the desired method, `GreaterThan`, as an argument to the call to the `BubbleSort()` method. The first version of C# required instantiation of the delegate, using the more verbose syntax shown in Listing 13.9.

LISTING 13.9: Passing a Delegate as a Parameter in C# 1.0

```
BubbleSort(items,
    new Comparer(GreaterThan));
```

In this case we use `Comparer` rather than `Func<int, int, bool>` because the latter wasn't available in C# 1.0.

Later versions support both syntaxes; throughout the remainder of the book we will show only the modern, concise syntax.

■ ADVANCED TOPIC

Delegate Internals

A delegate is actually a special kind of class. Although the C# standard does not specify exactly what the class hierarchy is, a delegate must always derive directly or indirectly from `System.Delegate`. In fact, in .NET, delegate types always derive from `System.MulticastDelegate`, which in turn derives from `System.Delegate`, as shown in Figure 13.1.

The first property is of type `System.Reflection.MethodInfo`. `MethodInfo` describes the signature of a method, including its name, parameters, and return type. In addition to `MethodInfo`, a delegate needs the instance of the object containing the method to invoke. This is the purpose of the second property, `Target`. In the case of a static method, `Target` corresponds to the type itself. The purpose of the `MulticastDelegate` class is the topic of the next chapter.

Note that all delegates are immutable; that is, you cannot change a delegate once you have created it. If you have a variable that contains a reference to a delegate and you want it to refer to a different method, you must create a new delegate and assign it to the variable.

3.0

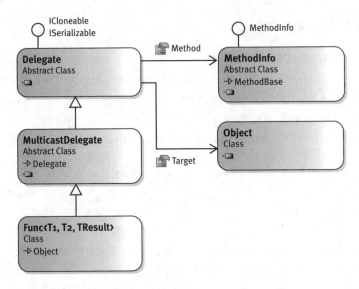

FIGURE 13.1: Delegate Types Object Model

Although all delegate data types derive indirectly from System .Delegate, the C# compiler does not allow you to declare a class that derives directly or indirectly from System.Delegate or System .MulticastDelegate. As a consequence, the code shown in Listing 13.10 is not valid.

LISTING 13.10: System.Delegate Cannot Explicitly Be a Base Class

```
// ERROR: Func<T1, T2, TResult> cannot
// inherit from special class System.Delegate
public class Func<T1, T2, TResult>: System.Delegate
{
    // ...
}
```

3.0

Passing the delegate to specify the sort order is a significantly more flexible strategy than using the approach described at the beginning of this chapter. By passing a delegate, you can change the sort order to be alphabetical simply by adding an alternative delegate to convert integers to strings as part of the comparison. Listing 13.11 shows a full listing that demonstrates alphabetical sorting, and Output 13.1 shows the results.

LISTING 13.11: Using a Different Func<int, int, bool> Compatible Method

```csharp
using System;
class DelegateSample
{
  public static void BubbleSort(
      int[] items, Func<int, int, bool> compare)
  {
      int i;
      int j;
      int temp;

      for (i = items.Length - 1; i >= 0; i--)
      {
          for (j = 1; j <= i; j++)
          {
              if (compare(items[j - 1], items[j]))
              {
                  temp = items[j - 1];
                  items[j - 1] = items[j];
                  items[j] = temp;
              }
          }
      }
  }

  public static bool GreaterThan(int first, int second)
  {
      return first > second;
  }

  public static bool AlphabeticalGreaterThan(
      int first, int second)
  {
      int comparison;
      comparison = (first.ToString().CompareTo(
          second.ToString()));

      return comparison > 0;
  }

  static void Main(string[] args)
  {
      int i;
      int[] items = new int[5];

      for (i=0; i<items.Length; i++)
      {
          Console.Write("Enter an integer: ");
          items[i] = int.Parse(Console.ReadLine());
      }
```

3.0

```
            BubbleSort(items, AlphabeticalGreaterThan);

        for (i = 0; i < items.Length; i++)
        {
            Console.WriteLine(items[i]);
        }
    }
}
```

OUTPUT 13.1

```
Enter an integer: 1
Enter an integer: 12
Enter an integer: 13
Enter an integer: 5
Enter an integer: 4
1
12
13
4
5
```

The alphabetical order is different from the numeric order. Even so, notice how simple it was to add this additional sort mechanism compared to the process used at the beginning of the chapter. The only changes to create the alphabetical sort order were the addition of the `AlphabeticalGreaterThan` method and then passing that method into the call to `BubbleSort()`.

Lambda Expressions

In Listings 13.7 and 13.10, we saw that you can convert the expressions `GreaterThan` and `AlphabeticalGreaterThan` to a delegate type that is compatible with the parameter types and the return type of the named method. You might have noticed that the declaration of the `GreaterThan` method—the code that says it is a public, static, `bool`-returning method with two parameters of type `int` named `first` and `second`—was considerably larger than the body of the method, which simply compared its two parameters and returned the result. It is unfortunate that so much ceremony must surround such a simple method merely so that it can be converted to a delegate type.

To address this concern, C# 2.0 introduced a far more compact syntax for creating a delegate, and C# 3.0 introduced several even more compact syntaxes than C# 2.0's syntax. The C# 2.0 feature is called **anonymous methods**, and the C# 3.0 feature is called **lambda expressions**. When referring generally to either syntax, we'll refer to them as **anonymous functions**. Both syntaxes are still legal, but for new code the lambda expression syntax is preferred over the anonymous method syntax. Throughout this book we generally use the lambda expression syntax except when specifically describing C# 2.0 anonymous methods.

Lambda expressions are themselves divided into two types: **statement lambdas** and **expression lambdas**. Figure 13.2 shows the hierarchical relationship between these terms.

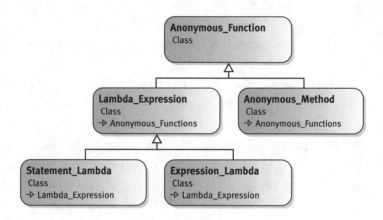

FIGURE 13.2: Anonymous Function Terminology

Statement Lambdas

The purpose of a lambda expression is to eliminate the hassle of declaring an entirely new member when you need to make a delegate from a very simple method. Several different forms of lambda expressions exist. A statement lambda, for example, consists of a formal parameter list, followed by the lambda operator =>, followed by a code block.

Listing 13.12 shows equivalent functionality to the call to BubbleSort from Listing 13.8, except that Listing 13.12 uses a statement lambda to represent the comparison method rather than creating a GreaterThan method. As you can see, much of the information that appeared in the GreaterThan method declaration is included in the statement lambda; the formal parameter declarations and the block are the same, but the method name and its modifiers are missing.

3.0

LISTING 13.12: Creating a Delegate with a Statement Lambda

```
// ...

    BubbleSort(items,
        (int first, int second) =>
        {
            return first < second;
        }
    );

// ...
```

When reading code that includes a lambda operator, you would replace the lambda operator with the words *go/goes to*. For example, in Listing 13.12, you would read the second `BubbleSort()` parameter as "integers `first` and `second` go to returning the result of `first` less than `second`."

As readers will observe, the syntax in Listing 13.12 is almost identical to that in Listing 13.8, apart from the fact that the comparison method is now found lexically where it is converted to the delegate type rather than being found elsewhere and looked up by name. The name of the method is missing, which explains why such methods are called *anonymous functions*. The return type is missing, but the compiler can see that the lambda expression is being converted to a delegate whose signature requires the return type `bool`. The compiler verifies that the expressions of every `return` statement in the statement lambda's block would be legal in a `bool`-returning method. The `public` modifier is missing; given that the method is no longer an accessible member of the containing class, there is no need to describe its accessibility. Similarly, the `static` modifier is no longer necessary. The amount of ceremony around the method is already greatly reduced.

The syntax is still needlessly verbose, however. We have deduced from the delegate type that the lambda expression must be `bool`-returning; we can similarly deduce that both parameters must be of type `int`, as shown in Listing 13.13.

LISTING 13.13: Omitting Parameter Types from Statement Lambdas

```
// ...

    BubbleSort(items,
        (first, second) =>
```

3.0

```
        {
            return first < second;
        }
    );
```
// ...

In general, explicitly declared parameter types are optional in all lambda expressions if the compiler can infer the types from the delegate that the lambda expression is being converted to. For situations when specifying the type makes code more readable, however, C# enables you to do so. In cases where inference is not possible, the C# language requires that the lambda parameter types be stated explicitly. If one lambda parameter type is specified explicitly, then all of them must be specified explicitly, and they must all match the delegate parameter types exactly.

Guidelines

CONSIDER omitting the types from lambda formal parameter lists when the types are obvious to the reader or when they are an insignificant detail.

One other means of reducing the syntax is possible, as shown in Listing 13.14: A lambda expression that has exactly one parameter whose type is inferred may omit the parentheses around the parameter list. If there are zero parameters or more than one parameter, or if the single parameter is explicitly typed, the lambda must have parentheses around the parameter list.

LISTING 13.14: Statement Lambdas with a Single Input Parameter

```
using System.Collections.Generic;
using System.Diagnostics;
using System.Linq;
    // ...
    IEnumerable<Process> processes = Process.GetProcesses().Where(
        process => { return process.WorkingSet64 > 1000000000; });
    // ...
```

In Listing 13.14, the Where() method returns a query for processes that have a physical memory utilization greater than 1 billion bytes. Contrast this with Listing 13.15, which has a parameterless statement lambda. The empty parameter list requires parentheses. Note also that in Listing 13.15, the body of the statement lambda includes multiple statements inside the statement block (via curly braces). Although a statement lambda can contain any number of statements, typically a statement lambda uses only two or three statements in its statement block.

LISTING 13.15: Parameterless Statement Lambdas

```
// ...
Func<string> getUserInput =
    () =>
    {
        string input;
        do
        {
            input = Console.ReadLine();
        }
        while(input.Trim().Length == 0);
        return input;
    };
// ...
```

Expression Lambdas

The statement lambda syntax is already much less verbose than the corresponding method declaration; as we've seen, it need not declare the method's name, accessibility, return type, or parameter types. Nevertheless, we can get even less verbose by using an expression lambda. In Listings 13.12, 13.13, and 13.14, we saw statement lambdas whose blocks consisted of a single return statement. What if we eliminated the ceremony around that? The only relevant information in such a lambda block is the expression that is returned. An expression lambda contains only that returned expression, with no statement block at all. Listing 13.16 is the same as Listing 13.12, except that it uses an expression lambda rather than a statement lambda.

LISTING 13.16: Passing a Delegate with an Expression Lambda

```
// ...
BubbleSort(items, (first, second) => first < second );
// ...
```

Generally, you would read the lambda operator => in an expression lambda the same way as you would a statement lambda: as *goes to* or *becomes,* although, in those cases where the delegate is a predicate, it is common to read the lambda operator as *such that* or *where.* You might read the lambda in Listing 13.16 as "first and second such that first is less than second."

Like the null literal, an anonymous function does not have any type associated with it; rather, its type is determined by the type it is being converted to. In other words, the lambda expressions we've seen so far are not intrinsically of the Func<int, int, bool> (or Comparer) type, but they are compatible with that type and may be converted to it. As a result, you cannot use the typeof() operator on an anonymous method, and calling GetType() is possible only after you convert the anonymous method to a particular type.

Table 13.1 provides additional lambda expression characteristics.

TABLE 13.1: Lambda Expression Notes and Examples

Statement	Example

Lambda expressions themselves do not have a type. Therefore, there are no members that can be accessed directly from a lambda expression, not even the methods of object.	`// ERROR: Operator "." cannot be applied to`
	`// operand of type "lambda expression"`
	`string s = ((int x) => x).ToString();`

Lambda expressions do not have a type and so cannot appear to the left of an is operator.	`// ERROR: The first operand of an "is" or "as"`
	`// operator may not be a lambda expression or`
	`// anonymous method`
	`bool b = ((int x) => x) is Func<int, int>;`

A lambda expression can be converted only to a compatible delegate type; here an int-returning lambda may not be converted to a delegate type that represents a bool-returning method.	`// ERROR: Lambda expression is not compatible`
	`// with Func<int, bool> type`
	`Func<int, bool> f = (int x) => x;`

A lambda expression does not have a type, so it cannot be used to infer the type of a local variable.	`// ERROR: Cannot assign lambda expression to`
	`// an implicitly typed local variable`
	`var v = x => x;`

3.0

continues

TABLE 13.1: Lambda Expression Notes and Examples (*continued*)

Statement	Example
Jump statements (break, goto, continue) inside lambda expressions cannot be used to jump to locations outside the lambda expression, and vice versa. Here the break statement inside the lambda would jump to the end of the switch statement outside the lambda.	```csharp // ERROR: Control cannot leave the body of an // anonymous method or lambda expression string[] args; Func<string> f; switch(args[0]) { case "/File": f = () => { if (!File.Exists(args[1])) break; return args[1]; }; // ... } ```
Parameters and locals introduced by a lambda expression are in scope only within the lambda body.	```csharp // ERROR: The name "first" does not // exist in the current context Func<int, int, bool> expression = (first, second) => first > second; first++; ```
The compiler's definite assignment analysis is unable to detect initialization of "outer" local variables in lambda expressions.	```csharp int number; Func<string, bool> f = text => int.TryParse(text, out number); if (f("1")) { // ERROR: Use of unassigned local variable System.Console.Write(number); } ```
	```csharp int number; Func<int, bool> isFortyTwo = x => 42 == (number = x); if (isFortyTwo(42)) { // ERROR: Use of unassigned local variable System.Console.Write(number); } ```

3.0

Anonymous Methods

Begin 2.0

Lambda expressions are not supported in C# 2.0. Instead, C# 2.0 uses a syntax called *anonymous methods*. An anonymous method is like a statement lambda, but without many of the features that make lambdas so compact. An anonymous method must explicitly type every parameter, and must have a statement block. Rather than using the lambda operator => between the parameter list and the code block, an anonymous method puts the keyword `delegate` before the parameter list, emphasizing that the anonymous method must be converted to a delegate type. Listing 13.17 shows the code from Listings 13.7, 13.12, and 13.15 rewritten to use an anonymous method.

LISTING 13.17: Passing an Anonymous Method in C# 2.0

```
// ...
BubbleSort(items,
    delegate(int first, int second)
    {
        return first < second;
    }
);
// ...
```

It is unfortunate that there are two very similar ways to define an anonymous function in C# 3.0 and later.

> ### Guidelines
>
> **AVOID** the anonymous method syntax in new code; prefer the more compact lambda expression syntax.

There is, however, one small feature that is supported in anonymous methods that is not supported in lambda expressions: Anonymous methods may omit their parameter list entirely in some circumstances.

▪ ADVANCED TOPIC

Parameterless Anonymous Methods

Unlike lambda expressions, anonymous methods may omit the parameter list entirely provided that the anonymous method body does not use any parameter and the delegate type requires only "value" parameters (i.e., it does not require the parameters to be marked as `out` or `ref`). For example, the anonymous method expression `delegate { return Console.ReadLine() != ""; }` is convertible to

3.0

2.0

End 2.0

any delegate type that requires a return type of bool regardless of the number of parameters the delegate requires. This feature is not used frequently, but you might encounter it when reading legacy code.

■ **ADVANCED TOPIC**

Why "Lambda" Expressions?

It is fairly obvious why anonymous methods are so named: They look very similar to method declarations but do not have a declared name associated with them. But where did the *lambda* in "lambda expressions" come from?

The idea of lambda expressions comes from the work of the logician Alonzo Church, who in the 1930s invented a technique called the *lambda calculus* for studying functions. In Church's notation, a function that takes a parameter *x* and results in an expression *y* is notated by prefixing the entire expression with a small Greek letter lambda and separating the parameter from the value with a dot. The C# lambda expression x=>y would be notated λx.y in Church's notation. Because it is inconvenient to use Greek letters in C# programs and because the dot already has many meanings in C#, the designers of C# chose to use the "fat arrow" notation rather than the original notation. The name lambda expression indicates that the theoretical underpinnings of the idea of anonymous functions are based on the lambda calculus, even though no letter lambda actually appears in the text.

Delegates Do Not Have Structural Equality

3.0

Begin 4.0

Delegate types in .NET do not exhibit **structural equality**. That is, you cannot convert a reference to an object of one delegate type to an unrelated delegate type, even if the formal parameters and return types of both delegates are identical. For example, you cannot assign a reference to a Comparer to a variable of type Func<int, int, bool> even though both delegate types represent methods that take two int parameters and return a bool. Unfortunately, the only way to use a delegate of a given type when a delegate of a structurally identical but unrelated delegate type is needed is to create a new delegate that refers to the `Invoke` method of the old delegate. For example, if you have a variable c of type `Comparer`, and you need to assign its value to a variable f of type `Func<int, int, bool>`, you can say `f = c.Invoke;`.

However, thanks to the variance support added in C# 4.0, it is possible to make reference conversions between some delegate types. Consider the following contravariant example: Because `void Action<in T>(T arg)` has the `in` type parameter modifier, it is possible to assign a reference to a delegate of type `Action<object>` to a variable of type `Action<string>`.

Many people find delegate contravariance confusing; just remember that an action that can act on every object can be used as an action that acts on any string. But the opposite is not true: An action that can act only on strings cannot act on every object. Similarly, every type in the `Func` family of delegates is covariant in its return type, as indicated by the `out` type parameter modifier on `TResult`. Therefore it is possible to assign a reference to a delegate of type `Func<string>` to a variable of type `Func<object>`.

Listing 13.18 shows examples of delegate covariance and contravariance.

LISTING 13.18: Using Variance for Delegates

```
// Contravariance
Action<object> broadAction =
  (object data) =>
  {
      Console.WriteLine(data);
  };
Action<string> narrowAction = broadAction;

// Covariance
Func<string> narrowFunction =
  () =>Console.ReadLine();
Func<object> broadFunction = narrowFunction;

// Contravariance and covariance combined
Func<object, string> func1 =
  (object data) => data.ToString();
Func<string, object> func2 = func1;
```

4.0

3.0

The last part of the listing combines both variance concepts into a single example, demonstrating how they can occur simultaneously if both `in` and `out` type parameters are involved.

End 4.0

Allowing reference conversions on generic delegate types was a key motivating scenario for adding covariant and contravariant conversions to C# 4.0. (The other was support for covariance to IEnumerable<out T>.)

■ ADVANCED TOPIC

Lambda Expression and Anonymous Method Internals

Lambda expressions (and anonymous methods) are not intrinsically built in to the CLR. Rather, when the compiler encounters an anonymous function, it translates it into special hidden classes, fields, and methods that implement the desired semantics. The C# compiler generates the implementation code for this pattern so that developers do not have to code it themselves. When given the code in Listing 13.12, 13.13, 13.16, or 13.17, the C# compiler generates CIL code that is similar to the C# code shown in Listing 13.19.

LISTING 13.19: C# Equivalent of CIL Generated by the Compiler for Lambda Expressions

```csharp
class DelegateSample
{
  // ...
  static void Main(string[] args)
  {
      int i;
      int[] items = new int[5];

      for (i=0; i<items.Length; i++)
      {
          Console.Write("Enter an integer:");
          items[i] = int.Parse(Console.ReadLine());
      }

      BubbleSort(items,
          DelegateSample.__AnonymousMethod_00000000);

      for (i = 0; i < items.Length; i++)
      {
          Console.WriteLine(items[i]);
      }

  }
```

3.0

```
    private static bool __AnonymousMethod_00000000(
        int first, int second)
    {
        return first < second;
    }

}
```

In this example, the compiler transforms an anonymous function into a separately declared static method, which is then instantiated as a delegate and passed as a parameter. Unsurprisingly, the compiler generates code that looks remarkably like the original code in Listing 13.8, which the anonymous function syntax was intended to streamline. However, the code transformation performed by the compiler can be considerably more complex than merely rewriting the anonymous function as a static method if outer variables are involved.

Outer Variables

Local variables declared outside a lambda expression (including parameters of the containing method) are called the **outer variables** of that lambda. (The this reference, though technically not a variable, is also considered to be an outer variable.) When a lambda body uses an outer variable, the variable is said to be **captured** (or, equivalently, **closed over**) by the lambda. In Listing 13.20, we use an outer variable to count how many times BubbleSort( ) performs a comparison. Output 13.2 shows the results of this listing.

LISTING 13.20: Using an Outer Variable in a Lambda Expression

```
class DelegateSample
{

    // ...

    static void Main(string[] args)
    {
        int i;
        int[] items = new int[5];
        int comparisonCount=0;

        for (i=0; i<items.Length; i++)
        {
            Console.Write("Enter an integer:");
            items[i] = int.Parse(Console.ReadLine());
        }
```

3.0

```
        BubbleSort(items,
            (int first, int second) =>
            {
                comparisonCount++;
                return first < second;
            }
        );

        for (i = 0; i < items.Length; i++)
        {
            Console.WriteLine(items[i]);
        }

        Console.WriteLine("Items were compared {0} times.",
                comparisonCount);
    }
}
```

OUTPUT 13.2

```
Enter an integer:5
Enter an integer:1
Enter an integer:4
Enter an integer:2
Enter an integer:3
5
4
3
2
1
Items were compared 10 times.
```

Note that comparisonCount appears outside the lambda expression and is incremented inside it. After calling the BubbleSort() method, comparisonCount is printed out to the console.

Normally, the lifetime of a local variable is tied to its scope; when control leaves the scope, the storage location associated with the variable is no longer valid. But a delegate created from a lambda that captures an outer variable might have a longer (or shorter) lifetime than the local variable normally would, and the delegate must be able to safely access the outer variable every time the delegate is invoked. Therefore, the lifetime of a captured variable is extended; it is guaranteed to live at least as long as the longest-lived delegate object capturing it. (And it may live even longer than that—precisely how the compiler generates code that ensures outer variable lifetimes are extended is an implementation detail and subject to change.)

The C# compiler takes care of generating CIL code that shares `comparisonCount` between the anonymous method and the method that declares it.

▪ ADVANCED TOPIC

Outer Variable CIL Implementation

The CIL code generated by the C# compiler for anonymous functions that capture outer variables is more complex than the code for a simple anonymous function that captures nothing. Listing 13.21 shows the C# equivalent of the CIL code used to implement outer variables for the code in Listing 13.20.

LISTING 13.21: C# Equivalent of CIL Code Generated by Compiler for Outer Variables

```csharp
class DelegateSample
{
    // ...
    private sealed class __LocalsDisplayClass_00000001
    {
        public int comparisonCount;
        public bool __AnonymousMethod_00000000(
            int first, int second)
        {
                comparisonCount++;
                return first < second;
        }
    }
    // ...
    static void Main(string[] args)
    {
        int i;
        __LocalsDisplayClass_00000001 locals =
            new __LocalsDisplayClass_00000001();
        locals.comparisonCount=0;
        int[] items = new int[5];

        for (i=0; i<items.Length; i++)
        {
            Console.Write("Enter an integer:");
            items[i] = int.Parse(Console.ReadLine());
        }

        BubbleSort(items, locals.__AnonymousMethod_00000000);
        for (i = 0; i < items.Length; i++)
        {
            Console.WriteLine(items[i]);
        }
```

3.0

```
        Console.WriteLine("Items were compared {0} times.",
                            locals.comparisonCount);
    }
}
```

Notice that the captured local variable is never "passed" anywhere and is never "copied" anywhere. Rather, the captured local variable (comparisonCount) is a single variable whose lifetime the compiler has extended by implementing it as an instance field rather than as a local variable. All usages of the local variable are rewritten to be usages of the field.

The generated class, __LocalsDisplayClass, is a **closure**—a data structure (class in C#) that contains an expression and the variables (public fields in C#) necessary to evaluate the expression.

Begin 5.0

▪ ADVANCED TOPIC

Accidentally Capturing Loop Variables

What do you think the output of Listing 13.22 should be?

LISTING 13.22: Capturing Loop Variables in C# 5.0

```
class CaptureLoop
{
  static void Main()
  {
      var items = new string[] { "Moe", "Larry", "Curly" };
      var actions = new List<Action>();
      foreach (string item in items)
      {
          actions.Add( ()=> { Console.WriteLine(item); } );
      }
      foreach (Action action in actions)
      {
          action();
      }
  }
}
```

3.0

Most people expect that the output will be as shown in Output 13.3, and in C# 5.0 it is. In previous versions of C#, however, the output is as shown in Output 13.4.

OUTPUT 13.3: C# 5.0 OUTPUT

```
Moe
Larry
Curly
```

OUTPUT 13.4: C# 4.0 OUTPUT

```
Curly
Curly
Curly
```

A lambda expression captures a variable and always uses the latest value of the variable; it does not capture and preserve the value that the variable had when the delegate was created. This is normally what you want—after all, the whole point of capturing comparisonCount in Listing 13.20 was to ensure that its latest value would be used when it was incremented. Loop variables are no different; when you capture a loop variable, every delegate captures the same loop variable. When the loop variable changes, every delegate that captured this loop variable sees the change. The C# 4.0 behavior is therefore justified but is almost never what the author of the code wants.

In C# 5.0, the C# language was changed so that the loop variable of a foreach loop is now considered to be a fresh variable every time the loop iterates; therefore, each delegate creation captures a different variable rather than all iterations sharing the same variable. This change was not applied to the for loop, however: If you write similar code using a for loop, any loop variable declared in the header of the for statement will be considered a single outer variable when captured. If you need to write code that works the same in both C# 5.0 and previous C# versions, use the pattern shown in Listing 13.23.

LISTING 13.23: Loop Variable Capture Workaround before C# 5.0

```csharp
class DoNotCaptureLoop
{
  static void Main()
  {
      var items = new string[] { "Moe", "Larry", "Curly" };
      var actions = new List<Action>();
      foreach (string item in items)
```

```
        {
            string _item = item;
            actions.Add(
                ()=> { Console.WriteLine(_item); } );
        }
        foreach (Action action in actions)
        {
            action();
        }
    }
}
```

Now there is clearly one fresh variable per loop iteration; each delegate is, in turn, closed over a different variable.

> **Guidelines**
>
> AVOID capturing loop variables in anonymous functions.

End 5.0

Expression Trees

Thus far we've seen that lambda expressions are a succinct syntax for declaring an "inline" method that can be converted to a delegate type. Expression lambdas (but not statement lambdas or anonymous methods) can also be converted to **expression trees**. A delegate is an object that enables you to pass around a method like any other object and invoke it at any time. An expression tree is an object that enables you to pass around the compiler's analysis of the lambda body. But why would you ever need that capability? Obviously, the compiler's analysis is useful to the compiler when generating the CIL, but why is it useful to the developer to have an object representing that analysis at execution time? Let's take a look at an example.

3.0

Using Lambda Expressions as Data

Consider the lambda expression in the following code:

```
persons.Where(
    person => person.Name.ToUpper() == "INIGO MONTOYA");
```

Suppose that persons is an array of Persons, and the formal parameter of the Where method that corresponds to the lambda expression argument is of delegate type Func<Person, bool>. The compiler emits a method that contains the code in the body of the lambda. It generates code that creates a delegate to the emitted method and passes the delegate to the `Where` method. The `Where` method returns a query object that, when executed, applies the delegate to each member of the array to determine the query results.

Now suppose that `persons` is not of type `Person[]` but rather is an object that represents a remote database table containing data on millions of people. Information about each row in the table can be streamed from the server to the client, and the client can then create a `Person` object corresponding to that row. The call to `Where` returns an object that represents the query. When the results of that query are requested on the client, how are the results determined?

One technique would be to transmit several million rows of data from the server to the client. You could create a `Person` object from each row, create a delegate from the lambda, and execute the delegate on every `Person`. This is conceptually no different from the array scenario, but it is far, far more expensive.

A second, much better technique is to somehow send the meaning of the lambda ("filter out every row that names a person other than Inigo Montoya") to the server. Database servers are optimized to rapidly perform this sort of filtering. The server can then choose to stream only the tiny number of matching rows to the client; instead of creating millions of `Person` objects and rejecting almost all of them, the client creates only those objects that already match the query, as determined by the server. But how does the meaning of the lambda get sent to the server?

This scenario is the motivation for adding expression trees to the language. Lambda expressions converted to expression trees become objects that represent data that describes the lambda expression rather than compiled code that implements an anonymous function. Since the expression tree represents data rather than compiled code, it is possible to analyze the lambda at execution time and use that information to construct a query that executes on a database, for example. The expression tree received by `Where()` might be converted into a SQL query that is passed to a database, as shown in Listing 13.24.

LISTING 13.24: Converting an Expression Tree to a SQL where Clause

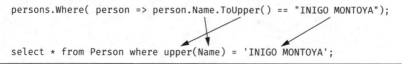

```
persons.Where( person => person.Name.ToUpper() == "INIGO MONTOYA");



select * from Person where upper(Name) = 'INIGO MONTOYA';
```

3.0

The expression tree passed to the `Where()` call says that the lambda argument consists of the following elements:

- A read of the `Name` property of a `Person` object
- A call to a `string` method called `ToUpper()`
- A constant value, `"INIGO MONTOYA"`
- An equality operator, `==`

The `Where()` method takes this data and converts it to the SQL `where` clause by examining the data and building a SQL query string. However, SQL is just one possibility; you can build an expression tree evaluator that converts expressions to any query language.

Expression Trees Are Object Graphs

At execution time, a lambda converted to an expression tree becomes an object graph containing objects from the `System.Linq.Expressions` namespace. The root object in the graph represents the lambda itself. This object refers to objects representing the parameters, a return type, and body expression, as shown in Figure 13.3. The object graph contains all the information that the compiler deduced about the lambda. That information can then be used at execution time to create a query. Alternatively, the root lambda expression has a method, `Compile`, that generates CIL on the fly and creates a delegate that implements the described lambda.

Figure 13.4 shows the types found in object graphs for a unary and binary expression in the body of a lambda.

A `UnaryExpression` represents an expression such as `–count`. It has a single child, `Operand`, of type `Expression`. A `BinaryExpression` has two child expressions, `Left` and `Right`. Both types have a `NodeType` property that identifies the specific operator, and both inherit from the base class `Expression`. There are another 30 or so expression types, such as `NewExpression`, `ParameterExpression`, `MethodCallExpression`, and `LoopExpression`, to represent (almost) every possible expression in C# and Visual Basic.

3.0

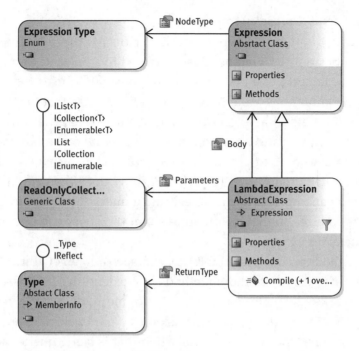

FIGURE 13.3: The Lambda Expression Tree Type

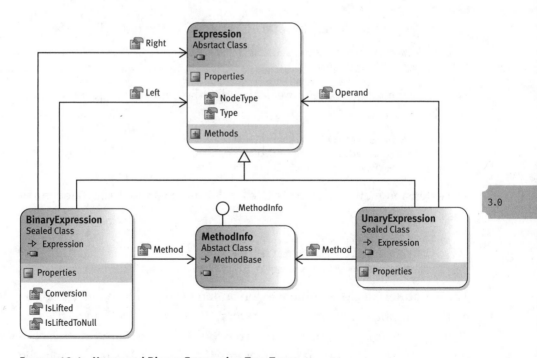

FIGURE 13.4: Unary and Binary Expression Tree Types

3.0

Delegates versus Expression Trees

The validity of a lambda expression is verified at compile time with a full semantic analysis, whether it is converted to a delegate or an expression tree. A lambda that is converted to a delegate causes the compiler to emit the lambda as a method and generates code that creates a delegate to that method at execution time. A lambda that is converted to an expression tree causes the compiler to generate code that creates an instance of LambdaExpression at execution time. But when using the Language Integrated Query (LINQ) API, how does the compiler know whether to generate a delegate, to execute a query locally, or to generate an expression tree so that information about the query can be sent to the remote database server?

The methods used to build LINQ queries, such as Where( ), are extension methods. The versions of those methods that extend the IEnumerable<T> interface take delegate parameters; the methods that extend the IQueryable<T> interface take expression tree parameters. The compiler, therefore, can use the type of the collection that is being queried to determine whether to create delegates or expression trees from lambdas supplied as arguments.

Consider, for example, the Where( ) method in the following code:

```
persons.Where( person => person.Name.ToUpper() ==
    "INIGO MONTOYA");
```

The extension method signature declared in the System.Linq.Enumerable class is

```
public IEnumerable<TSource> Where<TSource>(
    this IEnumerable<TSource> collection,
    Func<TSource, bool> predicate);
```

3.0

The extension method signature declared in the System.Linq.Queryable class is

```
public IQueryable<TSource> Where<TSource>(
    this IQueryable<TSource> collection,
    Expression<Func<TSource, bool>> predicate);
```

The compiler decides which extension method to use on the basis of the compile-time type of persons; if it is a type convertible to IQueryable<Person>, the method from System.Linq.Queryable is chosen. It converts the lambda to an expression tree. At execution time, the object referred to by persons receives the expression tree data and might use that data to build a SQL query, which is then passed to the database when the results of the query are requested. The result of the call to Where is an object that, when asked for query results, sends the query to the database and produces the results.

If persons cannot be converted implicitly to IQueryable<Person> but can be converted implicitly to IEnumerable<Person>, the method from System.Linq.Enumerable is chosen, and the lambda is converted to a delegate. The result of the call to Where is an object that, when asked for query results, applies the generated delegate as a predicate to every member of the collection and produces the results that match the predicate.

Examining an Expression Tree

As we've seen, converting a lambda expression to an Expression<TDelegate> creates an expression tree rather than a delegate. We saw previously in this chapter how to convert a lambda such as (x,y)=>x>y to a delegate type such as Func<int, int, bool>. To turn this same lambda into an expression tree, we simply convert it to Expression<Func<int, int, bool>>, as shown in Listing 13.25. We can then examine the generated object and display information about its structure, as well as that of a more complex expression tree.

Note that passing an instance of expression tree to Console .WriteLine() automatically converts the expression tree to a descriptive string form; the objects generated for expression trees all override ToString() so that you can see at a glance what the contents of an expression tree are when debugging.

LISTING 13.25: Examining an Expression Tree

3.0

```csharp
using System;
using System.Linq.Expressions;

public class Program
{
    public static void Main()
    {
        Expression<Func<int, int, bool>> expression;
        expression = (x, y) => x > y;
        Console.WriteLine("------------- {0} -------------",
            expression);
        PrintNode(expression.Body, 0);
        Console.WriteLine();
```

```csharp
        Console.WriteLine();
        expression = (x, y) => x * y > x + y;
        Console.WriteLine("------------- {0} -------------",
            expression);
        PrintNode(expression.Body, 0);
    }
    public static void PrintNode(Expression expression,
        int indent)
    {
        if (expression is BinaryExpression)
            PrintNode(expression as BinaryExpression, indent);
        else
            PrintSingle(expression, indent);
    }
    private static void PrintNode(BinaryExpression expression,
      int indent)
    {
        PrintNode(expression.Left, indent + 1);
        PrintSingle(expression, indent);
        PrintNode(expression.Right, indent + 1);
    }
    private static void PrintSingle(
        Expression expression, int indent)
    {
        Console.WriteLine("{0," + indent * 5 + "}{1}",
          "", NodeToString(expression));
    }
    private static string NodeToString(Expression expression)
    {
        switch (expression.NodeType)
        {
            case ExpressionType.Multiply:
                return "*";
            case ExpressionType.Add:
                return "+";
            case ExpressionType.Divide:
                return "/";
            case ExpressionType.Subtract:
                return "-";
            case ExpressionType.GreaterThan:
                return ">";
            case ExpressionType.LessThan:
                return "<";
            default:
                return expression.ToString() +
                    " (" + expression.NodeType.ToString() + ")";
        }
    }
}
```

In Output 13.5, we see that the Console.WriteLine() statements within Main() print out the body of the expression trees as text.

OUTPUT 13.5

```
------------- (x, y) => (x > y) -------------
    x (Parameter)
>
    y (Parameter)


------------- (x, y) => ((x * y) > (x + y)) -------------
        x (Parameter)
    *
        y (Parameter)
>
        x (Parameter)
    +
        y (Parameter)
```

The important point to note is that an expression tree is a collection of data, and by iterating over the data, it is possible to convert the data to another format; in this case we convert the expression tree to descriptive strings, but it could also be converted to expressions in another query language.

Using recursion, the PrintNode() function demonstrates that nodes in an expression tree are themselves trees containing zero or more child expression trees. The root tree that represents the lambda refers to the expression that is the body of the lambda with its Body property. Every expression tree node includes a NodeType property of enumerated type ExpressionType that describes what kind of expression it is. Numerous types of expressions exist: BinaryExpression, ConditionalExpression, LambdaExpression, MethodCallExpression, ParameterExpression, and ConstantExpression are examples. Each type derives from Expression.

Note that, although the expression tree library now contains objects to represent most of the statements of C# and Visual Basic, neither language supports the conversion of statement lambdas to expression trees. Only expression lambdas can be converted to expression trees.

3.0

SUMMARY

This chapter began with a discussion of delegates and their use as references to methods or callbacks. This powerful concept enables you to pass a set of instructions to call in a different location, rather than immediately, when coding the instructions.

The concept of lambda expressions is a syntax that supersedes (but does not eliminate) the C# 2.0 anonymous method syntax. These constructs allow programmers to assign a set of instructions to a variable directly, without defining an explicit method that contains the instructions. This construct provides significant flexibility for programming instructions dynamically within the method—a powerful concept that greatly simplifies the programming of collections through the LINQ API.

The chapter ended with a discussion of the concept of expression trees and a consideration of how they compile into objects that represent the semantic analysis of a lambda expression rather than the delegate implementation itself. This important feature supports such libraries as the Entity Framework and LINQ to XML—that is, libraries that interpret the expression tree and use it within contexts other than CIL.

Lambda expressions encompass both *statement lambdas* and *expression lambdas*. In other words, both statement lambdas and expression lambdas are types of lambda expressions.

One thing that the chapter mentioned but did not elaborate on was multicast delegates. The next chapter investigates multicast delegates in detail and explains how they enable the publish–subscribe pattern with events.

End 3.0

14

Events

I N CHAPTER 13, YOU SAW HOW TO REFERENCE A METHOD with an instance of a delegate type and invoke that method via the delegate. Delegates are the building blocks of a larger pattern called *publish–subscribe* or *observer*. The use of delegates for the publish–subscribe pattern is the focus of this chapter. Almost everything described in this chapter can be done using delegates alone. However, the event constructs that this chapter highlights provide additional encapsulation, making the publish–subscribe pattern easier to implement and less error-prone.

Begin 2.0

In the preceding chapter, all delegates referenced a single method. More broadly, a single delegate value can reference a whole collection of methods to be called in sequence; such a delegate is called a **multicast delegate**. Its application enables scenarios where notifications of single events, such as a change in object state, are published to multiple subscribers.

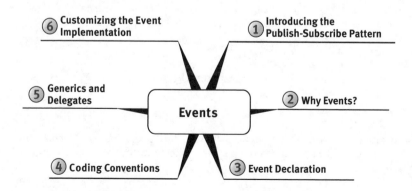

Although events existed in C# 1.0, the introduction of generics in C# 2.0 significantly changed the coding conventions because using a generic delegate data type meant that it was no longer necessary to declare a delegate for every possible event signature. For this reason, the chapter assumes a minimum of C# 2.0 throughout. Readers still living in the world of C# 1.0 can also use events, but they will have to declare their own delegate data types (as discussed in Chapter 13).

Coding the Publish-Subscribe Pattern with Multicast Delegates

Consider a temperature control, where a heater and a cooler are hooked up to the same thermostat. For the unit to turn on and off appropriately, you must notify the units of changes in temperature. One thermostat publishes temperature changes to multiple subscribers—the heating and cooling units. The next section investigates the code.[1]

Defining Subscriber Methods

Begin by defining the Heater and Cooler objects (see Listing 14.1).

LISTING 14.1: Heater and Cooler Event Subscriber Implementations

```
class Cooler
{
  public Cooler(float temperature)
  {
      Temperature = temperature;
  }
  // Cooler is activated when ambient temperature is higher than this
  public float Temperature { get; set; }

  // Notifies that the temperature changed on this instance
  public void OnTemperatureChanged(float newTemperature)
  {
      if (newTemperature > Temperature)
      {
          System.Console.WriteLine("Cooler: On");
      }
  }
```

2.0

1. In this example, we use the term *thermostat* because people more commonly think of it in the context of heating and cooling systems. Technically, *thermometer* would be more appropriate.

```
        else
        {
            System.Console.WriteLine("Cooler: Off");
        }
    }
}

class Heater
{
    public Heater(float temperature)
    {
        Temperature = temperature;
    }

    public float Temperature { get; set; }

    public void OnTemperatureChanged(float newTemperature)
    {
        if (newTemperature < Temperature)
        {
            System.Console.WriteLine("Heater: On");
        }
        else
        {
            System.Console.WriteLine("Heater: Off");
        }
    }
}
```

The two classes are essentially identical except for the temperature comparison. (In fact, you could eliminate one of the classes if you used a delegate to a comparison method within the OnTemperatureChanged method.) Each class stores the temperature at which the unit should be turned on. In addition, both classes provide an OnTemperatureChanged() method. Calling the OnTemperatureChanged() method is the means to indicate to the Heater and Cooler classes that the temperature has changed. The method implementation uses newTemperature to compare against the stored trigger temperature to determine whether to turn on the device.

The OnTemperatureChanged() methods are the subscriber (also called *listener*) methods. They must have the parameters and a return type that matches the delegate from the Thermostat class, which we discuss next.

2.0

Defining the Publisher

The Thermostat class is responsible for reporting temperature changes to the heater and cooler object instances. The Thermostat class code appears in Listing 14.2.

LISTING 14.2: Defining the Event Publisher, Thermostat

```csharp
public class Thermostat
{
  // Define the event publisher (initially without the sender)
  public Action<float> OnTemperatureChange { get; set; }

  public float CurrentTemperature { get; set; }
}
```

The Thermostat includes a property called OnTemperatureChange that is of the Action<float> delegate type. OnTemperatureChange stores a list of subscribers. Notice that only one delegate property is required to store all the subscribers. In other words, both the Cooler and the Heater instances will receive notifications of a change in the temperature from this single publisher.

The last member of Thermostat is the CurrentTemperature property. This property sets and retrieves the value of the current temperature reported by the Thermostat class.

Hooking Up the Publisher and Subscribers

Finally, we put all these pieces together in a Main() method. Listing 14.3 shows a sample of what Main() could look like.

LISTING 14.3: Connecting the Publisher and Subscribers

```csharp
class Program
{
  public static void Main()
  {
      Thermostat thermostat = new Thermostat();
      Heater heater = new Heater(60);
      Cooler cooler = new Cooler(80);
      string temperature;

      thermostat.OnTemperatureChange +=
          heater.OnTemperatureChanged;
      thermostat.OnTemperatureChange +=
          cooler.OnTemperatureChanged;
```

2.0

```
            Console.Write("Enter temperature: ");
            temperature = Console.ReadLine();
            thermostat.CurrentTemperature = int.Parse(temperature);
    }
}
```

The code in this listing has registered two subscribers (`heater` `.OnTemperatureChanged` and `cooler.OnTemperatureChanged`) to the `OnTemperatureChange` delegate by directly assigning them using the `+=` operator.

By taking the temperature value the user has entered as input, you can set the `CurrentTemperature` of `thermostat`. However, you have not yet written any code to publish the change temperature event to subscribers.

Invoking a Delegate

Every time the `CurrentTemperature` property on the `Thermostat` class changes, you want to **invoke the delegate** to notify the subscribers (`heater` and `cooler`) of the change in temperature. To achieve this goal, you must modify the `CurrentTemperature` property to save the new value and publish a notification to each subscriber. The code modification appears in Listing 14.4.

LISTING 14.4: Invoking a Delegate without Checking for null

```
public class Thermostat
{
  ...
  public float CurrentTemperature
  {
      get { return _CurrentTemperature; }
      set
      {
          if (value != CurrentTemperature)
          {
              _CurrentTemperature = value;

              // INCOMPLETE: Check for null needed
              // Call subscribers
              OnTemperatureChange(value);
          }
      }
  }
  private float _CurrentTemperature;
}
```

2.0

Now the assignment of CurrentTemperature includes some special logic to notify subscribers of changes in CurrentTemperature. The call to notify all subscribers is simply the single C# statement, OnTemperatureChange(value). This single statement publishes the temperature change to both the cooler and heater objects. Here, you see in practice that the ability to notify multiple subscribers using a single call is why delegates are more specifically known as multicast delegates, which are discussed further later in the chapter.

Check for null

One important part of event publishing code is missing from Listing 14.4. If no subscriber has registered to receive the notification, OnTemperatureChange would be null, and executing the OnTemperatureChange(value) statement would throw a NullReferenceException. To avoid this scenario, it is necessary to check for null before firing the event. Listing 14.5 demonstrates how to do this using C# 6.0's null conditional operator before calling Invoke().

LISTING 14.5: Invoking a Delegate

```csharp
public class Thermostat
{
    ...
    public float CurrentTemperature
    {
        get { return _CurrentTemperature; }
        set
        {
            if (value != CurrentTemperature)
            {
                _CurrentTemperature = value;
                // If there are any subscribers,
                // notify them of changes in temperature
                // by invoking said subscribers
                OnTemperatureChange?.Invoke(value);   // C# 6.0
            }
        }
    }
    private float _CurrentTemperature;
}
```

Notice the call to the Invoke() method that follows the null conditional. Although this method may be called using only a dot operator, there is little point, since that is the equivalent of calling the delegate directly (see OnTemperatureChange(value) in Listing 14.4). The important advantage underlying the null conditional operator is special logic to ensure that after checking for null, there is no possibility that a subscriber might invoke a stale handler (one that has changed after checking for null), leaving the delegate null again.

Unfortunately, no such special uninterruptable null-checking logic exists prior to C# 6.0. As such, the implementation is significantly more verbose in earlier C# versions, as shown in Listing 14.6.

LISTING 14.6: Invoking a Delegate with Null Check Prior to C# 6.0

```csharp
public class Thermostat
{
    ...
    public float CurrentTemperature
    {
        get{return _CurrentTemperature;}
        set
        {
            if (value != CurrentTemperature)
            {
                _CurrentTemperature = value;
                // If there are any subscribers,
                // notify them of changes in temperature
                // by invoking said subscribers
                Action<float> localOnChange =
                    OnTemperatureChange;
                if(localOnChange != null)
                {
                    // Call subscribers
                    localOnChange(value);
                }
            }
        }
    }
    private float _CurrentTemperature;
}
```

Instead of checking for null directly, this code first assigns OnTemperatureChange to a second delegate variable, localOnChange. This simple modification ensures that if all OnTemperatureChange subscribers are removed (by a different thread) between checking for null and sending the notification, you will not raise a NullReferenceException.

For the remainder of the book, all samples rely on the C# 6.0 null conditional operator for delegate invocation.

End 6.0

2.0

> ### Guidelines
>
> **DO** check that the value of a delegate is not null before invoking it.
>
> **DO** use the null conditional operator prior to calling Invoke( ) starting in C# 6.0.

▪ ADVANCED TOPIC

-= Operator for a Delegate Returns a New Instance

Given that a delegate is a reference type, it is perhaps somewhat surprising that assigning a local variable and then using that local variable is sufficient for making the null check thread-safe. Since localOnChange refers to the same location as OnTemperatureChange does, you might imagine that any changes in OnTemperatureChange would be reflected in localOnChange as well.

This is not the case because, effectively, any calls to OnTemperatureChange -= <subscriber> will not simply remove a delegate from OnTemperatureChange so that it contains one less delegate than before. Rather, such a call will assign an entirely new multicast delegate without having any effect on the original multicast delegate to which localOnChange also refers.

▪ ADVANCED TOPIC

Thread-Safe Delegate Invocation

If subscribers can be added and removed from the delegate on different threads, it is wise (as noted earlier) to conditionally invoke the delegate or copy the delegate reference into a local variable before checking it for null. Although this approach prevents the invocation of a null delegate, it does not avoid all possible race conditions. For example, one thread could make the copy, and then another thread could reset the delegate to null, and then the original thread could invoke the previous value of the delegate, thereby notifying a subscriber that is no longer on the list of subscribers. Subscribers in multithreaded programs should ensure that their code remains robust in this scenario; it is always possible that a "stale" subscriber will be invoked.

2.0

Delegate Operators

To combine the two subscribers in the Thermostat example, you used the
+= operator. This operator takes the first delegate and adds the second
delegate to the chain. Now, after the first delegate's method returns, the
second delegate is called. To remove delegates from a delegate chain, use
the -= operator, as shown in Listing 14.7.

LISTING 14.7: Using the += and -= Delegate Operators

```
// ...
Thermostat thermostat = new Thermostat();
Heater heater = new Heater(60);
Cooler cooler = new Cooler(80);

Action<float> delegate1;
Action<float> delegate2;
Action<float> delegate3;

delegate1 = heater.OnTemperatureChanged;
delegate2 = cooler.OnTemperatureChanged;

Console.WriteLine("Invoke both delegates:");
delegate3 = delegate1;
delegate3 += delegate2;
delegate3(90);

Console.WriteLine("Invoke only delegate2");
delegate3 -= delegate1;
delegate3(30);
// ...
```

The results of Listing 14.7 appear in Output 14.1.

OUTPUT 14.1

```
Invoke both delegates:
Heater: Off
Cooler: On
Invoke only delegate2
Cooler: Off
```

Furthermore, you can also use the + and – operators to combine delegates, as Listing 14.8 shows.

LISTING 14.8: Using the + and – Delegate Operators

2.0

```
// ...
Thermostat thermostat = new Thermostat();
Heater heater = new Heater(60);
Cooler cooler = new Cooler(80);
```

```
Action<float> delegate1;
Action<float> delegate2;
Action<float> delegate3;

// Note: Use new Action (cooler.OnTemperatureChanged)
// for C# 1.0 syntax
delegate1 = heater.OnTemperatureChanged;
delegate2 = cooler.OnTemperatureChanged;

Console.WriteLine("Combine delegates using + operator:");
delegate3 = delegate1 + delegate2;
delegate3(60);

Console.WriteLine("Uncombine delegates using - operator:");
delegate3 = delegate3 - delegate2;
delegate3(60);
// ...
```

Use of the assignment operator clears out all previous subscribers and allows you to replace them with new subscribers. This is an unfortunate characteristic of a delegate. It is simply too easy to mistakenly code an assignment when, in fact, the += operator is intended. The solution, called events, appears in the "Understanding Events" section later in this chapter.

Both the + and - operators and their assignment equivalents, += and -=, are implemented internally using the static methods System.Delegate.Combine() and System.Delegate.Remove(). These methods take two parameters of type delegate. The first method, Combine(), joins the two parameters so that the first parameter refers to the second within the list of delegates. The second, Remove(), searches through the chain of delegates specified in the first parameter and then removes the delegate specified by the second parameter.

One interesting thing to note about the Combine() method is that either or both of its parameters can be null. If one of them is null, Combine() returns the non-null parameter. If both are null, Combine() returns null. This explains why you can call thermostat .OnTemperatureChange += heater.OnTemperatureChanged; and not throw an exception, even if the value of thermostat.OnTemperatureChange is still null.

2.0

Sequential Invocation

Figure 14.1 highlights the sequential notification of both heater and cooler.

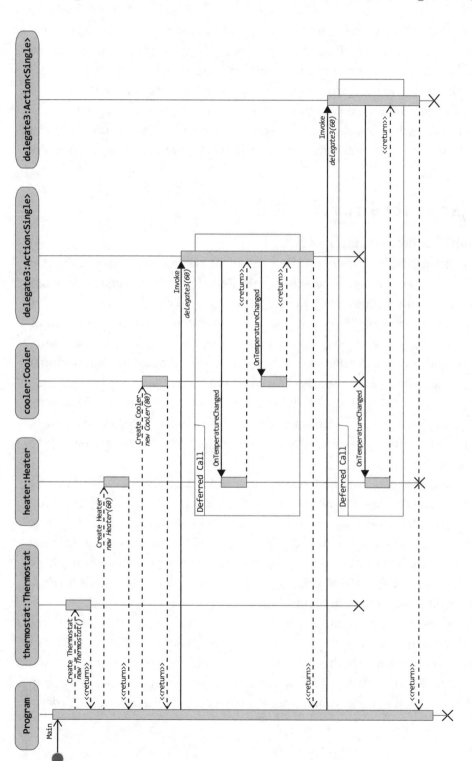

FIGURE 14.1: Delegate Invocation Sequence Diagram

Although you coded only a single call to OnTemperatureChange( ), the call is broadcast to both subscribers. Thus, with just one call, both cooler and heater are notified of the change in temperature. If you added more subscribers, they, too, would be notified by OnTemperatureChange( ).

Although a single call, OnTemperatureChange( ), caused the notification of each subscriber, the subscribers are still called sequentially, not simultaneously, because they are all called on the same thread of execution.

■ ADVANCED TOPIC

Multicast Delegate Internals

To understand how events work, you need to revisit the first examination of the System.Delegate type internals. Recall that the delegate keyword is an alias for a type derived from System.MulticastDelegate. In turn, System.MulticastDelegate is derived from System.Delegate, which, for its part, is composed of an object reference (needed for nonstatic methods) and a method reference. When you create a delegate, the compiler automatically employs the System.MulticastDelegate type rather than the System.Delegate type. The MulticastDelegate class includes an object reference and a method reference, just like its Delegate base class, but it also contains a reference to another System.MulticastDelegate object.

When you add a method to a multicast delegate, the MulticastDelegate class creates a new instance of the delegate type, stores the object reference and the method reference for the added method into the new instance, and adds the new delegate instance as the next item in a list of delegate instances. In effect, the MulticastDelegate class maintains a linked list of Delegate objects. Conceptually, you can represent the thermostat example as shown in Figure 14.2.

When invoking a multicast delegate, each delegate instance in the linked list is called sequentially. Generally, delegates are called in the order they were added, but this behavior is not specified within the Common Language Infrastructure (CLI) specification. Furthermore, it can be overridden. Therefore, programmers should not depend on an invocation order.

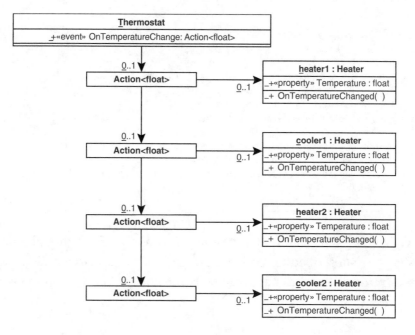

FIGURE 14.2: Multicast Delegates Chained Together

Error Handling

Error handling makes awareness of the sequential notification critical. If one subscriber throws an exception, later subscribers in the chain do not receive the notification. Consider, for example, what would happen if you changed Heater's OnTemperatureChanged() method so that it threw an exception, as shown in Listing 14.9.

LISTING 14.9: OnTemperatureChanged() Throwing an Exception

```csharp
class Program
{
  public static void Main()
  {
     Thermostat thermostat = new Thermostat();
     Heater heater = new Heater(60);
     Cooler cooler = new Cooler(80);
     string temperature;

     thermostat.OnTemperatureChange +=
        heater.OnTemperatureChanged;
     // Using C# 3.0. Change to anonymous method
```

Begin 3.0

2.0

```
// if using C# 2.0
thermostat.OnTemperatureChange +=
    (newTemperature) =>
        {
            throw new InvalidOperationException();
        };
thermostat.OnTemperatureChange +=
    cooler.OnTemperatureChanged;

Console.Write("Enter temperature: ");
temperature = Console.ReadLine();
thermostat.CurrentTemperature = int.Parse(temperature);
    }
}
```

Figure 14.3 shows an updated sequence diagram. Even though `cooler` and `heater` subscribed to receive messages, the lambda expression exception terminates the chain and prevents the `cooler` object from receiving notification.

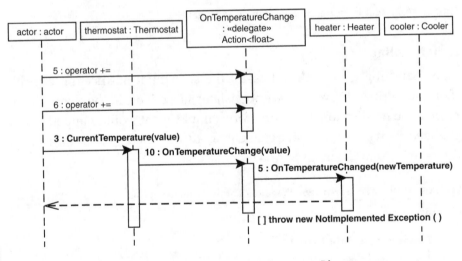

FIGURE 14.3: Delegate Invocation with Exception Sequence Diagram

To avoid this problem so that all subscribers receive notification, regardless of the behavior of earlier subscribers, you must manually enumerate through the list of subscribers and call them individually. Listing 14.10 shows the updates required in the `CurrentTemperature` property. The results appear in Output 14.2.

LISTING 14.10: Handling Exceptions from Subscribers

```csharp
public class Thermostat
{
    // Define the event publisher
    public Action<float> OnTemperatureChange;

    public float CurrentTemperature
    {
        get { return _CurrentTemperature; }
        set
        {
            if (value != CurrentTemperature)
            {
                _CurrentTemperature = value;
                Action<float> onTemperatureChange = OnTemperatureChange;
                if(onTemperatureChange != null)
                {
                    List<Exception> exceptionCollection =
                        new List<Exception>();
                    foreach (
                        Action<float> handler in
                        onTemperatureChange.GetInvocationList())
                    {
                        try
                        {
                            handler(value);
                        }
                        catch (Exception exception)
                        {
                            exceptionCollection.Add(exception);
                        }
                    }
                    if (exceptionCollection.Count > 0)
                    {
                        throw new AggregateException(
                            "There were exceptions thrown by
OnTemperatureChange Event subscribers.",
                            exceptionCollection);
                    }
                }
            }
        }
    }
    private float _CurrentTemperature;
}
```

OUTPUT 14.2

2.0

```
Enter temperature: 45
Heater: On
Error in the application
Cooler: Off
```

This listing demonstrates that you can retrieve a list of subscribers from a delegate's `GetInvocationList()` method. Enumerating over each item in this list returns the individual subscribers. If you then place each invocation of a subscriber within a try/catch block, you can handle any error conditions before continuing with the enumeration loop. In this example, even though the delegate subscriber throws an exception, `cooler` still receives notification of the temperature change. After all notifications have been sent, Listing 14.10 reports any exceptions by throwing an `AggregateException`, which wraps a collection of exceptions that are accessible by the `InnerExceptions` property. In this way, all exceptions are still reported and, at the same time, all subscribers are notified.

Parenthetically, no null conditional was used in this example, as a significant amount of code was dependent on a non-null delegate.

Method Returns and Pass-by-Reference

There is another scenario in which it is useful to iterate over the delegate invocation list instead of simply activating a notification directly. This scenario relates to delegates that either do not return `void` or have `ref` or `out` parameters. In the thermostat example, the `OnTemperatureChange` delegate is of type `Action<float>`, which returns `void` and has no `out` or `ref` parameters. As a result, no data is returned to the publisher. This consideration is important, because an invocation of a delegate potentially triggers notification to multiple subscribers. If each of the subscribers returns a value, it is ambiguous as to which subscriber's return value would be used.

If you changed `OnTemperatureChange` to return an enumeration value, indicating whether the device was on because of the temperature change, the new delegate would be of type `Func<float, Status>`, where `Status` was an enum with elements `On` and `Off`. All subscriber methods would have to use the same method signature as the delegate, and therefore, each would be required to return a status value. Also, since `OnTemperatureChange` might potentially correspond to a chain of delegates, it is necessary to follow the same pattern that you used for error handling. In other words, you must iterate through each delegate invocation list, using the `GetInvocationList()` method, to retrieve each individual return value. Similarly, delegate types that use `ref` and `out` parameters need special consideration. However, although it is possible to use this approach in exceptional circumstances, the guideline is to avoid this scenario entirely by only returning `void`.

2.0

Understanding Events

There are two key problems with the delegates as you have used them so far in this chapter. To overcome these issues, C# uses the keyword event. In this section, you will see why you would use events, and how they work.

Why Events?

This chapter and the preceding one covered all you need to know about how delegates work. Unfortunately, weaknesses in the delegate structure may inadvertently allow the programmer to introduce a bug. These issues relate to encapsulation that neither the subscription nor the publication of events can sufficiently control.

Encapsulating the Subscription

As demonstrated earlier, it is possible to assign one delegate to another using the assignment operator. Unfortunately, this capability introduces a common source for bugs. Consider Listing 14.11.

LISTING 14.11: Using the Assignment Operator = Rather Than +=

```
class Program
{
  public static void Main()
  {
      Thermostat thermostat = new Thermostat();
      Heater heater = new Heater(60);
      Cooler cooler = new Cooler(80);
      string temperature;

      // Note: Use new Action (cooler.OnTemperatureChanged)
      // if C# 1.0
      thermostat.OnTemperatureChange =
          heater.OnTemperatureChanged;

      // Bug: Assignment operator overrides
      // previous assignment
      thermostat.OnTemperatureChange =
          cooler.OnTemperatureChanged;

      Console.Write("Enter temperature: ");
      temperature = Console.ReadLine();
      thermostat.CurrentTemperature = int.Parse(temperature);
  }
}
```

2.0

Listing 14.11 is almost identical to Listing 14.7, except that instead of using the `+=` operator, you use a simple assignment operator. As a result, when code assigns `cooler.OnTemperatureChanged` to `OnTemperatureChange`, `heater.OnTemperatureChanged` is cleared out because an entirely new chain is assigned to replace the previous one. The potential for mistakenly using an assignment operator, when the `+=` assignment was intended, is so high that it would be preferable if the assignment operator were not even supported for objects except within the containing class. The `event` keyword provides this additional encapsulation so that you cannot inadvertently cancel other subscribers.

Encapsulating the Publication

The second important difference between delegates and events is that events ensure that only the containing class can trigger an event notification. Consider Listing 14.12.

LISTING 14.12: **Firing the Event from Outside the Events Container**

```
class Program
{
  public static void Main()
  {
      Thermostat thermostat = new Thermostat();
      Heater heater = new Heater(60);
      Cooler cooler = new Cooler(80);
      string temperature;

      // Note: Use new Action (cooler.OnTemperatureChanged)
      // if C# 1.0
      thermostat.OnTemperatureChange +=
          heater.OnTemperatureChanged;

      thermostat.OnTemperatureChange +=
          cooler.OnTemperatureChanged;

          thermostat.OnTemperatureChange(42);
    }
  }
```

In Listing 14.12, `Program` can invoke the `OnTemperatureChange` delegate even though the `CurrentTemperature` on `thermostat` did not change. `Program`, therefore, triggers a notification to all `thermostat` subscribers that the temperature changed, even though there was no change in the `thermostat` temperature. As before, the problem with the delegate

2.0

is that there is insufficient encapsulation. Thermostat should prevent any other class from being able to invoke the OnTemperatureChange delegate.

Declaring an Event

C# provides the event keyword to deal with both problems. Although seemingly like a field modifier, event defines a new type of member (see Listing 14.13).

LISTING 14.13: **Using the event Keyword with the Event-Coding Pattern**

```
public class Thermostat
{
    public class TemperatureArgs: System.EventArgs
    {
        public TemperatureArgs( float newTemperature )
        {
            NewTemperature = newTemperature;
        }

        public float NewTemperature { get; set; }
    }

    // Define the event publisher
    public event EventHandler<TemperatureArgs> OnTemperatureChange =
        delegate { };

    public float CurrentTemperature
    {
        ...
    }
    private float _CurrentTemperature;
}
```

The new Thermostat class has four changes relative to the original class. First, the OnTemperatureChange property has been removed, and OnTemperatureChange has instead been declared as a public field. This seems contrary to solving the earlier encapsulation problem. It would make more sense to increase the encapsulation, not decrease it by making a field public. However, the second change was to add the event keyword immediately before the field declaration. This simple change provides all the encapsulation needed. By adding the event keyword, you prevent use of the assignment operator on a public delegate field (e.g., thermostat .OnTemperatureChange = cooler.OnTemperatureChanged). In addition, only the containing class is able to invoke the delegate that

2.0

triggers the publication to all subscribers (e.g., disallowing `thermostat` `.OnTemperatureChange(42)` from outside the class). In other words, the `event` keyword provides the needed encapsulation that prevents any external class from publishing an event or unsubscribing previous subscribers it did not add. This resolves the two previously mentioned issues with plain delegates and is one of the key reasons for the inclusion of the `event` keyword in C#.

Another potential pitfall with plain delegates is that it is all too easy to forget to check for `null` (ideally using a null conditional in C# 6.0 code) before invoking the delegate. This omission may result in an unexpected `NullReferenceException`. Fortunately, the encapsulation that the `event` keyword provides enables an alternative possibility during declaration (or within the constructor), as shown in Listing 14.13. Notice that when declaring the event, we assign `delegate { }`—a non-null delegate, which does nothing. By assigning the empty delegate, we can raise the event without checking whether there are any subscribers. (This behavior is similar to assigning an array of zero items to a variable. Doing so allows the invocation of an array member without first checking whether the variable is `null`.) Of course, if there is any chance that the delegate could be reassigned with `null`, a check is still required. However, because the `event` keyword restricts assignment to occur only within the class, any reassignment of the delegate could occur only from within the class. Assuming `null` is never assigned, there will be no need to check for `null` whenever the code invokes the delegate.

Coding Conventions

All you need to do to gain the desired functionality is to change the original delegate variable declaration to a field and add the `event` keyword. With these two changes, you provide the necessary encapsulation and all other functionality remains the same. However, an additional change occurs in the delegate declaration in the code in Listing 14.13. To follow standard C# coding conventions, you should replace `Action<float>` with a new delegate type: `EventHandler<TemperatureArgs>`, a Common Language Runtime (CLR) type whose declaration is shown in Listing 14.14.

2.0

LISTING 14.14: The Generic Event Handler Type

```
public delegate void EventHandler<TEventArgs>(
    object sender, TEventArgs e);
```

The result is that the single temperature parameter in the `Action<TEventArgs>` delegate type is replaced with two new parameters—one for the publisher or "sender" and a second for the event data. This change is not something that the C# compiler will enforce, but passing two parameters of these types is the norm for a delegate intended for an event.

The first parameter, `sender`, contains an instance of the class that invoked the delegate. This is especially helpful if the same subscriber method registers with multiple events—for example, if the `heater.OnTemperatureChanged` event subscribes to two different `Thermostat` instances. In such a scenario, either `Thermostat` instance can trigger a call to `heater.OnTemperatureChanged`. To determine which instance of `Thermostat` triggered the event, you use the `sender` parameter from inside `Heater.OnTemperatureChanged()`. If the event is static, this option will not be available, so pass `null` for the `sender` argument value.

The second parameter, `TEventArgs e`, is specified as type `Thermostat.TemperatureArgs`. The important part about `TemperatureArgs`, at least as far as the coding convention goes, is that it derives from `System.EventArgs`. (In fact, derivation from `System.EventArgs` is something that the framework forced with a generic constraint until Microsoft .NET Framework 4.5.) The only significant property on `System.EventArgs` is `Empty`, which is used to indicate that there is no event data. When you derive `TemperatureArgs` from `System.EventArgs`, however, you add an additional property, `NewTemperature`, to pass the temperature from the thermostat to the subscribers.

To summarize the coding convention for events: The first argument, `sender`, is of type `object` and contains a reference to the object that invoked the delegate or `null` if the event is static. The second argument is of type `System.EventArgs` or something that derives from `System.EventArgs` but contains additional data about the event. You invoke the delegate exactly as before, except for the additional parameters. Listing 14.15 shows an example.

LISTING 14.15: Firing the Event Notification

```
public class Thermostat
{
  ...
  public float CurrentTemperature
  {
    get{return _CurrentTemperature;}
```

2.0

```
        set
        {
            if (value != CurrentTemperature)
            {
                _CurrentTemperature = value;
                // If there are any subscribers,
                // notify them of changes in temperature
                // by invoking said subscribers
                OnTemperatureChange?.Invoke(  // Using C# 6.0
                        this, new TemperatureArgs(value) );
            }
        }
    }
    private float _CurrentTemperature;
}
```

You usually specify the sender using the container class (this) because it is the only class that can invoke the delegate for events.

In this example, the subscriber could cast the sender parameter to Thermostat and access the current temperature that way, as well as via the TemperatureArgs instance. However, the current temperature on the Thermostat instance may change via a different thread. In the case of events that occur due to state changes, passing the previous value along with the new value is a pattern frequently used to control which state transitions are allowable.

Guidelines

DO check that the value of a delegate is not null before invoking it (possibly by using the null conditional operator in C# 6.0).

DO NOT pass null as the value of the sender for nonstatic events, but **DO** pass null as the same value for static events.

DO NOT pass null as the value of eventArgs argument.

DO use a delegate type of EventHandler<TEventArgs> for the events.

DO use System.EventArgs or a type that derives from System.EventArgs for a TEventArgs type.

CONSIDER using a subclass of System.EventArgs as the event argument type (TEventArgs) unless you are sure the event will never need to carry any data.

2.0

Generics and Delegates

The preceding section discussed that the guideline for defining a type for an event is to use a delegate type of EventHandler<TEventArgs>. In theory, any delegate type could be used, but by convention, the first parameter, sender, is of type object and the second parameter, e, should be of a type deriving from System.EventArgs. One of the more cumbersome aspects of delegates in C# 1.0 was that you had to declare a new delegate type whenever the parameters on the handler changed. Every creation of a new derivation from System.EventArgs (a relatively common occurrence) required the declaration of a new delegate data type that used the new EventArgs-derived type. For example, to use TemperatureArgs within the event notification code in Listing 14.15, it would be necessary to declare the delegate type TemperatureChangeHandler that has TemperatureArgs as a parameter (see Listing 14.16).

LISTING 14.16: **Using a Custom Delegate Type**

```csharp
public class Thermostat
{
  public class TemperatureArgs: System.EventArgs
  {
      public TemperatureArgs( float newTemperature )
      {
          NewTemperature = newTemperature;
      }

      public float NewTemperature
      {
          get { return _NewTemperature; }
          set { _NewTemperature = value; }
      }
      private float _NewTemperature;
  }

  public delegate void TemperatureChangeHandler(
      object sender, TemperatureArgs newTemperature);

  public event TemperatureChangeHandler
      OnTemperatureChange;

  public float CurrentTemperature
  {
      ...
  }
  private float _CurrentTemperature;
}
```

2.0

Although generally EventHandler<TEventArgs> is preferred over creating a custom delegate type such as TemperatureChangeHandler, there is one advantage associated with the latter type. Specifically, if a custom type is used, the parameter names can be specific to the event. In Listing 14.16, for example, when invoking the delegate to raise the event, the second parameter name will appear as newTemperature rather than as simply e.

Another reason why a custom delegate type might be used concerns parts of the CLR API that were defined prior to C# 2.0. As a result, it is not uncommon to encounter specific delegate types rather than the generic form on events coming from the CLR API. Regardless, in the majority of circumstances when using events in C# 2.0 and later, it is unnecessary to declare a custom delegate data type.

Guidelines

DO use System.EventHandler<T> instead of manually creating new delegate types for event handlers unless the parameter names of a custom type offer significant clarification.

■ ADVANCED TOPIC

Event Internals

Events restrict external classes from doing anything other than adding subscribing methods to the publisher via the += operator and then unsubscribing using the -= operator. In addition, they restrict classes, other than the containing class, from invoking the event. To do so, the C# compiler takes the public delegate variable with its event keyword modifier and declares the delegate as private. In addition, it adds a couple of methods and two special event blocks. Essentially, the event keyword is a C# shortcut for generating the appropriate encapsulation logic. Consider the example in the event declaration shown in Listing 14.17.

LISTING 14.17: Declaring the OnTemperatureChange Event

```csharp
public class Thermostat
{
    public event EventHandler<TemperatureArgs> OnTemperatureChange;

    ...
}
```

2.0

When the C# compiler encounters the event keyword, it generates CIL code equivalent to the C# code shown in Listing 14.18.

LISTING 14.18: C# Conceptual Equivalent of the Event CIL Code Generated by the Compiler

```csharp
public class Thermostat
{
    // ...
    // Declaring the delegate field to save the
    // list of subscribers
    private EventHandler<TemperatureArgs> _OnTemperatureChange;

    public void add_OnTemperatureChange(
        EventHandler<TemperatureArgs> handler)
    {
        System.Delegate.Combine(_OnTemperatureChange, handler);
    }

    public void remove_OnTemperatureChange(
        EventHandler<TemperatureArgs> handler)
    {
        System.Delegate.Remove(_OnTemperatureChange, handler);
    }

    public event EventHandler<TemperatureArgs> OnTemperatureChange
    {
        add
        {
            add_OnTemperatureChange(value)
        }
        remove
        {
            remove_OnTemperatureChange(value)
        }
    }
}
```

In other words, the code shown in Listing 14.17 is (conceptually) the C# shorthand that the compiler uses to trigger the code expansion shown in Listing 14.18. (The "conceptually" qualifier is needed because some details regarding thread synchronization have been eliminated for elucidation.)

The C# compiler first takes the original event definition and defines a private delegate variable in its place. As a result, the delegate becomes unavailable to any external class—even to classes derived from it.

Next, the C# compiler defines two methods, add_OnTemperatureChange() and remove_OnTemperatureChange(), in which the OnTemperatureChange

2.0

suffix is taken from the original name of the event. These methods are responsible for implementing the += and -= assignment operators, respectively. As Listing 14.18 shows, these methods are implemented using the static `System.Delegate.Combine()` and `System.Delegate.Remove()` methods, discussed earlier in the chapter. The first parameter passed to each of these methods is the private `EventHandler<TemperatureArgs>` delegate instance, `OnTemperatureChange`.

Perhaps the most curious part of the code generated from the `event` keyword is the last segment. The syntax is very similar to that of a property's getter and setter methods, except that the methods are called `add` and `remove`. The `add` block takes care of handling the `+=` operator on the event by passing the call to `add_OnTemperatureChange()`. In a similar manner, the `remove` block operator handles the `-=` operator by passing the call on to `remove_OnTemperatureChange`.

Take careful note of the similarities between this code and the code generated for a property. Recall that the C# implementation of a property is to create `get_<propertyname>` and `set_<propertyname>` and then to pass calls to the `get` and `set` blocks on to these methods. Clearly, the event syntax in such cases is very similar.

Another important characteristic to note about the generated CIL code is that the CIL equivalent of the `event` keyword remains in the CIL. In other words, an event is something that the CIL code recognizes explicitly; it is not just a C# construct. By keeping an equivalent `event` keyword in the CIL code, all languages and editors can provide special functionality because they can recognize the event as a special class member.

Customizing the Event Implementation

You can customize the code for `+=` and `-=` that the compiler generates. Consider, for example, changing the scope of the `OnTemperatureChange` delegate so that it is protected rather than private. This, of course, would allow classes derived from `Thermostat` to access the delegate directly instead of being limited to the same restrictions as external classes. To enable this behavior, C# allows the same property as the syntax shown in Listing 14.16. In other words, C# allows you to define custom `add` and `remove` blocks to provide a unique implementation for each aspect of the event encapsulation. Listing 14.19 provides an example.

2.0

LISTING 14.19: Custom add and remove Handlers

```
public class Thermostat
{
  public class TemperatureArgs: System.EventArgs
  {
    ...
  }

    // Define the event publisher
  public event EventHandler<TemperatureArgs> OnTemperatureChange
  {
      add
      {
        _OnTemperatureChange = (TemperatureChangeHandler)
        System.Delegate.Combine(value, _OnTemperatureChange);
      }
      remove
      {
        _OnTemperatureChange = (TemperatureChangeHandler)
        System.Delegate.Remove(_OnTemperatureChange, value);
      }
  }
  protected EventHandler<TemperatureArgs> _OnTemperatureChange;

  public float CurrentTemperature
  {
    ...
  }
  private float _CurrentTemperature;
}
```

In this case, the delegate that stores each subscriber, _OnTemperatureChange, was changed to `protected`. In addition, implementation of the add block switches around the delegate storage so that the last delegate added to the chain is the first delegate to receive a notification.

SUMMARY

Now that we have described events, it is worth mentioning that, in general, method references are the only cases where it is advisable to work with a delegate variable outside the context of an event. In other words, given the additional encapsulation features of an event and the ability to customize the implementation when necessary, the best practice is always to use events for the publish-subscribe pattern.

2.0

It may take a little practice before you can code events from scratch without referring to sample code. However, events are a critical foundation for the asynchronous, multithreaded coding of later chapters.

End 2.0

■ 15 ■
Collection Interfaces with Standard Query Operators

THE MOST SIGNIFICANT FEATURES ADDED in C# 3.0 were in collections attributable to a programming API called **Language Integrated Query (LINQ)**. Through a set of extension methods and lambda expressions, LINQ provides a far superior API for working with collections. In fact, in earlier editions of this book, the chapter on collections came immediately after the chapter on generics and just before the one on delegates. However, lambda expressions were so fundamental to LINQ that it is no longer possible to cover collections without first covering delegates (the basis of lambda expressions). Now that you have a solid foundation in lambda expressions from the preceding two chapters, we can delve into the details of collections—a topic that spans three chapters. In this chapter, the focus begins with **standard query operators**—a means of leveraging LINQ via direct invocation of extensions methods.

After introducing collection initializers, this chapter covers the various collection interfaces and explores how they relate to one another. This is the basis for understanding collections, so you should cover the material with diligence. The section on collection interfaces includes coverage of the IEnumerable<T> extension methods that were added in C# 3.0 to implement the standard query operators.

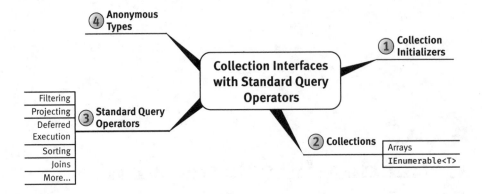

There are two categories of collection-related classes and interfaces: those that support generics and those that don't. This chapter primarily discusses the generic collection interfaces. You should use collection classes that don't support generics only when you are writing components that need to interoperate with earlier versions of the runtime. This is because everything that was available in the nongeneric form has a generic replacement that is strongly typed. Although the concepts still apply to both forms, we do not explicitly discuss the nongeneric versions.[1]

The chapter concludes with an in-depth discussion of anonymous types—topics that we covered only briefly in a few Advanced Topic sections in Chapter 3. The interesting thing about anonymous types is that they become eclipsed by C# 7.0's tuples—a topic we discuss further at the end of the chapter.

Collection Initializers

A **collection initializer** allows programmers to construct a collection with an initial set of members at instantiation time in a manner similar to array declaration. Before collection initialization was available, elements had to be explicitly added to a collection after the collection was instantiated—using something like `System.Collections.Generic`
`.ICollection<T>`'s `Add()` method. With collection initialization, the `Add()` calls are generated by the C# compiler rather than explicitly coded by the developer. Listing 15.1 shows how to initialize the collection using a collection initializer.

---

1. In fact, .NET Standards and .NET Core don't even include the nongeneric collections.

LISTING 15.1: Collection Initialization

```csharp
using System;
using System.Collections.Generic;

class Program
{
  static void Main()
  {
      List<string> sevenWorldBlunders;
      sevenWorldBlunders = new List<string>()
      {
          // Quotes from Ghandi
          "Wealth without work",
          "Pleasure without conscience",
          "Knowledge without character",
          "Commerce without morality",
          "Science without humanity",
          "Worship without sacrifice",
          "Politics without principle"
      };

      Print(sevenWorldBlunders);

  }

  private static void Print<T>(IEnumerable<T> items)
  {
      foreach (T item in items)
      {
          Console.WriteLine(item);
      }
  }
}
```

The syntax is similar not only to the array initialization but also to an object initializer with the curly braces following the constructor. If no parameters are passed in the constructor, the parentheses following the data type are optional (as they are with object initializers).

A few basic requirements are needed for a collection initializer to compile successfully. Ideally, the collection type to which a collection initializer is applied would be of a type that implements System .Collections.Generic.ICollection<T>. This ensures that the collection includes an Add() that the compiler-generated code can invoke. However, a relaxed version of the requirement also exists and simply demands that one or more Add() methods exist either as an extension method (C# 6.0) or as an instance method on a type that implements IEnumerable<T>—even if the collection doesn't implement ICollection<T>. The Add() methods

Begin 6.0

need to take parameters that are compatible with the values specified in the collection initializer.

For dictionaries, the collection initializer syntax is slightly more complex, because each element in the dictionary requires both the key and the value. This syntax is shown in Listing 15.2.

LISTING 15.2: Initializing a Dictionary<> with a Collection Initializer

```csharp
using System;
using System.Collections.Generic;
#if !PRECSHARP6
  // C# 6.0 or later
  Dictionary<string, ConsoleColor> colorMap =
      new Dictionary<string, ConsoleColor>
      {
          ["Error"] = ConsoleColor.Red,
          ["Warning"] = ConsoleColor.Yellow,
          ["Information"] = ConsoleColor.Green,
          ["Verbose"] = ConsoleColor.White
      };
#else
  // Before C# 6.0
  Dictionary<string, ConsoleColor> colorMap =
      new Dictionary<string, ConsoleColor>
      {
          { "Error", ConsoleColor.Red },
          { "Warning", ConsoleColor.Yellow },
          { "Information", ConsoleColor.Green },
          { "Verbose", ConsoleColor.White}
      };
#endif
```

This listing includes two different versions of the initialization. The first demonstrates a new syntax introduced in C# 6.0, which expresses the intent of a name/value pair by allowing the assignment operator to express which value is associated with which key. The second syntax (which still works with C# 6.0 or later) pairs the name and the value together using curly brackets.

End 6.0

Allowing initializers on collections that don't support ICollection<T> was important for two reasons. First, most collections (types that implement IEnumerable<T>) do not also implement ICollection<T>, which significantly reduces the usefulness of collection initializers. Second, matching on the method name and signature compatibility with the collection initializer items enables greater diversity in the items initialized into the collection. For example, the initializer now can support new DataStore(){ a, {b, c}} as long as there is one Add( ) method whose signature is compatible with a and a second Add( ) method whose signature is compatible with b, c.

What Makes a Class a Collection: `IEnumerable<T>`

By definition, a collection within .NET is a class that, at a minimum, implements `IEnumerable<T>` (or the nongeneric type `IEnumerable`). This interface is critical because implementing the methods of `IEnumerable<T>` is the minimum needed to support iterating over the collection.

Chapter 4 showed how to use a `foreach` statement to iterate over an array of elements. This syntax is simple and avoids the complication of having to know how many elements there are. The runtime does not directly support the `foreach` statement, however. Instead, the C# compiler transforms the code as described in this section.

foreach with Arrays

Listing 15.3 demonstrates a simple `foreach` loop iterating over an array of integers and then printing out each integer to the console.

LISTING 15.3: foreach with Arrays

```csharp
int[] array = new int[]{1, 2, 3, 4, 5, 6};

foreach (int item in array)
{
    Console.WriteLine(item);
}
```

From this code, the C# compiler creates a CIL equivalent of the `for` loop, as shown in Listing 15.4.

LISTING 15.4: Compiled Implementation of foreach with Arrays

```csharp
int[] tempArray;
int[] array = new int[]{1, 2, 3, 4, 5, 6};

tempArray = array;
for (int counter = 0; (counter < tempArray.Length); counter++)
{
    int item = tempArray[counter];

    Console.WriteLine(item);
}
```

In this example, note that foreach relies on support for the Length property and the index operator ([ ]). With the Length property, the C# compiler can use the for statement to iterate through each element in the array.

foreach with IEnumerable<T>

Although the code shown in Listing 15.4 works well on arrays where the length is fixed and the index operator is always supported, not all types of collections have a known number of elements. Furthermore, many of the collection classes, including the Stack<T>, Queue<T>, and Dictionary<Tkey, Tvalue> classes, do not support retrieving elements by index. Therefore, a more general approach of iterating over collections of elements is needed. The iterator pattern provides this capability. Assuming you can determine the first, next, and last elements, knowing the count and supporting retrieval of elements by index is unnecessary.

The System.Collections.Generic.IEnumerator<T> and nongeneric System.Collections.IEnumerator interfaces are designed to enable the iterator pattern for iterating over collections of elements, rather than the length–index pattern shown in Listing 15.4. A class diagram of their relationships appears in Figure 15.1.

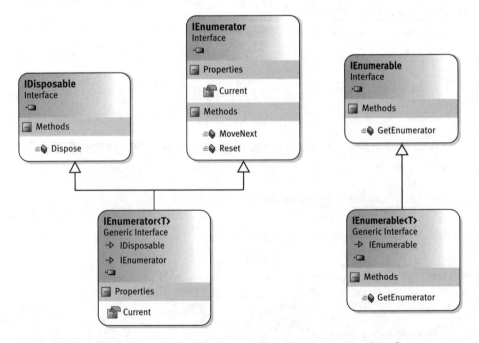

FIGURE 15.1: A Class Diagram of IEnumerator<T> and IEnumerator Interfaces

IEnumerator, which IEnumerator<T> derives from, includes three members. The first is bool MoveNext(). Using this method, you can move from one element within the collection to the next, while at the same time detecting when you have enumerated through every item. The second member, a read-only property called Current, returns the element currently in process. Current is overloaded in IEnumerator<T>, providing a type-specific implementation of it. With these two members on the collection class, it is possible to iterate over the collection simply using a while loop, as demonstrated in Listing 15.5. (The Reset() method usually throws a NotImplementedException, so it should never be called. If you need to restart an enumeration, just create a fresh enumerator.)

LISTING 15.5: Iterating over a Collection Using while

```
System.Collections.Generic.Stack<int> stack =
  new System.Collections.Generic.Stack<int>();
int number;
// ...

// This code is conceptual, not the actual code
while (stack.MoveNext())
{
  number = stack.Current;
  Console.WriteLine(number);
}
```

In Listing 15.5, the MoveNext() method returns false when it moves past the end of the collection. This replaces the need to count elements while looping.

Listing 15.5 uses a System.Collections.Generic.Stack<T> as the collection type. Numerous other collection types exist; this is just one example. The key trait of Stack<T> is its design as a last in, first out (LIFO) collection. Notice that the type parameter T identifies the type of all items within the collection. Collecting one type of object within a collection is a key characteristic of a generic collection. The programmer must know the data type within the collection when adding, removing, or accessing items within the collection.

The preceding example shows the gist of the C# compiler output, but it doesn't actually compile that way because it omits two important details concerning the implementation: interleaving and error handling.

State Is Shared

The problem with an implementation such as Listing 15.5 is that if two such loops interleaved each other—one foreach inside another, both using the same collection—the collection must maintain a state indicator of the current element so that when MoveNext() is called, the next element can be determined. In such a case, one interleaving loop can affect the other. (The same is true of loops executed by multiple threads.)

To overcome this problem, the collection classes do not support IEnumerator<T> and IEnumerator interfaces directly. As shown in Figure 15.1, there is a second interface, called IEnumerable<T>, whose only method is GetEnumerator(). The purpose of this method is to return an object that supports IEnumerator<T>. Instead of the collection class maintaining the state, a different class—usually a nested class, so that it has access to the internals of the collection—will support the IEnumerator<T> interface and will keep the state of the iteration loop. The enumerator is like a "cursor" or a "bookmark" in the sequence. You can have multiple bookmarks, and moving each of them enumerates over the collection independently of the other. Using this pattern, the C# equivalent of a foreach loop will look like the code shown in Listing 15.6.

LISTING 15.6: A Separate Enumerator Maintaining State during an Iteration

```
System.Collections.Generic.Stack<int> stack =
  new System.Collections.Generic.Stack<int>();
int number;
System.Collections.Generic.Stack<int>.Enumerator
  enumerator;

// ...

// If IEnumerable<T> is implemented explicitly,
// then a cast is required:
// ((IEnumerable<int>)stack).GetEnumerator();
enumerator = stack.GetEnumerator();
while (enumerator.MoveNext())
{
  number = enumerator.Current;
  Console.WriteLine(number);
}
```

■ ADVANCED TOPIC

Cleaning Up Following Iteration

Given that the classes that implement the IEnumerator<T> interface maintain the state, sometimes you need to clean up the state after it exits the loop (because either all iterations have completed or an exception is thrown). To achieve this, the IEnumerator<T> interface derives from IDisposable. Enumerators that implement IEnumerator do not necessarily implement IDisposable, but if they do, Dispose() will be called as well. This enables the calling of Dispose() after the foreach loop exits. The C# equivalent of the final Common Intermediate Language (CIL) code, therefore, looks like Listing 15.7.

LISTING 15.7: **Compiled Result of foreach on Collections**

```csharp
System.Collections.Generic.Stack<int> stack =
  new System.Collections.Generic.Stack<int>();
System.Collections.Generic.Stack<int>.Enumerator
  enumerator;
IDisposable disposable;

enumerator = stack.GetEnumerator();
try
{
  int number;
  while (enumerator.MoveNext())
  {
      number = enumerator.Current;
      Console.WriteLine(number);
  }
}
finally
{
  // Explicit cast used for IEnumerator<T>
  disposable = (IDisposable) enumerator;
  disposable.Dispose();

  // IEnumerator will use the as operator unless IDisposable
  // support is known at compile time
  // disposable = (enumerator as IDisposable);
  // if (disposable != null)
  // {
  //     disposable.Dispose();
  // }
}
```

Notice that because the IDisposable interface is supported by IEnumerator<T>, the using statement can simplify the code in Listing 15.7 to that shown in Listing 15.8.

LISTING 15.8: Error Handling and Resource Cleanup with using

```
System.Collections.Generic.Stack<int> stack =
  new System.Collections.Generic.Stack<int>();
int number;

using(
  System.Collections.Generic.Stack<int>.Enumerator
    enumerator = stack.GetEnumerator())
{
  while (enumerator.MoveNext())
  {
    number = enumerator.Current;
    Console.WriteLine(number);
  }
}
```

However, recall that the CIL does not directly support the using keyword. Thus the code in Listing 15.7 is actually a more accurate C# representation of the foreach CIL code.

■ ADVANCED TOPIC

foreach without IEnumerable

C# doesn't require that IEnumerable/IEnumerable<T> be implemented to iterate over a data type using foreach. Rather, the compiler uses a concept known as **duck typing**; it looks for a GetEnumerator() method that returns a type with a Current property and MoveNext() method. Duck typing involves searching by name rather than relying on an interface or explicit method call to the method. (The name "duck typing" comes from the whimsical idea that to be treated as a duck, the object must merely implement a Quack() method; it need not implement an IDuck interface.) If duck typing fails to find a suitable implementation of the enumerable pattern, the compiler checks whether the collection implements the interfaces.

Do Not Modify Collections during foreach Iteration

Chapter 4 showed that the compiler prevents assignment of the foreach variable (number). As is demonstrated in Listing 15.7, an assignment to number would not be a change to the collection element itself, so the C# compiler prevents such an assignment altogether.

In addition, neither the element count within a collection nor the items themselves can generally be modified during the execution of a foreach loop. If, for example, you called stack.Push(42) inside the foreach loop, it would be ambiguous whether the iterator should ignore or incorporate the change to stack—in other words, whether iterator should iterate over the newly added item or ignore it and assume the same state as when it was instantiated.

Because of this ambiguity, an exception of type System .InvalidOperationException is generally thrown upon accessing the enumerator if the collection is modified within a foreach loop, reporting that the collection was modified after the enumerator was instantiated.

Standard Query Operators

Begin 3.0

Besides the methods on System.Object, any type that implements IEnumerable<T> is required to implement only one other method, GetEnumerator(). Yet, doing so makes more than 50 methods available to all types implementing IEnumerable<T>, not including any overloading— and this happens without needing to explicitly implement any method except the GetEnumerator() method. The additional functionality is provided through C# 3.0's extension methods and resides in the class System.Linq.Enumerable. Therefore, including the using declarative for System.Linq is all it takes to make these methods available.

Each method on IEnumerable<T> is a **standard query operator**; it provides querying capability over the collection on which it operates. In the following sections, we examine some of the most prominent of these standard query operators. Many of these examples will depend on an Inventor and/or Patent class, both of which are defined in Listing 15.9.

LISTING 15.9: Sample Classes for Use with Standard Query Operators

```csharp
using System;
using System.Collections.Generic;
using System.Linq;

public class Patent
{
  // Title of the published application
  public string Title { get; set; }

  // The date the application was officially published
  public string YearOfPublication { get; set; }

  // A unique number assigned to published applications
  public string ApplicationNumber { get; set; }

  public long[] InventorIds { get; set; }

  public override string ToString()
  {
      return $"{ Title } ({ YearOfPublication })";
  }
}

public class Inventor
{
  public long Id { get; set; }
  public string Name { get; set; }
  public string City { get; set; }
  public string State { get; set; }
  public string Country { get; set; }

  public override string ToString()
  {
      return $"{ Name } ({ City }, { State })";
  }
}

class Program
{
  static void Main()
  {
    IEnumerable<Patent> patents = PatentData.Patents;
    Print(patents);

    Console.WriteLine();

    IEnumerable<Inventor> inventors = PatentData.Inventors;
    Print(inventors);
  }
```

3.0

```csharp
    private static void Print<T>(IEnumerable<T> items)
    {
        foreach (T item in items)
        {
            Console.WriteLine(item);
        }
    }
}

public static class PatentData
{
    public static readonly Inventor[] Inventors = new Inventor[]
        {
            new Inventor(){
                Name="Benjamin Franklin", City="Philadelphia",
                State="PA", Country="USA", Id=1 },
            new Inventor(){
                Name="Orville Wright", City="Kitty Hawk",
                State="NC", Country="USA", Id=2},
            new Inventor(){
                Name="Wilbur Wright", City="Kitty Hawk",
                State="NC", Country="USA", Id=3},
            new Inventor(){
                Name="Samuel Morse", City="New York",
                State="NY", Country="USA", Id=4},
            new Inventor(){
                Name="George Stephenson", City="Wylam",
                State="Northumberland", Country="UK", Id=5},
            new Inventor(){
                Name="John Michaelis", City="Chicago",
                State="IL", Country="USA", Id=6},
            new Inventor(){
                Name="Mary Phelps Jacob", City="New York",
                State="NY", Country="USA", Id=7},
        };

    public static readonly Patent[] Patents = new Patent[]
        {
            new Patent(){
                Title="Bifocals", YearOfPublication="1784",
                InventorIds=new long[] {1}},
            new Patent(){
                Title="Phonograph", YearOfPublication="1877",
                InventorIds=new long[] {1}},
            new Patent(){
                Title="Kinetoscope", YearOfPublication="1888",
                InventorIds=new long[] {1}},
            new Patent(){
                Title="Electrical Telegraph",
                YearOfPublication="1837",
                InventorIds=new long[] {4}},
```

3.0

```
            new Patent(){
                Title="Flying Machine", YearOfPublication="1903",
                InventorIds=new long[] {2,3}},
            new Patent(){
                Title="Steam Locomotive",
                YearOfPublication="1815",
                InventorIds=new long[] {5}},
            new Patent(){
                Title="Droplet Deposition Apparatus",
                YearOfPublication="1989",
                InventorIds=new long[] {6}},
            new Patent(){
                Title="Backless Brassiere",
                YearOfPublication="1914",
                InventorIds=new long[] {7}},
        };
    }
```

Listing 15.9 also provides a selection of sample data. Output 15.1 displays the results of running this code.

OUTPUT 15.1

```
Bifocals (1784)
Phonograph (1877)
Kinetoscope (1888)
Electrical Telegraph (1837)
Flying Machine (1903)
Steam Locomotive (1815)
Droplet Deposition Apparatus (1989)
Backless Brassiere (1914)

Benjamin Franklin (Philadelphia, PA)
Orville Wright (Kitty Hawk, NC)
Wilbur Wright (Kitty Hawk, NC)
Samuel Morse (New York, NY)
George Stephenson (Wylam, Northumberland)
John Michaelis (Chicago, IL)
Mary Phelps Jacob (New York, NY)
```

3.0

Filtering with Where()

To filter out data from a collection, we need to provide a filter method that returns true or false, indicating whether or not a particular element should be included. A delegate expression that takes an argument and returns a Boolean is called a **predicate**, and a collection's Where() method depends on predicates for identifying filter criteria, as shown in Listing 15.10. (Technically, the result of the Where() method is an **object** that encapsulates the operation of filtering a given sequence with a given predicate.) The results appear in Output 15.2.

LISTING 15.10: Filtering with System.Linq.Enumerable.Where( )

```csharp
using System;
using System.Collections.Generic;
using System.Linq;

class Program
{
  static void Main()
  {
      IEnumerable<Patent> patents = PatentData.Patents;
      patents = patents.Where(
          patent => patent.YearOfPublication.StartsWith("18"));
      Print(patents);
  }

  // ...
}
```

OUTPUT 15.2

```
Phonograph (1877)
Kinetoscope (1888)
Electrical Telegraph (1837)
Steam Locomotive (1815)
```

Notice that the code assigns the output of the Where( ) call back to IEnumerable<T>. In other words, the output of IEnumerable<T>.Where( ) is a new IEnumerable<T> collection. In Listing 15.10, it is IEnumerable<Patent>.

Less obvious is that the Where( ) expression argument has not necessarily been executed at assignment time. This is true for many of the standard query operators. In the case of Where( ), for example, the expression is passed in to the collection and "saved" but not executed. Instead, execution of the expression occurs only when it is necessary to begin iterating over the items within the collection. A foreach loop, for example, such as the one in Print( ) (in Listing 15.9), will trigger the expression to be evaluated for each item within the collection. At least conceptually, the Where( ) method should be understood as a means of specifying the query regarding what appears in the collection, not the actual work involved with iterating over to produce a new collection with potentially fewer items.

3.0

Projecting with Select()

Since the output from the IEnumerable<T>.Where() method is a new IEnumerable<T> collection, it is possible to again call a standard query operator on the same collection. For example, rather than just filtering the data from the original collection, we could transform the data (see Listing 15.11).

LISTING 15.11: Projection with System.Linq.Enumerable.Select()

```csharp
using System;
using System.Collections.Generic;
using System.Linq;

class Program
{
  static void Main()
  {
      IEnumerable<Patent> patents = PatentData.Patents;
      IEnumerable<Patent> patentsOf1800 = patents.Where(
          patent => patent.YearOfPublication.StartsWith("18"));
      IEnumerable<string> items = patentsOf1800.Select(
          patent => patent.ToString());

      Print(items);
  }

  // ...
}
```

In Listing 15.11, we create a new IEnumerable<string> collection. In this case, it just so happens that adding the Select() call doesn't change the output—but this is only because Print()'s Console.WriteLine() call used ToString() anyway. Obviously, a transform still occurred on each item from the Patent type of the original collection to the string type of the items collection.

Consider the example using System.IO.FileInfo in Listing 15.12.

LISTING 15.12: Projection with System.Linq.Enumerable.Select() and new

```csharp
// ...
IEnumerable<string> fileList = Directory.GetFiles(
    rootDirectory, searchPattern);
IEnumerable<FileInfo> files = fileList.Select(
    file => new FileInfo(file));
// ...
```

Here fileList is of type IEnumerable<string>. However, using the projection offered by Select, we can transform each item in the collection to a System.IO.FileInfo object.

Lastly, capitalizing on tuples, we could create an IEnumerable<T> collection where T is a tuple (see Listing 15.13 and Output 15.3).

LISTING 15.13: Projection to Tuple

```
// ...
IEnumerable<string> fileList = Directory.EnumerateFiles(
    rootDirectory, searchPattern);
IEnumerable<(string FileName, long Size)> items = fileList.Select(
    file =>
    {
        FileInfo fileInfo = new FileInfo(file);
        return (
            FileName: fileInfo.Name,
            Size: fileInfo.Length
        );
    });
// ...
```

OUTPUT 15.3

```
FileName = AssemblyInfo.cs, Size = 1704
FileName = CodeAnalysisRules.xml, Size = 735
FileName = CustomDictionary.xml, Size = 199
FileName = EssentialCSharp.sln, Size = 40415
FileName = EssentialCSharp.suo, Size = 454656
FileName = EssentialCSharp.vsmdi, Size = 499
FileName = EssentialCSharp.vssscc, Size = 256
FileName = intelliTechture.ConsoleTester.dll, Size = 24576
FileName = intelliTechture.ConsoleTester.pdb, Size = 30208
```

The output of an anonymous type automatically shows the property names and their values as part of the generated ToString() method associated with the anonymous type.

Projection using the Select() method is very powerful. We already saw how to filter a collection vertically (reducing the number of items in the collection) using the Where() standard query operator. Now, via the Select() standard query operator, we can also reduce the collection horizontally (making fewer columns) or transform the data entirely. In combination, Where() and Select() provide a means for extracting only those pieces of the original collection that are desirable for the current algorithm. These two methods alone provide a powerful collection manipulation API that would otherwise result in significantly more code that is less readable.

3.0

■ ADVANCED TOPIC

Running LINQ Queries in Parallel

With the abundance of computers having multiple processors and multiple cores within those processors, the ability to easily take advantage of the additional processing power becomes far more important. To do so, programs need to be changed to support multiple threads so that work can happen simultaneously on different CPUs within the computer. Listing 15.14 demonstrates one way to do this using Parallel LINQ (PLINQ).

LISTING 15.14: Executing LINQ Queries in Parallel

```
// ...
IEnumerable<string> fileList = Directory.EnumerageFiles(
    rootDirectory, searchPattern);
var items = fileList.AsParallel().Select(
    file =>
    {
        FileInfo fileInfo = new FileInfo(file);
        return new
        {
            FileName = fileInfo.Name,
            Size = fileInfo.Length
        };
    });
// ...
```

As Listing 15.14 shows, the change in code to enable parallel support is minimal. All that it uses is a Microsoft .NET Framework 4–introduced standard query operator, `AsParallel()`, on the static class `System.Linq .ParallelEnumerable`. Using this simple extension method, however, the runtime begins executing over the items within the `fileList` collection and returning the resultant objects in parallel. Each parallel operation in this case isn't particularly expensive (although it is relative to the other execution taking place), but consider CPU-intensive operations such as encryption or compression. Running the query in parallel across multiple CPUs can decrease execution time by a factor corresponding to the number of CPUs.

An important caveat to be aware of (and the reason why `AsParallel()` appears as an Advanced Topic rather than in the standard text) is that parallel execution can introduce race conditions, such that an operation on one thread can be intermingled with an operation on a different thread, causing data corruption. To avoid this problem, synchronization mechanisms are required on data with shared access from multiple threads to force the operations to be atomic where necessary. Synchronization itself, however, can introduce deadlocks that freeze the execution, further complicating the effective parallel programming.

More details on this and additional multithreading topics are provided in Chapters 19 and 20.

End 4.0

Counting Elements with Count()

Another query frequently performed on a collection of items is to retrieve the count. To support this type of query, LINQ includes the Count() extension method.

Listing 15.15 demonstrates that Count() is overloaded to simply count all elements (no parameters) or to take a predicate that counts only items identified by the predicate expression.

LISTING 15.15: Counting Items with Count()

```
using System;
using System.Collections.Generic;
using System.Linq;

class Program
{
  static void Main()
  {
      IEnumerable<Patent> patents = PatentData.Patents;
      Console.WriteLine($"Patent Count: { patents.Count() }");
      Console.WriteLine($@"Patent Count in 1800s: {
          patents.Count(patent =>
              patent.YearOfPublication.StartsWith("18"))
      }");
  }

  // ...
}
```

3.0

In spite of the apparent simplicity of the Count() statement, IEnumerable<T> has not changed, so the executed code still iterates over all the items in the collection. Whenever a Count property is directly available on the collection, it is preferable to use that rather than LINQ's Count() method (a subtle difference). Fortunately, ICollection<T> includes the Count property, so code that calls the Count() method on a collection that supports ICollection<T> will cast the collection and call Count directly. However, if ICollection<T> is not supported,

`Enumerable.Count()` will proceed to enumerate all the items in the collection rather than call the built-in `Count` mechanism. If the purpose of checking the count is just to see whether it is greater than zero (`if(patents.Count() > 0){...}`), the preferable approach would be to use the `Any()` operator (`if(patents.Any()){...}`). `Any()` attempts to iterate over only one of the items in the collection to return a true result, rather than iterating over the entire sequence.

Guidelines

DO use `System.Linq.Enumerable.Any()` rather than calling `patents.Count()` when checking if there are more than zero items.

DO use a collection's Count property (if available) in favor of calling the `System.Linq.Enumerable.Count()` method.

Deferred Execution

One of the most important concepts to remember when using LINQ is deferred execution. Consider the code in Listing 15.16 and the corresponding output in Output 15.4.

LISTING 15.16: Filtering with System.Linq.Enumerable.Where( )

```
using System;
using System.Collections.Generic;
using System.Linq;

// ...

    IEnumerable<Patent> patents = PatentData.Patents;
    bool result;
    patents = patents.Where(
        patent =>
        {
            if (result =
                patent.YearOfPublication.StartsWith("18"))
            {
                // Side effects like this in a predicate
                // are used here to demonstrate a
                // principle and should generally be
                // avoided
                Console.WriteLine("\t" + patent);
            }
            return result;
        });
```

3.0

```
Console.WriteLine("1. Patents prior to the 1900s are:");
foreach (Patent patent in patents)
{
}

Console.WriteLine();
Console.WriteLine(
    "2. A second listing of patents prior to the 1900s:");
Console.WriteLine(
    $@"    There are { patents.Count()
        } patents prior to 1900.");

Console.WriteLine();
Console.WriteLine(
    "3. A third listing of patents prior to the 1900s:");
patents = patents.ToArray();
Console.Write("    There are ");
Console.WriteLine(
    $"{ patents.Count() } patents prior to 1900.");

// ...
```

OUTPUT 15.4

```
1. Patents prior to the 1900s are:
        Phonograph (1877)
        Kinetoscope (1888)
        Electrical Telegraph (1837)
        Steam Locomotive (1815)

2. A second listing of patents prior to the 1900s:
        Phonograph (1877)
        Kinetoscope (1888)
        Electrical Telegraph (1837)
        Steam Locomotive (1815)
    There are 4 patents prior to 1900.

3. A third listing of patents prior to the 1900s:
        Phonograph (1877)
        Kinetoscope (1888)
        Electrical Telegraph (1837)
        Steam Locomotive (1815)
    There are 4 patents prior to 1900.
```

Notice that Console.WriteLine("1. Patents prior...) executes
before the lambda expression. This is a very important characteristic to
pay attention to because it is not obvious to those who are unaware of its
importance. In general, predicates should do exactly one thing—evaluate a
condition—and they should not have any side effects (even printing to the
console, as in this example).

3.0

To understand what is happening, recall that lambda expressions are delegates—references to methods—that can be passed around. In the context of LINQ and standard query operators, each lambda expression forms part of the overall query to be executed.

At the time of declaration, lambda expressions are not executed. In fact, it isn't until the lambda expressions are invoked that the code within them begins to execute. Figure 15.2 shows the sequence of operations.

As Figure 15.2 shows, three calls in Listing 15.14 trigger the lambda expression, and each time it is fairly implicit. If the lambda expression were expensive (such as a call to a database), it would therefore be important to minimize the lambda expression's execution.

First, the execution is triggered within the foreach loop. As we described earlier in the chapter, the foreach loop breaks down into a MoveNext() call, and each call results in the lambda expression's execution for each item in the original collection. While iterating, the runtime invokes the lambda expression for each item to determine whether the item satisfies the predicate.

Second, a call to Enumerable's Count() (the function) triggers the lambda expression for each item once more. Again, this is subtle behavior because Count (the property) is very common on collections that have not been queried with a standard query operator.

Third, the call to ToArray() (or ToList(), ToDictionary(), or ToLookup()) triggers the lambda expression for each item. However, converting the collection with one of these "To" methods is extremely helpful. Doing so returns a collection on which the standard query operator has already executed. In Listing 15.14, the conversion to an array means that when Length is called in the final Console.WriteLine(), the underlying object pointed to by patents is, in fact, an array (which obviously implements IEnumerable<T>); in turn, System.Array's implementation of Length is called and not System.Linq.Enumerable's implementation. Consequently, following a conversion to one of the collection types returned by a To method, it is generally safe to work with the collection (until another standard query operator is called). However, be aware that this will bring the entire result set into memory (it may have been backed by a database or file prior to this step). Furthermore, the To method will take a snapshot of the underlying data, such that no fresh results will be returned upon requerying the To method result.

3.0

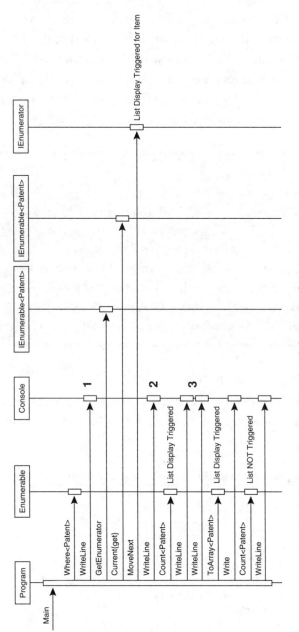

FIGURE 15.2: Sequence of Operations Invoking Lambda Expressions

3.0

We strongly encourage you to review the sequence diagram in Figure 15.2 along with the corresponding code and recognize that the deferred execution of standard query operators can result in extremely subtle triggering of the standard query operators; therefore, developers should use caution and seek to avoid unexpected calls. The query object represents the query, not the results. When you ask the query for the results, the whole query executes (perhaps even again) because the query object doesn't know that the results will be the same as they were during a previous execution (if one existed).

> **■ NOTE**
>
> To avoid such repeated execution, you must cache the data that the executed query retrieves. To do so, you assign the data to a local collection using one of the To collection methods. During the assignment call of a To method, the query obviously executes. However, iterating over the assigned collection after that point will not involve the query expression any further. In general, if you want the behavior of an in-memory collection snapshot, it is a best practice to assign a query expression to a cached collection to avoid unnecessary iterations.

Sorting with OrderBy( ) and ThenBy( )

Another common operation on a collection is to sort it. Sorting involves a call to `System.Linq.Enumerable`'s `OrderBy( )`, as shown in Listing 15.17 and Output 15.5.

LISTING 15.17: Ordering with System.Linq.Enumerable.OrderBy( )/ThenBy( )

```
using System;
using System.Collections.Generic;
using System.Linq;

// ...

    IEnumerable<Patent> items;
    Patent[] patents = PatentData.Patents;
    items = patents.OrderBy(
        patent => patent.YearOfPublication).ThenBy(
        patent => patent.Title);
    Print(items);
    Console.WriteLine();
```

3.0

```
items = patents.OrderByDescending(
    patent => patent.YearOfPublication).ThenByDescending(
    patent => patent.Title);
Print(items);
```

```
// ...
```

OUTPUT 15.5

```
Bifocals (1784)
Steam Locomotive (1815)
Electrical Telegraph (1837)
Phonograph (1877)
Kinetoscope (1888)
Flying Machine (1903)
Backless Brassiere (1914)
Droplet Deposition Apparatus (1989)

Droplet Deposition Apparatus (1989)
Backless Brassiere (1914)
Flying Machine (1903)
Kinetoscope (1888)
Phonograph (1877)
Electrical Telegraph (1837)
Steam Locomotive (1815)
Bifocals (1784)
```

The OrderBy() call takes a lambda expression that identifies the key on which to sort. In Listing 15.17, the initial sort uses the year that the patent was published.

However, notice that the OrderBy() call takes only a single parameter, which uses the name keySelector, to sort on. To sort on a second column, it is necessary to use a different method: ThenBy(). Similarly, code would use ThenBy() for any additional sorting.

OrderBy() returns an IOrderedEnumerable<T> interface, not an IEnumerable<T>. Furthermore, IOrderedEnumerable<T> derives from IEnumerable<T>, so all the standard query operators (including OrderBy()) are available on the OrderBy() return. However, repeated calls to OrderBy() would undo the work of the previous call such that the end result would sort by only the keySelector in the final OrderBy() call. For this reason, you should be careful not to call OrderBy() on a previous OrderBy() call.

Instead, you should specify additional sorting criteria using ThenBy(). Although ThenBy() is an extension method, it is not an extension of

3.0

IEnumerable<T> but rather of IOrderedEnumerable<T>. The method, also defined on System.Linq.Extensions.Enumerable, is declared as follows:

```
public static IOrderedEnumerable<TSource>
    ThenBy<TSource, TKey>(
        this IOrderedEnumerable<TSource> source,
        Func<TSource, TKey> keySelector)
```

In summary, use OrderBy() first, followed by zero or more calls to ThenBy() to provide additional sorting "columns." The methods OrderByDescending() and ThenByDescending() provide the same functionality except with descending order. Mixing and matching ascending and descending methods is not a problem, but if sorting further, use a ThenBy() call (either ascending or descending).

Two more important notes about sorting are warranted. First, the actual sort doesn't occur until you begin to access the members in the collection, at which point the entire query is processed. You can't sort unless you have all the items to sort, because you can't determine whether you have the first item. The fact that sorting is delayed until you begin to access the members is due to deferred execution, as we describe earlier in this chapter. Second, each subsequent call to sort the data (e.g., Orderby() followed by ThenBy() followed by ThenByDescending()) does involve additional calls to the keySelector lambda expression of the earlier sorting calls. In other words, a call to OrderBy() will call its corresponding keySelector lambda expression once you iterate over the collection. Furthermore, a subsequent call to ThenBy() will again make calls to OrderBy()'s keySelector.

Guidelines

DO NOT call an OrderBy() following a prior OrderBy() method call. Use ThenBy() to sequence items by more than one value.

■ **BEGINNER TOPIC**

Join Operations

Consider two collections of objects as shown in the Venn diagram in Figure 15.3. The left circle in the diagram includes all inventors, and the right circle contains all patents. The intersection includes both inventors and patents, and a line is formed for each case where there is a match of inventors to patents. As the diagram shows, each inventor may have multiple patents and each patent can have one or more inventors. Each patent has an inventor, but in some cases inventors do not yet have patents.

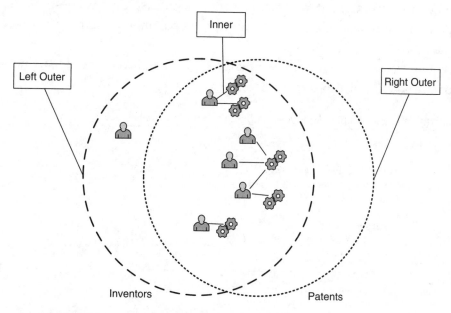

FIGURE 15.3: Venn Diagram of Inventor and Patent Collections

Matching up inventors within the intersection to patents is an **inner join**. The result is a collection of inventor/patent pairs in which both patents and inventions exist for a pair. A **left outer join** includes all the items within the left circle regardless of whether they have a corresponding patent. In this particular example, a **right outer join** would be the same as an inner join because there are no patents without inventors. Furthermore, the designation of left versus right is arbitrary, so there is really no distinction between left and outer joins. A **full outer join**, however, would include records from both outer sides; it is relatively rare to perform a full outer join.

Another important characteristic in the relationship between inventors and patents is that it is a **many-to-many** relationship. Each individual patent can have one or more inventors (e.g., the flying machine's invention by both Orville and Wilbur Wright). Furthermore, each inventor can have one or more patents (e.g., Benjamin Franklin's invention of both bifocals and the phonograph).

Another common relationship is a **one-to-many** relationship. For example, a company department may have many employees. However, each employee can belong to only one department at a time. (However, as is common with one-to-many relationships, adding the factor of time can transform them into many-to-many relationships. A particular employee may move from one department to another so that, over time, she could potentially be associated with multiple departments, making another many-to-many relationship.)

Listing 15.18 provides a sample listing of employee and department data, and Output 15.6 shows the results.

LISTING 15.18: Sample Employee and Department Data

```
public class Department
{
    public long Id { get; set; }
    public string Name { get; set; }
    public override string ToString()
    {
        return Name;
    }
}
```

```
public class Employee
{
    public int Id { get; set; }
    public string Name { get; set; }
    public string Title { get; set; }
    public int DepartmentId { get; set; }
    public override string ToString()
    {
        return $"{ Name } ({ Title })";
    }
}
```

```
public static class CorporateData
{
    public static readonly Department[] Departments =
        new Department[]
    {
        new Department(){
            Name="Corporate", Id=0},
        new Department(){
            Name="Human Resources", Id=1},
        new Department(){
            Name="Engineering", Id=2},
        new Department(){
            Name="Information Technology",
            Id=3},
```

3.0

```csharp
        new Department(){
            Name="Philanthropy",
            Id=4},
        new Department(){
            Name="Marketing",
            Id=5},
    };

    public static readonly Employee[] Employees = new Employee[]
        {
        new Employee(){
            Name="Mark Michaelis",
            Title="Chief Computer Nerd",
            DepartmentId = 0},
        new Employee(){
            Name="Michael Stokesbary",
            Title="Senior Computer Wizard",
            DepartmentId=2},
        new Employee(){
            Name="Brian Jones",
            Title="Enterprise Integration Guru",
            DepartmentId=2},
        new Employee(){
            Name="Anne Beard",
            Title="HR Director",
            DepartmentId=1},
        new Employee(){
            Name="Pat Dever",
            Title="Enterprise Architect",
            DepartmentId = 3},
        new Employee(){
            Name="Kevin Bost",
            Title="Programmer Extraordinaire",
            DepartmentId = 2},
        new Employee(){
            Name="Thomas Heavey",
            Title="Software Architect",
            DepartmentId = 2},
        new Employee(){
            Name="Eric Edmonds",
            Title="Philanthropy Coordinator",
            DepartmentId = 4}
    };
}


class Program
{
    static void Main()
    {
        IEnumerable<Department> departments =
            CorporateData.Departments;
        Print(departments);
```

3.0

```
                Console.WriteLine();

                IEnumerable<Employee> employees =
                    CorporateData.Employees;
                Print(employees);
        }

        private static void Print<T>(IEnumerable<T> items)
        {
            foreach (T item in items)
            {
                Console.WriteLine(item);
            }
        }
    }
}
```

OUTPUT 15.6

```
Corporate
Human Resources
Engineering
Information Technology
Philanthropy
Marketing

Mark Michaelis (Chief Computer Nerd)
Michael Stokesbary (Senior Computer Wizard)
Brian Jones (Enterprise Integration Guru)
Anne Beard (HR Director)
Pat Dever (Enterprise Architect)
Kevin Bost (Programmer Extraordinaire)
Thomas Heavey (Software Architect)
Eric Edmonds (Philanthropy Coordinator)
```

We use this data in the example in the following section on joining data.

Begin 7.0

Performing an Inner Join with Join( )

3.0

In the world of objects on the client side, relationships between objects are generally already set up. For example, the relationship between files and the directories in which they reside are preestablished with the DirectoryInfo.GetFiles( ) method and the FileInfo.Directory method, respectively. Frequently, however, this is not the case with data being loaded from nonobject stores. Instead, the data needs to be joined together so that you can navigate from one type of object to the next in a way that makes sense for the data.

Consider the example of employees and company departments. In Listing 15.19, we join each employee to his or her department and then list each employee with his or her corresponding department. Since each employee belongs to only one (and exactly one) department, the total number of items in the list is equal to the total number of employees—each employee appears only once (each employee is said to be **normalized**). Output 15.7 shows the results.

LISTING 15.19: An Inner Join Using System.Linq.Enumerable.Join()

```
using System;
using System.Linq;

// ...

        Department[] departments = CorporateData.Departments;
        Employee[] employees = CorporateData.Employees;

        IEnumerable<(int Id, string Name, string Title, Department
    Department)> items =
                employees.Join(
                    departments,
                    employee => employee.DepartmentId,
                    department => department.Id,
                    (employee, department) => (
                        employee.Id,
                        employee.Name,
                        employee.Title,
                        department
                    ));

        foreach (var item in items)
        {
            Console.WriteLine(
                $"{ item.Name } ({ item.Title })");
            Console.WriteLine("\t" + item.Department);
        }

    // ...
```

OUTPUT 15.7

```
Mark Michaelis (Chief Computer Nerd)
        Corporate
Michael Stokesbary (Senior Computer Wizard)
        Engineering
Brian Jones (Enterprise Integration Guru)
        Engineering
Anne Beard (HR Director)
        Human Resources
```

continues

OUTPUT 15.7 *continued*

```
Pat Dever (Enterprise Architect)
        Information Technology
Kevin Bost (Programmer Extraordinaire)
        Engineering
Thomas Heavey (Software Architect)
        Engineering
Eric Edmonds (Philanthropy Coordinator)
        Philanthropy
```

The first parameter for `Join()` has the name `inner`. It specifies the collection, `departments`, that `employees` joins to. The next two parameters are lambda expressions that specify how the two collections will connect. `employee => employee.DepartmentId` (with a parameter name of `outerKeySelector`) identifies that on each employee, the key will be `DepartmentId`. The next lambda expression (`department => department.Id`) specifies the `Department`'s `Id` property as the key—in other words, for each employee, join a department where `employee.DepartmentId` equals `department.Id`. The last parameter is the resultant item that is selected. In this case, it is a tuple with `Employee`'s `Id`, `Name`, and `Title` as well as a `Department` property with the joined department object.

Notice in the output that *Engineering* appears multiple times—once for each employee in `CorporateData`. In this case, the `Join()` call produces a **Cartesian product** between all the departments and all the employees such that a new record is created for every case where a record exists in both collections and the specified department IDs are the same. This type of join is an **inner join**.

The data could also be joined in reverse, such that `department` joins to each employee to list each department-to-employee match. Notice that the output includes more records than there are departments: There are multiple employees for each department, and the output is a record for each match. As we saw before, the Engineering department appears multiple times, once for each employee.

The code in Listing 15.20 (which produces Output 15.8) is similar to that in Listing 15.19, except that the objects, `Departments` and `Employees`, are reversed. The first parameter to `Join()` is `employees`, indicating what `departments` joins to. The next two parameters are lambda expressions that specify how the two collections will connect: `department => department.Id` for departments and `employee => employee.DepartmentId` for employees. As before, a join occurs whenever department.Id equals employee.EmployeeId. The final tuple parameter specifies a class with int Id, string Name, and Employee Employee items. (Specifying the names in the expression is optional but used here for clarity.)

7.0

LISTING 15.20: Another Inner Join with System.Linq.Enumerable.Join()

```csharp
using System;
using System.Linq;

// ...

    Department[] departments = CorporateData.Departments;
    Employee[] employees = CorporateData.Employees;

    IEnumerable<(long Id, string Name, Employee Employee)> items =
        departments.Join(
            employees,
            department => department.Id,
            employee => employee.DepartmentId,
            (department, employee) => (
                department.Id,
                department.Name,
                employee
            ));

    foreach (var item in items)
    {
        Console.WriteLine(item.Name);
        Console.WriteLine("\t" + item.Employee);
    }

// ...
```

OUTPUT 15.8

```
Corporate
        Mark Michaelis (Chief Computer Nerd)
Human Resources
        Anne Beard (HR Director)
Engineering
        Michael Stokesbary (Senior Computer Wizard)
Engineering
        Brian Jones (Enterprise Integration Guru)
Engineering
        Kevin Bost (Programmer Extraordinaire)
Engineering
        Thomas Heavey (Software Architect)
Information Technology
        Pat Dever (Enterprise Architect)
Philanthropy
        Eric Edmonds (Philanthropy Coordinator)
```

3.0

Grouping Results with GroupBy( )

7.0

In addition to ordering and joining a collection of objects, frequently you might want to group objects with like characteristics. For the employee data, you might want to group employees by department, region, job title, and so forth. Listing 15.21 shows an example of how to do this with the GroupBy( ) standard query operator (see Output 15.9 to view the output).

LISTING 15.21: Grouping Items Using System.Linq.Enumerable.GroupBy( )

```csharp
using System;
using System.Linq;

// ...

    IEnumerable<Employee> employees = CorporateData.Employees;

    IEnumerable<IGrouping<int, Employee>> groupedEmployees =
        employees.GroupBy((employee) => employee.DepartmentId);

    foreach(IGrouping<int, Employee> employeeGroup in
        groupedEmployees)
    {
        Console.WriteLine();
        foreach(Employee employee in employeeGroup)
        {
            Console.WriteLine("\t" + employee);
        }
        Console.WriteLine(
          "\tCount: " + employeeGroup.Count());
    }
// ...
```

OUTPUT 15.9

3.0

```
Mark Michaelis (Chief Computer Nerd)
    Count: 1

Michael Stokesbary (Senior Computer Wizard)
Brian Jones (Enterprise Integration Guru)
Kevin Bost (Programmer Extraordinaire)
Thomas Heavey (Software Architect)
    Count: 4

Anne Beard (HR Director)
    Count: 1

Pat Dever (Enterprise Architect)
    Count: 1

Eric Edmonds (Philanthropy Coordinator)
    Count: 1
```

Note that the items output from a GroupBy() call are of type IGrouping<TKey, TElement>, which has a property for the key that the query is grouping on (employee.DepartmentId). However, it does not have a property for the items within the group. Rather, IGrouping<TKey, TElement> derives from IEnumerable<T>, allowing for enumeration of the items within the group using a foreach statement or for aggregating the data into something such as a count of items (employeeGroup.Count()).

Implementing a One-to-Many Relationship with GroupJoin()

Listings 15.19 and 15.20 are virtually identical. Either Join() call could have produced the same output just by changing the tuple definition. When trying to create a list of employees, Listing 15.19 provides the correct result. Department ends up as an item of both tuples representing the joined employee. However, Listing 15.20 is not ideal. Given support for collections, a preferable representation of a department would have a collection of employees rather than a single tuple for each department–employee relationship. Listing 15.22 demonstrates; Output 15.10 shows the preferred output.

LISTING 15.22: Creating a Child Collection with System.Linq.Enumerable.GroupJoin()

```
using System;
using System.Linq;

// ...

    Department[] departments = CorporateData.Departments;
    Employee[] employees = CorporateData.Employees;

    IEnumerable<(long Id, string Name, IEnumerable<Employee> Employees)>
 items =
        departments.GroupJoin(
            employees,
            department => department.Id,
            employee => employee.DepartmentId,
            (department, departmentEmployees) => (
                department.Id,
                department.Name,
                departmentEmployees
            ));

    foreach (var item in items)
    {
        Console.WriteLine(item.Name);
```

```
    foreach (Employee employee in item.Employees)
    {
        Console.WriteLine("\t" + employee);
    }
}
```

7.0

`// ...`

OUTPUT 15.10

```
Corporate
        Mark Michaelis (Chief Computer Nerd)
Human Resources
        Anne Beard (HR Director)
Engineering
        Michael Stokesbary (Senior Computer Wizard)
        Brian Jones (Enterprise Integration Guru)
        Kevin Bost (Programmer Extraordinaire)
        Thomas Heavey (Software Architect)
Information Technology
        Pat Dever (Enterprise Architect)
Philanthropy
        Eric Edmonds (Philanthropy Coordinator)
```

To achieve the preferred result, we use `System.Linq.Enumerable`'s `GroupJoin()` method. The parameters are the same as those in Listing 15.19, except for the final tuple selected. In Listing 15.19, the lambda expression is of type `Func<Department, IEnumerable<Employee>, (long Id, string Name, IEnumerable<Employee> Employees)>`. Notice that we use the second type argument (`IEnumerable<Employee>`) to project the collection of employees for each department onto the resultant department tuple; thus each department in the resulting collection includes a list of the employees.

(Readers familiar with SQL will notice that, unlike `Join()`, `GroupJoin()` doesn't have a SQL equivalent because data returned by SQL is record based, not hierarchical.)

3.0

■ ADVANCED TOPIC

Implementing an Outer Join with GroupJoin()

The earlier inner joins are *equi-joins* because they are based on an equivalent evaluation of the keys. Records appear in the resultant collection only if there are objects in both collections. On occasion, however, it is desirable to create a record even if the corresponding object doesn't exist. For example, rather than leaving the Marketing department out from the final department list simply because it doesn't have any employees, it would be preferable if we included it with an empty employee list. To accomplish this, we perform a left outer join using a combination of both `GroupJoin()` and `SelectMany()` along with `DefaultIfEmpty()`. This is demonstrated in Listing 15.23 and Output 15.11.

LISTING 15.23: Implementing an Outer Join Using `GroupJoin()` with `SelectMany()`

```
using System;
using System.Linq;

// ...

    Department[] departments = CorporateData.Departments;
    Employee[] employees = CorporateData.Employees;

    var items = departments.GroupJoin(
        employees,
        department => department.Id,
        employee => employee.DepartmentId,
        (department, departmentEmployees) => new
        {
            department.Id,
            department.Name,
            Employees = departmentEmployees
        }).SelectMany(
            departmentRecord =>
                departmentRecord.Employees.DefaultIfEmpty(),
            (departmentRecord, employee) => new
                {
                    departmentRecord.Id,
                    departmentRecord.Name,
                    Employees =
                        departmentRecord.Employees
                }).Distinct();

    foreach (var item in items)
    {
        Console.WriteLine(item.Name);
        foreach (Employee employee in item.Employees)
        {
            Console.WriteLine("\t" + employee);
        }
    }

// ...
```

OUTPUT 15.11

```
Corporate
        Mark Michaelis (Chief Computer Nerd)
Human Resources
        Anne Beard (HR Director)
Engineering
        Michael Stokesbary (Senior Computer Wizard)
        Brian Jones (Enterprise Integration Guru)
        Kevin Bost (Programmer Extraordinaire)
        Thomas Heavey (Software Architect)
Information Technology
        Pat Dever (Enterprise Architect)
Philanthropy
        Eric Edmonds (Philanthropy Coordinator)
Marketing
```

Calling SelectMany( )

On occasion, you may have collections of collections. Listing 15.24 provides an example of such a scenario. The teams array contains two teams, each with a string array of players.

LISTING 15.24: Calling SelectMany()

```csharp
using System;
using System.Collections.Generic;
using System.Linq;

// ...

        (string Team, string[] Players)[] worldCup2006Finalists = new[]
        {
            (
                TeamName: "France",
                Players: new string[]
                {
                    "Fabien Barthez", "Gregory Coupet",
                    "Mickael Landreau", "Eric Abidal",
                    "Jean-Alain Boumsong", "Pascal Chimbonda",
                    "William Gallas", "Gael Givet",
                    "Willy Sagnol", "Mikael Silvestre",
                    "Lilian Thuram", "Vikash Dhorasoo",
                    "Alou Diarra", "Claude Makelele",
                    "Florent Malouda", "Patrick Vieira",
                    "Zinedine Zidane", "Djibril Cisse",
                    "Thierry Henry", "Franck Ribery",
                    "Louis Saha", "David Trezeguet",
                    "Sylvain Wiltord",
                }
            ),
```

```
        (
            TeamName: "Italy",
            Players: new string[]
            {
                "Gianluigi Buffon", "Angelo Peruzzi",
                "Marco Amelia", "Cristian Zaccardo",
                "Alessandro Nesta", "Gianluca Zambrotta",
                "Fabio Cannavaro", "Marco Materazzi",
                "Fabio Grosso", "Massimo Oddo",
                "Andrea Barzagli", "Andrea Pirlo",
                "Gennaro Gattuso", "Daniele De Rossi",
                "Mauro Camoranesi", "Simone Perrotta",
                "Simone Barone", "Luca Toni",
                "Alessandro Del Piero", "Francesco Totti",
                "Alberto Gilardino", "Filippo Inzaghi",
                "Vincenzo Iaquinta",
            }
        )
    };

    IEnumerable<string> players =
        worldCup2006Finalists.SelectMany(
            team => team.Players);

    Print(players);

// ...
```

The output from this listing has each player's name displayed on its own line in the order in which it appears in the code. The difference between `Select()` and `SelectMany()` is that `Select()` would return two items, one corresponding to each item in the original collection. `Select()` may project out a transform from the original type, but the number of items would not change. For example, `teams.Select(team => team.Players)` will return an `IEnumerable<string[]>`.

In contrast, `SelectMany()` iterates across each item identified by the lambda expression (the array selected by `Select()` earlier) and hoists out each item into a new collection that includes a union of all items within the child collection. Instead of two arrays of players, `SelectMany()` combines each array selected and produces a single collection of all items.

More Standard Query Operators

Listing 15.25 shows code that uses some of the simpler APIs enabled by `Enumerable`; Output 15.12 shows the results.

LISTING 15.25: More System.Linq.Enumerable Method Calls

```csharp
using System;
using System.Collections.Generic;
using System.Linq;
using System.Text;

class Program
{
  static void Main()
  {
      IEnumerable<object> stuff =
        new object[] { new object(), 1, 3, 5, 7, 9,
             "\"thing\"", Guid.NewGuid() };
      Print("Stuff: { stuff }");
      IEnumerable<int> even = new int[] { 0, 2, 4, 6, 8 };
      Print("Even integers: {0}", even);

      IEnumerable<int> odd = stuff.OfType<int>();
      Print("Odd integers: {0}", odd);

      IEnumerable<int> numbers = even.Union(odd);
      Print("Union of odd and even: {0}", numbers);

      Print("Union with even: {0}", numbers.Union(even));
      Print("Concat with odd: {0}", numbers.Concat(odd));
      Print("Intersection with even: {0}",
          numbers.Intersect(even));
      Print("Distinct: {0}", numbers.Concat(odd).Distinct());
      if (!numbers.SequenceEqual(
          numbers.Concat(odd).Distinct()))
      {
          throw new Exception("Unexpectedly unequal");
      }
      else
      {
          Console.WriteLine(
              @"Collection ""SequenceEquals""" +
                  $" {nameof(numbers)}.Concat(odd).Distinct())");
      }
      Print("Reverse: {0}", numbers.Reverse());
      Print("Average: {0}", numbers.Average());
      Print("Sum: {0}", numbers.Sum());
      Print("Max: {0}", numbers.Max());
      Print("Min: {0}", numbers.Min());
  }

  private static void Print<T>(
          string format, IEnumerable<T> items) =>
      Console.WriteLine(format, string.Join(
          ", ", items.Select(x => x.ToString())));
```

3.0

```csharp
    private static void Print<T>(string format, T item)
    {
        Console.WriteLine(format, item);
    }
}
```

OUTPUT 15.12

```
Stuff: System.Object, 1, 3, 5, 7, 9, "thing"
24c24a41-ee05-41b9-958e-50dd12e3981e
Even integers: 0, 2, 4, 6, 8
Odd integers: 1, 3, 5, 7, 9
Union of odd and even: 0, 2, 4, 6, 8, 1, 3, 5, 7, 9
Union with even: 0, 2, 4, 6, 8, 1, 3, 5, 7, 9
Concat with odd: 0, 2, 4, 6, 8, 1, 3, 5, 7, 9, 1, 3, 5, 7, 9
Intersection with even: 0, 2, 4, 6, 8
Distinct: 0, 2, 4, 6, 8, 1, 3, 5, 7, 9
Collection "SequenceEquals" numbers.Concat(odd).Distinct())
Reverse: 9, 7, 5, 3, 1, 8, 6, 4, 2, 0
Average: 4.5
Sum: 45
Max: 9
Min: 0
```

None of the API calls in Listing 15.25 requires a lambda expression. Tables 15.1 and 15.2 describe each method and provide an example. Included on System.Linq.Enumerable is a collection of aggregate functions that enumerate the collection and calculate a result (shown in Table 15.2). Count is one example of an aggregate function already shown in the chapter.

TABLE 15.1: Simpler Standard Query Operators

Comment Type	Description
OfType<T>()	Forms a query over a collection that returns only the items of a particular type, where the type is identified in the type parameter of the OfType<T>() method call.
Union()	Combines two collections to form a superset of all the items in both collections. The final collection does not include duplicate items even if the same item existed in both collections to start.
Concat()	Combines two collections to form a superset of both collections. Duplicate items are not removed from the resultant collection. Concat() will preserve the ordering. That is, concatenating {A, B} with {C, D} will produce {A, B, C, D}.

3.0

continues

TABLE 15.1: Simpler Standard Query Operators (*continued*)

Comment Type	Description
`Intersect()`	Extracts the collection of items that exist in both original collections.
`Distinct()`	Filters out duplicate items from a collection so that each item within the resultant collection is unique.
`SequenceEquals()`	Compares two collections and returns a Boolean indicating whether the collections are identical, including the order of items within the collection. (This is a very helpful message when testing expected results.)
`Reverse()`	Reverses the items within a collection so that they occur in reverse order when iterating over the collection.

TABLE 15.2: Aggregate Functions on System.Linq.Enumerable

Comment Type	Description
`Count()`	Provides a total count of the number of items within the collection
`Average()`	Calculates the average value for a numeric key selector
`Sum()`	Computes the sum values within a numeric collection
`Max()`	Determines the maximum value among a collection of numeric values
`Min()`	Determines the minimum value among a collection of numeric values

3.0

Note that each method listed in Tables 15.1 and 15.2 will trigger deferred execution.

■ ADVANCED TOPIC

Queryable Extensions for IQueryable<T>

One virtually identical interface to IEnumerable<T> is IQueryable<T>. Because IQueryable<T> derives from IEnumerable<T>, it has all the members of IEnumerable<T> but only those declared directly (e.g., GetEnumerator()). Extension methods are not inherited, so IQueryable<T> doesn't have any of the Enumerable extension methods. However, it has a similar extending class called System.Linq.Queryable that adds to IQueryable<T> almost all of the same methods that Enumerable added to IEnumerable<T>. Therefore, it provides a very similar programming interface.

What makes IQueryable<T> unique is that it enables custom LINQ providers. A LINQ provider subdivides expressions into their constituent parts. Once divided, the expression can be translated into another language, serialized for remote execution, injected with an asynchronous execution pattern, and much more. Essentially, LINQ providers allow for an interception mechanism into a standard collection API, and via this seemingly limitless functionality, behavior relating to the queries and collection can be injected.

For example, LINQ providers allow for the translation of a query expression from C# into SQL that is then executed on a remote database. In so doing, the C# programmer can remain in her primary object-oriented language and leave the translation to SQL to the underlying LINQ provider. Through this type of expression, programming languages can span the impedance mismatch between the object-oriented world and the relational database.

In the case of IQueryable<T>, vigilance regarding deferred execution is even more critical. Imagine, for example, a LINQ provider that returns data from a database. Rather than retrieving the data from a database regardless of the selection criteria, the lambda expression would provide an implementation of IQueryable<T> that possibly includes context information such as the connection string, but not the data itself. The data retrieval wouldn't occur until the call to GetEnumerator() or even MoveNext(). However, the GetEnumerator() call is generally implicit, such as when iterating over the collection with foreach or calling an Enumerable method such as Count<T>() or Cast<T>(). Obviously, cases such as this require developers to be wary of the subtle and repeated calls to any expensive operation that deferred execution might involve. For example, if calling GetEnumerator() involves a distributed call over the network to a database, it would be wise to avoid unintentional duplicate calls to iterations with Count() or foreach.

3.0

Anonymous Types with LINQ

C# 3.0 significantly improved support for handling collections of items using LINQ. What is amazing is that to support this advanced API, only eight new language enhancements were made. However, these enhancements are critical to why C# 3.0 was such a marvelous improvement to the language. Two such enhancements were anonymous types and implicit local variables. Even so, as of C# 7.0, anonymous types are essentially eclipsed by the introduction of C# tuple syntax. In fact, with the sixth edition of this book, all the LINQ samples that previously leveraged anonymous types were updated to use tuples instead. Even so, the remainder of the chapter covers the topic of anonymous types so that if you don't have access to C# 7.0 (or later) or you are working with code that was written prior to C# 7.0, you can still make sense of the anonymous type language feature. (If, however, you don't see yourself programming in a C# 6.0 or earlier world, you might consider skipping this section entirely.)

Anonymous Types

Anonymous types are data types that are declared by the compiler rather than through the explicit class definitions of Chapter 6. As with anonymous functions, when the compiler sees an anonymous type, it does the work to make that class for you and then lets you use it as though you had declared it explicitly. Listing 15.26 shows such a declaration.

LISTING 15.26: Implicit Local Variables with Anonymous Types

```
using System;

class Program
{
  static void Main()
  {
      var patent1 =
          new
          {
              Title = "Bifocals",
              YearOfPublication = "1784"
          };
      var patent2 =
          new
          {
              Title = "Phonograph",
              YearOfPublication = "1877"
          };
```

3.0

```
    var patent3 =
        new
        {
            patent1.Title,
            // Renamed to show property naming.
            Year = patent1.YearOfPublication
        };

Console.WriteLine(
    $"{ patent1.Title } ({ patent1.YearOfPublication })");
Console.WriteLine(
    $"{ patent2.Title } ({ patent2.YearOfPublication })");

Console.WriteLine();
Console.WriteLine(patent1);
Console.WriteLine(patent2);

Console.WriteLine();
Console.WriteLine(patent3);
    }
}
```

The corresponding output is shown in Output 15.13.

OUTPUT 15.13

```
Bifocals (1784)
Phonograph (1784)

{ Title = Bifocals, YearOfPublication = 1784 }
{ Title = Phonograph, YearOfPublication = 1877 }

{ Title = Bifocals, Year = 1784 }
```

Anonymous types are purely a C# feature, not a new kind of type in the runtime. When the compiler encounters the anonymous type syntax, it generates a CIL class with properties corresponding to the named values and data types in the anonymous type declaration.

3.0

■ BEGINNER TOPIC

Implicitly Typed Local Variables Reviewed (var)

Because an anonymous type has no name, it is not possible to declare a local variable as explicitly being of an anonymous type. Rather, the local variable's type is replaced with var. However, by no means does this indicate that implicitly typed variables are untyped. On the contrary, they are fully typed to the data type of the value they are assigned. If an implicitly typed variable is assigned an anonymous type, the underlying CIL code for the local variable declaration will be of the type generated by the compiler. Similarly, if the implicitly typed variable is assigned a `string`, its data type in the underlying CIL will be a `string`. In fact, there is no difference in the resultant CIL code for implicitly typed variables whose assignment is not an anonymous type (such as `string`) and those that are declared with an explicit type. If the declaration statement is `string text = "This is a test of the..."`, the resultant CIL code will be identical to an implicitly typed declaration, `var text = "This is a test of the..."`. The compiler determines the data type of the implicitly typed variable from the expression assigned. In an explicitly typed local variable with an initializer (`string s = "hello";`), the compiler first determines the type of s from the declared type on the left-hand side, then analyzes the right-hand side and verifies that the expression on the right-hand side is assignable to that type. In an implicitly typed local variable, the process is in some sense reversed. First the right-hand side is analyzed to determine its type, and then the "var" is logically replaced with that type.

Although C# does not include a name for the anonymous type, it is still strongly typed as well. For example, the properties of the type are fully accessible. In Listing 15.26, `patent1.Title` and `patent2.YearOfPublication` are called within the `Console.WriteLine` statement. Any attempts to call nonexistent members will result in compile-time errors. Even IntelliSense in IDEs such as Visual Studio works with the anonymous type.

You should use implicitly typed variable declarations sparingly. Obviously, for anonymous types, it is not possible to specify the data type, and the use of `var` is required. However, for cases where the data type is not an anonymous type, it is frequently preferable to use the explicit data type. As is the case generally, you should focus on making the semantics of the code more readable while at the same time using the compiler to verify that the resultant variable is of the type you expect. To accomplish this with implicitly typed local variables, use them only when the type assigned to the implicitly typed variable is entirely obvious. For example, in `var items = new Dictionary<string, List<Account>>();`, the resultant code is more succinct and readable. In contrast, when the type is not obvious, such as when a method return is assigned, developers should favor an explicit variable type declaration such as the following:

```
Dictionary<string, List<Account>> dictionary = GetAccounts();
```

Selecting into Anonymous Types with LINQ

Lastly, capitalizing on anonymous types, we could create an IEnumerable<T> collection where T is an anonymous type (see Listing 15.27 and Output 15.14).

LISTING 15.27: **Projection to an Anonymous Type**

```
// ...
IEnumerable<string> fileList = Directory.EnumerateFiles(
    rootDirectory, searchPattern);
var items = fileList.Select(
    file =>
    {
        FileInfo fileInfo = new FileInfo(file);
        return new
        {
            FileName = fileInfo.Name,
            Size = fileInfo.Length
        };
    });
// ...
```

OUTPUT 15.14

```
{ FileName = AssemblyInfo.cs, Size = 1704 }
{ FileName = CodeAnalysisRules.xml, Size = 735 }
{ FileName = CustomDictionary.xml, Size = 199 }
{ FileName = EssentialCSharp.sln, Size = 40415 }
{ FileName = EssentialCSharp.suo, Size = 454656 }
{ FileName = EssentialCSharp.vsmdi, Size = 499 }
{ FileName = EssentialCSharp.vsscc, Size = 256 }
{ FileName = intelliTechture.ConsoleTester.dll, Size = 24576 }
{ FileName = intelliTechture.ConsoleTester.pdb, Size = 30208 }
```

3.0

The output of an anonymous type automatically shows the property names and their values as part of the generated ToString() method associated with the anonymous type.

Projection using the Select() method is very powerful. We already saw how to filter a collection vertically (reducing the number of items in the collection) using the Where() standard query operator. Now, via the Select()

standard query operator, we can also reduce the collection horizontally (making fewer columns) or transform the data entirely. By adding support of anonymous types, we can `Select()` an arbitrary "object" extracting only those pieces of the original collection that are desirable for the current algorithm but without even having to declare a class to contain them.

More about Anonymous Types and Implicit Local Variables

In Listing 15.26, member names on the anonymous types are explicitly identified using the assignment of the value to the name for `patent1` and `patent2` (e.g., `Title = "Phonograph"`). However, if the value assigned is a property or field call, the name may default to the name of the field or property rather than explicitly specifying the value. `patent3`, for example, is defined using a property named `Title` rather than an assignment to an explicit name. As Output 15.13 shows, the resultant property name is determined, by the compiler, to match the property from where the value was retrieved.

   `patent1` and `patent2` both have the same property names with the same data types. Therefore, the C# compiler generates only one data type for these two anonymous declarations. `patent3`, however, forces the compiler to create a second anonymous type because the property name for the patent year is different from what it was in `patent1` and `patent2`. Furthermore, if the order of the properties were switched between `patent1` and `patent2`, these two anonymous types would also not be type-compatible. In other words, the requirements for two anonymous types to be type-compatible within the same assembly are a match in property names, data types, and order of properties. If these criteria are met, the types are compatible even if they appear in different methods or classes. Listing 15.28 demonstrates the type incompatibilities.

3.0

LISTING 15.28: Type Safety and Immutability of Anonymous Types

```csharp
class Program
{
  static void Main()
  {
      var patent1 =
          new
          {
              Title = "Bifocals",
              YearOfPublication = "1784"
          };
```

```
    var patent2 =
        new
        {
            YearOfPublication = "1877",
            Title = "Phonograph"
        };

    var patent3 =
        new
        {
            patent1.Title,
            Year = patent1.YearOfPublication
        };

    // ERROR: Cannot implicitly convert type
    //        'AnonymousType#1' to 'AnonymousType#2'
    patent1 = patent2;
    // ERROR: Cannot implicitly convert type
    //        'AnonymousType#3' to 'AnonymousType#2'
    patent1 = patent3;

    // ERROR: Property or indexer 'AnonymousType#1.Title'
    //        cannot be assigned to -- it is read-only
    patent1.Title = "Swiss Cheese";
    }
}
```

The resultant first two compile-time errors assert that the types are not compatible, so they will not successfully convert from one to the other.

The third compile-time error is caused by the reassignment of the `Title` property. Anonymous types are immutable, so it is a compile-time error to change a property on an anonymous type once it has been instantiated.

Although not shown in Listing 15.28, it is not possible to declare a method with an implicit data type parameter (`var`). Therefore, instances of anonymous types can be passed outside the method in which they are created in only two ways. First, if the method parameter is of type `object`, the anonymous type instance may be passed outside the method because the anonymous type will convert implicitly. A second way is to use method type inference, whereby the anonymous type instance is passed as a method type parameter that the compiler can successfully infer. Calling `void Method<T>(T parameter)` using `Function(patent1)`, therefore, would succeed, although the available operations on `parameter` within `Function()` are limited to those supported by `object`.

Although C# allows anonymous types such as the ones shown in Listing 15.26, it is generally not recommended that you define them in this way. Anonymous types provide critical functionality with C# 3.0 support for projections, such as joining/associating collections, as we discuss later in the chapter. However, generally you should reserve anonymous type definitions for circumstances where they are required, such as aggregation of data from multiple types.

Begin 7.0

At the time that anonymous methods were introduced, they were a breakthrough that solved an important problem: declaring a temporary type on the fly without the ceremony of having to declare a full type. Even so, there are several drawbacks, as I have detailed. Fortunately, C# 7.0 tuples have none of these drawbacks and, in fact, they essentially eclipse the need for using anonymous types altogether. Specifically, tuples have the following advantages over anonymous types:

- Provide a named type that can be used anywhere a type can be used, including declarations and type parameters
- Available outside the method in which they are instantiated
- Avoid type "pollution" with types that are generated but rarely used

One area that tuples differ from anonymous types is in the fact that anonymous types are reference types and tuples are value types. Whether this difference is advantageous to one approach or the other depends on the performance characteristics needed. If the tuple type is frequently copied and its memory footprint is more than 128 bits, a reference type is likely preferable. Otherwise, using a tuple will most likely be more performant—and a better choice to default to.

End 7.0

3.0

■ **ADVANCED TOPIC**

Anonymous Type Generation
Even though `Console.WriteLine()`'s implementation is to call `ToString()`, notice in Listing 15.26 that the output from `Console.WriteLine()` is not the default `ToString()`, which writes out the fully qualified data type name. Rather, the output is a list of `PropertyName = value` pairs, one for each property on the anonymous type. This occurs because the compiler overrides `ToString()` in the anonymous type code generation, so as to format the `ToString()` output as shown. Similarly, the generated type includes overriding implementations for `Equals()` and `GetHashCode()`.

The implementation of ToString() on its own is an important reason that variation in the order of properties causes a new data type to be generated. If two separate anonymous types, possibly in entirely separate types and even namespaces, were unified and then the order of properties changed, changes in the order of properties on one implementation would have noticeable and possibly unacceptable effects on the other's ToString() results. Furthermore, at execution time it is possible to reflect back on a type and examine the members on a type—even to call one of these members dynamically (determining at runtime which member to call). A variation in the order of members on two seemingly identical types could then trigger unexpected results. To avoid this problem, the C# designers decided to generate two different types.

■ ADVANCED TOPIC

Collection Initializers with Anonymous Types

You cannot have a collection initializer for an anonymous type, since the collection initializer requires a constructor call, and it is impossible to name the constructor. The workaround is to define a method such as static List<T> CreateList<T>(T t) { return new List<T>(); }. Method type inference allows the type parameter to be implied rather than specified explicitly, so this workaround successfully allows for the creation of a collection of anonymous types.

Another approach to initializing a collection of anonymous types is to use an array initializer. As it is not possible to specify the data type in the constructor, array initialization syntax allows for anonymous array initializers using new[ ] (see Listing 15.29).

3.0

LISTING 15.29: Initializing Anonymous Type Arrays

```
using System;
using System.Collections.Generic;
using System.Linq;

class Program
{
  static void Main()
  {
    var worldCup2006Finalists = new[]
    {
```

```
                        new
                        {
                            TeamName = "France",
                            Players = new string[]
                            {
                                "Fabien Barthez", "Gregory Coupet",
                                "Mickael Landreau", "Eric Abidal",
                                // ...
                            }
                        },
                        new
                        {
                            TeamName = "Italy",
                            Players = new string[]
                            {
                                "Gianluigi Buffon", "Angelo Peruzzi",
                                "Marco Amelia", "Cristian Zaccardo",
                                // ...
                            }
                        }
                };


                Print(worldCup2006Finalists);
            }

            private static void Print<T>(IEnumerable<T> items)
            {
                foreach (T item in items)
                {
                    Console.WriteLine(item);
                }
            }
        }
```

The resultant variable is an array of the anonymous type items, which
must be homogeneous because it is an array.

3.0

SUMMARY

This chapter described the internals of how the foreach loop works
and explained which interfaces are required for its execution. In addition, developers frequently filter a collection so that there are fewer items
and project the collection so that the items take a different form. Toward
that end, this chapter discussed the details of how to use the standard
query operators—LINQ introduced collection extension methods on the
System.Linq.Enumerable class—to perform collection manipulation.

In the introduction to standard query operators, we detailed the process of deferred execution and emphasized how developers should take care to avoid unintentionally reexecuting an expression via a subtle call that enumerates over the collection contents. The deferred execution and resultant implicit execution of standard query operators is a significant factor in code efficiency, especially when the query execution is expensive. Programmers should treat the query object as the query object, not the results, and expect the query to execute fully even if it executed already. The query object doesn't know that the results will be the same as they were during a previous execution.

Listing 15.23 appeared in an Advanced Topic section because of the complexity of calling multiple standard query operators one after the other. Although requirements for similar execution may be commonplace, it is not necessary to rely on standard query operators directly. C# 3.0 includes query expressions, a SQL-like syntax for manipulating collections in a way that is frequently easier to code and read, as we show in the next chapter.

The chapter ended with a detailed look at anonymous types and explained why tuples are, in fact, a preferable approach if you have C# 7.0 or later.

3.0

■ 16 ■

LINQ with Query Expressions

THE END OF CHAPTER 15 SHOWED A QUERY using standard query operators for GroupJoin(), SelectMany(), and Distinct(). The result was a statement that spanned multiple lines and was rather more complex and difficult to comprehend than statements typically written using only features of earlier versions of C#. Modern programs, which manipulate rich data sets, often require such complex queries; it would therefore be advantageous if the language made them easier to read. Domain-specific query languages such as SQL make it much easier to read and understand a query but lack the full power of the C# language. That is why the C# language designers added **query expressions** syntax to C# 3.0. With query expressions, many standard query operator expressions are transformed into more readable code, much like SQL.

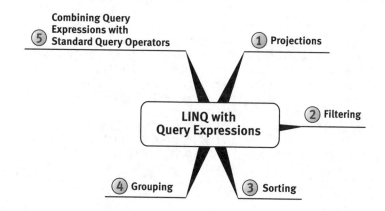

In this chapter, we introduce query expressions and use them to express many of the queries from the preceding chapter.

Introducing Query Expressions

Two of the operations that developers most frequently perform are **filtering** the collection to eliminate unwanted items and **projecting** the collection so that the items take a different form. For example, given a collection of files, we could filter it to create a new collection of only the files with a .cs extension or only the files larger than 1 million bytes. We could also project the file collection to create a new collection of paths to the directories where the files are located and the corresponding directory size. Query expressions provide straightforward syntaxes for both of these common operations. Listing 16.1 shows a query expression that filters a collection of strings; Output 16.1 shows the results.

LISTING 16.1: Simple Query Expression

```
using System;
using System.Collections.Generic;
using System.Linq;

// ...

static string[] Keywords = {
    "abstract", "add*", "alias*", "as", "ascending*",
    "async*", "await*", "base","bool", "break",
    "by*", "byte", "case", "catch", "char", "checked",
    "class", "const", "continue", "decimal", "default",
    "delegate", "descending*", "do", "double",
    "dynamic*", "else", "enum", "event", "equals*",
    "explicit", "extern", "false", "finally", "fixed",
    "from*", "float", "for", "foreach", "get*", "global*",
    "group*", "goto", "if", "implicit", "in", "int",
    "into*", "interface", "internal", "is", "lock", "long",
    "join*", "let*", "nameof*", "namespace", "new", "null",
    "object", "on*", "operator", "orderby*", "out",
    "override", "params", "partial*", "private", "protected",
    "public", "readonly", "ref", "remove*", "return", "sbyte",
    "sealed", "select*", "set*", "short", "sizeof",
    "stackalloc", "static", "string", "struct", "switch",
    "this", "throw", "true", "try", "typeof", "uint", "ulong",
    "unsafe", "ushort", "using", "value*", "var*", "virtual",
    "unchecked", "void", "volatile", "where*", "while", "yield*"};
```

3.0

```csharp
private static void ShowContextualKeywords1()
{
    IEnumerable<string> selection =
        from word in Keywords
            where !word.Contains('*')
            select word;

    foreach (string keyword in selection)
    {
        Console.Write(keyword + " ");
    }
}

// ...
```

OUTPUT 16.1

```
abstract as base bool break byte case catch char checked class const
continue decimal default delegate do double else enum event explicit
extern false finally fixed float for foreach goto if implicit in int
interface internal is lock long namespace new null object operator out
override params private protected public readonly ref return sbyte
sealed short sizeof stackalloc static string struct switch this throw
true try typeof uint ulong unchecked unsafe ushort using virtual void
volatile while
```

In this query expression, `selection` is assigned the collection of C# reserved keywords. The query expression in this example includes a `where` clause that filters out the noncontextual keywords.

Query expressions always begin with a `from` clause and end with a `select` clause or a `group` clause, identified by the `from`, `select`, or `group` contextual keyword, respectively. The identifier `word` in the `from` clause is called a **range variable**; it represents each item in the collection, much as the loop variable in a `foreach` loop represents each item in a collection.

Developers familiar with SQL will notice that query expressions have a syntax that is similar to that of SQL. This design was deliberate—it was intended that LINQ should be easy to learn for programmers who already know SQL. However, there are some obvious differences. The first difference that most SQL-experienced developers will notice is that the C# query expression shown here has the clauses in the following order: `from`, then `where`, then `select`. The equivalent SQL query puts the `SELECT` clause first, then the `FROM` clause, and finally the `WHERE` clause.

3.0

One reason for this change in sequence is to enable use of IntelliSense, the feature of the IDE whereby the editor produces helpful user interface elements such as drop-down lists that describe the members of a given object. Because from appears first and identifies the string array Keywords as the data source, the code editor can deduce that the range variable word is of type string. When you are entering the code into the editor and reach the dot following word, the editor will display only the members of string.

If the from clause appeared after the select, as it does in SQL, as you were typing in the query the editor would not know what the data type of word was, so it would not be able to display a list of word's members. In Listing 16.1, for example, it wouldn't be possible to predict that Contains() was a possible member of word.

The C# query expression order also more closely matches the order in which operations are logically performed. When evaluating the query, you begin by identifying the collection (described by the from clause), then filter out the unwanted items (with the where clause), and finally describe the desired result (with the select clause).

Finally, the C# query expression order ensures that the rules for "where" (range) variables are in scope are mostly consistent with the scoping rules for local variables. For example, a (range) variable must be declared by a clause (typically a from clause) before the variable can be used, much as a local variable must always be declared before it can be used.

Projection

The result of a query expression is a collection of type IEnumerable<T> or IQueryable<T>.[1] The actual type T is inferred from the select or group by clause. In Listing 16.1, for example, the compiler knows that Keywords is of type string[], which is convertible to IEnumerable<string>, and deduces that word is therefore of type string. The query ends with select word, which means the result of the query expression must be a collection of strings, so the type of the query expression is IEnumerable<string>.

3.0

---

1. The result of a query expression is, as a practical matter, almost always IEnumerable<T> or a type derived from it. It is legal, though somewhat perverse, to create an implementation of the query methods that return other types; there is no *requirement* in the language that the result of a query expression be convertible to IEnumerable<T>.

In this case, the "input" and the "output" of the query are both a collection of strings. However, the output type can be quite different from the input type if the expression in the `select` clause is of an entirely different type. Consider the query expression in Listing 16.2 and its corresponding output in Output 16.2.

LISTING 16.2: Projection Using Query Expressions

```csharp
using System;
using System.Collections.Generic;
using System.Linq;
using System.IO;

// ...

    static void List1(string rootDirectory, string searchPattern)
    {
        IEnumerable<string> fileNames = Directory.GetFiles(
            rootDirectory, searchPattern);
        IEnumerable<FileInfo> fileInfos =
            from fileName in fileNames
            select new FileInfo(fileName);

        foreach (FileInfo fileInfo in fileInfos)
        {
            Console.WriteLine(
                $@".{ fileInfo.Name } ({
                    fileInfo.LastWriteTime })");
        }
    }

// ...
```

OUTPUT 16.2

```
Account.cs (11/22/2011 11:56:11 AM)
Bill.cs (8/10/2011 9:33:55 PM)
Contact.cs (8/19/2011 11:40:30 PM)
Customer.cs (11/17/2011 2:02:52 AM)
Employee.cs (8/17/2011 1:33:22 AM)
Person.cs (10/22/2011 10:00:03 PM)
```

3.0

This query expression results in an `IEnumerable<FileInfo>` rather than the `IEnumerable<string>` data type returned by `Directory.GetFiles()`. The `select` clause of the query expression can potentially project out a data type that is different from what was collected by the `from` clause expression.

In this example, the type `FileInfo` was chosen because it has the two relevant fields needed for the desired output: the filename and the last write time. There might not be such a convenient type if you needed other information not captured in the `FileInfo` object. Tuples (or anonymous types prior to C# 7.0) provide a convenient and concise way to project the exact data you need without having to find or create an explicit type. Listing 16.3 provides output similar to that in Listing 16.2, but via tuple syntax rather than `FileInfo`.

LISTING 16.3: Tuples within Query Expressions

```csharp
using System;
using System.Collections.Generic;
using System.Linq;
using System.IO;

// ...

static void List2(string rootDirectory, string searchPattern)
{
    var fileNames =Directory.EnumerateFiles(
        rootDirectory, searchPattern)
    var fileResults =
        from fileName in fileNames
        select
        (
            Name: fileName,
            LastWriteTime: File.GetLastWriteTime(fileName)
        );

    foreach (var fileResult in fileResults)
    {
        Console.WriteLine(
            $@"{ fileResult.Name } ({
                fileResult.LastWriteTime })");
    }
}

// ...
```

In this example, the query projects out only the filename and its last file write time. A projection such as the one in Listing 16.3 makes little difference when working with something small, such as `FileInfo`. However, "horizontal" projection that filters down the amount of data associated with each item in the collection is extremely powerful when the amount of data is significant and retrieving it (perhaps from a different computer over the Internet) is expensive. Rather than retrieving all the data when a query executes, the use of a tuple (or an anonymous type before C# 7.0) enables the capability of storing and retrieving only the required data into the collection.

Imagine, for example, a large database that has tables with 30 or more columns. If there were no tuples, developers would be required either to use objects containing unnecessary information or to define small, specialized classes useful only for storing the specific data required. Instead, tuples enable support for types to be defined by the compiler— types that contain only the data needed for their immediate scenario. Other scenarios can have a different projection of only the properties needed for that scenario.

■ BEGINNER TOPIC

Deferred Execution with Query Expressions

Queries written using query expression notation exhibit deferred execution, just as the queries written in Chapter 15 did. Consider again the assignment of a query object to variable `selection` in Listing 16.1. The creation of the query and the assignment to the variable do not execute the query; rather, they simply build an object that represents the query. The method `word.Contains("*")` is not called when the query object is created. Rather, the query expression saves the selection criteria to be used when iterating over the collection identified by the `selection` variable.

To demonstrate this point, consider Listing 16.4 and the corresponding output (Output 16.3).

LISTING 16.4: Deferred Execution and Query Expressions (Example 1)

3.0

```csharp
using System;
using System.Collections.Generic;
using System.Linq;

// ...

    private static void ShowContextualKeywords2()
    {
        IEnumerable<string> selection = from word in Keywords
                                        where IsKeyword(word)
                                        select word;
        Console.WriteLine("Query created.");
```

```
        foreach (string keyword in selection)
        {
            // No space output here
            Console.Write(keyword);
        }
    }

    // The side effect of console output is included
    // in the predicate to demonstrate deferred execution;
    // predicates with side effects are a poor practice in
    // production code
    private static bool IsKeyword(string word)
    {
        if (word.Contains('*'))
        {
            Console.Write(" ");
            return true;
        }
        else
        {
            return false;
        }
    }
    // ...
```

OUTPUT 16.3

```
Query created.
add* alias* ascending* async* await* by* descending* dynamic*
equals* from* get* global* group* into* join* let* nameof* on*
orderby* partial* remove* select* set* value* var* where* yield*
```

In Listing 16.4, no space is output within the foreach loop. The side effect of printing a space when the predicate IsKeyword() is executed happens when the query is iterated over—not when the query is created. Thus, although selection is a collection (it is of type IEnumerable<T>, after all), at the time of assignment everything following the from clause comprises the selection criteria. Not until we begin to iterate over selection are the criteria applied.

Now consider a second example (see Listing 16.5 and Output 16.4).

LISTING 16.5: Deferred Execution and Query Expressions (Example 2)

```
using System;
using System.Collections.Generic;
using System.Linq;

// ...
```

3.0

```csharp
private static void CountContextualKeywords()
{
    int delegateInvocations = 0;
    Func<string, string> func =
        text=>
        {
            delegateInvocations++;
            return text;
        };

    IEnumerable<string> selection =
        from keyword in Keywords
        where keyword.Contains('*')
        select func(keyword);


    Console.WriteLine(
        $"1. delegateInvocations={ delegateInvocations }");

    // Executing count should invoke func once for
    // each item selected
    Console.WriteLine(
        $"2. Contextual keyword count={ selection.Count() }");

    Console.WriteLine(
        $"3. delegateInvocations={ delegateInvocations }");

    // Executing count should invoke func once for
    // each item selected
    Console.WriteLine(
        $"4. Contextual keyword count={ selection.Count() }");

    Console.WriteLine(
        $"5. delegateInvocations={ delegateInvocations }");

    // Cache the value so future counts will not trigger
    // another invocation of the query
    List<string> selectionCache = selection.ToList();

    Console.WriteLine(
        $"6. delegateInvocations={ delegateInvocations }");

    // Retrieve the count from the cached collection
    Console.WriteLine(
        $"7. selectionCache count={ selectionCache.Count() }");

    Console.WriteLine(
        $"8. delegateInvocations={ delegateInvocations }");

}

// ...
```

3.0

OUTPUT 16.4

```
1. delegateInvocations=0
2. Contextual keyword count=27
3. delegateInvocations=27
4. Contextual keyword count=27
5. delegateInvocations=54
6. delegateInvocations=81
7. selectionCache count=27
8. delegateInvocations=81
```

Rather than defining a separate method, Listing 16.5 uses a statement lambda that counts the number of times the method is called.

Three things in the output are remarkable. First, notice that after selection is assigned, DelegateInvocations remains at zero. At the time of assignment to selection, no iteration over Keywords is performed. If Keywords were a property, the property call would run—in other words, the from clause executes at the time of assignment. However, neither the projection, nor the filtering, nor anything after the from clause will execute until the code iterates over the values within selection. It is as though at the time of assignment, selection would more appropriately be called "query."

Once we call Count( ), however, a term such as *selection* or *items* that indicates a container or collection is appropriate because we begin to count the items within the collection. In other words, the variable selection serves a dual purpose of saving the query information and acting like a container from which the data is retrieved.

A second important characteristic to notice is that calling Count( ) twice causes func to again be invoked once on each item selected. Given that selection behaves both as a query and as a collection, requesting the count requires that the query be executed again by iterating over the IEnumerable<string> collection that selection refers to and counting the items. The C# compiler does not know whether anyone has modified the strings in the array such that the count would now be different, so the counting has to happen anew every time to ensure that the answer is correct and up-to-date. Similarly, a foreach loop over selection would trigger func to be called again for each item. The same is true of all the other extension methods provided via System.Linq.Enumerable.

3.0

■ ADVANCED TOPIC

Implementing Deferred Execution

Deferred execution is implemented by using delegates and expression trees. A delegate provides the ability to create and manipulate a reference to a method that contains an expression that can be invoked later. An expression tree similarly provides the ability to create and manipulate information about an expression that can be examined and manipulated later.

In Listing 16.5, the predicate expressions of the where clauses and the projection expressions of the select clauses are transformed by the compiler into expression lambdas, and then the lambdas are transformed into delegate creations. The result of the query expression is an object that holds onto references to these delegates. Only when the query results are iterated over does the query object actually execute the delegates.

Filtering

In Listing 16.1, we include a where clause that filters out reserved keywords but not contextual keywords. This where clause filters the collection "vertically"; if you think of the collection as a vertical list of items, the where clause makes that vertical list shorter so that the collection holds fewer items. The filter criteria are expressed with a **predicate**—a lambda expression that returns a bool such as word.Contains() (as in Listing 16.1) or File.GetLastWriteTime(file) < DateTime.Now.AddMonths(-1). The latter is shown in Listing 16.6, whose output appears in Output 16.5.

LISTING 16.6: Query Expression Filtering Using where

```csharp
using System;
using System.Collections.Generic;
using System.Linq;
using System.IO;

// ...

    static void FindMonthOldFiles(
        string rootDirectory, string searchPattern)
    {
        IEnumerable<FileInfo> files =
            from fileName in Directory.EnumerateFiles(
                rootDirectory, searchPattern)
            where File.GetLastWriteTime(fileName) <
                DateTime.Now.AddMonths(-1)
            select new FileInfo(fileName);
```

3.0

```
        foreach (FileInfo file in files)
        {
            // As simplification, current directory is
            // assumed to be a subdirectory of
            // rootDirectory
            string relativePath = file.FullName.Substring(
                    Environment.CurrentDirectory.Length);
            Console.WriteLine(
                $".{ relativePath } ({ file.LastWriteTime })");
        }
    }
// ...
```

OUTPUT 16.5

```
.\TestData\Bill.cs (8/10/2011 9:33:55 PM)
.\TestData\Contact.cs (8/19/2011 11:40:30 PM)
.\TestData\Employee.cs (8/17/2011 1:33:22 AM)
.\TestData\Person.cs (10/22/2011 10:00:03 PM)
```

Sorting

To order the items using a query expression, you can use the orderby clause, as shown in Listing 16.7.

LISTING 16.7: Sorting Using a Query Expression with an orderby Clause

```
using System;
using System.Collections.Generic;
using System.Linq;
using System.IO;

// ...
    static void ListByFileSize1(
        string rootDirectory, string searchPattern)
    {
        IEnumerable<string> fileNames =
            from fileName in Directory.EnumerateFiles(
                rootDirectory, searchPattern)
            orderby (new FileInfo(fileName)).Length descending,
                fileName
            select fileName;

        foreach (string fileName in fileNames)
        {
            Console.WriteLine(fileName);
        }
    }
// ...
```

3.0

Listing 16.7 uses the orderby clause to sort the files returned by Directory.GetFiles() first by file size in descending order, and then by filename in ascending order. Multiple sort criteria are separated by commas, such that first the items are ordered by size, and then, if the size is the same, they are ordered by filename. ascending and descending are contextual keywords indicating the sort order direction. Specifying the order as ascending or descending is optional; if the direction is omitted (as it is here on filename), the default is ascending.

The let Clause

Listing 16.8 includes a query that is very similar to the query in Listing 16.7, except that the type argument of IEnumerable<T> is FileInfo. Notice that there is a problem with this query: We have to redundantly create a FileInfo twice, in both the orderby clause and the select clause.

LISTING 16.8: Projecting a FileInfo Collection and Sorting by File Size

```csharp
using System;
using System.Collections.Generic;
using System.Linq;
using System.IO;

// ...
  static void ListByFileSize2(
      string rootDirectory, string searchPattern)
  {
      IEnumerable<FileInfo> files =
          from fileName in Directory.EnumerateFiles(
              rootDirectory, searchPattern)
          orderby new FileInfo(fileName).Length, fileName
          select new FileInfo(fileName);

      foreach (FileInfo file in files)
      {
          // As a simplification, the current directory
          // is assumed to be a subdirectory of
          // rootDirectory
          string relativePath = file.FullName.Substring(
              Environment.CurrentDirectory.Length);
          Console.WriteLine(
              $".{ relativePath }({ file.Length })");
      }
  }
// ...
```

3.0

Unfortunately, although the end result is correct, Listing 16.8 ends up instantiating a `FileInfo` object twice for each item in the source collection, which is wasteful and unnecessary. To avoid this kind of unnecessary and potentially expensive overhead, you can use a `let` clause, as demonstrated in Listing 16.9.

LISTING 16.9: Ordering the Results in a Query Expression

```csharp
// ...
IEnumerable<FileInfo> files =
    from fileName in Directory.EnumerateFiles(
        rootDirectory, searchPattern)
    let file = new FileInfo(fileName)
    orderby file.Length, fileName
    select file;
// ...
```

The `let` clause introduces a new range variable that can hold the value of an expression that is used throughout the remainder of the query expression. You can add as many `let` clauses as you like; simply add each as an additional clause to the query after the first `from` clause but before the final `select`/`group by` clause.

Grouping

A common data manipulation scenario is the grouping of related items. In SQL, this generally involves aggregating the items to produce a summary or total or other aggregate value. LINQ, however, is notably more expressive. LINQ expressions allow for individual items to be grouped into a series of subcollections, and those groups can then be associated with items in the collection being queried. For example, Listing 16.10 and Output 16.6 demonstrate how to group together the contextual keywords and the regular keywords.

3.0

LISTING 16.10: Grouping Together Query Results

```csharp
using System;
using System.Collections.Generic;
using System.Linq;

// ...
```

```
private static void GroupKeywords1()
{
    IEnumerable<IGrouping<bool, string>> selection =
        from word in Keywords
        group word by word.Contains('*');

    foreach (IGrouping<bool, string> wordGroup
        in selection)
    {
        Console.WriteLine(Environment.NewLine + "{0}:",
            wordGroup.Key ?
                "Contextual Keywords" : "Keywords");
        foreach (string keyword in wordGroup)
        {
            Console.Write(" " +
                (wordGroup.Key ?
                    keyword.Replace("*", null) : keyword));
        }
    }
}

// ...
```

OUTPUT 16.6

```
Keywords:
abstract as base bool break byte case catch char checked class
const continue decimal default delegate do double else enum event
explicit extern false finally fixed float for foreach goto if
implicit in int interface internal is lock long namespace new null
operator out override object params private protected public
readonly ref return sbyte sealed short sizeof stackalloc static
string struct switch this throw true try typeof uint ulong unsafe
ushort using virtual unchecked void volatile while
Contextual Keywords:
add alias ascending async await by descending dynamic equals from
get global group into join let nameof on orderby partial remove
select set value var where yield
```

There are several things to note in this listing. First, the query result is a sequence of elements of type IGrouping<bool, string>. The first type argument indicates that the "group key" expression following by was of type bool, and the second type argument indicates that the "group element" expression following group was of type string. That is, the query produces a sequence of groups where the Boolean key is the same for each string in the group.

Because a query with a group by clause produces a sequence of collections, the common pattern for iterating over the results is to create nested

3.0

foreach loops. In Listing 16.10, the outer loop iterates over the groupings and prints out the type of keyword as a header. The nested foreach loop prints each keyword in the group as an item below the header.

The result of this query expression is itself a sequence, which you can then query like any other sequence. Listing 16.11 and Output 16.7 show how to create an additional query that adds a projection onto a query that produces a sequence of groups. (The next section, on query continuations, shows a more pleasant syntax for adding more query clauses to a complete query.)

LISTING 16.11: Selecting a Tuple Following the group Clause

```csharp
using System;
using System.Collections.Generic;
using System.Linq;

// ...

    private static void GroupKeywords1()
    {
        IEnumerable<IGrouping<bool, string>> keywordGroups =
            from word in Keywords
            group word by word.Contains('*');

        IEnumerable<(bool IsContextualKeyword, IGrouping<bool, string> Items)>
            selection =
            from groups in keywordGroups
            select
            (
                IsContextualKeyword: groups.Key,
                Items: groups
            );

        foreach (
            (bool IsContextualKeyword, IGrouping<bool, string> Items)
                wordGroup in selection)
        {
            Console.WriteLine(Environment.NewLine + "{0}:",
                wordGroup.IsContextualKeyword ?
                    "Contextual Keywords" : "Keywords");
            foreach (string keyword in wordGroup.Items)
            {
                Console.Write(" " +
                    keyword.Replace("*", null));
            }
        }
    }

// ...
```

OUTPUT 16.7

```
Keywords:
abstract as base bool break byte case catch char checked class
const continue decimal default delegate do double else enum
event explicit extern false finally fixed float for foreach goto if
implicit in int interface internal is lock long namespace new null
operator out override object params private protected public
readonly ref return sbyte sealed short sizeof stackalloc static
string struct switch this throw true try typeof uint ulong unsafe
ushort using virtual unchecked void volatile while
Contextual Keywords:
add alias ascending async await by descending dynamic equals from
get global group into join let nameof on orderby partial remove
select set value var where yield
```

The group clause results in a query that produces a collection of IGrouping<TKey, TElement> objects—just as the GroupBy() standard query operator did (see Chapter 15). The select clause in the subsequent query uses a tuple to effectively rename IGrouping<TKey, TElement>.Key to IsContextualKeyword and to name the subcollection property Items. With this change, the nested foreach loop uses wordGroup.Items rather than wordGroup directly, as shown in Listing 16.10. Another potential item to add to the tuple would be a count of the items within the subcollection. This functionality is already available through LINQ's wordGroup.Items.Count() method, however, so the benefit of adding it to the anonymous type directly is questionable.

Query Continuation with into

As we saw in Listing 16.11, you can use an existing query as the input to a second query. However, it is not necessary to write an entirely new query expression when you want to use the results of one query as the input to another. You can extend any query with a **query continuation clause** using the contextual keyword into. A query continuation is nothing more than syntactic sugar for creating two queries and using the first as the input to the second. The range variable introduced by the into clause (groups in Listing 16.11) becomes the range variable for the remainder of the query; any previous range variables are logically a part of the earlier query and cannot be used in the query continuation. Listing 16.12 shows how to rewrite the code of Listing 16.11 to use a query continuation instead of two queries.

3.0

LISTING 16.12: Selecting without the Query Continuation

```csharp
using System;
using System.Collections.Generic;
using System.Linq;

// ...

    private static void GroupKeywords1()
    {
        IEnumerable<(bool IsContextualKeyword, IGrouping<bool, string> Items)>
            selection =
            from word in Keywords
            group word by word.Contains('*')
            into groups
                select
                (
                    IsContextualKeyword: groups.Key,
                    Items: groups
                );

    // ...

    }

// ...
```

The ability to run additional queries on the results of an existing query using into is not specific to queries ending with group clauses, but rather can be applied to all query expressions. Query continuation is simply a shorthand for writing query expressions that consume the results of other query expressions. You can think of into as a "pipeline operator," because it "pipes" the results of the first query into the second query. You can arbitrarily chain together many queries in this way.

Flattening Sequences of Sequences with Multiple from Clauses

3.0

It is often desirable to "flatten" a sequence of sequences into a single sequence. For example, each member of a sequence of customers might have an associated sequence of orders, or each member of a sequence of directories might have an associated sequence of files. The SelectMany sequence operator (discussed in Chapter 15) concatenates together all the subsequences; to do the same thing with query expression syntax, you can use multiple from clauses, as shown in Listing 16.13.

LISTING 16.13: **Multiple Selection**

```
var selection =
    from word in Keywords
    from character in word
    select character;
```

The preceding query will produce the sequence of characters a, b, s, t, r, a, c, t, a, d, d, *, a, l, i, a, ...

Multiple from clauses can also be used to produce the **Cartesian product**—the set of all possible combinations of several sequences—as shown in Listing 16.14.

LISTING 16.14: **Cartesian Product**

```
var numbers = new[] { 1, 2, 3 };
IEnumerable<(string Word, int Number)> product =
    from word in Keywords
    from number in numbers
    select (word, number);
```

This would produce a sequence of pairs (abstract, 1), (abstract, 2), (abstract, 3), (as, 1), (as, 2), ...

■ BEGINNER TOPIC

Distinct Members

Often, it is desirable to return only distinct (i.e., unique) items from within a collection, discarding any duplicates. Query expressions do not have explicit syntax for distinct members, but the functionality is available via the query operator Distinct(), which was introduced in Chapter 15. To apply a query operator to a query expression, the expression must be enclosed in parentheses so that the compiler does not think that the call to Distinct() is a part of the select clause. Listing 16.15 gives an example; Output 16.8 shows the results.

3.0

LISTING 16.15: **Obtaining Distinct Members from a Query Expression**

```
using System;
using System.Collections.Generic;
using System.Linq;

// ...
```

```
public static void ListMemberNames()
{
    IEnumerable<string> enumerableMethodNames = (
        from method in typeof(Enumerable).GetMembers(
            System.Reflection.BindingFlags.Static |
            System.Reflection.BindingFlags.Public)
        orderby method.Name
        select method.Name).Distinct();
    foreach(string method in enumerableMethodNames)
    {
        Console.Write($"{ method }, ");
    }
}
```

// ...

OUTPUT 16.8

```
Aggregate, All, Any, AsEnumerable, Average, Cast, Concat, Contains,
Count, DefaultIfEmpty, Distinct, ElementAt, ElementAtOrDefault,
Empty, Except, First, FirstOrDefault, GroupBy, GroupJoin,
Intersect, Join, Last, LastOrDefault, LongCount, Max, Min, OfType,
OrderBy, OrderByDescending, Range, Repeat, Reverse, Select,
SelectMany, SequenceEqual, Single, SingleOrDefault, Skip,
SkipWhile, Sum, Take, TakeWhile, ThenBy, ThenByDescending, ToArray,
ToDictionary, ToList, ToLookup, Union, Where, Zip,
```

In this example, `typeof(Enumerable).GetMembers()` returns a list of all the members (methods, properties, and so on) on `System.Linq` `.Enumerable`. However, many of these members are overloaded, sometimes more than once. Rather than displaying the same member multiple times, `Distinct()` is called from the query expression. This eliminates the duplicate names from the list. (We cover the details of `typeof()` and reflection [where methods like `GetMembers()` are available] in Chapter 18.)

3.0

Query Expressions Are Just Method Invocations

Somewhat surprisingly, adding query expressions to C# 3.0 required no changes to the Common Language Runtime (CLR) or to the Common Intermediate Language (CIL). Rather, the C# compiler simply translates query expressions into a series of method calls. Consider, for example, the query expression from Listing 16.1, a portion of which appears in Listing 16.16.

LISTING 16.16: Simple Query Expression

```
private static void ShowContextualKeywords1()
{
    IEnumerable<string> selection =
        from word in Keywords
            where word.Contains('*')
            select word;
    // ...
}
```

After compilation, the expression from Listing 16.16 is converted to an IEnumerable<T> extension method call from System.Linq.Enumerable, as shown in Listing 16.17.

LISTING 16.17: Query Expression Translated to Standard Query Operator Syntax

```
private static void ShowContextualKeywords3()
{
    IEnumerable<string> selection =
        Keywords.Where(word => word.Contains('*'));

    // ...
}
```

As discussed in Chapter 15, the lambda expression is then itself translated by the compiler to emit a method with the body of the lambda, and the usage of it becomes allocation of a delegate to that method.

Every query expression can (and must) be translated into method calls, but not every sequence of method calls has a corresponding query expression. For example, there is no query expression equivalent for the extension method TakeWhile<T>(Func<T, bool> predicate), which repeatedly returns items from the collection as long as the predicate returns true.

For those queries that do have both a method call form and a query expression form, which is better? This is a judgment call; some queries are better suited for query expressions, whereas others are more readable as method invocations.

3.0

> ### Guidelines
>
> **DO** use query expression syntax to make queries easier to read, particularly if they involve complex `from`, `let`, `join`, or `group` clauses.
>
> **CONSIDER** using the standard query operators (method call form) if the query involves operations that do not have a query expression syntax, such as `Count()`, `TakeWhile()`, or `Distinct()`.

SUMMARY

This chapter introduced a new syntax—namely, query expressions. Readers familiar with SQL will immediately see the similarities between query expressions and SQL. However, query expressions also introduce additional functionality, such as grouping into a hierarchical set of new objects, which is unavailable with SQL. All of the functionality of query expressions was already available via standard query operators, but query expressions frequently provide a simpler syntax for expressing such a query. Whether through standard query operators or query expression syntax, however, the end result is a significant improvement in the way developers can code against collection APIs—an improvement that ultimately provides a paradigm shift in the way object-oriented languages are able to interface with relational databases.

In the next chapter, we continue our discussion of collections by investigating some of the .NET framework collection types and exploring how to define custom collections.

End 3.0

■ 17 ■

Building Custom Collections

Chapter 15 covered the standard query operators—that is, the extension methods on IEnumerable<T> that provide methods common to all collections. However, these operators do not make all collections equally suited for all tasks; there is still a need for different collection types. Some collections are better suited to searching by key, whereas others are better suited to accessing items by position. Some collections act like queues: The first element in is the first out. Others are more like stacks: The first element in is the last out. Others are not ordered at all.

Begin 2.0

Mind map diagram: **Building Custom Collections**

- **5 Iterators** — Defining Syntax, yield, State, yield break
- **1 More Collection Interfaces** — ILIst<T>, IDictionary<TKey, TValue>, IComparable<T>, ICollection<T>
- **4 Returning null or an Empty Collection**
- **3 Providing an Index Operator**
- **2 Primary Collection Classes** — List<T>, Dictionary<TKey, TValue>, SortedDictionary<TKey, TValue> and SortedList<T>, Stack<T>, Queue<T>, LinkedList<T>

The .NET frameworks provide a plethora of collection types suited for many of the scenarios in which collections are needed. This chapter introduces some of these collection types and the interfaces they implement. It also describes how to create custom-built collections that support standard functionality, such as indexing. In addition, it explores the use of the `yield return` statement to create classes and methods that implement `IEnumerable<T>`. This C# 2.0 feature greatly simplifies implementation of collections that can be enumerated with the `foreach` statement.

Many nongeneric collection classes and interfaces are available in the Microsoft .NET Framework, but in general these exist today only for backward compatibility with code written before generics came into use. The generic collection types are both faster, because they avoid boxing costs, and more type-safe than the nongeneric collections. Thus, new code should almost always use the generic collection types exclusively. Throughout this book, we assume that you are primarily using generic collection types.

More Collection Interfaces

We've already seen how collections implement `IEnumerable<T>`, the primary interface that enables iteration over the elements of a collection. Many additional interfaces exist that are implemented by more complex collections. Figure 17.1 shows the hierarchy of interfaces implemented by collection classes.

These interfaces provide a standard way to perform common tasks such as iterating, indexing, and counting elements in a collection. This section examines these interfaces (at least all of the generic ones), starting at the bottom of Figure 17.1 and moving upward.

`IList<T>` versus `IDictionary<TKey, TValue>`

An English-language dictionary can be thought of as a collection of definitions. A specific definition can be rapidly accessed by looking up its associated "key"—that is, the word being defined. A dictionary collection class is similarly a collection of values, in which each value can be rapidly accessed by using its associated unique key. Note, however, that a language dictionary typically stores the definitions sorted alphabetically by key; a dictionary class might choose to do so but typically does not.

2.0

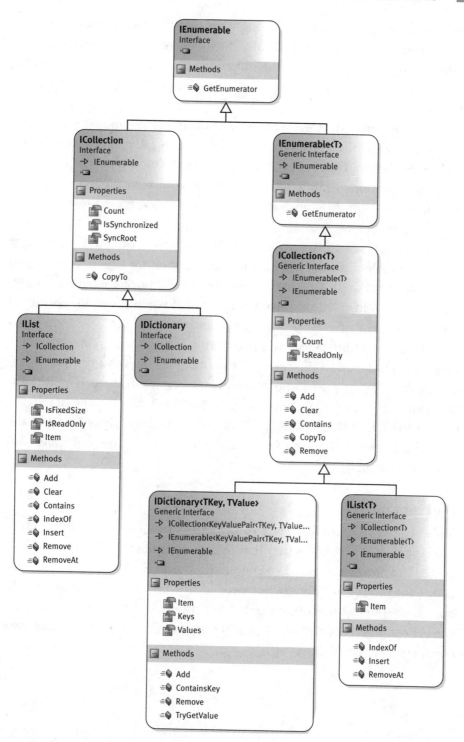

FIGURE 17.1: Collection Class Hierarchy

2.0

Dictionary collections are best thought of as an unordered list of keys and associated values unless specifically documented as being ordered. Similarly, one does not normally think of looking up "the sixth definition in the dictionary"; dictionary classes usually provide indexing only by key, not by position.

A list, by contrast, stores values in a specific order and accesses them by their position. In a sense, lists are just the special case of dictionaries where the "key" is always an integer and the "key set" is always a contiguous set of non-negative integers starting with zero. Nevertheless, that is a strong enough difference that it is worth having an entirely different type to represent it.

Thus, when selecting a collection class to solve some data storage or retrieval problem, the first two interfaces to look for are IList<T> and IDictionary<TKey, TValue>. These interfaces indicate whether the collection type is focused on retrieval of a value when given its positional index or retrieval of a value when given its associated key.

Both of these interfaces require that a class that implements them provide an indexer. In the case of IList<T>, the operand of the indexer corresponds to the position of the element being retrieved: The indexer takes an integer and gives you access to the nth element in the list. In the case of the IDictionary<TKey, TValue> interface, the operand of the indexer corresponds to the key associated with a value and gives you access to that value.

ICollection<T>

Both IList<T> and IDictionary<TKey, TValue> implement ICollection<T>. A collection that does not implement either IList<T> or IDictionary<TKey, TValue> will more than likely implement ICollection<T> (although not necessarily, because collections could implement the lesser requirement of IEnumerable or IEnumerable<T>). ICollection<T> is derived from IEnumerable<T> and includes two members: Count and CopyTo().

2.0

- The `Count` property returns the total number of elements in the collection. Initially, it might appear that this would be sufficient to iterate through each element in the collection using a `for` loop, but, in fact, the collection would also need to support retrieval by index, which the `ICollection<T>` interface does not include (although `IList<T>` does include it).

- The `CopyTo()` method provides the ability to convert the collection into an array. This method includes an `index` parameter so that you can specify where to insert elements in the target array. To use the method, you must initialize the array target with sufficient capacity, starting at the `index`, to contain all the elements in `ICollection<T>`.

Primary Collection Classes

Five key categories of collection classes exist, and they differ from one another in terms of how data is inserted, stored, and retrieved. Each generic class is located in the `System.Collections.Generic` namespace, and their nongeneric equivalents are found in the `System.Collections` namespace.

List Collections: `List<T>`

The `List<T>` class has properties similar to an array. The key difference is that these classes automatically expand as the number of elements increases. (In contrast, an array size is constant.) Furthermore, lists can shrink via explicit calls to `TrimToSize()` or `Capacity` (see Figure 17.2).

These classes are categorized as **list collections** whose distinguishing functionality is that each element can be individually accessed by index, just like an array. Therefore, you can set and access elements in the list collection classes using the index operator, where the index parameter value corresponds to the position of an element in the collection. Listing 17.1 shows an example, and Output 17.1 shows the results.

2.0

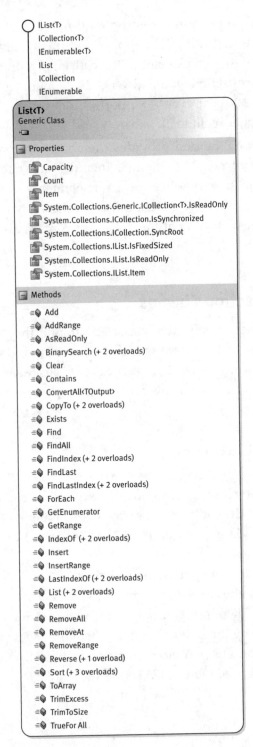

FIGURE 17.2: List<> Class Diagrams

LISTING 17.1: Using List<T>

```csharp
using System;
using System.Collections.Generic;

class Program
{
  static void Main()
  {
    List<string> list = new List<string>();

    // Lists automatically expand as elements
    // are added
    list.Add("Sneezy");
    list.Add("Happy");
    list.Add("Dopey");
    list.Add("Doc");
    list.Add("Sleepy");
    list.Add("Bashful");
    list.Add("Grumpy");

    list.Sort();

    Console.WriteLine(
        $"In alphabetical order { list[0] } is the "
        + $"first dwarf while { list[6] } is the last.");

    list.Remove("Grumpy");
  }
}
```

OUTPUT 17.1

```
In alphabetical order Bashful is the first dwarf while Sneezy is the last.
```

C# is zero-index based; therefore, index 0 in Listing 17.1 corresponds to the first element and index 6 indicates the seventh element. Retrieving elements by index does not involve a search. Rather, it entails a quick and simple "jump" operation to a location in memory.

A List<T> is an ordered collection; the Add() method appends the given item to the end of the list. Before the call to Sort() in Listing 17.1, "Sneezy" was first and "Grumpy" was last; after the call, the list is sorted into alphabetical order rather than the order in which items were added. Some collections automatically sort elements as they are added, but List<T> is not one of them; an explicit call to Sort() is required for the elements to be sorted.

2.0

To remove an element, you use the `Remove( )` or `RemoveAt( )` method to either remove a given element or remove whatever element is at a particular index, respectively.

■ ADVANCED TOPIC

Customizing Collection Sorting

You might have wondered how the `List<T>.Sort( )` method in Listing 17.1 knew how to sort the elements of the list into alphabetical order. The `string` type implements the `IComparable<string>` interface, which has one method, `CompareTo( )`. It returns an integer indicating whether the element passed is greater than, less than, or equal to the current element. If the element type implements the generic `IComparable<T>` interface (or the nongeneric `IComparable` interface), the sorting algorithm will, by default, use it to determine the sorted order.

But what if either the element type does not implement `IComparable<T>` or the default logic for comparing two things does not meet your needs? To specify a nondefault sort order, you can call the overload of `List<T>.Sort( )`, which takes `IComparer<T>` as an argument.

The difference between `IComparable<T>` and `IComparer<T>` is subtle but important. The first interface means, "I know how to compare *myself* to another instance of my type." The latter means, "I know how to compare *two things* of a given type."

The `IComparer<T>` interface is typically used when there are many different possible ways of sorting a data type and none is obviously the best. For example, you might have a collection of `Contact` objects that you sometimes want to sort by name, by location, by birthday, by geographic region, or by any number of other possibilities. Rather than choosing a sorting strategy and making the `Contact` class implement `IComparable<Contact>`, it might be wiser to create several different classes that implement `IComparer<Contact>`. Listing 17.2 shows a sample implementation of a `LastName, FirstName` comparison.

LISTING 17.2: Implementing IComparer<T>

```
class Contact
{
    public string FirstName { get; private set; }
    public string LastName { get; private set; }
```

2.0

```
  public Contact(string firstName, string lastName)
  {
    this.FirstName = firstName;
    this.LastName = lastName;
  }
}
```

```
using System;
using System.Collections.Generic;

class NameComparison : IComparer<Contact>
{
  public int Compare(Contact x, Contact y)
  {
    if (Object.ReferenceEquals(x, y))
      return 0;
    if (x == null)
      return 1;
    if (y == null)
      return -1;
    int result = StringCompare(x.LastName, y.LastName);
    if (result == 0)
      result = StringCompare(x.FirstName, y.FirstName);
    return result;
  }

  private static int StringCompare(string x, string y)
  {
    if (Object.ReferenceEquals(x, y))
      return 0;
    if (x == null)
      return 1;
    if (y == null)
      return -1;
    return x.CompareTo(y);
  }
}
```

To sort a List<Contact> by last name and then first name, you can call contactList.Sort(new NameComparer()).

Total Ordering

You are required to produce a **total order** when implementing IComparable<T> or IComparer<T>. Your implementation of CompareTo must provide a fully consistent ordering for any possible pair of items. This ordering is required to have a number of basic characteristics. For example, every element is required to be considered equal to itself. If an element X is considered to be equal to element Y, and element Y is considered to be equal to element Z, all three elements X, Y, and Z must be considered equal to one another. If an element X is considered to be greater than Y, Y must be considered to be less than X. And there must be no "transitivity paradoxes"—that is, you cannot have X greater than Y, Y greater than Z, and Z greater than X. If you fail to provide a total ordering, the action of the sort algorithm is undefined; it may produce a crazy ordering, it may crash, it may go into an infinite loop, and so on.

Notice, for example, how the comparer in Listing 17.2 ensures a total order, even if the arguments are null references. It would not be legal to say, "If either element is null, then return zero," for example, because then two non-null things could be equal to null but not equal to each other.

Guidelines

DO ensure that custom comparison logic produces a consistent "total order."

Searching a List<T>

To search List<T> for a particular element, you use the Contains(), IndexOf(), LastIndexOf(), and BinarySearch() methods. The first three methods search through the array, starting at the first element (or the last element for LastIndexOf()), and examine each element until the desired one is found. The execution time for these algorithms is proportional to the number of elements searched before a hit occurs. (Be aware that the collection classes do not require that all the elements within the collection are unique. If two or more elements in the collection are the same, IndexOf() returns the first index and LastIndexOf() returns the last index.)

BinarySearch() uses a much faster binary search algorithm but requires that the elements be sorted. A useful feature of the BinarySearch() method is that if the element is not found, a negative integer is returned. The bitwise complement (~) of this value is the index of the next element larger than the element being sought, or the total element count if there is no greater value. This provides a convenient means to insert new values into the list at the specific location so as to maintain sorting. Listing 17.3 provides an example.

2.0

LISTING 17.3: Using the Bitwise Complement of the BinarySearch() Result

```csharp
using System;
using System.Collections.Generic;

class Program
{
  static void Main()
  {
      List<string> list = new List<string>();
      int search;

      list.Add("public");
      list.Add("protected");
      list.Add("private");

      list.Sort();

      search = list.BinarySearch("protected internal");
      if (search < 0)
      {
        list.Insert(~search, "protected internal");
      }

      foreach (string accessModifier in list)
      {
          Console.WriteLine(accessModifier);
      }
  }
}
```

Beware that if the list is not first sorted, an element will not necessarily be found with this code, even if it is in the list. The results of Listing 17.3 appear in Output 17.2.

OUTPUT 17.2

```
private
protected
protected internal
public
```

■ **ADVANCED TOPIC**

Finding Multiple Items with FindAll()

Sometimes you must find multiple items within a list, and your search criteria are more complex than merely looking for specific values. To

2.0

support this scenario, System.Collections.Generic.List<T> includes a FindAll() method. FindAll() takes a parameter of type Predicate<T>, which is a reference to a method called a delegate. Listing 17.4 demonstrates how to use the FindAll() method.

LISTING 17.4: Demonstrating FindAll() and Its Predicate Parameter

```csharp
using System;
using System.Collections.Generic;

class Program
{
  static void Main()
  {
      List<int> list = new List<int>();
      list.Add(1);
      list.Add(2);
      list.Add(3);
      list.Add(2);

      List<int> results = list.FindAll(Even);

      foreach(int number in results)
      {
          Console.WriteLine(number);
      }
  }

  public static bool Even(int value) =>
      (value % 2) == 0;
}
```

In Listing 17.4's call to FindAll(), you pass a delegate instance, Even(). This method returns true when the integer argument value is even. FindAll() takes the delegate instance and calls into Even() for each item within the list (this listing uses C# 2.0's delegate type inferencing). Each time the return value is true, it adds it to a new List<T> instance and then returns this instance once it has checked each item within list. A complete discussion of delegates occurs in Chapter 13.

Dictionary Collections: Dictionary<TKey, TValue>

2.0

Another category of collection classes is the dictionary classes—specifically, Dictionary<TKey, TValue> (see Figure 17.3). Unlike the list collections, dictionary classes store name/value pairs. The name functions as a unique key that can be used to look up the corresponding element in a manner

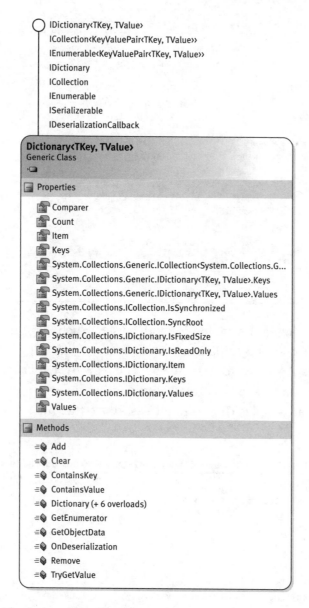

○ IDictionary<TKey, TValue>
ICollection<KeyValuePair<TKey, TValue>>
IEnumerable<KeyValuePair<TKey, TValue>>
IDictionary
ICollection
IEnumerable
ISerializable
IDeserializationCallback

Dictionary<TKey, TValue>
Generic Class

Properties

⚿ Comparer
⚿ Count
⚿ Item
⚿ Keys
⚿ System.Collections.Generic.ICollection<System.Collections.G...
⚿ System.Collections.Generic.IDictionary<TKey, TValue>.Keys
⚿ System.Collections.Generic.IDictionary<TKey, TValue>.Values
⚿ System.Collections.ICollection.IsSynchronized
⚿ System.Collections.ICollection.SyncRoot
⚿ System.Collections.IDictionary.IsFixedSize
⚿ System.Collections.IDictionary.IsReadOnly
⚿ System.Collections.IDictionary.Item
⚿ System.Collections.IDictionary.Keys
⚿ System.Collections.IDictionary.Values
⚿ Values

Methods

≡◆ Add
≡◆ Clear
≡◆ ContainsKey
≡◆ ContainsValue
≡◆ Dictionary (+ 6 overloads)
≡◆ GetEnumerator
≡◆ GetObjectData
≡◆ OnDeserialization
≡◆ Remove
≡◆ TryGetValue

FIGURE 17.3: Dictionary Class Diagrams

similar to that of using a primary key to access a record in a database. This adds some complexity to the access of dictionary elements, but because lookups by key are efficient operations, this is a useful collection. Note that the key may be any data type, not just a string or a numeric value.

 2.0

One option for inserting elements into a dictionary is to use the Add( ) method, passing both the key and the value, as shown in Listing 17.5.

LISTING 17.5: Adding Items to a Dictionary<TKey, TValue>

```
using System;
using System.Collections.Generic;

class Program
{
  static void Main()
  {
      // C# 6.0 (use {"Error", ConsoleColor.Red} pre-C# 6.0)
      var colorMap = new Dictionary<string, ConsoleColor>
          {
              ["Error"] = ConsoleColor.Red,
              ["Warning"] = ConsoleColor.Yellow,
              ["Information"] = ConsoleColor.Green
          };

      colorMap.Add("Verbose", ConsoleColor.White);
      // ...
  }
}
```

After initializing the dictionary with a C# 6.0 dictionary initializer (see the section "Collection Initializers" in Chapter 15), Listing 17.5 inserts the string a ConsoleColor of white for the key of "Verbose". If an element with the same key has already been added, an exception is thrown.

An alternative for adding elements is to use the indexer, as shown in Listing 17.6.

LISTING 17.6: Inserting Items in a Dictionary<TKey, TValue> Using the Index Operator

```
using System;
using System.Collections.Generic;

class Program
{
  static void Main()
  {
      // C# 6.0 (use {"Error", ConsoleColor.Red} pre-C# 6.0)
      var colorMap = new Dictionary<string, ConsoleColor>
          {
              ["Error"] = ConsoleColor.Red,
              ["Warning"] = ConsoleColor.Yellow,
              ["Information"] = ConsoleColor.Green
          };

      colorMap["Verbose"] = ConsoleColor.White;
      colorMap["Error"] = ConsoleColor.Cyan;

      // ...
  }
}
```

2.0

The first thing to observe in Listing 17.6 is that the index operator does not require an integer. Instead, the index operand type is specified by the first type argument (`string`), and the type of the value that is set or retrieved by the indexer is specified by the second type argument (`ConsoleColor`).

The second thing to notice in Listing 17.6 is that the same key ("`Error`") is used twice. In the first assignment, no dictionary value corresponds to the given key. When this happens, the dictionary collection classes insert a new value with the supplied key. In the second assignment, an element with the specified key already exists. Instead of inserting an additional element, the prior `ConsoleColor` value for the "`Error`" key is replaced with `ConsoleColor.Cyan`.

Attempting to read a value from a dictionary with a nonexistent key throws a `KeyNotFoundException`. The `ContainsKey()` method allows you to check whether a particular key is used before accessing its value, thereby avoiding the exception.

The `Dictionary<TKey, TValue>` is implemented as a *hash table*; this data structure provides extremely fast access when searching by key, regardless of the number of values stored in the dictionary. By contrast, checking whether there is a particular value in the dictionary collections is a time-consuming operation with linear performance characteristics, much like searching an unsorted list. To do this, you use the `ContainsValue()` method, which searches sequentially through each element in the collection.

You remove a dictionary element using the `Remove()` method, passing the key, not the element value.

Because both the key and the value are required to add a value to the dictionary, the loop variable of a `foreach` loop that enumerates elements of a dictionary must be `KeyValuePair<TKey, TValue>`. Listing 17.7 shows a snippet of code demonstrating the use of a `foreach` loop to enumerate the keys and values in a dictionary. The output appears in Output 17.3.

LISTING 17.7: Iterating over `Dictionary<TKey, TValue>` with `foreach`

```
using System;
using System.Collections.Generic;
```

2.0

```csharp
class Program
{
  static void Main()
  {
      // C# 6.0 (use {"Error", ConsoleColor.Red} pre-C# 6.0)
      Dictionary<string, ConsoleColor> colorMap =
          new Dictionary<string, ConsoleColor>
          {
              ["Error"] = ConsoleColor.Red,
              ["Warning"] = ConsoleColor.Yellow,
              ["Information"] = ConsoleColor.Green,
              ["Verbose"] = ConsoleColor.White
          };

      Print(colorMap);
  }

    private static void Print(
        IEnumerable<KeyValuePair<string, ConsoleColor>> items)
    {
        foreach (KeyValuePair<string, ConsoleColor> item in items)
        {
            Console.ForegroundColor = item.Value;
            Console.WriteLine(item.Key);
        }
    }
  }
}
```

OUTPUT 17.3

```
Error
Warning
Information
Verbose
```

Note that the order of the items shown here is the order in which the items were added to the dictionary, just as if they had been added to a list. Implementations of dictionaries will often enumerate the keys and values in the order in which they were added to the dictionary, but this feature is neither required nor documented, so you should not rely on it.

Guidelines

DO NOT make any unwarranted assumptions about the order in which elements of a collection will be enumerated. If the collection is not documented as enumerating its elements in a particular order, it is not guaranteed to produce elements in any particular order.

2.0

If you want to deal only with keys or only with elements within a dictionary class, they are available via the Keys and Values properties, respectively. The data type returned from these properties is of type ICollection<T>. The data returned by these properties is a reference to the data within the original dictionary collection rather than a copy; changes within the dictionary are automatically reflected in the collection returned by the Keys and Values properties.

■ ADVANCED TOPIC

Customizing Dictionary Equality

To determine whether a given key matches any existing key in the dictionary, the dictionary must be able to compare two keys for equality. This is analogous to the way that lists must be able to compare two items to determine their order. (For an example, see the Advanced Topic titled "Customizing Collection Sorting" earlier in this chapter.) By default, two instances of a value type are compared by checking whether they contain exactly the same data, and two instances of a reference type are compared to see whether both reference the same object. However, it is occasionally necessary to be able to compare two instances as equal even if they are not exactly the same value or exactly the same reference.

For example, suppose you wish to create a Dictionary<Contact, string> using the Contact type from Listing 17.2. However, you want any two Contact objects to compare as equal if they have the same first and last names, regardless of whether the two objects are reference equal. Much as you can provide an implementation of IComparer<T> to sort a list, so you can similarly provide an implementation of IEqualityComparer<T> to determine if two keys are to be considered equal. This interface requires two methods: one that returns whether two items are equal and one that returns a "hash code" that the dictionary can use to facilitate fast indexing. Listing 17.8 shows an example.

LISTING 17.8: Implementing IEqualityComparer<T>

```
using System;
using System.Collections.Generic;

class ContactEquality : IEqualityComparer<Contact>
{
  public bool Equals(Contact x, Contact y)
```

2.0

```
    {
        if (Object.ReferenceEquals(x, y))
            return true;
        if (x == null || y == null)
            return false;
        return x.LastName == y.LastName &&
            x.FirstName == y.FirstName;
    }

    public int GetHashCode(Contact x)
    {
        if (Object.ReferenceEquals(x, null))
            return 0;
        int h1 = x.FirstName == null ? 0 : x.FirstName.GetHashCode();
        int h2 = x.LastName == null ? 0 : x.LastName.GetHashCode();
        return h1 * 23 + h2;
    }
}
```

To create a dictionary that uses this equality comparer, you can use the constructor new `Dictionary<Contact, string>(new ContactEquality)`.

■ **BEGINNER TOPIC**

Requirements of Equality Comparisons

As discussed in Chapter 10, there are several important rules for the equality and hash code algorithms. Conformance to these rules is critical in the context of collections. Just as correctly sorting a list requires a custom ordering comparison to provide a total order, so too does a hash table require certain guarantees to be met by a custom equality comparison. The most important requirement is that if `Equals()` returns `true` for two objects, `GetHashCode()` must return the same value for those two objects. Note that the converse is not true: Two unequal items may have the same hash code. (Indeed, there *must* be two unequal items that have the same hash code because there are only 2^{32} possible hash codes but more than that many unequal objects!)

The second-most important requirement is that two calls to `GetHashCode()` on the same item must produce the same result for at least as long as the item is in the hash table. Note, however, that two objects that "look equal" are not required to give the same hash code in two separate runs of a program. For example, it is perfectly legal for a given contact to be assigned one hash code today, and two weeks later when you run the program a second time, for "the same" contact to be given a different hash code. Do not persist hash codes into a database and expect them to remain stable across different runs of a program.

Ideally, the result of GetHashCode() should appear to be random. That is, small changes to the input should cause large changes to the output, and the result should be distributed roughly evenly across all possible integer values. It is difficult, however, to devise a hash algorithm that is extremely fast and produces extremely well-distributed output; try to find a good middle ground.

Finally, GetHashCode() and Equals() must not throw exceptions. Notice how the code in Listing 17.8 is careful to never dereference a null reference, for example.

To summarize, here are the key principles:

- Equal objects must have equal hash codes.
- The hash code of an object should not change for the life of the instance (at least while it is in the hash table).
- The hashing algorithm should quickly produce a well-distributed hash.
- The hashing algorithm should avoid throwing exceptions in all possible object states.

Sorted Collections: SortedDictionary<TKey, TValue> and SortedList<T>

The sorted collection classes (see Figure 17.4) store their elements sorted by key for SortedDictionary<TKey, TValue> and by value for SortedList<T>. If we change the code in Listing 17.7 to use a SortedDictionary<string, string> instead of a Dictionary<string, string>, the output of the program is as appears in Output 17.4.

OUTPUT 17.4

```
Error
Information
Verbose
Warning
```

Note that the elements are sorted into order by key, not by value.

Because sorted collections must do extra work to maintain the sorted order of their elements, insertion and removal are typically slightly slower than insertion and removal of values in an unordered dictionary.

2.0

Because sorted collections must store their items in a particular order, it is possible to access values both by key and by index. To access a key or value by its index in the sorted list, use the `Keys` and `Values` properties. They return `IList<TKey>` and `IList<TValue>` instances, respectively; the resultant collection can be indexed like any other list.

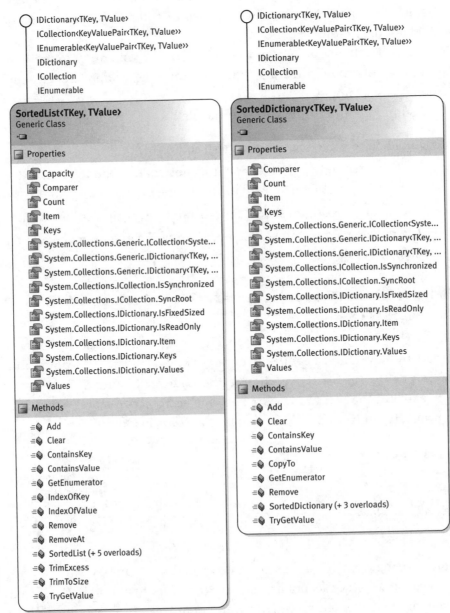

FIGURE 17.4: Sorted Collections

Stack Collections: Stack<T>

Chapter 12 discussed the stack collection classes (see Figure 17.5). The stack collection classes are designed as last in, first out (LIFO) collections. The two key methods are Push( ) and Pop( ).

- Push( ) inserts elements into the collection. The elements do not have to be unique.

- Pop( ) removes elements in the reverse order in which they were added.

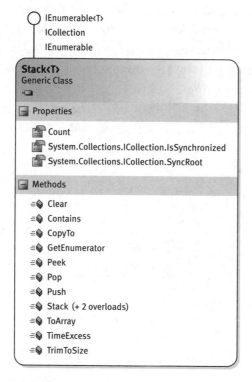

FIGURE 17.5: Stack<T> **Class Diagram**

To access the elements on the stack without modifying the stack, you use the Peek( ) and Contains( ) methods. The Peek( ) method returns the next element that Pop( ) will retrieve.

As with most collection classes, you use the Contains( ) method to determine whether an element exists anywhere in the stack. As with all collections, it is also possible to use a foreach loop to iterate over the elements in a stack. This allows you to access values from anywhere in

2.0

the stack. Note, however, that accessing a value via the foreach loop does not remove it from the stack—only Pop( ) provides this functionality.

Queue Collections: Queue<T>

Queue collection classes, shown in Figure 17.6, are identical to stack collection classes, except that they follow the ordering pattern of first in, first out (FIFO). In place of the Pop( ) and Push( ) methods are the Enqueue( ) and Dequeue( ) methods. The queue collection behaves like a pipe: You place objects into the queue at one end using the Enqueue( ) method and remove them from the other end using the Dequeue( ) method. As with stack collection classes, the objects do not have to be unique, and queue collection classes automatically increase in size as required. As a queue shrinks, it does not necessarily reclaim the storage space previously used, because that would make inserting a new element potentially more expensive. If you happen to know that a queue will remain the same size for a long time, however, you can hint to it that you would like to reclaim storage space by using the TrimToSize( ) method.

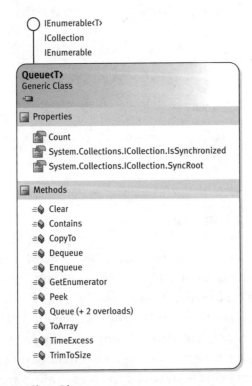

FIGURE 17.6: Queue<T> Class Diagram

2.0

Linked Lists: LinkedList<T>

System.Collections.Generic also supports a linked list collection that enables both forward and reverse traversal. Figure 17.7 shows the class diagram. (There is no corresponding nongeneric type.)

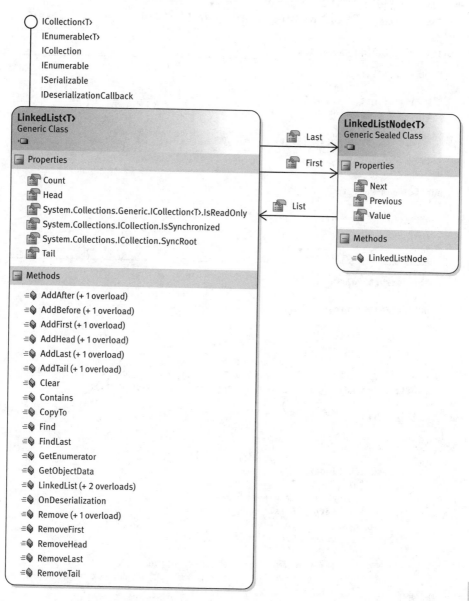

FIGURE 17.7: LinkedList<T> and LinkedListNode<T> Class Diagram

2.0

Providing an Indexer

Arrays, dictionaries, and lists all provide an **indexer** as a convenient way to get or set a member of a collection based on a key or index. As we've seen, to use the indexer you simply put the index (or indices) in square brackets after the collection name. It is possible to define your own indexer; Listing 17.9 shows an example using Pair<T>.

LISTING 17.9: Defining an Indexer

```csharp
interface IPair<T>
{
  T First { get;  }
  T Second { get;  }

  T this[PairItem index] { get; }
}
```

```csharp
public enum PairItem
{
    First,
    Second
}
```

```csharp
public struct Pair<T> : IPair<T>
{
  public Pair(T first, T second)
  {
    First = first;
    Second = second;
  }
  public T First { get; }  // C# 6.0 Getter-only Autoproperty
  public T Second { get; }  // C# 6.0 Getter-only Autoproperty

  public T this[PairItem index]
  {
    get
    {
        switch (index)
        {
            case PairItem.First:
                return First;
            case PairItem.Second:
                return Second;
            default :
                throw new NotImplementedException(
                    $"The enum { index.ToString() } has not been
                    implemented");
        }
    }
  }
}
```

An indexer is declared much as a property is declared, except that instead of the name of the property, you use the keyword `this` followed by a parameter list in square brackets. The body is also like a property, with `get` and `set` blocks. As Listing 17.9 shows, the parameter does not have to be an `int`. In fact, the index can take multiple parameters and can even be overloaded. This example uses an `enum` to reduce the likelihood that callers will supply an index for a nonexistent item.

The Common Intermediate Language (CIL) code that the C# compiler creates from an index operator is a special property called `Item` that takes an argument. Properties that accept arguments cannot be created explicitly in C#, so the `Item` property is unique in this aspect. Any additional member with the identifier `Item`, even if it has an entirely different signature, will conflict with the compiler-created member, so it will not be allowed.

■ **ADVANCED TOPIC**

Assigning the Indexer Property Name Using `IndexerName`

As indicated earlier, the CIL property name for an indexer defaults to `Item`. Using the `IndexerNameAttribute`, you can specify a different name, however. Listing 17.10, for example, changes the name to `"Entry"`.

LISTING 17.10: Changing the Indexer's Default Name

```
[System.Runtime.CompilerServices.IndexerName("Entry")]
public T this[params PairItem[] branches]
{
    // ...
}
```

This makes no difference to C# callers of the index, but it specifies the name for languages that do not support indexers directly.

This attribute is merely an instruction to the compiler to use a different name for the indexer; the attribute is not actually emitted into metadata by the compiler, so it is not available via reflection.

2.0

■**ADVANCED TOPIC**

Defining an Index Operator with Variable Parameters

An index operator can also take a variable parameter list. For example, Listing 17.11 defines an index operator for BinaryTree<T>, discussed in Chapter 12 (and again in the next section).

LISTING 17.11: Defining an Index Operator with Variable Parameters

```csharp
using System;

public class BinaryTree<T>
{

    // ...

    public BinaryTree<T> this[params PairItem[] branches]
    {
        get
        {
            BinaryTree<T> currentNode = this;

            // Allow either an empty array or null
            // to refer to the root node
            int totalLevels = branches?.Length ?? 0;
            int currentLevel = 0;

            while (currentLevel < totalLevels)
            {
                System.Diagnostics.Debug.Assert(branches != null,
                    $"{ nameof(branches) } != null");
                currentNode = currentNode.SubItems[
                    branches[currentLevel]];
                if (currentNode == null)
                {
                    // The binary tree at this location is null
                    throw new IndexOutOfRangeException();
                }
                currentLevel++;
            }
            return currentNode;
        }
    }
}
```

Each item within branches is a PairItem and indicates which branch to navigate down in the binary tree. For example,

```csharp
tree[PairItem.Second, PairItem.First].Value
```

will retrieve the value located at the second item in the first branch followed by the first branch within that branch.

Returning Null or an Empty Collection

When returning an array or collection, you must indicate that there are zero items by returning either null or a collection instance with no items. The better choice in general is to return a collection instance with no items. In so doing, you avoid forcing the caller to check for null before iterating over the items in the collection. For example, given a zero-size IEnumerable<T> collection, the caller can immediately and safely use a foreach loop over the collection without concern that the generated call to GetEnumerator() will throw a NullReferenceException. Consider using the Enumerable.Empty<T>() method to easily generate an empty collection of a given type.

One of the few times to deviate from this guideline is when null is intentionally indicating something different from zero items. For example, a collection of user names for a website might be null to indicate that an up-to-date collection could not be obtained for some reason; that is semantically different from an empty collection.

Guidelines

DO NOT represent an empty collection with a null reference.
CONSIDER using the Enumerable.Empty<T>() method instead.

Iterators

Chapter 15 went into detail on the internals of the foreach loop. This section discusses how to use **iterators** to create your own implementation of the IEnumerator<T>, IEnumerable<T>, and corresponding nongeneric interfaces for custom collections. Iterators provide clean syntax for specifying how to iterate over data in collection classes, especially using the foreach loop. The iterator allows end users of a collection to navigate its internal structure without knowledge of that structure.

▪ ADVANCED TOPIC

2.0

Origin of Iterators

In 1972, Barbara Liskov and a team of scientists at MIT began researching programming methodologies, focusing on user-defined data abstractions.

To prove much of their work, they created a language called CLU that had a concept called "clusters" (*CLU* being the first three letters of this term). Clusters were predecessors to the primary data abstraction that programmers use today: objects. During their research, the team realized that although they were able to use the CLU language to abstract some data representation away from end users of their types, they consistently found themselves having to reveal the inner structure of their data to allow others to intelligently consume it. The result of their consternation was the creation of a language construct called an *iterator*. (The CLU language offered many insights into what would eventually be popularized as object-oriented programming.)

If classes want to support iteration using the `foreach` loop construct, they must implement the enumerator pattern. As Chapter 15 describes, in C# the `foreach` loop construct is expanded by the compiler into the `while` loop construct based on the `IEnumerator<T>` interface that is retrieved from the `IEnumerable<T>` interface.

The problem with the enumeration pattern is that it can be cumbersome to implement manually, because it must maintain all the state necessary to describe the current position in the collection. This internal state may be simple for a list collection type class; the index of the current position suffices. In contrast, for data structures that require recursive traversal, such as binary trees, the state can be quite complicated. To mitigate the challenges associated with implementing this pattern, C# 2.0 included a construct that makes it easier for a class to dictate how the `foreach` loop iterates over its contents.

Defining an Iterator

Iterators are a means to implement methods of a class, and they are syntactic shortcuts for the more complex enumerator pattern. When the C# compiler encounters an iterator, it expands its contents into CIL code that implements the enumerator pattern. As such, there are no runtime dependencies for implementing iterators. Because the C# compiler handles implementation through CIL code generation, there is no real runtime performance benefit to using iterators. However, there is a substantial programmer productivity gain in choosing iterators over manual implementation of the enumerator pattern. To understand improvement, we first consider how an iterator is defined in code.

2.0

Iterator Syntax

An iterator provides shorthand implementation of iterator interfaces, the combination of the `IEnumerable<T>` and `IEnumerator<T>` interfaces. Listing 17.12 declares an iterator for the generic `BinaryTree<T>` type by creating a `GetEnumerator()` method. Next, you will add support for the iterator interfaces.

LISTING 17.12: Iterator Interfaces Pattern

```csharp
using System;
using System.Collections.Generic;

public class BinaryTree<T>:
    IEnumerable<T>
{
  public BinaryTree ( T value)
  {
      Value = value;
  }

  #region IEnumerable<T>
  public IEnumerator<T> GetEnumerator()
  {
      //...
  }
  #endregion IEnumerable<T>

  public T Value { get; }  // C# 6.0 Getter-only Autoproperty
  public Pair<BinaryTree<T>> SubItems { get; set; }
}

public struct Pair<T>
{
  public Pair(T first, T second) : this()
  {
      First = first;
      Second = second;
  }
  public T First { get; }  // C# 6.0 Getter-only Autoproperty
  public T Second { get; }  // C# 6.0 Getter-only Autoproperty
}
```

As Listing 17.12 shows, we need to provide an implementation for the `GetEnumerator()` method.

Yielding Values from an Iterator

2.0

Iterators are like functions, but instead of returning a single value, they *yield* a sequence of values, one at a time. In the case of `BinaryTree<T>`, the iterator yields a sequence of values of the type argument provided for T. If the nongeneric version of IEnumerator is used, the yielded values will instead be of type object.

To correctly implement the iterator pattern, you need to maintain some internal state to keep track of where you are while enumerating the collection. In the BinaryTree<T> case, you track which elements within the tree have already been enumerated and which are still to come. Iterators are transformed by the compiler into a "state machine" that keeps track of the current position and knows how to "move itself" to the next position.

The yield return statement yields a value each time an iterator encounters it; control immediately returns to the caller that requested the item. (An interesting point here is that control really does *immediately* return, unlike, ironically, the return statement. A return statement will run finally blocks along the way; yield return does not.) When the caller requests the next item, the code begins to execute immediately following the previously executed yield return statement. In Listing 17.13, you return the C# built-in data type keywords sequentially.

LISTING 17.13: Yielding Some C# Keywords Sequentially

```csharp
using System;
using System.Collections.Generic;

public class CSharpBuiltInTypes: IEnumerable<string>
{
    public IEnumerator<string> GetEnumerator()
    {
        yield return "object";
        yield return "byte";
        yield return "uint";
        yield return "ulong";
        yield return "float";
        yield return "char";
        yield return "bool";
        yield return "ushort";
        yield return "decimal";
        yield return "int";
        yield return "sbyte";
        yield return "short";
        yield return "long";
        yield return "void";
        yield return "double";
        yield return "string";
    }
```

2.0

```
        // The IEnumerable.GetEnumerator method is also required
        // because IEnumerable<T> derives from IEnumerable
    System.Collections.IEnumerator
        System.Collections.IEnumerable.GetEnumerator()
    {
        // Invoke IEnumerator<string> GetEnumerator() above
        return GetEnumerator();
    }
}

public class Program
{
    static void Main()
    {
        var keywords = new CSharpBuiltInTypes();
        foreach (string keyword in keywords)
        {
            Console.WriteLine(keyword);
        }
    }
}
```

The results of Listing 17.13 appear in Output 17.5.

OUTPUT 17.5

```
object
byte
uint
ulong
float
char
bool
ushort
decimal
int
sbyte
short
long
void
double
string
```

The output from this listing is a listing of the C# built-in types.

Iterators and State

When GetEnumerator() is first called in a foreach statement, such as foreach (string keyword in keywords) in Listing 17.13), an iterator object is created and its state is initialized to a special "start" state that represents the

2.0

fact that no code has executed in the iterator and, therefore, no values have been yielded yet. The iterator maintains its state as long as the foreach statement at the call site continues to execute. Every time the loop requests the next value, control enters the iterator and continues where it left off the previous time around the loop; the state information stored in the iterator object is used to determine where control must resume. When the foreach statement at the call site terminates, the iterator's state is no longer saved.

It is always safe to call GetEnumerator() again; "fresh" enumerator objects will be created when necessary.

Figure 17.8 shows a high-level sequence diagram of what takes place. Remember that the MoveNext() method appears on the IEnumerator<T> interface.

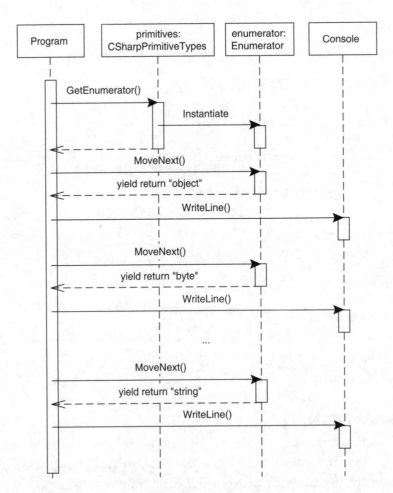

FIGURE 17.8: Sequence Diagram with yield return

2.0

In Listing 17.13, the `foreach` statement at the call site initiates a call to `GetEnumerator()` on the `CSharpBuiltInTypes` instance called `keywords`. Given the iterator instance (referenced by `iterator`), `foreach` begins each iteration with a call to `MoveNext()`. Within the iterator, you yield a value back to the `foreach` statement at the call site. After the `yield return` statement, the `GetEnumerator()` method seemingly pauses until the next `MoveNext()` request. Back at the loop body, the `foreach` statement displays the yielded value on the screen. It then loops back around and calls `MoveNext()` on the iterator again. Notice that the second time, control picks up at the second `yield return` statement. Once again, the `foreach` displays on the screen what `CSharpBuiltInTypes` yielded and starts the loop again. This process continues until there are no more `yield return` statements within the iterator. At that point, the `foreach` loop at the call site terminates because `MoveNext()` returns `false`.

More Iterator Examples

Before you modify `BinaryTree<T>`, you must modify `Pair<T>` to support the `IEnumerable<T>` interface using an iterator. Listing 17.14 is an example that yields each element in `Pair<T>`.

LISTING 17.14: Using yield to Implement BinaryTree<T>

```csharp
public struct Pair<T>: IPair<T>,
    IEnumerable<T>
{
  public Pair(T first, T second) : this()
  {
     First = first;
     Second = second;
  }
  public T First { get; }  // C# 6.0 Getter-only Autoproperty
  public T Second { get; }  // C# 6.0 Getter-only Autoproperty

  #region IEnumerable<T>
  public IEnumerator<T> GetEnumerator()
  {
     yield return First;
     yield return Second;
  }
  #endregion IEnumerable<T>

  #region IEnumerable Members
  System.Collections.IEnumerator
     System.Collections.IEnumerable.GetEnumerator()
```

2.0

```
    {
        return GetEnumerator();
    }
    #endregion
}
```

In Listing 17.14, the iteration over the Pair<T> data type loops twice: first through yield return First and then through yield return Second. Each time the yield return statement within GetEnumerator() is encountered, the state is saved and execution appears to "jump" out of the GetEnumerator() method context and into the loop body. When the second iteration starts, GetEnumerator() begins to execute again with the yield return Second statement.

System.Collections.Generic.IEnumerable<T> inherits from System.Collections.IEnumerable. Therefore, when implementing IEnumerable<T>, it is also necessary to implement IEnumerable. In Listing 17.14, you do so explicitly, and the implementation simply involves a call to IEnumerable<T>'s GetEnumerator() implementation. This call from IEnumerable.GetEnumerator() to IEnumerable<T>.GetEnumerator() will always work because of the type compatibility (via inheritance) between IEnumerable<T> and IEnumerable. Since the signatures for both GetEnumerator()s are identical (the return type does not distinguish a signature), one or both implementations must be explicit. Given the additional type safety offered by IEnumerable<T>'s version, you implement IEnumerable's implementation explicitly.

Listing 17.15 uses the Pair<T>.GetEnumerator() method and displays "Inigo" and "Montoya" on two consecutive lines.

LISTING 17.15: Using Pair<T>.GetEnumerator() via foreach

```
var fullname = new Pair<string>("Inigo", "Montoya");
foreach (string name in fullname)
{
    Console.WriteLine(name);
}
```

Notice that the call to GetEnumerator() is implicit within the foreach loop.

Placing a yield return within a Loop

It is not necessary to hardcode each yield return statement, as you did in both CSharpPrimitiveTypes and Pair<T>. Using the yield return statement, you can return values from inside a loop construct. Listing 17.16 uses a `foreach` loop. Each time the `foreach` within `GetEnumerator()` executes, it returns the next value.

LISTING 17.16: Placing `yield return` Statements within a Loop

```csharp
public class BinaryTree<T>: IEnumerable<T>
{
  // ...

  #region IEnumerable<T>
  public IEnumerator<T> GetEnumerator()
  {
      // Return the item at this node
      yield return Value;

      // Iterate through each of the elements in the pair
      foreach (BinaryTree<T> tree in SubItems)
      {
          if (tree != null)
          {
              // Since each element in the pair is a tree,
              // traverse the tree and yield each element
              foreach (T item in tree)
              {
                  yield return item;
              }
          }
      }
  }
  #endregion IEnumerable<T>

  #region IEnumerable Members
  System.Collections.IEnumerator
      System.Collections.IEnumerable.GetEnumerator()
  {
      return GetEnumerator();
  }
  #endregion
}
```

In Listing 17.16, the first iteration returns the root element within the binary tree. During the second iteration, you traverse the pair of subelements. If the subelement pair contains a non-null value, you traverse into that child node and yield its elements. Note that `foreach (T item in tree)` is a recursive call to a child node.

As observed with `CSharpBuiltInTypes` and `Pair<T>`, you can now iterate over `BinaryTree<T>` using a `foreach` loop. Listing 17.17 demonstrates this process, and Output 17.6 shows the results.

2.0

LISTING 17.17: Using foreach with BinaryTree<string>

```
// JFK
var jfkFamilyTree = new BinaryTree<string>(
    "John Fitzgerald Kennedy");

jfkFamilyTree.SubItems = new Pair<BinaryTree<string>>(
    new BinaryTree<string>("Joseph Patrick Kennedy"),
    new BinaryTree<string>("Rose Elizabeth Fitzgerald"));

// Grandparents (Father's side)
jfkFamilyTree.SubItems.First.SubItems =
    new Pair<BinaryTree<string>>(
    new BinaryTree<string>("Patrick Joseph Kennedy"),
    new BinaryTree<string>("Mary Augusta Hickey"));

// Grandparents (Mother's side)
jfkFamilyTree.SubItems.Second.SubItems =
    new Pair<BinaryTree<string>>(
    new BinaryTree<string>("John Francis Fitzgerald"),
    new BinaryTree<string>("Mary Josephine Hannon"));

foreach (string name in jfkFamilyTree)
{
    Console.WriteLine(name);
}
```

OUTPUT 17.6

```
John Fitzgerald Kennedy
Joseph Patrick Kennedy
Patrick Joseph Kennedy
Mary Augusta Hickey
Rose Elizabeth Fitzgerald
John Francis Fitzgerald
Mary Josephine Hannon
```

■ ADVANCED TOPIC

The Dangers of Recursive Iterators

The code in Listing 17.16 creates new "nested" iterators as it traverses the binary tree. As a consequence, when the value is yielded by a node, the value is yielded by the node's iterator, and then yielded by its parent's iterator, and then yielded by its parent's iterator, and so on, until it is finally yielded to the original loop by the root's iterator. A value that is n levels deep must actually pass its value up a chain of *n* iterators. If the binary tree is relatively shallow, this is not typically a problem; however, an imbalanced binary tree can be extremely deep and therefore expensive to iterate recursively.

Guidelines

CONSIDER using nonrecursive algorithms when iterating over potentially deep data structures.

■ BEGINNER TOPIC

struct versus class

An interesting side effect of defining Pair<T> as a struct rather than a class is that SubItems.First and SubItems.Second cannot be assigned directly, even if the setter were public. If you modify the setter to be public, the following will produce a compile error indicating that SubItems cannot be modified "because it is not a variable":

```
jfkFamilyTree.SubItems.First =
    new BinaryTree<string>("Joseph Patrick Kennedy");
```

The issue is that SubItems is a property of type Pair<T>, a struct. Therefore, when the property returns the value, a copy of SubItems is made, and assigning First on a copy that is promptly lost at the end of the statement would be misleading. Fortunately, the C# compiler prevents this error.

To overcome the issue, don't assign First (see the approach in Listing 17.17), use class rather than struct for Pair<T>, don't create a SubItems property and instead use a field, or provide properties in BinaryTree<T> that give direct access to SubItems members.

Canceling Further Iteration: yield break

Sometimes you might want to cancel further iteration. You can do so by including an if statement so that no further statements within the code are executed. However, you can also use yield break to cause MoveNext() to return false and control to return immediately to the caller and end the loop. Listing 17.18 shows an example of such a method.

2.0

LISTING 17.18: Escaping Iteration via `yield break`

```csharp
public System.Collections.Generic.IEnumerable<T>
    GetNotNullEnumerator()
{
    if((First == null) || (Second == null))
    {
        yield break;
    }
    yield return Second;
    yield return First;
}
```

This method cancels the iteration if either of the elements in the `Pair<T>` class is `null`.

A `yield break` statement is similar to placing a `return` statement at the top of a function when it is determined that there is no work to do. It is a way to exit from further iterations without surrounding all remaining code with an `if` block. As such, it allows multiple exits. Use it with caution, because a casual reading of the code may overlook the early exit.

■ **ADVANCED TOPIC**

How Iterators Work

When the C# compiler encounters an iterator, it expands the code into the appropriate CIL for the corresponding enumerator design pattern. In the generated code, the C# compiler first creates a nested private class to implement the `IEnumerator<T>` interface, along with its `Current` property and a `MoveNext()` method. The `Current` property returns a type corresponding to the return type of the iterator. Listing 17.14 of `Pair<T>` contains an iterator that returns a T type. The C# compiler examines the code contained within the iterator and creates the necessary code within the `MoveNext` method and the `Current` property to mimic its behavior. For the `Pair<T>` iterator, the C# compiler generates roughly equivalent code (see Listing 17.19).

LISTING 17.19: C# Equivalent of Compiler-Generated C# Code for Iterators

```csharp
using System;
using System.Collections.Generic;

public class Pair<T> : IPair<T>, IEnumerable<T>
{
    // ...
```

2.0

```csharp
// The iterator is expanded into the following
// code by the compiler
public virtual IEnumerator<T> GetEnumerator()
{
    __ListEnumerator result = new __ListEnumerator(0);
    result._Pair = this;
    return result;
}
public virtual System.Collections.IEnumerator
    System.Collections.IEnumerable.GetEnumerator()
{
    return new GetEnumerator();
}

private sealed class __ListEnumerator<T> : IEnumerator<T>
{
    public __ListEnumerator(int itemCount)
    {
        _ItemCount = itemCount;
    }

    Pair<T> _Pair;
    T _Current;
    int _ItemCount;

    public object Current
    {
        get
        {
            return _Current;
        }
    }

    public bool MoveNext()
    {
        switch (_ItemCount)
        {
            case 0:
                _Current = _Pair.First;
                _ItemCount++;
                return true;
            case 1:
                _Current = _Pair.Second;
                _ItemCount++;
                return true;
            default:
                return false;
        }
    }
}
}
```

2.0

Because the compiler takes the `yield return` statement and generates classes that correspond to what you probably would have written manually, iterators in C# exhibit the same performance characteristics as classes that implement the enumerator design pattern manually. Although there is no performance improvement, the gains in programmer productivity are significant.

■ ADVANCED TOPIC

Contextual Keywords

Many C# keywords are "reserved" and cannot be used as identifiers unless preceded with an @ sign. The `yield` keyword is a contextual keyword, not a reserved keyword; it is legal (though confusing) to declare a local variable called `yield`. In fact, all the keywords added to C# after version 1.0 have been contextual keywords; this helps prevent accidental breakages when upgrading existing programs to use new versions of the language.

Had the C# designers chosen to use `yield value;` instead of `yield return value;` as the syntax for an iterator to yield, a possible ambiguity would have been introduced: `yield(1+2);` now might be yielding a value, or it might be passing the value as an argument to a method called `yield`.

Since it was previously never legal to have the identifier `yield` appear immediately before `return` or `break`, the C# compiler knows that such a usage of `yield` must be as a keyword, not an identifier.

Creating Multiple Iterators in a Single Class

Previous iterator examples implemented `IEnumerable<T>` `.GetEnumerator()`—the method that `foreach` seeks implicitly. Sometimes you might want different iteration sequences, such as iterating in reverse, filtering the results, or iterating over an object projection other than the default. You can declare additional iterators in the class by encapsulating them within properties or methods that return `IEnumerable<T>` or `IEnumerable`. If you want to iterate over the elements of `Pair<T>` in reverse, for example, you could provide a `GetReverseEnumerator()` method, as shown in Listing 17.20.

2.0

LISTING 17.20: Using yield return in a Method That Returns IEnumerable<T>

```csharp
public struct Pair<T>: IEnumerable<T>
{
    // ...

    public IEnumerable<T> GetReverseEnumerator()
    {
        yield return Second;
        yield return First;
    }
    // ...
}

public void Main()
{
    var game = new Pair<string>("Redskins", "Eagles");
    foreach (string name in game.GetReverseEnumerator())
    {
        Console.WriteLine(name);
    }
}
```

Note that you return IEnumerable<T>, not IEnumerator<T>. This is different from IEnumerable<T>.GetEnumerator(), which returns IEnumerator<T>. The code in Main() demonstrates how to call GetReverseEnumerator() using a foreach loop.

yield Statement Requirements

You can use the yield return statement only in members that return an IEnumerator<T> or IEnumerable<T> type, or their nongeneric equivalents. Members whose bodies include a yield return statement may not have a simple return. If the member uses the yield return statement, the C# compiler generates the necessary code to maintain the state of the iterator. In contrast, if the member uses the return statement instead of yield return, the programmer is responsible for maintaining his own state machine and returning an instance of one of the iterator interfaces. Further, just as all code paths in a method with a return type must contain a return statement accompanied by a value (assuming they don't throw an exception), so all code paths in an iterator must contain a yield return statement if they are to return any data.

2.0

The following additional restrictions on the yield statement result in compiler errors if they are violated:

- The yield statement may appear only inside a method, a user-defined operator, or the get accessor of an indexer or property. The member must not take any ref or out parameter.

- The yield statement may not appear anywhere inside an anonymous method or lambda expression (see Chapter 13).

- The yield statement may not appear inside the catch and finally clauses of the try statement. Furthermore, a yield statement may appear in a try block only if there is no catch block.

SUMMARY

In this chapter, we reviewed the key collection classes and how they fit into categories according to the interfaces that they support. Each class focuses on inserting items into and retrieving items from the collection, using mechanisms such as by key, by index, or by FIFO or LIFO, to name a few. We also explored how to iterate over the collection. In addition, the chapter explained how to define custom collections with custom iterators for enumerating through items within the collection. (Iterators involve a contextual keyword, yield, that C# uses to generate underlying CIL code that implements the iterator pattern used by the foreach loop.)

In Chapter 18, we explore reflection, a topic briefly touched on earlier, albeit with little to no explanation. Reflection allows us to examine the structure of a type within CIL code at runtime.

End 2.0

∎ 18 ∎
Reflection, Attributes, and Dynamic Programming

ATTRIBUTES ARE A MEANS OF inserting additional metadata into an assembly and associating the metadata with a programming construct such as a class, method, or property. This chapter investigates the details surrounding attributes that are built into the framework and describes how to define custom attributes. To take advantage of custom attributes, it is necessary to identify them. This is handled through reflection. This chapter begins with a look at reflection, including how you can use it to dynamically bind at execution time based on member invocation by name (or metadata) at compile time. Reflection is frequently leveraged within tools such as a code generator. In addition, reflection is used at execution time when the call target is unknown.

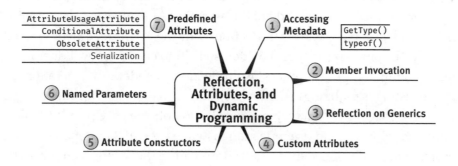

The chapter ends with a discussion of dynamic programming, a feature added in C# 4.0 that greatly simplifies working with data that is dynamic and requires execution-time rather than compile-time binding.

Reflection

Using reflection, it is possible to do the following.

- Access the metadata for types within an assembly. This includes constructs such as the full type name, member names, and any attributes decorating the construct.
- Dynamically invoke a type's members at runtime using the metadata, rather than a compile-time–defined binding.

Reflection is the process of examining the metadata within an assembly. Traditionally, when code compiles down to a machine language, all the metadata (such as type and method names) about the code is discarded. In contrast, when C# compiles into the Common Intermediate Language (CIL), it maintains most of the metadata about the code. Furthermore, using reflection, it is possible to enumerate through all the types within an assembly and search for those that match certain criteria. You access a type's metadata through instances of `System.Type`, and this object includes methods for enumerating the type instance's members. Additionally, it is possible to invoke those members on objects that are of the examined type.

The facility for reflection enables a host of new paradigms that otherwise are unavailable. For example, reflection enables you to enumerate over all the types within an assembly, along with their members, and in the process create stubs for documentation of the assembly API. You can then combine the metadata retrieved from reflection with the XML document created from XML comments (using the `/doc` switch) to create the API documentation. Similarly, programmers use reflection metadata to generate code for persisting (serializing) business objects into a database. It could also be used in a list control that displays a collection of objects. Given the collection, a list control could use reflection to iterate over all the properties of an object in the collection, defining a column within the list for each property. Furthermore, by invoking each property on each object, the list control could populate each row and column with the data contained in the object, even though the data type of the object is unknown at compile time.

XmlSerializer, ValueType, and the Microsoft .NET Framework's DataBinder are a few of the classes in the framework that use reflection for portions of their implementation as well.

Accessing Metadata Using System.Type

The key to reading a type's metadata is to obtain an instance of System.Type that represents the target type instance. System.Type provides all the methods for retrieving the information about a type. You can use it to answer questions such as the following:

- What is the type's name (Type.Name)?
- Is the type public (Type.IsPublic)?
- What is the type's base type (Type.BaseType)?
- Does the type support any interfaces (Type.GetInterfaces())?
- Which assembly is the type defined in (Type.Assembly)?
- What are a type's properties, methods, fields, and so on (Type .GetProperties(), Type.GetMethods(), Type.GetFields(), and so on)?
- Which attributes decorate a type (Type.GetCustomAttributes())?

There are more such members, but all of them provide information about a particular type. The key is to obtain a reference to a type's Type object, and the two primary ways to do so are through object.GetType() and typeof().

Note that the GetMethods() call does not return extension methods. These methods are available only as static members on the implementing type.

GetType()

object includes a GetType() member, and therefore, all types include this function. You call GetType() to retrieve an instance of System.Type corresponding to the original object. Listing 18.1 demonstrates this process, using a Type instance from DateTime. Output 18.1 shows the results.

LISTING 18.1: Using Type.GetProperties() to Obtain an Object's Public Properties

```csharp
DateTime dateTime = new DateTime();

Type type = dateTime.GetType();
foreach (
    System.Reflection.PropertyInfo property in
        type.GetProperties())
{
    Console.WriteLine(property.Name);
}
```

OUTPUT 18.1

```
Date
Day
DayOfWeek
DayOfYear
Hour
Kind
Millisecond
Minute
Month
Now
UtcNow
Second
Ticks
TimeOfDay
Today
Year
```

After calling GetType(), you iterate over each System.Reflection
.PropertyInfo instance returned from Type.GetProperties() and display the property names. The key to calling GetType() is that you must have an object instance. However, sometimes no such instance is available. Static classes, for example, cannot be instantiated, so there is no way to call GetType().

typeof()

Another way to retrieve a Type object is with the typeof expression. typeof binds at compile time to a particular Type instance, and it takes a type directly as a parameter. Listing 18.2 demonstrates the use of typeof with Enum.Parse().

LISTING 18.2: Using typeof() to Create a System.Type Instance

```csharp
using System.Diagnostics;
// ...
    ThreadPriorityLevel priority;
```

```
      priority = (ThreadPriorityLevel)Enum.Parse(
            typeof(ThreadPriorityLevel), "Idle");
 // ...
```

In this listing, Enum.Parse() takes a Type object identifying an enum and then converts a string to the specific enum value. In this case, it converts "Idle" to System.Diagnostics.ThreadPriorityLevel.Idle.

Similarly, Listing 18.3 in the next section uses the typeof expression inside the CompareTo(object obj) method to verify that the type of the obj parameter was indeed what was expected:

```
if(obj.GetType() != typeof(Contact)) { ... }
```

The typeof expression is resolved at compile time such that a type comparison—perhaps comparing the type returned from a call to GetType()—can determine if an object is of a specific type.

Member Invocation

The possibilities with reflection don't stop with retrieving the metadata. The next possible step is to take the metadata and dynamically invoke the members it references. Consider the possibility of defining a class to represent an application's command line.[1] The difficulty with a CommandLineInfo class such as this relates to populating the class with the actual command-line data that started the application. However, using reflection, you can map the command-line options to property names and then dynamically set the properties at runtime. Listing 18.3 demonstrates this process.

LISTING 18.3: Dynamically Invoking a Member

```
using System;
using System.Diagnostics;

public partial class Program
{
  public static void Main(string[] args)
  {
      string errorMessage;
      CommandLineInfo commandLine = new CommandLineInfo();
```

---

1. The .NET Standard 1.6 added the CommandLineUtils NuGet package that also provides a command-line parsing mechanism. For more information, see my MSDN article on the topic at http://itl.tc/sept2016.

```csharp
        if (!CommandLineHandler.TryParse(
            args, commandLine, out errorMessage))
        {
            Console.WriteLine(errorMessage);
            DisplayHelp();
        }

        if (commandLine.Help)
        {
            DisplayHelp();
        }
        else
        {
            if (commandLine.Priority !=
                ProcessPriorityClass.Normal)
            {
                // Change thread priority
            }

        }
        // ...

    }

    private static void DisplayHelp()
    {
        // Display the command-line help
        Console.WriteLine(
                "Compress.exe / Out:< file name > / Help \n"
                + "/ Priority:RealTime | High | "
                + "AboveNormal | Normal | BelowNormal | Idle");
    }
}
```

```csharp
using System;
using System.Diagnostics;

public partial class Program
{
    private class CommandLineInfo
    {
        public bool Help { get; set; }

        public string Out { get; set; }

        public ProcessPriorityClass Priority { get; set; }
            = ProcessPriorityClass.Normal;
    }
}
```

```csharp
using System;
using System.Diagnostics;
using System.Reflection;

public class CommandLineHandler
{
  public static void Parse(string[] args, object commandLine)
  {
      string errorMessage;
      if (!TryParse(args, commandLine, out errorMessage))
      {
          throw new ApplicationException(errorMessage);
      }
  }

  public static bool TryParse(string[] args, object commandLine,
      out string errorMessage)
  {
      bool success = false;
      errorMessage = null;
      foreach (string arg in args)
      {
          string option;
          if (arg[0] == '/' || arg[0] == '-')
          {
              string[] optionParts = arg.Split(
                  new char[] { ':' }, 2);

              // Remove the slash/dash
              option = optionParts[0].Remove(0, 1);
              PropertyInfo property =
                  commandLine.GetType().GetProperty(option,
                      BindingFlags.IgnoreCase |
                      BindingFlags.Instance |
                      BindingFlags.Public);
              if (property != null)
              {
                  if (property.PropertyType == typeof(bool))
                  {
                      // Last parameters for handling indexers
                      property.SetValue(
                          commandLine, true, null);
                      success = true;
                  }
                  else if (
                      property.PropertyType == typeof(string))
                  {
                      property.SetValue(
                          commandLine, optionParts[1], null);
                      success = true;
                  }
```

```csharp
                    else if (property.PropertyType.IsEnum)
                    {
                        try
                        {
                            property.SetValue(commandLine,
                                Enum.Parse(
                                    typeof(ProcessPriorityClass),
                                    optionParts[1], true),
                                null);
                            success = true;
                        }
                        catch (ArgumentException )
                        {
                            success = false;
                            errorMessage =
                                errorMessage =
                                    $@"The option '{
                                        optionParts[1]
                                        }' is invalid for '{
                                        option }'";
                        }
                    }
                    else
                    {
                        success = false;
                        errorMessage =
                            $@"Data type '{
                                property.PropertyType.ToString()
                                }' on {
                                commandLine.GetType().ToString()
                                } is not supported."
                    }
                }
                else
                {
                    success = false;
                    errorMessage =
                        $"Option '{ option }' is not supported.";
                }
            }
        }
        return success;
    }
}
```

Although Listing 18.3 is long, the code is relatively simple. `Main()` begins by instantiating a `CommandLineInfo` class. This type is defined specifically to contain the command-line data for this program. Each property corresponds to a command-line option for the program, where the command line is as shown in Output 18.2.

OUTPUT 18.2

```
Compress.exe /Out:<file name> /Help
    /Priority:RealTime|High|AboveNormal|Normal|BelowNormal|Idle
```

The `CommandLineInfo` object is passed to the `CommandLineHandler`'s `TryParse()` method. This method begins by enumerating through each option and separating out the option name (e.g., `Help` or `Out`). Once the name is determined, the code reflects on the `CommandLineInfo` object, looking for an instance property with the same name. If the property is found, it assigns the property using a call to `SetValue()` and specifies the data corresponding to the property type. (For arguments, this call accepts the object on which to set the value, the new value, and an additional `index` parameter that is `null` unless the property is an indexer.) This listing handles three property types: Boolean, string, and enum. In the case of enums, you parse the option value and assign the property the text's enum equivalent. Assuming the `TryParse()` call was successful, the method exits and the `CommandLineInfo` object is initialized with the data from the command line.

Interestingly, although `CommandLineInfo` is a private class nested within `Program`, `CommandLineHandler` has no trouble reflecting over it and even invoking its members. In other words, reflection can circumvent accessibility rules as long as appropriate permissions are established. If, for example, `Out` was private, it would still be possible for the `TryParse()` method to assign it a value. Because of this, it would be possible to move `CommandLineHandler` into a separate assembly and share it across multiple programs, each with its own `CommandLineInfo` class.

In this example, you invoke a member on `CommandLineInfo` using `PropertyInfo.SetValue()`. Not surprisingly, `PropertyInfo` also includes a `GetValue()` method for retrieving data from the property. For a method, however, there is a `MethodInfo` class with an `Invoke()` member. Both `MethodInfo` and `PropertyInfo` derive from `MemberInfo` (albeit indirectly), as shown in Figure 18.1.

The permissions (which are managed by a component of the runtime called Code Access Security [CAS]) are set up to allow private member invocation in this case because the program runs from the local computer. By default, locally installed programs are part of the trusted zone and have appropriate permissions granted. Programs run from a remote location will need to be explicitly granted such a right.

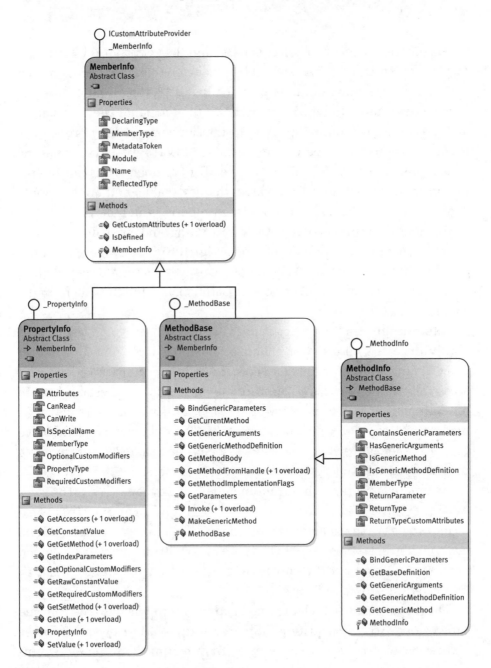

FIGURE 18.1: **MemberInfo Derived Classes**

Reflection on Generic Types

Begin 2.0

The introduction of generic types in version 2.0 of the Common Language Runtime (CLR) necessitated additional reflection features. Runtime reflection on generics determines whether a class or method contains a generic type and any type parameters or arguments it may include.

Determining the Type of Type Parameters

In the same way that you can use a typeof operator with nongeneric types to retrieve an instance of System.Type, so you can use the typeof operator on type parameters in a generic type or generic method. Listing 18.4 applies the typeof operator to the type parameter in the Add method of a Stack class.

LISTING 18.4: Declaring the Stack<T> Class

```
public class Stack<T>
{
    // ...
    public void Add(T i)
    {
        // ...
        Type t = typeof(T);
        // ...
    }
    // ...
}
```

Once you have an instance of the Type object for the type parameter, you may then use reflection on the type parameter itself to determine its behavior and tailor the Add method to the specific type more effectively.

Determining Whether a Class or Method Supports Generics

In the System.Type class for the version 2.0 release of the CLR, a handful of methods were added that determine whether a given type supports generic parameters and arguments. A generic argument is a type parameter supplied when a generic class is instantiated. You can determine whether a class or method contains generic parameters that have not yet been set by querying the Type.ContainsGenericParameters property, as demonstrated in Listing 18.5.

LISTING 18.5: Reflection with Generics

```csharp
using System;

public class Program
{
  static void Main()
  {
     Type type;
     type = typeof(System.Nullable<>);
     Console.WriteLine(type.ContainsGenericParameters);
     Console.WriteLine(type.IsGenericType);

     type = typeof(System.Nullable<DateTime>);
     Console.WriteLine(!type.ContainsGenericParameters);
     Console.WriteLine(type.IsGenericType);
  }
}
```

Output 18.3 shows the results of Listing 18.5.

OUTPUT 18.3

```
True
True
True
True
```

`Type.IsGenericType` is a Boolean property that evaluates whether a type is generic.

Obtaining Type Parameters for a Generic Class or Method

You can obtain a list of generic arguments, or type parameters, from a generic class by calling the `GetGenericArguments()` method. The result is an array of `System.Type` instances that corresponds to the order in which they are declared as type parameters of the generic class. Listing 18.6 reflects into a generic type and obtains each type parameter; Output 18.4 shows the results.

LISTING 18.6: Using Reflection with Generic Types

```csharp
using System;
using System.Collections.Generic;
```

2.0

```
public partial class Program
{
  public static void Main()
  {

    Stack<int> s = new Stack<int>();

    Type t = s.GetType();

    foreach(Type type in t.GetGenericArguments())
    {
      System.Console.WriteLine(
        "Type parameter: " + type.FullName);
    }
    // ...
  }
}
```

OUTPUT 18.4

```
Type parameter: System.Int32
```

End 2.0

nameof Operator

Begin 6.0

We briefly touched on the nameof operator in Chapter 11, where it was used to provide the name of a parameter in an argument exception:

```
throw new ArgumentException(
    "The argument did not represent a digit", nameof(textDigit));
```

Introduced in C# 6.0, this contextual keyword produces a constant string containing the unqualified name of whatever program element is specified as an argument. In this case, textDigit is a parameter to the method, so nameof(textDigit) returns "textDigit." (Given that this activity happens at compile time, nameof is not technically reflection. We include it here because ultimately it receives data about the assembly and its structure.)

You might ask what advantage is gained by using nameof(textDigit) over simply "textDigit" (especially given that the latter might even seem easier to use to some programmers). The advantages are twofold:

- The C# compiler ensures that the argument to the nameof operator is, in fact, a valid program element. This helps prevent errors when a program element name is changed, helps prevent misspellings, and so on.

- IDE tools work better with the nameof operator than with literal strings. For example, the "find all references" tool will find program elements mentioned in a nameof expression but not in a literal string. The automatic renaming refactoring also works better, and so on.

In the snippet given earlier, nameof(textDigit) produces the name of a parameter. However, the nameof operator works with any program element. For example, Listing 18.7 uses nameof to pass the property name to INotifyPropertyChanged.PropertyChanged.

LISTING 18.7: Dynamically Invoking a Member

```csharp
using System.ComponentModel;

public class Person : INotifyPropertyChanged
{
    public event PropertyChangedEventHandler PropertyChanged;
    public Person(string name)
    {
        Name = name;
    }
    private string _Name;
    public string Name
    {
        get { return _Name; }
        set
        {
            if (_Name != value)
            {
                _Name = value;
                // Using C# 6.0 conditional null reference
                PropertyChanged?.Invoke(
                    this,
                    new PropertyChangedEventArgs(
                        nameof(Name)));
            }
        }
    }
    // ...
}
```

Notice that whether only the unqualified "Name" is provided (because it's in scope) or the fully (or partially) qualified name such as Person.Name is used, the result is only the final identifier (the last element in a dotted name).

You can still use C# 5.0's CallerMemberName parameter attribute to obtain a property's name; see http://itl.tc/CallerMemberName for an example.

End 6.0

Attributes

Before delving into details on how to program attributes, we should consider a use case that demonstrates their utility. In the CommandLineHandler example in Listing 18.3, you dynamically set a class's properties based on the command-line option matching the property name. This approach is insufficient, however, when the command-line option is an invalid property name. /?, for example, cannot be supported. Furthermore, this mechanism doesn't provide any way of identifying which options are required versus which are optional.

Instead of relying on an exact match between the option name and the property name, you can use attributes to identify additional metadata about the decorated construct—in this case, the option that the attribute decorates. With attributes, you can decorate a property as Required and provide a /? option alias. In other words, attributes are a means of associating additional data with a property (and other constructs).

Attributes appear within square brackets preceding the construct they decorate. For example, you can modify the CommandLineInfo class to include attributes, as shown in Listing 18.8.

LISTING 18.8: Decorating a Property with an Attribute

```
class CommandLineInfo
{
    [CommandLineSwitchAlias("?")]
    public bool Help { get; set; }

    [CommandLineSwitchRequired]
    public string Out { get; set; }

    public System.Diagnostics.ProcessPriorityClass Priority
        { get; set; } =
            System.Diagnostics.ProcessPriorityClass.Normal;
}
```

In Listing 18.8, the Help and Out properties are decorated with attributes. The purpose of these attributes is to allow an alias of /? for /Help, and to indicate that /Out is a required parameter. The idea is that from within the CommandLineHandler.TryParse() method, you enable support for option aliases and, assuming the parsing was successful, you check that all required switches were specified.

There are two ways to combine attributes on the same construct. First, you can separate the attributes with commas within the same square brackets. Alternatively, you can place each attribute within its own square brackets. Listing 18.9 provides examples.

LISTING 18.9: Decorating a Property with Multiple Attributes

```
[CommandLineSwitchRequired]
[CommandLineSwitchAlias("FileName")]
    public string Out { get; set; }
```

```
[CommandLineSwitchRequired,
CommandLineSwitchAlias("FileName")]
    public string Out { get; set; }
```

In addition to decorating properties, developers can use attributes to decorate classes, interfaces, structs, enums, delegates, events, methods, constructors, fields, parameters, return values, assemblies, type parameters, and modules. For the majority of these cases, applying an attribute involves the same square bracket syntax shown in Listing 18.9. However, this syntax doesn't work for return values, assemblies, and modules.

Assembly attributes are used to add metadata about the assembly. Visual Studio's Project Wizard, for example, generates an `AssemblyInfo.cs` file that includes numerous attributes about the assembly. Listing 18.10 is an example of such a file.

LISTING 18.10: Assembly Attributes within `AssemblyInfo.cs`

```
using System.Reflection;
using System.Runtime.CompilerServices;
using System.Runtime.InteropServices;

// General information about an assembly is controlled
// through the following set of attributes. Change these
// attribute values to modify the information
// associated with an assembly.
[assembly: AssemblyTitle("CompressionLibrary")]
[assembly: AssemblyDescription("")]
[assembly: AssemblyConfiguration("")]
[assembly: AssemblyCompany("IntelliTect")]
[assembly: AssemblyProduct("Compression Library")]
[assembly: AssemblyCopyright("Copyright© IntelliTect 2006-2018")]
[assembly: AssemblyTrademark("")]
[assembly: AssemblyCulture("")]
```

```
// Setting ComVisible to false makes the types in this
// assembly not visible to COM components. If you need to
// access a type in this assembly from COM, set the ComVisible
// attribute to true on that type.
[assembly: ComVisible(false)]

// The following GUID is for the ID of the typelib
// if this project is exposed to COM
[assembly: Guid("417a9609-24ae-4323-b1d6-cef0f87a42c3")]

// Version information for an assembly consists
// of the following four values:
//
//       Major Version
//       Minor Version
//       Build Number
//       Revision
//
// You can specify all the values or you can
// default the Revision and Build Numbers
// by using the '*' as shown below:
// [assembly: AssemblyVersion("1.0.*")]
[assembly: AssemblyVersion("1.0.0.0")]
[assembly: AssemblyFileVersion("1.0.0.0")]
```

The `assembly` attributes define things such as the company, product, and assembly version number. Similar to `assembly`, identifying an attribute usage as `module` requires prefixing it with `module:`. The restriction on `assembly` and `module` attributes is that they must appear after the `using` directive but before any namespace or class declarations. The attributes in Listing 18.10 are generated by the Visual Studio Project Wizard and should be included in all projects to mark the resultant binaries with information about the contents of the executable or dynamic link library (DLL).

Return attributes, such as the one shown in Listing 18.11, appear before a method declaration but use the same type of syntax structure.

LISTING 18.11: Specifying a Return Attribute

```
[return: Description(
    "Returns true if the object is in a valid state.")]
public bool IsValid()
{
  // ...
  return true;
}
```

In addition to `assembly:` and `return:`, C# allows for explicit target identifications of `module:`, `class:`, and `method:`, corresponding to attributes that decorate the module, class, and method, respectively. `class:` and `method:`, however, are optional, as demonstrated earlier.

One of the conveniences of using attributes is that the language takes into consideration the attribute naming convention, which calls for `Attribute` to appear at the end of the name. However, in all the attribute *uses* in the preceding listings, no such suffix appears, despite the fact that each attribute used follows the naming convention. This is because although the full name (`DescriptionAttribute`, `AssemblyVersionAttribute`, and so on) is allowed when applying an attribute, C# makes the suffix optional. Generally, no such suffix appears when *applying* an attribute; rather, it appears only when defining one or using the attribute inline (such as `typeof(DescriptionAttribute)`).

Guidelines

DO apply `AssemblyVersionAttribute` to assemblies with public types.

CONSIDER applying the `AssemblyFileVersionAttribute` and `AssemblyCopyrightAttribute` to provide additional information about the assembly.

DO apply the following information assembly attributes:
`System.Reflection.AssemblyTitleAttribute`,
`System.Reflection.AssemblyCompanyAttribute`,
`System.Reflection.AssemblyProductAttribute`,
`System.Reflection.AssemblyDescriptionAttribute`,
`System.Reflection.AssemblyFileVersionAttribute`, and
`System.Reflection.AssemblyCopyrightAttribute`.

Custom Attributes

Defining a custom attribute is relatively trivial. Attributes are objects; therefore, to define an attribute, you need to define a class. The characteristic that turns a general class into an attribute is that it derives from `System.Attribute`. Consequently, you can create a `CommandLineSwitchRequiredAttribute` class, as shown in Listing 18.12.

LISTING 18.12: Defining a Custom Attribute

```
public class CommandLineSwitchRequiredAttribute : Attribute
{
}
```

With that simple definition, you now can use the attribute as demonstrated in Listing 18.8. So far, no code responds to the attribute; therefore, the `Out` property that includes the attribute will have no effect on command-line parsing.

> ### Guidelines
>
> DO name custom attribute classes with the suffix `Attribute`.

Looking for Attributes

In addition to providing properties for reflecting on a type's members, `Type` includes methods to retrieve the `Attributes` decorating that type. Similarly, all the reflection types (e.g., `PropertyInfo` and `MethodInfo`) include members for retrieving a list of attributes that decorate a type. Listing 18.13 defines a method to return a list of required switches that are missing from the command line.

LISTING 18.13: Retrieving a Custom Attribute

```
using System;
using System.Collections.Specialized;
using System.Reflection;

public class CommandLineSwitchRequiredAttribute : Attribute
{
  public static string[] GetMissingRequiredOptions(
      object commandLine)
  {
      List<string> missingOptions = new List<string>();
      PropertyInfo[] properties =
          commandLine.GetType().GetProperties();

      foreach (PropertyInfo property in properties)
      {
          Attribute[] attributes =
              (Attribute[])property.GetCustomAttributes(
                  typeof(CommandLineSwitchRequiredAttribute),
                  false);
```

```
            if ((attributes.Length > 0) &&
                (property.GetValue(commandLine, null) == null))
            {
                missingOptions.Add(property.Name);
            }
        }
        return missingOptions.ToArray();
    }
}
```

The code that checks for an attribute is relatively simple. Given a `PropertyInfo` object (obtained via reflection), you call `GetCustomAttributes()` and specify the attribute sought, then indicate whether to check any overloaded methods. (Alternatively, you can call the `GetCustomAttributes()` method without the attribute type to return all of the attributes.)

Although it is possible to place code for finding the `CommandLineSwitchRequiredAttribute` attribute within the `CommandLineHandler`'s code directly, it makes for better object encapsulation to place the code within the `CommandLineSwitchRequiredAttribute` class itself. This is frequently the pattern for custom attributes. What better location to place code for finding an attribute than in a static method on the attribute class?

Initializing an Attribute through a Constructor

The call to `GetCustomAttributes()` returns an array of objects that can be cast to an `Attribute` array. Because the attribute in our example didn't have any instance members, the only metadata information that it provided in the returned attribute was whether it appeared. Attributes can also encapsulate data, however. Listing 18.14 defines a `CommandLineAliasAttribute` attribute—a custom attribute that provides alias command-line options. For example, you can provide command-line support for /Help or /? as an abbreviation. Similarly, /S could provide an alias to /Subfolders that indicates the command should traverse all the subdirectories.

To support this functionality, you need to provide a constructor for the attribute. Specifically, for the alias, you need a constructor that takes a string argument. (Similarly, if you want to allow multiple aliases, you need to define an attribute that has a params string array for a parameter.)

LISTING 18.14: Providing an Attribute Constructor

```
public class CommandLineSwitchAliasAttribute : Attribute
{
  public CommandLineSwitchAliasAttribute(string alias)
  {
    Alias = alias;
  }

  public string Alias { get; private set; }
}


class CommandLineInfo
{
  [CommandLineSwitchAlias("?")]
  public bool Help { get; set; }

  // ...
}
```

When applying an attribute to a construct, only constant values and `typeof()` expressions are allowed as arguments. This constraint is intended to enable their serialization into the resultant CIL. It implies that an attribute constructor should require parameters of the appropriate types; creating a constructor that takes arguments of type `System.DateTime` would be of little value, as there are no `System.DateTime` constants in C#.

The objects returned from `PropertyInfo.GetCustomAttributes()` will be initialized with the specified constructor arguments, as demonstrated in Listing 18.15.

LISTING 18.15: Retrieving a Specific Attribute and Checking Its Initialization

```
PropertyInfo property =
    typeof(CommandLineInfo).GetProperty("Help");
CommandLineSwitchAliasAttribute attribute =
    (CommandLineSwitchAliasAttribute)
        property.GetCustomAttributes(
        typeof(CommandLineSwitchAliasAttribute), false)[0];
if(attribute.Alias == "?")
{
  Console.WriteLine("Help(?)");
};
```

Furthermore, as Listings 18.16 and 18.17 demonstrate, you can use similar code in a `GetSwitches()` method on `CommandLineAliasAttribute` that returns a dictionary collection of all the switches, including those from the property names, and associate each name with the corresponding attribute on the command-line object.

LISTING 18.16: Retrieving Custom Attribute Instances

```csharp
using System;
using System.Reflection;
using System.Collections.Generic;

public class CommandLineSwitchAliasAttribute : Attribute
{
  public CommandLineSwitchAliasAttribute(string alias)
  {
      Alias = alias;
  }

  public string Alias { get; set; }

  public static Dictionary<string, PropertyInfo> GetSwitches(
      object commandLine)
  {
      PropertyInfo[] properties = null;
      Dictionary<string, PropertyInfo> options =
          new Dictionary<string, PropertyInfo>();

      properties = commandLine.GetType().GetProperties(
          BindingFlags.Public | BindingFlags.NonPublic |
          BindingFlags.Instance);
      foreach (PropertyInfo property in properties)
      {
          options.Add(property.Name.ToLower(), property);
          foreach (CommandLineSwitchAliasAttribute attribute in
              property.GetCustomAttributes(
              typeof(CommandLineSwitchAliasAttribute), false))
          {
              options.Add(attribute.Alias.ToLower(), property);
          }
      }
      return options;
  }
}
```

LISTING 18.17: Updating CommandLineHandler.TryParse() to Handle Aliases

```csharp
using System;
using System.Reflection;
using System.Collections.Generic;

public class CommandLineHandler
{
  // ...
```

```csharp
public static bool TryParse(
    string[] args, object commandLine,
    out string errorMessage)
{

    bool success = false;
    errorMessage = null;

    Dictionary<string, PropertyInfo> options =
        CommandLineSwitchAliasAttribute.GetSwitches(
            commandLine);

    foreach (string arg in args)
    {
        PropertyInfo property;
        string option;
        if (arg[0] == '/' || arg[0] == '-')
        {
            string[] optionParts = arg.Split(
                new char[] { ':' }, 2);
            option = optionParts[0].Remove(0, 1).ToLower();

            if (options.TryGetValue(option, out property))
            {
                success = SetOption(
                    commandLine, property,
                    optionParts, ref errorMessage);
            }
            else
            {
                success = false;
                errorMessage =
                    $"Option '{ option }' is not supported.";
            }
        }
    }

    return success;
}


  private static bool SetOption(
      object commandLine, PropertyInfo property,
      string[] optionParts, ref string errorMessage)
  {
    bool success;

    if (property.PropertyType == typeof(bool))
    {
        // Last parameters for handling indexers
        property.SetValue(
            commandLine, true, null);
        success = true;
    }
```

```csharp
            else
            {

                if ((optionParts.Length < 2)
                    || optionParts[1] == ""
                    || optionParts[1] == ":")
                {
                    // No setting was provided for the switch
                    success = false;
                    errorMessage =
                        $"You must specify the value for the { property.Name }
option.";
                }
                else if (
                    property.PropertyType == typeof(string))
                {
                    property.SetValue(
                        commandLine, optionParts[1], null);
                    success = true;
                }
                else if (property.PropertyType.IsEnum)
                {
                    success = TryParseEnumSwitch(
                        commandLine, optionParts,
                        property, ref errorMessage);
                }
                else
                {
                    success = false;
                    errorMessage =
                        $@"Data type '{ property.PropertyType.ToString() }' on {
                            commandLine.GetType().ToString() } is not
supported.";
                }
            }
        }
        return success;
    }
}
```

System.AttributeUsageAttribute

Most attributes are intended to decorate only particular constructs. For example, it makes no sense to allow `CommandLineOptionAttribute` to decorate a class or an assembly. The attribute in those contexts would be meaningless. To avoid inappropriate use of an attribute, custom attributes can be decorated with `System.AttributeUsageAttribute` (yes, an attribute is decorating a custom attribute declaration). Listing 18.18 (for `CommandLineOptionAttribute`) demonstrates how to do this.

LISTING 18.18: Restricting the Constructs an Attribute Can Decorate

```
[AttributeUsage(AttributeTargets.Property)]
public class CommandLineSwitchAliasAttribute : Attribute
{
  // ...
}
```

If the attribute is used inappropriately, as it is in Listing 18.19, it will cause a compile-time error, as Output 18.5 demonstrates.

LISTING 18.19: AttributeUsageAttribute Restricting Where to Apply an Attribute

```
// ERROR: The attribute usage is restricted to properties
[CommandLineSwitchAlias("?")]
class CommandLineInfo
{
}
```

OUTPUT 18.5

```
...Program+CommandLineInfo.cs(24,17): error CS0592: Attribute
'CommandLineSwitchAlias' is not valid on this declaration type. It is
valid on 'property, indexer' declarations only.
```

`AttributeUsageAttribute`'s constructor takes an `AttributeTargets` flag. This enum provides a list of all possible targets that the runtime allows an attribute to decorate. For example, if you also allowed `CommandLineSwitchAliasAttribute` on a field, you would update the `AttributeUsageAttribute` class, as shown in Listing 18.20.

LISTING 18.20: Limiting an Attribute's Usage with **AttributeUsageAttribute**

```
// Restrict the attribute to properties and methods
[AttributeUsage(
    AttributeTargets.Field | AttributeTargets.Property)]
public class CommandLineSwitchAliasAttribute : Attribute
{
    // ...
}
```

Guidelines

DO apply the `AttributeUsageAttribute` class to custom attributes.

Named Parameters

In addition to restricting what an attribute can decorate, `AttributeUsageAttribute` provides a mechanism for allowing duplicates of the same attribute on a single construct. The syntax appears in Listing 18.21.

LISTING 18.21: Using a Named Parameter

```
[AttributeUsage(AttributeTargets.Property, AllowMultiple=true)]
public class CommandLineSwitchAliasAttribute : Attribute
{
    // ...
}
```

This syntax is different from the constructor initialization syntax discussed earlier. The `AllowMultiple` parameter is a **named parameter**, similar to the named parameter syntax used for optional method parameters (added in C# 4.0). Named parameters provide a mechanism for setting specific public properties and fields within the attribute constructor call, even though the constructor includes no corresponding parameters. The named attributes are optional designations, but they provide a means of setting additional instance data on the attribute without providing a constructor parameter for the purpose. In this case, `AttributeUsageAttribute` includes a public member called `AllowMultiple`. Therefore, you can set this member using a named parameter assignment when you use the attribute. Assigning named parameters must occur as the last portion of a constructor, following any explicitly declared constructor parameters.

Named parameters allow for assigning attribute data without providing constructors for every conceivable combination of which attribute properties are specified and which are not. Given that many of an attribute's properties may be optional, this is a useful construct in many cases.

■ BEGINNER TOPIC

FlagsAttribute

Chapter 9 introduced enums and included an Advanced Topic covering FlagsAttribute. This framework-defined attribute targets enums that represent flag type values. The Beginner Topic here also addresses FlagsAttribute, starting with the sample code shown in Listing 18.22.

LISTING 18.22: Using FlagsAttribute

```csharp
// FileAttributes defined in System.IO

[Flags]  // Decorating an enum with FlagsAttribute
public enum FileAttributes
{
  ReadOnly =        1<<0,      // 000000000000001
  Hidden =          1<<1,      // 000000000000010
  // ...
}
```

```csharp
using System;
using System.Diagnostics;
using System.IO;

class Program
{
  public static void Main()
  {
    // ...

      string fileName = @"enumtest.txt";
      FileInfo file = new FileInfo(fileName);

      file.Attributes = FileAttributes.Hidden |
          FileAttributes.ReadOnly;

      Console.WriteLine("\"{0}\" outputs as \"{1}\"",
          file.Attributes.ToString().Replace(",", " |"),
          file.Attributes);
```

```
            FileAttributes attributes =
                (FileAttributes)Enum.Parse(typeof(FileAttributes),
                file.Attributes.ToString());

            Console.WriteLine(attributes);

            // ...
        }
    }
```

Output 18.6 shows the results of Listing 18.22.

OUTPUT 18.6

```
"ReadOnly | Hidden" outputs as "ReadOnly, Hidden"
```

The flag documents that the enumeration values can be combined. Furthermore, it changes the behavior of the `ToString()` and `Parse()` methods. For example, calling `ToString()` on an enumeration that is decorated with `FlagsAttribute` writes out the strings for each enumeration flag that is set. In Listing 18.22, `file.Attributes.ToString()` returns "ReadOnly, Hidden" rather than the 3 it would have returned without the `FlagsAttribute` flag. If two enumeration values are the same, the `ToString()` call would return the first one. As mentioned earlier, however, you should use caution when relying on this outcome because it is not localizable.

Parsing a value from a string to the enumeration also works, provided each enumeration value identifier is separated by a comma.

Note that `FlagsAttribute` does not automatically assign the unique flag values or check that flags have unique values. The values of each enumeration item still must be assigned explicitly.

Predefined Attributes

The `AttributeUsageAttribute` attribute has a special characteristic that you haven't seen yet in the custom attributes you have created in this book. This attribute affects the behavior of the compiler, causing the compiler to sometimes report an error. Unlike the reflection code you wrote earlier for retrieving `CommandLineRequiredAttribute` and `CommandLineSwitchAliasAttribute`, `AttributeUsageAttribute` has no runtime code; instead, it has built-in compiler support.

AttributeUsageAttribute is a predefined attribute. Not only do such attributes provide additional metadata about the constructs they decorate, but the runtime and compiler also behave differently to facilitate these attributes' functionality. Attributes such as AttributeUsageAttribute, FlagsAttribute, ObsoleteAttribute, and ConditionalAttribute are examples of predefined attributes. They implement special behavior that only the CLI provider or compiler can offer because there are no extension points for additional noncustom attributes. In contrast, custom attributes are entirely passive. Listing 18.22 includes a couple of predefined attributes; Chapter 19 includes a few more.

System.ConditionalAttribute

Within a single assembly, the System.Diagnostics .ConditionalAttribute attribute behaves a little like the #if/#endif preprocessor identifier. However, instead of eliminating the CIL code from the assembly, System.Diagnostics.ConditionalAttribute will optionally cause the call to behave like a **no-op**, an instruction that does nothing. Listing 18.23 demonstrates the concept, and Output 18.7 shows the results.

LISTING 18.23: Using ConditionalAttribute to Eliminate a Call

```
#define CONDITION_A

using System;
using System.Diagnostics;

public class Program
{
  public static void Main()
  {
    Console.WriteLine("Begin...");
    MethodA();
    MethodB();
    Console.WriteLine("End...");
  }

  [Conditional("CONDITION_A")]
  static void MethodA()
  {
    Console.WriteLine("MethodA() executing...");
  }
```

```
    [Conditional("CONDITION_B")]
    static void MethodB()
    {
        Console.WriteLine("MethodB() executing...");
    }
}
```

OUTPUT 18.7

```
Begin...
MethodA() executing...
End...
```

This example defined `CONDITION_A`, so `MethodA()` executed normally. `CONDITION_B`, however, was not defined either through `#define` or by using the `csc.exe /Define` option. As a result, all calls to `Program.MethodB()` from within this assembly will do nothing.

Functionally, `ConditionalAttribute` is similar to placing an `#if`/`#endif` around the method invocation. The syntax is cleaner, however, because developers create the effect by adding the `ConditionalAttribute` attribute to the target method without making any changes to the caller itself.

The C# compiler notices the attribute on a called method during compilation, and assuming the preprocessor identifier exists, it eliminates any calls to the method. `ConditionalAttibute`, however, does not affect the compiled CIL code on the target method itself (besides the addition of the attribute metadata). Instead, it affects the call site during compilation by removing the calls. This further distinguishes `ConditionalAttribute` from `#if`/`#endif` when calling across assemblies. Because the decorated method is still compiled and included in the target assembly, the determination of whether to call a method is based not on the preprocessor identifier in the callee's assembly but rather on the caller's assembly. In other words, if you create a second assembly that defines `CONDITION_B`, any calls to `Program.MethodB()` from the second assembly will execute. This is a useful characteristic in many tracing and testing scenarios. In fact, calls to `System.Diagnostics.Trace` and `System.Diagnostics.Debug` use this trait with `ConditionalAttributes` on `TRACE` and `DEBUG` preprocessor identifiers.

Because methods don't execute whenever the preprocessor identifier is not defined, `ConditionalAttribute` may not be used on methods that include an out parameter or specify a return other than void. Doing so causes a compile-time error. This makes sense because potentially none of the code within the decorated method will execute, so it is unknown what to return to the caller. Similarly, properties cannot be decorated with ConditionalAttribute. The AttributeUsage (see the section titled "System.AttributeUsageAttribute" earlier in this chapter) for ConditionalAttribute[2] is AttributeTargets .Class and AttributeTargets.Method, which allows the attribute to be used on either a method or a class. However, the class usage is special because ConditionalAttribute is allowed only on System.Attribute-derived classes.

When ConditionalAttribute decorates a custom attribute, the latter can be retrieved via reflection only if the conditional string is defined in the calling assembly. Without such a conditional string, reflection that looks for the custom attribute will fail to find it.

System.ObsoleteAttribute

As mentioned earlier, predefined attributes affect the compiler's and/ or the runtime's behavior. ObsoleteAttribute provides another example of attributes affecting the compiler's behavior. Its purpose is to help with the versioning of code, providing a means of indicating to callers that a member or type is no longer current. Listing 18.24 is an example of ObsoleteAttribute usage. As Output 18.8 shows, any callers that compile code that invokes a member marked with ObsoleteAttribute will cause a compile-time warning, optionally an error.

LISTING 18.24: Using ObsoleteAttribute

```csharp
class Program
{
  public static void Main()
  {
      ObsoleteMethod();
  }

  [Obsolete]
  public static void ObsoleteMethod()
  {
  }
}
```

---

2. A feature started in Microsoft .NET Framework 2.0.

OUTPUT 18.8

```
c:\SampleCode\ObsoleteAttributeTest.cs(24,17): warning CS0612:
Program.ObsoleteMethod()' is obsolete
```

In this case, `ObsoleteAttribute` simply displays a warning. However, there are two additional constructors on the attribute. One of them, `ObsoleteAttribute(string message)`, appends the additional message argument to the compiler's obsolete message. The best practice for this message is to provide direction on what replaces the obsolete code. The second constructor is a `bool error` parameter that forces the warning to be recorded as an error instead.

`ObsoleteAttribute` allows third parties to notify developers of deprecated APIs. The warning (not an error) allows the original API to continue to work until the developer is able to update the calling code.

Serialization-Related Attributes

Using predefined attributes, the framework supports the capacity to serialize objects onto a stream so that they can be deserialized back into objects at a later time. This provides a means of easily saving a document type object to disk before shutting down an application. Later on, the document may be deserialized so that the user can continue to work on it.

Although an object can be relatively complex and can include links to many other types of objects that also need to be serialized, the serialization framework is easy to use. For an object to be serializable, the only requirement is that it includes a `System.SerializableAttribute`. Given the attribute, a formatter class reflects over the serializable object and copies it into a stream (see Listing 18.25).

LISTING 18.25: Saving a Document Using `System.SerializableAttribute`

```csharp
using System;
using System.IO;
using System.Runtime.Serialization.Formatters.Binary;

class Program
{
  public static void Main()
  {
      Stream stream;
      Document documentBefore = new Document();
```

```
        documentBefore.Title =
            "A cacophony of ramblings from my potpourri of notes";
        Document documentAfter;

        using (stream = File.Open(
            documentBefore.Title + ".bin", FileMode.Create))
        {
            BinaryFormatter formatter =
                new BinaryFormatter();
            formatter.Serialize(stream, documentBefore);
        }

        using (stream = File.Open(
            documentBefore.Title + ".bin", FileMode.Open))
        {
            BinaryFormatter formatter =
                new BinaryFormatter();
            documentAfter = (Document)formatter.Deserialize(
                stream);
        }

        Console.WriteLine(documentAfter.Title);
    }
}
```

```
// Serializable classes use SerializableAttribute
[Serializable]
class Document
{

    public string Title = null;
    public string Data = null;

    [NonSerialized]
    public long _WindowHandle = 0;

    class Image
    {
    }
    [NonSerialized]
    private Image Picture = new Image();
}
```

Output 18.9 shows the results of Listing 18.25.

OUTPUT 18.9

```
A cacophony of ramblings from my potpourri of notes
```

Listing 18.25 serializes and deserializes a Document object. Serialization involves instantiating a formatter (System.Runtime .Serialization.Formatters.Binary.BinaryFormatter, in this example) and calling Serialization() with the appropriate stream object. Deserializing the object simply involves calling the formatter's Deserialize() method, specifying the stream that contains the serialized object as an argument. However, given that the return from Deserialize() is of type object, you also need to cast it specifically to the type that was serialized.

Notice that serialization occurs for the entire object graph (all items associated with the serialized object [Document] via a field). Therefore, all fields in the object graph also must be serializable.

System.NonSerializable

Fields that are not serializable should be decorated with the System .NonSerializable attribute, which tells the serialization framework to ignore them. The same attribute should appear on fields that should not be persisted for use-case reasons. Passwords and Windows handles are good examples of fields that should not be serialized: Windows handles because they change each time a window is re-created, and passwords because data serialized into a stream is not encrypted and can be readily accessed. Consider the Notepad view of the serialized document in Figure 18.2.

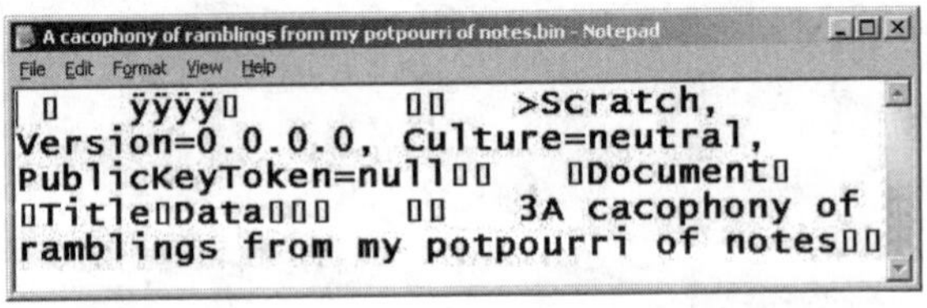

FIGURE 18.2: BinaryFormatter Does Not Encrypt Data

Listing 18.25 set the Title field, and the resultant *.BIN file includes the text in plain view.

Providing Custom Serialization

One way to add encryption is to provide custom serialization. Ignoring the complexities of encrypting and decrypting, this requires implementing the `ISerializable` interface in addition to using `SerializableAttribute`. The interface requires only the `GetObjectData()` method to be implemented. However, this is sufficient only for serialization. To support deserialization as well, it is necessary to provide a constructor that takes parameters of type `System.Runtime.Serialization.SerializationInfo` and `System.Runtime.Serialization.StreamingContext` (see Listing 18.26).

LISTING 18.26: Implementing System.Runtime.Serialization.ISerializable

```csharp
using System;
using System.Runtime.Serialization;

[Serializable]
class EncryptableDocument :
    ISerializable
{
    public EncryptableDocument(){ }

    enum Field
    {
        Title,
        Data
    }
    public string Title;
    public string Data;

    public static string Encrypt(string data)
    {
        string encryptedData = data;
        // Key-based encryption ...
        return encryptedData;
    }

    public static string Decrypt(string encryptedData)
    {
        string data = encryptedData;
        // Key-based decryption...
        return data;
    }
```

```
#region ISerializable Members
    public void GetObjectData(
    SerializationInfo info, StreamingContext context)
{
    info.AddValue(
        Field.Title.ToString(), Title);
    info.AddValue(
        Field.Data.ToString(), Encrypt(Data));
}

public EncryptableDocument(
    SerializationInfo info, StreamingContext context)
{
    Title = info.GetString(
        Field.Title.ToString());
    Data = Decrypt(info.GetString(
        Field.Data.ToString()));
}
#endregion
}
```

Essentially, the System.Runtime.Serialization.SerializationInfo object is a collection of name/value pairs. When serializing, the GetObject() implementation calls AddValue(). To reverse the process, you call one of the Get*() members. In this case, you encrypt and decrypt prior to serialization and deserialization, respectively.

Versioning the Serialization

One more serialization point deserves mention: versioning. Objects such as documents may be serialized using one version of an assembly and deserialized using a newer version; the reverse may also occur. If the programmer is not paying sufficient attention, however, version incompatibilities can easily be introduced in this process, sometimes unexpectedly. Consider the scenario shown in Table 18.1.

TABLE 18.1: Deserialization of a New Version Throws an Exception

Step	Description	Code

1	Define a class decorated with System.SerializableAttribute.	`[Serializable]`
		`class Document`
		`{`

2	Add a field or two (public or private) of any serializable type.	`    public string Title;`
		`    public string Data;`
		`}`

TABLE 18.1: Deserialization of a New Version Throws an Exception (*continued*)

Step	Description	Code
3	Serialize the object to a file called `*.v1.bin`.	```csharp‎Stream stream;‎Document documentBefore = new‎ Document();‎documentBefore.Title =‎ "A cacophony of ramblings from‎ ↳ my potpourri of notes";‎Document documentAfter;‎‎using (stream = File.Open(‎ documentBefore.Title + ".bin",‎ FileMode.Create))‎{‎ BinaryFormatter formatter =‎ new BinaryFormatter();‎ formatter.Serialize(‎ stream, documentBefore);‎}```
4	Add an additional field to the serializable class.	```csharp‎[Serializable]‎class Document‎{‎ public string Title;‎ public string Author;‎ public string Data;‎}```
5	Deserialize the `*v1.bin` file into the new object (`Document`) version.	```csharp‎using (stream = File.Open(‎ documentBefore.Title + ".bin",‎ FileMode.Open))‎{‎ BinaryFormatter formatter =‎ new BinaryFormatter();‎ documentAfter =‎ (Document)formatter.‎ ↳ Deserialize(‎ stream);‎}```

Surprisingly, even though all you did was add a new field, deserializing the original file throws a `System.Runtime.Serialization.SerializationException`. This is because the formatter looks for data corresponding to the new field within the stream. Failure to locate such data throws an exception.

Begin 2.0

End 2.0

To avoid this problem, the Microsoft .Net Framework 2.0 and later include a System.Runtime.Serialization.OptionalFieldAttribute. When backward compatibility is required, you must decorate serialized fields—even private ones—with OptionalFieldAttribute (unless, of course, a later version begins to require it).

■ ADVANCED TOPIC

System.SerializableAttribute and the CIL

In many ways, the serialization attributes behave just like custom attributes. At runtime, the formatter class searches for these attributes, and if the attributes exist, the classes are formatted appropriately. One of the characteristics that makes System.SerializableAttribute more than just a custom attribute, however, is that the CIL has a special header notation for serializable classes. Listing 18.27 shows the class header for the Person class in the CIL.

LISTING 18.27: The CIL for SerializableAttribute

```
class auto ansi serializable nested private
  beforefieldinit Person
  extends [mscorlib]System.Object
{
} // end of class Person
```

In contrast, attributes (including most predefined attributes) generally appear within a class definition (see Listing 18.28).

LISTING 18.28: The CIL for Attributes in General

```
.class private auto ansi beforefieldinit Person
     extends [mscorlib]System.Object
{
  .custom instance void CustomAttribute::.ctor() =
    ( 01 00 00 00 )
} // end of class Person
```

In Listing 18.28, CustomAttribute is the full name of the decorating attribute.

SerializableAttribute translates to a set bit within the metadata tables. This makes SerializableAttribute a **pseudoattribute**—that is, an attribute that sets bits or fields in the metadata tables.

Programming with Dynamic Objects

The introduction of dynamic objects in C# 4.0 simplified a host of programming scenarios and enabled several new ones previously not available. At its core, programming with dynamic objects enables developers to code operations using a dynamic dispatch mechanism that the runtime will resolve at execution time rather than the compiler verifying and binding to it at compile time.

Why? Many times, objects are inherently not statically typed. Examples include loading data from an XML/CSV file, a database table, the Internet Explorer DOM, or COM's `IDispatch` interface, or calling code in a dynamic language such as an IronPython object. C# 4.0's `Dynamic` object support provides a common solution for talking to runtime environments that don't necessarily have a compile-time–defined structure. In the initial implementation of dynamic objects in C# 4.0, four binding methods are available:

1. Using reflection against an underlying CLR type
2. Invoking a custom `IDynamicMetaObjectProvider` that makes available a `DynamicMetaObject`
3. Calling through the `IUnknown` and `IDispatch` interfaces of COM
4. Calling a type defined by dynamic languages such as IronPython

Of these four approaches, we will delve into the first two. The principles underlying them translate seamlessly to the remaining cases—COM interoperability and dynamic language interoperability.

Invoking Reflection Using `dynamic`

One of the key features of reflection is the ability to dynamically find and invoke a member on a type based on an execution-time identification of the member name or some other quality, such as an attribute (see Listing 18.3). However, C# 4.0's addition of dynamic objects provides a simpler way of invoking a member by reflection, assuming compile-time knowledge of the member signature. To reiterate, this restriction states that at compile time we need to know the member name along with the signature (the number of parameters and whether the specified parameters will be type-compatible with the signature). Listing 18.29 (with Output 18.10) provides an example.

LISTING 18.29: Dynamic Programming Using Reflection

```csharp
using System;

// ...
dynamic data =
  "Hello!  My name is Inigo Montoya";
Console.WriteLine(data);
data = (double)data.Length;
data = data * 3.5 + 28.6;
if(data == 2.4 + 112 + 26.2)
{
  Console.WriteLine(
      $"{ data } makes for a long triathlon.");
}
else
{
  data.NonExistentMethodCallStillCompiles();
}
// ...
```

OUTPUT 18.10

```
Hello!  My name is Inigo Montoya
140.6 makes for a long triathlon.
```

In this example, there is no explicit code for determining the object type, finding a particular `MemberInfo` instance, and then invoking it. Instead, data is declared as type `dynamic` and methods are called against it directly. At compile time, there is no check as to whether the members specified are available or even a check regarding which type underlies the dynamic object. Hence, it is possible at compile time to make any call so long as the syntax is valid. At compile time, it is irrelevant whether there is really a corresponding member.

However, type safety is not abandoned altogether. For standard CLR types (such as those used in Listing 18.29), the same type checker normally used at compile time for non-dynamic types is instead invoked at execution time for the `dynamic` type. Therefore, at execution time, if no such member is available, the call will result in a `Microsoft.CSharp.RuntimeBinder.RuntimeBinderException`.

Note that this capability is not nearly as flexible as the reflection described earlier in the chapter, although the API is undoubtedly simpler. The key difference when using a dynamic object is that it is necessary to identify the signature at compile time rather than determine things such as the member name at runtime (as we did when parsing the command-line arguments).

dynamic Principles and Behaviors

Listing 18.29 and the accompanying text reveal several characteristics of the dynamic data type:

- *dynamic is a directive to the compiler to generate code.*

  dynamic involves an interception mechanism so that when a dynamic call is encountered by the runtime, it can compile the request to CIL and then invoke the newly compiled call. (See the Advanced Topic titled "dynamic Uncovered" later in this chapter for more details.)

  The principle at work when a type is assigned to dynamic is to conceptually "wrap" the original type so that no compile-time validation occurs. Additionally, when a member is invoked at runtime, the wrapper intercepts the call and dispatches it appropriately (or rejects it). Calling GetType() on the dynamic object reveals the type underlying the dynamic instance—it does not return dynamic as a type.

- *Any type that converts to object will convert to dynamic.*

  In Listing 18.28, we successfully cast both a value type (double) and a reference type (string) to dynamic. In fact, all types can successfully be converted into a dynamic object. There is an implicit conversion from any reference type to dynamic. Similarly, there is an implicit conversion (a boxing conversion) from a value type to dynamic. In addition, there is an implicit conversion from dynamic to dynamic. This is perhaps obvious, but with dynamic this process is more complicated than simply copying the "pointer" (address) from one location to the next.

- *Successful conversion from dynamic to an alternative type depends on support in the underlying type.*

  Conversion from a dynamic object to a standard CLR type is an explicit cast (e.g., (double)data.Length). Not surprisingly, if the target type is a value type, an unboxing conversion is required. If the underlying type supports the conversion to the target type, the conversion from dynamic will also succeed.

4.0

- *The type underlying the dynamic type can change from one assignment to the next.*

  Unlike an implicitly typed variable (var), which cannot be reassigned to a different type, dynamic involves an interception mechanism for compilation before the underlying type's code is executed. Therefore, it is possible to successfully swap out the underlying type instance to an entirely different type. This will result in another interception call site that will need to be compiled before invocation.

- *Verification that the specified signature exists on the underlying type doesn't occur until runtime—but it does occur.*

  The compiler makes almost no verification of operations on a dynamic type, as the method call to person .NonExistentMethodCallStillCompiles() demonstrates. This step is left entirely to the work of the runtime when the code executes. Moreover, if the code never executes, even though surrounding code does (as with person .NonExistentMethodCallStillCompiles()), no verification and binding to the member will ever occur.

- *The result of any dynamic member invocation is of compile-time type dynamic.*

  A call to any member on a dynamic object will return a dynamic object. Therefore, calls such as data.ToString() will return a dynamic object rather than the underlying string type. However, at execution time, when GetType() is called on the dynamic object, an object representing the runtime type is returned.

- *If the member specified does not exist at runtime, the runtime will throw a Microsoft.CSharp.RuntimeBinder.RuntimeBinderException exception.*

  If an attempt to invoke a member at execution time does occur, the runtime will verify that the member call is truly valid (e.g., that the signatures are type-compatible in the case of reflection). If the method signatures are not compatible, the runtime will throw a Microsoft.CSharp.RuntimeBinder.RuntimeBinderException.

- *dynamic with reflection does not support extension methods.*

  Just like with reflection using System.Type, reflection using dynamic does not support extension methods. Invocation of extension methods is still available on the implementing type (e.g., `System.Linq.Enumerable`), just not on the extended type directly.

- *At its core, dynamic is a System.Object.*

  Given that any object can be successfully converted to dynamic, and that dynamic may be explicitly converted to a different object type, dynamic behaves like `System.Object`. Like `System.Object`, it even returns `null` for its default value (`default(dynamic)`), indicating it is a reference type. The special dynamic behavior of dynamic that distinguishes it from a `System.Object` appears only at compile time.

■ ADVANCED TOPIC

dynamic Uncovered

The CIL disassembler reveals that within the CIL, the dynamic type is actually a `System.Object`. In fact, without any invocations, declaration of the dynamic type is indistinguishable from `System.Object`. However, the difference becomes apparent when invoking a member. To invoke the member, the compiler declares a variable of type `System.Runtime.CompilerServices.CallSite<T>`. T varies on the basis of the member signature, but something simple such as the invocation of `ToString()` would require instantiation of the type `CallSite<Func<CallSite, object, string>>`, along with a method call with parameters of `CallSite site`, `object dynamicTarget`, and `string result`. site is the call site itself, dynamicTarget is the `object` on which the method call is invoked, and result is the underlying return value from the `ToString()` method call. Rather than instantiate `CallSite<Func<CallSite _site, object dynamicTarget, string result>>` directly, a `Create()` factory method is available for instantiating it. (`Create()` takes a parameter of type `Microsoft.CSharp.RuntimeBinder.CSharpConvertBinder`.) Given an instance of the `CallSite<T>`, the final step involves a call to `CallSite<T>.Target()` to invoke the actual member.

Under the covers at execution time, the framework uses reflection to look up members and to verify that the signatures match. Next, the runtime builds an expression tree that represents the dynamic expression as

4.0

defined by the call site. Once the expression tree is compiled, we have a CIL method body that is similar to what the compiler would have generated had the call not been dynamic. This CIL code is then cached in the call site, and the invocation occurs using a delegate invoke. As the CIL is now cached at the call site, the next invocation doesn't require all the reflection and compilation overhead again.

Why Dynamic Binding?

In addition to reflection, we can define custom types that we invoke dynamically. We might consider using dynamic invocation to retrieve the values of an XML element, for example. Rather than using the strongly typed syntax of Listing 18.30, using dynamic invocation we could call person.FirstName and person.LastName.

LISTING 18.30: Runtime Binding to XML Elements without dynamic

```csharp
using System;
using System.Xml.Linq;

// ...
XElement person = XElement.Parse(
    @"<Person>
        <FirstName>Inigo</FirstName>
        <LastName>Montoya</LastName>
</Person>");

Console.WriteLine("{0} {1}",
    person.Descendants("FirstName").FirstOrDefault().Value,
    person.Descendants("LastName").FirstOrDefault().Value);
// ...
```

Although the code in Listing 18.30 is not overly complex, compare it to Listing 18.31—an alternative approach that uses a dynamically typed object.

LISTING 18.31: Runtime Binding to XML Elements with dynamic

```csharp
using System;

// ...
dynamic person = DynamicXml.Parse(
    @"<Person>
        <FirstName>Inigo</FirstName>
        <LastName>Montoya</LastName>
    </Person>");

Console.WriteLine(
    $"{ person.FirstName } { person.LastName }");
// ...
```

The advantages are clear, but does that mean dynamic programming is preferable to static compilation?

Static Compilation versus Dynamic Programming

In Listing 18.31, we have the same functionality as in Listing 18.30, albeit with one very important difference: Listing 18.30 is entirely statically typed. Thus, at compile time, all types and their member signatures are verified with this approach. Method names are required to match, and all parameters are checked for type compatibility. This is a key feature of C# and something we have highlighted throughout the book.

In contrast, Listing 18.31 has virtually no statically typed code; the variable person is instead dynamic. As a result, there is no compile-time verification that person has a FirstName or LastName property—or any other members, for that matter. Furthermore, when coding within an IDE, there is no IntelliSense identifying any members on person.

The loss of typing would seem to result in a significant decrease in functionality. Why, then, is such a possibility even available in C#—a functionality that was added in C# 4.0, in fact?

To understand this apparent paradox, let's reexamine Listing 18.31. Notice the call to retrieve the "FirstName" element: Element .Descendants("LastName").FirstOrDefault().Value. The listing uses a string ("LastName") to identify the element name, but there is no compile-time verification that the string is correct. If the casing was inconsistent with the element name or if there was a space, the compile would still succeed, even though a NullReferenceException would occur with the call to the Value property. Furthermore, the compiler does not attempt to verify that the "FirstName" element even exists; if it doesn't, we would also get the NullReferenceException message. In other words, in spite of all the type-safety advantages, type safety doesn't offer many benefits when you're accessing the dynamic data stored within the XML element.

Listing 18.31 is no better than Listing 18.30 when it comes to compile-time verification of the element retrieval. If a case mismatch occurs or if the FirstName element didn't exist, there would still be an exception.[3] However, compare the call to access the first name in

4.0

---

3. You cannot use a space in the FirstName property call, but neither does XML support spaces in element names, so let's ignore this fact.

Listing 18.31 (person.FirstName) with the call in Listing 18.30. The call in the latter listing is undoubtedly significantly simpler.

In summary, there are situations in which type safety doesn't—and likely can't—make certain checks. In such cases, code that makes a dynamic call that is verified only at runtime, rather than also being verified at compile time, is significantly more readable and succinct. Obviously, if compile-time verification is possible, statically typed programming is preferred because readable and succinct APIs can accompany it. However, in the cases where it isn't effective, C# 4.0's dynamic capabilities enables programmers to write simpler code rather than emphasizing the purity of type safety.

Implementing a Custom Dynamic Object

Listing 18.31 included a method call to DynamicXml.Parse(...) that was essentially a factory method call for DynamicXml—a custom type rather than one built into the CLR framework. However, DynamicXml doesn't implement a FirstName or LastName property. To do so would break the dynamic support for retrieving data from the XML file at execution time rather than fostering compile-time-based implementation of the XML elements. In other words, DynamicXml does not use reflection for accessing its members but rather dynamically binds to the values based on the XML content.

The key to defining a custom dynamic type is implementation of the System.Dynamic.IDynamicMetaObjectProvider interface. Rather than implementing the interface from scratch, however, the preferred approach is to derive the custom dynamic type from System.Dynamic.DynamicObject. This provides default implementations for a host of members and allows you to override the ones that don't fit. Listing 18.32 shows the full implementation.

LISTING 18.32: Implementing a Custom Dynamic Object

```
using System;
using System.Dynamic;
using System.Xml.Linq;

public class DynamicXml : DynamicObject
{
    private XElement Element { get; set; }

    public DynamicXml(System.Xml.Linq.XElement element)
    {
        Element = element;
    }
}
```

```csharp
public static DynamicXml Parse(string text)
{
    return new DynamicXml(XElement.Parse(text));
}

public override bool TryGetMember(
    GetMemberBinder binder, out object result)
{
    bool success = false;
    result = null;
    XElement firstDescendant =
        Element.Descendants(binder.Name).FirstOrDefault();
    if (firstDescendant != null)
    {
        if (firstDescendant.Descendants().Count() > 0)
        {
            result = new DynamicXml(firstDescendant);
        }
        else
        {
            result = firstDescendant.Value;
        }
        success = true;
    }
    return success;
}

public override bool TrySetMember(
    SetMemberBinder binder, object value)
{
    bool success = false;
    XElement firstDescendant =
        Element.Descendants(binder.Name).FirstOrDefault();
    if (firstDescendant != null)
    {
        if (value.GetType() == typeof(XElement))
        {
            firstDescendant.ReplaceWith(value);
        }
        else
        {
            firstDescendant.Value = value.ToString();
        }
        success = true;
    }
    return success;
}
}
```

4.0

The key dynamic implementation methods for this use case are
TryGetMember() and TrySetMember() (assuming you want to assign

the elements as well). Only these two method implementations are necessary to support the invocation of the dynamic getter and setter properties. Furthermore, the implementations are straightforward. First, they examine the contained XElement, looking for an element with the same name as the binder.Name—the name of the member invoked. If a corresponding XML element exists, the value is retrieved (or set). The return value is set to true if the element exists and false if it doesn't. A return value of false will immediately cause the runtime to throw a Microsoft.CSharp.RuntimeBinder.RuntimeBinderException at the call site of the dynamic member invocation.

System.Dynamic.DynamicObject supports additional virtual methods if more dynamic invocations are required. Listing 18.33 produces a list of all overridable members.

LISTING 18.33: Overridable Members on System.Dynamic.DynamicObject

```
using System.Dynamic;

public class DynamicObject : IDynamicMetaObjectProvider
{
  protected DynamicObject();

  public virtual IEnumerable<string> GetDynamicMemberNames();
  public virtual DynamicMetaObject GetMetaObject(
      Expression parameter);
  public virtual bool TryBinaryOperation(
      BinaryOperationBinder binder, object arg,
          out object result);
  public virtual bool TryConvert(
      ConvertBinder binder, out object result);
  public virtual bool TryCreateInstance(
      CreateInstanceBinder binder, object[] args,
          out object result);
  public virtual bool TryDeleteIndex(
      DeleteIndexBinder binder, object[] indexes);
  public virtual bool TryDeleteMember(
      DeleteMemberBinder binder);
  public virtual bool TryGetIndex(
      GetIndexBinder binder, object[] indexes,
          out object result);
  public virtual bool TryGetMember(
      GetMemberBinder binder, out object result);
  public virtual bool TryInvoke(
      InvokeBinder binder, object[] args, out object result);
```

4.0

```
    public virtual bool TryInvokeMember(
        InvokeMemberBinder binder, object[] args,
            out object result);
    public virtual bool TrySetIndex(
        SetIndexBinder binder, object[] indexes, object value);
    public virtual bool TrySetMember(
        SetMemberBinder binder, object value);
    public virtual bool TryUnaryOperation(
        UnaryOperationBinder binder, out object result);
}
```

As Listing 18.33 shows, there are member implementations for everything—from casts and various operations, to index invocations. In addition, there is a method for retrieving all the possible member names: GetDynamicMemberNames().

End 4.0

SUMMARY

This chapter discussed how to use reflection to read the metadata that is compiled into the CIL. Using reflection, it is possible to provide a late binding in which the code to call is defined at execution time rather than at compile time. Although reflection is entirely feasible for deploying a dynamic system, it executes considerably more slowly than statically linked (compile-time), defined code. This tends to make it more prevalent and useful in development tools when performance is potentially not as critical.

Reflection also enables the retrieval of additional metadata decorating various constructs in the form of attributes. Typically, custom attributes are sought using reflection. You can define your own custom attributes that insert additional metadata of your own choosing into the CIL. At run-time, you can then retrieve this metadata and use it within the programming logic.

Many programmers view attributes as a precursor to a concept known as aspect-oriented programming, in which you add functionality through constructs such as attributes instead of manually implementing the functionality wherever it is needed. It will take some time before you see true aspects within C# (if ever); however, attributes provide a clear steppingstone in that direction, without creating a significant risk to the stability of the language.

Finally, this chapter included a feature introduced in C# 4.0—dynamic programming using the new type dynamic. This coverage included a discussion of why static binding, although preferred when the API is strongly typed, has limitations when working with dynamic data.

The next chapter looks at multithreading, where attributes are used for synchronization.

19

Multithreading

TWO SIGNIFICANT TRENDS OF THE PAST DECADE have had an enormous effect on the field of software development. First, the continued decrease in the cost of performing computations is no longer driven by increases in clock speed and transistor density, as illustrated by Figure 19.1. Rather, the cost of computation is now falling because it is economical to make hardware that has multiple CPUs.

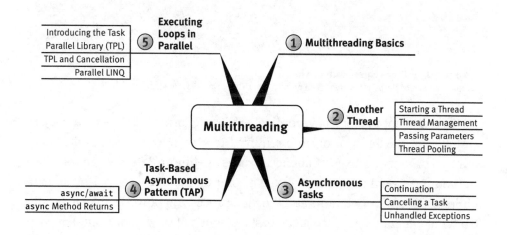

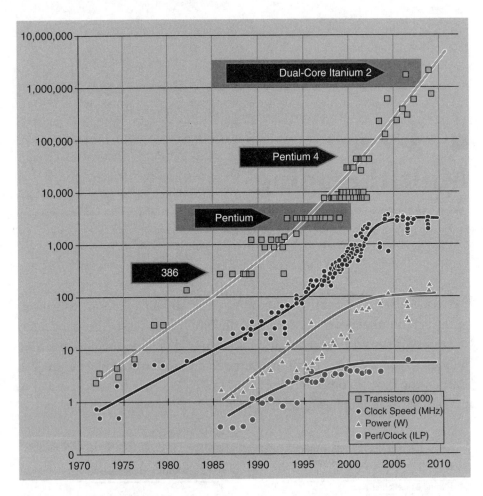

FIGURE 19.1: Clock Speeds over Time
(Graph compiled by Herb Sutter. Used with permission. Original at www.gotw.ca.)

Second, computations now routinely involve enormous **latency**. Latency is, simply put, the amount of time required to obtain a desired result. There are two principal causes of latency. **Processor-bound latency** occurs when the computational task is complex; if a computation requires performing 12 billion arithmetic operations and the total processing power available is only 6 billion operations per second, at least 2 seconds of processor-bound latency will be incurred between asking for the result and obtaining it. **I/O-bound latency**, by contrast, is latency incurred by the need to obtain data from an external source such as a disk drive, web server, and so on. Any computation that requires fetching data from a web server physically located far from the client machine will incur latency equivalent to millions of processor cycles.

These two trends together create an enormous challenge for modern software developers. Given that machines have more computing power than ever, how are we to make effective use of that power to deliver results to the user quickly and without compromising on the user experience? How do we avoid creating frustrating user interfaces that freeze up when a high-latency operation is triggered? Moreover, how do we go about splitting CPU-bound work among multiple processors to decrease the time required for the computation?

The standard technique for engineering software that keeps the user interface responsive and CPU utilization high is to write **multithreaded** programs that do multiple computations in parallel. Unfortunately, multithreading logic is notoriously difficult to get right; we spend the next two chapters exploring what makes multithreading difficult and learning how to use higher-level abstractions and new language features to ease that burden.

The higher-level abstractions we discuss are, first, the two principal components of the Parallel Extensions library that was released with .NET 4.0[1]—the **Task Parallel Library (TPL)** and **Parallel LINQ (PLINQ)**—and second, the **Task-based Asynchronous Pattern (TAP)** and its accompanying language support in C# 5.0 and later. Although we strongly encourage you to use these higher-level abstractions, we also cover some of the lower-level threading APIs from previous versions of the .NET runtime in this chapter. Additional multithreading patterns prior to C# 5.0 are available for download at https://IntelliTect.com/EssentialCSharp along with the chapters from *Essential C# 3.0*. Thus, if you want to fully understand the resources from multithreaded programming without the later features, you still have access to that material.

We start this chapter with a few beginner topics in case you are new to multithreading. Then we briefly discuss traditional thread manipulation without using the Parallel Extensions libraries to ensure that you have a basic understanding of thread manipulation; the following chapter goes into more details on that topic. We then spend most of this chapter covering the TPL, TAP, and PLINQ, in that order.

---

1. These libraries are available in .NET 3.5 by downloading the Reactive Extensions library for .NET 3.5.

Multithreading Basics

■ BEGINNER TOPIC

Multithreading Jargon

There is a lot of confusing jargon associated with multithreading, so let's define a few terms.

A **CPU** (central processing unit) or **core**[2] is the unit of hardware that actually executes a given program. Every machine has at least one CPU, though today multiple CPU machines are common. Many modern CPUs support **simultaneous multithreading** (which Intel trademarks as **Hyper-Threading**), a mode whereby a single CPU can appear as multiple "virtual" CPUs.

A **process** is a currently executing instance of a given program; the fundamental purpose of the operating system is to manage processes. Each process contains one or more threads. A process may be accessed programmatically by an instance of the `Process` class in the `System.Diagnostics` namespace.

C# programming at the level of statements and expressions is fundamentally about describing **flow of control**, and thus far in this book we've made the implicit assumption that a given program has only a single point of control. You can imagine the point of control as being a cursor that enters the text of your program at the `Main` method when you start it up, and then moves around the program as the various conditions, loops, method calls, and so on, are executed. A **thread** is this point of control. The `System.Threading` namespace contains the API for manipulating a thread, specifically, the `System.Threading.Thread` class.

A **single-threaded** program is one in which there is only one thread in the process. A **multithreaded** program has two or more threads in the process.

A piece of code is said to be **thread safe** if it behaves correctly when used in a multithreaded program. The **threading model** of a piece of code is the set of requirements that the code places upon its caller in exchange for guaranteeing thread safety. For example, the threading model of many

---

2. Technically, we ought to say that *CPU* always refers to the physical chip, and *core* may refer to a physical or virtual CPU. This distinction is unimportant for the purposes of this book, so we use these terms interchangeably.

classes is "static methods may be called from any thread, but instance methods may be called only from the thread that allocated the instance."

A **task** is a unit of potentially high-latency work that produces a resultant value or desired side effect. The distinction between tasks and threads is as follows: A task represents a job that needs to be performed, whereas a thread represents the worker that does the job. A task is useful only for its side effects and is represented by an instance of the Task class. A task used to produce a value of a given type is represented by the Task<T> class, which derives from the nongeneric Task type. These can be found in the System.Threading.Tasks namespace.

A **thread pool** is a collection of threads, along with logic for determining how to assign work to those threads. When your program has a task to perform, it can delegate a worker thread from the pool, assign the thread to perform the task, and then de-allocate it when the work completes, thereby making it available the next time additional work is requested.

■ **BEGINNER TOPIC**

The Why and How of Multithreading

There are two principal scenarios for multithreading: enabling multitasking and dealing with latency.

Users think nothing of running dozens of processes at the same time. They might have presentations and spreadsheets open for editing while at the same time they are browsing documents on the Internet, listening to music, receiving instant messages and email arrival notifications, and watching the little clock in the corner. Each of these processes has to continue to do its job even though it is not the only task the machine has to attend to. This kind of multitasking is usually implemented at the process level, but there are situations in which you want to do this sort of multitasking within single process.

For the purposes of this book, however, we will mostly be considering multithreading as a technique for dealing with latency. For example, to import a large file while simultaneously allowing a user to click Cancel, a developer creates an additional thread to perform the import. By performing the import on a different thread, the user can request cancellation instead of freezing the user interface until the import completes.

If enough cores are available that each thread can be assigned a core, each thread essentially gets its own little machine. However, more often than not, there are more threads than cores. Even the relatively common multicore machines of today still have only a handful of cores, while each process could quite possibly run dozens of threads.

To overcome the discrepancy between the numerous threads and the handful of cores, an operating system simulates multiple threads running concurrently by **time slicing**. The operating system switches execution from one thread to the next so quickly that it appears the threads are executing simultaneously. The period of time that the processor executes a particular thread before switching to another is the **time slice** or **quantum**. The act of changing which thread is executing in a given core is called a **context switch**.

The effect is similar to that of a fiber-optic telephone line in which the fiber-optic line represents the processor and each conversation represents a thread. A (single-mode) fiber-optic telephone line can send only one signal at a time, but many people can hold simultaneous conversations over the line. The fiber-optic channel is fast enough to switch between conversations so quickly that each conversation appears uninterrupted. Similarly, each thread of a multithreaded process appears to run continuously with other threads.

If two operations are running in parallel, via either true multicore parallelism or simulated parallelism using time slicing, they are said to be **concurrent**. To implement such concurrency, you invoke it **asynchronously**, such that both the execution and the completion of the invoked operation are separate from the control flow that invoked it. Concurrency, therefore, occurs when work dispatched asynchronously executes in parallel with the current control flow. **Parallel programming** is the act of taking a single problem and splitting it into pieces, whereby you **asynchronously** initiate the process of each piece such that the pieces can all be processed concurrently.

■ **BEGINNER TOPIC**

Performance Considerations

A thread that is servicing an I/O-bound operation can essentially be ignored by the operating system until the result is available from the I/O subsystem; switching away from an I/O-bound thread to a processor-bound thread results in more efficient processor utilization because the CPU is not idle while waiting for the I/O operation to complete.

However, context switching is not free; the current internal state of the CPU must be saved to memory, and the state associated with the new thread must be loaded. Similarly, if thread A is doing lots of work with one piece of memory, and thread B is doing lots of work with another piece of memory, context switching between them will likely mean that all of the data that was loaded into the cache from thread A will get replaced with the data from thread B (or vice versa). If there are too many threads, the switching overhead can begin to noticeably affect performance. Adding more threads will likely decrease performance further, to the point where the processor spends more time switching from one thread to another than it does accomplishing the work of each thread.

Even if we ignore the cost of context switching, time slicing itself can have a huge impact on performance. Suppose, for example, that you have two processor-bound high-latency tasks, each working out the average of two lists of 1 billion numbers each. Suppose the processor can perform 1 billion operations per second. If the two tasks are each associated with a thread, and the two threads each have their own core, obviously we can get both results in 1 second.

If, however, we have a single processor that the two threads share, time slicing will perform a few hundred thousand operations on one thread, then switch to the other thread, then switch back, and so on. Each task will consume a total of 1 second of processor time, and the results of both will therefore be available after 2 seconds, leading to an average completion time of 2 seconds. (Again, we are ignoring the cost of context switching.)

If we assigned those two tasks to a single thread that performed the first task and did not even start the second until after the first was completed, the result of the first task would be obtained in 1 second and the result of the subsequent task would be obtained 1 second after that, leading to an average time of 1.5 seconds (a task completes in either 1 or 2 seconds and therefore, on average, completes in 1.5 seconds).

Guidelines

DO NOT fall into the common error of believing that more threads always make code faster.

DO carefully measure performance when attempting to speed up processor-bound problems through multithreading.

■ BEGINNER TOPIC

Threading Problems

We've said several times that writing multithreaded programs is complex and difficult, but we have not said why. In a nutshell, the problem is that many of our reasonable assumptions that are true of single-threaded programs are violated in multithreaded programs. The issues include a lack of atomicity, race conditions, complex memory models, and deadlocks.

Most Operations Are Not Atomic

An atomic operation is one that always is observed to be either not started or already completed. Its state is never externally visible as "in progress." Consider, for example, this code fragment:

```
if (bankAccounts.Checking.Balance >= 1000.00m)
{
    bankAccounts.Checking.Balance -= 1000.00m;
    bankAccounts.Savings.Balance += 1000.00m;
}
```

This operation—checking for available funds and then conditionally debiting one account and crediting another—needs to be atomic. In other words, for it to execute correctly, we must ensure that there is never a moment when the operation can be observed to be partially completed. Imagine, for example, that two threads are running in this code concurrently. It is possible that both threads verify that there are sufficient funds in the account, and then both threads do a transfer of funds, even if there are only sufficient funds in the account to do the transfer once. And, in fact, the situation is considerably worse: There are *no* operations in this code fragment that are atomic! Even operations like compound addition/subtraction or reading and writing a property of decimal type are nonatomic operations in C#. As such, they can all be observed to be "partially complete" in multithreaded scenarios—only partially incremented or decremented. The observation of inconsistent state due to partially completed nonatomic operations is a special case of a more general problem, called a **race condition**.

Uncertainty Caused by Race Conditions

As we discussed earlier, concurrency is often simulated by time slicing. In the absence of special thread synchronization (which we discuss in detail the next chapter), the operating system can switch contexts between any two threads at any time of its choosing. As a consequence, when two threads are accessing the same object, which thread wins the race and gets to run first is unpredictable. If there are two threads running in the code fragment given previously, for example, it is possible that one thread might win the race and get all the way to the end before the second thread gets a chance to run. It is also possible that the context switch might happen after the first thread does the balance check, and the second thread might then win the race to get all the way to the end first.

The behavior of code that contains race conditions depends on the timing of context switches. This dependency introduces uncertainty concerning program execution. The order in which one instruction will execute relative to an instruction in a different thread is unknown. The worst of it is that code containing race conditions often will behave correctly 99.9 percent of the time, and then one time in a thousand a different thread wins the race due to an accident of timing. This unpredictability is what makes multithreaded programming so difficult.

Because such race conditions are difficult to replicate in the laboratory, much of the quality assurance of multithreaded code depends on long-running stress tests, specially designed code analysis tools, and a significant investment in code analysis and code review by experts. Perhaps more important than any of these is the discipline of keeping things as simple as possible. Often, in the name of hypothetical performance, a developer will try to avoid the simple approach of using a lock and go for lower-level primitives such as interlocked operations and volatiles, which makes it much more likely that their code is wrong. "Keep it simple" is possibly one of the most important guidelines of good multithreaded programming.

Chapter 20 is about techniques for dealing with race conditions.

Memory Models Are Complex

The existence of race conditions, where two points of control can "race" through a piece of code at unpredictable and inconsistent speeds, is bad enough, but it gets worse. Consider two threads that are running on two different processors but are accessing the same fields of some object. Modern processors do not actually access main memory every time you use a variable. Rather, they make a local copy in special cache memory on the processor; these caches are then periodically synchronized with main memory. This means that two threads that read from and write to the same location on two different processors can, in fact, be failing to observe each other's updates to that memory or observing inconsistent results. Essentially what we have here is a race condition that depends on when processors choose to synchronize their caches.

Locking Leads to Deadlocks

Clearly there must exist mechanisms to make nonatomic operations into atomic operations, to instruct the operating system to schedule threads so as to avoid races, and to ensure that processor caches are synchronized when necessary. The primary mechanism used to solve all these problems in C# programs is the lock statement. This statement allows the developer to identify a section of code as "critical" code that only one thread may be in at one time; if multiple threads try to enter the critical section, the operating system will suspend[3] all but one. The operating system also ensures that processor caches are synchronized properly upon encountering a lock.

However, locks introduce problems of their own (along with performance overhead). Most notably, if the order of lock acquisition between threads varies, a **deadlock** could occur such that threads freeze, each waiting for the other to release its lock.

For example, consider Figure 19.2.

Thread A	Thread B
Acquires a lock on A	Acquires a lock on B
Requests a lock on B	Requests a lock on A
Deadlocks, waiting for B	Deadlocks, waiting for A

Time

FIGURE 19.2: Deadlock Timeline

At this point, each thread is waiting on the other thread before proceeding, so each thread is blocked, leading to an overall deadlock in the execution of that code.

We discuss various locking techniques in detail in Chapter 20.

---

3. Either by putting the thread to sleep, spinning the thread, or spinning the thread before putting it back into sleep mode and repeating.

> ## Guidelines
>
> **DO NOT** make an unwarranted assumption that any operation that is atomic in regular code will be atomic in multithreaded code.
>
> **DO NOT** assume that all threads will observe all side effects of operations on shared memory in a consistent order.
>
> **DO** ensure that code that concurrently holds multiple locks always acquires them in the same order.
>
> **AVOID** all race conditions—that is, conditions where program behavior depends on how the operating system chooses to schedule threads.

Working with System.Threading

The Parallel Extensions library is extraordinarily useful because it allows you to manipulate a higher-level abstraction, the task, rather than working directly with threads. However, you might need to work with code written before the TPL and PLINQ were available (prior to .NET 4.0), or you might have a programming problem not directly addressed by them. In this section, we briefly cover some of the basic underlying APIs for directly manipulating threads.

Asynchronous Operations with System.Threading.Thread

The operating system implements threads and provides various unmanaged APIs to create and manage those threads. The Common Language Runtime (CLR) wraps these unmanaged threads and exposes them in managed code via the System.Threading.Thread class, an instance of which represents a point of control in the program. As mentioned earlier, you can think of a thread as a worker that independently follows the instructions that make up your program.

Listing 19.1 provides an example. The independent point of control is represented by an instance of Thread that runs concurrently. A thread needs to know which code to run when it starts up, so its constructor takes a delegate that refers to the code that is to be executed. In this case, we convert a method group, DoWork, to the appropriate delegate type, ThreadStart. We then start the thread running by calling Start(). While the new thread is running, the main thread attempts to print 10,000 hyphens to the console. We instruct the main thread to then wait for the worker thread to complete its work by calling Join(). The result is shown in Output 19.1.

LISTING 19.1: Starting a Method Using System.Threading.Thread

```csharp
using System;
using System.Threading;

public class RunningASeparateThread
{
  public const int Repetitions = 1000;

  public static void Main()
  {
      ThreadStart threadStart = DoWork;
      Thread thread = new Thread(threadStart);
      thread.Start();
      for(int count = 0; count < Repetitions; count++)
      {
          Console.Write('-');
      }
      thread.Join();
  }

  public static void DoWork()
  {
      for(int count = 0; count < Repetitions; count++)
      {
          Console.Write('+');
      }
  }
}
```

OUTPUT 19.1

```
+++++++++++++++++++++++++++++----------------------------------------
---------------------------------------------------------------------
---------------------------------------------------------------------
---------------------------------------------------------------------
---------------------------------------------------------------------
---------------------------------------------------------------+++++
+++++++++++++++++++++++++++++++++++++++++++++++++++++++++++++++++++++
+++++++++++++++++++++++++++++++++++++++++++++++++++++++++++++++++++++
+++++++++++++++++++++++++++++++++++++++++++++++++++++++++++++++++++++
+++++++++++++++++++++++++++++++++++++++++++++++++++++++++++++++++++++
+++++++++++++++++++++++++++++++++++++++++++++++++++++++++++++++++++++
+++++++++++++++++++++++++++-------------------------------------------
---------------------------------------------------------------------
---------------------------------------------------------------------
---------------------------------------------------------------------
-----------------------------------------+++++++++++++++++++
+++++++++++++++++++++++++++++++++++++++++++++++++++++++++++++++++++++
+++++++++++++++++++++++++++++++++++++++++++++++++++++++++++++++++++++
+++++++++++++++++++++++++++++++++++++++++++++++++++++++++++++++++++++
+++++++++++++++++++++++++++++++++++++++++++++++++++++++++++++++++++++
+++++++++++++++++++++++++++++++++++++++++++++++++++++++++++++++++++++
+++++++++++++++++-----------------------------------------------------
---------------------------------------------------------------------
------------------------------------+++++++++++++++++++++++++
+++++++++++++++++++++++++++++++++++++++++++++++++++++++++++++++++++++
+++++++++++++++++++++++++++++++++++++++++++++++
```

As you can see, the threads appear to be taking turns executing, each printing out a few hundred characters before the context switches. The two loops are running in parallel rather than the first one running to completion before the second one begins, as it would if the delegate had been executed synchronously.

For code to run under the context of a different thread, you need a delegate of type `ThreadStart` or `ParameterizedThreadStart` to identify the code to execute. (The latter allows for a single parameter of type `object`; both are found in the `System.Threading` namespace.) Given a `Thread` instance created using the thread-start delegate constructor, you can start the thread executing with a call to `thread.Start()`. (Listing 19.1 creates a variable of type `ThreadStart` explicitly to show the delegate type in the source code. The method group `DoWork` could have been passed directly to the thread constructor.) The call to `Thread.Start()` tells the operating system to begin concurrent execution of the new thread; control on the main thread immediately returns from the call and executes the `for` loop in the `Main()` method. The threads are now independent, and neither waits for the other until the call to `Join()`.

Thread Management

Threads include several methods and properties for managing their execution. Here are some of the basic ones:

- As we saw in Listing 19.1, you can cause one thread to wait for another with `Join()`. This tells the operating system to suspend execution of the current thread until the other thread is terminated. The `Join()` method is overloaded to take either an `int` or a `TimeSpan` to support a maximum time to wait for thread completion before continuing execution.

- By default, a new thread is a *foreground* thread; the operating system will terminate a process when all its foreground threads are complete. You can mark a thread as a *background* thread by setting the `IsBackground` property to `true`. The operating system will then allow the process to be terminated even if the background thread is still running. However, it is still a good idea to ensure that all threads are not terminated and instead to exit cleanly before the process exits; see the section "Canceling a Task" later in this chapter for more details.

- Every thread has an associated priority, which you can change by setting the `Priority` property to a new `ThreadPriority` enum value. The possible values are `Lowest`, `BelowNormal`, `Normal`, `AboveNormal`, and `Highest`. The operating system prefers to schedule time slices to higher-priority threads. Be careful; if you set the priorities incorrectly, you can end up with "starvation" situations where one high-priority thread prevents many low-priority threads from ever running.

- If you simply want to know whether a thread is still alive or has finished all of its work, you can use the Boolean `IsAlive` property. A more informative picture of a thread's state is accessible through the `ThreadState` property. The `ThreadState` enum values are `Aborted`, `AbortRequested`, `Background`, `Running`, `Stopped`, `StopRequested`, `Suspended`, `SuspendRequested`, `Unstarted`, and `WaitSleepJoin`. These are flags; some of these values can be combined.

There are two commonly used—and commonly abused—methods for controlling threads that deserve to be discussed in their own sections: `Sleep()` and `Abort()` (the latter is not available on .NET Core).

Do Not Put Threads to Sleep in Production Code

The static `Thread.Sleep(...)` method puts the current thread to sleep, essentially telling the operating system not to schedule any time slices to this thread until the given amount of time has passed. A single parameter—either a number of milliseconds or a `TimeSpan`—specifies how long the operating system will wait before continuing execution. While it is waiting, the operating system will, of course, schedule time slices for any other threads that might be waiting their turn to execute. This might sound like a sensible thing to do, but it is a "bad code smell" that indicates the design of the program could probably be better.

Threads are often put to sleep to try to synchronize a thread with some event in time. However, the operating system does not guarantee any level of precision in its timing. That is, if you say, "Put this thread to sleep for 123 milliseconds," the operating system will put it to sleep for *at least* 123 milliseconds, and possibly much longer. The actual amount of time between the thread going to sleep and then waking up again is not deterministic and can be arbitrarily long. Do not attempt to use `Thread.Sleep()` as a high-precision timer, because it is not.

Worse, `Thread.Sleep()` is often used as a "poor man's synchronization system." That is, if you have some unit of asynchronous work, and the current thread cannot proceed until that work is done, you might be tempted to put the thread to sleep for much longer than you think the asynchronous work will take, in the hopes that it will be finished when the current thread wakes up. This is a bad idea: Asynchronous work, by its very nature, can take longer than you think. Use proper thread synchronization mechanisms, described in the next chapter, to synchronize threads. (We'll give an example of this sort of abuse in Listing 19.2.)

Putting a thread to sleep is also a bad programming practice because it means that the sleeping thread is, obviously, unresponsive to attempts to run code on it. If you put the main thread of a Windows application to sleep, that thread will no longer be processing messages from the user interface and will therefore appear to be hung.

More generally, putting a thread to sleep is a bad programming practice because the whole point of allocating an expensive resource like a thread is to get work out of that resource. You wouldn't pay an employee to sleep, so do not pay the price of allocating an expensive thread only to put it to sleep for millions or billions of processor cycles.

That said, there are some valid uses of `Thread.Sleep()`. First, putting a thread to sleep with a time delay of zero tells the operating system "the current thread is politely giving up the rest of its quantum to another thread if there is one that can use it." The polite thread will then be scheduled normally, without any further delay. Second, `Thread.Sleep()` is commonly used in test code to simulate a thread that is working on some high-latency operation without actually having to burn a processor doing some pointless arithmetic. Other uses in production code should be reviewed carefully to ensure that there is not a better way to obtain the desired effect.

In task-based asynchronous programming in C# 5, you can use the `await` operator on the result of the `Task.Delay()` method to introduce an asynchronous delay without blocking the current thread. See the "Timers" section in Chapter 20 for further detail.

Guidelines

AVOID calling `Thread.Sleep()` in production code.

Do Not Abort Threads in Production Code

The Thread object has an Abort() method (although not available on .NET Core) that, when executed, attempts to destroy the thread. It does so by causing the runtime to throw a ThreadAbortException in the thread; this exception can be caught, but even if it is caught and ignored, it is automatically rethrown to try to ensure that the thread is, in fact, destroyed. There are many reasons why it is a very bad idea to attempt to abort a thread. Here are some of them:

- The method promises only to *try* to abort the thread; there is no guarantee that it will succeed. For example, the runtime will not attempt to cause a ThreadAbortException if the point of control of the thread is currently inside a finally block (because critical cleanup code could be running right now and should not be interrupted) or is in unmanaged code (because doing so could corrupt the CLR itself). Rather, the CLR defers throwing the exception until control leaves the finally block or returns to managed code. But there is no guarantee that this ever happens. The thread being aborted might contain an infinite loop inside a finally block. (Ironically, the fact that the thread has an infinite loop might be the reason you are attempting to abort it in the first place.)

- The aborted thread might be in critical code protected by a lock statement. (See Chapter 20 for details.) Unlike a finally block, a lock will not prevent the exception. The critical code will be interrupted halfway through by the exception, and the lock object will be automatically released, allowing other code that is waiting on the lock object to enter the critical section and observe the state of the halfway-executed code. The whole point of locking is to prevent that scenario, so aborting a thread can transform what looks like thread-safe code into dangerously incorrect code.

- The CLR guarantees that its internal data structures will never be corrupted if a thread is aborted, but the Base Class Library (BCL) does not make this guarantee. Aborting a thread can leave any of your data structures or the BCL's data structures in an arbitrarily bad state if the exception is thrown at the wrong time. Code running on other threads, or in the finally blocks of the aborted thread, can see this corrupted state and crash or behave badly.

In short, you should never abort a thread unless you are doing so as a last resort; ideally you should abort a thread only as part of a larger emergency shutdown whereby the entire AppDomain or the entire process is being destroyed. Fortunately, task-based asynchrony uses a more robust and safer cooperative cancellation pattern to terminate a thread when results are no longer needed, as discussed in the next major section, "Asynchronous Tasks."

Guidelines

AVOID aborting a thread in production code; doing so will yield unpredictable results and can destabilize a program.

Thread Pooling

As we discussed earlier, in the Beginner Topic titled "Performance Considerations," it is possible for an excess of threads to negatively impact performance. Threads are expensive resources, thread context switching is not free, and running two jobs in simulated parallelism via time slicing can be significantly slower than running them one after the other.

To mitigate these problems, the BCL provides a thread pool. Instead of allocating threads directly, you can tell the thread pool which work you want to perform. When the work is finished, rather than the thread terminating and being destroyed, it is returned to the pool, saving on the cost of allocating a new thread when more work comes along. Listing 19.2 shows how to do the same thing as Listing 19.1, but this time with a pooled thread.

LISTING 19.2: Using ThreadPool Instead of Instantiating Threads Explicitly

```csharp
using System;
using System.Threading;

public class Program
{
  public const int Repetitions = 1000;
  public static void Main()
  {
      ThreadPool.QueueUserWorkItem(DoWork, '+');

      for(int count = 0; count < Repetitions; count++)
      {
          Console.Write('-');
      }
```

```
        // Pause until the thread completes.
        // This is for illustrative purposes; do not
        // use Thread.Sleep for synchronization in
        // production code.
        Thread.Sleep(1000);
    }
    public static void DoWork(object state)
    {
        for(int count = 0; count < Repetitions; count++)
        {
            Console.Write(state);
        }
    }
}
```

The output of Listing 19.2 is similar to Output 19.1—that is, an intermingling of periods and hyphens. If we had a lot of different jobs to perform asynchronously, this pooling technique would provide more efficient execution on single-processor and multiprocessor computers. The efficiency is achieved by reusing threads over and over rather than reconstructing them for every asynchronous call. Unfortunately, thread pool use is not without its pitfalls: There are still performance and synchronization problems to consider when using a thread pool.

To make efficient use of processors, the thread pool assumes that all the work you schedule on the thread pool will finish in a timely manner so that the thread can be returned to the thread pool and reused by another task. The thread pool also assumes that all the work will be of a relatively short duration (i.e., consuming milliseconds or seconds of processor time, not hours or days). By making this assumption, it can ensure that each processor is working full out on a task and not inefficiently time-slicing multiple tasks, as described in the Beginner Topic on performance. The thread pool attempts to prevent excessive time slicing by ensuring that thread creation is "throttled" so that no one processor is oversubscribed with too many threads. Of course, as a consequence, consuming all threads within the pool can delay execution of queued-up work. If all the threads in the pool are consumed by long-running or I/O-bound work, the queued-up work will be delayed.

Unlike Thread and Task, which are objects that you can manipulate directly, the thread pool does not provide a reference to the thread used to execute a given piece of work. This prevents the calling thread from synchronizing with, or controlling, the worker thread via the thread management functions described earlier in the chapter. In Listing 19.2 we use the poor man's synchronization that we earlier discouraged; this would be a bad idea in production code because we do not actually know how long the work will take to complete.

In short, the thread pool does its job well, but that job does not include providing services to deal with long-running jobs or jobs that need to be synchronized with the main thread or with one another. What we really need to do is build a higher-level abstraction that can use threads and thread pools as an implementation detail; that abstraction is implemented by the TPL, which is the topic of most of the rest of this chapter.

For more details on other techniques for managing worker threads that were commonly used prior to .NET 4, see the *Essential C# 3.0* multithreading chapters at https://IntelliTect.com/EssentialCSharp.

Guidelines

DO use the thread pool to efficiently assign processor time to processor-bound tasks.

AVOID allocating a pooled worker thread to a task that is I/O bound or long-running; use TPL instead.

Asynchronous Tasks

Begin 4.0

Multithreaded programming includes the following complexities:

1. *Monitoring an asynchronous operation state for completion:* This includes determining when an asynchronous operation has completed, preferably not by polling the thread's state or by blocking and waiting.

2. *Thread pooling:* This avoids the significant cost of starting and tearing down threads. In addition, thread pooling avoids the creation of too many threads, such that the system spends more time switching threads than running them.

3. *Avoiding deadlocks:* This involves preventing the occurrence of deadlocks while attempting to protect the data from simultaneous access by two different threads.

4. *Providing atomicity across operations and synchronizing data access:* Adding synchronization around groups of operations ensures that operations execute as a single unit and that they are appropriately interrupted by another thread. Locking is provided so that two different threads do not access the data simultaneously.

Furthermore, anytime a method is long running, multithreaded programming will probably be required—that is, invoking the long-running method asynchronously. As developers write more multithreaded code, a common set of scenarios and programming patterns for handling those scenarios emerges.

C# 5.0 enhanced the programmability of one such pattern—TAP—by leveraging the TPL from .NET 4.0 and enhancing the C# language with new constructs to support it. This and the following section delve into the details of the TPL on its own and then the TPL with the `async`/`await` contextual keywords that simplify TAP programming.

From Thread to Task

Creating a thread is a relatively expensive operation, and each thread consumes a large amount (1 megabyte, by default, on Windows for example) of virtual memory. We saw earlier in this chapter that it is potentially more efficient to use a thread pool to allocate threads when needed, assign asynchronous work to the thread, run the work to completion, and then reuse the thread for subsequent asynchronous work rather than destroying the thread when the work is complete and creating a new one later.

In Microsoft .NET Framework 4 and later, instead of creating an operating system thread each time asynchronous work is started, the TPL creates a `Task` and tells the **task scheduler** that there is asynchronous work to perform. A task scheduler might use many different strategies to fulfill this purpose, but by default it requests a worker thread from the thread pool. The thread pool, as we've seen already, might decide that it is more efficient to run the task later, after some currently executing tasks have completed, or it might decide to schedule the task's worker thread to a particular processor. The thread pool determines whether it is more efficient to create an entirely new thread or to reuse an existing thread that previously finished executing.

By abstracting the concept of asynchronous work into the Task object, the TPL provides an object that represents asynchronous work and provides an object-oriented API for interacting with that work. Moreover, by providing an object that represents the unit of work, the TPL enables programmatically building up workflows by composing small tasks into larger ones, as we'll see.

A task is an object that encapsulates work that executes asynchronously. This should sound familiar: A *delegate* is also an object that represents code. The difference between a task and a delegate is that delegates are **synchronous** and tasks are **asynchronous**. Executing a delegate, say, an Action, immediately transfers the point of control of the current thread to the delegate's code; control does not return to the caller until the delegate is finished. By contrast, starting a task almost immediately returns control to the caller, no matter how much work the task must perform. The task executes asynchronously, typically on another thread (though, as we will see later in this chapter, it is possible and even beneficial to execute tasks asynchronously with only one thread). A task essentially transforms a delegate from a synchronous to an asynchronous execution pattern.

Introducing Asynchronous Tasks

You know when a delegate is done executing on the current thread because the caller cannot do anything until the delegate is done. But how do you know when a task is done, and how do you get the result, if there is one? Consider the example of turning a synchronous delegate into an asynchronous task. We'll do the same thing we did with threads in Listing 19.1 and thread pools in Listing 19.2, but this time with tasks: The worker thread will write periods to the console, while the main thread writes hyphens.

Starting the task obtains a thread from the thread pool, creating a second point of control, and executes the delegate on that thread. The point of control on the main thread continues normally after the call to start the task (Task.Run()). The results of Listing 19.3 are almost identical to Output 19.1.

LISTING 19.3: Invoking an Asynchronous Task

```
using System;
using System.Threading.Tasks;
```

```csharp
public class Program
{
  public static void Main()
  {
      const int Repetitions = 10000;
      // Use Task.Factory.StartNew<string>() for
      // TPL prior to .NET 4.5
      Task task = Task.Run(() =>
          {
              for(int count = 0;
                  count < Repetitions; count++)
              {
                  Console.Write('-');
              }
          });
      for(int count = 0; count < Repetitions; count++)
      {
          Console.Write('+');
      }

      // Wait until the Task completes
      task.Wait();
  }
}
```

The code that is to run in a new thread is defined in the delegate (of type `Action` in this case) passed to the `Task.Run()` method. This delegate (in the form of a lambda expression) prints out dashes to the console repeatedly. The loop that follows the starting of the task is almost identical, except that it displays plus signs.

4.0

Notice that following the call to `Task.Run()` the `Action` passed as the argument immediately starts executing. The `Task` is said to be "hot," meaning that it has already been triggered to start executing—as opposed to a "cold" task, which needs to be explicitly started before the asynchronous work begins.

Although a `Task` can also be instantiated in a cold state via the `Task` constructor, doing so is generally appropriate only as an implementation detail internal to an API that returns an already running (hot) `Task`, one triggered by a call to `Task.Start()`.

Notice that the exact state of a hot task is indeterminate immediately following the call to `Run()`. The behavior is determined by a combination of the operating system and its load, the .NET framework, and the accompanying task library. The combination determines whether `Run()` chooses to execute the task's worker thread immediately or delay it until additional resources are available. In fact, it is possible that the hot task is already finished by the time the code on the calling thread gets its turn to execute again. The call to `Wait()` forces the main thread to wait until all the work assigned to the task has completed executing. This is analogous to calling `Join()` on the worker thread, as we did in Listing 19.1.

In this scenario, we have a single task, but it is also possible for many tasks to be running asynchronously. It is common to have a set of tasks where you want to wait for all of them to complete, or for any one of them to complete, before continuing execution of the current thread. The `Task.WaitAll()` and `Task.WaitAny()` methods do so.

So far, we've seen how a task can take an `Action` and run it asynchronously. But what if the work executed in the task returns a result? We can use the `Task<T>` type to run a `Func<T>` asynchronously. When executing a delegate synchronously, we know that control will not return until the result is available. When executing a `Task<T>` asynchronously, we can poll it from one thread to see if it is done, and fetch the result when it is.[4] Listing 19.4 demonstrates how to do so in a console application. Note that this sample uses a `PiCalculator.Calculate()` method that we will delve into further in the section "Executing Loop Iterations in Parallel."

LISTING 19.4: Polling a Task<T>

```
using System;
using System.Threading.Tasks;

public class Program
{
  public static void Main()
  {
    // Use Task.Factory.StartNew<string>() for
    // TPL prior to .NET 4.5
    Task<string> task =
        Task.Run<string>(
            () => PiCalculator.Calculate(100));
```

4.0

---

4. Exercise caution when using this polling technique. When creating a task from a delegate, as we have here, the task will be scheduled to run on a worker thread from the thread pool. As a consequence, the current thread will loop until the work is complete on the worker thread. This technique works, but it might consume CPU resources unnecessarily. Such a polling technique is dangerously broken if, instead of scheduling the task to run on a worker thread, you schedule the task to execute in the future on the current thread. Since the current thread is in a loop polling the task, it will loop forever because the task will not complete until the current thread exits the loop.

```csharp
    foreach(
        char busySymbol in Utility.BusySymbols())
    {
        if(task.IsCompleted)
        {
            Console.Write('\b');
            break;
        }
        Console.Write(busySymbol);
    }

    Console.WriteLine();

    Console.WriteLine(task.Result);
    System.Diagnostics.Trace.Assert(
        task.IsCompleted);
    }
}


public class PiCalculator
{
    public static string Calculate(int digits = 100)
    {
        // ...
    }
}


public class Utility
{
    public static IEnumerable<char> BusySymbols()
    {
        string busySymbols = @"-\|/-\|/";
        int next = 0;
        while(true)
        {
            yield return busySymbols[next];
            next = (next + 1) % busySymbols.Length;
            yield return '\b';
        }
    }
}
```

This listing shows that the data type of the task is Task<string>. The generic type includes a Result property from which to retrieve the value returned by the Func<string> that the Task<string> executes.

Note that Listing 19.4 does not make a call to Wait(). Instead, reading from the Result property automatically causes the current thread to block until the result is available, if it isn't already; in this case we know that it will already be complete when the result is fetched.

In addition to the `IsCompleted` and `Result` properties on `Task<T>`, several others are worth noting:

- The `IsCompleted` property is set to `true` when a task completes, whether it completed normally or faulted (i.e., ended because it threw an exception). More detailed information on the status of a task can be obtained by reading the `Status` property, which returns a value of type `TaskStatus`. Possible values are `Created`, `WaitingForActivation`, `WaitingToRun`, `Running`, `WaitingForChildrenToComplete`, `RanToCompletion`, `Canceled`, and `Faulted`. `IsCompleted` is true whenever the `Status` is `RanToCompletion`, `Canceled`, or `Faulted`. Of course, if the task is running on another thread and you read the status as running, the status could change to completed at any time, including immediately after you read the value of the property. The same is true of many other states—even `Created` could potentially change if a different thread starts it. Only `RanToCompletion`, `Canceled`, and `Faulted` can be considered final states that no longer can be transitioned.

- A task can be uniquely identified by the value of the `Id` property. The static `Task.CurrentId` property provides the identifier for the currently executing `Task` (i.e., the task that is executing the `Task.CurrentId` call). These properties are especially useful when debugging. 4.0

- You can use the `AsyncState` to associate additional data with a task. For example, imagine a `List<T>` whose values will be computed by various tasks. Each task could contain the index of the value in the `AsyncState` property. This way, when the task completes, the code can index into the list using the `AsyncState` (first casting it to an `int`).[5]

We discuss other useful properties later in this chapter under "Canceling a Task."

---

5. Be careful when using tasks to asynchronously mutate collections. The tasks might be running on worker threads, and the collection might not be thread safe. It is safer to fill in the collection from the main thread after the tasks are completed.

Task Continuation

We've talked several times about the control flow of a program without ever saying what the most fundamental nature of control flow is: *Control flow determines what happens next.* When you have a simple control flow like `Console.WriteLine(x.ToString());`, the control flow tells you that when `ToString` completes normally, the next thing that will happen is a call to `WriteLine` with the value returned as the argument. The concept of "what happens next" is called **continuation**; each point in a control flow has a continuation. In our example, the continuation of `ToString` is `WriteLine` (and the continuation of `WriteLine` is whatever code runs in the next statement). The idea of continuation is so elementary to C# programming that most programmers don't even think about it; it's part of the invisible air that they breathe. The act of C# programming is the act of constructing continuation upon continuation until the control flow of the entire program is complete.

Notice that the continuation of a given piece of code in a normal C# program will be executed *immediately* upon the completion of that code. When `ToString()` returns, the point of control on the current thread immediately does a synchronous call to `WriteLine`. Notice also that there are actually two possible continuations of a given piece of code: the *normal* continuation and the *exceptional* continuation that will be executed if the current piece of code throws an exception.

Asynchronous method calls, such as starting a `Task`, add an additional dimension to the control flow. With an asynchronous `Task` invocation, the control flow goes immediately to the statement after the `Task.Start()`, while at the same time, it begins executing within the body of the `Task` delegate. In other words, what happens next when asynchrony is involved is multidimensional. Unlike with exceptions where the continuation is just a different path, with asynchrony continuation is an additional, parallel path.

Asynchronous tasks also allow composition of larger tasks out of smaller tasks by describing asynchronous continuations. Just as with regular control flow, a task can have different continuations to handle error situations, and tasks can be melded together by manipulating their continuations. There are several techniques for doing so, the most explicit of which is the `ContinueWith()` method (see Listing 19.5 and its corresponding output, Output 19.2).

LISTING 19.5: Calling Task.ContinueWith()

```csharp
using System;
using System.Threading.Tasks;

public class Program
{
  public static void Main()
  {
    Console.WriteLine("Before");
    // Use Task.Factory.StartNew<string>() for
    // TPL prior to .NET 4.5
    Task taskA =
        Task.Run( () =>
            Console.WriteLine("Starting..."))
        .ContinueWith(antecedent =>
            Console.WriteLine("Continuing A..."));
    Task taskB = taskA.ContinueWith( antecedent =>
        Console.WriteLine("Continuing B..."));
    Task taskC = taskA.ContinueWith( antecedent =>
        Console.WriteLine("Continuing C..."));
    Task.WaitAll(taskB, taskC);
    Console.WriteLine("Finished!");
  }
}
```

OUTPUT 19.2

```
Before
Starting...
Continuing A...
Continuing C...
Continuing B...
Finished!
```

4.0

The ContinueWith() method enables "chaining" two tasks together, such that when the predecessor task—the **antecedent task**—completes, the second task—the **continuation task**—is automatically started asynchronously. In Listing 19.5, for example, Console.WriteLine("Starting...") is the antecedent task body and Console.WriteLine("Continuing A...") is its continuation task body. The continuation task takes a Task as its argument (antecedent), thereby allowing the continuation task's code to access the antecedent task's completion state. When the antecedent task is completed, the continuation task starts automatically, asynchronously executing the second delegate and passing the just-completed antecedent task as an argument to that delegate. Furthermore, since the ContinueWith()

method returns a Task as well, that Task can be used as the antecedent of yet another Task, and so on, forming a continuation chain of Tasks that can be arbitrarily long.

If you call ContinueWith() twice on the same antecedent task (as Listing 19.5 shows with taskB and taskC representing continuation tasks for taskA), the antecedent task (taskA) has two continuation tasks, and when the antecedent task completes, both continuation tasks will be executed asynchronously. Notice that the order of execution of the continuation tasks from a single antecedent is indeterminate at compile time. Output 19.2 happens to show taskC executing before taskB, but in a second execution of the program, the order might be reversed. However, taskA will always execute before taskB and taskC because the latter are continuation tasks of taskA and therefore can't start before taskA completes. Similarly, the Console.WriteLine("Starting...") delegate will always execute to completion before taskA (Console.WriteLine("Continuing A...")) because the latter is a continuation task of the former. Furthermore, Finished! will always appear last because of the call to Task.WaitAll(taskB, taskC) that blocks the control flow from continuing until both taskB and taskC complete.

Many different overloads of ContinueWith() are possible, and some of them take a TaskContinuationOptions value to tweak the behavior of the continuation chain. These values are flags, so they can be combined using the logical OR operator (|). A brief description of some of the possible flag values appears in Table 19.1; see the online MSDN documentation[6] for more details.

TABLE 19.1: List of Available TaskContinuationOptions Enums

Enum	Description
None	This is the default behavior. The continuation task will be executed when the antecedent task completes, regardless of its task status.

6. MSDN .NET Framework Developer Center, http://msdn.microsoft.com/en-us/library/system.threading.tasks.taskcontinuationoptions(v=vs.110).aspx

TABLE 19.1: List of Available TaskContinuationOptions Enums (*continued*)

Enum	Description
PreferFairness	If two tasks were both asynchronously started, one before the other, there is no guarantee that the one that was started first actually gets to run first. This flag asks the task scheduler to try to increase the likelihood that the first task started is the first task to execute—something that is particularly relevant when the two tasks you describe are created from different thread pool threads.
LongRunning	This tells the task scheduler that the task is likely to be an I/O-bound high-latency task. The scheduler can then allow other queued work to be processed rather than starved because of the long-running task. This option should be used sparingly.
AttachedToParent	This specifies that a task should attempt to attach to a parent task within the task hierarchy.
DenyChildAttach (.NET 4.5)	This throws an exception if creation of a child task is attempted. If code within the continuation tries to use AttachedToParent, it will behave as if there was no parent.
NotOnRanToCompletion*	This specifies that the continuation task should not be scheduled if its antecedent ran to completion. This option is not valid for multitask continuations.
NotOnFaulted*	This specifies that the continuation task should not be scheduled if its antecedent threw an unhandled exception. This option is not valid for multitask continuations.
OnlyOnCanceled*	This specifies that the continuation task should be scheduled only if its antecedent was canceled. This option is not valid for multitask continuations.

4.0

continues

TABLE 19.1: List of Available TaskContinuationOptions Enums (*continued*)

Enum	Description
NotOnCanceled*	This specifies that the continuation task should not be scheduled if its antecedent was canceled. This option is not valid for multitask continuations.
OnlyOnFaulted*	This specifies that the continuation task should be scheduled only if its antecedent threw an unhandled exception. This option is not valid for multitask continuations.
OnlyOnRanToCompletion*	This specifies that the continuation task should be scheduled only if its antecedent ran to completion. This option is not valid for multitask continuations.
ExecuteSynchronously	This specifies that the continuation task should be executed synchronously. With this option specified, the continuation the schedule will attempt to execute the work on is the same thread that causes the antecedent task to transition into its final state. If the antecedent is already complete when the continuation is created, the continuation will run on the thread creating the continuation.
HideScheduler (.NET 4.5)	This prevents the ambient scheduler from being seen as the current scheduler in the created task. This means that operations like Run/StartNew and ContinueWith that are performed in the created task will see TaskScheduler.Default (null) as the current scheduler. This is useful when continuation should run on a particular scheduler, but the continuation is calling out to additional code that should not schedule work on the same scheduler.

4.0

TABLE 19.1: List of Available TaskContinuationOptions Enums (*continued*)

Enum	Description
LazyCancellation (.NET 4.5)	This causes the continuation to delay monitoring the supplied cancellation token for a cancellation request until the antecedent has completed. Consider tasks t1, t2, and t3, where the latter is a continuation of the former. If t2 is canceled before t1 completes, it is possible that t3 could start before t1 completes. Setting LazyCancellation avoids this.
RunContinuationsAsynchronously (.NET 4.6)	When a task is created with the RunContinuationsAsynchronously option, that tells the task that it should force its continuations to run asynchronously. Even if the task is itself a continuation, this option does not affect how that task is run, only how continuations from it are run. A continuation task can be created with both TaskContinuationOptions.ExecuteSynchronously and TaskContinuationOptions.RunContinuationsAsynchronously. The former causes the continuation to execute synchronously when its antecedent completes, and causes the continuation's continuations to run asynchronously when the continuation completes.

4.0

In Table 19.1, the items denoted with a star (*) indicate under which conditions the continuation task will be executed; thus they are particularly useful for creating continuations that act like event handlers for the antecedent task's behavior. Listing 19.6 demonstrates how an antecedent task can be given multiple continuations that execute conditionally, depending on how the antecedent task completed.

LISTING 19.6: Registering for Notifications of Task Behavior with ContinueWith()

```
using System;
using System.Threading.Tasks;
using System.Diagnostics;
using AddisonWesley.Michaelis.EssentialCSharp.Shared;
```

```
public class Program
{
  public static void Main()
  {
      // Use Task.Factory.StartNew<string>() for
      // TPL prior to .NET 4.5
      Task<string> task =
          Task.Run<string>(
              () => PiCalculator.Calculate(10));

      Task faultedTask = task.ContinueWith(
          (antecedentTask) =>
          {
              Trace.Assert(antecedentTask.IsFaulted);
              Console.WriteLine(
                  "Task State: Faulted");
          },
          TaskContinuationOptions.OnlyOnFaulted);

      Task canceledTask = task.ContinueWith(
          (antecedentTask) =>
          {
              Trace.Assert(antecedentTask.IsCanceled);
              Console.WriteLine(
                  "Task State: Canceled");
          },
          TaskContinuationOptions.OnlyOnCanceled);

      Task completedTask = task.ContinueWith(
          (antecedentTask) =>
          {
              Trace.Assert(antecedentTask.IsCompleted);
              Console.WriteLine(
                  "Task State: Completed");
          }, TaskContinuationOptions.
                OnlyOnRanToCompletion);

      completedTask.Wait();
  }
}
```

In this listing, we effectively register *listeners* for *events* on the antecedent's task so that when the task completes normally or abnormally, the particular "listening" task will begin executing. This is a powerful capability, particularly if the original task is a fire-and-forget task—that is, a task that we start, hook up to continuation tasks, and then never refer to again.

In Listing 19.6, notice that the final `Wait()` call is on `completedTask`, not on `task`—the original antecedent task created with `Task.Run()`. Although each delegate's `antecedentTask` is a reference to the antecedent task (`task`), from outside the delegate listeners we can effectively discard the reference to the original `task`. We can then rely solely on the continuation tasks that begin executing asynchronously without any need for follow-up code that checks the status of the original `task`.

In this case, we call `completedTask.Wait()` so that the main thread does not exit the program before the completed output appears (see Output 19.3).

OUTPUT 19.3

```
Task State: Completed.
```

In this case, invoking `completedTask.Wait()` is somewhat contrived because we know that the original task will complete successfully. However, invoking `Wait()` on `canceledTask` or `faultedTask` will result in an exception. Those continuation tasks run only if the antecedent task is canceled or throws an exception; given that will not happen in this program, those tasks will never be scheduled to run, and waiting for them to complete would throw an exception. The continuation options in Listing 19.3 happen to be mutually exclusive, so when the antecedent task runs to completion and the task associated with `completedTask` executes, the task scheduler automatically cancels the tasks associated with `canceledTask` and `faultedTask`. The canceled tasks end with their state set to `Canceled`. Therefore, calling `Wait()` (or any other invocation that would cause the current thread to wait for a task completion) on either of these tasks will throw an exception indicating that they are canceled.

A less contrived approach might be to call `Task.WaitAny(` `completedTask, canceledTask, faultedTask)`, which will throw an `AggregateException` that then needs to be handled.

Unhandled Exception Handling on Task with `AggregateException`

When calling a method synchronously, we can wrap it in a try block with a catch clause to identify to the compiler which code we want to execute when an exception occurs. This does not work with an asynchronous call, however. We cannot simply wrap a try block around a call to `Start()` to catch an exception, because control immediately returns from the call, and control will then leave the try block, possibly long before the exception occurs on the worker thread. One solution is to wrap the body of the task delegate with a try/catch block. Exceptions thrown on and subsequently caught by the worker thread will consequently not present problems, as a try block will work normally on the worker thread. This is not the case, however, for unhandled exceptions—those that the worker thread does not catch.

Generally (starting with version 2.0[7] of the CLR), unhandled exceptions on any thread are treated as fatal, trigger the operating system error reporting dialog, and cause the application to terminate abnormally. All exceptions on all threads must be caught, and if they are not, the application is not allowed to continue to run. (For some advanced techniques for dealing with unhandled exceptions, see the upcoming Advanced Topic titled "Dealing with Unhandled Exceptions on a Thread.") Fortunately, this is not the case, however, for unhandled exceptions in an asynchronously running task. Rather, the task scheduler inserts a catchall exception handler around the delegate so that if the task throws an otherwise unhandled exception, the catchall handler will catch it and record the details of the exception in the task, avoiding any trigger of the CLR automatically terminating the process.

As we saw in Listing 19.6, one technique for dealing with a faulted task is to explicitly create a continuation task that is the fault handler for that task; the task scheduler will automatically schedule the continuation when it detects that the antecedent task threw an unhandled exception. If no such handler is present, however, and `Wait()` (or an attempt to get the `Result`) executes on a faulted task, an `AggregateException` will be thrown (see Listing 19.7 and Output 19.4).

LISTING 19.7: Handling a Task's Unhandled Exception

```
using System;
using System.Threading.Tasks;

public class Program
{
```

---

7. In version 1.0 of the CLR, an unhandled exception on a worker thread terminated the thread but not the application. As a result, it was possible for a buggy program to have all its worker threads die, but the main thread would continue to run, even though the program was no longer doing any work. This is a confusing situation for users to be in; it is better to signal to the user that the application is in a bad state and terminate it before it can do any more harm.

```csharp
public static void Main()
{
    // Use Task.Factory.StartNew<string>() for
    // TPL prior to .NET 4.5
    Task task = Task.Run(() =>
    {
        throw new InvalidOperationException();
    });

    try
    {
        task.Wait();
    }
    catch(AggregateException exception)
    {
        exception.Handle(eachException =>
            {
                Console.WriteLine(
                    $"ERROR: { eachException.Message }");
                return true;
            });
    }
}
```

OUTPUT 19.4

```
ERROR: Operation is not valid due to the current state of the object.
```

4.0

The aggregate exception is so called because it may contain many exceptions collected from one or more faulted tasks. Imagine, for example, asynchronously executing ten tasks in parallel and five of them throwing exceptions. To report all five exceptions and have them handled in a single catch block, the framework uses the `AggregateException` as a means of collecting the exceptions and reporting them as a single exception. Furthermore, since it is unknown at compile time whether a worker task will throw one or more exceptions, an unhandled faulted task will always throw an `AggregateException`. Listing 19.7 and Output 19.4 demonstrate this behavior. Even though the unhandled exception thrown on the worker thread was of type `InvalidOperationException`, the type of the exception caught on the main thread is still an `AggregateException`. Also, as expected, to catch the exception requires an `AggregateException` catch block.

A list of the exceptions contained within an `AggregateException` is available from the `InnerExceptions` property. As a result, you can iterate over this property to examine each exception and determine the appropriate course of action. Alternatively, and as shown in Listing 19.7, you can use the `AggregateException.Handle()` method, specifying an expression to execute against each individual exception contained within the `AggregateException`. One important characteristic of the `Handle()` method to consider, however, is that it is a predicate. As such, the predicate should return `true` for any exceptions that the `Handle()` delegate successfully addresses. If any exception handling invocation returns `false` for an exception, the `Handle()` method will throw a new `AggregateException` that contains the composite list of such corresponding exceptions.

You can also observe the state of a faulted task without causing the exception to be rethrown on the current thread by simply looking at the `Exception` property of the task. Listing 19.8 demonstrates this approach by waiting for the completion of a fault continuation of a task[8] that we know will throw an exception.

LISTING 19.8: Observing Unhandled Exceptions on a Task Using ContinueWith()

```
using System;
using System.Diagnostics;
using System.Threading.Tasks;

public class Program
{
  public static void Main()
  {
      bool parentTaskFaulted = false;
      Task task = new Task(() =>
          {
              throw new InvalidOperationException();
          });
      Task continuationTask = task.ContinueWith(
          (antecedentTask) =>
          {
              parentTaskFaulted =
                  antecedentTask.IsFaulted;
          }, TaskContinuationOptions.OnlyOnFaulted);
```

---

8. As we discussed earlier, waiting for a fault continuation to complete is a strange thing to do because most of the time it will never be scheduled to run in the first place. This code is provided for illustrative purposes only.

```
        task.Start();
        continuationTask.Wait();
        Trace.Assert(parentTaskFaulted);
        Trace.Assert(task.IsFaulted);
        task.Exception.Handle(eachException =>
        {
            Console.WriteLine(
                $"ERROR: { eachException.Message }");
            return true;
        });
    }
}
```

Notice that to retrieve the unhandled exception on the original task, we use the Exception property. The result is output identical to Output 19.4.

If an exception that occurs within a task goes entirely unobserved—that is, (1) it isn't caught from within the task; (2) the completion of the task is never observed, via Wait(), Result, or accessing the Exception property, for example; and (c) the faulted ContinueWith() is never observed—then the exception is likely to go unhandled entirely, resulting in a process-wide unhandled exception. In .NET 4.0, such a faulted task would get rethrown by the finalizer thread and likely crash the process. In contrast, in .NET 4.5, the crashing has been suppressed (although the CLR can be configured for the crashing behavior if preferred).

In either case, you can register for an unhandled task exception via the TaskScheduler.UnobservedTaskException event.

4.0

■ ADVANCED TOPIC

Dealing with Unhandled Exceptions on a Thread

As we discussed earlier, an unhandled exception on any thread by default causes the application to shut down. An unhandled exception is a fatal, unexpected bug, and the exception may have occurred because a crucial data structure is corrupt. You therefore have no idea what the program could possibly be doing, so the safest thing to do is to shut down the whole thing immediately.

Ideally, no programs would ever throw unhandled exceptions on any thread; programs that do so have bugs, and the best course of action is to find and fix the bug before the software is shipped to customers. However, rather than shutting down an application as soon as possible when an unhandled exception occurs, it is often desirable to save any working data and/or log the exception for error reporting and future debugging. This requires a mechanism to register notifications of unhandled exceptions.

With both the Microsoft .NET Framework and .NET Core 2.0 (or later), every AppDomain provides such a mechanism, and to observe the unhandled exceptions that occur in an AppDomain, you must add a handler to the UnhandledException event. The UnhandledException event will fire for all unhandled exceptions on threads within the application domain, whether it is the main thread or a worker thread. Note that the purpose of this mechanism is notification; it does not permit the application to recover from the unhandled exception and continue executing. After the event handlers run, the application will display the Operating Systems Error Reporting dialog, and then the application will exit. (For console applications, the exception details will also appear on the console.)

In Listing 19.9, we show how to create a second thread that throws an exception, which is then handled by the application domain's unhandled exception event handler. For demonstration purposes, to ensure that thread timing issues do not come into play, we insert some artificial delays using Thread.Sleep. Output 19.5 shows the results.

LISTING 19.9: Registering for Unhandled Exceptions

```
using System;
using System.Diagnostics;
using System.Threading;

public class Program
{
  public static Stopwatch clock = new Stopwatch();
  public static void Main()
  {
    try
    {
      clock.Start();
      // Register a callback to receive notifications
      // of any unhandled exception
      AppDomain.CurrentDomain.UnhandledException +=
        (s, e) =>
          {
            Message("Event handler starting");
            Delay(4000);
          };
```

4.0

```
Thread thread = new Thread(() =>
{
  Message("Throwing exception.");
  throw new Exception();
});
thread.Start();

Delay(2000);
}
finally
{
  Message("Finally block running.");
}
}

static void Delay(int i)
{
  Message($"Sleeping for {i} ms");
  Thread.Sleep(i);
  Message("Awake");
}

static void Message(string text)
{
  Console.WriteLine("{0}:{1:0000}:{2}",
    Thread.CurrentThread.ManagedThreadId,
    clock.ElapsedMilliseconds, text);
}
}
```

4.0

OUTPUT 19.5

```
3:0047:Throwing exception.
3:0052:Unhandled exception handler starting.
3:0055:Sleeping for 4000 ms
1:0058:Sleeping for 2000 ms
1:2059:Awake
1:2060:Finally block running.
3:4059:Awake
Unhandled Exception: System.Exception: Exception of type 'System.
Exception' was thrown.
```

As you can see in Output 19.5, the new thread is assigned thread ID 3 and the main thread is assigned thread ID 1. The operating system schedules thread 3 to run for a while; it throws an unhandled exception, the event handler is invoked, and it goes to sleep. Soon thereafter, the operating system realizes that thread 1 can be scheduled, but its code immediately puts it to sleep. Thread 1 wakes up first and runs the finally block, and then

2 seconds later thread 3 wakes up, and the unhandled exception finally crashes the process.

This sequence of events—the event handler executing, and the process crashing after it is finished—is typical but not guaranteed. The moment there is an unhandled exception in your program, all bets are off; the program is now in an unknown and potentially very unstable state, so its behavior can be unpredictable. In this case, as you can see, the CLR allows the main thread to continue running and executing its finally block, even though it knows that by the time control gets to the finally block, another thread is in the AppDomain's unhandled exception event handler.

To emphasize this fact, try changing the delays so that the main thread sleeps longer than the event handler. In that scenario, the finally block will never execute! The process will be destroyed by the unhandled exception before thread 1 wakes up. You can also get different results depending on whether the exception-throwing thread is or is not created by the thread pool. The best practice, therefore, is to avoid all possible unhandled exceptions, whether they occur in worker threads or in the main thread.

How does this pertain to tasks? What if there are unfinished tasks hanging around the system when you want to shut it down? We look at task cancellation in the next section.

Guidelines

AVOID writing programs that produce unhandled exceptions on any thread.

CONSIDER registering an unhandled exception event handler for debugging, logging, and emergency shutdown purposes.

DO cancel unfinished tasks rather than allowing them to run during application shutdown.

Canceling a Task

Earlier in this chapter, we described why it's a bad idea to rudely abort a thread so as to cancel a task being performed by that thread. The TPL uses **cooperative cancellation**, a far more polite, robust, and reliable technique for safely canceling a task that is no longer needed. A task that supports cancellation monitors a `CancellationToken` object (found in the `System.Threading` namespace) by periodically polling it to see if a cancellation request has been issued. Listing 19.10 demonstrates both the cancellation request and the response to the request. Output 19.6 shows the results.

LISTING 19.10: Canceling a Task Using CancellationToken

```csharp
using System;
using System.Threading;
using System.Threading.Tasks;
using AddisonWesley.Michaelis.EssentialCSharp.Shared;

public class Program
{
  public static void Main()
  {
      string stars =
          "*".PadRight(Console.WindowWidth-1, '*');
      Console.WriteLine("Push ENTER to exit.");

      CancellationTokenSource cancellationTokenSource=
          new CancellationTokenSource();
      // Use Task.Factory.StartNew<string>() for
      // TPL prior to .NET 4.5
      Task task = Task.Run(
          () =>
              WritePi(cancellationTokenSource.Token),
                  cancellationTokenSource.Token);

      // Wait for the user's input
      Console.ReadLine();

      cancellationTokenSource.Cancel();
      Console.WriteLine(stars);
      task.Wait();
      Console.WriteLine();
  }

  private static void WritePi(
      CancellationToken cancellationToken)
  {
      const int batchSize = 1;
      string piSection = string.Empty;
      int i = 0;

      while(!cancellationToken.IsCancellationRequested
          || i == int.MaxValue)
      {
          piSection = PiCalculator.Calculate(
              batchSize, (i++) * batchSize);
          Console.Write(piSection);
      }
  }
}
```

4.0

OUTPUT 19.6

```
Push ENTER to exit.
3.1415926535897932384626433832795028841971693993751058209749445922307816
406286208998628034825342117067982148086513282306647093844609550582223172
5359408128481117450
**********************************************************************************
2
```

After starting the task, a `Console.Read()` blocks the main thread. At the same time, the task continues to execute, calculating the next digit of pi and printing it out. Once the user presses Enter, the execution encounters a call to `CancellationTokenSource.Cancel()`. In Listing 19.10, we split the call to `task.Cancel()` from the call to `task.Wait()` and print out a line of asterisks in between. The purpose of this step is to show that quite possibly an additional iteration will occur before the cancellation token is observed—hence the additional 2 in Output 19.6 following the stars. The 2 appears because the `CancellationTokenSource.Cancel()` doesn't rudely stop the task from executing. The task keeps on running until it checks the token, and politely shuts down when it sees that the owner of the token is requesting cancellation of the task.

The `Cancel()` call effectively sets the `IsCancellationRequested` property on all cancellation tokens copied from `CancellationTokenSource .Token`. There are a few things to note, however:

4.0

- A `CancellationToken`, not a `CancellationTokenSource`, is given to the asynchronous task. A `CancellationToken` enables polling for a cancellation request; the `CancellationTokenSource` provides the token and signals it when it is canceled (see Figure 19.3). By passing the `CancellationToken` rather than the `CancellationTokenSource`, we don't have to worry about thread synchronization issues on the `CancellationTokenSource` because the latter remains accessible to only the original thread.

- A `CancellationToken` is a struct, so it is copied by value. The value returned by `CancellationTokenSource.Token` produces a copy of the token. The fact that `CancellationToken` is a value type and a copy is created results in thread safe access to `CancellationTokenSource.Token`—it is available only from within the `WritePi()` method.

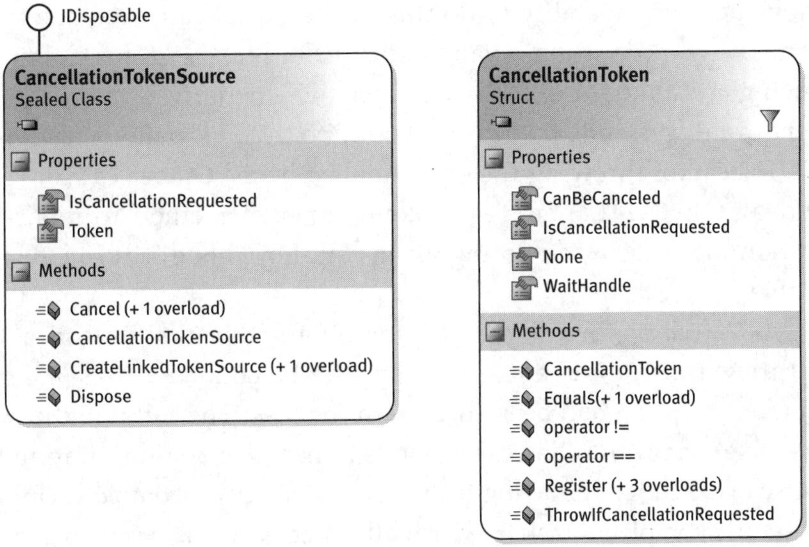

FIGURE 19.3: CancellationTokenSource and CancellationToken Class Diagrams

To monitor the IsCancellationRequested property, a copy of the CancellationToken (retrieved from CancellationTokenSource.Token) is passed to the task. In Listing 19.9, we then occasionally check the IsCancellationRequested property on the CancellationToken parameter; in this case, we check after each digit calculation. If IsCancellationRequested returns true, the while loop exits. Unlike a thread abort, which would throw an exception at essentially a random point, we exit the loop using normal control flow. We guarantee that the code is responsive to cancellation requests by polling frequently.

One other point to note about the CancellationToken is the overloaded Register() method. Via this method, you can register an action that will be invoked whenever the token is canceled. In other words, calling the Register() method subscribes to a listener delegate on the corresponding CancellationTokenSource's Cancel().

Given that canceling before completing is the expected behavior in this program, the code in Listing 19.9 does not throw a System.Threading.Tasks.TaskCanceledException. As a consequence, task.Status will return TaskStatus.RanToCompletion—providing no indication that the work of the task was, in fact, canceled. In this example, there is no need for such an indication; however, the TPL does include the capability to do this. If the cancel call were disruptive in some way—preventing a valid result from returning, for example—throwing a `TaskCanceledException` (which derives from `System .OperationCanceledException`) would be the TPL pattern for reporting it. Instead of throwing the exception explicitly, `CancellationToken` includes a `ThrowIfCancellationRequested()` method to report the exception more easily, assuming an instance of `CancellationToken` is available.

If you attempt to call `Wait()` (or obtain the `Result`) on a task that threw `TaskCanceledException`, the behavior is the same as if any other exception had been thrown in the task: The call will throw an `AggregateException`. The exception is a means of communicating that the state of execution following the task is potentially incomplete. Unlike a successfully completed task in which all expected work executed successfully, a canceled task potentially has partially completed work—the state of the work is untrusted.

This example demonstrates how a long-running processor-bound operation (calculating pi almost indefinitely) can monitor for a cancellation request and respond if one occurs. There are some cases, however, when cancellation can occur without explicitly coding for it within the target task. For example, the `Parallel` class discussed later in the chapter offers such a behavior by default.

4.0

Begin 5.0

Task.Run(): A Shortcut and Simplification to Task.Factory.StartNew()

In .NET 4.0, the general practice for obtaining a task was to call `Task .Factory.StartNew()`. In .NET 4.5, a simpler calling structure was provided in `Task.Run()`. Like `Task.Run()`, `Task.Factory.StartNew()` could be used in C# 4.0 scenarios to invoke CPU-intensive methods that require an additional thread to be created.

Given .NET 4.5, `Task.Run()` should be used by default unless it proves insufficient. For example, if you need to control the task with `TaskCreationOptions`, if you need to specify an alternative scheduler, or if, for performance reasons, you want to pass in object state, you should consider using `Task.Factory.StartNew()`. Only in rare cases, where you need to separate creation from scheduling, should constructor instantiation followed by a call to `Start()` be considered.

Listing 19.11 provides an example of using `Task.Factory.StartNew()`.

LISTING 19.11: Using Task.Factory.StartNew()

```csharp
public Task<string> CalculatePiAsync(int digits)
{
  return Task.Factory.StartNew<string>(
      () => CalculatePi(digits));
}

private string CalculatePi(int digits)
{
    // ...
}
```

End 5.0

Long-Running Tasks

As we discussed earlier in the commentary on Listing 19.2, the thread pool assumes that work items will be processor bound and relatively short-lived; it makes these assumptions to effectively throttle the number of threads created. This prevents both overallocation of expensive thread resources and oversubscription of processors that would lead to excessive context switching and time slicing.

But what if the developer knows that a task will be long-running and, therefore, will hold on to an underlying thread resource for a long time? In this case, the developer can notify the scheduler that the task is unlikely to complete its work anytime soon. This has two effects. First, it hints to the scheduler that perhaps a dedicated thread ought to be created specifically for this task rather than attempting to use a thread from the thread pool. Second, it hints to the scheduler that perhaps this would be a good time to allow more tasks to be scheduled than there are processors to handle them. This will cause more time slicing to happen, which is a good thing. We do not want one long-running task to hog an entire processor and prevent shorter-running tasks from using it. The short-running tasks will be able to use their time slice to finish a large percentage of their work, and the long-running task is unlikely to notice the relatively slight delays caused by sharing a processor with other tasks. To accomplish this, use the `TaskCreationOptions.LongRunning` option when calling `StartNew()`, as shown in Listing 19.12. (`Task.Run()` does not support a `TaskCreationOptions` parameter.)

4.0

LISTING 19.12: Cooperatively Executing Long-Running Tasks

```
using System.Threading.Tasks;

// ...

    Task task = Task.Factory.StartNew(
        () =>
            WritePi(cancellationTokenSource.Token),
                TaskCreationOptions.LongRunning);

// ...
```

Guidelines

DO inform the task factory that a newly created task is likely to be long-running so that it can manage it appropriately.

DO use `TaskCreationOptions.LongRunning` sparingly.

Tasks Are Disposable

Note that `Task` also supports `IDisposable`. This is necessary because `Task` may allocate a `WaitHandle` when waiting for it to complete; since `WaitHandle` supports `IDisposable`, `Task` also supports `IDisposable` in accordance with best practices. However, note that the preceding code samples do not include a `Dispose()` call, nor do they rely on such a call implicitly via the `using` statement. The listings instead rely on an automatic `WaitHandle` finalizer invocation when the program exits.

This approach leads to two notable results. First, the handles live longer and hence consume more resources than they ought to. Second, the garbage collector is slightly less efficient because finalized objects survive into the next generation. However, both of these concerns are inconsequential in the `Task` case unless an extraordinarily large number of tasks are being finalized. Therefore, even though technically speaking all code should be disposing of tasks, you needn't bother to do so unless performance metrics require it and it's easy—that is, if you're certain that `Task`s have completed and no other code is using them.

The Task-based Asynchronous Pattern

As we've seen so far, tasks provide a better abstraction for the manipulation of asynchronous work than threads do. Tasks are automatically scheduled to the right number of threads, and large tasks can be composed by chaining together small tasks, just as large programs can be composed from multiple small methods.

However, there are some drawbacks to tasks. The principal difficulty with tasks is that they turn your program logic "inside out." To illustrate this, we first consider a synchronous method that is blocked on an I/O-bound, high-latency operation—a web request. Next, we compare it to an asynchronous version prior to C# 5.0 and TAP. Lastly, we revise the same example by using C# 5.0 (and higher) and the async/await contextual keywords.

Synchronously Invoking a High-Latency Operation

In Listing 19.13, the code uses a WebRequest to download a web page and display its size. If the operation fails, an exception is thrown.

LISTING 19.13: A Synchronous Web Request

```
using System;
using System.IO;
using System.Net;
using System.Linq;

public class Program
{
  public static void Main(string[] args)
  {
      string url = "http://www.IntelliTect.com";
      if(args.Length > 0)
      {
          url = args[0];
      }

      try
      {
          Console.Write(url);
          WebRequest webRequest =
              WebRequest.Create(url);

          WebResponse response =
              webRequest.GetResponse();

          Console.Write(".....");

          using(StreamReader reader =
              new StreamReader(
                  response.GetResponseStream()))
          {
```

4.0

```
                string text =
                    reader.ReadToEnd();
                Console.WriteLine(
                    FormatBytes(text.Length));
            }
        }
        catch(WebException)
        {
            // ...
        }
        catch(IOException )
        {
            // ...
        }
        catch(NotSupportedException )
        {
            // ...
        }
    }

    static public string FormatBytes(long bytes)
    {
        string[] magnitudes =
            new string[] { "GB", "MB", "KB", "Bytes" };
        long max =
            (long)Math.Pow(1024, magnitudes.Length);

        return string.Format("{1:##.##} {0}",
            magnitudes.FirstOrDefault(
                magnitude =>
                    bytes > (max /= 1024)) ?? "0 Bytes",
                (decimal)bytes / (decimal)max);
    }
}
```

4.0

The logic in Listing 19.13 is relatively straightforward—using common C# idioms like try/catch blocks and return statements to describe the control flow. Given a WebRequest, this code calls GetResponse() to download the page. To gain stream access to the page, it calls GetResponseStream() and assigns the result to a StreamReader. Finally, it reads to the end of the stream with ReadToEnd() to determine the size of the page and then print it out to the screen.

The problem with this approach is, of course, that the calling thread is blocked until the I/O operation completes; this is wasting a thread that could be doing useful work while the asynchronous operation executes. For this reason, we cannot, for example, execute any other code, such as code that indicates progress.

Asynchronously Invoking a High-Latency Operation Using the TPL

To address this problem, Listing 19.14 takes a similar approach but instead
uses task-based asynchrony with the TPL.

LISTING 19.14: An Asynchronous Web Request

```csharp
using System;
using System.IO;
using System.Net;
using System.Linq;
using System.Threading.Tasks;
using System.Runtime.ExceptionServices;

public class Program
{
  public static void Main(string[] args)
  {
      string url = "http://www.IntelliTect.com";
      if(args.Length > 0)
      {
          url = args[0];
      }

      Console.Write(url);

      Task task = WriteWebRequestSizeAsync(url);

      try
      {
          while(!task.Wait(100))
          {
              Console.Write(".");
          }
      }
      catch(AggregateException exception)
      {
          exception = exception.Flatten();
          try
          {
              exception.Handle(innerException =>
              {
                  // Rethrowing rather than using
                  // if condition on the type
                  ExceptionDispatchInfo.Capture(
                      exception.InnerException)
                      .Throw();
                  return true;
              });
          }
          catch(WebException)
          {
              // ...
          }
```

4.0

```
        catch(IOException )
        {
            // ...
        }
        catch(NotSupportedException )
        {
            // ...
        }
    }
}


private static Task WriteWebRequestSizeAsync(
    string url)
{
    StreamReader reader = null;
    WebRequest webRequest =
        WebRequest.Create(url);

    Task task =
        webRequest.GetResponseAsync()
    .ContinueWith( antecedent =>
    {
        WebResponse response =
            antecedent.Result;

        reader =
            new StreamReader(
                response.GetResponseStream());
        return reader.ReadToEndAsync();
    })
    .Unwrap()
    .ContinueWith(antecedent =>
    {
        if(reader != null) reader.Dispose();
        string text = antecedent.Result;
        Console.WriteLine(
            FormatBytes(text.Length));
    });

    return task;
}

    // ...
}
```

4.0

Unlike Listing 19.13, when Listing 19.14 executes, it prints periods to the console while the page is downloading. The result is that instead of simply printing four periods (. . . .) to the console, Listing 19.14 is able to continuously print periods for as long as it takes to download the file, read it from the stream, and determine its size.

Unfortunately, this asynchrony comes at the cost of complexity. Interspersed throughout the code is TPL-related code that interrupts the flow. Rather than simply following the `WebRequest.GetResponseAsync()` call with steps to retrieve the `StreamReader` and call `ReadToEndAsync()`, the asynchronous version of the code requires `ContinueWith()` statements. The first `ContinueWith()` statement identifies what to execute after the `WebRequest.GetResponseAsync()`. Notice that the `return` statement in the first `ContinueWith()` expression returns `StreamReader.ReadToEndAsync()`, which returns another `Task`.

Without the `Unwrap()` call, therefore, the antecedent in the second `ContinueWith()` statement is a `Task<Task<string>>`, which alone indicates the complexity. As a result, it is necessary to call `Result` twice—once on the `antecedent` directly and a second time on the `Task<string>.Result` property `antecedent.Result` returned, with the latter blocking subsequent execution until the `ReadToEnd()` operation completes. To avoid the `Task<Task<TResult>>` structure, we preface the call to `ContinueWith()` with a call to `Unwrap()`, thereby shedding the outer `Task` and appropriately handling any errors or cancellation requests.

The complexity doesn't stop with `Tasks` and `ContinueWith()`, however: The exception handling adds an entirely new dimension to the complexity. As mentioned earlier, the TPL generally throws an `AggregateException` exception because of the possibility that an asynchronous operation could encounter multiple exceptions. However, because we are calling the `Result` property from within `ContinueWith()` blocks, it is possible that inside the worker thread we might also throw an `AggregateException`.

As you learned earlier in the chapter, there are multiple ways to handle these exceptions:

1. We can add continuation tasks to all `*Async` methods that return a task along with each `ContinueWith()` method call. However, doing so would prevent us from using the fluid API in which the `ContinueWith()` statements are chained together one after the other. Furthermore, this would force us to deeply embed error-handling logic into the control flow rather than simply relying on exception handling.

2. We can surround each delegate body with a try/catch block so that no exceptions go unhandled from the task. Unfortunately,

4.0

this approach is less than ideal as well. First, some exceptions (like those triggered when calling antecedent.Result) will throw an AggregateException from which we will need to unwrap the InnerException(s) to handle them individually. Upon unwrapping them, we either rethrow them so as to catch a specific type or conditionally check for the type of the exception separately from any other catch blocks (even catch blocks for the same type). Second, each delegate body will require its own separate try/catch handler, even if some of the exception types between blocks are the same. Third, Main's call to task.Wait() could still throw an exception because WebRequest.GetResponseAsync() could potentially throw an exception, and there is no way to surround it with a try/catch block. Therefore, there is no way to eliminate the try/catch block in Main that surrounds task.Wait().

3. We can ignore all exception handling from within WriteWebRequestSizeAsync() and instead rely solely on the try/catch block that surrounds Main's task.Wait(). Given that we know the exception will be an AggregateException, we can have a catch for only that exception. Within the catch block, we can handle the exception by calling AggregateException.Handle() and throwing each exception using the Exception-Dispatch-Info object so as not to lose the original stack trace. These exceptions are then caught by the expected exception handlers and addressed accordingly. Notice, however, that before handling the Aggregate-Exception's InnerExceptions, we first call AggregateException.Flatten(). This step addresses the issue of an AggregateException wrapping inner exceptions that are also of type AggregateException (and so on). By calling Flatten(), we ensure that all exceptions are moved to the first level and all contained AggregateExceptions are removed.

As shown in Listing 19.14, option 3 is probably the preferred approach because it keeps the exception handling outside the control flow for the most part. This doesn't eliminate the error-handling complexity entirely; rather, it simply minimizes the occasions on which it is interspersed within the regular control flow.

Although the asynchronous version in Listing 19.14 has almost the same logical control flow as the synchronous version in Listing 19.13, both versions attempt to download a resource from a server, and if the download succeeds, the result is returned. (If the download fails, the exception's type is interrogated to determine the right course of action.) However, clearly the asynchronous version of Listing 19.14 is significantly more difficult to read, understand, and change than the corresponding synchronous version in Listing 19.13. Unlike the synchronous version, which uses standard control flow statements, the asynchronous version is forced to create multiple lambda expressions to express the continuation logic in the form of delegates.

And this is a fairly simple example! Imagine what the asynchronous code would look like if, for example, the synchronous code contained a loop that retried the operation three times if it failed, if it tried to contact multiple different servers, if it took a collection of resources rather than a single one, or if all of these possible features occurred together. Adding those features to the synchronous version would be straightforward, but it is not at all clear how to do so in the asynchronous version. Rewriting synchronous methods into asynchronous methods by explicitly specifying the continuation of each task gets very complicated very quickly even if the synchronous continuations are what appear to be very simple control flows.

The Task-based Asynchronous Pattern with `async` and `await`

Fortunately, it turns out that it is not too difficult to write a computer program that does these complex code transformations for you. The designers of the C# language realized this need would crop up, and they added such a capability to the C# 5.0 compiler. Starting with C# 5.0, you can rewrite the synchronous program given earlier into an asynchronous program much more easily using TAP; the C# compiler then does the tedious work of transforming your method into a series of task continuations. Listing 19.15 shows how to rewrite Listing 19.13 into an asynchronous method without the major structural changes of Listing 19.14.

LISTING 19.15: An Asynchronous Web Request Using the Task-based Asynchronous Pattern

```
using System;
using System.IO;
using System.Net;
using System.Linq;
using System.Threading.Tasks;
```

```csharp
public class Program
{
  private static async Task WriteWebRequestSizeAsync(
    string url)
  {
    try
    {
      WebRequest webRequest =
          WebRequest.Create(url);
      WebResponse response =
          await webRequest.GetResponseAsync();
      using(StreamReader reader =
          new StreamReader(
              response.GetResponseStream()))
      {
          string text =
              await reader.ReadToEndAsync();
          Console.WriteLine(
              FormatBytes(text.Length));
      }
    }
    catch(WebException)
    {
        // ...
    }
    catch(IOException )
    {
        // ...
    }
    catch(NotSupportedException )
    {
        // ...
    }
  }

  public static void Main(string[] args)
  {
      string url = "http://www.IntelliTect.com";
      if(args.Length > 0)
      {
          url = args[0];
      }

      Console.Write(url);

      Task task = WriteWebRequestSizeAsync(url);

      while(!task.Wait(100))
      {
          Console.Write(".");
      }
  }

  // ...

}
```

Notice the small differences between Listing 19.13 and Listing 19.15. First, we refactor the body of the web request functionality into a new method (`WriteWebRequestSizeAsync()`) and add the new contextual keyword `async` to the method's declaration. A method decorated with this keyword must return `void`, `Task`, `Task<T>`, or, as of C# 7.0, `ValueTask<T>`.[9] In this case, since there is no data returned by the body of the method but we still want the capability of returning information about the asynchronous activity to the caller, `WriteWebRequestSizeAsync()` returns `Task`. Notice the method name suffix is `Async`; this suffix is not necessary, but it is conventional to mark asynchronous methods this way so as to identify their asynchronous behavior. Finally, everywhere there is an asynchronous equivalent for the synchronous method, we insert the new contextual keyword `await` before invoking the asynchronous version.

Begin 7.0

End 7.0

Notice that nothing else changes between Listings 19.13 and 19.15. The asynchronous method versions seemingly still return the same data types as before—despite that each actually returns a `Task<T>`. This is not via some magical implicit cast, either. `GetResponseAsync()` is declared as follows:

```
public virtual Task<WebResponse> GetResponseAsync() { ... }
```

At the call site, we assign the return value to `WebResponse`:

```
WebResponse response = await webRequest.GetResponseAsync()
```

The `async` contextual keyword plays a critical role by signaling to the compiler that it should rewrite the expression into a state machine that represents all the control flow we saw in Listing 19.14 (and more).

4.0

Also notice the try/catch logic improvements over Listing 19.14 that appear in Listing 19.15. In Listing 19.15, there is no catching an `AggregateException`. The `catch` clause continues to catch the exact type of exception expected, with no unwrapping of the inner exceptions required. To accomplish this, the await rewrite logic takes the first exception from the task and throws that exception—hence, that is the exception that is caught. (In contracts, when you invoke a task's `Wait()` method, the exceptions are gathered into an `AggregateException` and the aggregate exception is thrown.) The aim is to make the asynchronous code look as much as possible like the synchronous code.

---

9. Technically, you can also return any type that implements a `GetAwaiter` method. See the Advanced Topic titled "Awaiting Non-`Task<T>` or Values" later in the chapter.

To better explain the control flow, Table 19.2 shows each task in a separate column along with the execution that occurs on each task. There are a couple of important misconceptions that the table helps to dismiss:

- **Misconception #1: A method decorated with the `async` keyword is automatically executed on a worker thread when called.** This is absolutely not true; the method is executed normally, on the calling thread, and if the implementation doesn't await any incomplete awaitable tasks, it will complete synchronously on the same thread. It's the method's implementation that is responsible for starting any asynchronous work. Just using the `async` keyword does not change where the method's code executes. Also, there is nothing unusual about a call to an `async` method from the caller's perspective; it is a method typed as returning a `Task`, it is called normally, and it returns an object of its return type normally.

- **Misconception #2: The `await` keyword causes the current thread to block until the awaited task is completed.** That is also absolutely not true. If you want the current thread to block until the task completes, call the `Wait()` method, as we have already described. In fact, the `Main` thread does so repeatedly while waiting for the other tasks to complete. Each time `task.Wait(100)`, it blocks. However, once this call completes, the body of the while loop executes concurrently with the other tasks—not synchronously. The `await` keyword evaluates the expression that follows it, which is usually of type `Task` or `Task<T>`, adds a continuation to the resultant task, and then *immediately* returns control to the caller. The creation of the task has started asynchronous work; the `await` keyword means that the developer wishes the caller of this method to continue executing its work on this thread while the asynchronous work is processed. At some point after that asynchronous work is complete, execution will resume at the point of control following the `await` expression.

In fact, the principal reasons why the `async` keyword exists in the first place are twofold. First, it makes it crystal clear to the reader of the code that the method that follows will be automatically rewritten by the compiler. Second, it informs the compiler that usages of the `await` contextual keyword in the method are to be treated as asynchronous control flow and not as an ordinary identifier.

TABLE 19.2: Control Flow within Each Task

Description	Main() Thread	GetResponseAsync() Task	ReadToEndAsync() Task

Execution flows normally into Main and up through the first Console.Write() statement.	`string url =`
	`"http://www.IntelliTect.com";`
	`if(args.Length > 0)`
	`{`		

A call is made to WriteWebRequestSizeAsync(), so control flows into that method as it would normally.	`    url = args[0];` `}`		

Instructions within WriteWebRequestSizeAsync() execute normally (still on the Main() thread), including the call to WebRequest.Create(url).	`Console.Write(url);`
	
	`Task task =`
	`    WriteWebRequestSizeAsync(url);`
	`WebRequest webRequest =`
	`    WebRequest.Create(url);`		

The first await modifier begins, generating a new Task on which the GetResponseAsync() can execute. Assuming it didn't execute almost instantaneously, the control flow returns to Main() and begins executing the while loop.	`while(!task.Wait(100))`
	`{`
	
	`    Console.Write(".");`
	`}`
		`WebResponse response =`
		`    await webRequest.`
		⮑`GetResponseAsync();`
		`StreamReader reader =`
		`    new StreamReader(`
		`        response.`
		⮑`GetResponseStream()));`	

Once the GetResponseAsync() task completes, execution within the same task continues with the implicit assignment of the said task's result to the response variable. Then the StreamReader is instantiated from the response.			

Upon the occurrence of another await, another task is created, this time to execute ReadToEndAsync(). (All the while, Main's while loop continues executing.)			`string text =`
			`    (await reader`
			⮑`.ReadToEndAsync());`
			`Console.WriteLine(`
			`    FormatBytes(text.`
			⮑`Length));`

Upon completion of the ReadToEndAsync() task, the result is assigned to text, whose Length is then displayed on the console.			
Finally, task.Wait() returns true and the process executes.			

4.0

Begin 7.0

Starting with C# 7.1, it is possible to have an `async Main` method. As a result, Listing 19.15's `Main` signature could be `private static async Task Main(string[] args)`, and we could change the `WriteWebRequestSizeAsync` invocation to `await WriteWebRequestSizeAsync(url)`. The disadvantage in this case would be that we could no longer have a timeout (`task.Wait(100)`).

Returns from async Methods

When language support for TAP was added to C# 5.0, only three possible data types could be returned: `void`, `Task`, and `Task<T>`. Of these options, `Task`/`Task<T>` comes with a disadvantage, and `void` is practically a non-option.

Introducing async Return of ValueTask<T>

We use asynchronous methods for long-running, high-latency operations. And (obviously), since `Task`/`Task<T>` is the return, we always need to obtain one of these objects to return. The alternative, to return `null`, would force callers to always check for `null` before invoking the method—an unreasonable and frustrating API from a usability perspective. Generally, the cost to create a `Task`/`Task<T>` is insignificant in comparison to the long-running, high-latency operation.

4.0

What happens, though, if the operation can be short-circuited and a result returned immediately? Consider, for example, compressing a buffer. If the amount of data is significant, performing the operation asynchronously makes sense. If, however, data is 0-length, then the operation can return immediately, and obtaining a (cached or new instance of) `Task`/`Task<T>` is pointless because there is no need for a task when the operation completes immediately. Unfortunately, there was no alternative when `async`/`await` was introduced in C# 5.0. However, C# 7.0 added support for arbitrary types that meet certain criteria—namely, support for a `GetAwaiter()` method, as detailed in the Advanced Topic titled "Awaiting Non-`Task<T>` or Values." For example, C# 7.0-related .NET frameworks include `ValueTask<T>`, a value type that scales down to support lightweight instantiation when a long-running operation can be short-circuited or that supports the full functionality of a task otherwise. Listing 19.16 provides an example of file compression but escaping via `ValueTask<T>` if the compression can be short-circuited.

LISTING 19.16: Returning ValueTask<T> from an async Method

```csharp
using System;
using System.IO;
using System.Net;
using System.Linq;
using System.Threading.Tasks;

public class Program
{
    private static async ValueTask<byte[]> CompressAsync(byte[] buffer)
    {
        if (buffer.Length == 0)
        {
            return buffer;
        }
        using (MemoryStream memoryStream = new MemoryStream())
        using (System.IO.Compression.GZipStream gZipStream =
            new System.IO.Compression.GZipStream(
                memoryStream, System.IO.Compression.CompressionMode.
Compress))
        {
            await gZipStream.WriteAsync(buffer, 0, buffer.Length);
            buffer = memoryStream.ToArray();
        }

        return buffer;
    }
    // ...
}
```

Notice that even though an asynchronous method, such as GZipStream.WriteAsync(), might return Task<T>, the await implementation still works within a ValueTask<T> returning method. In Listing 19.16, for example, changing the return from ValueTask<T> to Task<T> involves no other code changes.

ValueTask<T> begs the question of when to use it versus Task/ Task<T>. If your operation doesn't return a value, just use Task (there is no nongeneric ValueTask<T> because it has no benefit). If your operation is likely to complete asynchronously, or if it's not possible to cache tasks for common result values, Task<T> is also preferred. If, however, the operation is likely to complete synchronously and you can't reasonably cache all common return values, ValueTask<T> might be appropriate. For example, there's generally no benefit to returning ValueTask<bool> instead of Task<bool>, because you can easily cache a Task<bool> for both true and false values—and in fact, the async infrastructure does this automatically. In other words, when returning an asynchronous `Task<bool>` method that completes synchronously, a cached result `Task<bool>` will return regardless.

7.0

Returning void from an Asynchronous Method

The last return option available for an `async` method is `void`—a method henceforth referred to as an **async void method**. However, `async void` methods should generally be avoided. Unlike when returning a `Task`/`Task<T>`, when there is a return, it is indeterminate when a method completes executing, and if an exception occurs, returning `void` means there is no such container to report an exception. In the exception case, any exception that is thrown on an `async void` method likely ends up on the UI `SynchronizationContext`—effectively an unhandled exception (see the Advanced Topic titled "Dealing with Unhandled Exceptions on a Thread").

If `async void` methods should be generally avoided, why are they allowed in the first place? It's because `async void` methods can be used to enable `async` event handlers. As discussed in Chapter 14, an event should be declared as an `EventHandler<T>` where `EventHandler<T>` has a signature of

```
void EventHandler<TEventArgs>(object sender, TEventArgs e)
```

4.0

Therefore, to fit the convention of an event matching the `EventHandler<T>` signature, an `async` event needs to return `void`. One might suggest changing the convention, but (as discussed in Chapter 14) there could be multiple subscribers and retrieving the return from multiple subscribers is nonintuitive and cumbersome. For this reason, the guideline is to avoid `async void` methods unless they are subscribers to an event handler—in which case they should not throw exceptions. Alternatively, you should provide a synchronization context to receive notifications of synchronization events such as the scheduling of work (e.g., `Task.Run()`) and, perhaps more important, unhandled exceptions. Listing 19.17 and the accompanying Output 19.7 provide an example of how to do this.

LISTING 19.17: Catching an Exception from an async void Method

```
using System;
using System.Threading;
using System.Threading.Tasks;
```

```csharp
public class AsyncSynchronizationContext : SynchronizationContext
{
    public Exception Exception { get; set; }
    public ManualResetEventSlim ResetEvent { get;} = new
        ManualResetEventSlim();

    public override void Send(SendOrPostCallback callback, object state)
    {
        try
        {
            Console.WriteLine($@"Send notification invoked...(Thread ID: {
                Thread.CurrentThread.ManagedThreadId})");
            callback(state);
        }
        catch (Exception exception)
        {
            Exception = exception;
#if !WithOutUsingResetEvent
            ResetEvent.Set();
#endif
        }
    }

    public override void Post(SendOrPostCallback callback, object state)
    {
        try
        {
            Console.WriteLine($@"Post notification invoked...(Thread ID: {
                Thread.CurrentThread.ManagedThreadId})");
            callback(state);
        }
        catch (Exception exception)
        {
            Exception = exception;
#if !WithOutUsingResetEvent
            ResetEvent.Set();
#endif
        }
    }
}

public class Program
{
    static bool EventTriggered { get; set; }

    public const string ExpectedExceptionMessage = "Expected Exception";
    public static void Main()
    {

        AsyncSynchronizationContext synchronizationContext =
            new AsyncSynchronizationContext();
        SynchronizationContext.
            SetSynchronizationContext(synchronizationContext);
```

```
        try
        {

            OnEvent(null, null);

    #if WithOutUsingResetEvent
            Task.Delay(1000);  //
    #else
            synchronizationContext.ResetEvent.Wait();
    #endif

            if(synchronizationContext.Exception != null)
            {
                Console.WriteLine($@"Throwing expected exception....(Thread
ID: {
                Thread.CurrentThread.ManagedThreadId})");
                System.Runtime.ExceptionServices.ExceptionDispatchInfo.
Capture(
                    synchronizationContext.Exception).Throw();
            }
        }
        catch(Exception exception)
        {
            Console.WriteLine($@"{exception} thrown as expected.(Thread ID: {
                Thread.CurrentThread.ManagedThreadId})");
        }
    }

    static async void OnEvent(object sender, EventArgs eventArgs)
    {
        Console.WriteLine($@"Invoking Task.Run...(Thread ID: {
                Thread.CurrentThread.ManagedThreadId})");
        await Task.Run(()=>
        {
            Console.WriteLine($@"Running task... (Thread ID: {
                Thread.CurrentThread.ManagedThreadId})");
            throw new Exception(ExpectedExceptionMessage);
        });
    }
}
```

OUTPUT 19.7

```
Invoking Task.Run...(Thread ID: 8)
Running task... (Thread ID: 9)
Post notification invoked...(Thread ID: 8)
Post notification invoked...(Thread ID: 8)
Throwing expected exception....(Thread ID: 8)
System.Exception: Expected Exception
   at AddisonWesley.Michaelis.EssentialCSharp.Chapter19.
Listing19_17.Program.Main() in
...Listing19.17.AsyncVoidReturn.cs:line 80 thrown as expected.(Thread ID: 8)
```

The code executes procedurally up until the await `Task.Run()` invocation within `OnEvent()` starts. Following its completion, control is passed to the `Post()` method within `AsyncSynchronizationContext`. After the execution and completion of the `Post()` invocation, the `Console.WriteLine("throw Exception...")` executes, and then an exception is thrown. This exception is captured by the `AsyncSynchronizationContext.Post()` method and passed back into `Main()`.

In this example, we use a `Task.Delay()` call to ensure the program doesn't end before the `Task.Run()` invocation but, as shown in the next chapter, a `ManualResetEventSlim` would be the preferred approach.

Asynchronous Lambdas and Local Functions

Just as a lambda expression converted to a delegate can be used as a concise syntax for declaring a normal method, so C# 5.0 (and later) also allows lambdas containing `await` expressions to be converted to delegates. To do so, just precede the lambda expression with the `async` keyword. In Listing 19.18, we rewrite the `GetResourceAsync()` method from Listing 19.15 from an `async` method to an `async` lambda.

LISTING 19.18: An Asynchronous Client-Server Interaction as a Lambda Expression

```csharp
using System;
using System.IO;
using System.Net;
using System.Linq;
using System.Threading.Tasks;

public class Program
{

  public static void Main(string[] args)
  {
      string url = "http://www.IntelliTect.com";
      if(args.Length > 0)
      {
          url = args[0];
      }

      Console.Write(url);

      Func<string, Task> writeWebRequestSizeAsync =
          async (string webRequestUrl) =>
```

4.0

```
        {
            // Error handling ommitted for
            // elucidation
            WebRequest webRequest =
                WebRequest.Create(url);

            WebResponse response =
                await webRequest.GetResponseAsync();
            using(StreamReader reader =
                new StreamReader(
                    response.GetResponseStream()))
            {
                string text =
                    (await reader.ReadToEndAsync());
                Console.WriteLine(
                    FormatBytes(text.Length));
            }
        };
```

```
    Task task = writeWebRequestSizeAsync(url);
```

```
        while (!task.Wait(100))
        {
            Console.Write(".");
        }
    }

    // ...


}
```

4.0

Begin 7.0

Similarly, the same can be achieved in C# 7.0 or later with a local function. For example, in Listing 19.18, you could change the lambda expression header (everything up to and including the => operator) to:

```
async Task WriteWebRequestSizeAsync(string webRequestUrl)
```

leaving everything in the body, including the curly braces, unchanged.

Note that an `async` lambda expression has exactly the same restrictions as the named `async` method:

- An `async` lambda expression must be converted to a delegate whose return type is `void`, `Task`, `Task<T>`, or, as of C# 7.0, `ValueTask<T>`.
- The lambda is rewritten so that `return` statements become signals that the task returned by the lambda has completed with the given result.
- Execution within the lambda expression occurs synchronously until the first `await` on an incomplete awaitable is executed.

- All instructions following the `await` will execute as continuations on the return from the invoked asynchronous method (or, if the awaitable is already complete, will be simply executed synchronously rather than as continuations).

- An `async` lambda expression can be invoked with an `await` (not shown in Listing 19.18).

End 7.0

■ ADVANCED TOPIC

Implementing a Custom Asynchronous Method

Implementing an asynchronous method by relying on other asynchronous methods (which, in turn, rely on more asynchronous methods) is relatively easy with the `await` keyword. However, at some point in the call hierarchy, it becomes necessary to write a "leaf" asynchronous `Task`-returning method. Consider, for example, an asynchronous method for running a command-line program with the eventual goal that the output could be accessed. Such a method would be declared as follows:

```
static public Task<Process> RunProcessAsync(string filename)
```

The simplest implementation would, of course, be to rely on `Task`.`Run()` again and call both the `System.Diagnostics.Process`'s `Start()` and `WaitForExit()` methods. However, creating an additional thread in the current process is unnecessary when the invoked process itself will have its own collection of one or more threads. To implement the `RunProcessAsync()` method and return to the caller's synchronization context when the invoked process completes, we can rely on a `TaskCompletionSource<T>` object, as shown in Listing 19.19.

4.0

LISTING 19.19: Implementing a Custom Asynchronous Method

```
using System.Diagnostics;
using System.Threading;
using System.Threading.Tasks;
class Program
{
    static public Task<Process> RunProcessAsync(
        string fileName,
        string arguments = null,
        CancellationToken cancellationToken =
            default(CancellationToken))
```

```
    {
        TaskCompletionSource<Process> taskCS =
            new TaskCompletionSource<Process>();

        Process process = new Process()
        {
            StartInfo = new ProcessStartInfo(fileName)
            {
                UseShellExecute = false,
                Arguments = arguments
            },
            EnableRaisingEvents = true
        };

        process.Exited += (sender, localEventArgs) =>
        {
            taskCS.SetResult(process);
        };

        cancellationToken
            .ThrowIfCancellationRequested();

        process.Start();

        cancellationToken.Register(() =>
        {
            process.CloseMainWindow();
        });

        return taskCS.Task;
    }

    // ...
}
```

4.0

Ignore the highlighting for the moment and instead focus on the pattern of using an event for notification when the process completes. Since `System.Diagnostics.Process` includes a notification upon exit, we register for this notification and use it as a callback from which we can invoke `TaskCompletionSource.SetResult()`. The code in Listing 19.19 follows a fairly common pattern that you can use to create an asynchronous method without having to resort to `Task.Run()`.

Another important characteristic that an `async` method might require is cancellation. TAP relies on the same methods for cancellation as the TPL does—namely, a `System.Threading.CancellationToken`. Listing 19.19 highlights the code necessary to support cancellation. In this example, we allow for canceling before the process ever starts, as well as an attempt to close the application's main window (if there is one). A more aggressive approach would be to call `Process.Kill()`, but this method could potentially cause problems for the program that is executing.

Notice that we don't register for the cancellation event until after the process is started. This avoids any race conditions that might occur if cancellation is triggered before the process actually begins.

One last feature to consider supporting is a progress update. Listing 19.20 is the full version of `RunProcessAsync()` with just such an update.

LISTING 19.20: **Implementing a Custom Asynchronous Method with Progress Support**

```csharp
using System;
using System.Diagnostics;
using System.Threading;
using System.Threading.Tasks;
class Program
{
    static public Task<Process> RunProcessAsync(
        string fileName,
        string arguments = null,
        CancellationToken cancellationToken =
            default(CancellationToken),
        IProgress<ProcessProgressEventArgs> progress =
            null,
        object objectState = null)
    {
        TaskCompletionSource<Process> taskCS =
            new TaskCompletionSource<Process>();

        Process process = new Process()
        {
            StartInfo = new ProcessStartInfo(fileName)
            {
                UseShellExecute = false,
                Arguments = arguments,
                RedirectStandardOutput =
                    progress != null
            },
            EnableRaisingEvents = true
        };

        process.Exited += (sender, localEventArgs) =>
        {
            taskCS.SetResult(process);
        };
```

4.0

```
        if(progress != null)
        {
            process.OutputDataReceived +=
                (sender, localEventArgs) =>
                {
                    progress.Report(
                        new ProcessProgressEventArgs(
                            localEventArgs.Data,
                            objectState));
                };
        }

        if(cancellationToken.IsCancellationRequested)
        {
            cancellationToken
                .ThrowIfCancellationRequested();
        }

        process.Start();

        if(progress != null)
        {
            process.BeginOutputReadLine();
        }

        cancellationToken.Register(() =>
        {
            process.CloseMainWindow();
            cancellationToken
                .ThrowIfCancellationRequested();
        });

        return taskCS.Task;
    }
    // ...
}


class ProcessProgressEventArgs
{
    // ...
}
```

■ ADVANCED TOPIC

Awaiting Non-Task<T> or Values

Generally, the expression that follows the await keyword is of either type
Task or type Task<T>. In the examples of await shown so far in this chapter, the expressions that follow the keyword have all returned Task<T>.

From a syntax perspective, an `await` operating on type `Task` is essentially the equivalent of an expression that returns `void`. In fact, because the compiler does not even know whether the task has a result, much less which type it is, such an expression is classified in the same way as a call to a `void`-returning method; that is, you can use it only in a statement context. Listing 19.21 shows some `await` expressions used as statement expressions.

LISTING 19.21: An `await` Expression May Be a Statement Expression

```csharp
async Task<int> DoStuffAsync()
{
  await DoSomethingAsync();
  await DoSomethingElseAsync();
  return await GetAnIntegerAsync() + 1;
}
```

Here we presume that the first methods return a `Task` rather than a `Task<T>`. Since there is no result value associated with the first two tasks, awaiting them produces no value; thus the expression must appear as a statement. The third task is presumably of type `Task<int>`, and its value can be used in the computation of the value of the task returned by `DoStuffAsync()`.

This Advanced Topic begins with the word *Generally*—a deliberate injection of incertitude. In fact, the exact rule regarding the return type that `await` requires is more generic than just `Task` or `Task<T>`. Rather, it requires that the type support a `GetAwaiter`. This method produces an object that has certain properties and methods needed by the compiler's rewriting logic. This makes the system extensible by third parties.[10] If you want to design your own non-`Task`-based asynchrony system that uses some other type to represent asynchronous work, however, you can do so and still use the `await` syntax.

Note, however, until C# 7.0's introduction of `ValueTask<T>`, it was not possible to make `async` methods return something other than `void`, `Task`, or `Task<T>`, no matter which type is awaited inside the method.

---

10. This technique of allowing third-party extension by looking for a particular method by its signature is used in two other C# features: LINQ looks for methods like `Select()` and `Where()` by name to implement the `select` and `where` contextual keywords, and the `foreach` loop does not require that the collection implement `IEnumerable`, just that it have an appropriate `GetEnumerator()` method.

Wrapping your head around precisely what is happening in an `async` method can be difficult, but it is far less difficult than trying to figure out what asynchronous code written with explicit continuations in lambdas is doing. The key points to remember are as follows:

- When control reaches an `await` keyword, the expression that follows it produces a task.[11] Control then returns to the caller so that it can continue to do work while the task completes asynchronously.

- Some time after the task completes, control resumes at the point following the `await`. If the awaited task produces a result, that result is then obtained. If it faulted, the exception is thrown.

- A `return` statement in an `async` method causes the task associated with the method invocation to become completed; if the `return` statement has a value, the value returned becomes the result of the task.

Task Schedulers and the Synchronization Context

On occasion, this chapter has mentioned the task scheduler and its role in determining how to assign work to threads efficiently. Programmatically, the task scheduler is an instance of the `System.Threading .Tasks.TaskScheduler`. This class, by default, uses the thread pool to schedule tasks appropriately, determining how to safely and efficiently execute them—when to reuse them, dispose them, or create additional ones.

It is possible to create your own task scheduler that makes different choices about how to schedule tasks by deriving a new type from the `TaskScheduler` class. You can obtain a `TaskScheduler` that will schedule a task to the current thread (or, more precisely, to the **synchronization context** associated with the current thread), rather than to a different worker thread, by using the static `FromCurrentSynchronizationContext()` method.[12]

The synchronization context under which a task executes and, in turn, the continuation task(s) execute(s), is important because the awaiting task consults the synchronization context (assuming there is one) so that a task can execute efficiently and safely. Listing 19.22 (along with Output 19.8)

---

11. Technically, it is an awaitable type, as described in the Advanced Topic titled "Awaiting Non-Task<T> Values."

12. For an example, see Listing C.8 in *Multithreading Patterns Prior to C# 5.0*, available at https://IntelliTect.com/EssentialCSharp.

is similar to Listing 19.5 except that it also prints out the thread ID when it displays the message.

LISTING 19.22: Calling Task.ContinueWith()

```csharp
using System;
using System.Threading;
using System.Threading.Tasks;

public class Program
{
  public static void Main()
  {
      DisplayStatus("Before");
      Task taskA =
          Task.Run(() =>
                DisplayStatus("Starting..."))
          .ContinueWith( antecedent =>
                DisplayStatus("Continuing A..."));
      Task taskB = taskA.ContinueWith( antecedent =>
          DisplayStatus("Continuing B..."));
      Task taskC = taskA.ContinueWith( antecedent =>
          DisplayStatus("Continuing C..."));
      Task.WaitAll(taskB, taskC);
      DisplayStatus("Finished!");
  }

  private static void DisplayStatus(string message)
  {
      string text = string.Format(
              $@"{ Thread.CurrentThread.ManagedThreadId
                }: { message }");
      Console.WriteLine(text);
  }
}
```

OUTPUT 19.8

```
1: Before
3: Starting...
4: Continuing A...
3: Continuing C...
4: Continuing B...
1: Finished!
```

What is noteworthy about this output is that the thread ID changes sometimes and gets repeated at other times. In this kind of plain console application, the synchronization context (accessible from SynchronizationContext.Current) is null—the default synchronization context causes the thread pool to handle thread allocation instead. This explains why the thread ID changes between tasks: Sometimes the thread pool determines that it is more efficient to use a new thread, and sometimes it decides that the best course of action is to reuse an existing thread.

Fortunately, the synchronization context gets set automatically for types of applications where that is critical. For example, if the code creating tasks is running in a thread created by ASP.NET, the thread will have a synchronization context of type `AspNetSynchronizationContext` associated with it. In contrast, if your code is running in a thread created in a Windows UI application (Windows Presentation Foundation [WPF] or Windows Forms), the thread will have an instance of `DispatcherSynchronizationContext` associated with it. (For console applications, there is no synchronization context by default.) Since the TPL consults the synchronization context and the synchronization context varies depending on the circumstances of the execution, the TPL is able to schedule continuations executing in contexts that are both efficient and safe.

To modify the code so that the synchronization context is leveraged instead, you must (1) set the synchronization context and (2) use `async/await` so that the synchronization context is consulted.[13]

It is possible to define custom synchronization contexts and to work with existing synchronization contexts to improve their performance in some specific scenarios. However, describing how to do so is beyond the scope of this text.

4.0

async/await with the Windows UI

One place where synchronization is especially important is in the context of UI and Web programming. With the Windows UI, for example, a message pump processes messages such as mouse click and move events. Furthermore, the UI is single-threaded, so that interaction with any UI components (e.g., a text box) must always occur from the single UI thread. One of the key advantages of the `async/await` pattern is that it leverages the synchronization context to ensure that continuation work—work that appears after the `await` statement—will always execute on the same synchronization task that invoked the `await` statement. This approach is of significant

---

13. For a simple example of how to set the synchronization context of a thread and how to use a task scheduler to schedule a task to that thread, see Listing C.8 in *Multithreading Patterns Prior to C# 5.0*, available at https://IntelliTect.com/EssentialCSharp.

value because it eliminates the need to explicitly switch back to the UI thread to update a control.

To better appreciate this benefit, consider the example of a UI event for a button click in WPF, as shown in Listing 19.23.

LISTING 19.23: Synchronous High-Latency Invocation in WPF

```csharp
using System;

private void PingButton_Click(
  object sender, RoutedEventArgs e)
{
  StatusLabel.Content = "Pinging...";
  UpdateLayout();
  Ping ping = new Ping();
  PingReply pingReply =
      ping.Send("www.IntelliTect.com");
  StatusLabel.Text = pingReply.Status.ToString();
}
```

Given that `StatusLabel` is a WPF `System.Windows.Controls` `.TextBlock` control and we have updated the `Content` property twice within the `PingButton_Click()` event subscriber, it would be a reasonable assumption that first "Pinging..." would be displayed until `Ping.Send()` returned, and then the label would be updated with the status of the `Send()` reply. As those experienced with Windows UI frameworks well know, this is not, in fact, what happens. Rather, a message is posted to the Windows message pump to update the content with "Pinging...," but because the UI thread is busy executing the `PingButton_Click()` method, the Windows message pump is not processed. By the time the UI thread frees up to look at the Windows message pump, a second `Text` property update request has been queued and the only message that the user is able to observe is the final status.

To fix this problem using TAP, we change the code highlighted in Listing 19.24.

LISTING 19.24: Synchronous High-Latency Invocation in WPF Using await

```csharp
using System;
async private void PingButton_Click(
  object sender, RoutedEventArgs e)
{
  StatusLabel.Content = "Pinging...";
  UpdateLayout();
```

4.0

```
    Ping ping = new Ping();
    PingReply pingReply =
        await ping.SendPingAsync("www.IntelliTect.com");
    StatusLabel.Text = pingReply.Status.ToString();
}
```

This change offers two advantages. First, the asynchronous nature of the ping call frees up the caller thread to return to the Windows message pump caller's synchronization context, and it processes the update to `StatusLabel.Content` so that "Pinging..." appears to the user. Second, when awaiting `ping.SendTaskAsync()` completes, it will always execute on the same synchronization context as the caller. Also, because the synchronization context is specifically appropriate for Windows UI, it is single-threaded, and therefore, the return will always be to the same thread—the UI thread. In other words, rather than immediately executing the continuation task, the TPL consults the synchronization context, which instead posts a message regarding the continuation work to the message pump. Next, because the UI thread monitors the message pump, upon picking up the continuation work message, it invokes the code following the `await` call. (As a result, the invocation of the continuation code is on the same thread as the caller that processed the message pump.)

There is a key code readability feature built into the TAP language pattern. Notice in Listing 19.24 that the call to return `pingReply.Status` appears to flow naturally after the `await`, providing a clear indication that it will execute immediately following the previous line. However, writing what really happens from scratch would be far less understandable for multiple reasons.

await Operators

There is no limitation on the number of times that `await` can be placed into a single method. In fact, such statements are not limited to appearing one after another. Rather, `await` statements can be placed into loops and processed consecutively one after the other, thereby following a natural control flow the way code appears. Consider the example in Listing 19.25.

LISTING 19.25: Iterating over an Await Operation

```csharp
async private void PingButton_Click(
  object sender, RoutedEventArgs e)
{
  List<string> urls = new List<string>()
    {
      "www.habitat-spokane.org",
      "www.partnersintl.org",
      "www.iassist.org",
      "www.fh.org",
      "www.worldvision.org"
    };
  IPStatus status;

  Func<string, Task<IPStatus>> func =
    async (localUrl) =>
      {
        Ping ping = new Ping();
        PingReply pingReply =
          await ping.SendPingAsync(localUrl);
        return pingReply.Status;
      };

  StatusLabel.Content = "Pinging…";

  foreach(string url in urls)
  {
    status = await func(url);
    StatusLabel.Text =
      $@"{ url }: { status.ToString() } ({
        Thread.CurrentThread.ManagedThreadId })";
  }
}
```

4.0

Regardless of whether the `await` statements occur within an iteration or as separate entries, they will execute serially, one after the other and in the same order they were invoked from the calling thread. The underlying implementation is to string them together in the semantic equivalent of `Task.ContinueWith()` except that all of the code between the `await` operators will execute in the caller's synchronization context.

Support for TAP from the UI is one of the key scenarios that led to TAP's creation. A second scenario takes place on the server, when a request comes in from a client to query an entire table's worth of data from the database. As querying the data could be time-consuming, a new thread should be created rather than consuming one from the limited number allocated to the thread pool. The problem with this approach is that the work to query from the database is executing entirely on another machine. There is no reason to block an entire thread given that the thread is generally not active anyway.

To summarize, TAP was created to address these key problems:

- There is a need to allow long-running activities to occur without blocking the UI thread.

- Creating a new thread (or `Task`) for non–CPU-intensive work is relatively expensive when you consider that all the thread is doing is waiting for the activity to complete.

- When the activity completes (either by using a new thread or via a callback), it is frequently necessary to make a thread synchronization context switch back to the original caller that initiated the activity.

- TAP provides a new pattern that works for both CPU-intensive and non–CPU-intensive asynchronous invocations—one that all .NET languages support explicitly.

Begin 7.0

4.0

End 7.0

Parenthetically, in C# 5.0 and 6.0 there was a restriction that awaits couldn't appear within exception handling `catch` or `finally` statements. However, this restriction has been removed starting with C# 7.0. This is a helpful improvement when you consider that you likely might want to log the exception from the outermost exception handler in the call stack and logging is a relatively expensive operation such that doing so with an asynchronous await is desirable.

Executing Loop Iterations in Parallel

Consider the `for` loop statement and associated code shown in Listing 19.26 and the corresponding output, Output 19.9. The listing calls a method for calculating a section of the decimal expansion of pi, where the parameters are the number of digits and the digit to start with. The actual calculation is not germane to the discussion. What is interesting about this calculation is that it is *embarrassingly parallelizable*; that is, it is remarkably easy to split up a large task—say, computing 1 million decimal digits of pi—into any desired number of smaller tasks that can all be run in parallel. These types of computations are the easiest ones to speed up by adding parallelism.

LISTING 19.26: For Loop Synchronously Calculating Pi in Sections

```csharp
using System;
using AddisonWesley.Michaelis.EssentialCSharp.Shared;

class Program
{
  const int TotalDigits = 100;
  const int BatchSize = 10;

  static void Main()
  {
      string pi = null;
      const int iterations = TotalDigits / BatchSize;
      for(int i = 0; i < iterations; i++)
      {
          pi += PiCalculator.Calculate(
              BatchSize, i * BatchSize);
      }

      Console.WriteLine(pi);
  }
}
```

```csharp
using System;

class PiCalculator
{
  public static string Calculate(
      int digits, int startingAt)
  {
      // ...
  }

  // ...
}
```

OUTPUT 19.9

```
>3.1415926535897932384626433832795028841971693993751058209749445923078164062862089986280348253421170679821480865132823066470938446095505822317253594081284811174502841027019385211055596446229489549303819644288109756659334461284756482337867831652712019091456485669234603486104543266482133936072602491412737245870066063155881748815209209628292540917153643678925903600113305305488204665213841469519415116094330572703657595919530921861173819326117931051185480744623799627495673518857527248912279381830119491
```

The for loop executes each iteration synchronously and sequentially. However, because the pi calculation algorithm splits the pi calculation into independent pieces, it is not necessary to compute the pieces sequentially as long as the results are appended in the right order. Imagine what would happen if you could have all the iterations of this loop run concurrently: Each processor could take a single iteration and execute it in parallel with other processors executing other iterations. Given the simultaneous execution of iterations, we could decrease the execution time more and more based on the number of processors.

The TPL provides a convenient method, `Parallel.For()`, that does precisely that. Listing 19.27 shows how to modify the sequential, single-threaded program in Listing 19.26 to use the helper method.

LISTING 19.27: For Loop Calculating Pi in Sections in Parallel

```csharp
using System;
using System.Threading.Tasks;
using AddisonWesley.Michaelis.EssentialCSharp.Shared;

// ...

class Program
{
  static void Main()
  {
      string pi = null;
      const int iterations = TotalDigits / BatchSize;
      string[] sections = new string[iterations];
      Parallel.For(0, iterations, (i) =>
      {
          sections[i] = PiCalculator.Calculate(
              BatchSize, i * BatchSize);
      });
      pi = string.Join("", sections);
      Console.WriteLine(pi);
  }
}
```

The output for Listing 19.27 is identical to Output 19.9; however, the execution time is significantly faster if you have multiple CPUs (and possibly slower if you do not). The `Parallel.For()` API is designed to look similar to a standard `for` loop. The first parameter is the `fromInclusive` value, the second is the `toExclusive` value, and the last is the `Action<int>` to perform as the loop body. When using an expression lambda for the action, the code looks similar to a `for` loop statement except that now each iteration may execute in parallel. As with the `for` loop, the call to `Parallel.For()` will not complete until all iterations are complete. In other words, by the time execution reaches the `string.Join()` statement, all sections of pi will have been calculated.

Note that the code for combining the various sections of pi no longer occurs inside the iteration (`action`) in Listing 19.27. As sections of the pi calculation will very likely not complete sequentially, appending a section whenever an iteration completes will likely append them out of order. Even if sequence was not a problem, there is still a potential race condition because the `+=` operator is not atomic. To address both problems, each section of pi is stored into an array, and no two or more iterations will access a single element within the array simultaneously. Only once all sections of pi are calculated does `string.Join()` combine them. In other words, we postpone concatenating the sections until after the `Parallel.For()` loop has completed. This avoids any race condition caused by sections not yet calculated or sections concatenating out of order.

The TPL uses the same sorts of thread pooling techniques that it uses for task scheduling to ensure good performance of the parallel loop: It will try to ensure that CPUs are not overscheduled, and so on.

Guidelines

DO use parallel loops when the computations performed can be easily split up into many mutually independent processor-bound computations that can be executed in any order on any thread.

4.0

The TPL also provides a similar parallel version of the `foreach` statement, as shown in Listing 19.28.

LISTING 19.28: Parallel Execution of a foreach Loop

```csharp
using System;
using System.Collections.Generic;
using System.IO;
using System.Threading.Tasks;

class Program
{
  // ...
  static void EncryptFiles(
      string directoryPath, string searchPattern)
  {
      IEnumerable<string> files = Directory.EnumerateFiles(
          directoryPath, searchPattern,
          SearchOption.AllDirectories);
```

```
        Parallel.ForEach(files, (fileName) =>
        {
            Encrypt(fileName);
        });
    }
    // ...
}
```

In this example, we call a method that encrypts each file within the `files` collection. It does so in parallel, executing as many threads as the TPL determines is efficient.

∎ ADVANCED TOPIC

How the TPL Tunes Its Own Performance

The default scheduler within the TPL targets the thread pool, resulting in a variety of heuristics to try to ensure that the right number of threads are executing at any one time. Two of the heuristics it uses are **hill climbing** and **work stealing**.

The hill climbing algorithm involves creating threads to run tasks, and then monitoring the performance of those tasks to try to experimentally determine the point at which adding more threads begins making performance worse. Once that point is reached, the number of threads can then be decreased back to the number that produced the best performance.

The TPL associates top-level tasks that are waiting to be executed with no particular thread. If, however, a task running on a thread itself creates another task, the newly created task is associated with that thread automatically. When the new child task is eventually scheduled to run, it usually runs on the same thread as the task that created it. The work stealing algorithm identifies threads that have an unusually large or unusually small amount of pending work; a thread that has too few tasks associated with it will sometimes "steal" not-yet-executed tasks from threads that have too many tasks waiting to run.

The key feature of these algorithms is that they enable the TPL to dynamically tune its own performance to mitigate processor overscheduling and underscheduling and to balance the work among the available processors.

The TPL generally does a good job of tuning its own performance, but you can help it do a better job by providing hints about the best course of action. Specifying the TPL `TaskCreationOptions.LongRunning` option described earlier in the section "Long-Running Tasks" is an example of such a hint. You can also explicitly tell the task scheduler how many threads you think would be best to service a parallel loop; see the Advanced Topic titled "Parallel Loop Options" later in the chapter for more details.

■ **BEGINNER TOPIC**

Parallel Loop Exception Handling with AggregateException

We know already that the TPL catches and saves exceptions associated with tasks in an `AggregateException`, because a given task might have several exceptions obtained from its subtasks. This is also the case with parallel execution of loops: Each iteration could have produced an exception, so the exceptions need to be gathered up into one aggregating exception. Consider the example in Listing 19.29 and its output in Output 19.10.

LISTING 19.29: Unhandled Exception Handling for Parallel Iterations

```csharp
using System;
using System.Collections.Generic;
using System.IO;
using System.Threading;
using System.Threading.Tasks;

class Program
{
  // ...
  static void EncryptFiles(
      string directoryPath, string searchPattern)
  {
      IEnumerable<string> files = Directory.EnumerateFiles(
          directoryPath, searchPattern,
          SearchOption.AllDirectories);
      try
      {
          Parallel.ForEach(files, (fileName) =>
          {
              Encrypt(fileName);
          });
      }
      catch(AggregateException exception)
      {
          Console.WriteLine(
              "ERROR: {0}:",
              exception.GetType().Name);
```

4.0

```
        foreach(Exception item in
            exception.InnerExceptions)
        {
            Console.WriteLine("  {0} - {1}",
                item.GetType().Name, item.Message);
        }
    }
}
// ...
}
```

OUTPUT 19.10

```
ERROR: AggregateException:
  UnauthorizedAccessException - Attempted to perform an unauthorized
↳operation.
  UnauthorizedAccessException - Attempted to perform an unauthorized
↳operation.
  UnauthorizedAccessException - Attempted to perform an unauthorized
↳operation.
```

Output 19.10 shows that three exceptions occurred while executing the `Parallel.ForEach<T>(...)` loop. However, in the code, there is only one catch of type `System.AggregateException`. The `UnauthorizedAccessException`s were retrieved from the `InnerExceptions` property on the `AggregateException`. With a `Parallel.ForEach<T>()` loop, each iteration could potentially throw an exception, so the `System.AggregateException` thrown by the method call will contain each of those exceptions within its `InnerExceptions` property.

Canceling a Parallel Loop

Unlike a task, which requires an explicit call if it is to block until it completes, a parallel loop executes iterations in parallel but does not itself return until the entire parallel loop completes. Canceling a parallel loop, therefore, generally involves invocation of the cancellation request from a thread other than the one executing the parallel loop. In Listing 19.30, we invoke `Parallel.ForEach<T>()` using `Task.Run()`. In this manner, not only does the query execute in parallel, but it also executes asynchronously, allowing the code to prompt the user to "Push ENTER to exit."

LISTING 19.30: Canceling a Parallel Loop

```csharp
using System;
using System.Collections.Generic;
using System.IO;
using System.Threading;
using System.Threading.Tasks;

public class Program
{
  // ...

  static void EncryptFiles(
      string directoryPath, string searchPattern)
  {

      string stars =
          "*".PadRight(Console.WindowWidth-1, '*');

      IEnumerable<string> files = Directory.GetFiles(
          directoryPath, searchPattern,
          SearchOption.AllDirectories);

      CancellationTokenSource cts =
          new CancellationTokenSource();
      ParallelOptions parallelOptions =
          new ParallelOptions
              { CancellationToken = cts.Token };
      cts.Token.Register(
          () => Console.WriteLine("Canceling..."));

      Console.WriteLine("Push ENTER to exit.");

      Task task = Task.Run(() =>
          {
              try
              {
                  Parallel.ForEach(
                      files, parallelOptions,
                      (fileName, loopState) =>
                          {
                              Encrypt(fileName);
                          });
              }
              catch(OperationCanceledException){}
          });

      // Wait for the user's input
      Console.Read();
```

4.0

```
      // Cancel the query
      cts.Cancel();
      Console.Write(stars);
      task.Wait();
  }
}
```

The parallel loops use the same cancellation token pattern that tasks use. The token obtained from a `CancellationTokenSource` is associated with the parallel loop by calling an overload of the `ForEach()` method that has a parameter of type `ParallelOptions`. This object contains the cancellation token.

Note that if you cancel a parallel loop operation, any iterations that have not started yet are prevented from starting by checking the `IsCancellationRequested` property. Existing executing iterations will run to their respective termination points. Furthermore, calling `Cancel()` even after all iterations have completed will still cause the registered cancel event (via `cts.Token.Register()`) to execute.

The only means by which the `ForEach()` method is able to acknowledge that the loop has been canceled is via the `OperationCanceledException`. Given that cancellation in this example is expected, the exception is caught and ignored, allowing the application to display "Canceling...," followed by a line of stars before exiting.

4.0

■ ADVANCED TOPIC

Parallel Loop Options

Although not generally necessary, it is possible to control the maximum degree of parallelism (i.e., the number of threads that are scheduled to run at the same time) via the `ParallelOptions` parameter on overloads of both the `Parallel.For()` and `Parallel.ForEach<T>()` loops. In some specific cases, the developer may know more about the particular algorithm or circumstance such that changing the maximum degree of parallelism makes sense. These circumstances include the following:

- Scenarios where you want to disable parallelism to make debugging or analysis easier. Setting the maximum degree of parallelism to 1 ensures that the loop iterations do not run concurrently.

- Scenarios where you know ahead of time that the degree of parallelism will be gated on an external factor such as a hardware constraint. For example, if your parallel operation involves using multiple USB ports, it is possible that there is no point in creating more threads than there are available ports.

- Scenarios with really long-running loop iterations (e.g., minutes or hours). The thread pool can't distinguish long-running iterations from blocked operations, so it could end up introducing many new threads, all of which will be consumed by the `for` loop. This can result in incremental thread growth over time, resulting in a huge number of threads in the process.

And so on. To control the maximum degree of parallelism, use the `MaxDegreeOfParallelism` property on the `ParallelOptions` object.

You can also use the `ParallelOptions` object's `TaskScheduler` property to specify a custom task scheduler to use to schedule the tasks associated with each iteration. For example, you might have an asynchronous event handler that responds to the user's click of a Next button. If the user clicks the button several times, you might want to use a custom task scheduler that prioritizes the most recently created task rather than prioritizing the task that has waited the longest. The task scheduler provides a means of specifying how the tasks will execute in relation to one another.

The `ParallelOptions` object also has a `CancellationToken` property that provides a mechanism to communicate to the loop that no further iterations should start. Additionally, the body of an iteration can watch the cancellation token to determine if an early exit from the iteration is in order.

4.0

■ ADVANCED TOPIC

Breaking a Parallel Loop

Like a standard `for` loop, the `Parallel.For()` loop supports the concept of "breaking" to exit the loop and canceling any further iterations. In the context of parallel `for` execution, however, a break signifies that no *new* iterations following the breaking iteration should start. All currently executing iterations, however, will run to completion.

To break a parallel loop, you can provide a cancellation token and cancel it on another thread, as described in the preceding Advanced Topic.

You can also use an overload of the `Parallel.For()` method whose body delegate takes two parameters: the index and a `ParallelLoopState` object. An iteration that wishes to break the loop can call the `Break()` or `Stop()` method on the loop state object passed to the delegate. The `Break()` method indicates that no more iterations with index values higher than the current value need to execute; the `Stop()` method indicates that no more iterations need to run at all.

For example, suppose you have a `Parallel.For()` loop that is performing ten iterations in parallel. Some of those iterations might run faster than others, and the task scheduler does not guarantee that they will run in any particular order. Suppose the first iteration has completed; iterations 3, 5, 7, and 9 are "in flight," scheduled to four different threads; and iterations 5 and 7 both call `Break()`. In this scenario, iterations 6 and 8 will never start, but iterations 2 and 4 will still be scheduled to run. Iterations 3 and 9 will run to completion because they were already started when the break happened.

The `Parallel.For()` and `Parallel.ForEach<T>()` methods return a reference to a `ParallelLoopResult` object that contains useful information about what happened during the loop. This result object has the following properties:

- `IsCompleted` returns a Boolean indicating whether all iterations started.
- `LowestBreakIteration` identifies the lowest iteration that executed a break. The value is of type `long?`, where a value of null indicates no break statement was encountered.

Returning to the ten-iteration example, the `IsCompleted` property will return `false` and the `LowestBreakIteration` will return a value of 5.

Running LINQ Queries in Parallel

Just as it is possible to execute a loop in parallel using `Parallel.For()`, so it is also possible to execute LINQ queries in parallel using the Parallel LINQ API (PLINQ, for short). An example of a simple nonparallel LINQ expression is shown in Listing 19.31; in Listing 19.32, we modify it to run in parallel.

LISTING 19.31: LINQ Select()

```
using System.Collections.Generic;
using System.Linq;

class Cryptographer
{
  // ...
  public List<string>
    Encrypt(IEnumerable<string> data)
  {
      return data.Select(
          item => Encrypt(item)).ToList();
  }
  // ...
}
```

In Listing 19.31, a LINQ query uses the Select() standard query operator to encrypt each string within a sequence of strings and convert the resultant sequence to a list. This seems like an embarrassingly parallel operation; each encryption is likely to be a high-latency processor-bound operation that could be farmed out to a worker thread on another CPU.

Listing 19.32 shows how to modify Listing 19.31 so that the code that encrypts the strings is executed in parallel.

LISTING 19.32: Parallel LINQ Select()

```
using System.Linq;

class Cryptographer
{
  // ...
  public List<string> Encrypt (IEnumerable<string> data)
  {
      return data.AsParallel().Select(
          item => Encrypt(item)).ToList();
  }
  // ...
}
```

4.0

As Listing 19.32 shows, the change to enable parallel support is extremely small! All that it uses is a standard query operator, AsParallel(), which can be found on the static class System.Linq.ParallelEnumerable. This simple extension method tells the runtime that it can execute the query in parallel. The result is that on machines with multiple available CPUs, the total time taken to execute the query can be significantly shorter.

System.Linq.ParallelEnumerable, the engine that was introduced in Microsoft .NET Framework 4.0 to enable PLINQ, includes a superset of the query operators available on System.Linq.Enumerable. Thus, it provided the API that enabled the possible performance improvements for all of the common query operators, including those used for sorting, filtering (Where()), projecting (Select()), joining, grouping, and aggregating. Listing 19.33 shows how to do a parallel sort.

LISTING 19.33: Parallel LINQ with Standard Query Operators

```
// ...
    OrderedParallelQuery<string> parallelGroups =
        data.AsParallel().OrderBy(item => item);

    // Show the total count of items still
    // matches the original count
    System.Diagnostics.Trace.Assert(
        data.Count == parallelGroups.Sum(
            item => item.Count()));
// ...
```

As Listing 19.33 shows, invoking the parallel version simply involves a call to the AsParallel() extension method. Notice that the type of the result returned by the parallel standard query operators is either ParallelQuery<T> or OrderedParallelQuery<T>; both inform the compiler that it should continue to use the parallel versions of the standard query operations that are available.

Given that query expressions are simply a syntactic sugar for the method call form of the query used in Listings 19.30 and 19.31, you can just as easily use AsParallel() with the expression form. Listing 19.34 shows an example of executing a grouping operation in parallel using query expression syntax.

LISTING 19.34: Parallel LINQ with Query Expressions

```
// ...
    ParallelQuery<IGrouping<char, string>> parallelGroups;
    parallelGroups =
        from text in data.AsParallel()
        orderby text
        group text by text[0];
```

```
// Show the total count of items still
// matches the original count
System.Diagnostics.Trace.Assert(
    data.Count == parallelGroups.Sum(
        item => item.Count()));
// ...
```

As you saw in the previous examples, converting a query or iteration loop to execute in parallel is simple. There is one significant caveat, however: As we will discuss in depth in Chapter 20, you must take care not to allow multiple threads to inappropriately access and modify the same memory simultaneously. Doing so will cause a race condition.

As we saw earlier in this chapter, the `Parallel.For()` and `Parallel.ForEach<T>` methods will gather up any exceptions thrown during the parallel iterations and then throw one aggregating exception containing all of the original exceptions. PLINQ operations are no different. That is, they also have the potential of returning multiple exceptions for exactly the same reason: When the query logic is run on each element in parallel, the code executing on each element can independently throw an exception. Unsurprisingly, PLINQ deals with this situation in exactly the same way as do parallel loops and the TPL: Exceptions thrown during parallel queries are accessible via the `InnerExceptions` property of the `AggregateException`. Therefore, wrapping a PLINQ query in a try/catch block with the exception type of `System.AggregateException` will successfully handle any exceptions within each iteration that were unhandled.

Canceling a PLINQ Query

As expected, the cancellation request pattern is also available on PLINQ queries. Listing 19.35 (with Output 19.11) provides an example. Like the parallel loops, canceled PLINQ queries will throw a `System .OperationCanceledException`. Also like the parallel loops, executing a PLINQ query is a synchronous operation on the invoking thread. Thus, a common technique is to wrap the parallel query in a task that runs on another thread so that the current thread can cancel it if necessary—the same solution used in Listing 19.30.

LISTING 19.35: **Canceling a PLINQ Query**

```csharp
using System;
using System.Collections.Generic;
using System.Linq;
using System.Threading;
using System.Threading.Tasks;

public class Program
{

  public static List<string> ParallelEncrypt(
      List<string> data,
      CancellationToken cancellationToken)
  {
      return data.AsParallel().WithCancellation(
          cancellationToken).Select(
              (item) => Encrypt(item)).ToList();
  }

  public static void Main()
  {
      ConsoleColor originalColor = Console.ForegroundColor;
      List<string> data = Utility.GetData(100000).ToList();

      CancellationTokenSource cts =
          new CancellationTokenSource();

      Console.WriteLine("Push ENTER to Exit.");

      // Use Task.Factory.StartNew<string>() for
      // TPL prior to .NET 4.5
      Task task = Task.Run(() =>
      {
          data = ParallelEncrypt(data, cts.Token);
      }, cts.Token);

      // Wait for the user's input
      Console.Read();

      if (!task.IsCompleted)
      {
          cts.Cancel();
          try { task.Wait(); }
          catch (AggregateException exception)
          {
              Console.ForegroundColor = ConsoleColor.Red;
              TaskCanceledException taskCanceledException =
                  (TaskCanceledException)exception.Flatten()
                  .InnerExceptions
                  .FirstOrDefault(
                  innerException =>
                      innerException.GetType() ==
                      typeof(TaskCanceledException));
```

4.0

```
        if(taskCanceledException != null){
            Console.WriteLine($@"Cancelled: {
                taskCanceledException.Message }");
        }
        else
        {
            // ...
        }
    }
}
else
{
    task.Wait();
    Console.ForegroundColor = ConsoleColor.Green;
    Console.Write("Completed successfully");
}
Console.ForegroundColor = originalColor;
    }
}
```

OUTPUT 19.11

```
Cancelled: A task was canceled.
```

As with a parallel loop or task, canceling a PLINQ query requires a
CancellationToken, which is available from a CancellationTokenSource.
However, rather than overloading every PLINQ query to support the cancellation token, the ParallelQuery<T> object returned by IEnumerable's
AsParallel() method includes a WithCancellation() extension method
that simply takes a CancellationToken. As a result, calling Cancel() on
the CancellationTokenSource object will request the parallel query to
cancel—because it checks the IsCancellationRequested property on the
CancellationToken.

As mentioned, canceling a PLINQ query will throw an exception in
place of returning the complete result. One common technique for dealing
with a possibly canceled PLINQ query is to wrap the query in a try block
and catch the OperationCanceledException. A second common technique, used in Listing 19.35, is to pass the CancellationToken both to
ParallelEncrypt() and as a second parameter on Run(). This will cause
task.Wait() to throw an AggregateException whose InnerException
property will be set to a TaskCanceledException. The aggregating
exception can then be caught, just as you would catch any other exception
from a parallel operation.

4.0

SUMMARY

In this chapter, we started by examining the basic parts of multithreaded programs: the Thread class, which represents an independent point of control in a program, and the ThreadPool, which encourages efficient allocation and scheduling of threads to multiple CPUs. However, these APIs are low-level entities that are difficult to work with directly. Starting with Version 4.0, the Microsoft .NET Framework provides the Parallel Extensions library, which includes the Task Parallel Library (TPL) and Parallel LINQ (PLINQ). Both provide new APIs for creating and scheduling units of work represented by Task objects, executing loops in parallel using Parallel.For() and Parallel.ForEach(), and automatically parallelizing LINQ queries with AsParallel().

We also discussed how C# 5.0 (and later) makes programming complex workflows with Task objects much easier by automatically rewriting your programs to manage the continuation "wiring" that composes larger tasks out of smaller tasks.

At the beginning of this chapter, we briefly glossed over some of the difficult problems that developers often face when writing multithreaded programs: atomicity problems, deadlocks, and other race conditions that introduce uncertainty and bad behavior into multithreaded programs. The standard way to avoid these problems is to carefully write code that uses locks to synchronize access to shared resources; this is the topic of the next chapter.

End 4.0

■ 20 ■
Thread Synchronization

I N CHAPTER 19, WE DISCUSSED the details of multithreaded programming using the Task Parallel Library (TPL) and Parallel LINQ (PLINQ). One topic we specifically avoided, however, was thread synchronization, which prevents race conditions while avoiding deadlocks. Thread synchronization is the topic of this chapter.

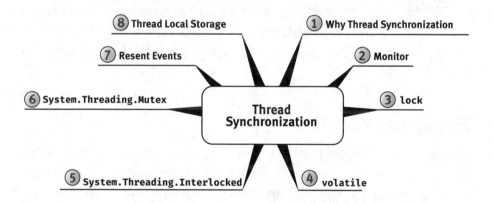

We begin with a multithreaded example with no thread synchronization around shared data—resulting in a race condition in which data integrity is lost. This discussion serves as the introduction for why we need thread synchronization. It is followed by coverage of myriad mechanisms and best practices for doing it.

Prior editions of this book included a significant section on additional multithreading patterns and another on various timer callback mechanisms. With the introduction of the async/await pattern, however, those approaches have essentially been replaced unless you are programming with frameworks prior to C# 5.0/.NET 4.5. However, pre-C# 5.0 material is still available from this book's website: https://IntelliTect.com/EssentialCSharp.

This entire chapter uses the TPL, so the samples cannot be compiled on frameworks prior to Microsoft .NET Framework 4. However, unless specifically identified as a Microsoft .NET Framework 4 API, the only reason for the Microsoft .NET Framework 4 restriction is the use of the System.Threading.Tasks.Task class to execute the asynchronous operation. Modifying the code to instantiate a System.Threading.Thread and use a Thread.Join() to wait for the thread to execute will allow the vast majority of samples to compile on earlier frameworks.

That being said, the specific API for starting tasks throughout this chapter is the .NET 4.5 (or later) System.Threading.Tasks .Task.Run(). As we discussed in Chapter 19, this method is preferred over System.Threading.Tasks.Task.Factory.StartNew() because it is simpler and sufficient for the majority of scenarios. If you are limited to .NET 4, you can replace Task.Run() with Task.Factory.StartNew() without any additional modifications. (For this reason, the chapter does not explicitly highlight such code as .NET 4.5–specific code when only this method is used.)

Why Synchronization?

Running a new thread is a relatively simple programming task. What makes multithreaded programming difficult, however, is identifying which data multiple threads can safely access simultaneously. The program must synchronize such data to prevent simultaneous access, thereby creating the "safety." Consider Listing 20.1.

LISTING 20.1: Unsynchronized State

```
using System;
using System.Threading.Tasks;
```

```
public class Program
{
    const int _Total = int.MaxValue;
    static long _Count = 0;

    public static void Main()
    {
        // Use Task.Factory.StartNew for .NET 4.0
        Task task = Task.Run(()=>Decrement());

        // Increment
        for(int i = 0; i < _Total; i++)
        {
            _Count++;
        }

        task.Wait();
        Console.WriteLine("Count = {0}", _Count);
    }

    static void Decrement()
    {
        // Decrement
        for(int i = 0; i < _Total; i++)
        {
            _Count--;
        }
    }
}
```

One possible result of Listing 20.1 appears in Output 20.1.

OUTPUT 20.1

```
Count = 113449949
```

The important thing to note about Listing 20.1 is that the output is not 0. It would have been if Decrement() was called directly (sequentially). However, when calling Decrement() asynchronously, a race condition occurs because the individual steps within _Count++ and _Count-- statements intermingle. (As discussed in the Beginner Topic titled "Multithreading Jargon" in Chapter 19, a single statement in C# will likely involve multiple steps.) Consider the sample execution in Table 20.1.

TABLE 20.1: Sample Pseudocode Execution

Main Thread	Decrement Thread	Count
. . .	. . .	. . .
Copy the value 0 out of _Count.		0
Increment the copied value (0), resulting in 1.		0
Copy the resultant value (1) into _Count.		1
Copy the value 1 out of _Count.		1
	Copy the value 1 out of _Count.	1
Increment the copied value (1), resulting in 2.		1
Copy the resultant value (2) into _Count.		2
	Decrement the copied value (1), resulting in 0.	2
	Copy the resultant value (0) into _Count.	0
. . .	. . .	. . .

Table 20.1 shows a parallel execution (or a thread context switch) by the transition of instructions appearing from one column to the other. The value of _Count after a particular line has completed appears in the last column. In this sample execution, _Count++ executes twice and _Count-- occurs once. However, the resultant _Count value is 0, not 1. Copying a result back to _Count essentially wipes out any _Count value changes that have occurred since the read of _Count on the same thread.

The problem in Listing 20.1 is a race condition, where multiple threads have simultaneous access to the same data elements. As this sample execution demonstrates, allowing multiple threads to access the same data elements is likely to undermine data integrity, even on a single-processor computer. To remedy this potential problem, the code needs synchronization around the data. Code or data synchronized for simultaneous access by multiple threads is **thread-safe**.

There is one important point to note about atomicity of reading and writing to variables. The runtime guarantees that a type whose size is no bigger than a native (pointer-size) integer will not be read or written partially. With a 64-bit operating system, therefore, reads and writes to a `long` (64 bits) will be atomic. However, reads and writes to a 128-bit variable such as `decimal` may not be atomic. Therefore, write operations to change a `decimal` variable may be interrupted after copying only 32 bits, resulting in the reading of an incorrect value, known as a **torn read**.

■ BEGINNER TOPIC

Multiple Threads and Local Variables

Note that it is not necessary to synchronize local variables. Local variables are loaded onto the stack, and each thread has its own logical stack. Therefore, each local variable has its own instance for each method call. By default, local variables are not shared across method calls; likewise, they are not shared among multiple threads.

However, this does not mean local variables are entirely without concurrency issues—after all, code could easily expose the local variable to multiple threads.[1] A parallel `for` loop that shares a local variable between iterations, for example, will expose the variable to concurrent access and a race condition (see Listing 20.2).

LISTING 20.2: Unsynchronized Local Variables

```
using System;
using System.Threading.Tasks;

public class Program
{
  public static void Main()
  {
      int x = 0;
      Parallel.For(0, int.MaxValue, i =>
```

---

1. While at the C# level it's a local, at the Common Intermediate Language level it's a field— and fields can be accessed from multiple threads.

```
        {
            x++;
            x--;
        });
        Console.WriteLine("Count = {0}", x);
    }
}
```

In this example, x (a local variable) is accessed within a parallel for loop, so multiple threads will modify it simultaneously, creating a race condition very similar to that in Listing 20.1. The output is unlikely to yield the value 0 even though x is incremented and decremented the same number of times.

Synchronization Using `Monitor`

Begin 4.0

To synchronize multiple threads so that they cannot execute particular sections of code simultaneously, you can use a **monitor** to block the second thread from entering a protected code section before the first thread has exited that section. The monitor functionality is part of a class called `System.Threading.Monitor`, and the beginning and end of protected code sections are marked with calls to the static methods `Monitor.Enter()` and `Monitor.Exit()`, respectively.

Listing 20.3 demonstrates synchronization using the `Monitor` class explicitly. As this listing shows, it is important that all code between calls to `Monitor.Enter()` and `Monitor.Exit()` be surrounded with a try/finally block. Without this block, an exception could occur within the protected section and `Monitor.Exit()` may never be called, thereby blocking other threads indefinitely.

LISTING 20.3: Synchronizing with a Monitor Explicitly

```csharp
using System;
using System.Threading;
using System.Threading.Tasks;

public class Program
{
    readonly static object _Sync = new object();
    const int _Total = int.MaxValue;
    static long _Count = 0;
```

```
public static void Main()
{
    // Use Task.Factory.StartNew for .NET 4.0
    Task task = Task.Run(()=>Decrement());

    // Increment
    for(int i = 0; i < _Total; i++)
    {
        bool lockTaken = false;
        try
        {
            Monitor.Enter(_Sync, ref lockTaken);
            _Count++;
        }
        finally
        {
            if (lockTaken)
            {
                Monitor.Exit(_Sync);
            }
        }
    }

    task.Wait();
    Console.WriteLine($"Count = {_Count}");
}

static void Decrement()
{
    for(int i = 0; i < _Total; i++)
    {
        bool lockTaken = false;
        try
        {
            Monitor.Enter(_Sync, ref lockTaken);
            _Count--;
        }
        finally
        {
            if(lockTaken)
            {
                Monitor.Exit(_Sync);
            }
        }
    }
}
}
```

4.0

The results of Listing 20.3 appear in Output 20.2.

OUTPUT 20.2

```
Count = 0
```

Note that calls to `Monitor.Enter()` and `Monitor.Exit()` are associated with each other by sharing the same object reference passed as the parameter (in this case, `_Sync`). The `Monitor.Enter()` overload method that takes the `lockTaken` parameter was added to the framework only in .NET 4.0. Before that, no such `lockTaken` parameter was available and there was no way to reliably catch an exception that occurred between the `Monitor.Enter()` and the try block. Placing the try block immediately following the `Monitor.Enter()` call was reliable in release code because the just-in-time compiler, or JIT, prevented any such asynchronous exception from sneaking in. However, anything other than a try block immediately following the `Monitor.Enter()`, including any instructions that the compiler might have injected within debug code, could prevent the JIT from reliably returning execution within the try block. Therefore, if an exception did occur, it would leak the lock (the lock remained acquired) rather than executing the finally block and releasing it—likely causing a deadlock when another thread tried to acquire the lock. In summary, in versions of the framework prior to .NET 4.0, you should always follow `Monitor.Enter()` with a try/finally `{Monitor.Exit(_Sync))}` block.

`Monitor` also supports a `Pulse()` method for allowing a thread to enter the *ready queue*, indicating it is up next for execution. This is a common means of synchronizing producer–consumer patterns so that no "consume" occurs until there has been a "produce." The producer thread that owns the monitor (by calling `Monitor.Enter()`) calls `Monitor.Pulse()` to signal the consumer thread (which may already have called `Monitor.Enter()`) that an item is available for consumption and that it should get ready. For a single `Pulse()` call, only one thread (the consumer thread, in this case) can enter the ready queue. When the producer thread calls `Monitor.Exit()`, the consumer thread takes the lock (`Monitor.Enter()` completes) and enters the critical section to begin consuming the item. Once the consumer processes the waiting item, it calls `Exit()`, thus allowing the producer (currently blocked with `Monitor.Enter()`) to produce again. In this example, only one thread can enter the ready queue at a time, ensuring that there is no consumption without production, and vice versa.

End 4.0

Using the `lock` Keyword

Because of the frequent need for synchronization using `Monitor` in multithreaded code, and because the try/finally block can easily be forgotten, C# provides a special keyword to handle this locking synchronization pattern. Listing 20.4 demonstrates the use of the lock keyword, and Output 20.3 shows the results.

LISTING 20.4: Synchronization Using the lock Keyword

```csharp
using System;
using System.Threading;
using System.Threading.Tasks;

public class Program
{
    readonly static object _Sync = new object();
    const int _Total = int.MaxValue;
    static long _Count = 0;

    public static void Main()
    {
        // Use Task.Factory.StartNew for .NET 4.0
        Task task = Task.Run(()=>Decrement());

        // Increment
        for(int i = 0; i < _Total; i++)
        {
            lock(_Sync)
            {
                _Count++;
            }
        }

        task.Wait();
        Console.WriteLine($"Count = {_Count}");
    }

    static void Decrement()
    {
        for(int i = 0; i < _Total; i++)
        {
            lock(_Sync)
            {
                _Count--;
            }
        }
    }
}
```

OUTPUT 20.3

```
Count = 0
```

By locking the section of code accessing _Count (using either lock or Monitor), you make the Main() and Decrement() methods thread-safe, meaning they can be safely called from multiple threads simultaneously. (Prior to C# 4.0, the concept was the same but the compiler-emitted code depended on the lockTaken-less Monitor.Enter() method, and the Monitor.Enter() called was emitted before the try block.)

The price of synchronization is a reduction in performance. Listing 20.5, for example, takes an order of magnitude longer to execute than Listing 20.1 does, which demonstrates lock's relatively slow execution compared to the execution of incrementing and decrementing the count.

Even when lock is insignificant in comparison with the work it synchronizes, programmers should avoid indiscriminate synchronization so as to avoid the possibility of deadlocks and unnecessary synchronization on multiprocessor computers that could instead be executing code in parallel. The general best practice for object design is to synchronize *mutable static* state and not any instance data. (There is no need to synchronize something that never changes.) Programmers who allow multiple threads to access a particular object must provide synchronization for the object. Any class that explicitly deals with threads is likely to want to make instances thread-safe to some extent.

Begin 7.1

■ BEGINNER TOPIC

Task Return with No await

In Listing 20.1, although Task.Run(()=>Decrement()) returns a Task, the await operator is not used. The reason for this is that until C# 7.1, Main() doesn't support the use of async. Given C# 7.1, however, the code can be refactored to use the async/await pattern, as shown in Listing 20.5.

LISTING 20.5: async Main() with C# 7.1

```
using System;
using System.Threading.Tasks;

public class Program
{
    readonly static object _Sync = new object();
    const int _Total = int.MaxValue;
    static long _Count = 0;
```

```
public static async Task Main()
{
    // Use Task.Factory.StartNew for .NET 4.0
    Task task = Task.Run(()=>Decrement());

    // Increment
    for(int i = 0; i < _Total; i++)
    {
        lock(_Sync)
        {
            _Count++;
        }
    }

    await task;
    Console.WriteLine($"Count = {_Count}");
}

static void Decrement()
{
    for(int i = 0; i < _Total; i++)
    {
        lock(_Sync)
        {
            _Count--;
        }
    }
}
}
```

End 7.1

Choosing a Lock Object

Whether or not the lock keyword or the Monitor class is explicitly used, it is crucial that programmers carefully select the lock object.

In the previous examples, the synchronization variable, _Sync, is declared as both private and read-only. It is declared as read-only to ensure that the value is not changed between calls to Monitor.Enter() and Monitor.Exit(). This allows correlation between entering and exiting the synchronized block.

Similarly, the code declares _Sync as private so that no synchronization block outside the class can synchronize the same object instance, causing the code to block.

If the data is public, the synchronization object may be public so that other classes can synchronize using the same object instance. However, this makes it harder to avoid deadlock. Fortunately, the need for this pattern is rare. For public data, it is instead preferable to leave synchronization entirely outside the class, allowing the calling code to take locks with its own synchronization object.

It's important that the synchronization object not be a value type. If the lock keyword is used on a value type, the compiler will report an error. (In the case of accessing the System.Threading.Monitor class explicitly [not via lock], no such error will occur at compile time. Instead, the code will throw an exception with the call to Monitor.Exit(), indicating there was no corresponding Monitor.Enter() call.) The issue is that when using a value type, the runtime makes a copy of the value, places it in the heap (boxing occurs), and passes the boxed value to Monitor.Enter(). Similarly, Monitor.Exit() receives a boxed copy of the original variable. The result is that Monitor.Enter() and Monitor.Exit() receive different synchronization object instances so that no correlation between the two calls occurs.

Why to Avoid Locking on this, typeof(type), and string

One seemingly reasonable pattern is to lock on the this keyword for instance data in a class and on the type instance obtained from typeof(type) (e.g., typeof(MyType)) for static data. Such a pattern provides a synchronization target for all states associated with a particular object instance when this is used and for all static data for a type when typeof(type) is used. The problem is that the synchronization target that this (or typeof(type)) points to could participate in the synchronization target for an entirely different synchronization block created in an unrelated block of code. In other words, although only the code within the instance itself can block using the this keyword, the caller that created the instance can pass that instance to a synchronization lock.

The result is that two different synchronization blocks that synchronize two entirely different sets of data could block each other. Although perhaps unlikely, sharing the same synchronization target could have an unintended performance impact and, in extreme cases, could even cause a deadlock. Instead of locking on this or even typeof(type), it is better to define a private, read-only field on which no one will block except for the class that has access to it.

Another lock type to avoid is string because of string interning. If the same string constant appears within multiple locations, it is likely that all locations will refer to the same instance, making the scope of the lock much broader than expected.

In summary, you should use a per-synchronization context instance of type `object` for the lock target.

> **Guidelines**
>
> **AVOID** locking on `this`, `typeof()`, or a `string`.
>
> **DO** declare a separate, read-only synchronization variable of type `object` for the synchronization target.

■ ADVANCED TOPIC

Avoid Synchronizing with `MethodImplAttribute`

One synchronization mechanism that was introduced in .NET 1.0 was the `MethodImplAttribute`. Used in conjunction with the `MethodImplOptions.Synchronized` method, this attribute marks a method as synchronized so that only one thread can execute the method at a time. To achieve this, the JIT essentially treats the method as though it was surrounded by `lock(this)` or, in the case of a static method, locks on the type. Such an implementation means that, in fact, the method and all other methods on the same class, decorated with the same attribute and enum parameter, are synchronized—rather than each method being synchronized relative to itself. In other words, given two or more methods on the same class decorated with the attribute, only one of them will be able to execute at a time, and the one executing will block all calls by other threads to itself or to any other method in the class with the same decoration. Furthermore, since the synchronization is on `this` (or even worse, on the type), it suffers the same detriments as `lock(this)` (or worse, for the static) discussed in the preceding section. As a result, it is a best practice to avoid the attribute altogether.

> **Guidelines**
>
> **AVOID** using the `MethodImplAttribute` for synchronization.

Declaring Fields as `volatile`

On occasion, the compiler or CPU may optimize code in such a way that the instructions do not occur in the exact order they are coded, or some instructions are optimized out. Such optimizations are innocuous when code executes on one thread. However, with multiple threads, such optimizations may have unintended consequences because the optimizations may change the order of execution of a field's read or write operations relative to an alternate thread's access to the same field.

One way to stabilize this behavior is to declare fields using the `volatile` keyword. This keyword forces all reads and writes to the volatile field to occur at the exact location the code identifies instead of at some other location that the optimization produces. The `volatile` modifier identifies that the field is susceptible to modification by the hardware, operating system, or another thread. As such, the data is "volatile," and the keyword instructs the compilers and runtime to handle it more exactly. (See http://bit.ly/CSharpReorderingOptimizations for further details.)

In general, the use of the `volatile` modifier is rare and fraught with complications that will likely lead to incorrect usage. Using `lock` is preferred to the `volatile` modifier unless you are absolutely certain about the `volatile` usage.

Using the System.Threading.Interlocked Class

The mutual exclusion pattern described so far provides the minimum set of tools for handling synchronization within a process (application domain). However, synchronization with `System.Threading.Monitor` is a relatively expensive operation, and an alternative solution that the processor supports directly targets specific synchronization patterns.

Listing 20.6 sets `_Data` to a new value as long as the preceding value was `null`. As indicated by the method name, this pattern is the compare/exchange pattern. Instead of manually placing a lock around behaviorally equivalent compare and exchange code, the `Interlocked.CompareExchange()` method provides a built-in method for a synchronous operation that does the same check for a value (`null`) and updates the first parameter if the value is equal to the second parameter. Table 20.2 shows other synchronization methods supported by `Interlocked`.

LISTING 20.6: Synchronization Using System.Threading.Interlocked

```csharp
public class SynchronizationUsingInterlocked
{
    private static object _Data;

    // Initialize data if not yet assigned
    static void Initialize(object newValue)
    {
        // If _Data is null, then set it to newValue
        Interlocked.CompareExchange(
            ref _Data, newValue, null);
    }

    // ...
}
```

TABLE 20.2: Interlocked's Synchronization-Related Methods

Begin 2.0

Method Signature	Description

`public static T CompareExchange<T>(`
`   T location,`
`   T value,`
`   T comparand`
`);`
	Checks location for the value in comparand. If the values are equal, it sets location to value and returns the original data stored in location.

`public static T Exchange<T>(`
`   T location,`
`   T value`
`);`
	Assigns location with value and returns the previous value.

`public static int Decrement(`
`   ref int location`
`);`
	Decrements location by 1. It is equivalent to the prefix -- operator, except Decrement() is thread-safe.

`public static int Increment(`
`   ref int location`
`);`
	Increments location by 1. It is equivalent to the prefix ++ operator, except Increment() is thread-safe.

`public static int Add(`
`   ref int location,`
`   int value`
`);`
	Adds value to location and assigns location the result. It is equivalent to the += operator

`public static long Read(`
`   ref long location`
`);`
	Returns a 64-bit value in a single atomic operation.

End 2.0

Most of these methods are overloaded with additional data type signatures, such as support for `long`. Table 20.2 provides the general signatures and descriptions.

Note that you can use `Increment()` and `Decrement()` in place of the synchronized `++` and `--` operators from Listing 20.5, and doing so will yield better performance. Also note that if a different thread accessed `_Count` using a non-interlocked method, the two accesses would not be synchronized correctly.

Event Notification with Multiple Threads

One area where developers often overlook synchronization is when firing events. The unsafe thread code for publishing an event is similar to Listing 20.7.

LISTING 20.7: Firing an Event Notification

```
// Not thread-safe
if(OnTemperatureChanged != null)
{
  // Call subscribers
  OnTemperatureChanged(
      this, new TemperatureEventArgs(value) );
}
```

This code is valid as long as there is no race condition between this method and the event subscribers. However, the code is not atomic, so multiple threads could introduce a race condition. It is possible that between the time when `OnTemperatureChange` is checked for `null` and when the event is actually fired, `OnTemperatureChange` could be set to `null`, thereby throwing a `NullReferenceException`. In other words, if multiple threads could potentially access a delegate simultaneously, it is necessary to synchronize the assignment and firing of the delegate.

The C# 6.0 solution to this dilemma is trivial. All that is necessary is to use the null-conditional operator:

```
OnTemperature?.Invoke(
    this, new TemperatureEventArgs( value ) );
```

The null-conditional operator is specifically designed to be atomic, so this invocation of the delegate is, in fact, atomic. The key, obviously, is to remember to make use of the null-conditional operator.

Although it requires more code, thread-safe delegate invocation prior to C# 6.0 isn't especially difficult, either. This approach works because the operators for adding and removing listeners are thread-safe and static (operator overloading is done with static methods). To correct Listing 20.7 and make it thread-safe, assign a copy, check the copy for null, and fire the copy (see Listing 20.8).

LISTING 20.8: Thread-Safe Event Notification

```
// ...
TemperatureChangedHandler localOnChange =
    OnTemperatureChanged;
if(localOnChanged != null)
{
  // Call subscribers
  localOnChanged(
      this, new TemperatureEventArgs(value) );
}
// ...
```

Given that a delegate is a reference type, it is perhaps surprising that assigning a local variable and then firing with the local variable is sufficient for making the null check thread-safe. As localOnChange points to the same location that OnTemperatureChange points to, you might think that any changes in OnTemperatureChange would be reflected in localOnChange as well.

However, this is not the case: Any calls to OnTemperatureChange += <listener> will not add a new delegate to OnTemperatureChange but rather will assign it an entirely new multicast delegate without having any effect on the original multicast delegate to which localOnChange also points. This makes the code thread-safe because only one thread will access the localOnChange instance, and OnTemperatureChange will be an entirely new instance if listeners are added or removed.

Synchronization Design Best Practices

Along with the complexities of multithreaded programming come several best practices for handling those complexities.

Avoiding Deadlock

With the introduction of synchronization comes the potential for deadlock. Deadlock occurs when two or more threads wait for one another to release a synchronization lock. For example, suppose Thread 1 requests a lock on _Sync1, and then later requests a lock on _Sync2 before releasing the lock on _Sync1. At the same time, Thread 2 requests a lock on _Sync2, followed by a lock on _Sync1, before releasing the lock on _Sync2. This sets the stage for the deadlock. The deadlock actually occurs if both Thread 1 and Thread 2 successfully acquire their initial locks (_Sync1 and _Sync2, respectively) before obtaining their second locks.

For a deadlock to occur, four fundamental conditions must be met:

1. *Mutual exclusion:* One thread (ThreadA) exclusively owns a resource such that no other thread (ThreadB) can acquire the same resource.

2. *Hold and wait:* One thread (ThreadA) with a mutual exclusion is waiting to acquire a resource held by another thread (ThreadB).

3. *No preemption:* The resource held by a thread (ThreadA) cannot be forcibly removed (ThreadA needs to release its own locked resource).

4. *Circular wait condition:* Two or more threads form a circular chain such that they lock on the same two or more resources, and each waits on the resource held by the next thread in the chain.

Removing any one of these conditions will prevent the deadlock.

A scenario likely to cause a deadlock is when two or more threads request exclusive ownership on the same two or more synchronization targets (resources) and the locks are requested in different orders. This situation can be avoided when developers are careful to ensure that multiple lock acquisitions always occur in the same order. Another cause of a deadlock is locks that are not **reentrant**. When a lock from one thread can block the same thread—that is, when it re-requests the same lock—the lock is not reentrant. For example, if ThreadA acquires a lock and then re-requests the same lock but is blocked because the lock is already owned (by itself), the lock is not reentrant and the additional request will deadlock.

The code generated by the lock keyword (with the underlying Monitor class) is reentrant. However, as we shall see in the "More Synchronization Types" section, some lock types are not reentrant.

When to Provide Synchronization

As we discussed earlier, all static data should be thread-safe. Therefore, synchronization needs to surround static data that is mutable. Generally, programmers should declare private static variables and then provide public methods for modifying the data. Such methods should internally handle the synchronization if multithreaded access is possible.

In contrast, instance state is not expected to include synchronization. Synchronization may significantly decrease performance and increase the chance of a lock contention or deadlock. With the exception of classes that are explicitly designed for multithreaded access, programmers sharing objects across multiple threads are expected to handle their own synchronization of the data being shared.

Avoiding Unnecessary Locking

Without compromising data integrity, programmers should avoid unnecessary synchronization where possible. For example, you should use immutable types between threads so that no synchronization is necessary (this approach has proved invaluable in functional programming languages such as F#). Similarly, you should avoid locking on thread-safe operations such as simple reads and writes of values smaller than a native (pointer-size) integer, as such operations are automatically atomic.

Guidelines

DO NOT request exclusive ownership on the same two or more synchronization targets in different orders.

DO ensure that code that concurrently holds multiple locks always acquires them in the same order.

DO encapsulate mutable static data in public APIs with synchronization logic.

AVOID synchronization on simple reading or writing of values no bigger than a native (pointer-size) integer, as such operations are automatically atomic.

More Synchronization Types

In addition to `System.Threading.Monitor` and `System.Threading.Interlocked`, several more synchronization techniques are available.

Begin 2.0

Using System.Threading.Mutex

System.Threading.Mutex is similar in concept to the System.Threading
.Monitor class (without the Pulse() method support), except that the lock
keyword does not use it, and Mutexes can be named so that they support synchronization across multiple processes. Using the Mutex class, you can synchronize access to a file or some other cross-process resource. Since Mutex is a
cross-process resource, .NET 2.0 added support to allow for setting the access
control via a System.Security.AccessControl.MutexSecurity object. One
use for the Mutex class is to limit an application so that it cannot run multiple
times simultaneously, as Listing 20.9 demonstrates.

LISTING 20.9: Creating a Single Instance Application

```csharp
using System;
using System.Threading;
using System.Reflection;

public class Program
{
  public static void Main()
  {
      // Indicates whether this is the first
      // application instance
      bool firstApplicationInstance;

      // Obtain the mutex name from the full
      // assembly name
      string mutexName =
          Assembly.GetEntryAssembly().FullName;

      using(Mutex mutex = new Mutex(false, mutexName,
          out firstApplicationInstance))
      {

          if(!firstApplicationInstance)
          {
              Console.WriteLine(
                  "This application is already running.");
          }
          else
          {
              Console.WriteLine("ENTER to shut down");
              Console.ReadLine();
          }
      }
  }
}
```

The results from running the first instance of the application appear in Output 20.4.

OUTPUT 20.4

```
ENTER to shut down
```

The results of the second instance of the application while the first instance is still running appear in Output 20.5.

OUTPUT 20.5

```
This application is already running.
```

In this case, the application can run only once on the machine, even if it is launched by different users. To restrict the instances to once per user, add `System.Environment.UserName` (which requires the Microsoft .NET Framework or .NET Standard 2.0) as a suffix when assigning the `mutexName`.

`Mutex` derives from `System.Threading.WaitHandle`, so it includes the `WaitAll()`, `WaitAny()`, and `SignalAndWait()` methods. These methods allow it to acquire multiple locks automatically—something `Monitor` does not support.

End 2.0

WaitHandle

The base class for `Mutex` is a `System.Threading.WaitHandle`. This is a fundamental synchronization class used by the `Mutex`, `EventWaitHandle`, and `Semaphore` synchronization classes. The key methods on a `WaitHandle` are the `WaitOne()` methods. These methods block execution until the `WaitHandle` instance is signaled or set. The `WaitOne()` methods include several overloads allowing for an indefinite wait: `void WaitOne()`, a millisecond-timed wait; `bool WaitOne(int milliseconds)`; and `bool WaitOne(TimeSpan timeout)`, a `TimeSpan` wait. The versions that return a Boolean will return a value of `true` whenever the `WaitHandle` is signaled before the timeout.

In addition to the `WaitHandle` instance methods, there are two key static members: `WaitAll()` and `WaitAny()`. Like their instance cousins, these static members support timeouts. In addition, they take a collection of WaitHandles, in the form of an array, so that they can respond to signals coming from within the collection.

Note that WaitHandle contains a handle (of type SafeWaitHandle) that implements IDisposable. As such, care is needed to ensure that WaitHandles are disposed when they are no longer needed.

Reset Events: *ManualResetEvent and ManualResetEventSlim*

Begin 4.0

One way to control uncertainty about when particular instructions in a thread will execute relative to instructions in another thread is with reset events. In spite of the term *events*, reset events have nothing to do with C# delegates and events. Instead, reset events are a way to force code to wait for the execution of another thread until the other thread signals. They are especially useful for testing multithreaded code because it is possible to wait for a particular state before verifying the results.

The reset event types are System.Threading.ManualResetEvent and the Microsoft .NET Framework 4–added lightweight version, System .Threading.ManualResetEventSlim. (As discussed in the upcoming Advanced Topic titled "Favor ManualResetEvent and Semaphores over AutoResetEvent," there is a third type, System.Threading .AutoResetEvent, but programmers should avoid it in favor of one of the first two.) The key methods on the reset events are Set() and Wait() (called WaitOne() on ManualResetEvent). Calling the Wait() method will cause a thread to block until a different thread calls Set() or until the wait period times out. Listing 20.10 demonstrates how this works, and Output 20.6 shows the results.

LISTING 20.10: Waiting for ManualResetEventSlim

```csharp
using System;
using System.Threading;
using System.Threading.Tasks;

public class Program
{
    static ManualResetEventSlim MainSignaledResetEvent;
    static ManualResetEventSlim DoWorkSignaledResetEvent;
```

```csharp
public static void DoWork()
{
    Console.WriteLine("DoWork() started....");
    DoWorkSignaledResetEvent.Set();
    MainSignaledResetEvent.Wait();
    Console.WriteLine("DoWork() ending....");
}

public static void Main()
{
    using(MainSignaledResetEvent =
        new ManualResetEventSlim())
    using (DoWorkSignaledResetEvent =
        new ManualResetEventSlim())
    {
        Console.WriteLine(
            "Application started....");
        Console.WriteLine("Starting task....");

        // Use Task.Factory.StartNew for .NET 4.0
        Task task = Task.Run(()=>DoWork());

        // Block until DoWork() has started
        DoWorkSignaledResetEvent.Wait();
        Console.WriteLine(
            " Waiting while thread executes...");
        MainSignaledResetEvent.Set();
        task.Wait();
        Console.WriteLine("Thread completed");
        Console.WriteLine(
            "Application shutting down....");
    }
}
```

4.0

OUTPUT 20.6

```
Application started....
Starting thread....
DoWork() started....
Waiting while thread executes...
DoWork() ending....
Thread completed
Application shutting down....
```

Listing 20.10 begins by instantiating and starting a new Task. Table 20.3 shows the execution path in which each column represents a thread. In cases where code appears on the same row, it is indeterminate which side executes first.

TABLE 20.3: Execution Path with `ManualResetEvent` Synchronization

Main()	DoWork()
...	
Console.WriteLine("Application started....");	
Task task = new Task(DoWork);	
Console.WriteLine("Starting thread....");	
task.Start();	
DoWorkSignaledResetEvent.Wait();	Console.WriteLine("DoWork() started....");
	DoWorkSignaledResetEvent.Set();
Console.WriteLine("Thread executing...");	MainSignaledResetEvent.Wait();
MainSignaledResetEvent.Set();	
task.Wait();	Console.WriteLine("DoWork() ending....");
Console.WriteLine("Thread completed");	
Console.WriteLine("Application exiting....");	

Calling a reset event's `Wait()` method (for a `ManualResetEvent`, it is called `WaitOne()`) blocks the calling thread until another thread signals and allows the blocked thread to continue. Instead of blocking indefinitely, `Wait()`/`WaitOne()` overrides include a parameter, either in milliseconds or as a `TimeSpan` object, for the maximum amount of time to block. When specifying a timeout period, the return from `WaitOne()` will be `false` if the timeout occurs before the reset event is signaled. `ManualResetEvent.Wait()` also includes a version that takes a cancellation token, allowing for cancellation requests as discussed in Chapter 19.

The difference between `ManualResetEventSlim` and `ManualResetEvent` is that the latter uses kernel synchronization by default whereas the former is optimized to avoid trips to the kernel except as a last resort. Thus, `ManualResetEventSlim` is more performant even though it could possibly use more CPU cycles. For this reason, you should use `ManualResetEventSlim` in general unless waiting on multiple events or across processes is required.

Notice that reset events implement `IDisposable`, so they should be disposed when they are no longer needed. In Listing 20.10, we do this via a `using` statement. (`CancellationTokenSource` contains a `ManualResetEvent`, which is why it, too, implements `IDisposable`.)

Although not exactly the same, `System.Threading.Monitor`'s `Wait()` and `Pulse()` methods provide similar functionality to reset events in some circumstances.

■ ADVANCED TOPIC

Favor ManualResetEvent and Semaphores over AutoResetEvent

There is a third reset event, `System.Threading.AutoResetEvent`, that, like `ManualResetEvent`, allows one thread to signal (with a call to `Set()`) another thread that this first thread has reached a certain location in the code. The difference is that the `AutoResetEvent` unblocks only one thread's `Wait()` call: After the first thread passes through the auto-reset gate, it goes back to locked. With the auto-reset event, it is all too easy to mistakenly code the producer thread with more iterations than the consumer thread. Therefore, use of `Monitor`'s `Wait()`/`Pulse()` pattern or use a semaphore (if fewer than *n* threads can participate in a particular block) is generally preferred.

In contrast to an `AutoResetEvent`, the `ManualResetEvent` won't return to the unsignaled state until `Reset()` is called explicitly.

Semaphore/SemaphoreSlim and CountdownEvent

`Semaphore` and `SemaphoreSlim` have the same performance differences as `ManualResetEvent` and `ManualResetEventSlim`. Unlike `ManualResetEvent`/`ManualResetEventSlim`, which provide a lock (like a gate) that is either open or closed, semaphores restrict only *N* calls to pass within a critical section simultaneously. The semaphore essentially keeps a count of the pool of resources. When this count reaches zero, it blocks any further access to the pool until one of the resources is returned, making it available for the next blocked request that is queued.

`CountdownEvent` is much like a semaphore, except it achieves the opposite synchronization. That is, rather than protecting further access to a pool of resources that are all used up, the `CountdownEvent` allows access only once the count reaches zero. Consider, for example, a parallel operation that downloads a multitude of stock quotes. Only when all of the quotes are downloaded can a particular search algorithm execute. The `CountdownEvent` may be used for synchronizing the search algorithm, decrementing the count as each stock is downloading, and then releasing the search to start once the count reaches zero.

Notice that `SemaphoreSlim` and `CountdownEvent` were introduced with Microsoft .NET Framework 4. In .NET 4.5, the former includes a `SemaphoreSlim.WaitAsync()` method so that the Task-based Asynchronous Pattern (TAP) can be used when waiting to enter the semaphore.

Concurrent Collection Classes

Another series of classes introduced with Microsoft .NET Framework 4 is the concurrent collection classes. These classes are especially designed to include built-in synchronization code so that they can support simultaneous access by multiple threads without concern for race conditions. A list of the concurrent collection classes appears in Table 20.4.

TABLE 20.4: Concurrent Collection Classes

Collection Class	Description
`BlockingCollection<T>`	Provides a blocking collection that enables producer/consumer scenarios in which producers write data into the collection while consumers read the data. This class provides a generic collection type that synchronizes add and remove operations without concern for the back-end storage (whether a queue, stack, list, or something else). `BlockingCollection<T>` provides blocking and bounding support for collections that implement the `IProducerConsumerCollection<T>` interface.
`ConcurrentBag<T>`*	A thread-safe unordered collection of T type objects.

TABLE 20.4: Concurrent Collection Classes (*continued*)

Collection Class	Description
`ConcurrentDictionary<TKey, TValue>`	A thread-safe dictionary; a collection of keys and values.
`ConcurrentQueue<T>`*	A thread-safe queue supporting first in, first out (FIFO) semantics on objects of type T.
`ConcurrentStack<T>`*	A thread-safe stack supporting first in, last out (FILO) semantics on objects of type T.

* Collection classes that implement `IProducerConsumerCollection<T>`.

A common pattern enabled by concurrent collections is support for thread-safe access by producers and consumers. Classes that implement `IProducerConsumerCollection<T>` (identified by * in Table 20.4) are specifically designed to provide such support. This enables one or more classes to be pumping data into the collection while a different set reads it out, removing it. The order in which data is added and removed is determined by the individual collection classes that implement the `IProducerConsumerCollection<T>` interface.

Although it is not built into the out-of-the-box .NET/Dotnet Core Frameworks, an additional immutable collection library is available as a NuGet package reference, called `System.Collections.Immutable`. The advantage of the immutable collection is that it can be passed freely between threads without concern for either deadlocks or interim updates. As immutable collections cannot be modified, interim updates won't occur; thus such collections are automatically thread-safe (so there is no need to lock access). For more information, see http://itl.tc/SystemCollectionsImmutable.

4.0

Thread Local Storage

In some cases, using synchronization locks can lead to unacceptable performance and scalability restrictions. In other instances, providing synchronization around a particular data element may be too complex, especially when it is added after the original coding.

One alternative solution to synchronization is isolation, and one method for implementing isolation is **thread local storage**. With thread local storage, each thread has its own dedicated instance of a variable.

As a result, there is no need for synchronization, as there is no point in synchronizing data that occurs within only a single thread's context. Two examples of thread local storage implementations are ThreadLocal<T> and ThreadStaticAttribute.

ThreadLocal<T>

Use of thread local storage with Microsoft .NET Framework 4 or later involves declaring a field (or variable, in the case of closure by the compiler) of type ThreadLocal<T>. The result is a different instance of the field for each thread, as demonstrated in Listing 20.11 and Output 20.7. Note that a different instance exists even if the field is static.

LISTING 20.11: Using ThreadLocal<T> for Thread Local Storage

```csharp
using System;
using System.Threading;

public class Program
{
    static ThreadLocal<double> _Count =
        new ThreadLocal<double>(() => 0.01134);

    public static double Count
    {
        get { return _Count.Value; }
        set { _Count.Value = value; }
    }

    public static void Main()
    {
        Thread thread = new Thread(Decrement);
        thread.Start();

        // Increment
        for(double i = 0; i < short.MaxValue; i++)
        {
            Count++;
        }

        thread.Join();
        Console.WriteLine("Main Count = {0}", Count);
    }

    static void Decrement()
    {
        Count = -Count;
```

4.0

```
    for (double i = 0; i < short.MaxValue; i++)
    {
        Count--;
    }
    Console.WriteLine(
        "Decrement Count = {0}", Count);
  }
 }
```

OUTPUT 20.7

```
Decrement Count = -32767.01134
Main Count = 32767.01134
```

As Output 20.7 demonstrates, the value of Count for the thread executing Main() is never decremented by the thread executing Decrement(). For Main()'s thread, the initial value is 0.01134 and the final value is 32767.01134. Decrement() has similar values, except that they are negative. As Count is based on the static field of type ThreadLocal<T>, the thread running Main() and the thread running Decrement() have independent values stored in _Count.Value.

End 4.0

Thread Local Storage with ThreadStaticAttribute

Decorating a static field with a ThreadStaticAttribute, as in Listing 20.12, is a second way to designate a static variable as an instance per thread. This technique has a few caveats relative to ThreadLocal<T>, but it also has the advantage of being available prior to Microsoft .NET Framework 4. (Also, since ThreadLocal<T> is based on the ThreadStaticAttribute, it would consume less memory and give a slight performance advantage given frequently enough repeated small iterations.)

LISTING 20.12: Using ThreadStaticAttribute for Thread Local Storage

```
using System;
using System.Threading;

public class Program
{
    [ThreadStatic]
    static double _Count = 0.01134;
    public static double Count
    {
        get { return Program._Count; }
        set { Program._Count = value; }
    }
```

```
public static void Main()
{
    Thread thread = new Thread(Decrement);
    thread.Start();

    // Increment
    for(int i = 0; i < short.MaxValue; i++)
    {
        Count++;
    }

    thread.Join();
    Console.WriteLine("Main Count = {0}", Count);
}

static void Decrement()
{
    for(int i = 0; i < short.MaxValue; i++)
    {
        Count--;
    }
    Console.WriteLine("Decrement Count = {0}", Count);
}
```

The results of Listing 20.12 appear in Output 20.8.

OUTPUT 20.8

```
Decrement Count = -32767
Main Count = 32767.01134
```

As in Listing 20.11, the value of Count for the thread executing Main()
is never decremented by the thread executing Decrement(). For Main()'s
thread, the initial value is a negative _Total and the final value is 0. In
other words, with ThreadStaticAttribute the value of Count for each
thread is specific to the thread and not accessible across threads.

Notice that unlike with Listing 20.11, the value displayed for the decrement count does not have any decimal digits, indicating it was never
initialized to 0.01134. Although the value of _Count is assigned during
declaration—private double _Count = 0.01134 in this example—only
the thread static instance associated with the thread running the static
constructor will be initialized. In Listing 20.12, only the thread executing
Main() will have a thread local storage variable initialized to 0.01134.
The value of _Count that Decrement() decrements will always be

initialized to 0 (default(double) since _Count is an double). Similarly, if a constructor initializes a thread local storage field, only the constructor calling that thread will initialize the thread local storage instance. For this reason, it is a good practice to initialize a thread local storage field within the method that each thread initially calls. However, this is not always reasonable, especially in connection with async, in which different pieces of computation might run on different threads, resulting in unexpectedly differing thread local storage values on each piece.

The decision to use thread local storage requires some degree of cost–benefit analysis. For example, consider using thread local storage for a database connection. Depending on the database management system, database connections are relatively expensive, so creating a connection for every thread could be costly. Similarly, locking a connection so that all database calls are synchronized places a significantly lower ceiling on scalability. Each pattern has its costs and benefits, and the best choice depends largely on the individual implementation.

Another reason to use thread local storage is to make commonly needed context information available to other methods without explicitly passing the data via parameters. For example, if multiple methods in the call stack require user security information, you can pass the data using thread local storage fields instead of as parameters. This technique keeps APIs cleaner while still making the information available to methods in a thread-safe manner. Such an approach requires that you ensure the thread local data is always set—a step that is especially important on Tasks or other thread pool threads because the underlying threads are reused.

Timers

Begin 5.0

On occasion, it is necessary to delay code execution for a specific period of time or to register for a notification after a specific period of time. Examples include refreshing the screen at a specific period rather than immediately when frequent data changes occur. One approach to implementing timers is to leverage the async/await pattern of C# 5.0 and the Task.Delay() method added in .NET 4.5. As we pointed out in Chapter 19, one key feature of TAP is that the code executing after an async call will continue in a supported thread context, thereby avoiding any UI cross-threading issues. Listing 20.13 provides an example of how to use the Task.Delay() method.

LISTING 20.13: Using Task.Delay() as a Timer

```csharp
using System;
using System.Threading.Tasks;

public class Pomodoro
{
    // ...

    private static async Task TickAsync(
        System.Threading.CancellationToken token)
    {
        for(int minute = 0; minute < 25; minute++)
        {
            DisplayMinuteTicker(minute);
            for(int second = 0; second < 60; second++)
            {
                await Task.Delay(1000);
                if(token.IsCancellationRequested) break;
                DisplaySecondTicker();
            }
            if(token.IsCancellationRequested) break;
        }
    }
}
```

The call to Task.Delay(1000) will set a countdown timer that triggers after 1 second and executes the continuation code that appears after it.

Fortunately, in C# 5.0, TAP's use of the synchronization context specifically addressed executing UI-related code exclusively on the UI thread. Prior to that, it was necessary to use specific timer classes that were UI-thread-safe—or could be configured as such. Timers such as System.Windows.Forms.Timer, System.Windows.Threading .DispatcherTimer, and System.Timers.Timer (if configured appropriately) are UI-thread-friendly. Others, such as System.Threading.Timer, are optimized for performance.

End 5.0

■ADVANCED TOPIC

Controlling the COM Threading Model with the STAThreadAttribute

With COM, four different apartment-threading models determine the threading rules relating to calls between COM objects. Fortunately, these rules—and the complexity that accompanied them—have disappeared from .NET as long as the program invokes no COM components. The general approach to handling COM interoperability issues is to place all .NET components within the main, single-threaded apartment by decorating a process's `Main` method with the `System.STAThreadAttribute`. In so doing, it is not necessary to cross apartment boundaries to invoke the majority of COM components. Furthermore, apartment initialization does not occur unless a COM interop call is made. The caveat to this approach is that all other threads (including those of `Task`) will default to using a multithreaded apartment (MTA). In turn, care needs to be taken when invoking COM components from other threads besides the main one.

COM interop is not necessarily an explicit action by the developer. Microsoft implemented many of the components within the Microsoft .NET Framework by creating a runtime callable wrapper (RCW) rather than rewriting all the COM functionality within managed code. As a result, COM calls are often made unknowingly. To ensure that these calls are always made from a single-threaded apartment, it is generally a good practice to decorate the main method of all Windows Forms executables with the `System.STAThreadAttribute`.

SUMMARY

In this chapter, we looked at various synchronization mechanisms and saw how a variety of classes are available to protect against race conditions. Coverage included the `lock` keyword, which leverages `System.Threading.Monitor` under the covers. Other synchronization classes include `System.Threading.Interlocked`, `System.Threading.Mutext`, `System.Threading.WaitHandle`, reset events, semaphores, and the concurrent collection classes.

In spite of all the progress made in improving multithreaded programming between early versions of .NET and today, synchronization of multithreaded programming remains complicated with numerous pitfalls. To avoid these sand traps, several best practices have been identified. They include consistently acquiring synchronization targets in the same order and wrapping static members with synchronization logic.

Before closing the chapter, we considered the `Task.Delay()` method, a .NET 4.5 introduced API for implementing a timer based on TAP.

The next chapter investigates another complex .NET technology: that of marshalling calls out of .NET and into unmanaged code using P/Invoke. In addition, it introduces a concept known as unsafe code, which C# uses to access memory pointers directly, as unmanaged code does (e.g., C++).

21

Platform Interoperability and Unsafe Code

C# HAS GREAT CAPABILITIES especially when you consider that the underlying framework is entirely managed. Sometimes, however, you do need to escape out of all the safety that C# provides and step back into the world of memory addresses and pointers. C# supports this action in two significant ways. The first option is to go through Platform Invoke (P/Invoke) and calls into APIs exposed by unmanaged dynamic link libraries (DLLs). The second way is through **unsafe code**, which enables access to memory pointers and addresses.

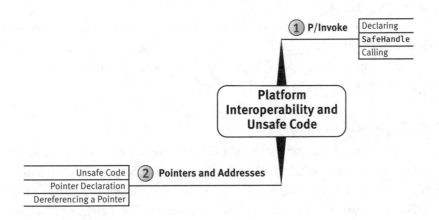

The majority of the chapter discusses interoperability with unmanaged code and the use of unsafe code. This discussion culminates with a small program that determines the processor ID of a computer. The code requires that you do the following:

1. Call into an operating system DLL and request allocation of a portion of memory for executing instructions.
2. Write some assembler instructions into the allocated area.
3. Inject an address location into the assembler instructions.
4. Execute the assembler code.

Aside from the P/Invoke and unsafe constructs covered here, the complete listing demonstrates the full power of C# and the fact that the capabilities of unmanaged code are still accessible from C# and managed code.

Platform Invoke

Whether a developer is trying to call a library of existing unmanaged code, accessing unmanaged code in the operating system not exposed in any managed API, or trying to achieve maximum performance for an algorithm by avoiding the runtime overhead of type checking and garbage collection, at some point there must be a call into unmanaged code. The Common Language Infrastructure (CLI) provides this capability through P/Invoke. With P/Invoke, you can make API calls into exported functions of unmanaged DLLs.

The APIs invoked in this section are Windows APIs. Although the same APIs are not available on other platforms, developers can still use P/Invoke for APIs native to their operating systems or for calls into their own DLLs. The guidelines and syntax are the same.

Declaring External Functions

Once the target function is identified, the next step of P/Invoke is to declare the function with managed code. Just as with all regular methods that belong to a class, you need to declare the targeted API within the context of a class, but by using the `extern` modifier. Listing 21.1 demonstrates how to do this.

LISTING 21.1: Declaring an External Method

```
using System;
using System.Runtime.InteropServices;
class VirtualMemoryManager
{
  [DllImport("kernel32.dll", EntryPoint="GetCurrentProcess")]
  internal static extern IntPtr GetCurrentProcessHandle();
}
```

In this case, the class is `VirtualMemoryManager`, because it will contain functions associated with managing memory. (This particular function is available directly off the `System.Diagnostics.Processor` class, so there is no need to declare it in real code.) Note that the method returns an `IntPtr`; this type is explained in the next section.

The `extern` methods never include any body and are (almost) always static. Instead of a method body, the `DllImport` attribute, which accompanies the method declaration, points to the implementation. At a minimum, the attribute needs the name of the DLL that defines the function. The runtime determines the function name from the method name, although you can override this default using the `EntryPoint` named parameter to provide the function name. (The .NET framework will automatically attempt calls to the Unicode [...W] or ASCII [...A] API version.)

It this case, the external function, `GetCurrentProcess()`, retrieves a pseudohandle for the current process that you will use in the call for virtual memory allocation. Here's the unmanaged declaration:

```
HANDLE GetCurrentProcess();
```

Parameter Data Types

Assuming the developer has identified the targeted DLL and exported function, the most difficult step is identifying or creating the managed data types that correspond to the unmanaged types in the external function.[1] Listing 21.2 shows a more difficult API.

---

1. One particularly helpful resource for declaring Win32 APIs is www.pinvoke.net. It provides a great starting point for many APIs, helping you avoid some of the subtle problems that can arise when coding an external API call from scratch.

LISTING 21.2: The `VirtualAllocEx()` API

```
LPVOID VirtualAllocEx(
    HANDLE hProcess,      // The handle to a process. The
                          // function allocates memory within
                          // the virtual address space of this
                          // process.
    LPVOID lpAddress,     // The pointer that specifies a
                          // desired starting address for the
                          // region of pages that you want to
                          // allocate. If lpAddress is NULL,
                          // the function determines where to
                          // allocate the region.
    SIZE_T dwSize,        // The size of the region of memory to
                          // allocate, in bytes. If lpAddress
                          // is NULL, the function rounds dwSize
                          // up to the next page boundary.
    DWORD flAllocationType, // The type of memory allocation
    DWORD flProtect);     // The type of memory allocation
```

`VirtualAllocEx()` allocates virtual memory that the operating system specifically designates for execution or data. To call it, you need corresponding definitions in managed code for each data type; although common in Win32 programming, `HANDLE`, `LPVOID`, `SIZE_T`, and `DWORD` are undefined in the CLI managed code. The declaration in C# for `VirtualAllocEx()`, therefore, is shown in Listing 21.3.

LISTING 21.3: Declaring the `VirtualAllocEx()` API in C#

```csharp
using System;
using System.Runtime.InteropServices;
class VirtualMemoryManager
{
  [DllImport("kernel32.dll")]
  internal static extern IntPtr GetCurrentProcess();

  [DllImport("kernel32.dll", SetLastError = true)]
  private static extern IntPtr VirtualAllocEx(
      IntPtr hProcess,
      IntPtr lpAddress,
      IntPtr dwSize,
      AllocationType flAllocationType,
      uint flProtect);
}
```

One distinct characteristic of managed code is that primitive data types such as `int` do not change their size on the basis of the processor. Whether the processor is 16, 32, or 64 bits, `int` is always 32 bits. In unmanaged code, however, memory pointers will vary depending on the processor. Therefore, instead of mapping types such as HANDLE and LPVOID simply to ints, you need to map to System.IntPtr, whose size will vary depending on the processor memory layout. This example also uses an AllocationType enum, which we discuss in the section "Simplifying API Calls with Wrappers" later in this chapter.

An interesting point to note about Listing 21.3 is that IntPtr is useful not just for pointers; that is, it is useful for other things such as quantities. IntPtr does not mean just "pointer stored in an integer"; it also means "integer that is the size of a pointer." An IntPtr need not contain a pointer but simply needs to contain something the size of a pointer. Lots of things are the size of a pointer but are nevertheless not pointers.

Using ref Rather Than Pointers

Frequently, unmanaged code uses pointers for pass-by-reference parameters. In these cases, P/Invoke doesn't require that you map the data type to a pointer in managed code. Instead, you map the corresponding parameters to ref (or out, depending on whether the parameter is in/out or just out). In Listing 21.4, lpflOldProtect, whose data type is PDWORD, is an example that returns the "pointer to a variable that receives the previous access protection of the first page in the specified region of pages."[2]

LISTING 21.4: Using ref and out Rather Than Pointers

```
class VirtualMemoryManager
{
  // ...
  [DllImport("kernel32.dll", SetLastError = true)]
  static extern bool VirtualProtectEx(
      IntPtr hProcess, IntPtr lpAddress,
      IntPtr dwSize, uint flNewProtect,
      ref uint lpflOldProtect);
}
```

Despite that lpflOldProtect is documented as [out] (even though the signature doesn't enforce it), the description goes on to mention that the parameter must point to a valid variable and not NULL. This inconsistency is confusing, but commonly encountered. The guideline is

---

2. MSDN documentation.

to use ref rather than out for P/Invoke type parameters since the callee can always ignore the data passed with ref, but the converse will not necessarily succeed.

The other parameters are virtually the same as VirtualAllocEx() except that the lpAddress is the address returned from VirtualAllocEx(). In addition, flNewProtect specifies the exact type of memory protection: page execute, page read-only, and so on.

Using StructLayoutAttribute for Sequential Layout

Some APIs involve types that have no corresponding managed type. Calling these types requires redeclaration of the type in managed code. You declare the unmanaged COLORREF struct, for example, in managed code (see Listing 21.5).

LISTING 21.5: Declaring Types from Unmanaged Structs

```csharp
[StructLayout(LayoutKind.Sequential)]
struct ColorRef
{
  public byte Red;
  public byte Green;
  public byte Blue;
  // Turn off warning about not accessing Unused
  #pragma warning disable 414
  private byte Unused;
  #pragma warning restore 414

  public ColorRef(byte red, byte green, byte blue)
  {
      Blue = blue;
      Green = green;
      Red = red;
      Unused = 0;
  }
}
```

Various Microsoft Windows color APIs use COLORREF to represent RGB colors (i.e., levels of red, green, and blue).

The key in this declaration is StructLayoutAttribute. By default, managed code can optimize the memory layouts of types, so layouts may not be sequential from one field to the next. To force sequential layouts so that a type maps directly and can be copied bit for bit (blitted) from managed to unmanaged code, and vice versa, you add the

`StructLayoutAttribute` with the `LayoutKind.Sequential` enum value. (This is also useful when writing data to and from filestreams where a sequential layout may be expected.)

Since the unmanaged (C++) definition for `struct` does not map to the C# definition, there is not a direct mapping of unmanaged struct to managed struct. Instead, developers should follow the usual C# guidelines about whether the type should behave like a value or a reference type, and whether the size is small (approximately less than 16 bytes).

Error Handling

One inconvenient aspect of Win32 API programming is the fact that the APIs frequently report errors in inconsistent ways. For example, some APIs return a value (`0`, `1`, `false`, and so on) to indicate an error, whereas others set an out parameter in some way. Furthermore, the details of what went wrong require additional calls to the `GetLastError()` API and then an additional call to `FormatMessage()` to retrieve an error message corresponding to the error. In summary, Win32 error reporting in unmanaged code seldom occurs via exceptions.

Fortunately, the P/Invoke designers provided a mechanism for error handling. To enable it, if the `SetLastError` named parameter of the `DllImport` attribute is `true`, it is possible to instantiate a `System.ComponentModel.Win32Exception()` that is automatically initialized with the Win32 error data immediately following the P/Invoke call (see Listing 21.6).

LISTING 21.6: Win32 Error Handling

```
class VirtualMemoryManager
{
  [DllImport("kernel32.dll", ", SetLastError = true)]
  private static extern IntPtr VirtualAllocEx(
      IntPtr hProcess,
      IntPtr lpAddress,
      IntPtr dwSize,
      AllocationType flAllocationType,
      uint flProtect);

  // ...
  [DllImport("kernel32.dll", SetLastError = true)]
  static extern bool VirtualProtectEx(
      IntPtr hProcess, IntPtr lpAddress,
      IntPtr dwSize, uint flNewProtect,
      ref uint lpflOldProtect);
```

```csharp
[Flags]
private enum AllocationType : uint
{
    // ...
}

[Flags]
private enum ProtectionOptions
{
    // ...
}

[Flags]
private enum MemoryFreeType
{
    // ...
}

public static IntPtr AllocExecutionBlock(
    int size, IntPtr hProcess)
{
    IntPtr codeBytesPtr;
    codeBytesPtr = VirtualAllocEx(
        hProcess, IntPtr.Zero,
        (IntPtr)size,
        AllocationType.Reserve | AllocationType.Commit,
        (uint)ProtectionOptions.PageExecuteReadWrite);

    if (codeBytesPtr == IntPtr.Zero)
    {
        throw new System.ComponentModel.Win32Exception();
    }

    uint lpflOldProtect = 0;
    if (!VirtualProtectEx(
        hProcess, codeBytesPtr,
        (IntPtr)size,
        (uint)ProtectionOptions.PageExecuteReadWrite,
        ref lpflOldProtect))
    {
        throw new System.ComponentModel.Win32Exception();
    }
    return codeBytesPtr;
}

public static IntPtr AllocExecutionBlock(int size)
{
    return AllocExecutionBlock(
        size, GetCurrentProcessHandle());
}
}
```

This code enables developers to provide the custom error checking that each API uses while still reporting the error in a standard manner.

Listings 21.1 and 21.3 declared the P/Invoke methods as internal or private. Except for the simplest of APIs, wrapping methods in public wrappers that reduce the complexity of the P/Invoke API calls is a good guideline that increases API usability and moves toward object-oriented type structure. The `AllocExecutionBlock()` declaration in Listing 21.6 provides a good example of this approach.

> ## Guidelines
>
> **DO** create public managed wrappers around unmanaged methods that use the conventions of managed code, such as structured exception handling.

Using SafeHandle

Begin 2.0

Frequently, P/Invoke involves a resource, such as a handle, that code needs to clean up after using. Instead of requiring developers to remember this step is necessary and manually code it each time, it is helpful to provide a class that implements `IDisposable` and a finalizer. In Listing 21.7, for example, the address returned after `VirtualAllocEx()` and `VirtualProtectEx()` requires a follow-up call to `VirtualFreeEx()`. To provide built-in support for this process, you define a `VirtualMemoryPtr` class that derives from `System.Runtime.InteropServices.SafeHandle`.

LISTING 21.7: Managed Resources Using SafeHandle

```
public class VirtualMemoryPtr :
  System.Runtime.InteropServices.SafeHandle
{
  public VirtualMemoryPtr(int memorySize) :
      base(IntPtr.Zero, true)
  {
      ProcessHandle =
          VirtualMemoryManager.GetCurrentProcessHandle();
      MemorySize = (IntPtr)memorySize;
      AllocatedPointer =
          VirtualMemoryManager.AllocExecutionBlock(
          memorySize, ProcessHandle);
      Disposed = false;
  }
```

```csharp
    public readonly IntPtr AllocatedPointer;
    readonly IntPtr ProcessHandle;
    readonly IntPtr MemorySize;
    bool Disposed;

    public static implicit operator IntPtr(
        VirtualMemoryPtr virtualMemoryPointer)
    {
        return virtualMemoryPointer.AllocatedPointer;
    }

    // SafeHandle abstract member
    public override bool IsInvalid
    {
        get
        {
            return Disposed;
        }
    }

    // SafeHandle abstract member
    protected override bool ReleaseHandle()
    {
        if (!Disposed)
        {
            Disposed = true;
            GC.SuppressFinalize(this);
            VirtualMemoryManager.VirtualFreeEx(ProcessHandle,
                AllocatedPointer, MemorySize);
        }
        return true;
    }
}
```

System.Runtime.InteropServices.SafeHandle includes the abstract members IsInvalid and ReleaseHandle(). You place your cleanup code in the latter; the former indicates whether this code has executed yet.

With VirtualMemoryPtr, you can allocate memory simply by instantiating the type and specifying the needed memory allocation.

Calling External Functions

Once you declare the P/Invoke functions, you invoke them just as you would any other class member. The key, however, is that the imported DLL must be in the path, including the executable directory, so that it can be successfully loaded. Listings 21.6 and 21.7 demonstrate this approach. However, they rely on some constants.

End 2.0

Since `flAllocationType` and `flProtect` are flags, it is a good practice to provide constants or enums for each. Instead of expecting the caller to define these constants or enums, encapsulation suggests you provide them as part of the API declaration, as shown in Listing 21.8.

LISTING 21.8: Encapsulating the APIs Together

```
class VirtualMemoryManager
{
  // ...

  /// <summary>
  /// The type of memory allocation. This parameter must
  /// contain one of the following values.
  /// </summary>
  [Flags]
  private enum AllocationType : uint
  {
      /// <summary>
      /// Allocates physical storage in memory or in the
      /// paging file on disk for the specified reserved
      /// memory pages. The function initializes the memory
      /// to zero.
      /// </summary>
      Commit = 0x1000,
      /// <summary>
      /// Reserves a range of the process's virtual address
      /// space without allocating any actual physical
      /// storage in memory or in the paging file on disk
      /// </summary>
      Reserve = 0x2000,
      /// <summary>
      /// Indicates that data in the memory range specified by
      /// lpAddress and dwSize is no longer of interest. The
      /// pages should not be read from or written to the
      /// paging file. However, the memory block will be used
      /// again later, so it should not be decommitted. This
      /// value cannot be used with any other value.
      /// </summary>
      Reset = 0x80000,
      /// <summary>
      /// Allocates physical memory with read-write access.
      /// This value is solely for use with Address Windowing
      /// Extensions (AWE) memory.
      /// </summary>
      Physical = 0x400000,
      /// <summary>
      /// Allocates memory at the highest possible address
      /// </summary>
      TopDown = 0x100000,
  }
```

```
    /// <summary>
    /// The memory protection for the region of pages to be
    /// allocated
    /// </summary>
    [Flags]
    private enum ProtectionOptions : uint
    {
        /// <summary>
        /// Enables execute access to the committed region of
        /// pages. An attempt to read or write to the committed
        /// region results in an access violation.
        /// </summary>
        Execute = 0x10,
        /// <summary>
        /// Enables execute and read access to the committed
        /// region of pages. An attempt to write to the
        /// committed region results in an access violation.
        /// </summary>
        PageExecuteRead = 0x20,
        /// <summary>
        /// Enables execute, read, and write access to the
        /// committed region of pages
        /// </summary>
        PageExecuteReadWrite = 0x40,
        // ...
    }


    /// <summary>
    /// The type of free operation
    /// </summary>
    [Flags]
    private enum MemoryFreeType : uint
    {
        /// <summary>
        /// Decommits the specified region of committed pages.
        /// After the operation, the pages are in the reserved
        /// state.
        /// </summary>
        Decommit = 0x4000,
        /// <summary>
        /// Releases the specified region of pages. After this
        /// operation, the pages are in the free state.
        /// </summary>
        Release = 0x8000
    }

    // ...
}
```

The advantage of enums is that they group together the various values.
Furthermore, they can limit the scope to nothing else besides these values.

Simplifying API Calls with Wrappers

Whether it is error handling, structs, or constant values, one goal of effective API developers is to provide a simplified managed API that wraps the underlying Win32 API. For example, Listing 21.9 overloads VirtualFreeEx() with public versions that simplify the call.

LISTING 21.9: **Wrapping the Underlying API**

```
class VirtualMemoryManager
{
  // ...

  [DllImport("kernel32.dll", SetLastError = true)]
  static extern bool VirtualFreeEx(
      IntPtr hProcess, IntPtr lpAddress,
      IntPtr dwSize, IntPtr dwFreeType);
  public static bool VirtualFreeEx(
      IntPtr hProcess, IntPtr lpAddress,
      IntPtr dwSize)
  {
      bool result = VirtualFreeEx(
          hProcess, lpAddress, dwSize,
          (IntPtr)MemoryFreeType.Decommit);
      if (!result)
      {
          throw new System.ComponentModel.Win32Exception();
      }
      return result;
  }
  public static bool VirtualFreeEx(
      IntPtr lpAddress, IntPtr dwSize)
  {
      return VirtualFreeEx(
          GetCurrentProcessHandle(), lpAddress, dwSize);
  }

  [DllImport("kernel32", SetLastError = true)]
  static extern IntPtr VirtualAllocEx(
      IntPtr hProcess,
      IntPtr lpAddress,
      IntPtr dwSize,
      AllocationType flAllocationType,
      uint flProtect);

  // ...
}
```

Function Pointers Map to Delegates

One last key point related to P/Invoke is that function pointers in unmanaged code map to delegates in managed code. To set up a timer, for example, you would provide a function pointer that the timer could call back on, once it had expired. Specifically, you would pass a delegate instance that matches the signature of the callback.

Guidelines

Given the idiosyncrasies of P/Invoke, there are several guidelines to aid in the process of writing such code.

> ### Guidelines
>
> **DO NOT** unnecessarily replicate existing managed classes that already perform the function of the unmanaged API.
>
> **DO** declare extern methods as private or internal.
>
> **DO** provide public wrapper methods that use managed conventions such as structured exception handling, use of enums for special values, and so on.
>
> **DO** simplify the wrapper methods by choosing default values for unnecessary parameters.
>
> **DO** use the SetLastErrorAttribute on Windows to turn APIs that use SetLastError error codes into methods that throw Win32Exception.
>
> **DO** extend SafeHandle or implement IDisposable and create a finalizer to ensure that unmanaged resources can be cleaned up effectively.
>
> **DO** use delegate types that match the signature of the desired method when an unmanaged API requires a function pointer.
>
> **DO** use ref parameters rather than pointer types when possible.

Pointers and Addresses

On occasion, developers may want to access and work with memory, and with pointers to memory locations, directly. This is necessary, for example, for certain operating system interactions as well as with certain types of time-critical algorithms. To support this capability, C# requires use of the unsafe code construct.

Unsafe Code

One of C#'s great features is the fact that it is strongly typed and supports type checking throughout the runtime execution. What makes this feature especially beneficial is that it is possible to circumvent this support and manipulate memory and addresses directly. You would do so when working with things such as memory-mapped devices, for example, or if you wanted to implement time-critical algorithms. The key is to designate a portion of the code as unsafe.

Unsafe code is an explicit code block and compilation option, as shown in Listing 21.10. The unsafe modifier has no effect on the generated CIL code itself but rather is simply a directive to the compiler to permit pointer and address manipulation within the unsafe block. Furthermore, *unsafe* does not imply *unmanaged*.

LISTING 21.10: Designating a Method for Unsafe Code

```
class Program
{
  unsafe static int Main(string[] args)
  {
      // ...
  }
}
```

You can use unsafe as a modifier to the type or to specific members within the type.

In addition, C# allows unsafe as a statement that flags a code block to allow unsafe code (see Listing 21.11).

LISTING 21.11: Designating a Code Block for Unsafe Code

```
class Program
{
  static int Main(string[] args)
  {
    unsafe
    {
        // ...
    }
  }
}
```

Code within the unsafe block can include unsafe constructs such as pointers.

> **■ NOTE**
>
> It is necessary to explicitly indicate to the compiler that unsafe code is supported.

When writing unsafe code, your code becomes vulnerable to the possibility of buffer overflows and similar outcomes that may potentially expose security holes. For this reason, it is necessary to explicitly notify the compiler that unsafe code occurs. To accomplish this, set the `AllowUnsafeBlocks` to `true` in your CSPROJ file. See Listing 21.12.

LISTING 21.12: Invalid Referent Type Example

```xml
<Project Sdk="Microsoft.NET.Sdk">
  <PropertyGroup>
    <OutputType>Exe</OutputType>
    <TargetFramework>netcoreapp1.0</TargetFramework>
    <ProductName>Chapter20</ProductName>
    <WarningLevel>2</WarningLevel>
    <AllowUnsafeBlocks>True</AllowUnsafeBlocks>
  </PropertyGroup>
  <Import Project="..\Versioning.targets" />
  <ItemGroup>
    <ProjectReference Include="..\SharedCode\SharedCode.csproj" />
  </ItemGroup>
</Project>
```

Alternatively, you can pass the property on the command line when running `dotnet build` (see Output 20.1).

OUTPUT 21.1

```
dotnet build /property:AllowUnsafeBlocks=True
```

Or, if invoking C# compiler directly, you need the `/unsafe` switch (see Output 21.2).

OUTPUT 21.2

```
csc.exe /unsafe Program.cs
```

With Visual Studio, you can activate this feature by checking the Allow Unsafe Code check box from the Build tab of the Project Properties window.

The /unsafe switch enables you to directly manipulate memory and execute instructions that are unmanaged. Requiring /unsafe, therefore, makes exposure to potential security vulnerabilities that such code might introduce explicit. With great power comes great responsibility.

Pointer Declaration

Now that you have marked a code block as unsafe, it is time to look at how to write unsafe code. First, unsafe code allows the declaration of a pointer. Consider the following example:

```
byte* pData;
```

Assuming pData is not null, its value points to a location that contains one or more sequential bytes; the value of pData represents the memory address of the bytes. The type specified before the * is the **referent type**, or the type located where the value of the pointer refers. In this example, pData is the pointer and byte is the referent type, as shown in Figure 21.1.

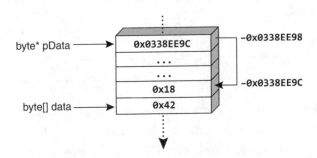

FIGURE 21.1: Pointers Contain the Address of the Data

Because pointers are simply integers that happen to refer to a memory address, they are not subject to garbage collection. C# does not allow referent types other than **unmanaged types**, which are types that are not reference types, are not generics, and do not contain reference types. Therefore, the following command is not valid:

```
string* pMessage;
```

Likewise, this command is not valid:

```
ServiceStatus* pStatus;
```

where ServiceStatus is defined as shown in Listing 21.13. The problem, once again, is that ServiceStatus includes a string field.

Language Contrast: C/C++—Pointer Declaration

In C/C++, multiple pointers within the same declaration are declared as follows:

```
int *p1, *p2;
```

Notice the * on p2; this makes p2 an int* rather than an int. In contrast, C# always places the * with the data type:

```
int* p1, p2;
```

The result is two variables of type int*. The syntax matches that of declaring multiple arrays in a single statement:

```
int[] array1, array2;
```

Pointers are an entirely new category of type. Unlike structs, enums, and classes, pointers don't ultimately derive from System.Object and are not even convertible to System.Object. Instead, they are convertible (explicitly) to System.IntPtr (which can be converted to System.Object).

LISTING 21.13: Invalid Referent Type Example

```
struct ServiceStatus
{
  int State;
  string Description;  // Description is a reference type
}
```

In addition to custom structs that contain only unmanaged types, valid referent types include enums, predefined value types (sbyte, byte, short, ushort, int, uint, long, ulong, char, float, double, decimal, and bool), and pointer types (such as byte**). Lastly, valid syntax includes void* pointers, which represent pointers to an unknown type.

Assigning a Pointer

Once code defines a pointer, it needs to assign a value before accessing it. Just like reference types, pointers can hold the value null; this is their default value. The value stored by the pointer is the address of a location. Therefore, to assign the pointer, you must first retrieve the address of the data.

You could explicitly cast an integer or a long into a pointer, but this rarely occurs without a means of determining the address of a particular data value at execution time. Instead, you need to use the address operator (&) to retrieve the address of the value type:

```
byte* pData = &bytes[0];  // Compile error
```

The problem is that in a managed environment, data can move, thereby invalidating the address. The error message is "You can only take the address of [an] unfixed expression inside a fixed statement initializer." In this case, the byte referenced appears within an array, and an array is a reference type (a movable type). Reference types appear on the heap and are subject to garbage collection or relocation. A similar problem occurs when referring to a value type field on a movable type:

```
int* a = &"message".Length;
```

Either way, to assign an address of some data requires the following:

- The data must be classified as a variable.
- The data must be an unmanaged type.
- The variable needs to be classified as fixed, not movable.

If the data is an unmanaged variable type but is not fixed, use the fixed statement to fix a movable variable.

Fixing Data

To retrieve the address of a movable data item, it is necessary to fix, or pin, the data, as demonstrated in Listing 21.14.

LISTING 21.14: Fixed Statement

```
byte[] bytes = new byte[24];
fixed (byte* pData = &bytes[0]) // pData = bytes also allowed
{
  // ...
}
```

Within the code block of a fixed statement, the assigned data will not move. In this example, bytes will remain at the same address, at least until the end of the fixed statement.

The fixed statement requires the declaration of the pointer variable within its scope. This avoids accessing the variable outside the fixed statement, when the data is no longer fixed. However, it is your responsibility as a programmer to ensure that you do not assign the pointer to another variable that survives beyond the scope of the fixed statement—possibly in an API call, for example. Unsafe code is called "unsafe" for a reason; you are required to ensure that you use the pointers safely rather than relying on the runtime to enforce safety on your behalf. Similarly, using `ref` or `out` parameters will be problematic for data that will not survive beyond the method call.

Since a string is an invalid referent type, it would appear invalid to define pointers to strings. However, as in C++, internally a string is a pointer to the first character of an array of characters, and it is possible to declare pointers to characters using `char*`. Therefore, C# allows for declaring a pointer of type `char*` and assigning it to a string within a fixed statement. The fixed statement prevents the movement of the string during the life of the pointer. Similarly, it allows any movable type that supports an implicit conversion to a pointer of another type, given a fixed statement.

You can replace the verbose assignment of `&bytes[0]` with the abbreviated `bytes`, as shown in Listing 21.15.

LISTING 21.15: Fixed Statement without Address or Array Indexer

```
byte[] bytes = new byte[24];
fixed (byte* pData = bytes)
{
  // ...
}
```

Depending on the frequency and time needed for their execution, fixed statements may have the potential to cause fragmentation in the heap because the garbage collector cannot compact fixed objects. To reduce this problem, the best practice is to pin blocks early in the execution and to pin fewer large blocks rather than many small blocks. Unfortunately, this preference has to be tempered with the practice of pinning as little as possible for as short a time as possible, so as to minimize the chance that a collection will happen during the time that the data is pinned. To some extent, .NET 2.0 reduces this problem through its inclusion of some additional fragmentation-aware code.

It is possible that you might need to fix an object in place in one method body and have it remain fixed until another method is called; this is not possible with the `fixed` statement. If you are in this unfortunate situation, you can use methods on the `GCHandle` object to fix an object in place indefinitely. You should do so only if it is absolutely necessary, however; fixing an object for a long time makes it highly likely that the garbage collector will be unable to efficiently compact memory.

Allocating on the Stack

You should use the `fixed` statement on an array to prevent the garbage collector from moving the data. However, an alternative is to allocate the array on the call stack. Stack allocated data is not subject to garbage collection or to the finalizer patterns that accompany it. Like referent types, the requirement is that the `stackalloc` data is an array of unmanaged types. For example, instead of allocating an array of bytes on the heap, you can place it onto the call stack, as shown in Listing 21.16.

LISTING 21.16: Allocating Data on the Call Stack

```
byte* bytes = stackalloc byte[42];
```

Because the data type is an array of unmanaged types, the runtime can allocate a fixed buffer size for the array and then restore that buffer once the pointer goes out of scope. Specifically, it allocates `sizeof(T) * E`, where E is the array size and T is the referent type. Given the requirement of using `stackalloc` only on an array of unmanaged types, the runtime restores the buffer back to the system by simply unwinding the stack, thereby eliminating the complexities of iterating over the f-reachable queue (see, in Chapter 10, the section titled "Garbage Collection" and the discussion of finalization) and compacting reachable data. Therefore, there is no way to explicitly free `stackalloc` data.

The stack is a precious resource. Although it is small, running out of stack space will have a big effect—namely, the program will crash. For this reason, you should make every effort to avoid running out stack space. If a program does run out of stack space, the best thing that can happen is for the program to shut down/crash immediately. Generally, programs have less than 1MB of stack space (possibly a lot less). Therefore, take great care to avoid allocating arbitrarily sized buffers on the stack.

Dereferencing a Pointer

Accessing the data stored in a variable of a type referred to by a pointer requires that you dereference the pointer, placing the indirection operator prior to the expression. `byte data = *pData;`, for example, dereferences the location of the `byte` referred to by `pData` and produces a variable of type `byte`. The variable provides read/write access to the single `byte` at that location.

Using this principle in unsafe code allows the unorthodox behavior of modifying the "immutable" string, as shown in Listing 21.17. In no way is this strategy recommended, even though it does expose the potential of low-level memory manipulation.

LISTING 21.17: Modifying an Immutable String

```
string text = "S5280ft";
Console.Write("{0} = ", text);
unsafe  // Requires /unsafe switch
{
  fixed (char* pText = text)
  {
      char* p = pText;
      *++p = 'm';
      *++p = 'i';
      *++p = 'l';
      *++p = 'e';
      *++p = ' ';
      *++p = ' ';
  }
}
Console.WriteLine(text);
```

The results of Listing 21.17 appear in Output 21.3.

OUTPUT 21.3

```
S5280ft = Smile
```

In this case, you take the original address and increment it by the size of the referent type (`sizeof(char)`), using the preincrement operator. Next, you dereference the address using the indirection operator and then assign the location with a different character. Similarly, using the + and – operators on a pointer changes the address by the * `sizeof(T)` operand, where T is the referent type.

Similarly, the comparison operators (==, !=, <, >, <=, and >=) work to compare pointers, translating effectively to the comparison of address location values.

One restriction on the dereferencing operator is the inability to dereference a void*. The void* data type represents a pointer to an unknown type. Since the data type is unknown, it can't be dereferenced to produce a variable. Instead, to access the data referenced by a void*, you must convert it to any other pointer type and then dereference the later type.

You can achieve the same behavior as implemented in Listing 21.17 by using the index operator rather than the indirection operator (see Listing 21.18).

LISTING 21.18: Modifying an Immutable String with the Index Operator in Unsafe Code

```
string text;
text = "S5280ft";
Console.Write("{0} = ", text);

unsafe  // Requires /unsafe switch
{
  fixed (char* pText = text)
  {
      pText[1] = 'm';
      pText[2] = 'i';
      pText[3] = 'l';
      pText[4] = 'e';
      pText[5] = ' ';
      pText[6] = ' ';
  }
}
Console.WriteLine(text);
```

The results of Listing 21.18 appear in Output 21.4.

OUTPUT 21.4

```
S5280ft = Smile
```

Modifications such as those in Listing 21.17 and Listing 21.18 can lead to unexpected behavior. For example, if you reassigned text to "S5280ft" following the Console.WriteLine() statement and then redisplayed text, the output would still be Smile because the address of two equal string literals is optimized to one string literal referenced by both variables. In spite of the apparent assignment

```
text = "S5280ft";
```

after the unsafe code in Listing 21.17, the internals of the string assignment are an address assignment of the modified "S5280ft" location, so text is never set to the intended value.

Accessing the Member of a Referent Type

Dereferencing a pointer produces a variable of the pointer's underlying type. You can then access the members of the underlying type using the member access dot operator in the usual way. However, the rules of operator precedence require that *x.y means *(x.y), which is probably not what you intended. If x is a pointer, the correct code is (*x).y, which is an unpleasant syntax. To make it easier to access members of a dereferenced pointer, C# provides a special member access operator: x->y is a shorthand for (*x).y, as shown in Listing 21.19.

LISTING 21.19: Directly Accessing a Referent Type's Members

```
unsafe
{
  Angle angle = new Angle(30, 18, 0);
  Angle* pAngle = &angle;
  System.Console.WriteLine("{0}° {1}' {2}\"",
      pAngle->Hours, pAngle->Minutes, pAngle->Seconds);
}
```

The results of Listing 21.19 appear in Output 21.5.

OUTPUT 21.5

```
30° 18' 0
```

Executing Unsafe Code via a Delegate

As promised at the beginning of this chapter, we finish up with a full working example of what is likely the most "unsafe" thing you can do in C#: obtain a pointer to a block of memory, fill it with the bytes of machine code, make a delegate that refers to the new code, and execute it. In this example, we use assembly code to determine the processor ID. If run on a Windows machine, it prints the processor ID. Listing 21.20 shows how to do it.

LISTING 21.20: Designating a Block for Unsafe Code

```
using System;
using System.Runtime.InteropServices;
using System.Text;
```

```csharp
class Program
{
  public unsafe delegate void MethodInvoker(byte* buffer);

  public unsafe static int ChapterMain()
  {
      if (RuntimeInformation.IsOSPlatform(OSPlatform.Windows))
      {
          unsafe
          {
              byte[] codeBytes = new byte[] {
              0x49, 0x89, 0xd8,         // mov     %rbx,%r8
              0x49, 0x89, 0xc9,         // mov     %rcx,%r9
              0x48, 0x31, 0xc0,         // xor     %rax,%rax
              0x0f, 0xa2,               // cpuid
              0x4c, 0x89, 0xc8,         // mov     %r9,%rax
              0x89, 0x18,               // mov     %ebx,0x0(%rax)
              0x89, 0x50, 0x04,         // mov     %edx,0x4(%rax)
              0x89, 0x48, 0x08,         // mov     %ecx,0x8(%rax)
              0x4c, 0x89, 0xc3,         // mov     %r8,%rbx
              0xc3                      // retq
        };

              byte[] buffer = new byte[12];

              using (VirtualMemoryPtr codeBytesPtr =
                  new VirtualMemoryPtr(codeBytes.Length))
              {
                  Marshal.Copy(
                      codeBytes, 0,
                      codeBytesPtr, codeBytes.Length);

                  MethodInvoker method =
Marshal.GetDelegateForFunctionPointer<MethodInvoker>(codeBytesPtr);
                  fixed (byte* newBuffer = &buffer[0])
                  {
                      method(newBuffer);
                  }
              }
              Console.Write("Processor Id: ");
              Console.WriteLine(ASCIIEncoding.ASCII.GetChars(buffer));
          } // unsafe
      }
      else
      {
          Console.WriteLine("This sample is only valid for Windows");
      }
      return 0;
  }
}
```

The results of Listing 21.20 appear in Output 21.6.

OUTPUT 21.6

```
Processor Id: GenuineIntel
```

SUMMARY

As demonstrated throughout this book, C# offers great power, flexibility, consistency, and a fantastic structure. This chapter highlighted the ability of C# programs to perform very low-level machine-code operations.

Before we end the book, Chapter 22 briefly describes the underlying execution framework and shifts the focus from the C# language to the broader context in which C# programs execute.

■ 22 ■
The Common Language Infrastructure

ONE OF THE FIRST ITEMS that C# PROGRAMMERS ENCOUNTER beyond the syntax is the context under which a C# program executes. This chapter discusses the underpinnings of how C# handles memory allocation and de-allocation, type checking, interoperability with other languages, cross-platform execution, and support for programming metadata. In other words, this chapter investigates the Common Language Infrastructure on which C# relies both at compile time and during execution. It covers the execution engine that governs a C# program at runtime and considers how C# fits into a broader set of languages that are governed by the same execution engine. Because of C#'s close ties with this infrastructure, most of the features that come with the infrastructure are made available to C#.

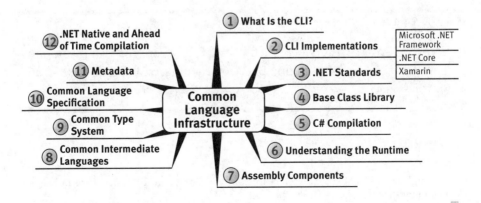

Defining the Common Language Infrastructure

Instead of generating instructions that a processor can interpret directly, the C# compiler generates instructions in an intermediate language, the **Common Intermediate Language (CIL)**. A second compilation step occurs, generally at execution time, converting the CIL to **machine code** that the processor can understand. Conversion to machine code is still not sufficient for code execution, however. It is also necessary for a C# program to execute under the context of an agent. The agent responsible for managing the execution of a C# program is the **Virtual Execution System (VES)**, generally more casually referred to as the **runtime**. (Note that the runtime in this context does not refer to a time, such as execution time; rather, the runtime—the Virtual Execution System—is an agent responsible for managing the execution of a C# program.) The runtime is responsible for loading and running programs and providing additional services (security, garbage collection, and so on) to the program as it executes.

The specifications for the CIL and the runtime are contained within an international standard known as the **Common Language Infrastructure (CLI)**.[1] The CLI is a key specification for understanding the context in which a C# program executes and how it can seamlessly interact with other programs and libraries, even when they are written in other languages. Note that the CLI does not prescribe the implementation for the standard but rather identifies the requirements for how a CLI framework should behave once it conforms to the standard. This provides CLI implementers with the flexibility to innovate where necessary while still providing enough structure that programs created by one CLI implementation can execute on a different implementation and even on a different operating system.

> **■ NOTE**
>
> Note the similarity between the CIL and CLI acronyms and the names they stand for. Distinguishing between them now will help you avoid confusion later.

---

1. Throughout the chapter, CLI refers to Common Language Infrastructure rather than command-line interface as in Dotnet CLI.

Contained within the CLI standard are specifications for the following:

- The Virtual Execution System
- The Common Intermediate Language
- The Common Type System
- The Common Language Specification
- Metadata
- The framework

This chapter broadens your view of C# to include the CLI, which is critical to how C# programs operate and interact with programs and with the operating system.

CLI Implementations

The primary implementations of the CLI today are .NET Core, which runs on Windows, as well as UNIX/Linux and Mac OS; the .NET Framework for Windows; and Xamarin, which is intended for iOS, Mac OS, and Android applications. Each implementation of the CLI includes a C# compiler and a set of framework class libraries; the version of C# supported by each, as well as the exact set of classes in the libraries, varies considerably, and many implementations are now only of historical interest. Table 22.1 describes these implementations.

TABLE 22.1: Implementations of the CLI

Compiler	Description
Microsoft .NET Framework	This traditional (and first) version of the CLR is for creating applications that run on Windows. It includes support for Windows Presentation Foundation, Windows Forms, and ASP.NET. It uses the .NET Framework Base Class Library (BCL).
.NET Core/CoreCLR	The .NET Core project, as the name implies, contains the core functionality common to all new implementations of .NET. It is an open source and platform-portable rewrite of the .NET Framework designed for high-performance applications. The CoreCLR is the implementation of the CLR for this project. At time of this book's writing, .NET Core 2.0 has been released for Windows, macOS, Linux, FreeBSD, and NetBSD. See https://github.com/dotnet/coreclr for more details.

continues

TABLE 22.1: Implementations of the CLI (*continued*)

Compiler	Description
Xamarin	Xamarin is a set of development tools and platform-portable .NET framework libraries as well as an implementation of the CLR that helps developers to create applications that run on Microsoft Windows, iOS, Mac OS, and Android platforms with a very high degree of code reuse. Xamarin uses the Mono BCL.
Microsoft Silverlight	This cross-platform implementation of the CLI was for creating browser-based web client applications. Microsoft stopped developing Silverlight in 2013.
.NET Compact Framework	This is a trimmed-down implementation of the .NET Framework designed to run on PDAs, phones, and the Xbox 360. The XNA library and tools for developing Xbox 360 applications are based on the Compact Framework 2.0 release; Microsoft stopped development of XNA in 2013.
.NET Micro Framework	The Micro Framework is Microsoft's open source implementation of the CLI for devices so resource constrained that they cannot run the compact framework.
Mono	Mono is an open source, cross-platform implementation of the CLI for many UNIX-based operating systems, mobile operating systems such as Android, and game consoles such as PlayStation and Xbox.
DotGNU Portable.NET	This effort to create a cross-platform implementation of the CLI was decommissioned in 2012.
Shared Source CLI (Rotor)	Between 2001 and 2006, Microsoft released shared-source reference implementations of the CLI licensed for noncommercial use.

While the list is extensive considering the work required to implement the CLI, there are three frameworks that are the most relevant going forward.

Microsoft .NET Framework

The **Microsoft .NET Framework** was the first .NET CLI implementation (released in February 2000). As such, it is the most mature framework with the largest API set. It supports building web, console, and Microsoft

Windows client applications. The biggest limitation of the .NET Framework is that it runs on Microsoft Windows only—in fact, it is bundled with Microsoft Windows. There are numerous sub-frameworks included with the Microsoft .NET Framework, the most prominent of which are:

- **.NET Framework Base Class Library (BCL):** Provides types representing the built-in CLI data types, which include support for file IO, fundamental collections classes, custom attributes, string manipulation, and more. The BCL provides the definition for each of the C# native types such as `int` and `string`.

- **ASP.NET:** Used to build websites and web-based APIs. This framework forms the foundation of Microsoft-based websites since its release in 2002 but is slowly being usurped by its replacement, ASP.NET Core, which provides operating system portability along with significant performance improvements and an updated API with greater pattern consistency.

- **Windows Presentation Foundation (WPF):** A graphical user interface framework used to build rich UI applications that run on Microsoft Windows. WPF provides not only a set of UI components but also a declarative language called the **eXtended Application Markup Language** (**XAML**) that enables a hierarchical definition of an application's user interface.

You will frequently hear the Microsoft .NET Framework referred to simply as the **.NET Framework**. Notice the capital *F*, which distinguishes it from a generic implementation of the CLI and the term *.NET framework*.

.NET Core

.NET Core is the cross-platform implementation of the .NET CLI going forward. Furthermore, .NET Core is an open source rewrite of the .NET Framework with a focus on high performance and cross-platform compatibility.

.NET Core consists of the .NET Core Runtime (Core CLR), .NET Core framework libraries, as well as a set of Dotnet command-line tools that can be used to create and build all available application scenarios. The combination of these components are included in the .NET Core SDK. If you've followed along with this book's samples, you've been using .NET Core and the Dotnet tools already.

The .NET Core API is compatible with existing .NET Framework, Xamarin, and Mono implementations via .NET Standard, which is discussed in further detail later in the chapter.

The current focus of .NET Core is to build high-performant and portable console applications as well as to serve as the .NET Foundation for ASP.NET Core and Windows 10 Universal Windows Platform (UWP) applications. Additional frameworks are emerging from .NET Core as more and more operating systems are supported.

Xamarin

This cross-platform development tool includes application UI development support for Android, Mac OS, and iOS and (with the release of .NET Standard 2.0) the capability of building **Universal Windows Applications**, which can run on Windows 10, Windows 10 Mobile, Xbox One, and HoloLens. What makes Xamarin especially powerful is that the same code base can be used to produce platform-native–looking user interfaces on each of the operating systems supported.

.NET Standard

Historically, it has been quite difficult to write a library of C# code that can be used on multiple operating systems or even different .NET frameworks on the same operating system. The problem was that the framework APIs on each framework had different classes available (and/or methods in those classes). The .NET Standard solves this issue by defining a common set of .NET APIs each framework must implement to be compliant with a specified version of the .NET standard. This uniformity ensures that developers have a consistent set of APIs available to them across each .NET framework that is compliant with the .NET Standard version they target. If you wish to write your core application logic once and ensure that it can be used in any modern implementation of .NET, the easiest way to do so is to create a .NET Standard library project (available as a project type in Visual Studio 2017 or from the class library template with the Dotnet CLI). The .NET Core compiler will ensure that any code in the library references only classes and methods common to the version of the .NET Standard you target.

Class library authors should think carefully when choosing which standard to support. The higher the version number of the .NET Standard you target, the less you need to worry about writing your own implementation of APIs that might be missing in lower .NET Standard versions. However, the disadvantage of targeting a higher .NET Standard version is that it will not be as portable across different .NET frameworks. If you wish your library to work with .NET Core 1.0, for example, then you will need to target .NET Standard 1.6 and consequently will not have access to all the reflection APIs that are common to the Microsoft .NET Framework. To summarize this dichotomy: Target higher .NET Standard versions if you are lazy and lower .NET Standard versions if portability is more important than reducing your workload.

For more information, including the mapping of .NET framework implementations and their versions to their corresponding .NET Standard version, see http://itl.tc/NETStandard.

Base Class Library

In addition to providing a runtime environment in which CIL code can execute, the CLI defines a core set of class libraries that programs may employ, called the **Base Class Library**. The class libraries contained in the BCL provide foundational types and APIs, allowing programs to interact with the runtime and underlying operating system in a consistent manner. The BCL includes support for collections, simple file access, some security, fundamental data types (`string`, among others), streams, and the like.

Similarly, a Microsoft-specific library called the **Framework Class Library (FCL)** includes support for rich client user interfaces, web user interfaces, database access, distributed communication, and more.

C# Compilation to Machine Code

The `HelloWorld` program listing in Chapter 1 is obviously C# code, and you compiled it for execution using the C# compiler. However, the processor still cannot directly interpret compiled C# code. An additional compilation step is required to convert the result of C# compilation into machine code. Furthermore, the execution requires the involvement of an agent that adds more services to the C# program—services that it was not necessary to code for explicitly.

All computer languages define syntax and semantics for programming. Since languages such as C and C++ compile to machine code, the platform for these languages is the underlying operating system and machine instruction set, be it Microsoft Windows, Linux, macOS, or something else. In contrast, with languages such as C#, the underlying context is the runtime (or VES).

CIL is what the C# compiler produces after compiling. It is termed a *common intermediate language* because an additional step is required to transform the CIL into something that processors can understand. Figure 22.1 shows the process.

In other words, C# compilation requires two steps:

1. Conversion from C# to CIL by the C# compiler
2. Conversion from CIL to instructions that the processor can execute

The runtime understands CIL statements and compiles them to machine code. Generally, a **component** within the runtime performs this compilation from CIL to machine code. This component is the **just-in-time (JIT) compiler**, and **jitting** can occur when the program is installed or executed. Most CLI implementations favor execution-time compilation of the CIL, but the CLI does not specify when the compilation needs to occur. In fact, the CLI even allows the CIL to be interpreted rather than compiled, like the way many scripting languages work. In addition, .NET includes a tool called NGEN that enables compilation to machine code prior to running the program. This preexecution-time compilation needs to take place on the computer on which the program will be executing because it will evaluate the machine characteristics (processor, memory, and so on) as part of its effort to generate more efficient code. The advantage of using NGEN at installation (or at any time prior to execution) is that you can reduce the need for the jitter to run at startup, thereby decreasing startup time.

As of Visual Studio 2015, the C# compiler also supports .NET native compilation, whereby the C# code is compiled into native machine code when creating a deployed version of the application, much like using the NGEN tool. Universal Windows Applications make use of this feature.

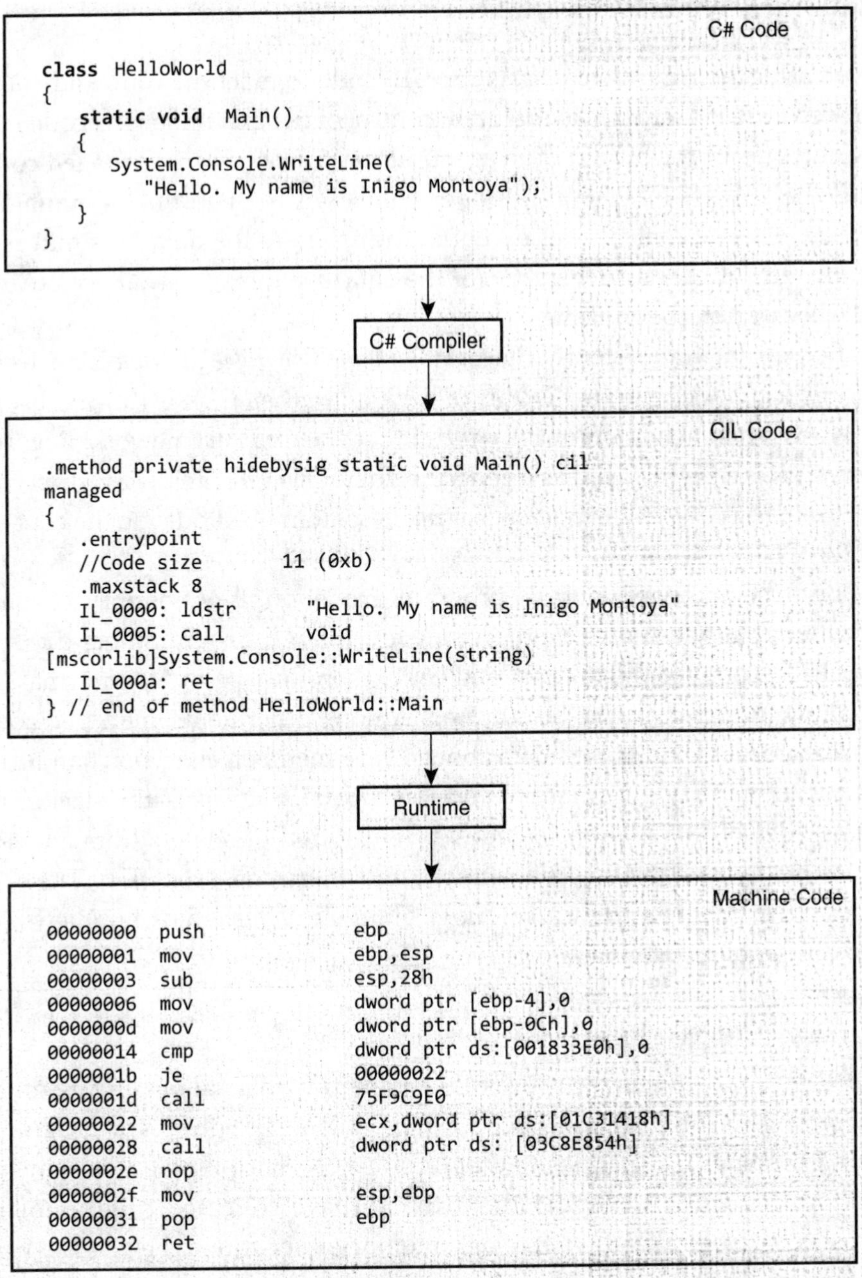

```
                                                         C# Code
class HelloWorld
{
    static void  Main()
    {
        System.Console.WriteLine(
            "Hello. My name is Inigo Montoya");
    }
}
```

```
C# Compiler
```

```
                                                         CIL Code
.method private hidebysig static void Main() cil
managed
{
    .entrypoint
    //Code size        11 (0xb)
    .maxstack 8
    IL_0000: ldstr       "Hello. My name is Inigo Montoya"
    IL_0005: call        void
[mscorlib]System.Console::WriteLine(string)
    IL_000a: ret
} // end of method HelloWorld::Main
```

```
Runtime
```

```
                                                         Machine Code
00000000    push            ebp
00000001    mov             ebp,esp
00000003    sub             esp,28h
00000006    mov             dword ptr [ebp-4],0
0000000d    mov             dword ptr [ebp-0Ch],0
00000014    cmp             dword ptr ds:[001833E0h],0
0000001b    je              00000022
0000001d    call            75F9C9E0
00000022    mov             ecx,dword ptr ds:[01C31418h]
00000028    call            dword ptr ds: [03C8E854h]
0000002e    nop
0000002f    mov             esp,ebp
00000031    pop             ebp
00000032    ret
```

FIGURE 22.1: Compiling C# to Machine Code

Runtime

Even after the runtime converts the CIL code to machine code and starts to execute it, it continues to maintain control of the execution. The code that executes under the context of an agent such as the runtime is **managed code**, and the process of executing under control of the runtime is **managed execution**. The control over execution transfers to the data; this makes it **managed data** because memory for the data is automatically allocated and de-allocated by the runtime.

Somewhat inconsistently, the term *Common Language Runtime* is not technically a generic term that is part of the CLI. Rather, CLR is the Microsoft-specific implementation of the runtime for the .NET framework. Regardless, CLR is casually used as a generic term for *runtime*, and the technically accurate term, *Virtual Execution System*, is seldom used outside the context of the CLI specification.

Because an agent controls program execution, it is possible to inject additional services into a program, even though programmers did not explicitly code for them. Managed code, therefore, provides information to allow these services to be attached. Among other items, managed code enables the location of metadata about a type member, exception handling, access to security information, and the capability to walk the stack. The remainder of this section includes a description of some additional services made available via the runtime and managed execution. The CLI does not explicitly require all of them, but the established CLI frameworks have an implementation of each.

Garbage Collection

Garbage collection is the process of automatically de-allocating memory according to the program's needs. It represents a significant programming problem for languages that don't have an automated system for performing this cleanup. Without the garbage collector, programmers must remember to always free any memory allocations they make. Forgetting to do so, or doing so repeatedly for the same memory allocation, introduces memory leaks or corruption into the program—something exacerbated by long-running programs such as web servers. Because of the runtime's built-in support for garbage collection, programmers targeting runtime execution can focus on adding program features rather than on the "plumbing" related to memory management.

Language Contrast: C++—Deterministic Destruction

The exact mechanics for how the garbage collector works are not part of the CLI specification; therefore, each implementation can take a slightly different approach. (In fact, garbage collection is one item not explicitly required by the CLI.) One key concept with which C++ programmers may need to become familiar is the notion that garbage-collected objects are not necessarily collected **deterministically** (at well-defined, compile-time–known locations). In fact, objects can be garbage-collected anytime between when they are last accessed and when the program shuts down. This includes collection prior to falling out of scope and collection well after an object instance is accessible by the code.

The garbage collector takes responsibility only for handling memory management; that is, it does not provide an automated system for managing resources unrelated to memory. Therefore, if an explicit action to free a resource (other than memory) is required, programmers using that resource should utilize special CLI-compatible programming patterns that will aid in the cleanup of those resources (see Chapter 10).

Garbage Collection on .NET

Most implementations of the CLI use a generational, compacting, mark-and-sweep–based algorithm to reclaim memory. It is "generational" because objects that have lived for only a short period will be cleaned up sooner than objects that have already survived garbage collection sweeps because they were still in use. This convention conforms to the general pattern of memory allocation that objects that have been around longer will continue to outlive objects that have only recently been instantiated.

Additionally, the .NET garbage collector uses a mark-and-sweep algorithm. During each garbage collection execution, it marks objects that are to be de-allocated and compacts together the objects that remain so that there is no "dirty" space between them. The use of compression to fill in the space left by de-allocated objects often results in faster instantiation of new objects (than is possible with unmanaged code), because it is not necessary to search through memory to locate space for a new allocation. Compression also decreases the chance of paging because more objects are located in the same page, which improves performance as well.

The garbage collector takes into consideration the resources on the machine and the demand on those resources at execution time. For example, if memory on the computer is still largely untapped, the garbage collector is less likely to run and take time to clean up those resources. This optimization is rarely taken by execution environments and languages that are not based on garbage collection.

Type Safety

One of the key advantages the runtime offers is checking conversions between types, known as **type checking**. Via type checking, the runtime prevents programmers from unintentionally introducing invalid casts that can lead to buffer overrun vulnerabilities. Such vulnerabilities are one of the most common means of breaking into a computer system, and having the runtime automatically prevent these holes from opening is a significant gain.[2] Type checking provided by the runtime ensures the following:

- Both the variables and the data that the variables refer to are typed, and the type of the variable is compatible with the type of the data to which it refers.
- It is possible to locally analyze a type (without analyzing all of the code in which the type is used) to determine which permissions will be required to execute that type's members.
- Each type has a compile-time–defined set of methods and the data they contain. The runtime enforces rules about which classes can access those methods and data. Methods marked as "private," for example, are accessible only by the containing type.

■ **ADVANCED TOPIC**

Circumventing Encapsulation and Access Modifiers

Given appropriate permissions, it is possible to circumvent encapsulation and access modifiers via a mechanism known as **reflection**. Reflection provides late binding by enabling support for browsing through a type's members, looking up the names of particular constructs within an object's metadata, and invoking the type's members.

---

2. Assuming you are not the unscrupulous type who is looking for such vulnerabilities.

Platform Portability

C# programs are **platform-portable, supporting execution across different operating systems (cross-platform support)**—that is, capable of running on multiple operating systems and executing on different CLI implementations. Portability in this context is not limited to recompiling source code for each platform, but rather, a single CLI module compiled for one framework can run on any CLI-compatible framework without needing to be recompiled. This portability occurs because the work of porting the code lies in the hands of the runtime implementation rather than the application developer (thanks to the .NET Standard). The restriction is, of course, that no platform-specific APIs can be used in your cross-platform code. When developing a cross-platform application, developers can package, or refactor, common code into cross-platform compatible libraries and then call the libraries from platform-specific code to reduce the total amount of code required to support cross-platform applications.

Performance

Many programmers accustomed to writing unmanaged code will correctly point out that managed environments impose overhead on applications, no matter how simple they are. The trade-off is one of increased development productivity and reduced bugs in managed code versus runtime performance. The same dichotomy emerged as programming went from assembler to higher-level languages such as C, and from structured programming to object-oriented development. In the majority of scenarios, development productivity wins out, especially as the speed and reduced price of hardware surpass the demands of applications. Time spent on architectural design is much more likely to yield big performance gains than the complexities of low-level development. In the climate of security holes caused by buffer overruns, managed execution is even more compelling.

Undoubtedly, certain development scenarios (e.g., device drivers) may not yet fit with managed execution. However, as managed execution increases in capability and sophistication, many of these performance considerations will likely vanish. Unmanaged execution will then be reserved for development where precise control or circumvention of the runtime is deemed necessary.[3]

Furthermore, the runtime introduces several factors that can contribute to improved performance over native compilation. For example, because translation to machine code takes place on the destination machine, the resultant compiled code matches the processor and memory layout of that machine, resulting in performance gains generally not leveraged by nonjitted languages. Also, the runtime is able to respond to execution conditions that direct compilation to machine code rarely takes into account. If, for example, the box has more memory than is required, unmanaged languages will still de-allocate their memory at deterministic, compile-time–defined execution points in the code. Alternatively, JIT-compiled languages will need to de-allocate memory only when it is running low or when the program is shutting down. Even though jitting can add a compile step to the execution process, code efficiencies that a jitter can insert may lead to improved performance rivaling that of programs compiled directly to machine code. Ultimately, CLI programs are not necessarily faster than non-CLI programs, but their performance is competitive.

Assemblies, Manifests, and Modules

Included in the CLI is the specification of the CIL output from a source language compiler, usually an assembly. In addition to the CIL instructions themselves, an assembly includes a **manifest** that is made up of the following components:

- The types that an assembly defines and imports
- Version information about the assembly itself
- Additional files the assembly depends on
- Security permissions for the assembly

---

3. Indeed, Microsoft has indicated that managed development will be the predominant means of writing applications for its Windows platform in the future, even for those applications that are integrated with the operating system.

The manifest is essentially a header to the assembly, providing all the information about what an assembly is composed of, along with the information that uniquely identifies it.

Assemblies can be class libraries or the executables themselves, and one assembly can reference other assemblies (which, in turn, can reference more assemblies), thereby establishing an application composed of many components rather than existing as one large, monolithic program. This is an important feature that modern programming frameworks take for granted, because it significantly improves maintainability and allows a single component to be shared across multiple programs.

In addition to the manifest, an assembly contains the CIL code within one or more modules. Generally, the assembly and the manifest are combined into a single file, as was the case with `HelloWorld.exe` in Chapter 1. However, it is possible to place modules into their own separate files and then use an assembly linker (`al.exe`) to create an assembly file that includes a manifest that references each module.[4] This approach not only provides another means of breaking a program into components but also enables the development of one assembly using multiple source languages.

Casually, the terms *module* and *assembly* are somewhat interchangeable. However, the term *assembly* is predominant for those talking about CLI-compatible programs or libraries. Figure 22.2 depicts the various component terms.

Note that both assemblies and modules can also reference files such as resource files that have been localized to a particular language. Although it is rare, two different assemblies can reference the same module or file.

Even though an assembly can include multiple modules and files, the entire group of files has only one version number, which is placed in the assembly manifest. Therefore, the smallest versionable component within an application is the assembly, even if that assembly is composed of multiple files. If you change any of the referenced files—even to release a patch—without updating the assembly manifest, you will violate the integrity of the manifest and the entire assembly itself. As a result, assemblies form the logical construct of a component or unit of deployment.

---

4. This is partly because one of the primary CLI IDEs, Visual Studio .NET, lacks functionality for working with assemblies composed of multiple modules. Current implementations of Visual Studio .NET do not have integrated tools for building multimodule assemblies, and when they use such assemblies, IntelliSense does not fully function.

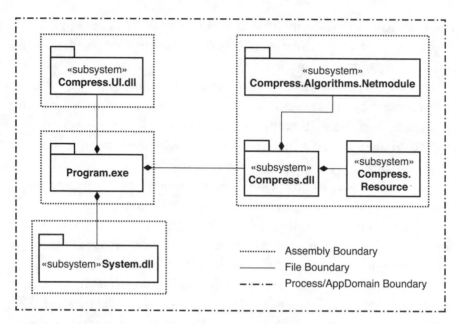

FIGURE 22.2: Assemblies with the Modules and Files They Reference

> **■ NOTE**
>
> Assemblies—not the individual modules that compose them—form the smallest unit that can be versioned and installed.

Even though an assembly (the logical construct) could consist of multiple modules, most assemblies contain only one. Furthermore, Microsoft now provides an `ILMerge.exe` utility for combining multiple modules and their manifests into a single file assembly.

Because the manifest includes a reference to all the files an assembly depends on, it is possible to use the manifest to determine an assembly's dependencies. Furthermore, at execution time, the runtime needs to examine only the manifest to determine which files it requires. Only tool vendors distributing libraries shared by multiple applications (e.g., Microsoft) need to register those files at deployment time. This makes deployment significantly easier. Often, deployment of a CLI-based application is referred to as **xcopy deployment**, after the Windows `xcopy` command that simply copies files to a selected destination.

Language Contrast: COM DLL Registration

Unlike Microsoft's COM files of the past, CLI assemblies rarely require any type of registration. Instead, it is possible to deploy applications by copying all the files that compose a program into a particular directory and then executing the program.

Common Intermediate Language

In keeping with the Common Language Infrastructure name, another important feature of the CIL and the CLI is to support the interaction of multiple languages within the same application (instead of portability of source code across multiple operating systems). As a result, the CIL is the intermediate language not only for C#, but also for many other languages, including Visual Basic .NET, the Java-like language J#, some incantations of Smalltalk, C++, and a host of others (more than 20 at the time of this writing, including versions of COBOL and FORTRAN). Languages that compile to the CIL are termed **source languages**, and each has a custom compiler that converts the source language to the CIL. Once compiled to the CIL, the source language is insignificant. This powerful feature enables the development of libraries by different development groups across multiple organizations, without concern for the language choice of a particular group. Thus, the CIL enables programming language interoperability as well as operating system portability.

▪ NOTE

A powerful feature of the CLI is its support for multiple languages. This support enables the creation of programs using multiple languages and the accessibility of libraries written in one language from code written in a different language.

Common Type System

Regardless of the programming language, the resultant program operates internally on data types; therefore, the CLI includes the **Common Type System (CTS)**. The CTS defines how types are structured and laid out in memory, as well as the concepts and behaviors that surround types. It includes type manipulation directives alongside the information about the data stored within the type. The CTS standard applies to how types appear and behave at the external boundary of a language because the purpose of the CTS is to achieve interoperability between languages. It is the responsibility of the runtime at execution time to enforce the contracts established by the CTS.

Within the CTS, types are classified into two categories:

- **Values** are bit patterns used to represent basic types, such as integers and characters, as well as more complex data in the form of structures. Each value type corresponds to a separate type designation not stored within the bits themselves. The separate type designation refers to the type definition that provides the meaning of each bit within the value and the operations that the value supports.
- **Objects** contain within them the object's type designation. (This helps in enabling type checking.) Objects have identity that makes each instance unique. Furthermore, objects have slots that can store other types (either values or object references). Unlike with values, changing the contents of a slot does not change the identity of the object.

These two categories of types translate directly to C# syntax that provides a means of declaring each type.

Common Language Specification

Since the language integration advantages provided by the CTS generally outweigh the costs of implementing it, the majority of source languages support the CTS. However, there is also a subset of CTS language conformance called the **Common Language Specification (CLS)**, whose focus is on library implementations. The CLS is intended for library developers and provides them with standards for writing libraries that are accessible from the majority of source languages, regardless of whether the source languages using the library are CTS-compliant. It is called the *Common Language Specification* because it is intended to also encourage CLI languages to provide a means of creating interoperable libraries, or libraries that are accessible from other languages.

For example, although it is perfectly reasonable for a language to provide support for an unsigned integer, such a type is not included as part of the CLS. Therefore, developers implementing a class library should not externally expose unsigned integers because doing so would cause the library to be less accessible from CLS-compliant source languages that do not support unsigned integers. Ideally, then, any libraries that are to be accessible from multiple languages should conform to the CLS. Note that the CLS is not concerned with types that are not exposed externally to the assembly.

Also note that it is possible to have the compiler issue a warning when you create an API that is not CLS-compliant. To accomplish this, you use the assembly attribute `System.CLSCompliant` and specify a value of `true` for the parameter.

Metadata

In addition to execution instructions, CIL code includes **metadata** about the types and files included in a program. The metadata includes the following items:

- A description of each type within a program or class library
- The manifest information containing data about the program itself, along with the libraries it depends on
- Custom attributes embedded in the code, providing additional information about the constructs the attributes decorate

The metadata is not a cursory, nonessential add-on to the CIL. Rather, it represents a core component of the CLI implementation. It provides the representation and the behavior information about a type and includes location information about which assembly contains a particular type definition. It serves a key role in saving data from the compiler and making it accessible at execution time to debuggers and the runtime. This data not only is available in the CIL code but also is accessible during machine code execution so that the runtime can continue to make any necessary type checks.

Metadata provides a mechanism for the runtime to handle a mixture of native and managed code execution. Also, it increases code and execution robustness because it smooths the migration from one library version to the next, replacing compile-time–defined binding with a load-time implementation.

All header information about a library and its dependencies is found in a portion of the metadata known as the manifest. As a result, the manifest portion of the metadata enables developers to determine a module's dependencies, including information about particular versions of the dependencies and signatures indicating who created the module. At execution time, the runtime uses the manifest to determine which dependent libraries to load, whether the libraries or the main program has been tampered with, and whether assemblies are missing.

The metadata also contains **custom attributes** that may decorate the code. Attributes provide additional metadata about CIL instructions that are accessible via the program at execution time.

Metadata is available at execution time by a mechanism known as **reflection**. With reflection, it is possible to look up a type or its member at execution time and then invoke that member or determine whether a construct is decorated with a particular attribute. This provides **late binding**, in which the system determines which code to execute at execution time rather than at compile time. Reflection can even be used for generating documentation by iterating through metadata and copying it into a help document of some kind (see Chapter 18).

.NET Native and Ahead of Time Compilation

The .NET Native feature (supported by .NET Core and recent .NET Framework implementations) creates a platform-specific executable. This is referred to as ahead of time (AOT) compilation.

.NET Native allows programmers to continue to code in C# while achieving native code performance and faster startup times by eliminating the need to JIT compile code.

When .NET Native compiles an application, the .NET FCL is statically linked to the application; .NET Framework runtime components optimized for static precompilation are included as well. These specially built components are optimized for .NET Native and provide improved performance over the standard .NET runtime. The compilation step does not change your application in any way. You are free to use all the constructs and APIs of .NET, as well as depend on managed memory and memory cleanup, since .NET Native will include all components of the .NET Framework in your executable.

SUMMARY

This chapter described many new terms and acronyms that are important for understanding the context under which C# programs run. The preponderance of three-letter acronyms can be confusing. Table 22.2 provides a summary list of the terms and acronyms that are part of the CLI.

TABLE 22.2: Common C#-Related Acronyms

Acronym	Definition	Description
.NET	None	Microsoft's implementation of the entire CLI stack. Includes the CLR, CIL, and various languages, all of which are CLS-compliant.
BCL	Base Class Library	The portion of the CLI specification that defines the collection, threading, console, and other base classes necessary to build virtually all programs.
C#	None	A programming language. Separate from the CLI standard is a C# Language Specification, also ratified by the ECMA and ISO standards bodies.
CIL (IL)	Common Intermediate Language	The language of the CLI specification that defines the instructions for the code executable on implementations of the CLI. It is sometimes also referred to as IL or Microsoft IL (MSIL) to distinguish it from other intermediate languages. (To indicate that it is a standard broader than Microsoft, CIL is preferred over MSIL and even IL.)
CLI	Common Language Infrastructure	The specification that defines the intermediate language, base classes, and behavioral characteristics that enable implementers to create Virtual Execution Systems and compilers in which source languages are interoperable on top of a common execution environment.

continues

TABLE 22.2: Common C#-Related Acronyms (*continued*)

Acronym	Definition	Description
CLR	Common Language Runtime	Microsoft's implementation of the runtime, as defined in the CLI specification.
CLS	Common Language Specification	The portion of the CLI specification that defines the core subset of features that source languages *must* support to be executable on runtimes implemented according to the CLI specification.
CTS	Common Type System	A standard generally implemented by CLI-compliant languages that defines the representation and behavior of types that the language exposes visibly outside a module. It includes concepts for how types can be combined to form new types.
FCL	.NET Framework Class Library	The class library that makes up Microsoft's .NET Framework. It includes Microsoft's implementation of the BCL as well as a large library of classes for such things as web development, distributed communication, database access, and rich client user interface development, among others.
VES (runtime)	Virtual Execution System	An agent that manages the execution of a program that is compiled for the CLI.

Index

Index of 7.0 Topics

Index of 6.0 Topics

Index of 5.0 Topics

Credits

Item	Title	Attribution
Figure 1.1	The New Project dialog	Courtesy of Microsoft Corporation.
Figure 1.2	Dialog that shows the Program.cs file	Courtesy of Microsoft Corporation.
Figure 4.5	Collapsed Region in Microsoft Visual Studio .NET	Courtesy of Microsoft Corporation.
Figure 10.2	The Project Menu	Courtesy of Microsoft Corporation.
Figure 10.3	The Browse Filter	Courtesy of Microsoft Corporation.
Figure 10.4	XML Comments as Tips in Visual Studio IDE	Courtesy of Microsoft Corporation.
Output 12.1	Output of a Program Similar to the Etch A Sketch Game	Courtesy of Microsoft Corporation.
Output 12.2	Implementing Undo with a Generic Stack Class	Courtesy of Microsoft Corporation.
Figure 18.2	BinaryFormatter Does Not Encrypt Data	Courtesy of Microsoft Corporation.
Figure 19.1	Clock Speeds over Time	Graph compiled by Herb Sutter Used with permission. Original at www.gotw.ca.
Figure 19.3	CancellationTokenSource and CancellationToken Class Diagrams	Courtesy of Microsoft Corporation.

IntelliTect

Passionate Hard Work, Courageous Honesty, Innovative Excellence

IntelliTect Corporation is a high-end software architecture and development consulting firm based in Spokane, Washington. The company provides architecture consulting, full life-cycle software development, and training that enables its customers to solve the most challenging of problems. IntelliTect has expert principal and senior engineers specializing in the latest Microsoft technologies, including cloud computing, Big Data and AI, Microsoft .NET, Visual Studio Team Services, Office365/SharePoint, and Enterprise Application Integration.

IntelliTect uses best practice application life-cycle management to deliver quality software solutions on time, on scope, and within budget. IntelliTect specializes in the following services:

- Software development training, consulting, and implementation using a wide variety of software including C#, .NET, SQL Server, Oracle, and Visual Studio Team Services (VSTS), delivered on premises or using cloud services including Azure, Amazon Web Services, and the Google Cloud Platform.

- IntelliTect conducts software architecture workshops tailored to our client needs. Services include designing services-oriented architectures, security assessments, project scoping, and solution deployment blueprints.

- IntelliTect enables companies to achieve efficient and effective collaboration with enterprise content management (ECM). Services include Office365/SharePoint consulting, training, deployment, intranet portals, and custom application development.

- For the integration and migration of large enterprise applications as well as business-to-business transactions, IntelliTect develops cloud, BizTalk, and SQL Server Integration Services (SSIS) integration solutions. Cloud solutions include Azure Data Factory, Logic Apps, and Functions and Application Services; BizTalk integrations include the use of line-of-business adapters and the Enterprise Service Bus (ESB).

IntelliTect personnel serve on numerous Microsoft Advisory Boards, publish frequently, and present at conferences including TechEd, DevConnections, and VSLive.

IntelliTect is committed to devoting a significant portion of its profits to the fight against extreme poverty around the world.